I0796098

ALSO BY JACK CHEEVERS

Act of War: Lyndon Johnson, North Korea, and the Capture of the Spy Ship Pueblo

KENNEDY'S COUP

A White House Plot, a Saigon Murder, and America's Descent into Vietnam

JACK CHEEVERS

SIMON & SCHUSTER

New York Amsterdam/Antwerp London

Toronto Melbourne/Sydney New Delhi

Simon & Schuster
1230 Avenue of the Americas
New York, NY 10020

First Simon & Schuster hardcover edition February 2026

Interior design by Wendy Blum
Endpaper: Map by David Lindroth

Manufactured in the United States of America

10 9 8 7 6 5 4 3 2 1

Library of Congress Control Number: 2025945414

ISBN 978-1-6680-8240-9
ISBN 978-1-6680-8242-3 (ebook)

For my uncle:

Second Lieutenant Robert E. Hartenstein,
United States Army Air Forces. Navigator, B-26 bomber,
452nd Bomber Squadron, 322nd Bomber Group (Medium).

Killed in action on November 28, 1944, as his aircraft attacked ground targets in support of American combat troops pushing into Germany.

Bobby was twenty-two.

—

Ad vitam aeternam

CONTENTS

"Great blunders are often made,
like large ropes, of a multitude of fibers."

—

Victor Hugo, *Les Misérables*

CHAPTER 1

A MASSACRE IN EDEN

JOHN HELBLE LOVED to drift along the Perfume River at night. For practically nothing he could rent a sampan and a Vietnamese boatman would steer him out into the middle of the wide, slow-moving stream. From there the low outlines of the old imperial capital of Hue were faintly visible along both banks, north and south. Helble floated on the calm, black water in near silence, past places where long-ago emperors marshaled armies, wrote poetry, and frolicked with concubines. Dim lights shone from both shores, but there was little traffic noise, for in 1963 few people in Hue drove after dark.

Helble, the twenty-nine-year-old American consul in Hue, had many visitors from Saigon, often fellow State Department officers and their wives. They came north ostensibly on official business, but really to tour the Citadel, the unimaginably luxurious home of the Nguyen emperors, and the overgrown but still magnificent imperial tombs nearby. Helble's entertainment program usually included a nighttime sampan outing on the Perfume. He and his guests glided up and down the river, no particular destination in mind, as smaller, canoe-like vessels, their prows lit by lanterns, pulled alongside, offering Vietnamese delicacies cooked on the spot. There were various stories about how the Perfume got its name, but the best one was that it had been scented by orchids falling into its waters far upstream, in the foothills of the Annamite Mountains.

Helble would always remember the languorous beauty of those quiet nights on the Perfume River. But when he arrived on its south bank one hot day in May 1963, he wasn't playing tour guide; he was investigating a massacre.

With its French doors and colorful border of tropical flowers, the South Vietnamese government radio station next to the river seemed an unlikely spot for bloodshed. But on the manic night of May 8, 1963, several thousand Hue residents, most of them Buddhists, had surrounded the station, demanding that it devote airtime to a commemoration of Buddha's birthday. The station manager refused, and soldiers and militiamen moved in with rifles, concussion grenades, and armored vehicles. Gunfire erupted, along with violent explosions. The terrified crowd fled in all directions, leaving behind seven lifeless bodies. An eighth person died later.

Helble looked around the station the next day for anything that might shed light on what had happened. He found a bullet hole in a drainpipe attached to the building, and other damage probably caused by concussion grenades. But it wasn't clear what triggered the violence or who was responsible.

For the past two years, Helble had been trying to understand why things happened the way they did in Hue. Though he spoke fluent Vietnamese and had many acquaintances in the lovely city of 100,000, he had yet to figure out its power structure and how it worked. In some ways, Hue resembled a Sicilian hill town, placid and picturesque on the surface, but rigidly controlled behind the scenes by the Mafia. The insular little city had no newspapers, minimal crime, and—at least until the May 8 slaughter—a docile population.

Helble, his wife, and their young son had come to Hue in the spring of 1961, as the South Vietnamese government strained to put down a worsening insurgency by communist guerrillas called Viet Cong. In those days, the conflict seldom intruded into Hue, although Helble occasionally heard firefights between the VC and local police at a guard post on the far side of a large rice paddy behind his house.

The war was fought mostly in the countryside, and a big part of Helble's job was to travel around South Vietnam's seven northernmost provinces, picking up information on local military, political, and economic conditions, and reporting it to his superiors at the U.S. embassy in Saigon. He roamed his mostly rural region in a Willys jeep, with a submachine gun known as a Swedish K on the seat beside him. His assistant at the consulate had acquired the weapon by trading a case of rum to an American military adviser, who was part of a growing contingent brought in to help the South Vietnamese army fight the VC.

Stationed four hundred miles away from his nearest boss, Helble had a large degree of autonomy, and that suited him just fine. He liked adventure and was unfazed by the dangers of circuit-riding through Viet Cong–haunted countryside. Gregarious, perceptive, and immensely curious, he was an ideal man for the Hue consulate, which functioned as a U.S. observation post for the upper third of South Vietnam, directly below the demilitarized zone that separated it from communist North Vietnam.

A native of the mill town of Appleton, Wisconsin, Helble graduated from the University of Wisconsin and soon afterward joined the State Department. He underwent Vietnamese-language training and found himself at the bustling Saigon embassy in the summer of 1960. Within a few months, he learned just how volatile South Vietnam could be.

In November 1960, rebel paratroopers stormed into Saigon and tried to overthrow South Vietnam's authoritarian president, Ngo Dinh Diem. The attackers surrounded Diem's residence, Independence Palace, in the heart of Saigon. Helble heard about the incipient coup early in the morning and blithely decided to walk past the besieged palace on his way to work, noting anything that might be useful to the embassy.

In front of the palace, he found paratroopers taking cover behind trees. Wrecked jeeps and soldiers' corpses lay in the street. An intense firefight suddenly broke out between the attackers and troops defending the palace. Helble jumped over a low wall around a nearby villa, pressing himself flat on the ground behind it. As it happened, the house was occupied by William Colby, chief of the Central Intelligence Agency station in Saigon, and his wife and their four children. "John, what the hell are you doing down there?" Colby shouted from a balcony. Helble scampered inside the house. The CIA executive was anxious to get to the embassy to carry out his duties and asked his unexpected guest to stay with his family. Helble agreed.

For the next thirty-six hours, Helble carefully observed the fighting and telephoned blow-by-blow reports to the embassy. He watched as rebel troops, tanks, and armored personnel carriers exchanged fire with loyal soldiers around the palace, wincing as stray bullets shattered windows in Colby's home. Artillery shells arced overhead and threw up geysers of dirt on the palace's parklike grounds.

When a group of mutinous soldiers set up a command post in the front yard, Helble went out and talked to the young lieutenant in charge, asking if Colby's wife and kids could safely leave their house. The lieutenant then marched up to the palace's front gate with a white flag, talked to someone inside, and came back and told Helble: "OK, you can take them out now. We have agreed that there will be no firing." Colby's family slipped away unharmed. Diem ultimately survived the attempted coup, calling in loyal troops from outlying areas to save him.

HELBLE FIGURED HIS INTREPID reporting from the villa led to his promotion to Hue over a more experienced foreign service officer who'd been tagged to go there.

His consular district was huge, covering thousands of square miles, with varied terrain that included beautiful white sand beaches on the South China Sea, thickly forested highlands populated by primitive tribespeople, and spooky jungles and mountains along the Laotian border that concealed dangerous animals as well as dangerous men. In his early days as consul, he was oblivious to the very real hazards of traveling in his new domain.

When Helble first arrived in Hue, the departing consul, a high-spirited man named Tom Barnes, put him in a jeep and took him on a five-day orientation tour.

Their destination was Kontum, a market town in the mountainous Central Highlands. They started off by driving south along coastal Highway 1, one of the few paved roads in the region, and then west to Pleiku, a crossroads town and home to a major South Vietnamese army base. Normally, travelers made their way to Pleiku and then took an established road north to Kontum. But Barnes knew a shortcut, and the two Americans swerved off the main road onto a muddy track that led into the forest.

They soon reached a village inhabited by mountain tribespeople. There they met a French priest who'd lived with the mountaineers for many years and reported that the Viet Cong were active in the area. The Americans got back in their jeep and continued along the isolated route, winding through mountain forests for hours as daylight faded. They finally arrived in Kontum after dark, parked in the American military compound, and joined some U.S. Army advisers at a bar. One of them asked why the two diplomats were getting in from Pleiku so late. Helble replied that they hadn't come from Pleiku; they'd taken the shortcut through the mountains. Silence descended on the bar. One of the advisers exclaimed, "You did *what*? Nobody's been down that track for years. It's totally insecure."

On a different trip, Helble had to slam on his brakes to avoid running smack-dab into a Viet Cong ambush in Quang Ngai Province. Just ahead, guerrillas on both sides of the road were shooting at South Vietnamese militiamen who'd been riding in a truck. Helble jumped into a ditch and crawled over to the militiamen, getting off a few shots from his .38-caliber revolver, which wasn't very effective for combat. (After that, he took the Swedish K with him.) The communists broke off the attack and melted into the landscape.

One way to foil VC attackers was to drive fast. Helble was doing that on another day in Quang Ngai as he approached a steep ramp that led onto a short, steel-frame bridge. He hit the ramp at about thirty miles per hour, bumped across the bridge, and was racing away when he heard a loud explosion behind him. Checking his rearview mirror, he saw the bridge gone and pieces of it falling from the sky. He figured he'd been moving just quickly enough to thwart the hidden guerrilla who'd detonated the mine.

Helble nevertheless enjoyed rambling about his consular district, typically spending one week in Hue and the next on the road.

The scenery along the way could be humdrum, such as the scrublands and rice paddies bordering Highway 1, adorned only by an occasional clutch of banana trees. Or it could be breathtaking, like the thrilling vistas along the narrow thirteen-mile road that wound through the Hai Van Pass—Ocean Cloud Pass—in mountains bordering the South China Sea. Helble traversed the pass on his frequent trips to Danang, where he consulted with American and South Vietnamese military authorities.

In the coastal lowlands, he often stopped to talk with farmers in their paddies, asking about crop yields and whether Diem's government was doing enough to help them. (It took him a while to adjust to the sight of a barefoot farmer, standing atop an earthen irrigation dike, his pants rolled up to his knees and multiple leeches attached to his blood-streaked legs.) Pulling into a village or town, he'd seek out the headman to discuss the economy or how the war was going in that district. As poor as they were, the rural Vietnamese were gracious hosts, offering their visitor a can of warm beer or soda pop. After a long, dusty day of careening over dirt and gravel roads, Helble gulped the drink gratefully.

As his tour wore on, it became more and more dangerous for an American to traipse around the boonies on his own. The VC stepped up their attacks, and the young diplomat occasionally was forced to accept, at the insistence of worried local officials, an escort of armed soldiers. By 1963, he was doing much of his travel aboard small, single-engine airplanes with CIA pilots. Flying was faster, and certainly safer, than driving, and Helble liked getting the pilots to buzz his house in Hue as the plane headed for a short landing strip in the Citadel.

Thus alerted, his wife would hurry out to the airfield to collect her husband.

HUE HAD LONG BEEN the cultural and intellectual wellspring of Vietnam. With its backdrop of pine-covered hills, it was a somnolent old city of scholars and warriors, exquisite gardens and abandoned palaces, drowsing in memories of its glorious imperial past.

In the early 1960s, it was a quiet, conservative place. Sampans brought a daily catch of fresh fish up the Perfume River from a lagoon near the South China Sea. Schoolgirls rode bicycles while wearing white ao dai gowns with split side panels that streamed behind them, making them look like swallows in flight. Young men and women bustled about the Hue University campus, where a team of West German doctors was helping to establish a medical school. There was little nightlife, no dance halls, and only a single bar, the Green Door. Hue's people were the proud puritans of South Vietnam, differing considerably from the less restrained Saigonese in dress, speech, manner, and attitudes. They regarded their countrymen to the south as lazy, undisciplined, and badly corrupted by money and foreign influences, and themselves as the less affluent but high-minded conservators of the nation's heritage and values.

"We have," a Hue resident wryly told an American journalist, "one of the most enormous superiority complexes on earth."

The most intriguing feature of the landscape was the Citadel, a walled mini-city surrounded by moats that had been the home of the emperors and their enormous courts. At its core was the Forbidden Purple City, a smaller replica of Beijing's Forbidden City, where the thirteen successive emperors of the Nguyen dynasty lived in a dreamworld of extraordinary beauty and luxury, attended by scores of wives and sometimes hundreds of concubines, plus a corps of imperial eunuchs.

The Nguyen lords were entertained by paramours and rare animals in their royal palaces and gardens, or dancers and actors in their private theater. Elsewhere in the Citadel were court offices and homes for high-ranking government and military officials and their families. Inside its walls were guardhouses, stables, war elephants, caged tigers, and arms storehouses. The extensive grounds were once adorned with lovely lakes, ornamental bridges, and perfectly landscaped flora. (In the nineteenth century, Emperor Minh Mang put eight thousand soldiers to work on the magnificent Tim Tam gardens and an accompanying lake.) Ponds and canals within the royal fortress were dotted with white lotuses, the Buddhist symbol of spiritual and bodily purity.

The emperors' armies were backed on the battlefield by elephants, which could impale enemy soldiers with their tusks and scatter cavalry with their terrifying trumpets. The animals became royal favorites and emblems of imperial power. In a specially built arena, elephants and tigers battled to the death for the amusement of emperors and their guests. (The elephants routinely won, since royal keepers blunted the tigers' teeth and claws.) French travelers wrote of these ferocious clashes with awe and revulsion, comparing them to the feral spectacles in ancient Rome's Colosseum.

The emperors were long gone by 1963. But they had a successor of sorts in an enigmatic, potbellied figure named Ngo Dinh Can, a younger brother of President Diem.

Although he held no government office, Can ruled Hue and the rest of upper South Vietnam like a viceroy. Rarely seen in public, he lived with his bedridden ninety-one-year-old mother in a house enclosed by high walls topped with triple strands of electrified wire. Can directed his own secret police force, known as the Special Action Group, which had a reputation for crushing the Viet Cong and noncommunist political rivals with equal ruthlessness. Through a network of informants and sycophants, he stayed abreast of all significant political and military developments in his region. "He had his agents everywhere," said one U.S. diplomat. Without Can's blessing, no one got an important government job or won a seat in the National Assembly.

Pragmatic and down-to-earth, he liked to be called "Uncle Can" and was said to have a sparkling wit. He kept close tabs on popular aspirations and attitudes toward Diem's regime, and was seen as generally sympathetic to common people.

But Can tolerated no dissent. While his brother's political antagonists in Saigon were sometimes allowed to make speeches and be quoted in newspapers, in Can's satrapy no such insubordination was permitted. His political organization had a hand in most major economic development projects in the region, and he was believed to control the lucrative trade in cassia, a cinnamon-like spice. He told one associate that his family had salted away $7 million in foreign banks and that if things went bad, they and their friends could sail away from South Vietnam in five ships they owned.

Can disliked foreigners and dodged each of the eager young American consuls who arrived in Hue every few years and sought an audience with him. He pleaded ill health or insisted he was only a private citizen, with no official role in government. He did, however, send the Americans interesting gifts. One of Helble's predecessors received the stuffed head of a gaur, a large horned bovine similar to a bison, as a going-away present. The last U.S. consul who managed to get inside Can's home, in 1959, described it as "bizarre," citing such trappings as two enormous stuffed tigers, a stuffed leopard, and numerous cages filled with raucous birds. A Vietnamese official who'd accompanied the American explained that Can was very fond of animals because he had no wife or children.

Helble, too, tried to speak with Can, but was told to submit questions in writing; he did so and got back only pabulum. But everywhere he went, he felt Can's unseen presence.

He sensed it every time he tried to talk with a Vietnamese about local politics or the government, only to have that person gingerly steer the conversation to another topic. Hue was filled with police and soldiers, but they kept a low profile, which was all they really needed to do. The people of Hue knew who was in charge and how they were expected to act.

LONG BEFORE JOHN HELBLE and other Americans came to Vietnam, it was conquered and colonized by the French. During the latter half of the nineteenth century, France gradually seized control of what became known as French Indochina, composed of the modern-day states of Vietnam, Cambodia, and Laos.

In 1885, French soldiers sacked Hue, killing as many as 1,500 Vietnamese and forcing the young Nguyen emperor, Ham Nghi, to flee into the countryside with his regents. The French took over the imperial capital and ran the country for their own benefit until Ho Chi Minh's communist guerrilla army forced them out in 1954.

Hue still carried a vivid colonial imprint when Helble arrived. The splendid former French governor-general's mansion graced the city's French Quarter, on the south side of the Perfume River, where Hue's most affluent families resided. Also on the south side was the French-built, raspberry-colored railroad station. The glamorous Cercle Sportif de Hue country club, where colons once played tennis on grass courts and sipped cocktails at the poolside bar, was shuttered, but bore ghostly witness to the charms of colonial life.

Helble and his wife, Joan, also got a taste of upper-crust living. They moved into a spacious French Quarter villa and hired four servants, including a cook, a gardener, and a nursemaid for their little son, and, in the fall of 1961, a newborn daughter.

A bridge enthusiast, Helble hosted weekly games at his house with Jerry Greiner, a CIA agent who was under cover as Helble's "vice-consul." Another regular was Jan Berlin, a U.S. Army doctor who sometimes accompanied Helble on his jeep jaunts in the countryside. The men drank cognac and smoked Philippine cigars as Helble carefully tallied their scores. He also enjoyed taking his family to a gorgeous beach on the South China Sea. Only a handful of other American couples lived in Hue, and Helble and his wife sometimes joined them at a firing range as they honed their shooting skills in case of a Viet Cong attack on their homes or offices.

Helble liked Hue and the Vietnamese, and accepted their cultural idiosyncrasies with easygoing Midwestern tolerance. For instance, he dined on a number of occasions with the rotund, jocular rector of Hue University, a Jesuit priest named Cao Van Luan. Father Luan loved playing a puckish practical joke on his foreign guests: he served them cooked dog meat, without telling them in advance.

Helble didn't mind eating dog, although it wouldn't be his first choice on a restaurant menu, and was sometimes present at Father Luan's dinners with other Americans. When they finished their meal, the newcomers often remarked, "Father, that was a delicious dish. What was that?" The priest would smile slyly and say, "Dog." The guests sometimes didn't catch what he said at first, or didn't believe their ears. Many of them then beelined for the front yard, making sounds that indicated the meal might not have been so appetizing after all.

Helble loved sports, especially games played with a racket: tennis, badminton, racquetball. Soon after moving into his villa, he poured blacktop in his backyard, put up a net and lights, and began organizing badminton games and tournaments.

The games had a dual purpose: they were partly for fun and partly a way for Helble to better understand Hue's political and social anatomy. Most of those he invited were government bureaucrats or professors and students from the university. As players batted the shuttlecock back and forth, Helble chatted quietly on the sidelines with those not playing. He asked bureaucrats about their jobs and students about their professors, as obliquely and discreetly as possible. "You always had to be somewhat circumspect in how you approached it," he recalled. Helble held several games a week and several tournaments a year, gleaning valuable information and becoming a first-rate badminton player in the bargain.

Helble had other ploys for collecting information as well. For their first Christmas in Hue, he and Joan decided to throw a dinner dance party, even though it was known that Can, the city's unofficial overlord, didn't approve of dancing. Helble had heard that some Hue residents who'd been educated in Europe or the United States chafed at restrictions on dancing and other Western-style entertainments, and he wanted to find out who they were. So he and Joan invited a couple dozen Vietnamese, including members of the local power structure, to their home.

The Helbles cranked up their record player with Herb Alpert and the Tijuana Brass and Les Elgart's dance band. But only a few Vietnamese couples showed up, and they stayed off the dance floor. The party looked like a bust, but the Helbles gamely went ahead with dinner. Afterward, one of the Vietnamese couples excused themselves and left. It was still early, so Helble put on more records and the place suddenly sprang to life. The remaining couples moved onto the dance floor and had a blast. They explained to Helble why they were all so inhibited at first: the gentleman who'd just departed was Can's right-hand man, and "no one was crazy enough to dance in his presence."

IN THE TWO YEARS preceding the radio station massacre, Helble had noticed an intensifying competition between Hue's two main religious groups, Buddhists and Catholics.

Hue was the de facto capital of South Vietnamese Buddhism. Leading monks lived there and worshiped at Tu Dam Pagoda, with its striking tower resembling a stack of giant mushrooms. About 70 percent of South Vietnam's population identified, at least nominally, as Buddhist, and Buddhist festivals and processions were commonplace in Hue.

While Catholics made up only 10 to 12 percent of South Vietnam's people, they had outsize influence in Hue. The city was the family seat of President Diem, an ardent Catholic who, in his youth, had studied to be a priest. In 1961, the Vatican appointed Diem's older brother, Ngo Dinh Thuc, as Hue's archbishop. Strong-willed and self-righteous, Thuc moved forcefully to raise Catholicism's profile in the city, constructing a large church and renovating the Hue cathedral. Even Can, the Ngo clan's least devout member, was a weekly churchgoer and lived in Hue's Catholic quarter, Phu Cam.

Helble watched as the two faiths tried to outdo one another on holy days, ratcheting up the size and splendor of their celebrations. If the Catholics held a big procession to mark one of their sacred days, the Buddhists staged an even grander one when their turn came. Though heavily outnumbered, Catholics consistently put on good shows of strength. When Archbishop Thuc's new church was dedicated in 1962, for instance, many government officials came up from Saigon for the ceremony.

Indeed, Buddhists complained to Helble that Diem's regime had for years consistently favored Catholics. Hue University faculty members bent over backward to please Thuc, believing, as Helble put it in a report to the State Department, that the influential prelate "can break the University if he sees fit." And Helble had seen evidence of direct government assistance to the Catholic community. Shortly after he moved to Hue, construction began on a Catholic seminary near his house. Helble saw five South Vietnamese army trucks bringing fill material to the building site. Two years later, the work was still underway, with the same trucks helping. Local residents told him that army trucks were also used to build the new church.

THE MAY 8 MASSACRE stirred deep anger among Buddhists in Hue. Even some Catholics were upset at the tactics government troops had used against people at the radio station.

Helble had his diplomatic position to consider, and didn't want to be seen as taking too close an interest in what the Diem government surely regarded as an internal matter. But he did conduct his own circumspect investigation, quietly talking to Buddhist leaders and the few anti-regime dissidents he could find. He gathered official reports on the killings from Vietnamese police and military sources, and spoke with Major Dang Sy, commander of the government troops at Radio Hue. A Catholic, the officer had become the primary villain in what was shaping up as a major scandal.

In a lengthy cable to the State Department, Helble said he tried to verify all of the events preceding the massacre, but conceded that his report might not be completely accurate. The incident began, he wrote, on May 7, when Hue police asked local Buddhists to take down flags hoisted in celebration of Wesak, an annual holy day commemorating the birth, enlightenment, and death of Buddha. The cops, however, met with "considerable popular resistance."

The next morning, the Buddhists held their traditional Wesak parade and a ceremony at Tu Dam Pagoda. During the ceremony a monk named Tri Quang delivered a fiery speech attacking the Diem government for ordering the removal of Buddhist flags and discriminating against Buddhists. "Now is the time to fight!" he exhorted his listeners.

That evening, a large crowd gathered at Tu Dam for a traditional flower dance. But the performance was canceled and the crowd headed for the radio station by the river. By 8 p.m., as many as four thousand people were outside the building.

At that point, Helble acknowledged, the details of what happened got fuzzy. Tri Quang went to the radio station and demanded either that a tape of his morning speech be broadcast, or that he be allowed to repeat the speech on the air live. But the station manager refused, whether because the speech hadn't been cleared by government censors or because there was no room in the program lineup, Helble couldn't say. Tri Quang then addressed the crowd over a loudspeaker, urging them to remain calm even though he'd been denied airtime. The province chief circulated among the people, pleading with them to go home.

But they didn't and the authorities eventually lost patience. Many police officers appeared, along with two companies of soldiers and militiamen and eight armored scout cars and U.S.-supplied armored personnel carriers. Fire trucks arrived and tried to disperse the crowd by spraying water. The hoses, however, didn't have enough pressure to push people back and many actually enjoyed the cool streams on a hot night. Eyewitnesses said the protesters engaged in no violence, although two youths scrambled onto the radio station's roof and planted a Buddhist flag, shouting, "Victory!"

Loudspeaker appeals and tear gas volleys also failed to break up the crowd. At about 10:45 p.m. the security forces all began firing their guns in the air, creating a frightening racket that went on for about one minute. Several earsplitting explosions occurred at about the same time. Armored vehicles rolled forward into the demonstrators, and terrified men, women, and children began running and stumbling. When the bedlam subsided, seven mangled corpses lay outside the radio station. Six of the dead were children or youths. About fifteen other people were taken to local hospitals and dispensaries for treatment.

Two eyewitnesses later said they saw a soldier pitch a concussion grenade onto the radio station's concrete porch, where several people died. Though the devices weren't designed to kill, a U.S. Army doctor who viewed the victims told Helble their wounds could have been caused by such grenades going off "in the midst of a closely-packed crowd." The doctor also believed that two children had been crushed to death beneath armored vehicles.

The government claimed that Viet Cong agents caused the fatalities by hurling plastic explosives into the crowd. But that story, Helble reported to his superiors, was "greeted with incredulity" by the people of Hue. "They were amazed," he wrote, "that the Government would try to cover up the incident in such a manner when it seemed everyone clearly knew the real truth."

STREET PROTESTS SWEPT THE city over the next few days. On the morning after the massacre, about eight hundred people, many of them young and chanting, "Kill us, kill us!," marched to the train station, where the province chief stood on a sound truck with the monk Tri Quang by his side. The province chief told the crowd that the soldiers and militiamen took the actions they did in order to suppress Viet Cong agitators. When an American helicopter appeared overhead, a machine gun protruding from its side door, protesters cried out, "Go ahead, drop the bombs!" But at Tri Quang's behest, they dispersed peacefully.

That afternoon, the charismatic monk, with his shaved head and large, intense eyes, addressed several thousand people again gathered at the radio station. He said he'd call a mass meeting soon, but that if they didn't go home immediately, he'd "fast unto death." The crowd broke up without incident.

Helble had gone to one of the demonstrations in an effort to gauge the level of popular support for the Buddhists and get more details of their grievances. But he figured he was under surveillance and didn't want Can's men to see him on the streets too much. He found out that several Americans from other U.S. government agencies in Hue were going to protests as well. All of them were tall white men who stood out very visibly among the Vietnamese.

For instance, Jerry Greiner, the CIA officer, was a six-foot-three former college football linebacker and heavyweight boxer. Someone showed Helble a laugh-out-loud photo of Greiner trying, with no success, to conceal his bulk behind a streetlight pole. Helble instructed Greiner and the others to stay away from the demonstrations and gave one of the consulate's Vietnamese employees a crash course in how to use a Rolleiflex camera. That way, Helble could keep a low profile and still find out the size of the crowds and what their banners said.

The Buddhists called another mass meeting at Tu Dam on May 10. Police and troops lined the roads leading to the pagoda. Thousands of protesters began arriving, many waving Buddhist flags in open defiance of a regime ban on them. Others carried signs and banners that read "Long live the Buddhist religion," "Ready to sacrifice blood," and "The international Buddhist flag will never go down." Tri Quang took the stage and told his listeners they could fly their flags and he'd bear the consequences. He urged them to remain peaceful, carry no weapons, and be vigilant against Viet Cong attempts to infiltrate their ranks. When he asked the people whether they'd follow his leadership, they roared their assent.

Tri Quang and other prominent monks then outlined five demands to the Diem government that were soon to become highly contentious. They wanted Diem to lift restrictions on the Buddhist flag and repeal a French-era law they said made it difficult to acquire property for Buddhist schools, temples, and other facilities. They demanded that the government stop "arresting and terrorizing" Buddhists, and that monks be guaranteed the freedom to preach. Lastly, Tri Quang and the other leaders demanded punishment for those responsible for the massacre and compensation for victims' families.

Two days later, what Helble described as a "goon squad" of about ten men struck back, beating up several people in various places around the city. The victims seemed to have been picked at random, although most were young. Two of them were assaulted in a coffee shop in Hue's central market as nearby police did nothing. The only plausible explanation Helble heard was that Can was trying to reestablish some semblance of control by intimidating the population.

Tensions nonetheless eased in Hue as the days passed. Authorities ended a nighttime curfew and Buddhist leaders toned down their rhetoric. A mass meeting of eight thousand people at Tu Dam on May 21 was completely peaceful, with speakers avoiding attacks on the government and no inflammatory banners or signs appearing in the crowd.

But something had changed, and the people sensed it. The cloak of invincibility that had covered Can, and by extension Diem, was badly torn, if not completely shredded. Buddhists had long been submissive to the powers that be, focused as they were on attaining nirvana rather than concessions from the regime. Over the course of a few spring days, however, they'd learned to their surprise that they could parade through the streets, defy government rules, make anti-government speeches, and not face brutal repression. The authorities certainly had lashed out with deadly force at the radio station, but later seemed to back off as more demonstrations unfolded.

In contrast to the rigidly hierarchical Catholic Church, Buddhism in South Vietnam was known for its loose organization and the broad autonomy it granted to individual pagodas. But the protests had galvanized Buddhists with a new sense of unity and pride. The scale of the demonstrations, along with participants' willingness to risk being arrested or even shot, showed the urgency and popularity of the Buddhist cause. A profound psychological liberation was taking place in Hue. There were still thugs on the streets ready to attack people if they got out of line, but there were many more Buddhists, and they weren't backing down. The old mindset that the people had to remain meek and voiceless was disintegrating.

The May marches and rallies also marked the emergence of a formidable new Buddhist leader: Tri Quang. In the past, monks were visible mostly during their ethereal street processions, in flowing black or gray robes, to and from their pagodas. Tri Quang cut sharply against that passive, disengaged image. A powerful orator and shrewd strategist, he seemed to have a mesmeric grip on the crowds he addressed. When he told people to quiet down, they immediately went silent. When he told them to raise their banners and placards, they instantly did so. When he told them to go home, they obeyed without question.

Almost overnight, the little-known monk had become a sort of Buddhist Spartacus. He'd astutely guided the Hue protests since the beginning, using them to publicize his claims that the Diem regime persecuted Buddhists while helping Catholics. Tri Quang threatened that if the government didn't satisfy the five Buddhist demands, he and other monks would launch a hunger strike. Buddhists had reached the point of no return with the regime, and "more martyrs would be created," if necessary, to achieve their goals. Not only were ordinary Buddhists behind him, he declared, but also many military and government officers.

Helble sent a long, insightful cable to his superiors summarizing the memorable month of May. He'd never seen such a compelling "rice-roots" movement since arriving in Vietnam, he wrote; the people of Hue seemed stunned by their newfound strength. The Diem regime's insistence that the Viet Cong caused the massacre had cost it all credibility in Hue. No one believed that story, and few now trusted the government to tell the truth about anything.

The killings and their aftermath also had implications for the United States, Helble wrote. The Buddhist leaders and other dissidents he'd talked with didn't blame the Americans for what had happened. On the contrary, many in Hue believed that Americans sympathized with their cause. But the United States could lose its good reputation if it didn't modify its blanket support of the regime, Helble predicted. If Diem took more bloody action against the Buddhists, the U.S. government might wind up branded as an accessory, in light of all the advisers, equipment, and other aid it was providing his security forces.

Diem, meanwhile, acceded to only one of the Buddhists' demands—he compensated the victims' families ten thousand piastres, or about $142, apiece—while sloughing off the others. Helble's report warned: "Should the Buddhists persist, as it appears they will from this vantage point, and the [government] continues to resist any real compromise, as their past performances would indicate they may, the pressure could mount to serious proportions."

His words were as prophetic as they were understated.

CHAPTER 2

STRANGER IN A STRANGE LAND

WHILE HELBLE KEPT an eye on Buddhist restiveness in Hue, his boss, U.S. Ambassador Frederick Nolting, was preparing for a vacation cruise on the Aegean Sea with his family.

Nolting was eager for the break after serving for two strenuous years as President John F. Kennedy's envoy to South Vietnam. The ambassador, his wife, and their two youngest daughters were to first fly from Saigon to New Delhi, where they'd visit the Taj Mahal. The next stop was Cairo and a two-day voyage up the Nile. From there they'd go on to Athens to meet their two oldest daughters, both students at Wellesley College. The whole clan then would board a rented Greek fishing boat and spend ten days exploring the island-strewn, azure waters that once nourished the city-states of ancient Greece.

A tall Virginian with a country-doctor manner and a PhD in philosophy, Nolting had taken charge of the U.S. embassy in Saigon in May 1961. He was under instructions from Kennedy to establish a relationship of mutual trust and cooperation with Diem, South Vietnam's headstrong, fiercely nationalistic president. Nolting soon found himself overseeing the massive Kennedy administration effort, launched at the end of that year, to provide South Vietnam with enough military and economic assistance to prevail over the Viet Cong.

Signs of the expanding U.S. presence were hard to miss in Saigon. American cargo ships unloaded arms and heavy equipment at docks on the Saigon River. U.S. military personnel stepped off air-conditioned Boeing 707 jets into the furnace-like heat at Tan Son Nhut airport. Air Force transport planes discharged tons of radar equipment, electric generators, trucks, Quonset huts, and other materials. Crew-cut American pilots, rural-development specialists, police trainers, and intelligence operatives thronged the humid tropical streets.

Within a few months, the American program—dubbed Operation Beef-Up—began to show results. In rice paddies, tangled jungles, and rugged mountains, U.S. Army advisers accompanied South Vietnamese troops into battle, recommending the best tactics to pursue and kill Viet Cong fighters. American helicopters gave government soldiers extraordinary mobility, depositing them practically on top of startled enemy units. Fast-moving, U.S.-made M113 armored personnel carriers chased guerrillas across the countryside like jackrabbits. Bearing nineteen troops, the ten-ton amphibious vehicles galloped over dry terrain at forty miles per hour and churned across canals and flooded rice fields at up to twenty miles per hour. Any VC caught in the open were mowed down by the vehicles' .50-caliber machine guns.

Meanwhile, American planes blasted guerrillas with rockets, bombs, and cannons. They dropped canisters of napalm, a nightmarish weapon made of jellied gasoline that enveloped its victims in flames and sucked the oxygen out of the air around them; those who weren't burned to death died of suffocation.

By early 1963, the number of U.S. military personnel in South Vietnam had jumped to more than 11,300, including 3,000 combat advisers, from 875 at the start of JFK's presidency.

Yet the tough, resilient Viet Cong adapted to helicopters and armored personnel carriers, developing new tactics to cope with both. To the bafflement of the Americans, VC combat groups, while suffering severe casualties, somehow grew bigger, from company to battalion size. The guerrillas gradually replaced their homemade shotguns and old French bolt-action rifles with modern semiautomatic rifles, machine guns, and mortars. Many of the new weapons were American, captured from South Vietnamese forces, while others were Chinese- and Soviet-made, smuggled over jungle trails from Laos and Cambodia, or landed from boats in one of the innumerable small bays, lagoons, and river mouths along South Vietnam's serpentine, 1,500-mile coast.

The U.S. advisory program, too, had its limitations. Many of the Americans living with and advising South Vietnamese combat units were top-notch, gung ho officers who got along well with their counterparts and believed they were helping to improve their fighting capabilities.

Others felt they were doing little good. The tonal Vietnamese language was difficult to learn and few advisers ever mastered it. Miffed that foreigners thought they didn't know how to fight on their own soil, South Vietnamese commanders often ignored the Americans' advice; some stopped communicating altogether. "We were often hopelessly baffled and frequently misunderstood," remembered Martin Dockery, who as a twenty-three-year-old Army lieutenant worked with a South Vietnamese battalion and wrote a book about his experiences, pointedly titled *Lost in Translation*. "Not a day went by that I did not find certain situations confusing. I was never entirely certain of what I was being told or what was happening."

One top South Vietnamese general judged the advisers' overall impact as "marginal at best."

Nolting nonetheless believed that slow but steady progress was being made in the war as Washington combined its military help with a wide variety of civilian assistance programs. In rural provinces, where small boys rode water buffalo in the rice paddies and impoverished villages broiled in the sun, American aid workers were helping to build schools, roads, medical clinics, bridges, water wells, and airstrips. The idea was to win the peasants' "hearts and minds" by demonstrating the many benefits that would flow if they sided with the government against the Viet Cong.

The centerpiece of the military-civilian effort in the countryside was the "strategic hamlet" program, led by another of Diem's brothers, the Machiavellian intellectual Ngo Dinh Nhu. Strategic hamlets were clusters of houses enclosed by barbed-wire fences, moats, and rows of sharpened stakes, and protected by local militiamen. Nhu hoped to quickly prod most of the rural population into the fortified communities, cutting the VC off from their main sources of food, recruits, intelligence, and "tax" revenues. By mid-1963, some seven thousand strategic hamlets had been built, with more than 8 million of South Vietnam's 14 million people living in them, or so the government claimed. Nolting felt the mushrooming numbers indicated that the Diem regime was gaining control of the disputed countryside.

General Paul Harkins, the relentlessly optimistic, West Point–educated commander of U.S. military operations in South Vietnam, was fond of saying that the war might be over by the end of that year. Such glib pronouncements made Nolting cringe, but he, too, believed that the tide had turned against the communists. On a wall inside the U.S. embassy was a *Peanuts* cartoon that summed up the prevailing official outlook. The caption read: "How can we lose when we're so sincere?"

The war was never far from Saigon in the spring of 1963. Fighter-bombers and helicopters bristling with rockets and machine guns crisscrossed the skies above the steamy metropolis of 2 million people. Outgoing mortar fire could be heard on the city's outskirts; at night, brilliant white flares and artillery flashes pierced the deep blackness on the far side of the Saigon River. Viet Cong terrorists tossed bombs into crowded restaurants and bars, leaving blown-out walls and awful carnage among GIs and Vietnamese civilians alike.

Nolting had seen the results of VC viciousness in the countryside as well. In one village he visited, the communists had murdered some peasants and hung them "like scarecrows" as a warning to others. In September 1961, he traveled to a rural province and met the vigorous young man who was the top government official there. The following week, the Viet Cong beheaded the province chief in front of his wife and children. Nolting wondered if his visit had somehow triggered the cruel execution.

AT FIFTY-ONE, "FRITZ" NOLTING was a veteran diplomat with a soft voice, a gentle sense of humor, and seemingly limitless energy.

Within a few months of arriving, he'd visited much of South Vietnam, tramping through dusty villages and muddy rice paddies, often alongside the stout, much shorter Diem. He was well-liked by subordinates, who described him as thoughtful, kind, and dedicated. "There was," noted a younger colleague, "an appealing, elemental decency and openness about the man." Nolting spent long hours at the embassy, tucked into a shabby former bank building near the Saigon River, chain-smoking in his office as he wrestled with a host of issues and problems.

At his ambassadorial residence, with its graceful porte cochere and high walls topped with broken glass, Nolting liked to play the piano and sing hymns and spirituals, although he'd sometimes pound out an exuberant rendition of "Camptown Races." He and his family played tennis and swam in the pool at the elegant Cercle Sportif Saigonnais country club. A devout Episcopalian, Nolting attended services every Sunday. His youngest daughter, Jane, remembered him as someone who always tried to bring cheer into others' lives, although his own seemed touched with melancholy. "He had a little bit of a gloomy side to him," she said. "He was very emotional and he would cry sometimes at unexpected moments."

After only two months in Saigon, Nolting was the target of a VC assassination attempt as he was chauffeured back to the embassy after lunch at home. Two youths on a motorbike pulled alongside his Mercury sedan at a busy intersection and tossed a homemade bomb into the back seat. "I threw it out while it was still sputtering," Nolting recalled. He jumped out of the car, yelling at nearby schoolchildren to run, while his "damn-fool bodyguard" fired his gun at the fleeing terrorists in a crowded area. Nolting then picked up the explosive device and heaved it farther away; it failed to detonate. He ordered his guard to stop shooting and realized he was "shaking like a leaf."

The ambassador reported the incident to the State Department, asking that no fuss be made and saying of himself and his Saigon colleagues: "We here are unanimous on the proposition that we will not be bluffed, or terrorized, out of the necessary work to be done here." Nolting and Harkins both received so many death threats that they turned them into a black-humor game, keeping weekly scorecards.

THE SCION OF AN old-line Virginia family that lost much of its wealth in the Depression, Nolting obtained a bachelor's degree in history from the University of Virginia in 1933. For the next five years he worked at his father's investment firm, selling municipal bonds and trying to help some of his dad's clients who lost money in the 1929 crash. He then returned to UVA, earning a master's degree in philosophy in 1940. The following year he was awarded a second master's in the same subject at Harvard, where he took classes from the famed British philosopher and social critic Bertrand Russell.

After the Japanese attacked Pearl Harbor, Nolting entered the Navy as a lieutenant junior grade and trained as a gunnery officer. He subsequently commanded an antiaircraft gun crew aboard a Liberty ship, the SS *Roger Williams*, which participated in Operation Dragoon, the allied invasion of southern France in August 1944. During an hour-long air attack off Algiers, Nolting's twenty-six-man crew shot down an enemy plane. "Lt. Nolting is cool under fire, efficient, and conscientious," the ship's master wrote. "As the only Naval officer aboard, Lt. Nolting is a real credit to the Navy." Nolting left the Navy in 1946 with two Bronze Stars and the rank of lieutenant commander.

He joined the State Department that same year and worked as a special assistant to two formidable secretaries of state, Dean Acheson and John Foster Dulles, acquiring a reputation as a comer. Nolting and his wife also bought Sully, a sixty-five-acre former plantation and manor house in Chantilly, Virginia, where he reveled in tending his hayfields and a small cattle herd in his off-hours. In 1955, he was posted to Paris as a member of the U.S. Mission to NATO, eventually rising to deputy chief.

Nolting moved past many of his contemporaries on the career ladder and, in 1961, Kennedy's secretary of state, Dean Rusk, selected him for the South Vietnam ambassadorship. His predecessor in Saigon, the dyspeptic Elbridge Durbrow, had played bad cop with Diem, making so many hard-nosed demands for reform of South Vietnam's increasingly unpopular government that Diem came close to banning him from Independence Palace. Kennedy told Nolting to take the opposite tack, offering friendly counsel and easing the tensions stirred by Durbrow's table pounding.

Not long after Nolting took over in Saigon, Diem requested American help against the VC, who were killing government officials by the hundreds in the countryside. Nolting accepted the Saigon job on condition that he be brought home after two years, so his younger girls could live stateside again. Rusk agreed, observing that South Vietnam was so close to collapse that Nolting would probably find himself back home in six months.

Nolting had no special qualifications for the Saigon assignment. He didn't speak Vietnamese and had never been to the country. Other than briefings in Washington and some hasty reading, he knew little about Vietnam's politics, culture, and history, much less about communist revolutionary warfare and how to counteract it.

To help him in Saigon he brought along a State Department colleague, William Trueheart, as his chief deputy. The two men had known each other for most of their lives and attended the University of Virginia together. (Trueheart, too, studied philosophy.) Trueheart had been in Nolting's wedding party, and the ambassador was the godfather to Trueheart's two young sons. But what Trueheart called "this beautiful friendship" would be ruined in the coming months as the Kennedy administration abruptly turned against Diem, putting the two old friends at bitter odds.

Nolting loved being Kennedy's emissary in Saigon—he called it the most exciting and gratifying job he ever had. He was "100 percent in favor" of American intervention in South Vietnam. He didn't think the struggle with the Viet Cong could be won by purely military means; instead, Washington and Saigon would have to employ a range of military, political, economic, social, "and above all, moral" tactics to win.

While Washington had been pressuring Diem for years to democratize and decentralize his government, Nolting believed any progress South Vietnam made would come slowly. The country had never had a democratic form of government and to expect one to develop in a short period, he believed, was unrealistic. Nolting thought Diem wanted to foster democracy in the long run, and had taken some steps in that direction, but the United States shouldn't expect much more from an underdeveloped nation embroiled in an existential war. Building South Vietnam into a strong, independent state would take years, perhaps decades, and Nolting wondered if Congress, the press, and the American people had that much patience and perseverance.

NOLTING RAN INTO HIS first bureaucratic crisis in Saigon toward the end of 1961. The Pentagon was creating a new organization—Military Assistance Command, Vietnam, or MACV—to oversee the rapid influx of U.S. military men and matériel. General Harkins was put in charge. He was awarded a fourth star, giving him essentially the same rank in the military as Nolting held in the State Department.

Nolting and Trueheart worried that the advent of MACV meant that military aspects of the war would be emphasized at the expense of political and economic aspects, a concern that proved to be well-founded. Nolting was so upset about the formation of MACV that Trueheart thought he'd resign. But it turned out that the ambassador and Harkins got along splendidly, having few disagreements, and Nolting put his qualms aside.

Through MACV the Kennedy administration sharply ramped up its support for Diem in spite of his poor reputation among many U.S. diplomats and military officials who'd dealt with him in the past.

Since Diem became prime minister in 1954, he'd been the target of complaints that he was a dictator who used police-state methods to control his people; routinely ignored U.S. advice intended to make his government more effective; meddled in his army's operations for political reasons; and was congenitally unable to delegate authority (to the point that he personally reviewed passport applications). Critics viewed him as almost irrationally suspicious, ever more remote from his people, and increasingly dependent for political guidance on his family, especially his widely disliked brother Nhu and his adder-tongued wife, Madame Nhu.

Two weeks into his tenure, Nolting got an opportunity to size up Diem for himself. The ambassador and his family were invited to join the president at his villa in Dalat, a tranquil resort town set amid cool, fragrant pine forests in the Central Highlands that attracted those seeking to escape Saigon's brutal heat and humidity. Diem was there along with Madame Nhu and her four children. (Nhu was off on a hunting trip.)

One of Diem's quirks was his staggering verbosity. He was infamous among foreign diplomats and journalists for talking for hours on end, leaving his listeners, barely able to get a word in, on the verge of unconsciousness in the stuffy warmth of Independence Palace. Some Americans speculated that these verbal marathons were Diem's way of holding off uncomfortable questions from visitors. But one U.S. official who knew him well believed Diem was trying to educate Americans, whom he felt knew far too little about his country. Diem's first session with Nolting was no exception, as he launched into a monologue that lasted six hours.

Nolting found Diem's words fascinating. The South Vietnamese leader walked the U.S. ambassador through his country's long history, starting with ancient times and the turbulent one thousand years of Chinese rule. He talked of the French colonial era, lasting nearly a century, and the savage eight-year war between France and the communist-led Viet Minh, forerunners of the Viet Cong, who finally defeated French troops at Dien Bien Phu.

Diem also explained South Vietnam's different ethnic groups and their problems, and how North Vietnam, under the communist leader Ho Chi Minh, had covertly boosted its military aid to the VC, infiltrating weapons, supplies, and trained men into the south. Diem and Nolting conversed in French, chain-smoking and drinking endless cups of tepid tea. Despite his reputation for ceaseless verbiage, Diem stopped often to answer the ambassador's questions and occasionally laughed at himself.

Nolting began to form an impression of the talkative president as an extraordinary person, courageous and utterly dedicated to preserving and strengthening his tormented land. When the men finally finished, Madame Nhu's nine-year-old son entertained Nolting and his family by playing Mozart on the piano.

After the Dalat weekend, Nolting began to accompany Diem on his frequent trips to rural areas. They'd board an airplane or helicopter, usually around 5 a.m., and take off for some provincial capital, army post, or obscure village. The destinations were sometimes so remote that the last leg of a trip had to be made on foot or in a small boat.

Diem ran Nolting ragged, making two or three such expeditions each week. They traveled to the VC-infested Camau Peninsula at the country's southern tip, where most of the charcoal for South Vietnamese cook pots came from; the tense demilitarized zone; and the Central Highlands, where primitive tribesmen known as Montagnards (French for *mountaineers*) still hunted with bows and arrows.

Diem had served as a province chief in the 1920s and early 1930s, and was intensely interested in rural problems. He enjoyed meeting farmers and villagers and discussing their needs and concerns: land rents, water supplies, availability of seeds and fertilizer, condition of local roads and canals. He was a fountain of ideas for improvement and was especially proud of his government's agricultural stations, which taught peasants how to raise fruit and nut trees, build fishponds, and grow mushrooms in stacks of rice straw.

Diem didn't perform well as a speaker before large crowds. But Nolting saw that he was very effective with small groups of peasants, informal and sympathetic, listening to complaints and often settling disputes on the spot. He bowed politely to his constituents, rather than shaking hands or slapping backs as an American politician would, and complained of the elaborate ceremonies and dinners put on for him by fawning local officials.

"There was a real rapport and mutual respect between President Diem and the large majority of the rural people," Nolting later wrote. "Unfortunately, this was not true of the 'intellectuals' of Saigon. Maybe that's why Diem was always eager to visit the countryside."

DESPITE THEIR VERY DIFFERENT backgrounds, the genteel Virginian and the loquacious Asian head of state had much in common and got along famously. Both were well educated, devoted to public service, and deeply interested in philosophy, religion, and all things farm-related. Nolting's daughter Jane described them as "really, really, really soulmates," adding: "It was a surprise to both of them, I'm sure."

The ambassador made a point of also getting to know Nhu, who, as Diem's closest confidant and chief political counselor (underlings addressed him as "Monsieur le Conseiller"), was the second most powerful man in South Vietnam. Nolting and Nhu immersed themselves in lengthy discussions of existentialism and the philosopher Immanuel Kant, and Nhu invited the American on a tiger hunt.

Tigers are nocturnal and hunters typically pursued them at night. Donning a miner's helmet with a headlamp, Nolting ventured into the mountains with Nhu, an avid hunter and an excellent shot. They walked for hours through the pitch-blackness, identifying different animals by the color their eyes reflected: yellowish for a deer or water buffalo; reddish for a tiger. Together, they bagged a couple of deer, a bobcat, and a "large skunk-like animal," but no tigers. At the end of the hunt, they stretched out on blankets, and Nhu, almost as garrulous as his older brother, outlined his vision for South Vietnam at length.

Thrilled by the excursion, Nolting told his family all about it. "He came back very excited about going out into the woods at night," recalled Jane. "He took it like any gentleman would take an exciting adventure."

In 1962, Nolting's mother died in a Virginia hospital before he was able to get home to her. Hearing the news, Diem showed up at the ambassador's residence, alone and wearing a black suit of mourning. Nolting's wife quietly withdrew as the two men sat in the living room, saying nothing for a long time. Diem looked genuinely grief-stricken, and Nolting was touched by his empathic presence.

By then, Nolting was firmly in Diem's corner. He liked and admired the determined president, and became Diem's strongest advocate within the U.S. government. Diem had his flaws, the ambassador knew: He was a proud and overly sensitive man with a messianic belief in his ability to govern his country better than anyone else (a conviction Nolting felt wasn't entirely unjustified). He was unbelievably long-winded and had no earthly idea of how to deal with American newsmen, resulting in many unflattering news stories. With his unwavering faith in his own talents and innate suspiciousness toward subordinates, Diem refused to hand much authority to others, making his government rigidly centralized and inefficient.

Yet Nolting also viewed Diem as a man of great integrity, passionately devoted to the cause of a free Vietnam. As far as the ambassador could tell, he was the only South Vietnamese political figure capable of winning the war against the VC. If he was an authoritarian, he was a benevolent one who cared deeply about his people's welfare. He never acted out of cruelty or venality. He agonized over decisions he had to make, always searching for the moral rather than the expedient course, and didn't even seem to enjoy the exercise of power. He once told Nolting his dream had been to become a Catholic monk; he'd gone into politics only because he believed his country needed him.

Kennedy had asked Nolting to evaluate whether Diem was someone Washington could work with and, in a July 1961 cable, the ambassador returned his verdict: the U.S. government should back the doughty South Vietnamese leader "to the hilt." Diem and Nhu, in turn, had high regard for the American emissary. As Nhu told a U.S. newsman at a cocktail party: "Your ambassador is the first one who has ever understood us."

Diem's gravest problem, as Nolting saw it, was trying to foster democracy in an Asian peasant society with no real experience of representative government. South Vietnam had a constitution, a National Assembly, and a court system, but these institutions had only existed since the mid-1950s and were far from strong or independent enough to support a vigorous democratic process in the Western sense.

In cable after cable, Washington instructed Nolting to prod Diem to broaden his government, to bring in other respected figures who could enhance his standing with his people. But the ambassador discovered that many South Vietnamese who could fill such a role—lawyers, doctors, academics, businessmen—held Diem in contempt. They attacked him in letters to Saigon newspapers and in café conversations with American journalists. To Nolting, they seemed like an unusually cliquish group; many had been trained in Paris and lorded their advanced degrees over those with less education. Nolting felt they should put their talents to use helping their president instead of sniping at him. When Diem asked if he knew anyone who'd be a good addition to his government, the American produced a list of names. Diem read it and said, "If you can persuade any of these people to serve, I would be delighted to have them in my government."

The ambassador approached every person on his list, but all of them turned him down. Several said they wouldn't work under Diem, since he wasn't as well educated as them or had ranked lower in school. One man said he'd serve only if he were appointed minister of the interior, with complete control of the police and no interference from Diem. After Nolting reported the results of his survey to Diem, the president said, "You see, that is my problem."

The ambassador told friends that when he pestered Diem to make all the changes that Washington constantly demanded, amid a dangerous war, he felt like a surgeon trying to perform an appendectomy on a man carrying a heavy trunk up a staircase.

NOLTING KEPT TRYING NEVERTHELESS. Day after day, month after month, he met with Diem or members of his government, pressing for improvements that Washington wanted in exchange for its military and economic aid. Nolting was soft spoken, but made his points forcefully when necessary. And he scored some victories. For instance, after many delays, the Saigon government in April 1963 launched a U.S.-recommended amnesty program for VC fighters, calling it *Chieu Hoi*, or "Open Arms." The number of VC defections rose, and some high-ranking guerrilla officers crossed over to the government side.

But Diem had his own ideas about how much influence Washington should have in his country, and he was mulishly resistant to many American wishes.

His compulsion to keep the United States at arm's length was rooted in his personal history. Much of his adult life had been devoted to getting the French out of Vietnam and guiding his country to independence. The last remnants of the French Expeditionary Corps had hauled down the Tricolor and departed in 1956, but Diem remained highly sensitive to even the appearance of foreign domination.

The main VC propaganda line against him, in fact, was that the French colonialists had simply been replaced by American neocolonialists, and that Diem was America's puppet. In order to deflect such broadsides, Diem often rejected Washington's demands for reforms even as he accepted more U.S. advisers and aid dollars. (One astute observer described him as a puppet who pulled his own strings.) But the more American aid Diem took, the more the VC attacked him as Washington's lackey, labeling him *My-Diem*, meaning "American Diem."

The touchy issue of South Vietnamese sovereignty erupted into the open in May 1963, when *The Washington Post* ran a front-page interview with Nhu in which the political counselor made the startling statement that American personnel in South Vietnam should be cut by 50 percent. Diem and Nhu had been desperate for U.S. help in 1961, when the Viet Cong were threatening to overwhelm them. But they grew steadily less happy as more Americans streamed in. "If you bring in the American dog," Diem groused to a journalist, "you must accept American fleas." Now, nearly two years after their SOS, the brothers believed they were winning the war and the Americans had become a serious political irritant.

Indeed, U.S. advisers had injected themselves into all manner of South Vietnamese public and private activities, including radio broadcasting, harbor management, air traffic control, taxation, highway construction, and industrial development. On top of that, American military advisers were sprinkled throughout the South Vietnamese army, from corps level down to company level. U.S. advisers also worked with each of the country's forty-one province chiefs, helping them deploy Civil Guard and village militia units, which were suffering the heaviest casualties against the VC. Both the State Department and the CIA had Vietnamese-speaking agents circulating about the country, picking up political and economic intelligence.

Yet another group of Americans was assisting the strategic hamlet program.

Most of them were young men handling an array of tasks with imagination and verve for the U.S. Operations Mission, the embassy's economic aid arm. Under the hard-driving, idealistic leadership of Rufus Phillips, a former Yale football player and ex–CIA agent, the USOM men helped rural people build schools, roads, bridges, pigpens, fishponds, and other facilities. They gave farmers faster-growing varieties of rice along with seed and fertilizers for fruit and vegetable crops.

Their main job was to check on the progress of strategic hamlet construction. Since some provinces had hundreds of hamlets, the USOM agents were frequently on the road, often traveling through VC-dominated areas. They were shot at and had narrow escapes as mines blew up vehicles in government convoys.

Diem and Nhu had long been suspicious of American intentions, and the rising numbers of U.S. military advisers, civilian technicians, and rural aid workers did nothing to allay their misgivings. They worried that the ever-expanding network of Americans throughout their government and military could one day be used to unseat them.

The South Vietnamese president complained to Nolting that Washington was trying to take over his government and turn the country into a "protectorate," just as the French had. In some provinces, the peasants thought the energetic Americans actually *were* the government. Since Americans usually controlled the money, materials, and equipment for backcountry improvement projects, Diem said, his officials felt as inferior as they had under the French, who rarely allowed the Vietnamese to rise much beyond low-level fonctionnaire positions in the colonial civil service.

WHAT GAVE DIEM AND Nhu the most pause was the U.S. Special Forces teams training and arming Montagnards in remote parts of the Central Highlands.

The nomadic tribes were descendants of some of the earliest peoples to occupy the region that later became Vietnam, Laos, and Cambodia. Primitive and superstitious, they'd wandered their homelands in the mountains and high plateaus for centuries, slashing and burning patches of forest or jungle to plant their rice, and moving on when the soil wore out. About 700,000 Montagnards in South Vietnam were divided into numerous tribes. Although they constituted only 5 percent of the country's population, their traditional lands covered 60 percent of its territory.

The tribal people staged thundering elephant races and loved to drink a potent, sour-tasting wine made from rice. Visitors to their villages were met with great hospitality and handed bamboo straws through which to drink the wine from large earthen jugs. Besides farming, tribal people hunted game with crossbows and blowguns.

Ethnic Vietnamese, living mostly in lowlands along the central coast or in the Mekong Delta, feared the highland regions, associating them with disease, wild animals, and evil spirits. The Vietnamese had nothing in common with the darker-skinned highland nomads and referred to them as *moi*, or savages. The mountain people reciprocated the disdain in full.

As exploitative as they were of the Vietnamese, the French had treated the Montagnards with paternalism and protectiveness. They designated tribal areas as autonomous regions, relatively free of central government control. When Diem took over, he tried to reach out to the tribes, a potential strategic asset in the war against the VC. The mountaineers were tough, wily fighters completely at ease in their rugged territories, some of which straddled communist infiltration routes. Diem granted tribal people South Vietnamese citizenship and eliminated the word *moi* from official documents, replacing it with *compatriotes montagnards* ("mountain compatriots"). But his government also made some serious missteps with them, such as banning their traditional crossbows.

The mountain dwellers didn't like the Viet Cong any more than they did the South Vietnamese; both groups were, after all, Vietnamese. But with VC guerrillas forcibly taking their food and livestock, and sometimes using them as slave labor, thousands of tribespeople abandoned their lands for government-controlled zones, often burning their crops and killing their animals to deny them to the communists.

By mid-1962, U.S. Special Forces had trained and armed 35,000 members of the Rhade tribe. American soldiers got along well with the highland dwellers, giving them medical care and helping with construction projects. But Saigon feared the possible consequences of arming the tribesmen, who wanted autonomy from the South Vietnamese government, and worried that it would be difficult to take U.S.-supplied weapons away from them.

"The Americans," complained one of Diem's generals, "have put an army at my back."

Diem assigned the head of his own Special Forces to spy on the American soldiers despite repeated U.S. assurances that they weren't inciting tribespeople to rebel. But, as a State Department expert pointed out, the training program was undermined by "the general Vietnamese tendency to regard the Montagnards as somewhat less than human." Tensions between the South Vietnamese and the Rhade would boil over into a deadly tribal uprising in 1964.

Diem and Nhu acknowledged that U.S. personnel, military and civilian, often spurred their own officials to work harder and achieve more. But the Americans also reported instances of corruption or abusive treatment of peasants that they witnessed, generating hostility from the accused Vietnamese officials.

One USOM worker, for example, stopped to gas his car near a bus station in Binh Dinh Province on the central coast. He saw people standing in lines to buy tickets. South Vietnamese soldiers kept cutting to the front of the lines, shoving the civilians out of their way and into the mud. "Civilian reaction was one of obvious hate," the American reported.

Farther on, he saw a blind beggar woman being led by a child. "When she approached soldiers waiting to board a bus," the aid worker observed, "one of them pushed her down into the mud, actually knocking her down; the other soldiers around him laughed at this." Again, onlookers glared angrily at the soldiers. Such incidents undercut support for the Diem regime in the countryside, and Americans urged the president over and over to restrain his soldiers and petty officials from physically abusing rural people, extorting money from them, or forcing them to work on public works projects without pay.

Nhu's griping in *The Washington Post* about the number of Americans in his country provoked a predictable uproar in Congress and the U.S. press. A State Department official characterized his remarks as "incomprehensible," and Nolting was instructed to have Diem muzzle his brother. Nhu's infelicitous comments heightened Kennedy's fear that such outbursts would damage his Vietnam policy in the eyes of Congress and the American public. (He told a press conference he'd be happy to pull some advisers out of South Vietnam the day after Diem's government made an official request.)

But the controversy illustrated how U.S. policy had unintentionally sucked Diem into a vicious cycle. The can-do Americans wanted more leverage over Diem's government and his conduct of the war in exchange for their burgeoning assistance programs, which cost $1 million per day. Diem took the aid, knowing that he lost a little more face with his own people every time another American stepped off a jet at Tan Son Nhut airport. As North Vietnam's premier, Pham Van Dong, concisely explained to an interviewer:

> Monsieur Diem's position is quite difficult. He is unpopular, and the more unpopular he is, the more American aid he will require to stay in power. And the more American aid he receives, the more he will look like the puppet of the Americans, and the less likely he is to win popular support.

ALTHOUGH NOLTING WAS CONVINCED that U.S. policies were working, some of his colleagues, in both Saigon and Washington, worried that Diem's ongoing refusal to overhaul his government was weakening the war effort. They were also beginning to view the low-key, gentlemanly ambassador as part of the problem.

Despite Washington's demands for reform, the regime's repressive grip was as tight as ever. Saigon newspapers labored under heavy censorship. Diem had imprisoned or forced into exile many of his noncommunist political opponents, and his secret police inspired terror among the populace. Nevertheless, Nolting kept up his nonstop defense of Diem. To the ambassador's critics, his seemingly blind loyalty indicated that he'd become an apologist for the South Vietnamese leader and was no longer properly representing U.S. interests.

Nolting certainly was doing everything he could to protect his friend at

Independence Palace. He felt that while Diem's government was improving, it remained shaky and that criticism, especially by Americans, only made it more vulnerable to the communists.

At one point, the ambassador learned that the chief of the USOM Public Safety Division, Frank Walton, had privately told a group of people in Washington that "things are going very badly" in Vietnam. Under Walton, an able former deputy chief of the Los Angeles Police Department, the Public Safety Division trained South Vietnamese police and militiamen. He'd told his Washington audience, among other things, that he was troubled by the use of U.S.-made napalm in bombing attacks, which often killed innocent peasants and created new VC recruits in the countryside. Incredulous at Walton's blunt remarks, Nolting wanted him removed, but a State Department superior told him to leave Walton alone.

The ambassador also tried to keep under wraps a forthcoming U.S. Governmental Accountability Office report that was "severely critical" of American aid programs in South Vietnam and certain "personalities" in Diem's government—a clear reference to Nhu and his wife. The GAO also suggested that Saigon hadn't acted in good faith in negotiations with Washington.

Nolting warned that if released publicly, the report would erode U.S. public support for the regime and generate more coup plots against Diem. (The State Department replied that it would try to classify sections of the report unflattering to the South Vietnamese leader.)

And when the CIA discovered that someone in Diem's government was planning to assassinate him, Nolting told the agency to pass its information along to the president. Diem swiftly arrested twenty army officers he believed were involved in the plot.

Although Secretary of State Rusk had recently praised Nolting, telling him in a letter to "keep up the good work," the ambassador sensed that unseen forces in Washington were lining up against him.

Chatting with a young embassy officer, Nolting said cryptically that "he had enemies in Washington who would use anything to get him." Nolting's instructions to build a "bridge of confidence" to Diem hadn't changed. He started to feel, however, that Kennedy administration officials were growing impatient with both Diem and U.S. diplomats still trying to carry out the policy of mutual trust and collaboration.

Nolting also became aware that some of his own subordinates in Saigon were criticizing his kid-glove handling of Diem in surreptitious telegrams to Washington. One day he had an unpleasant conversation with John Anspacher, a public affairs officer with the U.S. Information Service.

Anspacher believed that rather than acting as a bulldog for Washington, Nolting had become a lapdog for Diem. "Every time he went over to the palace, he was given a shopping list and he never argued about it," Anspacher said. "He never tried to tell Diem what was right and what was wrong." Anspacher had begun to think the United States wasn't fighting the Viet Cong so much as it was fighting its own ally's chief of state. Anspacher had previously worked under Durbrow, whose hardball approach toward Diem he admired.

Anspacher told Nolting he'd recently attended a dinner at which some prominent South Vietnamese complained that things in their country were going from bad to worse. They wanted Nolting to take a tougher stance with Diem, but said they couldn't get an appointment to speak with the ambassador. Anspacher described the Vietnamese critics as "the loyal opposition" and urged Nolting to meet with them. But Nolting refused, saying, "The president wouldn't like it." Anspacher asked which president he was referring to; Nolting said President Diem. Anspacher then snapped: "Mr. Ambassador, you don't work for President Diem. It doesn't make any difference whether he likes it or not. What matters is the president you work for: Kennedy."

Anspacher felt so strongly about the matter that he quietly met in Washington with several others from the Saigon embassy staff, including the chief political counselor, Joseph Mendenhall, who also thought Nolting was too accommodating. The group went to the White House and grumbled to Walt Rostow, Kennedy's deputy national security assistant.

But Nolting had far more influential detractors than Anspacher. One was Michael Forrestal, a member of Kennedy's National Security Council staff who functioned as his point man on Vietnam.

"Ambassador Nolting had gotten himself into a deeply unfortunate position of being so thoroughly identified with the Diem regime that he had lost his capacity to influence President Diem," Forrestal recalled. "A number of people from Washington had gone over to Saigon . . . and had observed Nolting with Diem. It was quite clear that Nolting respected Diem, but the reverse wasn't true. And you had a very strong impression that our ambassador had gotten himself to the point where Diem no longer really believed or took seriously what he said."

The ambassador began to feel a distinct shift in the Washington policy winds in March 1963, when the man who'd soon become his most vehement disparager, Averell Harriman, was appointed Kennedy's undersecretary of state for political affairs, the State Department's number three job. Harriman and Nolting had locked horns before, and within a few months they'd be engaged in one of the fiercest, most consequential bureaucratic struggles of the Vietnam War.

THE SON OF A ruthless railroad baron, Averell Harriman had enjoyed a colorful and highly successful career as an international businessman, diplomat, and politician.

As a younger man, he bought steel mills in Poland and manganese mines in Soviet Georgia, and controlled one of the largest steamship fleets in the world. Bold, hugely ambitious, and a canny negotiator, he helped create the aviation conglomerate that spawned Pan American Airways and American Airlines. By age thirty two, he sat on the boards of fifty-four corporations.

As his wealth burgeoned in the high-flying 1920s, Harriman became a polo fanatic, touring California clubs and becoming one of the country's top players. Though humorless and parsimonious in the way very rich people sometimes are, he acquired a reputation as a playboy, aided by his raven hair, athletic good looks, and seemingly permanent tan.

He switched to the Democratic Party in 1932 and worked for President Roosevelt's National Recovery Administration. After the United States entered World War II, FDR tapped him to expedite the shipment of American war matériel to beleaguered Britain and the Soviet Union under the Lend-Lease program. Harriman haggled with Stalin and played bezique with Churchill.

In 1943, FDR appointed him ambassador to the Soviet Union and he attended most of the Allies' wartime conferences. In 1946, he served as ambassador to Britain for about six months before President Harry Truman named him secretary of commerce. Harriman went to Paris in 1948 as supervisor of the Marshall Plan, which channeled billions of dollars into rebuilding the war-shattered cities and industries of Western Europe.

He was elected governor of New York in 1954, but ousted after one term by Republican Nelson Rockefeller in a landslide defeat that left him deeply embittered. Blaming others for his loss, Harriman "was like a wounded animal," recalled one friend, "flailing, snarling, snapping at everybody." He'd hoped to become president one day, but failed to win the Democratic nomination in 1952 and again in 1956.

Always drawn to power, Harriman anxiously courted JFK during and after the 1960 presidential campaign, but was given a position in the new administration—ambassador-at-large—somewhat below his station as a Democratic eminence. Despite passing him over for a more prominent role in his State Department, Kennedy valued Harriman's long track record of negotiating with foreign heads of state, numerous contacts in the Soviet Union and around the world, and adroitness at dealing with the press. Soon Harriman was assigned to resolve one of Kennedy's most pressing foreign policy crises: the dangerous little war in Laos, a picture-book land of elephants, peaceful farmers, and cloud-piercing mountains.

President Dwight Eisenhower's administration had tried to create a pro-U.S. bastion there by backing a right-wing general, Phoumi Nosavan, against communist Pathet Lao guerrillas and North Vietnamese troops. While Phoumi's U.S.-equipped forces held parts of southern Laos, the Pathet Lao controlled much of the northern and eastern parts of the country. Phoumi, however, proved to be a particularly inept military leader, and the communists made steady inroads into his territory.

Eisenhower had warned Kennedy that the fall of Laos would mean the collapse of all of Southeast Asia, and urged him to dispatch American troops if necessary to hold it. (Eisenhower popularized the "domino theory" that if one Southeast Asian nation fell to communist domination, others inevitably would topple as well.) But Kennedy viewed landlocked Laos as a difficult and dangerous place to wage war, far from American naval and air power and wedged between North Vietnam and China, both of which could easily funnel more troops into the fray. Kennedy instead wanted a ceasefire followed by international negotiations to form a coalition government that would include representatives of Phoumi, the Pathet Lao, and Souvanna Phouma, a longtime neutralist leader.

Kennedy handed Harriman the difficult task of hammering out a deal. The indefatigable ambassador-at-large traveled thousands of miles and knocked heads in a variety of foreign capitals in an aggressive effort to forge an agreement that would relieve the pressure on Kennedy to take military action.

In September 1961, Harriman flew to Saigon to persuade Diem to sign on. But the South Vietnamese leader balked, worrying that a coalition government in Laos would do nothing to stop Hanoi from infiltrating soldiers and supplies into his country over what Americans would come to know as the Ho Chi Minh Trail. Then little more than a skein of primitive footpaths, the trail ran through tall, jungled mountains and steep ravines in eastern Laos—territory firmly held by communist forces. Diem also was concerned that creating a coalition government in Laos would cause the Americans to push for a similar arrangement for South Vietnam, which he felt would lead inevitably to a communist takeover.

Convening with Harriman in a small, overheated room at his palace, Diem, as usual, spoke at almost interminable length, going back to his experiences with Ho Chi Minh's communists in the 1930s, and their history of bad faith and broken promises. Diem didn't trust them to abide by a key requirement of Harriman's deal: withdrawal of all foreign troops from Laos.

Harriman wore a hearing aid and had the churlish habit of ostentatiously turning it off when he was bored by something an underling was telling him. As Diem droned on, Harriman clicked off his earpiece, closed his eyes, and appeared to fall asleep.

Diem noticed Harriman's inattention with annoyance, but kept talking. Nolting, sitting next to Harriman on a sofa, nudged him. Harriman suddenly snapped into action, saying the Soviets had assured him that all of the communist parties to the covenant, including the North Vietnamese, would adhere to its terms. Although it's not clear whether he was authorized to do so, Harriman added a harrowing threat: "If you do not sign this treaty, you will lose American support. You have to choose."

Both Diem and Nolting viewed the Laos agreement as unenforceable, setting off what Nolting described as several "rather hot and heavy" confrontations between him and Harriman. When Harriman said he had a "fingertips feeling" that the Soviets would adequately police the pact, Nolting retorted that his fingertips told him just the opposite.

Nolting eventually knuckled under, against his better judgment, and urged Diem to sign in order not to lose Kennedy's backing. The U.S. president badly wanted a coalition, or neutral government, and Harriman was determined to get it at all costs. The encounter left bad blood all around. Harriman himself had doubts about his "good bad deal," which turned out to be simply bad.

SIGNED IN JULY 1962 at Geneva, the Declaration on the Neutrality of Laos began to fall apart almost immediately.

Diem and Nolting's fears of communist perfidy were borne out in full. While the United States pulled its 666 military advisers out of Laos, and halted CIA weapons drops to Hmong tribesmen bravely fighting the communists, the North Vietnamese kept virtually all of their estimated 10,000 soldiers in Laos, ensuring Hanoi's continued mastery of infiltration routes in the eastern portion of the country. Nolting allowed himself a measure of grim satisfaction when American military officers began referring to the Ho Chi Minh Trail as the "Averell Harriman Memorial Highway." In coming years, the North Vietnamese would improve and widen the trail system to such a degree that their tanks were able to drive down it en route to final victory over South Vietnam's army in 1975.

The Geneva agreement did, however, permit Kennedy to back away from the Laos conflict without committing U.S. combat forces, and Harriman's star rose in the administration.

His appointment as undersecretary for political affairs made him one of the most powerful figures in the State Department. His hearing-aid antics amused Kennedy, and the seventy-one-year-old Harriman acquired the nickname "the Crocodile" due to his penchant for figuratively biting the heads off staffers who weren't prepared to answer his rapid-fire questions. Harriman loved the nickname, which made him seem tough to the dynamic men around Kennedy, many of them decades younger than him, and he proudly displayed a small brass crocodile on his desk. An aura of action and excitement surrounded him, and he attracted a circle of devotees.

In February 1963, Harriman wrote Nolting a letter questioning whether he'd cultivated enough relationships with Diem's noncommunist political opponents as a way of gaining leverage on him. Harriman said working with oppositionists would give Washington more options in the event of an anti-Diem coup or other change of government. Nolting reacted with ill-concealed irritation. "I must confess to being somewhat astonished by the implication that we are living in cocoons here," he wrote back. The embassy was in contact with dozens of dissidents, he wrote, including bankers, doctors, labor leaders, lawyers, and professors.

But Nolting warned that giving too much encouragement to Diem's political enemies could stimulate his overthrow. The ambassador added pointedly that he "would not find it possible to be an agent in a change in U.S. policy away from forthright support" of Diem and his government.

Harriman also was apprehensive about the increasingly tense relationship between the embassy and the small group of American journalists in Saigon. The Kennedy administration was taking a beating in the press as Diem refused to reform, the VC intensified their attacks, and casualties among American servicemen rose. Nolting's own press officer characterized the embassy's relations with American reporters as "indescribably bad."

Nolting admitted that the growing animus between the embassy and newsmen was the "Achilles heel of our operation here." But he complained in another letter to Harriman that journalists were only interested in covering the war effort and its problems, and usually ignored "good news" stories like the opening of a new school or hospital wing in the provinces.

He spoke often to reporters, he wrote, trying to convince them to give Diem the benefit of the doubt instead of writing up every stumble by his government and army. They ignored his pleas, relentlessly criticizing the South Vietnamese leader and complicating U.S. relations with him and his government. Journalists "caused me great alarm and pain," Nolting grumbled. "They were undermining the thing all the time, constantly."

The ambassador never seemed to grasp that while it might be his job to succor Diem, it wasn't the newsmen's; their job was to inform their readers back home whether American policies in Vietnam were working or not. "Fritz Nolting is one of the finest human beings I've ever met," one of his aides later reflected, "but he didn't have the foggiest idea of how to deal with the press." In a bid to end-run the obstreperous press pack in Saigon, Nolting proposed coming home for several weeks so he could give speeches and confer with newspaper publishers and top editors in the United States. But Harriman said no; the ambassador had too much to do in Saigon.

HIS MOST IMMEDIATE TASK was to contain the widening ripples from the Hue massacre. The State Department worried that Diem would lash out with draconian action against the Buddhists, making matters worse. Nolting delayed his vacation for a couple of weeks, hoping he could nudge Diem toward conciliation. To publicize their claims of government persecution, the Buddhists planned to stage demonstrations in Saigon and Hue; violence could easily flare.

Diem met with Buddhist leaders on May 15, but didn't give much ground. Buddhists and Catholics were both guilty of "disorderly use" of religious flags, he told his visitors. He refused to discipline any government officials over the killings or stop arresting Buddhist protesters in Hue, saying "subversive elements" could take advantage of any suspension of police action. When the Buddhists asked him to guarantee that they could freely practice their beliefs, he called them "damn fools" for not knowing that freedom of religion was enshrined in South Vietnam's constitution.

Three days later, Nolting discussed the Buddhists with Diem for two hours. The ambassador urged him to make a clear-cut public statement that his security forces were to blame for the massacre. Diem refused. He was convinced, he told Nolting, that the VC or other agitators had thrown explosives that killed the protesters, and that Buddhist leaders in Hue had provoked the entire incident.

Nolting found Diem's attitude troubling but understandable: He was trying to avoid doing something that might make him look weak. But his regime was moving too slowly and grudgingly to defuse the situation, which Diem seemed to take far less seriously than the U.S. embassy did. Nolting told the president he hoped he wasn't underestimating his people's anger over the Hue deaths.

On May 21, about four hundred monks marched from Cholon, Saigon's Chinatown, to Xa Loi Pagoda, a few blocks from Diem's palace, to commemorate the Hue massacre. Xa Loi, the city's biggest temple, was now the buzzing headquarters for Buddhist organizing activities. A police jeep led the monks' procession and numerous unarmed cops were in evidence along the route. There was "commendable restraint on both sides," Nolting cabled Washington, and no one was hurt or arrested.

Nolting felt the situation had calmed down enough that he and his family could safely leave on their vacation. But his wife, Lindsay, was uneasy.

Vietnamese friends kept asking exactly when she and her husband were going and coming back; Lindsay suggested they cruise the Aegean some other time. Her husband dissuaded her, arguing that the tickets were paid for, their two older daughters were already in Greece, and the State Department had cut his travel orders. If anything happened in Saigon, Nolting's good friend and deputy, Trueheart, was to contact him through the U.S. embassy in Athens or anywhere else along his travel route.

Everything was arranged; it was time to go.

The Noltings flew out of Saigon on May 23. Looking back in sorrow on that departure many years later, the ambassador wrote: "I could not have made a worse mistake."

CHAPTER 3

"A BASKET OF CRABS": SAIGON 1954

AMERICANS USUALLY DESCRIBED Diem as short, although, at five feet, four inches tall, he was of average height for a Vietnamese man.

He was stoutly built, with a round, smoothly placid face and "the dreamy eyes of a mystic," in the words of one American. His gleaming black hair was carefully oiled and combed, and he habitually wore a white sharkskin suit with baggy white pants, a style the Vietnamese picked up from the colonial French. He had a rolling, toes-out way of walking, inevitably leading some Americans to refer to him as "the Penguin."

A lifelong bachelor, Diem lived in his lavish palace as austerely as a cloistered monk. He slept on an old army cot in a small room with no air-conditioning. His office was equally spartan—a table and two chairs—and he usually worked there fifteen or sixteen hours a day. His memory was encyclopedic; not only could he reel off the names of dozens of his province chiefs but the names of their fathers and grandfathers as well.

Long pledged to chastity, he was shy and uncomfortable around women. Foreign diplomats and journalists often commented on what they regarded as his humorlessness and lack of personal magnetism. While he usually projected an air of Asian tranquility and self-possession, he was a bundle of nervous energy with an explosive temper. In meetings he often lit one cigarette after another and drummed his fingers. An aide once saw him kick a tray of food out of a servant's hands because it didn't contain exactly what he wanted for lunch.

South Vietnam's leader was an unusual admixture of East and West: a devout Roman Catholic imbued with Confucian ethics ruling a largely Buddhist nation. He made no secret of his Catholicism. He inserted biblical references into speeches and frequently attended Mass at Saigon's great, redbrick Notre Dame Cathedral, sitting not in the regular pews but near the altar, closely following the ceremony as the archbishop bowed toward him. Like many Vietnamese, he also embraced Confucianism, with its emphasis on obedience to family, the immutability of the social and political order, and subordination of individual rights to collective welfare. He proclaimed Confucius's birthday a state holiday and liked to display his knowledge of the ancient Chinese texts that underlay Confucian philosophy, absorbed by the Vietnamese from Chinese conquerors a thousand years earlier.

From an early age, Diem believed he was destined to lead his country and save it from communism (one American journalist called this a "grade-A Messiah complex"). After surviving multiple attempts to overthrow or assassinate him, he was convinced he was God's instrument in Vietnam. Though thoroughly marinated in Vietnamese tradition, Diem wanted to build a modern state as quickly as possible. He was determined to wipe out all traces of colonialism and make rapid improvements in the economy, education system, and agricultural practices.

Born in Hue in 1901, Diem was the son of a mandarin and spent his early years amid the imperial court, luxuriously ensconced in the Citadel. Mandarins were powerful court officials who handled day-to-day matters of the realm. Selected on the basis of competitive exams that tested their knowledge of classical Confucian literature and the Chinese language, they were generally divided into two specialties: those who ran government affairs and those who oversaw military matters. But the French took over the imperial government when they occupied Hue in the late nineteenth century. The emperor and his mandarins were permitted to keep their positions, but lost almost all of their authority.

Diem's father was Ngo Dinh Kha, a respected mandarin-scholar and committed Roman Catholic. Kha raised his six sons and two daughters in an atmosphere of "militant Catholicism," taking them to Mass almost every morning. In the evenings, the children knelt together and said their prayers; their parents then sang them to sleep with the "Ave Maria."

At the time of Diem's birth, Kha served as grand chamberlain to Emperor Thanh Thai, who reigned as a powerless front man while the French governor-general made all important decisions. Kha supervised the imperial household as well as the imperial cavalry. He made daily inspection tours of the Citadel on horseback, cantering through that still-enchanted world with Diem often in tow. The boy was fascinated by the royal stables, elephant barn, and especially a pavilion that housed the royal chariots, elaborately decorated with images of dragons, birds, and turtles. Once used in war, the chariots bore royal parties on tiger hunts. But the Citadel also served as a billet for French soldiers, an ever-present symbol of Vietnamese weakness and humiliation.

The French deposed Thanh Thai in 1907, and later exiled him to Réunion Island in the Indian Ocean. Because he was the only mandarin to oppose the action, Kha went to prison. Released after a long illness, he moved his family to a plot of land he owned in a village outside Hue. Kha began cultivating rice, and Diem and his siblings learned to live with much less than they had at the Citadel.

An unusually studious child, Diem surrounded his cot with "a palisade of all types of books" and read at night by candlelight. Even as a boy he was stubborn and given to emotional outbursts, sometimes screaming at others to get his way. "He had to really pull himself together in order to control his rage," remembered his older brother Thuc, later to become Hue's Catholic archbishop. On the other hand, Diem often made family members laugh with his gift for mimicry.

Kha strove to instill a strong spirit of patriotism in his children, regaling them with stories of Vietnamese heroes of the past. His home was often a gathering place for prominent nationalists—mandarins, provincial officials, and intellectuals—who quietly discussed what could be done to end

French depredations. Kha was adamant that violence not be used against the occupiers, but many Vietnamese were losing patience and an era of bloody revolts was not far away. Diem often listened to the men's hopeful talk of national independence and freedom, discussions that had a powerful impact on his developing mind.

DIEM LABORED IN THE family rice paddies alongside his siblings and went on long, exploratory horseback rides in the countryside. He attended l'Ecole Pellerin, a Catholic primary school in Hue where classes were taught in French, Latin, and classical Chinese. Even as a youth, he was deeply devout, spending hours in prayer and meditation. At fifteen, he thought seriously of becoming a priest and studied briefly at a Catholic seminary. According to Thuc, Diem had to withdraw because he was allergic to fish, an unavoidable staple in the diet of novitiates. (Thuc thought his younger brother too unworldly and "too unyielding" for the church in any event.) Diem did swear to remain celibate, a promise that friends believed he kept throughout his life.

When he was seventeen, Diem entered the prestigious School of Law and Administration, which trained promising young men for service in the colonial bureaucracy. Graduating first in his class in 1921, he rose rapidly thereafter. He worked first as a district chief in his home province and nearby Quang Tri Province. He supervised nearly three hundred villages, riding a horse from one to the next, wearing formal robes and a conical straw hat as he collected taxes, inspected public works, and settled peasant disputes.

In 1930, he was appointed governor of Ninh Thuan Province on the central coast. It was a time when many Vietnamese nationalists, angry after decades of French exploitation, were primed for rebellion. The French had done a great deal to develop Vietnam, building railroads, bridges, and beautiful public edifices; digging canals; and draining swamplands for cultivation. They created vast plantations for rice, tea, and rubber. Most profits from such enterprises, however, went into French pockets, while Vietnamese workers were often rewarded with contempt and brutality.

Although the French improved Vietnam's infrastructure, they badly weakened its social structure. They demolished the Vietnamese monarchy, dismantled the strong Vietnamese educational system, and implanted the alien religion of Catholicism. Peasants were subjected to onerous taxes and forced to work without pay on canals and other public works projects, often for twelve hours a day. Some were beaten to death. Tens of thousands of Vietnamese were shipped off to other French colonies in New Caledonia, New Hebrides, and Réunion Island to work on plantations and in mines.

Vietnamese from all walks of life, from unskilled laborers to professionals, were routinely victims of racist insults and acts of violence by colons, who were often the dregs of metropolitan France. "Here we give refuge to the miscreant and the worthless, the spongers and thieves," wrote French novelist Claude Farrère. "Those who settle in Indochina do not know how to work in France. Those who trade in Indochina were bankrupt. Those who lord it over the scholar mandarin flunk out of college. And those who sit in judgment and condemn have perhaps themselves been judged and condemned." The French deployed their feared security police, the Sûreté Générale, to round up suspected revolutionaries, many of whom were sent to the prison island of Poulo Condor, known as "the colonial Bastille," in the South China Sea.

Some of the worst colonial cruelties took place on rubber plantations in the Terre Rouge (Red Earth) region, stretching in a wide band from Bien Hoa, about twenty miles northeast of Saigon, to Cambodia. In 1930, more than thirty thousand laborers worked on twenty-five such plantations. Early each morning these men and women trudged into the long rows of rubber trees carrying a special knife with which they cut away a thin spiral strip of bark, allowing latex to drip into a bowl attached to a tree's trunk. They labored ten to twelve hours a day, lived in squalid barracks, and were fed inadequate portions of unnourishing food. Many were worked to exhaustion or became ill from dysentery, malaria, and beriberi. Those too sick to work were taken into the forest and left to die.

About five thousand peasants worked on the big Phu Rieng rubber plantation in conditions little better than what slaves endured in the American South. Their windowless, steel-roofed barracks became as hot as ovens in the tropical sun. Under a brutal overseer, a former French Foreign Legion captain, workers were beaten bloody with bamboo rods; women were raped.

"The most common forms of punishment were to make the person drop his pants, then beat him on the buttocks, or beat his feet until the soles were in ribbons," wrote one man who survived a stint at the Michelin-owned plantation. "After a beating, the worker would be locked up in a dark room, legs shackled, and left without food for two or three days. Some people were forgotten there until they died of thirst." Small groups of workers were sometimes able to flee these Stygian circumstances, while others escaped only by hanging themselves from trees. In 1930, the workers launched a strike and took over the plantation for several days until French soldiers forced them back into the rubber groves to resume their toil.

Protest demonstrations and rebellions erupted by the score during the early 1930s. Ho Chi Minh's newly formed Indochinese Communist Party helped organize revolts in two provinces, with peasants briefly establishing Bolshevik-style soviets. Alarmed at the scale of the disorders, the French responded with a breathtakingly vicious crackdown. The French air force bombed civilian protesters, with casualties running into the thousands. The Sûreté made wholesale arrests of communists and noncommunist nationalists alike.

Diem had studied communist leaflets, books, and newspapers since his days as a district chief in the 1920s, when he first noticed communist organizers at work in the villages. He developed a counterstrategy, parading captured communist agents in rags and telling the villagers: "They say they stand for poor people. Well, let them dress like it." He also broke up a communist plot to seize his provincial capital, a success that led to his appointment as chief of a larger province.

In an effort to calm the agitated populace, the French decided to reconstitute the monarchy in a carefully circumscribed way. They brought back the eighteen-year-old emperor, Bao Dai, from France, where he'd been raised by a French family and educated in French schools. Bao Dai was sent on a tour of the areas roiled by uprisings and allowed to choose his own government ministers. In 1933, he picked Diem as his chief minister. But when the French rejected some of Diem's proposed reforms, including creation of a national assembly, he quit, commenting that to remain in his post under such conditions would be a "deplorable comedy."

The resignation cemented his lasting reputation for uncompromising nationalism and integrity.

DIEM KEPT A LOW profile for the rest of the 1930s, staying in touch with other fervent nationalists in Hue and Saigon and studying ways in which the Vietnamese might expel the French.

He met frequently with the revered historian Phan Boi Chau, a longtime advocate of armed liberation who the French had convicted of sedition and sentenced to house arrest in Hue. Meeting for hours at a stretch at Chau's home or aboard a sampan on the Perfume River, the two men discussed the reasons for the failure of the many attempted revolts against the French.

In 1938, the Vatican elevated Diem's brother Thuc to bishop of the Vinh Long diocese. Diem accompanied him on a tour of Catholic communities during which Thuc gave speeches to large and enthusiastic crowds, often paying filial homage to their then-deceased father, who was widely respected for his unbending nationalism. In his spare time, Diem indulged in his favorite pastimes: reading, horseback riding, hunting, growing flowers, and photography. The Sûreté kept him under surveillance.

Vietnam underwent more upheaval in 1940 after the German army invaded and occupied much of France. The unoccupied portion was administered by the pro-Nazi Vichy government, which permitted Japan, Germany's ally, to establish air bases and other military facilities in Vietnam.

Diem and other Vietnamese nationalists had long regarded Japan as a model for Asian nations that sought to modernize without first undergoing a degrading interregnum of European colonization. Realizing that Japan was now the real power in Vietnam, Diem contacted a variety of Japanese military and civilian officials. He also set up an underground political party, the Association for the Revitalization of Greater Vietnam, hoping to bring together all of the nationalist groups under his leadership. When French police began arresting party members in 1944, Diem managed to escape with the help of the Japanese consul in Hue, who slipped him out of town dressed as a Japanese army officer. Diem made his way to Saigon, living for several months under Japanese military protection.

As the war in the Pacific turned against the Japanese, they seized control of Vietnam in March 1945, arresting and interning French officials and soldiers. The Japanese allowed Bao Dai to remain as their puppet emperor, and he asked Diem to become his prime minister and form a new government. Diem initially refused, but soon regretted his decision, perhaps believing the Japanese would ultimately grant the country independence. It was too late, however; Bao Dai gave the job to another man.

When Japan surrendered to the Allies in August 1945, Ho Chi Minh moved quickly to fill the power vacuum in Vietnam. He proclaimed his own government based in Hanoi and asked Bao Dai to abdicate his throne in order to help legitimize the new regime. Diem was horrified. Still in Saigon, he disguised himself and boarded a train for Hue in an effort to stop Bao Dai from abandoning his position. But Viet Minh agents kidnapped Diem before he reached Bao Dai and held him for months at a series of secret locations in jungles and mountains.

Wracked by dysentery and malaria, Diem nearly died. The Viet Minh also murdered his oldest brother, Ngo Dinh Khoi, who, like Diem, had served under the French as a provincial governor and was active in breaking up communist groups. Khoi and his son were buried alive. For good measure, the Viet Minh burned down Diem's house in Hue, destroying his library of ten thousand books.

In February 1946, Diem was brought to Hanoi for an audience with Ho, who apologized for Khoi's killing and asked Diem to join his new government.

Diem refused, bluntly calling Ho a "criminal," but was allowed to leave unmolested, perhaps because the communist leader didn't want to alienate Diem's Catholic and nationalist supporters. At the end of that year, Ho's guerrilla army went to war against the French in a bid to achieve full independence for Vietnam. The war would drag on for eight brutal years, leaving as many as a million Vietnamese dead.

After giving up his throne and briefly serving as a powerless "special adviser" to Ho, Bao Dai retreated into comfortable exile in Hong Kong. The French managed to drive the Viet Minh out of Hanoi in the early stages of the war, and wanted Bao Dai back as their colonial emperor. Diem and other nationalists pleaded with him to demand unfettered independence in exchange. But in 1949, Bao Dai signed an agreement with the French that gave only partial autonomy to a newly created Associated State of Vietnam, with Paris retaining control of its military, foreign relations, customs, currency, and other key national functions. Bao Dai became its chief of state.

DIEM HAD REACHED A political and personal crossroads. He'd tried hard to create a "third force," an alternative to both French colonialism and Ho's communism. But with war raging between the French and Viet Minh, travel was dangerous and both sides were hostile to his message. French police continued to harass him; the Viet Minh targeted him for assassination. In 1950, Diem decided to visit Japan, the United States, and Europe in hopes of drumming up support for his cause.

The global political scene had changed dramatically by then. In China, Mao Zedong's guerrillas had emerged victorious after a long struggle with nationalist forces under Chiang Kai-shek. North Korea invaded South Korea, inaugurating a bitter war between communist troops and United Nations forces led by the United States. The Soviets had successfully tested their first atomic bomb. The U.S. government was putting into effect a new policy to "contain" communism, while a hard-drinking U.S. senator from Wisconsin, Joe McCarthy, made baseless charges that Washington was riddled with communist spies, stirring public fear.

Accompanied by his brother Thuc, Diem inspected American factories during a tour set up by the State Department, and moved on to Rome and then France, where he conferred again with Bao Dai. By the fall of 1950, he was back in the United States. He spent the next two and a half years living in Maryknoll seminaries in New York and New Jersey, thanks to Thuc's Catholic connections.

In 1950, President Harry Truman began channeling American military aid to the French in their fight against the Viet Minh, but Diem wanted Washington to shift its aid to noncommunist Vietnamese nationalists. He argued that U.S. support of the despised colonial regime was pushing Vietnamese into the arms of Ho's communists, a line that resonated well in McCarthy-era Washington.

Diem met with a host of American academics, religious figures, politicians, and other prominent people, some of whom would become important backers in the future. He had audiences with Francis Cardinal Spellman, the influential archbishop of New York, and William Donovan, leader of the famed Office of Strategic Services, which fielded commando teams that fought in occupied Europe and the Far East during World War II. He was introduced to Supreme Court Justice William O. Douglas and a rising young congressman from Massachusetts, John F. Kennedy.

Many of those he met were favorably impressed with the passionate Catholic patriot. Mike Mansfield, a Democratic senator from Montana and former professor of Asian history, came away from a lunch with him feeling that if anyone could hold Vietnam, "it was somebody like Ngo Dinh Diem." Diem went back to France in 1953, trying to persuade the large Vietnamese community there that a third-force government, with himself at the helm, was the best option for their homeland.

While Diem sought support in Europe and America, Ho's troops continued their grinding war against the French. In May 1954, triumphant Viet Minh soldiers raised their bloodred, yellow-starred battle flag over the defeated French garrison at Dien Bien Phu, in an obscure mountain valley in Vietnam's wild, northwestern corner. More than ten thousand French soldiers became prisoners. It was one of history's greatest military upsets, a stunning victory by Asian peasants over a European army equipped with modern weapons and backed by airpower, and it effectively knocked an exhausted France out of the war. The day after the French surrender, international negotiations began in Geneva to end the conflict.

The following month, Diem met with Bao Dai at the ex-emperor's château outside Cannes on the French Riviera. A shrewd and intelligent man, Bao Dai had been torn for years between his impulse to be a good leader of his people and France's steadfast refusal to ever let him inhabit that role. After Diem quit as his top minister in 1933, Bao Dai retreated into a sybaritic lifestyle. He kept his hand in Vietnamese politics, but he was never able to stand up to French power, and his personal pleasures and comforts were paramount.

Bao Dai once again asked Diem to serve as prime minister. He knew he wouldn't have French backing much longer and Diem, with his U.S. connections, might be able to induce Washington to provide assistance. Diem accepted Bao Dai's offer, but on the condition that he be granted sweeping civil and military powers. Bao Dai, in turn, made his new premier swear an oath that he wouldn't use those powers to depose him. American officials generally approved of Diem, although the U.S. ambassador in Paris, Douglas Dillon, condescendingly described him as a "Yogi-like mystic" who'd likely be pleading for more U.S. aid soon.

The Geneva negotiators announced in July 1954 that a ceasefire had been agreed upon. Although the Viet Minh controlled about three-quarters of Vietnam, the country would be split roughly in half at the 17th parallel. French forces would withdraw south of that line, while Ho's would move north of it. For three hundred days, people would be allowed to move freely from one "regroupment zone" to the other. In two years, an election was to be held to rejoin both halves of Vietnam under a single leader—a contest most observers expected Ho to easily win. Meanwhile, Ho's capital would remain in Hanoi; Diem's new government would be headquartered in Saigon.

BY THE TIME THE Geneva Accords were signed, Diem was already back in Saigon. After nearly four years abroad, he returned home on a French jetliner from Paris on June 25. He greeted a knot of Vietnamese, French, and American officials who came to welcome him at Tan Son Nhut airport and then stepped into a waiting limousine.

The road from the airport to downtown Saigon was lined with thousands of excited spectators, many of whom had waited for hours in the hot sun for a glimpse of their new premier. But the people were in a festive mood and didn't seem to mind.

Standing among them was an American, Colonel Edward Lansdale. The U.S. embassy listed him as an air force attaché, but in fact he headed a special CIA team whose mission was to strengthen Diem and his fledgling government by any means available. Lansdale wanted to gauge the crowd's reaction to their new leader, but Diem's big black car, preceded by a phalanx of police motorcycles with sirens screaming, zoomed past, denying spectators any real contact with him. Obviously disappointed, they drifted away.

A onetime San Francisco advertising man who sported an Errol Flynn–style mustache, Lansdale was well-known within the CIA for devising innovative political and military tactics that helped the Philippine army put down a persistent rebellion by communist guerrillas known as Hukbalahaps. He went on to help elect a staunchly anti-communist defense minister, Ramon Magsaysay, as president of the Philippines in 1953. On the eve of Lansdale's departure for South Vietnam, CIA director Allen Dulles urged him to "find another Magsaysay."

After Diem's motorcade flashed past, Lansdale wondered if the new prime minister was getting the right political advice. He should've driven slowly along in an open car, the American felt, or walked among his people, giving them a chance to see him, touch him, shout their admiration and affection. Lansdale spent the rest of that day writing Diem a memo suggesting ways to organize his government and army. But he doubted that Diem had the necessary political instincts to rally popular support for his ambitious nation-building program.

The CIA agent apparently wasn't aware that Diem was rushing to get to downtown Saigon, where he was to make a speech to another large crowd that awaited him: labor activists, members of the city's large Chinese community, and civil servants who'd been given the afternoon off to attend. The event had been organized by his brother Nhu, a cunning strategist who quickly became Diem's most trusted adviser. Diem mingled happily with his followers, smiling and shaking hands, and then got behind the microphone.

"In this critical situation, I will act decisively," he pledged to the throng. "I will move with determination to open a path to national salvation. A total revolution will be implemented in every facet of the life and organization of the nation."

The situation Diem faced was nothing if not critical. Eight years of war had left extensive destruction throughout the country. Highways, railroads, and inland waterways were severely damaged throughout South Vietnam. More than a million acres of rice-growing land were abandoned and overgrown, rural landowners having fled gunfire and bombs for the relative safety of Saigon and other cities. Rubber production and fishery output had plummeted. As the Viet Minh withdrew north, they did their best to add to the devastation. They dynamited bridges, tore down telegraph lines, pulled up railroad tracks, and made roads impassable by digging deep ditches across them.

The government was in equally poor shape. One-quarter of the soldiers in South Vietnam's new national army had deserted. The loyalties of the rest were unclear; wags chuckled that Diem ruled little more than his palace grounds. South Vietnam's treasury was nearly empty; Diem barely had enough money to keep his new regime going for a month.

In the wake of Dien Bien Phu, frightened French business owners, technicians, and government workers sold their possessions and scurried home to France. Investment capital all but dried up. The French had employed many Vietnamese in colonial government offices, but never allowed them to make significant decisions or rise much higher than clerks. Many of these timorous functionaries remained after Diem took over, and he had great difficulty making his government run properly.

Diem regarded the Geneva peace deal as a disaster for South Vietnam, and his government didn't sign the agreements. While he'd retain the rich rice lands of the Mekong Delta, Ho Chi Minh got the mineral resources and small industrial base of the north. Diem also worried that the French army's withdrawal from Ho's territory meant that the communists would soon overwhelm many Catholic communities there. He flew to Hanoi and appealed to French commanders to stay longer, but they refused.

THE GENEVA ACCORDS DID, however, contain a silver lining for Diem: the provision that people could move freely between north and south within the three-hundred-day window. Beginning in late July, that clause unleashed a vast and dramatic exodus as roughly 900,000 North Vietnamese frantically sought to reach South Vietnam before the deadline. The bulk of them were Catholic and would constitute a steely pillar of political support for Diem in the future.

Thousands of northerners began streaming into Hanoi and the nearby port of Haiphong. They lugged cook pots, clothes, and anything else that could be slung over a shoulder pole; some carried loved ones on their backs. They were exhausted and afraid; the majority were women, children, and the elderly. Entire villages packed up and left, often at the direction of a headman or Catholic priest. Overwhelmed by their numbers, the South Vietnamese and French requested American help in feeding, providing medical care, and transporting the refugees south.

The U.S. Navy assembled an armada of seventy-eight ships for what was dubbed Operation Passage to Freedom. Most were cargo vessels or large landing craft of the kind that delivered tanks and trucks on World War II invasion beaches. The first transport, the USS *Menard*, left Haiphong on August 16, 1954, jammed with two thousand North Vietnamese. Emigrants were whisked away as fast as they could be loaded.

During the thousand-mile voyage south, American sailors fed families, played with children, and screened Hollywood comedies for the refugees who, though they spoke no English, giggled and guffawed at the universal language of slapstick. Navy doctors treated thousands who were ill and attended scores of births. American ships made a total of five hundred trips in three hundred days.

About 650,000 of the evacuees were Catholic, while about 200,000 were Buddhist. Most undertook the perilous journey out of fear that they wouldn't be able to practice their faith or would have their property confiscated by the communists.

Lansdale heightened their anxiety with a clever campaign of black propaganda. At his behest, South Vietnamese soldiers in civilian clothes traveled through the north spreading the false rumor that Ho Chi Minh had let in Chinese troops, who were raping women. Lansdale's men printed and distributed a phony leaflet that instructed Hanoi residents how to "behave" when Viet Minh troops marched in and took over from the French. Shop owners were ordered to prepare a list of their goods so communist authorities would know what to seize. Shortly after the broadsides were handed out, refugee registration tripled and the value of the Viet Minh currency dropped by half.

The extraordinary outflow of humanity from North Vietnam yielded a propaganda bonanza for Diem and the United States, as newspapers and magazines played up hair-raising accounts of destitute people risking everything to escape the descending yoke of communism. (By contrast, only about ninety thousand people moved from south to north, most of them Viet Minh cadres and their families.)

As the number of émigrés soared, the Viet Minh began trying to block their exit.

Ho's agents spread their own propaganda, such as that U.S. sailors planned to throw their passengers overboard to the sharks. Horror stories multiplied, particularly in the U.S. Catholic press, of the Viet Minh beating, torturing, and gunning down priests and their parishioners who tried to leave. (Some tales strained credibility. One, possibly planted by Lansdale, claimed that communists pierced children's eardrums with chopsticks so they could no longer hear Catholic teachings.)

When the Viet Minh closed roads to Hanoi and Haiphong, desperate refugees began risking an ocean voyage in sampans and bamboo rafts. In just a few months, French patrol boats rescued ten thousand people from the sea. But many others drowned when their flimsy vessels broke up in rough water.

IN 1954, THE FRENCH had an expression to describe Saigon: *un panier des crabes*, a "basket of crabs," a place where people were always at each other's throats.

The phrase carried a note of Gallic condescension, but also a large grain of truth. In the near-anarchy that prevailed in the months following the Geneva conference, Diem's capital was indeed a hotbed of intrigue and ruthless competition for power. Diem was one of the toughest crabs in the basket, but he was surrounded by others with claws extended in his direction.

His patron and ostensible boss, Bao Dai, would soon be plotting to remove him as premier. A criminal gang called the Binh Xuyen—which, incredibly, controlled both the local and national police—wanted to expand its power. The countryside teemed with thousands of well-armed soldiers loyal not to Diem's shaky government but to religious splinter groups that had political ambitions of their own. And the French, who still dominated South Vietnam's economy, were eager to replace the deeply Francophobic Diem with a more pliant leader who'd serve their interests after their last troops sailed for home.

One possibility was General Nguyen Van Hinh, chief of staff of the nascent South Vietnamese armed forces. A handsome ladies' man, Hinh was among the many Frenchified Vietnamese who held high rank in South Vietnam's military. He had a French wife, French citizenship, and a second commission as a colonel in the French air force.

Hinh believed Diem was incapable of leading the nation and openly schemed to unseat him. Diem tried to fire the general, but he refused to relinquish his command, ringing his headquarters with tanks. He sent armored cars to blare anti-government slogans over loudspeakers as they circled Diem's palace. Hinh boasted to friends that once he'd disposed of Diem, he'd take the premier's fiery sister-in-law, Madame Nhu, as his concubine. (Confronting the general at a party, Madame Nhu told him he didn't "have the guts" to depose Diem and even if he did, he'd never possess her because "I will claw your throat out first.") In his most peculiar effort to rattle Diem, Hinh circled the palace over and over on a motor scooter.

American officials told the mutinous general he'd lose U.S. aid if he kept up his antics. Unabashed, Hinh kept setting "dates" for his anticipated coup and laughing uproariously when each date passed with no action. U.S. officials weren't sure how seriously to take his threats.

Hinh invited Lansdale to dine with him one evening at his residence. When the American arrived, he found a hive of apparent coup preparations, as messengers ran in and out and Hinh's field commanders pored over maps of Saigon. The general insisted the action would take place the next day. The quick-witted Lansdale said that was too bad because he was leaving for

Manila that night and wanted to take Hinh and some of his officers along. Lansdale apologized for the short notice, but the jaunt would include a tour of Manila's best nightclubs. Hinh replied that he couldn't go, given the circumstances, but that three of his aides were welcome to. Lansdale quickly rustled up a C-47 transport plane and he and Hinh's men winged their way to the Philippines.

When Lansdale returned to Saigon, he learned that the coup hadn't taken place; Hinh explained implausibly that he'd forgotten his absent aides were needed to pull it off. Perhaps embarrassed at his military commander's increasingly inane behavior, Bao Dai called him to Paris in November, and Hinh never returned to South Vietnam.

WITH HINH DECLAWED, DIEM still faced the Binh Xuyen gangsters and two armed religious sects: the Cao Dai and the Hoa Hao, which together had about 2 million followers and forty thousand troops. The religious groups dominated large swaths of the countryside south and west of Saigon in almost feudal fashion, taxing peasants, but also protecting them in their fields. Both faiths wanted to keep running their lucrative fiefdoms without interference from a strong central government.

The Caodaists were based in Tay Ninh, a provincial capital about sixty-five miles northwest of Saigon. There they'd built a massive, twin-towered temple that novelist Graham Greene aptly described as a "Walt Disney fantasia of the East." Within its high-ceilinged nave were green dragons slithering around pink pillars and a glittery blue sphere, resembling a giant disco ball, adorned with an all-seeing, all-knowing eye, the faith's primary symbol. Haloed figures of the eclectic Cao Dai pantheon—including Buddha, Jesus, Victor Hugo, Joan of Arc, Pericles, and Sun Yat-sen—lined the walls. Caodaism's hierarchy modeled itself on the Catholic Church, complete with a "pope," bishops, priests, and nuns.

Concentrated in the Mekong Delta, the Hoa Haos embraced an amalgam of Buddhism, ancestor worship, animistic rites, and Confucianism. They were led by Huynh Phu So, an itinerant Buddhist healer and prophet known as the "Mad Monk." A mesmerizing speaker, So accurately predicted the fall of France in 1940 and the Japanese invasion of Indochina. His auguries and emphasis on austere living and personal salvation attracted many followers and so worried the French that they tried to exile him to Laos. During and after World War II, So and his fiercely independent disciples took up arms against the Japanese, the French, and the Viet Minh; Ho Chi Minh's agents murdered him in 1947.

Diem's most cutthroat adversaries, the Binh Xuyen, had evolved from a small band of river pirates into a well-heeled criminal syndicate that owned casinos, hotels, and rubber plantations, along with a huge Saigon brothel, the Hall of Mirrors, that employed 1,200 prostitutes. The gang ran the city's opium dens, had interests in bus companies and commercial fishing, and even set retail pork prices. One Binh Xuyen gangster was Saigon's police chief; another headed the national security police, the Sûreté. Like the sects, the Binh Xuyen had its own army, with 3,500 troops in Saigon.

Its leader was an illiterate ex-chauffeur and prison escapee named Le Van Vien. Renowned for his cruelty and venality, the bullnecked Vien lived in a heavily guarded compound just across the Arroyo Chinois, a waterway that formed part of the city's southern boundary. Dreadful rumors about him abounded; according to one, those who failed to pay him protection money wound up as kibble for the tiger in his private zoo.

Unlike American mobsters, the Binh Xuyen operated in a strikingly open manner. Its green beret–wearing soldiers collected "road safety taxes" from farmers and travelers coming into Saigon, and a government minister presided at the dedication of the Hall of Mirrors. By 1954, Vien was reputed to be the city's wealthiest man.

Emerging from the swamps and marshes south of Saigon in the 1920s, the Binh Xuyen preyed on sampans and junks bringing rice and other products to the city's river docks. They supplemented their income with occasional forays into Cholon to rob or kidnap wealthy Chinese merchants for ransom. Pursued by police, the river pirates disappeared into the nearly impenetrable mangrove swamps of the Rung Sat, or Forest of Assassins.

Like many young Vietnamese, Vien had been swept up in the wave of nationalism that engulfed the country after World War II, joining the Viet

Minh in the struggle to stop the French from reestablishing colonial control. But Viet Minh leaders came to view Vien as too independent and tried to assassinate him. The gang chieftain dodged the trap and in retaliation made a deal with the French: the Binh Xuyen would expose underground Viet Minh cells in Saigon in exchange for a "zone of influence" in Cholon. The gangsters joined French police in a highly effective sweep, and Viet Minh grenade-tossing and other terror attacks declined sharply.

French military intelligence also cut Vien in on Operation X, in which poppies harvested in North Vietnam and Laos were brought into Saigon to be refined into opium and sold to addicts. In 1954, Vien was said to have paid Bao Dai $1 million to take over the Saigon police and the Sûreté. He also funneled a slice of his profits from opium and prostitution to the ex-emperor, to help him savor the sweet life on the Riviera.

Vien's most glittering possession was the Grande Monde, an enormous gambling and entertainment establishment in Cholon. Behind its high yellow walls noodle peddlers and taxi drivers squandered their daily pittances at card tables and roulette wheels alongside businessmen, French legionnaires, and bejeweled courtesans. When gamblers tired of losing money, they could watch a Chinese theater performance, consult an astrologer, enjoy a champagne dinner, see a boxing match, or dance to a jazz band on a floor almost as big as an American football field.

The Grande Monde had opened in 1946 at the direction of the French governor-general, who viewed licensing it as a perfectly legitimate way to help underwrite the burgeoning costs of reoccupying Vietnam. It was soon said to be the most profitable casino in Asia.

DIEM KNEW HE COULDN'T govern a country where mobsters supervised the police and militarized religious groups ran their own ministates.

He tried to appease the Cao Dai and Hoa Hao, giving each sect four cabinet seats out of the total of fourteen in his government. Using CIA funds, he bribed sect commanders to bring their troops into the Vietnamese National Army.

But sooner or later, Diem believed, he'd have to use force to break the

Binh Xuyen and the sects. South Vietnam would never be truly independent until it shook off the insidious influences of gangsters, armed ecstatics, and the French. In addition, the premier was under growing pressure from his nationalist supporters, who were frustrated at his lack of progress in getting the French out of the country. Tens of thousands of French soldiers remained in South Vietnam. The longer they stayed, the weaker Diem looked.

American and French officials warned Diem that pitched combat with his antagonists would wreak unspeakable destruction on Saigon's densely populated neighborhoods, and could even touch off civil war. But in January 1955, the premier moved toward an open clash with the Binh Xuyen, refusing to renew the Grande Monde's operating license and forcing it to close.

Leaning against his Cadillac, flanked by his hoods, Vien, the gang chieftain, watched sullenly one night as the last customer strolled out of his casino. "Under brush-cut hair, his face was pitted and swarthy, his eyes like stones in the lamplight," recorded a British journalist. Vien uttered something in Vietnamese, which an aide translated in a soft voice for the newspaperman: "We are going to teach Mr. Diem the four truths."

FOR YEARS THE FRENCH had been arming and paying the Binh Xuyen and the sects to fight the Viet Minh. When Paris abruptly cut off the subsidies in early 1955, Diem refused to continue them with U.S. aid dollars, which the Americans were now giving directly to his government. The Binh Xuyen had plenty of cash from various underworld enterprises to pay their soldiers. But the Cao Dai and Hoa Hao were in a bind; as their money ran out, their unpaid troops might simply pack up and go home.

The sects conferred with the Binh Xuyen in March and decided to demand a bigger say in Diem's government. They created the United Front of Nationalist Forces and issued an ultimatum, giving the premier five days to reorganize his cabinet, although they never specified exactly what they wanted it to look like. If he failed to comply, the front threatened, "All South Vietnam will be put to blood and fire."

Diem not only ignored the ultimatum, he made a provocative countermove, ordering his army to clear the Binh Xuyen out of municipal police headquarters and installing his own police chief. The maneuver was carried out peacefully and, a few days later, the premier dropped the other shoe. He told his defense minister he was sending the army to evict the gangsters from Sûreté headquarters as well. The minister promptly quit in protest and the French pleaded with Diem to postpone the move, which he reluctantly agreed to do.

The Binh Xuyen, however, had had enough. Shortly after midnight on March 29, 1955, they began mortaring Independence Palace. As explosions shook the well-tended grounds, Diem rushed outside in his pajamas to comfort wounded palace guards and make sure the rest were ready to repulse a ground assault. At about the same time, Binh Xuyen soldiers attacked municipal police headquarters in Cholon. The gangsters also launched an assault on Vietnamese army headquarters, located nearby.

At his house a few blocks from the palace, Lansdale was jolted awake by the loud crump of mortar shells exploding. He also heard the deep *tock-tock-tock* of machine guns and realized Diem's infantry was engaged in combat somewhere. He got a call through to the prime minister, who said Binh Xuyen green berets were pouring heavy fire into police headquarters. Truckloads of national soldiers racing to reinforce the cops had been ambushed on Boulevard Gallieni, the broad artery connecting Saigon with Cholon. French tanks, Diem claimed, were blocking additional reinforcements. The prime minister worried that his police would be overrun unless help arrived soon.

Hopping into his car to go see for himself, Lansdale soon came to a traffic circle where a convoy of Vietnamese troop trucks had been halted by French light tanks. Vietnamese officers were angrily arguing with French officers; the noise from nearby firefights was deafening.

The Vietnamese demanded to be let through, saying the besieged police needed them now. The French refused. Lansdale joined the argument, whipping out a notebook and demanding the French officers' names. They replied that he'd better clear out before their tanks cleared him out.

Lansdale sped to the home of General J. Lawton Collins, the U.S. special presidential envoy to South Vietnam and his immediate boss. The CIA operative told Collins what he'd seen and said the French army appeared to be deliberately helping the Binh Xuyen. Lansdale was appalled; to him, it was as if the U.S. Army was helping Al Capone take over Chicago.

One of the Army's most senior officers, Collins had seen enough bloodshed to last several lifetimes. He'd commanded an infantry division during bitter World War II fighting against the Japanese on Guadalcanal and the Solomon Islands. General Eisenhower picked him to lead one of the two American army corps that landed in Normandy on D-Day; Collins's forces later spearheaded the crucial breakout at Saint-Lô. During the Korean War Collins served as Army chief of staff. After Eisenhower became president, he gave Collins the Vietnam assignment in November 1954. As Eisenhower's personal representative, Collins was supposed to be in Saigon only a few months, until a regular ambassador arrived.

Collins listened to Lansdale and then explained that he'd just been in touch with General Paul Ely, the French commissioner-general and commander of French forces. They agreed that the killing must stop immediately. Ely was trying to contact Diem and Vien, to have them order their men to disengage. French tanks had moved into the streets to enforce a ceasefire. Just four hours after it began, the battle was over. Casualties were relatively light: 26 killed, 112 wounded.

AN UNEASY FEELING OF suspended animation settled over Saigon. The city took on the appearance of an armed camp: behind sandbag walls and barbed-wire barricades, Binh Xuyen and national army strongpoints bristled with guns. The French had about thirty thousand soldiers and four hundred tanks in Saigon, and they corralled the Vietnamese army and Binh Xuyen in separate areas.

Diem, however, was determined to finish the gangsters. His men had fought well and morale was high. The Cao Dai and Hoa Hao seemed to be backing away from the United Front, and in any event most sect troops were too far away from Saigon to be of any use.

But it was far from certain that Diem could beat the Binh Xuyen. Collins was concerned that sustained fighting might lead to an army revolt, as soldiers objected to killing fellow Vietnamese. The CIA reported that Diem's own commanders believed the gangster army "is currently capable of isolating and controlling Saigon."

With the ceasefire holding, Diem pursued his bribe-and-conquer strategy, trying to peel more sect commanders away from the rebel coalition. He gave at least $100,000 to a Cao Dai commander in exchange for integrating his eight thousand soldiers into the national army. The Binh Xuyen were spreading money around as well. The Cao Dai pope, for example, received a new Cadillac as an incentive to stick with the United Front.

On the surface, life went on as usual in Saigon. Fashionable Saigonese packed the Rue Catinat, the city's elegant dining and shopping thoroughfare. But a sense of impending cataclysm could be felt everywhere. Gunfire between Binh Xuyen and national troops was a daily occurrence. Heavily armed gangsters rode around in jeeps, and ugly reports surfaced that they'd disemboweled a squad of captured government soldiers. Bloated corpses floated down the Arroyo Chinois, hands tied, bullet holes behind the ears.

On April 26, Diem executed an artful, if goading, end run around his archenemies. The Binh Xuyen still occupied Sûreté headquarters on Rue Catinat, inside the French defense perimeter. Diem declared he was forming a completely new national police agency, to be headquartered on Boulevard Gallieni. More than half of the Binh Xuyen Sûreté's seven hundred employees quickly defected to Diem's new Sûreté. The following day, Diem's Sûreté chief announced he was halting Binh Xuyen patrols in Saigon.

Vien's response wasn't long in coming. On April 28, mortar shells again began crashing into Independence Palace. Diem telephoned General Ely, saying the Binh Xuyen had broken the ceasefire and his palace was under attack; the prime minister was ordering his army to fight back. Ely warned Diem that he'd hold him responsible for the bloodshed that inevitably would result from street fighting. Diem hung up.

Binh Xuyen soldiers began pushing out of Cholon toward central Saigon along Boulevard Gallieni. Tens of thousands of people lived in the area; many fled on bicycles, carrying any possessions they could, as national troops took up positions behind trees and hastily erected barricades. Flocks of civilians milled around on the streets, unsure what to do. They ran into nearby buildings whenever gunfire flared and came back out during lulls. An elderly woman pulling a half-naked child by the hand pleaded in broken French, "Where to go? Where to go?"

Mortar shells began falling near army headquarters in a Cholon slum where thousands of North Vietnamese refugees lived in miserable huts. The dwellings caught fire and flames spread rapidly. Firemen in gold and silver helmets tried to extinguish the blazes but were driven off by more mortar detonations.

Binh Xuyen reinforcements crossed the Arroyo Chinois into Cholon that night and tried to drive a wedge between army and police headquarters on Boulevard Gallieni. Diem's soldiers fought fiercely, knocking the gangsters out of their strongholds at the Grande Monde casino and a high school.

Fighting spilled into the next day. Clouds of choking black smoke hung over the city; hundreds of people had already been killed. Diem summoned Lansdale to the palace, gouged with shell holes. The prime minister looked exhausted and close to tears. Under ferocious pressure for months, he'd just received a harshly worded telegram from Bao Dai, calling him a monster for plunging South Vietnam into fratricidal warfare. The chief of state ordered Diem to come to France right away.

Diem looked at his CIA friend imploringly. Crammed into a small alcove in Diem's bedroom, the two men were so close their knees touched. Lansdale calmly counseled the premier to review every action he'd taken during the crisis, and ask himself if each step had been justified and principled. Diem recounted the whole sequence, concluding that he'd had no choice: a government that turned its police services over to criminals could never serve the people's interests. If it was to have any legitimacy, Diem's regime had to crush the Binh Xuyen. After a lengthy discussion, Lansdale asked if Diem was sure of his decision. "I know I'm doing the right thing!" the premier exulted. He decided to defy Bao Dai's summons and continue the battle to rid his capital of gangsters.

But the Eisenhower administration's support for Diem was wavering.

Several days earlier, General Collins had flown to Washington to make his case against Diem in person.

Collins had at first supported Diem. But as the months wore on and the political crises piled up, he lost confidence in the prime minister. He watched in consternation as Diem's defense minister quit, along with all eight sect members of his government, to protest the fighting.

In multiple cables to Washington, Collins laid out a catalog of Diem's sins and shortcomings that would be echoed by other American officials for years to come. Although the premier was a model of courage, honesty, and determination, Collins also viewed him as stubborn, uncompromising, focused on trivial matters instead of important ones, and increasingly isolated by his dependence on his brother Nhu and other family members for advice. He didn't seem able to handle other strong-willed politicians; Collins felt he lacked the skills to be a national leader.

In meetings at the State Department and the Pentagon, Collins argued that the U.S. government should dump Diem and back another anti-communist politician. Collins lunched with Eisenhower, relating examples of what he considered Diem's bad judgment, including his plan to attack the Binh Xuyen–held Sûreté headquarters, which could have produced numerous civilian casualties. "This fellow is impossible," Collins told the president.

Collins also met with Secretary of State John Foster Dulles, a strong Diem advocate. Dulles was reluctant to pull the plug on the South Vietnamese leader, but finally acceded to Collins's line of reasoning. He sent telegrams to the U.S. embassies in Saigon and Paris, indicating that Washington was ready to work with France to replace Diem.

Lansdale, however, thought that would be a perilous mistake and fired off cables urging Washington to stick with Diem. One message, cosigned by the top U.S. military official in Saigon, Lieutenant General John O'Daniel, said the Vietnamese army "appears [to] have capability, morale and desire to finish Binh Xuyen now" and warned, "Any change in leadership or command at this time could result in chaos." Lansdale's reports were just the ammunition Dulles needed. He issued a "blocking cable" to the Saigon and Paris embassies, ordering that no action be taken on his previous dispatch.

The battle, meanwhile, was turning decisively in Diem's favor.

His soldiers drove the Binh Xuyen back over the Arroyo Chinois toward their fortified headquarters. By early May, the Battle of Saigon was largely over. As Collins and Ely had predicted, the cost in blood and devastation was high. More than five hundred civilians were dead; another twenty thousand were homeless. Shelling and fires wrecked entire blocks in one of Saigon's poorest districts. People without shelter were forced to camp out in parks and other open areas.

Nevertheless, Diem had succeeded in destroying Vien's criminal empire. National troops were chasing the remnants of the gangster army back to their old haunts in the Forest of Assassins. The Grande Monde had burned to the ground; Vien's villa was a bombed-out shambles. His oldest son, commander of the green berets, died from a stomach wound. Vien remained at large, but soon slipped out of South Vietnam for a comfortable life as a wealthy exile in Paris.

The battle taught Diem some powerful lessons: Military force was sometimes justified to put down domestic political antagonists. American advice—such as Collins's admonition to make peace with the Binh Xuyen and the sects—sometimes had to be ignored. And above all, the premier should never waver in his belief in the righteousness of his own cause.

Diem applied these axioms again and again over the next several years as he consolidated his power and brought dissidents and political rivals to heel. But the same precepts would lead him fatally astray during his final crisis.

CHAPTER 4

"DIEMOCRACY" AND ITS DISCONTENTS

WITH THE BATTLE of Saigon won, Diem's popularity soared. Soldiers from the sect armies surrendered in large numbers following the Binh Xuyen's defeat. (The Cao Dai pope fled to Cambodia.) In May 1955, the French agreed to move their troops out of Saigon to coastal embarkation points, leaving Vietnamese in control of the city for the first time in decades. South Vietnamese were thrilled to see their strong nationalist premier in action. "At that time, we were all behind Diem: the army, civil service, and the farmers out in the villages," recalled Tran Van Don, a top military aide to the president.

In the provinces Diem was hailed as a conquering hero. Most Viet Minh fighters had pulled out of South Vietnam's villages and towns, and Diem's army was moving in behind them, trying to establish Saigon's authority. Diem sometimes accompanied his soldiers.

On the Camau Peninsula, at the country's southern tip, "just about every man, woman, and child in Camau town turned out to greet him," Lansdale wrote. People waved excitedly and called out to him; troops in an honor guard broke ranks to cheer him. When his plane circled the port city of Qui Nhon on the central coast, people raced to the airfield to meet him. Well-wishers hoisted him to their shoulders and a great cheer went up. Diem was startled at first, grabbing his bearers' hair to steady himself, but soon was savoring the adulation. His plane was mobbed by fifty thousand people in the central coast town of Tuy Hoa, an impressive turnout in an area dominated for years by the Viet Minh.

Returning from such forays Diem "seemed revitalized, bubbling over with new energy," recalled Lansdale. "He had received a heady dose of genuinely demonstrated popularity."

Among Diem's highest priorities was to scrub South Vietnamese society of every corrosive vestige of French colonialism. One early effort was his "anti–four vices" campaign against opium smoking, gambling, prostitution, and alcoholism. By stamping out such depravities, the prime minister hoped to begin a "moral rearmament" of his people, reigniting in them traditional values of discipline, honesty, responsibility, and sacrifice—and forging a right-minded citizenry for his new independent state.

In Saigon, famous under the French for its tempting assortment of recherché pleasures, Diem attacked with puritanical vengeance. His anti-vice drive kicked off at a public square when a white-suited official set fire to a large pile of opium pipes, pornographic magazines, and playing cards. Police shut down five hundred opium dens. Diem buried strip clubs under a blizzard of new regulations, causing many to close. He converted the big Paradise brothel—where three hundred prostitutes cavorted in mirrored cubicles—into a rehabilitation center that trained sex workers as nurses and seamstresses.

THERE WAS ONE OTHER debilitating legacy of French rule to be erased: Diem's onetime benefactor, the ex-emperor Bao Dai.

When the French ran his government, Bao Dai had few duties beyond conducting ritual ceremonies to honor ancestors. Known for his pursuit of luxurious indulgences, he dashed about Hue in expensive cars, played tennis and golf, and went sailing on the South China Sea. He built two lavish villas surrounded by large estates stocked with his favorite game, which he hunted from the back of an elephant. He was a familiar face in the casinos of Cannes, wagering large sums. Although a Buddhist, he married a devout Catholic and kept multiple mistresses.

By the early 1950s, many Vietnamese saw him as fatally compromised by his passivity and serial collaboration with French colonialists, Japanese militarists, Ho's communists, and, most recently, Binh Xuyen gangsters. Diem learned that amid his desperate battle against the Binh Xuyen, Bao Dai had plotted with the French to oust him.

The prime minister turned the tables in July 1955, announcing a referendum in which South Vietnam's voters could choose whether to keep Bao Dai as their head of state or replace him with Diem. If they picked Diem, he would then proclaim a republic, ridding South Vietnam of its tarnished former monarch and creating the framework, for the first time, of a representative government.

From his château outside Cannes, Bao Dai angrily revoked Diem's premiership. Diem ignored this latest decree from the absentee leader and set an October date for the referendum. He and Nhu then uncorked a furious campaign of vilification against Bao Dai, the themes of which were quickly picked up by newspapers and radio.

Mocking effigies of the former emperor appeared on the streets of Saigon and elsewhere, along with posters attacking him as the "puppet king selling his country" and "master keeper of gambling dens and brothels." One Saigon newspaper memorably labeled him a "dung beetle who sold his country for personal glory" as it inaugurated a three-week series of articles exposing his lush love life. Bao Dai remained lethargically on the Riviera, not bothering to defend himself in his native land.

In drafting the referendum, Diem cleverly linked deposing Bao Dai with the widely popular notion of establishing a government headed by an elected head of state. Lansdale had urged him not to simply overthrow Bao Dai, but instead put the matter to a popular vote in order to invest the results with as much legitimacy as possible. The CIA operative also cautioned against stuffing ballot boxes or otherwise tampering with the referendum. But Diem couldn't resist. His agents lurked near polling places, leaning on people to vote the right way and beating up some who didn't.

Since many South Vietnamese were illiterate, the ballots carried side-by-side photos of Diem and Bao Dai. Voters were to tear the ballots in half and cast the portion picturing their candidate. The ballots depicted a smiling Diem enfolded by enthusiastic supporters, while the photo of a dour Bao Dai looked like it was taken in a police lineup.

When the votes were tallied, Diem had racked up 98 percent, a margin of victory so absurd that, in the words of one U.S. official, it "would have made a Tammany Hall boss blush." The CIA concluded that the plebiscite had been marred by "substantial government manipulation," noting that the number of votes cast in Saigon exceeded the number of registered voters there by 150,000.

In any event, Diem had gotten himself elected president of the new Republic of Vietnam. But unscrupulous electioneering wasn't the only sign that he already was embracing an autocratic style of governing. In June 1955, the CIA reported that he was arresting rival politicians. Two months after the Bao Dai referendum, government agents detained Dr. Phan Quang Dan, a Saigon physician with a Harvard doctorate who was well on his way to becoming Diem's best-known critic. Dr. Dan's arrest caused even Lansdale to complain to CIA headquarters that "the government is using force as a substitute for good leadership."

WITH THE ARMY AND police finally under his control, Diem set out to uproot what remained of the communist political apparatus in South Vietnam.

After the 1954 ceasefire, most Viet Minh and their families moved north. But some five thousand elite cadres stayed behind, carefully hiding their guns, explosives, radios, and other equipment. They were confident they could take over Diem's government, not by violent means but by electing communists and left-wing sympathizers to the National Assembly. They organized demonstrations and agitated openly in Saigon and elsewhere, calling for a coalition government and reunification with the north.

Diem went after the stay-behind agents with his "Anti-Communist Denunciation Campaign." Citizens were exhorted at government-sponsored rallies to publicly renounce communism and point out Hanoi's operatives in their midst. Since they conducted their political work overtly, communists were easy to identify, and Diem's police and soldiers arrested or killed many of them.

The dragnet swept up many innocents, however. Some were nationalists who'd fought with the Viet Minh, but parted ways after learning of Ho's true goals; others merely had a relative in the communist-led resistance. Some were simply Bao Dai supporters. As the anti-communist campaign rolled on, people made false denunciations to settle old grudges, injure a business rival, or grab a neighbor's land; corrupt government officials exacted bribes by threatening to incriminate someone. In 1956, Diem exacerbated the situation with a new edict allowing the indefinite detention of anyone who could even vaguely be labeled a "subversive."

Between the detention law and the denunciation campaign, thousands of blameless people wound up in prison. Diem's police beat and tortured people; some were victims of extrajudicial killings. Lansdale reported to CIA headquarters an informant's claim that seven thousand political prisoners were locked up in Saigon's Chi Hoa prison by early 1956.

The anti-communist onslaught generated a great deal of ill-feeling toward the regime, especially among peasants. Diem didn't particularly care. He believed that he'd inherited the "mandate of heaven," an ancient Confucian concept that held that a sovereign was the mediator between heaven and earth, entitled to rule as long as he was personally virtuous and his reign benefited the people. If the sovereign ruled badly, the people had the right to withdraw the mandate of heaven.

Diem believed the mandate was firmly in his deserving hands and therefore public approval didn't matter; he needed only a loyal army and an administrative apparatus to govern. Indeed, he thought the people of South Vietnam owed him "a sacred respect" as their brave and morally correct leader.

THE CIA TRIED TO nudge him toward a more populist style, as Lansdale had done with Ramon Magsaysay in the Philippines. But the agency concluded that Diem's inability to establish an "essential rapport" with his people was his government's most serious shortcoming. Paul Harwood, a CIA operative who was close to Nhu, urged him to get his brother to ditch his colonial-style sharkskin suits in favor of traditional Vietnamese garb, but Diem wouldn't change his wardrobe. Groping for ways to bond him more closely with his public, CIA headquarters suggested that Diem be given elocution lessons.

The CIA also worked closely with Nhu, the most powerful behind-the-scenes figure in South Vietnam.

Thin, self-assured, darkly handsome, and like his older brother a garrulous chain-smoker, Nhu was the regime's chief political strategist and house intellectual. In addition, he ran Diem's secret police and intelligence-gathering organizations. Fascinated by communist organizing techniques, Nhu created the Can Lao, a secret political party, complete with communist-style cells and cadres, which kept close watch on dissidents and potential rivals in the army, government, and business community. The Can Lao also operated secret jails for political prisoners, including one in a most improbable location: the lovely Saigon Zoo and Botanical Gardens, where some detainees underwent torture in Room P-40.

With his intellectual arrogance and mirthless smile, Nhu elicited widely different reactions from Americans. Harwood regarded him as witty, sociable, and genuinely interested in finding ways to strengthen his brother's government. Lansdale disliked him, describing him as a "Mussolini-type character" who "reveled in this secret type of government control of the people, and slowly attempted to evolve a Fascist-type state." A visiting American academic got a vivid demonstration of Nhu's sinister aura when the political counselor strode confidently into a gathering of well-heeled Saigonese at a private home. The other guests immediately scattered to the far end of the room, like frightened seals fleeing the sudden appearance of an orca.

As a student in Paris in the mid-1930s, Nhu attended the École Nationale des Chartes, a prestigious training ground for archivists and librarians. He organized other Vietnamese students to support the Socialist politician Léon Blum, who became prime minister of France's Popular Front government in 1936. Nhu later returned to Vietnam, landed a job at the National Library in Hanoi, and got married. He and his young wife settled first in

Hue and then in Dalat, the charming Central Highlands resort town, where he indulged his passion for cultivating orchids. He also threw himself into politics, working relentlessly to build a base of support for Diem among Catholics and others. He was active in the labor movement and published a political journal, *Society*, which backed trade unions.

He almost always deferred to his older brother; Diem in turn deeply valued Nhu's political ideas and judgments. Nhu loved political intrigue, both to advance Diem's agenda and foil anyone scheming to undermine the president. (At one point, Nhu and his wife hid behind a silk screen so they could eavesdrop on Diem's exchanges with a visiting U.S. congressional delegation.)

Diem tended to place absolute faith in anything Nhu told him, accepting his brother's views over those of other palace advisers. "If one hundred people would come in and say it's raining outside, and Nhu comes in and says it's not, he'd believe Nhu," recalled an American who knew both men.

Nhu supported his brother as he moved on multiple fronts to concentrate government authority in his hands. Diem abolished the powerful regional governors and handpicked his own province chiefs. He took one action that Lansdale regarded as catastrophic, replacing locally elected village councils with his own appointees. This violated a centuries-old tradition of village autonomy ("the emperor's writ stops at the village gate") that had been respected even by the French. What was worse, Diem's nominees frequently were city dwellers or Catholics from Central Vietnam (or both), overseeing resentful Buddhist peasants in the Mekong Delta or other southern regions.

Diem also refused to participate in the 1956 election prescribed by the Geneva agreements and intended to reunify North and South Vietnam, arguing that Ho Chi Minh would never allow free and fair elections in the north. Washington backed Diem's position.

After decades of repression, many of Diem's constituents thirsted for democracy. According to Lansdale, it was the number one topic of conversation at sidewalk food stands, favorite spots for South Vietnamese to exchange news and opinions. The CIA agent spent hours explaining the U.S. Constitution to Diem and outlining how Filipino leaders maintained a democratic government even under the stresses of the Huk insurgency.

Under constant pressure from Washington to reform, Diem often told Americans that he favored introducing representative government in South Vietnam. His plan was to build democracy from the bottom up, starting with strategic hamlets and eventually letting their inhabitants elect local leaders. But democratic freedoms had to be carefully rationed, he believed, since the communists would take advantage of them to subvert his government. ("If we open the window, not only the sunlight but many bad things fly in also," Madame Nhu explained to a foreign journalist.) Widespread illiteracy was an impediment; many people couldn't read a ballot. Montagnard languages didn't even have a word that meant "democracy."

Diem backed the drafting of a constitution and formation of a national assembly, and those stances provided a glint of hope that he might permit democratic institutions to take root. However, the legislature created in 1956 was widely regarded as a rubber stamp for the president. And while the constitution contained some progressive features—workers had the right to unionize, for example—it also gave Diem tremendous power, including the ability to suspend civil rights in order to "meet the legitimate demands of public security and order."

Close observers of the regime began to speak of "Diemocracy"—a government with the trappings of democracy, but not the substance.

DESPITE HIS DISCOURAGING LURCH toward autocracy, many people considered Diem a remarkable success given the hurdles he'd faced.

By 1957, French troops were gone. Many northern refugees were resettled in new, government-supported communities in the Central Highlands and Mekong Delta. Diem was strengthening his civil administration and armed forces, rebuilding South Vietnam's war-battered infrastructure, and at least providing the country with some political stability.

With generous aid from the United States, his regime in its first three years repaired 6,214 miles of roads and 186 miles of railroads. It dredged roughly 13 million cubic yards of mud from clogged canals and rehabilitated major irrigation systems. New universities opened in Saigon and Hue, and the government planned medical and veterinary schools as well.

The South Vietnamese economy rebounded vigorously after the French war. Rice production almost doubled from 2.6 million tons in 1954 to 5 million tons in 1959. Rubber production rose steadily. Fishermen quadrupled their catch, from 52,000 tons in 1955 to 212,000 tons in 1961. The south began to mine coal and produce fibers like kenaf and jute for industrial use. Hospitals, clinics, and maternity stations sprung up in the countryside.

Diem worked closely in many of these endeavors with the U.S. government, which was eager to bulwark his country against Ho's north as part of its global strategy to contain communism.

American economists, public health experts, and construction engineers poured into Saigon. Michigan State University helped to set up a school to train government administrators and law enforcement officers. By 1956, U.S. assistance came to $270 million annually, making South Vietnam one of the highest per capita recipients of American foreign aid in the world.

The Eisenhower administration—on the verge of dumping the South Vietnamese leader just a couple of years before—now lionized him as "an example for people everywhere who hate tyranny and love freedom." Influential U.S. magazines amplified the theme of Diem as anti-communist idol. *Life* dubbed him "The Tough Miracle Man of Vietnam," while *Reader's Digest*—with a monthly circulation close to 10 million—hailed him as the "Biggest Little Man in Asia." Gushing that "a wholly unexpected political miracle has occurred in South Vietnam," *Foreign Affairs* declared that "history may yet adjudge Diem as one of the great figures of twentieth century Asia."

The hero worship culminated in Eisenhower's invitation for Diem to visit the United States.

A couple of months before Diem was scheduled to arrive, Nhu and his wife flew to Washington to test the waters, with plane tickets purchased by the CIA. Although Nhu held no official position, he met in March 1957 with Eisenhower, Secretary of State John Foster Dulles, CIA director Allen Dulles, and several senators. Allen Dulles hosted a dinner for the Nhus at the Alibi Club, a private men's club in Washington, where Madame Nhu reveled in the attention paid her by the CIA chief and various State Department and Pentagon notables. Nhu wasn't happy with his wife's performance, but the couple's CIA escort, Paul Harwood, enthused that she exploited her vivacity and good looks to become "the star of the evening."

Diem's American visit in May 1957 was a smashing success. Eisenhower accorded the South Vietnamese chief of state the unusual honor of personally greeting him at Washington's National Airport. The two presidents rode into the capital together in an open limousine as fifty thousand well-wishers and spectators lined the route. One local journalist noted Diem's stone-faced reaction to the crowds, but gave it a gracious spin, writing that the visitor's "air of modest solemnity was far more impressive than any grinning, arm-waving performance could have been."

The next day, Diem addressed a joint session of Congress, shrewdly striking exactly the right balance between gratitude and determination as he thanked Americans for their "generous and unselfish assistance" and pledged to continue his fight against communism. The legislators repeatedly interrupted his speech with lusty applause and gave him a standing ovation. Washington newspapers were no less smitten. The *Post* ran a four-page profile under the headline "Diệm—Symbol of Free New Asia," while *The Evening Star* proclaimed "Welcome to a Champion."

Diem headed next for New York City, where he received an even warmer welcome as 250,000 people turned out for a ticker-tape parade in his honor along Broadway. Mayor Robert Wagner hosted a reception at City Hall, extolling Diem as "a man to whom freedom is the very breath of life." Diem later attended a glittering dinner at the Ambassador Hotel; the master of ceremonies was Henry Luce, head of the Time-Life publishing empire, and the guests included Eleanor Roosevelt, John D. Rockefeller Jr., and Senator John F. Kennedy. Diem also attended Mass at St. Patrick's Cathedral with Cardinal Spellman, now a close ally, and visited the Maryknoll seminary in Ossining, New York, where he'd stayed a few years earlier as a little-known Vietnamese gadfly.

Prior to his arrival in Washington, the State Department had discreetly circulated a protocol memo urging U.S. officials not to raise the issue of Diem's authoritarian abuses, including his penchant for imprisoning dissidents, noting that "he is most sensitive to such charges." Indeed, when asked at a New York press conference about political prisoners in his country, Diem mendaciously said there were none.

One notable exception to the hosanna chorus in Congress and the media was the usually pro-Diem *Life* magazine, which observed: "For all its electoral and constitutional show, South Vietnam appears in many ways to be as much of a police state as its Vietminh rival to the north, and Diem may easily be mistaken for another dictator." But most American publications and officials had only praise for the gallant anti-communist paladin.

Diem's visit marked the apogee of his reputation in the United States. As news stories about his antidemocratic excesses multiplied and surviving communist cadres launched a small but determined insurgency, his prestige slipped into a long, steady decline.

BACK HOME IN SAIGON, Diem returned to quashing his opponents.

Noncommunist activists were jailed along with communists, whistleblowers who complained about government corruption, even Buddhist monks and Catholic priests.

One of those imprisoned was Dr. Tran Van Do, Diem's first foreign minister and a man with a towering reputation for integrity. He was jailed after breaking with Diem over his growing authoritarianism. Another was Y Bham, a Rhade tribesman and leader of the Montagnard autonomy movement. Prisoners were often held without trial for years in what one historian described as "grim climactic and health conditions [that] insured a high casualty rate." The regime admitted that it imprisoned 48,000 people between 1954 and 1960, although some observers said the real figure was far higher.

Journalists were another target. Diem and Nhu regarded the news media not as an independent watchdog institution but as an arm of the state, a tool for imposing the government line on the public. Saigon's twenty newspapers labored under strict censorship; anyone who bucked the rules was headed for trouble.

Editors were instructed what to publish in regular "guidance" memos from regime officials, who sometimes wrote their editorials for them. Newspapers had to submit their page layouts, prior to publication, to a team of twelve censors, who often returned them with blank spaces where articles offensive to the palace had been cut out. Editors were told to fill the spaces with something else. The government controlled both the supply of newsprint and the agency that distributed papers to newsstands. (The national police chief ran the distribution agency.) Anyone brave or foolish enough to defy the censors could find themselves without newsprint for their presses or unable to sell their papers on the street.

In some cases, the regime simply shut down newspapers or arrested journalists. A Catholic weekly was suppressed in 1957 after it suggested that public enthusiasm for Diem had waned. In 1958, the publisher of a Saigon daily, *Thoi Luan*, was sentenced to ten months in prison after he warned readers of the "threat posed by Diem's policies that alienated the people." Things occasionally got rougher when the police or a government-incited mob wrecked a newspaper's office and presses.

Many of the newsmen and others languishing in prison had been arrested by Nhu's secret police, euphemistically called the Service des Etudes Politiques et Sociales (Political and Social Studies Service). SEPES engaged in both espionage and counterintelligence operations, and had broad authority to investigate almost anybody and anything, from the conduct of local elections to the behavior of a cabinet minister or army general.

SEPES was run by a tiny, conspiratorial man with a huge smile named Dr. Tran Kim Tuyen. Standing less than five feet tall and weighing under one hundred pounds, Tuyen was a Catholic from northern Vietnam, a onetime seminarian who played the violin, read Proust, and had completed all but his final year of medical school. (He was universally called a "doctor" even though he never practiced medicine.) Tuyen exuded the shy, modest manner of a Confucian scholar, down to the long, carefully tended fingernail on his left pinkie finger. Once Nhu's private secretary, Tuyen had known his boss since his Hanoi days in the 1940s and was considered one of the regime's most loyal adherents.

But appearances in South Vietnam were often deceptive, and Tuyen was no exception. For beneath the secret-policeman exterior was a would-be reformer, acutely aware of the need to liberalize the regime before it was overthrown.

With so much power in Diem's hands, many South Vietnamese hoped that he'd feel confident enough to allow a certain measure of true democratic competition in the 1959 National Assembly elections. Yet there was widespread fear of communist subversion. Diem's security chief warned that the Viet Cong were planning "extensive interference" with voting in Saigon and adjoining provinces; thousands of troops were posted in the city to stop it.

Diem's grassroots political organization, the National Revolutionary Movement, laid on a massive public education campaign, with posters, banners, and rallies, claiming that the assembly elections would contrast sharply with communist-style elections. The large field of candidates—625 in all—included Nhu and his wife, who both held assembly seats. The most high-profile candidate was Phan Quang Dan, the Saigon physician and ardent Diem critic. Short, stocky, and uncompromisingly blunt, the forty-one-year-old Dan was a different breed of politician than the elderly intellectuals who made up much of the regime's noncommunist opposition.

But Diem's control mechanisms soon clicked into action. One hundred and sixty-five candidates were disqualified by government screening commissions set up to ensure that only the "right" candidates appeared on the ballot. Another seventy candidates withdrew; reports surfaced that some had been threatened. On Election Day, government agents carefully monitored trends in the voting, and soldiers were called in to cast ballots for government-backed candidates who seemed in danger of losing.

Predictably, the results were a landslide for the palace (87 of the 123 new assemblymen were pro-Diem). A subsequent CIA analysis called the election "the dirtiest and most openly rigged of all" nationwide contests under Diem. Despite the government manipulation, Dr. Dan was elected in a Saigon district by a large margin. But while he was on his way to the assembly's opening session, he was arrested, charged with election fraud, and prevented from taking his seat.

***LIFE* MAGAZINE HAD BEEN** quite right: Diem and Nhu had indeed created a state that in some ways was a mirror image of Ho Chi Minh's.

The South Vietnamese government was too clumsy and inefficient to be as ruthlessly totalitarian as Ho's, but there were strong similarities. Thousands of political dissidents were in prison. Censors kept the press under tight control. Opposition political parties had been suppressed, election outcomes were predetermined, and secret police used fear and night arrests to enforce loyalty to the leader. Ho's communist regime, however, had one element that Diem's lacked: an official ideology.

Nhu tried to rectify that by reviving a doctrine called "personalism," espoused in the 1930s by the French Catholic philosopher Emmanuel Mounier. Though it had lapsed into obscurity, personalism was an important intellectual force in Depression-era France as Catholic thinkers sought a middle ground between the chaotic individualism of capitalism and the regimented collectivism of Marxism.

Mounier believed that unfettered capitalism, yoked to the Western ideal of individual freedom, had reduced man to anarchic selfishness, pursuing his own narrow goals as he isolated and alienated himself from society. Communism, on the other hand, exploited man as a powerless cipher in a totalitarian state, stripping him of humanity and spiritual values. Personalism attempted to steer between the two poles, allowing people to reach their potential as creative human beings while they worked with others to bene fit their social group. Mounier thus made a distinction between the liberal concept of the "individual" and his idea of the "whole person," who could flourish in his own life while helping to promote the collective good.

Nhu returned from his Paris student days an avid personalist. He and Diem believed that Mounier's doctrine was compatible with Confucianism and Buddhism, and could serve as the philosophical foundation for their plans to modernize South Vietnam. They saw personalism, with its emphasis on personal struggle and responsibility to the group, as an ideal vehicle for motivating people, particularly the rural masses, to work and sacrifice together, building schools, clinics, and other public projects with little or no government assistance. Personalism was taught in schools, books on personalism were published, personalist posters sprouted in cities and towns. Civil servants and military officers were sent to a personalist training academy overseen by Diem's brother, then-Bishop Thuc.

But the Ngos' efforts to develop a dogma that could compete with communism never caught on. Most South Vietnamese didn't seem to understand Nhu's abstruse explanations of personalism (even Nolting admitted he fell asleep as Nhu expounded on it after a tiger hunt), and the few that did resented it as a fundamentally Catholic creed.

Americans who tried to comprehend personalism tended to see it as a rationale for an all-powerful state to demand subservience and extract free labor from peasants. Moreover, the palace's use of torture, detention without trial, censorship, and other dictatorial methods didn't square very well with the concept of letting individuals flourish to their fullest potential.

Many South Vietnamese also took offense at what they viewed as the regime's attempts to impose a Catholic moral code on a more relaxed Buddhist society.

In 1958, the National Assembly passed the controversial "family law," which banned polygamy and concubinage, practices tolerated in Vietnam for centuries. The law also prohibited divorce, except in "exceptionally unhappy" cases in which Diem himself had to be consulted. The new proscriptions were pushed through the assembly by Madame Nhu, a self-declared champion of women's rights. Among other things, her law eliminated men's right to unilaterally declare themselves divorced, forcing their wives to return to their parents.

Gossips said Madame Nhu had a personal stake in the matter since her older sister, Le Chi, had abandoned a loveless marriage for an open affair with a French big-game hunter. The situation was especially sensitive because the sister's cuckolded husband served as Diem's secretary of the interior. The palace banished both Le Chi's husband and lover to France; the lover later claimed Madame Nhu had ordered someone to inject him with cholera.

The whole fiasco led observers to conclude that Madame Nhu was now such a powerful figure in the palace that she could get rid of anyone, no matter how close they were to Diem.

SHE CERTAINLY WAS THE most intriguing figure in the palace.

Brave, beautiful, fiercely anti-communist, and ardently feminist, she was also haughty, impatient, and hungry for power. Photographers often captured her in her trademark tight silk dresses, towering bouffant, and long, scarlet-lacquered nails. (The French journalist Jean Lacouture indelibly described her as fitting as snugly in a silk frock as "a dagger in its sheath.")

She functioned as a first lady for the bachelor Diem. While there was never any sexual relationship between the two, Madame Nhu talked to and comforted the president after long days of work, charming him and easing his tensions. She also needled and argued vociferously with him about the efficacy of government policies and the suitability of government ministers, and she sometimes prevailed.

Her chronic coquettishness with influential men triggered rumors of infidelity and her venomous tongue was legendary. She once said of Diem to an astonished American journalist: "The president is like a child, and sometimes I get so angry with him I could slap him." At any hour of the day or night, she might pick up the phone and upbraid a general, government sachem, or foreign newsman over some perceived wrongdoing or shortcoming. She wrote in her diary: "Intelligence breeds ambition, but isn't it terrible when one has to work with idiots to carry out great plans? God must have created those idiots to test me." Her waspish personality and calculated sensuality saddled her with a nickname embraced by Vietnamese and Americans alike: the Dragon Lady.

Born in Hanoi in 1924, Madame Nhu was raised by affluent parents who named her Tran Le Xuan, or "beautiful spring." Her father, Tran Van Chuong, was a lawyer in the French colonial administration, a wealthy landowner, and the son of a provincial governor; her mother, a renowned beauty from Hue, was a princess in the imperial family.

Much of Le Xuan's childhood was spent at her family's grand manor, staffed by twenty servants, in Hanoi's French Quarter. Her mother loved to host opulent salons in her home, in the manner of the grande dames of Paris.

Influential French, Vietnamese, and—after the fall of France in 1940—Japanese men were invited to discuss literature, art, and politics. According to French police files, Madame Chuong enjoyed affairs with multiple men, including a Japanese diplomat who betrayed his French wife for her. (Diem later added both of his sister-in-law's parents to his nepotistic oligarchy: Tran Van Chuong became South Vietnam's ambassador to the United States; Madame Chuong became her country's observer at the United Nations.)

One day in the garden of her family home, fifteen-year-old Le Xuan met Ngo Dinh Nhu, the smiling, good-looking scion of a noted Hue family who'd just returned from Paris and begun a new job at the Hanoi library. Nhu was then nearly thirty. After a three-year engagement, the couple married and moved to Hue; in deference to her new husband, Le Xuan, a Buddhist, converted to Catholicism.

When war broke out between the French and Viet Minh, the Nhus found themselves in serious jeopardy. Nhu had been trying to assemble a network of noncommunist political activists and, in December 1946, raggedly dressed Viet Minh soldiers showed up at his house, looking for him. He hid upstairs and slipped away at night.

Madame Nhu boldly invited the Viet Minh in to await her husband's return; instead, they seized her, her infant daughter, and three female relatives and herded them out of town along with a procession of other people. Madame Nhu and her family members were held for three months at a farmhouse, living on rice, milk, and sardines. When bombing by French warplanes came too close, the Viet Minh let the captives go.

Madame Nhu reunited with her husband in Dalat. But Nhu was absorbed in his political work and often disappeared without a word, leaving his wife to her own devices. She spent time with her cousin Bao Dai, playing bridge and picnicking in the countryside.

Nhu asked his wife to come with him to Saigon in 1953 as he drummed up more support for Diem. Madame Nhu pitched in by organizing a boisterous—and dangerous—street demonstration by four thousand northern refugees against the Binh Xuyen in September 1954. One person was killed and others injured when the gangster-controlled Saigon police tried to break up the crowd. As cops with guns drawn closed in on her, she hopped into a car and sped away, calling out: "Arrest me if you can!"

But there was deep sadness in Madame's life. She'd never been in love with the older Nhu and their marriage was a cold one. He was frequently away from her, working long hours with Diem, traveling to distant places, or hunting. Nhu admitted to cheating on her.

In 1956, she was elected to the National Assembly and began her crusade to improve the lot of Vietnamese women. She commissioned a memorial statue on the Saigon waterfront of the heroic Trung sisters, who raised an army against the invading Chinese during the time of Christ and later drowned themselves in a river rather than surrender to the hated foreigners. But Saigonese noticed that the sculptor, whether out of fear or servility, replaced the faces of the Trungs with those of Madame and her oldest daughter.

Such self-aggrandizement, coupled with the regime's heavy-handed repression, began to generate a serious backlash by the late 1950s.

"Discontent in both official and private circles in South Vietnam with President Diem's one-man rule is growing threat to government stability," warned an assessment prepared for Eisenhower's National Security Council in September 1958. "A major source of dissatisfaction is Diem's brother, Ngo Dinh Nhu, who heads the president's tight circle of advisers and is widely feared and hated."

An attempt to assassinate Diem at a provincial fair in 1957 was followed by another attempt the next year, when paratroopers opened fire on his airplane. American officials in Saigon and Washington began to divide into two camps: those who believed that only a tough-minded autocrat could hold the new nation together, and those who felt that Diem's increasingly antidemocratic rule made it more and more difficult to justify U.S. support for him.

WHILE DISSIDENTS GRUMBLED ABOUT Diem in Saigon cafés, communist cadres were desperately trying to elude his police and soldiers in the countryside.

The regime's Anti-Communist Denunciation Campaign was highly effective, wiping out nearly the entire communist network in the south by 1959. Many cadres fled with their families to jungle or forest hideouts. Some lived in tunnels, emerging only at night. On the Camau Peninsula, a major Viet Minh base area during the French war, cadres took refuge in the U Minh Forest, a vast tangle of mangrove swamps notorious for malaria and other diseases. The anti-communist drive "truly and efficiently destroyed our Party," according to a notebook captured from a high-ranking political officer. After membership plunged from one thousand to six in Gia Dinh Province, adjacent to Saigon, the local communist party secretary committed suicide. Diem began calling party activists "Viet Cong," or Vietnamese communists, to belittle them and make clear their political goals.

Facing extermination, the VC fought back. Poorly armed and few in number, they initially limited their attacks to small, isolated military outposts. North Vietnam reinforced them, sending trained cadres and supplies into the south over the Ho Chi Minh Trail. The VC began to assassinate government officials in rural areas in what they dubbed their "extermination of traitors" campaign. Teachers, health workers, police officers, and youth leaders were gunned down, disemboweled, or beheaded, often in front of their families or other terrified villagers.

The VC used terror as a political tool, sparingly and selectively. A terrorist act rarely was committed unless it advanced a political goal. The insurgents targeted the most effective and popular local officials as well as the most corrupt, abusive ones, whose elimination often pleased local peasants. Sometimes the killers went after a religious figure with strong anti-communist views, or a villager with a reputation for integrity who could be expected to resist them. A Catholic priest was stabbed to death with bamboo spears. Four young men were beheaded and their heads nailed to a bridge for locals to see.

In Long An Province, a richly productive rice-growing area that wrapped around Saigon to the south and west, the VC murdered twenty-six hamlet chiefs, police officers, and others during the 1960 Tet holidays, normally a joyous time of family reunions and ancestor worship. The communists planned to kill many more officials, but some of the intended victims found out and fled their homes and offices before the assassins arrived. That was precisely the VC's goal: to undermine and ultimately paralyze the Saigon government in the countryside by killing or scaring off its agents and administrators. In all, the Viet Cong killed an estimated 1,500 regime officials in 1960.

As rural officials were slain or ran away, the government had more difficulty collecting taxes and recruiting soldiers. Farmers no longer gave information to troops and police looking for local VC. Government administrators couldn't travel safely in the provinces, and Diem's rural-improvement programs began to break down. The Viet Cong killed or kidnapped so many DDT sprayers—and promised to kill any replacements—that the malaria-eradication program collapsed. By murdering teachers, the guerrillas forced the closure of 200 primary schools in 1960, interrupting the education of some 25,000 kids. Sometimes the VC wrecked a program simply by spreading lies about it. When the government tried to introduce a nutritious and fast-growing species of fish—tilapia—the communists told peasants that eating it caused leprosy.

THE ANTI-TILAPIA CAMPAIGN WAS but one example of the VC's expert use of propaganda to erode the Saigon government's legitimacy in rural areas.

The communists worked continuously to exploit peasant grievances against Saigon. VC cadres organized "misery telling" sessions at which hundreds of rural people were encouraged to voice their resentment toward Diem's regime for imposing taxes, enforcing land rents, and drafting their sons into the army when they were needed at home to work the crops. Peasants were encouraged to stop paying taxes and land rents, burn their government-issued identity cards, and hoist VC flags.

The communists also took advantage of peasants' hunger for farmland.

Since the days of the French, landownership had been concentrated in the hands of a relative few, with millions of peasants forced to rent land, often at exorbitant prices, or work as low-paid laborers on someone else's property. Diem came up with a program to redistribute land, but it was relatively conservative and took several years to get underway. Peasants had to pay for the parcels they received and only about 10 percent of them nationwide benefited from the program.

By contrast, the communists simply seized land from its owners, many of them absentee, and gave it to poor people for free.

The Viet Cong told the delighted new owners that the government would try to take away their acreage, but they could defend it by joining the guerrillas and harassing or killing troops who tried to enter their village. Anxious peasants then helped to destroy bridges, tear up roads, and block canals to impede army movements. Of course, the communists never mentioned that if they succeeded in taking over South Vietnam, the peasants' land would be taken from them and collectivized, as had happened in the north.

As the VC gradually pushed Saigon's representatives out of rural areas, they set up their own government, complete with schools, health clinics, and tax collectors. The guerrillas played a game with the French managers of rubber plantations, ostensibly "kidnapping" them and later releasing them in exchange for "ransom" payments. That way the French didn't arouse the government's ire by directly paying VC taxes. In December 1960, the guerrillas' political arm, the National Liberation Front, was founded and began organizing students, workers, professional people, and others.

The communists also extended their terror campaign from the countryside into Saigon. Boys as young as twelve were recruited to heave grenades into restaurants, bars, and stalled traffic. Bicycle frames stuffed with explosives blew up in the streets. People grew afraid to sit on patios, go to the movies, or shop in outdoor markets.

The strife began to disrupt the South Vietnamese economy. Rice production, after peaking in 1959, began to decline as the VC intercepted shipments headed for urban areas; by mid-1961, South Vietnam had no more surplus rice to export. Production of sugarcane, coconuts, and tobacco began to drop. (With French plantation owners surreptitiously paying off the VC, rubber production kept rising.)

Yet the regime remained strongly entrenched. In April 1960, eighteen prominent noncommunist politicians gathered at Saigon's Caravelle Hotel and issued a sweeping indictment of Diem's abuses and failings. Their manifesto called on him to liberalize his government, promote democracy, guarantee basic civil rights, and recognize opposition parties. Diem and Nhu rejected the demands and jailed most of the "Caravellistas." A roundup of anti-government students, doctors, lawyers, and professors followed.

THE SITUATION FINALLY BOILED over on November 11, 1960, when three battalions of mutinous paratroopers slipped into Saigon and surrounded Independence Palace. (This was the incident that sent John Helble jumping over a wall on his way to work.)

The paratroopers opened fire with machine guns on Diem's bedroom at 3 a.m. Palace guards fought back, but it soon became clear that reinforcements were needed. Diem and Dr. Tuyen, the secret police chief, began making urgent phone calls to loyal troop commanders outside Saigon.

News of the mutiny spread through the city as the sun rose. But the rebels hadn't thought through their attempted coup very well. No other military units joined them, and they had no real plan for running the government if they succeeded. Dissident politicians arrived at the insurgents' command post to help them articulate a political program. Among them was Dr. Dan, the vocal Diem critic who'd been denied his National Assembly seat.

The attack on the palace bogged down and the two sides began to negotiate. The rebels demanded more aggressive military action against the Viet Cong. Diem agreed and went on the radio promising to dissolve his government and allow his generals to establish a junta. But he used the talks to buy time as he, Nhu, and Tuyen worked the phones to bring reliable troops into Saigon to save them.

Thirty-six hours after the revolt began, combat units from the Mekong Delta entered the city and encircled the outnumbered paratroopers. Rebel officers fled and their uprising collapsed.

Though it failed, the insurrection reverberated widely in South Vietnam. While Diem had publicly pledged to reform his government, he merely reshuffled his cabinet and continued his repressive ways, using the attempted putsch as a pretext to arrest even more opposition figures. But his broken promise, one astute observer noted, amounted to a "psychological coup de grace to Diem's reputation as a nationalist leader of honesty and integrity." Because the president had "lowered himself" by parleying with the rebels, Madame Nhu was more convinced than ever he was a milksop. "I am disgusted with him," she wrote angrily in her diary.

The uprising also bolstered Diem and Nhu's doubts about the strength of the U.S. commitment to them. Throughout the late 1950s, the Americans had steadfastly supported the regime with military and economic aid. In the 1960 crisis, however, they backed away: with rebel troops outside Independence Palace, the embassy made it clear in phone calls with Diem that Washington wouldn't take sides.

Diem's police soon came for Dr. Dan, arresting him at his office along with his nurse, secretary, and even patients in his waiting room. He was taken to the secret prison at the Saigon Zoo and placed in a windowless cell, about six feet long and four and a half feet wide. The cell swarmed with mosquitoes; the only place to sleep was the dirt floor.

At night, he was blindfolded, tied to a bench, and tortured. Wires were attached to his fingers and toes, and someone cranked an electricity generator. "The shock made me shout, and when I opened my mouth, they poured water down my throat," Dan recalled. "They wanted to make me suffer." The torturers asked questions as they worked on him: Which army officers did he talk to? Who were his American contacts? The sessions started at 9 p.m. and often dragged on until three in the morning.

Slumped in his cell, alone and not knowing what had become of his wife and three children, the physician wasn't sure he could hold on to his sanity. In the blackness he prayed and tried to make plans for the future. The only sounds he heard were the cries of others being tortured. Some had their fingers nailed to a table.

According to Dan, one day his cell door opened and Nhu walked in. He suspected Dan of having connections to certain army generals. "You must tell me everything," Nhu said. "If you refuse, we will use the electric shock. If that doesn't work, we'll use the water torture. If that doesn't loosen your tongue, we'll suspend you head down and beat you. And if those don't work, we have many, many other methods."

Dan replied that if the regime had evidence against him, he should be put on trial. Nhu only scoffed. "There's no justice here," he said. Dan had two choices: cooperate and live, or resist and die.

"If you oppose us, we'll destroy you," said the president's brother.

Dan was eventually chained to the deck of a boat in a driving rain and taken to the old French prison island, Poulo Condor, in the South China Sea.

THE VIET CONG, MEANWHILE, escalated their military attacks.

In January 1960, about two hundred guerrillas overran a South Vietnamese army regimental headquarters in Tay Ninh Province near the Cambodian border, inflicting sixty-six casualties and capturing enough weapons and ammunition to arm five hundred men. In March, VC units ambushed three South Vietnamese battalions conducting separate sweep operations near the Cambodian frontier, forcing all of them to retreat.

Ambassador Durbrow reported to Washington that the Viet Cong now had three thousand full-time guerrillas. Like the Viet Minh before them, the VC operated as self-sufficiently as possible. They captured or manufactured their weapons, slept in hammocks slung from trees instead of barracks, and grew their own food. Most of their soldiers were recruited in the south.

What really distinguished the Viet Cong from conventional armies was their emphasis on political organizing. In the early 1960s, their main-force units engaged in military missions only one day per month, on average. The rest of their time was spent in training, propaganda activities, growing rice and other food, and political indoctrination classes.

They had no tanks, trucks, artillery, or aircraft. But they were disciplined and motivated. Their tactics were creative and, unlike Diem's forces, they learned from their mistakes. Badly armed in the beginning, the Viet Cong quickly acquired better weapons—often U.S.-made—by attacking isolated, mud-walled forts defended by Diem's ill-trained rural militia. So many of these old, French-built outposts were overrun that American military advisers began calling them "VC supply depots" and urging Diem to dismantle them. He refused.

The communists often spent days or weeks practicing an attack, down to the smallest details. They were particularly adept at ambushes, catching South Vietnamese infantry patrols or vehicle convoys in devastating cross fires. When the unit under attack called for help, the VC ambushed the relief force. Full-time guerrillas—known to Americans as "hardhats" for their helmets made of tightly woven straw—were backed up by farmers who were part-time guerrillas, tilling their fields by day and fighting by night. Wearing the same black cotton blouses and shorts that peasants wore, the VC were all but impossible to distinguish from the rural population.

BY CONTRAST, SOUTH VIETNAM'S army—formally called the Army of the Republic of Vietnam—was a conventional military force to its marrow.

Largely shaped by American advisers in the late 1950s, the ARVN was a smaller version of the U.S. Army, organized into corps, divisions, regiments, and so forth. In a war that called for small, mobile units to pursue fast-moving guerrillas in difficult terrain, the ARVN was road-bound by tanks and trucks, burdened with inexperienced commanders, and reluctant to patrol at night, when the VC generally operated.

The senior U.S. military adviser in Saigon from 1955 to 1960 was Lieutenant General Samuel Williams. The Pentagon warned Williams that North Vietnam was likely to launch a Korea-style invasion of the south due to Diem's refusal to take part in the 1956 reunification election. Williams took the admonition seriously, working hard to build up South Vietnam's defenses at the 17th parallel.

Under his direction, the ARVN was structured so it could link up smoothly with arriving U.S. combat units when an invasion came. The ARVN built up its reservoir of tanks and artillery, and South Vietnamese officers went to U.S. Army schools to learn about armored warfare and how to block the expected cross-border invasion. Williams continued to beef up the ARVN even after a consensus developed among U.S. intelligence analysts that Ho Chi Minh wasn't planning to invade after all.

Both Williams and Diem believed that the Viet Cong's rural attacks represented their "last gasp" as government forces got closer to wiping them out. Diem thought the conflict could be solved by military means, although Nhu believed a mainly political approach was needed. The president favored a large, conventional army, but some of his military leaders wanted to make the ARVN a lighter, more flexible counterguerrilla force. (One general argued that 105-millimeter artillery should be eliminated altogether, since it made ARVN troops reluctant to patrol beyond the guns' twelve-thousand-yard range.)

In the meantime, the ARVN was making the same mistakes the French had: clinging to roads instead of aggressively patrolling in rice fields, swamps, and jungles; squandering its mobility and striking power by guarding static facilities like bridges and government buildings; and conceding freedom of movement to the VC at night.

Besides its conventional structure and tactics, the ARVN was plagued by inexperienced commanders. While many top officers had served under the French, few ever reached field grade and some weren't qualified to command large infantry formations.

Even the best ARVN leaders, moreover, faced frequent interference from the palace. Diem and Nhu were forever shifting combat units from place to place in order to stymie potential coups. They kept a close watch on the selection and promotion of high-ranking officers, valuing them more for their perceived loyalty than their military skills. Those considered politically unreliable were sidelined. Of the seventeen ARVN generals in 1961, only six commanded combat troops. (One general, in charge of the malaria-eradication program, was mockingly called "the mosquito general.")

Religion was sometimes a litmus test, too. One general recalled being summoned to Hue by Diem and Archbishop Thuc, who demanded: "Do you know that one of your colonels . . . openly displays anti-Catholic feelings?" The general said he doubted that, but was silently angry about being held responsible for a subordinate's alleged religious biases.

Yet for all of that the ARVN was quite capable of winning battles. Many younger officers and noncoms were good leaders, and South Vietnamese units could be lethally effective when properly deployed. American advisers were impressed by the endurance and stoicism of ARVN soldiers, who tried to hide their pain when wounded. They obeyed orders without question and often displayed courage on the battlefield.

TO WESTERN EYES, HOWEVER, the ARVN was nothing if not a peculiar army.

It was filled with draftees, mostly country boys who until recently had been tending water buffaloes and rice shoots. The South Vietnamese seemed to find humor in almost any situation, and often laughed and talked even while under fire. It was customary for Vietnamese friends to hold hands, and some soldiers did so while on patrol, making them easier targets for the VC.

The ARVN didn't provide food to troops in the field. Instead, they received an allowance to buy what they wanted from local sellers and cook it to taste. Units on the march invariably stopped at midday to make lunch and take the traditional Vietnamese siesta, lasting up to three hours. Those not napping flirted with local women or foraged for more to eat. The system worked if the troops got paid on time. If they didn't, they simply took what they wanted. They stole chickens and ducks, giving their peasant owners another grievance against the government.

An ARVN battalion moving overland could be almost as noisy and colorful as a circus coming to town.

Tied to soldiers' field packs were pots and pans, clanging loudly, and live poultry, squawking wildly. Day and night, the troops smoked, talked, rattled, laughed, and shouted. If they spent more than a few days in the field, their wives, children, and girlfriends often came out to meet them. One American adviser witnessed several such affectionate reunions (although he worried that if the soldiers' women knew where they were, so did the VC). When an ARVN platoon was airlifted from one base to another, the soldiers' families, household wares, and barnyard animals went along with them. A U.S. pilot recalled having to transport so many pigs, water buffaloes, chickens, and ducks that he began leaving his plane's cargo ramp open in flight to ventilate the stench.

Cultural differences aside, ARVN units often exhibited a marked lack of aggressiveness, despite the constant goading of their American advisers to close with the enemy. Their noisiness while on the move sometimes seemed calculated to alert VC troops in the hope that they'd melt away and a battle could be avoided. The South Vietnamese stayed on their bases and didn't patrol much at night, giving the VC free rein to terrorize unprotected villages. Large-scale ARVN sweep operations, involving thousands of soldiers trying to flush VC fighters out of a specific area, were clamorous and slow, and the communists were usually gone by the time government troops arrived.

ARVN battle planners often gave the VC an escape hatch, attacking an enemy unit from three sides but leaving the fourth side open. (U.S. combat advisers bitterly dubbed this "the three-sided Vietnamese square.") While Diem denied it, some Americans believed he'd ordered his commanders to avoid casualties out of fear of another army revolt as deaths and injuries mounted.

Many draftees simply saw no reason to fight hard and risk their lives for an unpopular regime. Many also were deeply afraid of the VC. Colonel Daniel Boone Porter, the top U.S. Army adviser to the ARVN's IV Corps in the Mekong Delta, concluded that South Vietnamese soldiers had either experienced or heard about so many ferocious enemy ambushes that they became "obsessed with the idea that the Viet Cong were invincible." By contrast, government troops rarely set ambushes, convinced that even trapped VC fighters would slug their way out and kill the ambushers.

To make matters worse, Diem's soldiers often abused the rural folk they were supposed to protect, especially in areas where peasants were considered sympathetic to the VC.

Troops roughed up or tortured them for information on the enemy, a practice that one American described as "tragically stupid," since it alienated the very people the army needed on its side. Farmers who panicked and ran were shot. Rather than enter a village and carefully search it, ARVN units sometimes simply attacked it. If anything incriminating was found in a peasant's house, the dwelling was burned down.

Villagers were forced to walk at the head of troop columns, setting off any mines or booby traps the guerrillas had planted. The ARVN routinely used artillery to "interdict" VC movements, firing at random from miles away, often from dawn to dusk, killing some villagers and terrifying the rest. These practices contrasted sharply with the VC, who were trained to treat peasants with respect. They paid for any food they took and helped peasants work their fields, making them more likely to provide intelligence on the ARVN.

More and more South Vietnamese joined the communists. From a mid-1959 low of about 5,000 members, party ranks shot up to almost 35,000 by late 1961.

AS THE WAR HEATED up, Madame Nhu decided that life in Saigon was becoming altogether too frivolous.

She reacted by shepherding her "social purification law" through the National Assembly. The law banned dancing, prostitution, cockfighting, fortune-telling, contraception, even underwire bras. Thirty-odd popular songs were outlawed on the grounds that they were too "sentimental" for a nation at war, ironically angering ARVN soldiers, who loved listening to and singing along with such tunes on transistor radios.

The dance ban stirred the strongest popular reaction. The Dragon Lady declared that South Vietnamese were already "dancing with death" in their struggle with the Viet Cong, and that was enough dancing. She sent police into the streets to make sure no one was shaking a leg, either in public or private. But many Vietnamese loved to boogie, and Chubby Checker's hit song "The Twist" had touched off a dance craze among Saigonese. Dance halls and nightclubs locked their doors and became "twisteasies." Vietnamese teenagers defied the ban by organizing secret twist parties in each other's homes. Vietnamese and American adults posted servants outdoors to watch for snoopy cops as they turned up the dance music for their party guests.

In her graceless efforts to impose austere wartime virtue on her people, Madame Nhu made herself one of South Vietnam's most despised figures.

Buddhists interpreted her new restrictions as yet another attempt to inflict a rigid Catholic code of behavior on them. Madame, wrote an American academic who knew her well, "is as brilliant, vivacious, bitchy, and brutal in her Borgia-like fashion as ever—and with (charitably) the purest of intentions she is succeeding in alienating substantial segments of the population from her brother-in-law's regime at a time when it needs the enthusiastic support of everyone." Nhu joined his wife's crusade, requiring Diem's cabinet ministers to participate in communist-style "criticism/self-criticism" sessions, and encouraging them to confess their marital problems and strive to reach new heights of personal rectitude.

Many Vietnamese still regarded Diem with respect and even affection, although they were saddened that a once-promising nationalist leader had gone so badly astray. The Nhus, however, were widely loathed, especially among Saigon's politically conscious classes: businessmen, civil servants, military officers, and intellectuals. That abhorrence manifested itself in a host of nasty rumors, ranging from financial corruption to personal perversion.

The most vicious tales were aimed at Madame, who'd become, noted a foreign diplomat, "the object of more envy and disputes than Cleopatra herself." One story claimed that she'd looted all the gold from the Bank of Vietnam and lured Nolting into smuggling it out of South Vietnam in the form of a solid-gold statue of herself. She purportedly owned a coffee plantation in Brazil and a movie theater in Paris, and her wealth was secreted in Swiss bank accounts. She was sleeping with Diem and had had a longtime affair with a prominent, French-born general. American aid to South Vietnam was a payoff for her sexual favors. Nhu, too, was the subject of scandalous whispers, often involving alleged financial manipulations by his Can Lao Party. He was said not to care about his wife's indiscretions because he smoked so much opium.

The rumors were so numerous and so malicious that the couple took out newspaper ads to refute them. At a press conference, Nhu volunteered that "my wife has no bank account." He was referring to rampant scuttlebutt that Madame had secretly transferred funds abroad, even though none of the newsmen present had raised the subject. Such denials only fanned the flames, and the Nhus eventually stopped issuing them. Alarmed by the intensity of the rumormongering and the political damage it caused, Durbrow quietly instructed the CIA to investigate the Nhus' alleged foreign holdings. But, he said, the agency found "no verification whatsoever, not even hints about it."

DESPITE THE GOSSIP AND resentment, both Nhus managed to build their own independent power bases.

Nhu was "supreme leader" of the Republican Youth, a paramilitary organization that claimed a membership of more than 1.3 million men and women between eighteen and thirty-five years old, mostly in rural areas. Its stated purpose was the "full development of young people's needs in the social, intellectual, and spiritual fields," but its real goal was to build an armed youth movement for the Ngo family in the countryside. Nhu often appeared at Republican Youth rallies in the group's regulation uniform of blue beret, blue shirt, and blue slacks. The CIA trained its members, but warned that it resembled the Hitler Youth.

Madame Nhu had two groups of her own. One was the Women's Solidarity Movement, with a reputed 2 million members, many of them wives of civil servants and military officers who had little choice but to join. The other was her personal army, the Women's Paramilitary Corps, created in 1962 to train thousands of young women for combat. Saigon newspapers were full of stories and photographs of lithe females in rakish bush hats and trim blue coveralls, leaping over walls and squeezing off rounds on rifle ranges. Few if any ever got into combat, but they were quite photogenic in parades. Madame's teenage daughter, Le Thuy, was a member; an American journalist once saw her shoot balloons out of a man's hand with a .45-caliber pistol from ninety feet away.

But the Ngos' position grew more precarious as resentment toward them deepened within South Vietnam's military. Many officers were furious at Diem for his promotion policies and constant reshuffling of combat units, and blamed him for the ineffective war effort.

In February 1962, two rogue air force pilots attacked Independence Palace, where the Nhu family lived with Diem. Flying American-made AD-6 Skyraiders, the pilots circled the palace at low altitude, dropping bombs and napalm and strafing it with rockets and cannons. South Vietnamese navy vessels moored in the Saigon River opened fire on the airmen; one crash-landed in the river, the other flew to asylum in Cambodia.

The pilots had concentrated their attack on the palace's west wing, which housed the Nhus and their four children. A Chinese governess was killed by a falling beam while trying to protect the Nhus' youngest child. Hurrying to put on a dressing gown, Madame Nhu plunged through a hole in her bedroom floor and fell two stories onto a pile of broken wood, twisted iron, and hot ash, suffering third-degree burns and deep lacerations on an arm. When her husband, searching frantically through the smoke and rubble, finally found her, she fainted in his arms.

A bomb crashed through the ceiling of Diem's bedroom, but failed to go off. He made a brief radio address, urging the public to stay calm and giving thanks to "divine providence" for sparing him. Two hours after the bombing, he received a group of foreign diplomats, joking with them and seeming unruffled. But in a private moment with General Harkins, Diem admitted his fear that "sometime I'm going to get shot right in the back of the neck."

BY THE SPRING OF 1963, after nine years in power, Diem's government had hardened into a sclerotic family clique with fading public support.

Incompetence and political interference weakened his army. Diem and his relatives had alienated virtually every segment of South Vietnamese society. Many once-supportive nationalists had given up on him and become what the French derisively called *attentistes*, uncommitted fence-sitters, waiting to see which way the struggle between the regime and the Viet Cong would go before taking a side.

Diem was becoming more isolated, more authoritarian, and more reliant on his family for support and advice. The personality traits that helped him triumph during the Battle of Saigon had become liabilities. Stubborn determination had calcified into obstinacy; principled conviction had soured into self-righteousness.

But he was still in charge, and held levers of power that could keep him in charge.

CHAPTER 5

A FIERCE TRIBE OF TRUTH SEEKERS

AS HE STEPPED off his plane at Tan Son Nhut airport, David Halberstam was convinced he'd been delivered to South Vietnam as surely by fate as by jetliner.

At twenty-eight, Halberstam was a rising star at America's most influential newspaper, *The New York Times.* Boisterous, opinionated, and boyishly extroverted, he'd quickly establish himself as the dominant personality in the small but talented group of American news reporters stationed in Saigon.

The rangy Harvard graduate made no bones about his prodigious ego, joking to friends about an editor's remark that "David is almost as good a reporter as he thinks he is." He could reduce noisy restaurants and cocktail parties to stunned silence with booming denunciations of government officials, his fist slamming a table for emphasis. With his thick-framed glasses, caterpillar eyebrows, and big grin, he was a brilliant brat, as vocally combative with his New York bosses as he was with dissembling bureaucrats. Halberstam would soon be haunting the U.S. embassy, buttonholing anyone and everyone for news leads, and traveling widely in the countryside, talking with American advisers who saw the war at mud level.

It was easy to take sides for or against Diem when Halberstam arrived in Saigon in September 1962. Many Americans there, both military and civilian, had quietly turned against the president, believing his government was too weak and unpopular to win the war, and too repressive to deserve U.S. support. Others thought the tough, experienced Diem was the only person who could hold his people and army together against the VC.

Halberstam soon joined the critics' ranks, setting himself against not only Diem but against Nolting and Harkins as well. Passionate about digging up hard truths, the young *Times* man developed a deep and enduring anger toward both U.S. officials, seeing them as part of what he called "the lying machine" that was trying to whitewash the difficulties Americans were encountering in the war.

While most other Saigon journalists aimed to be neutral observers, Halberstam harbored a crusader's zeal. "He was quite different from the rest of us," said his friend Horst Faas, a photographer for the Associated Press news service. "He believed in his duty to change things."

Halberstam's judgments about people and events could be savagely harsh. Yet he had a sophisticated grasp of both politics and military strategy, and his Saigon-datelined stories would boldly contradict Washington's official optimism about the war in a manner that had little precedent in American journalism. Before his fifteen-month stint in South Vietnam was over, he'd be vilified as soft on communism, a weak sister who cried at the sight of dead Viet Cong, and a conscious subverter of American foreign policy. An irritated JFK would try to get him yanked out of South Vietnam. But the torrent of insightful front-page news stories and Sunday analysis pieces that rushed from Halberstam's battered portable typewriter would create a remarkably full and vivid portrait of the Diem regime and earn their author a Pulitzer Prize.

Riding from the airport into Saigon for the first time, Halberstam sensed the beauty of South Vietnam as well as the dark turbulence just beneath the surface. Troops were everywhere. He knew this assignment would be exciting, difficult, the opportunity of a lifetime. He'd begged his editors to send him and now here he was.

"Never as in that moment had life seemed so real to me," he later wrote. "I had finally arrived at the place where I was always destined to go."

AFTER GRADUATING FROM HARVARD in 1955, Halberstam didn't migrate with other Ivy Leaguers to New York or Washington for entry-level jobs at a television network or other big, prestigious news organization that promised good pay and rapid advancement. Instead, he headed for the smallest daily newspaper in Mississippi, the West Point *Daily Times Leader*, circulation four thousand, because it offered something far more interesting: a front-row seat covering the civil rights upheaval in the Deep South. But the cub reporter quit after an editor killed his story about people in the rigidly segregated town joining the supremacist White Citizens' Council.

Halberstam soon landed a new job with *The Nashville Tennessean*, which gave him much more latitude to cover civil rights. On the side, he wrote uncommonly good freelance articles for *The Reporter*, a small but well-regarded newsmagazine. His work attracted the attention of James Reston, *The New York Times*'s Washington bureau chief, who hired him in 1960.

Halberstam came to South Vietnam with the same conventional Cold War views that many Americans held in the early 1960s. Communist imperialism had to be stopped, he believed, and the United States had the power and moral obligation to stop it. No less than other Americans, Halberstam had been moved by President Kennedy's words about the necessity for America to win the "long twilight struggle" against the Soviet Union and China. He firmly supported U.S. efforts to help South Vietnam defeat the Viet Cong. But his experiences to come would lead him to radically rethink whether Washington and its Vietnamese ally could win the war.

By the fall of 1962, relations between U.S. journalists and the Diem regime had sunk to what one American official described as "an abysmal low." Things weren't much better between the reporters and the U.S. embassy, which was continually trying to put a positive spin on the regime's shortcomings. On the day Halberstam got to Saigon, he attended a going-away party for a *Newsweek* reporter, François Sully.

A debonair, high-living Frenchman, Sully had come to Vietnam as a paratrooper in 1947. He stayed on and, after a failed career as a tea planter, became a war correspondent. Since he believed the Americans were making many of the same mistakes the French had, Sully's reporting on the war bore a sharper edge than that of most U.S. correspondents, aggravating both Diem and Nolting. When the latter challenged one of his stories, asking, "Why, Monsieur Sully, do you always see the hole in the doughnut?" the Frenchman merrily rejoined, "Because, Monsieur l'Ambassadeur, there is a hole in the doughnut."

Diem had already banned *Newsweek* from South Vietnam newsstands. But Sully moved into the palace's crosshairs for the final time with a dispatch headlined "Vietnam: The Unpleasant Truth."

Characterizing the war as "a losing proposition," Sully's story quoted Bernard Fall, a respected historian of the French and U.S. interventions in Vietnam, as saying the Americans were teaching the ARVN conventional military tactics that wouldn't work against the guerrillas. An anonymous South Vietnamese officer told Sully the war was being lost because the government wasn't doing enough to protect the peasants. But what really set Madame Nhu off was a caption below a photo of her cherished Women's Paramilitary Corps. It read: "Female militia in Saigon: the enemy has more drive and enthusiasm."

It made no difference to Madame Nhu that the offending words about the women she called "my little darlings" had been written not by Sully but by an editor in New York. She launched a wrathful campaign of insults and phony charges against Sully through Saigon's regime-friendly press, which excoriated him variously as a VC spy, an opium smuggler, a French spy, and a fancier of orgies.

More ominously, three secret police agents in black leather jackets began to follow him. Despite pleas from his fellow journalists and Nolting that he be allowed to stay, Sully was expelled from South Vietnam on September 9.

LIKE MANY WESTERNERS, HALBERSTAM fell quickly under Saigon's spell.

The great humid city was stupendous, churning and fermenting under the equatorial sun. The monsoon season, which lashed and drenched Saigon with rain for half the year, was ending; the dry season, with its scorching heat, was about to begin. Wartime Saigon was exotic and romantic and electric, with just enough danger in the air to make a young bachelor feel marvelously alive.

Long known as the Paris of the East, it was a captivating metropolis of broad boulevards, lovely shade trees, and brilliant flowers. Fine French, Chinese, and Vietnamese restaurants abounded, along with pleasant sidewalk cafés, elegant nightclubs, and ice cream parlors filled with teenagers defying the Dragon Lady by doing the twist, from the waist up, in the booths. As in Hue, French influence was widely visible, especially in handsome colonial-era public buildings such as the opera house and upper-class neighborhoods of large, airy villas behind high walls splashed with bougainvillea and flowering mimosa.

The first thing Westerners usually noticed was the blast-furnace heat. Next was the smell: "an unfamiliar, exotic, sickly sweet mixture of tropical fruits, flowers, sea breezes, rotting vegetation, diesel fumes, piss, gunpowder, and cordite," as an American soldier described it. Then there was the colorfully horrendous traffic. Downtown streets were clogged with jeeps, motor scooters, army trucks, ox-drawn carts, bicycles (both pedaled and motorized, with as many as five adults and children hanging on), small blue-and-yellow Renault cabs that looked like oversize ladybugs, and bicycle taxis known as cyclo-pousses, in which passengers sat on a sort of wheeled love seat while a Vietnamese pedaled away from behind.

White-uniformed traffic policemen standing on daintily canopied platforms seemed to have little control over drivers careening down streets and around traffic circles. Pedestrians took their lives in their hands whenever they tried to cross a road; one U.S. journalist was knocked down and had his arm broken by a speeding motorcyclist. Weaving skillfully through the bedlam were young women perched primly on Lambretta or Vespa motor scooters.

Diem's capital was a place of striking sights and customs. On street corners excited schoolboys staged cricket fights in arenas made of cookie tins. Sidewalk dentists pulled bad teeth (without benefit of anesthesia) for ten cents a pop. Amid the stifling midday heat, office workers streamed home for lunch and a nap, while cyclo-pousse drivers curled up on their love seats for their own siestas. Monkey meat was among the delicacies for sale in the jam-packed central market. Noodle peddlers ambled through the streets, clicking sticks together to announce their presence. Thousands of porters—men and women, young and old—scurried along with shoulder poles bearing heavy baskets of food, water, charcoal, construction materials, and sometimes VC contraband.

A newcomer could water-ski on the Saigon River, ride horses at the Cercle Hippique, enjoy a swim and a gin fizz at the Cercle Sportif Saigonnais, or shop at stores awash in high-end consumer goods, many of them U.S.-subsidized imports. Because Saigon was relatively close to the equator, dusk came at about 7 p.m. year-round. Lanterns were lit and streets filled with the tinkling of bicycle bells as workers pedaled home, some with long baguettes tied to their bike baskets. Sidewalk food stands gave off mouthwatering smells of grilled pork patties, beef wrapped in betel leaves, steaming noodle soups called pho, and curry spiced with cassia.

Restaurants were inexpensive and excellent. Gourmands considered the Arc-en-Ciel in Cholon the best Chinese restaurant in Southeast Asia. At the end of the evening, the well-heeled congregated at the rooftop bar of the Majestic Hotel, enjoying a pastis and cool breezes off the Saigon River. Restless men boarded riverfront junks that served as floating brothels.

While much of Diem's capital sparkled with ornaments of prosperity, there was a second Saigon, a shadow city rife with poverty and misery.

Twenty-five percent of Saigon's workers were unemployed, a rate comparable to the worst depths of the Depression in America. On the city's outskirts lay slums where hovels slapped together from plywood, tar paper, and flattened beer cans had no electricity or running water. Human waste was emptied into the street or a reeking canal, and destitute inhabitants often had little more than a day's supply of rice and fish. Police frequently checked their identity cards and barged into their huts searching for VC.

Those without a home crawled into hammocks at night with handheld radios, consoling themselves with sentimental Vietnamese folk music.

For many Americans, however, the city was an exotic adventure. The U.S. military established an officers' club on the roof of the Rex Hotel, in the middle of the city, with grilled steaks and cold beer always on tap. High-heeled Vietnamese hostesses waved U.S. servicemen into nightclubs and bars with names like Blue Moon, Starlight, and OK Corral. American couples threw so many cocktail parties that a local women's club did a thriving business renting out martini glasses.

HALBERSTAM WAS FASCINATED BY all of it. He spent his first days in Saigon picking other journalists' brains, developing contacts among U.S. and South Vietnamese officials, and exploring the manifold charms of his new beat.

He discovered "Radio Catinat," a tongue-in-cheek reference to gossip about the regime exchanged in the restaurants, bars, and sidewalk cafés that lined Rue Catinat. (Diem had renamed it Tu Do, or Freedom Street, but most foreign reporters stuck with the more evocative French name.) Diem and Nhu despised the dissidents and intellectuals who whiled away their days in cafés sipping coffee and retailing rumors about the Ngo family's alleged plundering. But newsmen found the eateries useful places to pick up tips and background information, some of which was even true.

With his long, self-confident strides, Halberstam visited the Radio Catinat hot spots: the sidewalk café outside the Continental Hotel; Cheap Charlie's restaurant; and Givral, known for its delicious pastries and ice cream. He especially liked Brodard's, a low-priced hash house where he inhaled gargantuan lunches to fuel his hypersonic metabolism: a steak, french fries, shrimp, soup, another steak, and two slices of pie with ice cream, washed down with two glasses of milk and an iced coffee.

While making his rounds Halberstam met a slight, smiling Vietnamese who held court every afternoon at Givral and was reputed to be the best news source in Saigon.

Pham Xuan An presented himself as a journalist who'd attended a Southern California community college and seemed to know everyone in town. He was smart and funny, referring to himself self-deprecatingly as a "docteur de sexologie," "professeur de coup d'etat," or "commander of military dog training," a reference to the pet German shepherd that always lay at his feet. Then employed by the Reuters news agency, An would later work for *Time* magazine and as an assistant to Robert Shaplen, the respected Asia correspondent for *The New Yorker*. Halberstam wrote admiringly that An had the "best military contacts in the country" and was part of a "small but first-rate intelligence network" of knowledgeable reporters.

What Halberstam didn't know was that the witty, outgoing An was also a resourceful Viet Cong spy. And he'd soon play a key role in alerting Western newsmen to a dramatic VC battlefield victory over a much larger ARVN force, leading to a spate of devastating news stories in U.S. newspapers.

IN EARLY OCTOBER, HALBERSTAM jumped out of a helicopter hovering low over a Mekong Delta rice paddy with an ARVN infantry squad. He sank almost up to his chin in the murky, rotor-whipped water.

A hundred yards ahead was a row of trees, the squad's first objective. Such tree lines sometimes concealed disciplined VC troops, waiting for the enemy to come close enough to be cut down in the first volley. Halberstam began slogging toward the trees, feeling exposed and scared. His boots kept getting stuck in the muddy bottom; his throat went dry as sand. He was acutely aware of being the tallest target in the water.

But the trees held no communists this time, and the soldiers moved into a nearby village. Only a handful of women and children were there; the men had all fled, except for an old man with a wispy beard. Younger males often ran off at the ARVN's approach, worried they'd be accused of being VC and, if not beaten or shot, at least dragged off to local army headquarters for interrogation.

Halberstam watched as an ARVN captain questioned two women about the guerrillas. One said none were in the area, but the other admitted a communist unit had been there the day before, offering the villagers tea and showing off captured U.S. weapons.

By late morning, with the punishing sun high in the sky, the soldiers took a break, sipping milk from coconuts they'd sliced open. They watched as American-built T-28 airplanes bombed and machine-gunned a nearby village. It turned out that VC troops operating in the area had brutally and efficiently ambushed a company of elite ARVN Rangers. Thirty Rangers were dead, and others wounded.

Halberstam's squad entered the blasted village that afternoon, encountering scenes that would long fester in the journalist's memory.

A weeping man emerged from his charred hut. "In one hand he held a dead piglet, in the other a dead baby," Halberstam later wrote. Farther on was a corpse under a poncho. The reporter later saw a terrified old man bowing before Vietnamese and American officers as he claimed he'd never heard of the Viet Cong.

Halberstam tramped with the troops for several more miles, but they made no contact with the VC. By the end of his first day in the delta, he'd learned two things. First was the difficulty of pursuing guerrillas in this region, flat and green from the air, but on the ground crisscrossed by canals, upon which the VC often slipped away in sampans, and studded with mangrove swamps, sugarcane fields, and thickets of coconut trees that made natural hiding places. It was bandit country, easy for even larger VC units to disappear in. The other lesson was how onerous the war was for the average peasant, his village invaded by the ARVN during the day and the VC at night, always having to bow and scrape before whichever armed men appeared outside his dwelling.

Sunburned and exhausted, Halberstam returned that night to the headquarters of the ARVN Seventh Division, located outside the small city of My Tho, about forty miles south of Saigon. The unit the newsman accompanied that day was part of the Seventh, which patrolled the fecund, well-populated rice lands of the northern Mekong Delta. While the southern delta, where the Twenty-First Division operated, was largely under VC control, the northern delta was considered a toss-up, with government troops as likely to win out as the communists.

THOUGH DESPERATE FOR SLEEP, Halberstam fell into what turned into an all-night conversation with Lieutenant Colonel John Paul Vann, senior U.S. adviser to the Seventh Division.

A short, red-faced bulldog of a man, the thirty-seven-year-old Virginian was fast becoming a legend in Vietnam for his mastery of small-unit tactics and almost unhinged lack of concern for his own safety. Despite the risk of ambush or capture, he investigated dirt roads the guerrillas used not by flying over them in a spotter plane but by driving them in a jeep. He made a point of going on night patrols with ARVN squads once or twice a week, hoping by his example to persuade the Vietnamese commander he worked with to pursue the VC after dark more often.

Vann was regarded as one of the best infantry advisers in Vietnam. When the VC began ambushing the Ranger company that day, he'd dispatched reinforcements and, characteristically, flew into the battle himself aboard a transport helicopter that was hit by furious ground fire. An American gunner beside him was killed and most of the dozen ARVN soldiers aboard were killed or wounded. Perforated with thirty-nine bullet holes, Vann's chopper crashed, but he walked away with only a minor shrapnel wound.

Vann's experiences had given him profound respect for the enemy. The VC always carried their dead away with them, he told Halberstam, partly out of consideration for their comrades, partly to deny the ARVN any sense of accomplishment by making it hard to accurately count casualties. While only a year or two ago the VC fought with homemade weapons or old French rifles, they now had the same small arms the ARVN used, captured in battle or stolen off the Saigon docks. As they slipped away from a firefight, the communists even picked up expended bullet casings, to be refilled and used again.

The most worrisome development, Vann said, was the enemy's reaction to newly introduced U.S. helicopters.

At first, the VC had cut and run whenever the choppers appeared, only to be slaughtered by airborne gunners. But they'd learned from experience and changed tactics accordingly. Now they held fast in defensive positions.

In short, the VC had largely lost their fear of helicopters, Vann said. It was a sign that the U.S. intervention might not be working. And it also meant, he added with disdain, that the Pentagon, while giving lip service to winning hearts and minds, would react by giving the South Vietnamese more conventional military technology, more heavy equipment, more firepower—exactly what wasn't needed.

What was needed, he insisted, was more emphasis on fighting the way the VC did.

"This is a political war and it calls for the utmost discrimination in killing," he told Halberstam. "The best weapon for killing is a knife, but I'm afraid we can't do it that way. The next best is a rifle. The worst is an airplane, and after that the worst is artillery. You have to know who you are killing."

The ARVN's increasing reliance on artillery and air strikes was counterproductive, Vann said. Had Halberstam noticed the topography around the villages he marched through that day? They were surrounded by dense tree lines, similar to the difficult-to-penetrate hedgerows of Normandy. When the ARVN approached, Viet Cong soldiers moved from villages into tree lines for concealment and protection. When necessary, they headed to nearby canals, where sampans waited to evacuate them. Or they simply ducked under the water's surface, breathing through bamboo straws until government troops passed by.

But aircraft pilots and artillery spotters, Vann continued, preferred visible targets, so they fired not on tree lines but on villages, where they could see buildings and people. Since the VC usually had already left a village under attack, the only people killed were ordinary peasants, usually women, children, and old men who lived there. And every time the government killed an innocent, it made it that much easier for the VC to recruit angry relatives and friends into their ranks. Hearts and minds were closed forever.

Halberstam cultivated many sources during his Vietnam sojourn, but none was more important than John Paul Vann. Not only had Vann given him a first-rate seminar about why the VC were making progress against the much larger, more powerful South Vietnamese army, he continued to provide background information and insight into the war as time went on. Halberstam was delighted at his luck in finding Vann, and his stories began to reflect the colonel's influence. While Halberstam's initial dispatches contained a degree of optimism about the ARVN, that soon changed. The headlines indicated his new direction:

Vietnam War a Frustrating Hunt for an Elusive Foe (Oct. 9, 1962)
Viet Cong Maintain Strength Despite Set-Backs (Oct. 11, 1962)
U.S. Deeply Involved in the Uncertain Struggle for Vietnam (Oct. 21, 1962)

Halberstam went back to the Mekong Delta again and again. It was the cockpit of the war, easy to get to from Saigon by taxi or helicopter. He gradually built up a network of sources among younger U.S. military men—captains, majors, and colonels serving as field advisers to ARVN combat units—and spent so much time in the delta that they inducted him into the "Blackfoot Club," reserved for those whose feet were darkened by mud seeping into their boots as they tromped through rice paddies and scrublands.

As the son of a surgeon who served in the U.S. Army Air Corps during World War II, Halberstam had great respect for the American military and admired many of the advisers he encountered. They weren't rabid war-lovers; they were the cream of the U.S. Army, tough and well-trained, yet fired by a sense of high purpose. Many were West Pointers; most were volunteers. They believed that America's presence in Vietnam was necessary and right, even noble. Halberstam saw the combat advisers, with their selfless determination to help the South Vietnamese, as akin to Peace Corps volunteers.

Most of them gave Halberstam the company line at first: the ARVN was doing well, victory was within our grasp. As the reporter visited them over and over, however, he sensed their optimism faltering.

These men were anything but Willie-and-Joe-style complainers and malcontents. But their ARVN counterparts often ignored their fighting advice. The South Vietnamese failed to take advantage of good tactical intelligence; they shied away from making contact with the enemy and failed to pursue him when they did. Worse, when the advisers reported these problems to General Harkins and his headquarters staff, they often found themselves getting brushed off.

So they turned to Halberstam. He didn't print their names, but their hard-won observations often made their way into his stories. And his stories rarely were ignored at the White House and the Pentagon.

AN INTENSELY SOCIAL ANIMAL, Halberstam loved to hang out with fellow journalists.

In 1962, only a handful of American and other Western newsmen worked full-time in Saigon. The major wire services—Associated Press, United Press International, Reuters, and Agence France-Presse—had resident correspondents. But *The New York Times*, Halberstam's employer, was the only U.S. newspaper to maintain a full-time correspondent there.

Halberstam had met most of the reporters at François Sully's going-away party. One of the most memorable was Malcolm Browne, the thirty-one-year-old chief of the Associated Press bureau.

Even in a profession known for its eccentrics, Browne stood out. A native of New York's Greenwich Village, he'd worked as a chemist before the Army drafted him in the late 1950s and sent him to South Korea, where he worked on *Stars and Stripes*, a newspaper that covers the U.S. military. His red hair was styled in a low-slung pompadour and his body was so skinny it seemed to have only two dimensions. He wore a ring embossed with a skull and a solid-gold bracelet that he thought, probably naively, he could barter if the VC captured him.

Below his pant cuffs peeked the bright red socks he wore every day and everywhere, whether he was headed to a VIP interview or an ARVN sweep in the delta. On a wall in the cramped AP office he hung a withered human hand, souvenir of a VC ambush, and a bamboo canteen stained dark red, presumably with the blood of the guerrilla who last drank from it—arresting reminders of the brutal war being fought beyond the comfortable confines of Saigon. When other newsmen headed for crowded restaurants and bars in the evening, Browne demurred, preferring to retreat to his one-room apartment above the AP office and listen to thundering Wagnerian operas.

The wire-service loner was entranced by Vietnam, calling it "the greatest love I ever had, and the greatest I ever will." He thought Diem could win the war, although only after a long, costly struggle. Madame Nhu frightened him. The first lady, Browne wrote, "could crush a political opponent with the flick of an eyelash, and often did. Even while smiling demurely, her eyes often shone with a deadly hardness that could mean prison or death for someone."

Watching her harangue a crowd of supporters, Browne was reminded of a pagan goddess demanding a blood sacrifice in an old Hollywood movie. He was sure she wouldn't hesitate to have Western journalists assassinated if she got the chance.

Browne chain-smoked—four packs a day—and typed with a furious "two-finger tattoo," punching out reams of short, just-the-facts-ma'am stories the AP transmitted to hundreds of client newspapers and radio and TV stations in the United States and other countries. A younger AP colleague, Peter Arnett, a New Zealander soon to make his own mark in Vietnam, remembered Browne's intensity, "a blaze in his eyes," as he worked. Browne was hardly a stylish writer, but he was smart and hardworking and produced reliably factual copy.

He was exposed to what he called the Kennedy administration's "love of stealth" shortly after coming to South Vietnam in November 1961. On his third day in the country, he drove up to South Vietnamese air force headquarters at Bien Hoa, about twenty miles northeast of Saigon. The U.S. Air Force had a significant presence there, and Browne wanted to investigate rumors that American pilots, who were supposed to be limited to training, were actually flying combat missions.

As he pulled up to the base gate, two Vietnamese military policemen barred his way; an American MP stood behind them. Undeterred, Browne strolled around the base perimeter and spotted two T-28 aircraft with South Vietnamese air force markings. The planes were taxiing and Browne could see clearly into their cockpits: both were piloted by Caucasians. He also got a good look at the pilot of a Skyraider, another U.S.-made, propeller-driven craft bearing South Vietnamese insignia. The Skyraider had bombs in its wing racks and, again, a Caucasian at the controls.

Browne began taking photographs, but the MPs pounced on him. They seized his camera, ripped out the film, and marched him off for a security check. He was soon released and returned to Saigon, where he knocked out his story, believing what he'd seen demonstrated that his countrymen were directly waging war in South Vietnam, not merely acting as advisers and trainers.

Browne soon witnessed another example of Washington's attempts to play down U.S. involvement in the war. One morning in December 1961, he was having coffee and croissants on Rue Catinat when he noticed a huge ship looming over the riverfront at the foot of the street. It was the aircraft ferry USNS *Core*, bearing thirty-two H-21 "Shawnee" troop-carrying helicopters and about four hundred American pilots, gunners, and ground crewmen. The *Core*'s arrival marked one of the first deployments under Operation Beef-Up.

Browne joined a half dozen other reporters at the dock, but an MP refused to answer their questions. They proceeded to the downtown office of the U.S. Information Service and asked a press officer what he could tell them.

"Aircraft carrier? What aircraft carrier? I don't see any aircraft carrier," the man replied with a smirk.

After several months of such experiences, Browne distilled what he'd learned into a twenty-four-page mimeographed handbook, *A Short Guide to News Coverage in Vietnam*, that he gave to AP employees new to Saigon.

Extracting news from government sources in South Vietnam "requires aggressiveness, resourcefulness and at times methods uncomfortably close to those used by professional intelligence units," he wrote. "You can expect very little help from most official sources and news comes the hard way. Correspondents in Vietnam are regarded by the Saigon Government as 'scabby sheep' and treated accordingly."

Browne advised newcomers to be skeptical of information from the regime, especially when it involved military operations. "Beware of claims of military victories; this is not the kind of war from which real victories turn up often on either side. Saigon and Hanoi are equally extravagant in their claims." In fact, newsmen should personally count enemy bodies on the battlefield rather than accept inflated killed-in-action statistics from government spokesmen.

He also recommended that greenhorns ask for two flak jackets when they boarded a helicopter—one to wear and one to sit on—and noted that belts and ropes made good tourniquets for gunshot wounds. If newbies chose to carry a pistol in the field, they should never try to shoot it out with the VC, since they "outnumber you and generally pack Tommy guns."

Cocktail parties at foreign embassies could be good venues to pick up information, although not always. British diplomats were very well informed but tight-lipped, while the value of information derived from U.S. embassy sources was "variable." The French and Polish knew little, but at least the Poles threw good parties. Browne appended a list of "certain officials who can be counted to tell bald-faced 180-degree whoppers nearly every time."

HALBERSTAM LIKED TO WORK with wire-service reporters, exchanging facts and tips, and hoped to forge a partnership with Browne. But Browne didn't want outside newsmen cluttering up his little office, eating up his time and that of his subordinates. When the *Times* reporter asked for workspace in the AP office, Browne turned him down.

Halberstam then gravitated to Neil Sheehan, the brooding, twenty-six-year-old workaholic who served as the one-man Saigon bureau for United Press International.

Sheehan had grown up on his family's dairy farm outside Holyoke, Massachusetts. Deciding early on that he didn't want a life of milking cows and shoveling manure, Sheehan earned scholarships first to prep school and then to Harvard. Six foot two, dark-haired, and trimly handsome, he indulged his love of poetry by joining the university's literary magazine, the *Advocate*. He also developed a drinking problem that plagued him for several years. Following one bibulous party for the magazine's staff, Sheehan drunkenly heaved a typewriter through a closed, second-story window. He narrowly escaped expulsion.

Graduating in 1958 with honors but no idea of what to do with his life, Sheehan shocked his literary friends by enlisting. He was assigned to the Army Security Agency, which eavesdropped on phone calls and radio messages in foreign countries, and sent to language school in Monterey, California, to learn Arabic. But after he was arrested for public inebriation, the army shipped him to South Korea, where he worked on his division's newspaper, *The Bayonet*, while stationed near the dangerous demilitarized zone separating the south from communist North Korea.

Sheehan's drinking worsened. Night after freezing night, he hit the bar at the enlisted men's club until closing time and then staggered back to his barracks, moaning, "Mother of God, mother of God" as he fell into his ice-cold bunk. A sympathetic sergeant thought a change of scenery might do him good and arranged a transfer to Tokyo.

There Sheehan landed a job on *Stars and Stripes* and put booze behind him. But he relapsed hard toward the end of his tour, wandering around at night guzzling sake from two-and-a-half-liter bottles. An Army buddy would go out searching for Sheehan, down back alleys and into sketchy neighborhoods, until he found him, blacked out and sprawled on the ground, an empty bottle nearby.

When a badly hungover Sheehan slunk into the *Stars and Stripes* office one morning, a sergeant he worked with snapped, "You're drunk again." "I can't help it," Sheehan blurted. "I'm an alcoholic." The sergeant took him that night to an Alcoholics Anonymous meeting. He stopped drinking and never fell off the wagon again.

Discharged from the Army, Sheehan parlayed his military newspaper experience into a $75-a-week job with UPI, which dispatched him to Saigon in April 1962. Sheehan was thrilled. Like many young American men of the era, he'd been raised on John Wayne movies and Ernest Hemingway novels. He saw war as a "glorious adventure" and believed completely in the rightness of American goals in South Vietnam.

In Saigon, the young wire reporter found a role model in Homer Bigart, then the resident *New York Times* correspondent.

Bigart had been reporting on wars and other conflicts for twenty years, and many considered him the premier war correspondent of his time. The winner of two Pulitzer Prizes, he'd covered World War II in both the European and Pacific theaters, the Korean War, and France's doomed struggle to reclaim its Vietnam colony.

Bigart was famous among his peers for asking endless, naive-sounding questions at press conferences until exasperated briefers finally coughed up more information than they'd intended. He didn't necessarily buy into Cold War shibboleths, especially the idea that the United States should support foreign despots, no matter how loathsome, as long as they spouted anti-communism. At fifty-four, Bigart was overweight, cranky, and suspicious of almost everything that came out of government officials' mouths; when frustrated or upset, he stuttered.

He detested South Vietnam, seeing it as malevolent and corrupt, and his reporting on the regime was as perceptive as it was relentlessly critical. In one front-page story he coined the phrase "sink or swim with Ngo Dinh Diem" to describe what he regarded as Washington's perilously shortsighted policy of uncritical, open-ended support for the South Vietnamese president.

Just before he finally departed Vietnam in July 1962, Bigart made a last foray into the Mekong Delta to witness the ARVN in action. Sheehan tagged along. ARVN commanders claimed to have a major VC unit trapped, but not a shot was fired nor a guerrilla spotted for two days as Bigart and Sheehan slogged through mud and underbrush along with government soldiers.

Eventually the other correspondents went home; Bigart deluged ARVN press officers with his usual simple-sounding questions. Finally, Sheehan had had enough. There was no story here, he told Bigart; no shooting, no bodies. They should just go back to Saigon like everyone else.

But the shrewd, middle-aged warhorse saw a deeper meaning in the ARVN's inability to find and close with the enemy, and what that implied for the costly U.S. military advisory program.

"No story, kid?" Bigart said, glaring at Sheehan. "It doesn't work. That's the story, k-k-kid. It doesn't *work*."

HALBERSTAM QUICKLY FOUND HIS footing on his new beat, traveling to different parts of South Vietnam and churning out a string of penetrating stories.

He wrote about the VC disrupting life in Saigon by attacking shipments of charcoal from the Camau Peninsula, reducing the capital's supply of cooking fuel. He accompanied an ARVN battalion in the Central Highlands as it freed about one hundred Montagnards the VC had captured and were using as slaves to grow food.

In a perceptive analysis piece in late October, Halberstam noted the many difficulties of fighting the communists. With no front lines in the war, it was hard to find the enemy and nearly impossible to distinguish guerrillas from innocent peasants. While the VC were "lean and hungry," experienced at political warfare, and willing to sustain whatever losses were necessary to win, he wrote, the Diem regime "has yet to demonstrate much appeal to large elements of its own people." Thanks to the infusion of U.S. aid, the war seemed to be going better than it had a year earlier, "when it was going very badly indeed." But with little reliable information on enemy strengths and weaknesses, it was difficult to know whether the Saigon army was winning or losing. And if the U.S. advisory program failed, Halberstam concluded, Washington might have few alternatives besides "the open commitment of American combat troops."

In late October, Halberstam and other newsmen got a revealing look into how much Diem feared his own people. The occasion was the annual National Day parade in Saigon, held to commemorate the 1955 referendum in which Diem ousted Bao Dai.

The parade route stretched for several blocks along a wide boulevard next to the Saigon River. A reviewing stand was set up in the middle. For several weeks, carefully chosen military units had been practicing in Saigon, bringing the war effort to a near standstill in some outlying areas. Armored personnel carriers had trundled in from delta combat zones despite the pleas of American advisers to keep them in action in the field.

Diem was clearly worried about another coup attempt and had taken extensive precautions to protect himself. Sealed off from regular traffic, the parade zone swarmed with cops. Security men swept for explosives. Members of Diem's Presidential Guard and other elite units had been issued uniforms only that morning, and checked multiple times since then to prevent them from secreting guns or grenades in their clothing.

Fighter-bombers circled to the south of the city, but had been prohibited from flying over it in order to preclude another effort to rain bombs on the president. Tanks were stationed at key intersections, engines rumbling and radios crackling, ready to intercept any rebel units that might try to capture or kill him.

Journalists were told to be in their seats by 7 a.m. As they arrived, they noticed something strange: police were turning away thousands of ordinary citizens who wanted to see the parade. After surviving multiple assassination and coup attempts, Diem was taking no chances with his constituents. Only government officials and their families, foreign visitors, and other special guests were permitted. When a reporter asked Nolting what he thought of the public's exclusion, the ambassador refused to believe it.

Diem showed up after most guests had been seated. He received salutes from his military leaders and heard the playing of a song titled "President Ngo Should Live Forever." (The Nhus stayed away, under a family policy of never appearing together in public in case of attack.)

The parade began, featuring about one thousand members of Madame Nhu's paramilitary women marching briskly with brand-new American carbines and submachine guns (which, according to a U.S. official, had been diverted from the ARVN without permission). Then came long lines of Nhu's blue-uniformed Republican Youth, although most of them looked to Halberstam like middle-aged government workers. Despite the lengthy preparations, the procession was over in minutes; combat units brought into Saigon were ordered back to fighting the VC.

DIEM AND THE NHUS loathed American journalists, the most irritating fleas that had ridden in with the American dog.

The president and his brother believed that the U.S. government controlled the reporters, just as they managed the South Vietnamese press, and were furious that Washington didn't keep its scribblers on a tighter leash. So, the regime took action on its own. U.S. newsmen began complaining of taps on their phones and police agents on their tails. When reporters brought their stories to the government telegraph office to be transmitted home to their editors, copies were quietly passed to the palace.

The regime's anti-press campaign grew bolder after the *Newsweek* correspondent, François Sully, was expelled. Saigon newspapers spread a story that *The New York Times* had taken a $40,000 bribe to print an interview with an official of the VC's National Liberation Front. Madame Nhu charged that the *Times* was part of "an international Communist-inspired conspiracy" to undermine South Vietnam, and that American newsmen were shills for Hanoi. She snapped at one U.S. reporter that her country wasn't required to observe "your crazy freedoms."

In early November, the regime kicked out a second reporter, James Robinson of NBC News, after he told a palace interpreter that a maundering, three-hour interview with Diem was a "waste of time." A few days later, Nhu told an American visitor that any newsman who dared to bad-mouth the regime or the war effort would be expelled.

Top U.S. civilian and military officials knew that their Vietnam policies depended on the support of Congress and the public and that, even though most Americans were paying little attention to South Vietnam, critical news stories could erode support for the war. Yet their approach to press relations was surprisingly ham-handed.

Although some junior U.S. diplomats had friendly contacts with reporters, who were about the same age and sometimes had similar educational backgrounds, older, top-level officials often treated them as much like scabby sheep as the Saigon government did, rarely inviting them to lunch or embassy functions. Since ranking U.S. officials thought reporters couldn't be trusted, they didn't trade information with them, a routine transaction at American missions in other parts of the world that usually benefited both parties.

Some American officials treated journalists with frank disdain. One day in the Central Highlands Halberstam ran into General Maxwell Taylor, the newly appointed chairman of the Joint Chiefs of Staff. Taylor was on a whirlwind tour of strategic hamlets and bare-chested Montagnard tribesmen squatted nearby, watching silently. The newsman walked up to the four-star general, stuck out his hand in greeting, and said: "General Taylor, David Halberstam of *The New York Times*."

Taylor turned on his heel and walked away without a word. Halberstam, for once speechless, felt like he'd been slapped in the face.

Nolting met with reporters often, and even claimed to like them. But he was in an impossible position, trying to carry out contradictory marching orders from Washington that bounced back and forth between downplaying U.S. participation in the war and wanting to be more honest and open with journalists.

Nolting knew Diem was as seriously flawed as his government. Yet the ambassador was convinced that the war was being won, albeit slowly, and that the regime was worth salvaging. He saw Diem taking positive steps, such as using U.S. aid to open new surgical wings at provincial hospitals. In discussions with journalists and fellow diplomats, Nolting deliberately confined himself to cheery optimism in order to "help create a new and winning psychology."

Despite his pleas for patience and understanding, the press focused mostly on Diem's failings, and the ambassador found it hard to conceal his resentment.

He refused to try to protect Robinson, the NBC reporter, from expulsion. In a cable to the State Department, he condescendingly described the Saigon-based correspondents as novices no more skilled or discerning than stateside reporters covering an "earthquake or Hollywood divorce."

Nolting's relationship with Halberstam descended into mutual acrimony. The ambassador felt that Halberstam's increasingly pointed stories fell on American public opinion "like drops of acid," slowly eating away at support for Diem and the war effort. The *Times* reporter, Nolting claimed in a memoir, was the leader of a group of newsmen that congregated at the Caravelle Hotel bar and whose self-appointed mission was to "get Diem." Halberstam in turn believed that Nolting saw him and his colleagues as "the enemy" and, many years after leaving Vietnam, mocked him during a TV interview as ignorant, arrogant, and "a great snob."

One day Halberstam met the ambassador in his office. After some pleasantries, he asked whether Nolting was as troubled as he was by the ARVN's problems in the delta. Halberstam had just spent a week there and picked up nothing but negative reports from American advisers. He tried to share his information with Nolting, but the ambassador grew irritated, then angry.

"How dare you challenge the word of men like Paul Harkins!" he declared.

Face flushed, Nolting stood up behind his desk. He asked whether Halberstam had attended a recent press conference featuring a high-level defector, a VC colonel who claimed he broke with the communists because the ARVN was "the wave of the future." But prior to the event, Halberstam received a warning from one of his sources, Colonel Bryce Denno, senior adviser to the ARVN First Division, based in Danang.

Denno knew the VC officer defected for personal reasons and told Halberstam that Saigon authorities might try "to sell you a bill of goods" about him. The reporter decided not to file a story about the press conference because he couldn't figure out how to write what Denno told him without burning him as a source. He told Nolting only that he hadn't gone to the press conference.

The ambassador erupted: "You come in here and challenge the word of our generals, but you don't even cover the most important press conference we have this year! Get out! Get out!" By then Halberstam was angry, too, shouting as he left the office that "it was all goddam lies" and that the VC colonel had privately criticized the ARVN as incompetent.

It was a telling moment: a U.S. ambassador angrily kicking a representative of America's most powerful newspaper—a paper that JFK and many others in Washington read carefully every day—out of his office. Nolting eventually got to the point that he refused to speak to Halberstam.

ONE OF NOLTING'S METHODS for trying to strengthen Diem's standing with his people was always to emphasize South Vietnam's role in the war, especially when things went well, while de-emphasizing America's. When talking to the press, the ambassador sought to keep Diem and the ARVN in the foreground, and U.S. advisers and aid in the background. Thus, he and other U.S. diplomats and military commanders generally deferred to Saigon whenever a news announcement was to be made.

The problem was that Diem's government refused to release much useful information. In October 1962, ARVN officers were ordered to respond only to written questions from reporters, and then only after their Saigon superiors approved the answers. The result was that Halberstam and other journalists got virtually nothing from Diem's officers in Saigon or in the field, unless they spoke anonymously.

During World War II, U.S. military leaders, including General George Patton, often gave American newsmen a heads-up on major operations before they happened. The reporters understood the need for secrecy, and deliberate violations were almost unheard of. But Harkins went along with Diem's tell-them-nothing policy, refusing to provide tips on upcoming missions even when American servicemen were involved.

Shut off from official sources in Saigon, Halberstam and other reporters went looking elsewhere. They hit a jackpot in the form of junior and mid-level embassy officers, U.S. infantry advisers like Denno and Vann, helicopter pilots who operated throughout the country, and aggrieved members of Diem's government.

The infantry advisers knew all about the ARVN and its shortcomings, and the pilots shuttled back and forth to battlefields and often were happy to give detailed accounts of what happened when Diem's soldiers engaged the VC. If Harkins and his staff in Saigon wouldn't talk candidly, the mud-streaked Americans who lived with South Vietnamese units in the field were willing to open up, especially when a reporter came out and got dirty with them in the paddies and swamps.

A particularly valuable source was Major Ivan Slavich, a U.S. Army pilot who came to South Vietnam in late 1962 with the first wave of UH-1B "Huey" helicopters, the fast, heavily armed gunships that became one of the most recognizable symbols of the Vietnam War.

A swashbuckling former paratrooper and Marine from San Francisco, Slavich gladly took reporters everywhere in his chopper. If they couldn't make it to Tan Son Nhut before the birds lifted off, Slavich and his crews told them what happened during the operation when they flew back.

"After Ivan came in, you just couldn't bullshit us anymore," Halberstam recalled. "We could find out anything."

Slavich enjoyed the newsmen's roistering company and spent off-duty time with them, too. Halberstam was flying back to Saigon with him one day when the pilot asked if he wanted to have dinner. Halberstam said yes. Slavich then decided to invite another journalist, Mert Perry, a freelancer working for *Time* magazine. He got on the radio and told the military operator to dial Perry's number.

"Sir!" Slavich barked when Perry answered the phone in the apartment he shared with his wife. "The U.S. Army wishes to invite Mr. and Mrs. Perry to join Major Slavich and Mr. Halberstam for dinner." And off they all went to a fine restaurant that night.

Indeed, that surreal quality permeated the newsmen's lives: they'd see people get napalmed and machine-gunned in the delta during the day and then dine sumptuously at a Saigon restaurant, perhaps in the company of an attractive Vietnamese woman, that night. Malcolm Browne once survived a terrifying helicopter crash in the afternoon and spent the evening in black tie at the Caravelle Hotel, listening appreciatively to a singer from Paris.

TWO WEEKS BEFORE THANKSGIVING 1962, the South Vietnamese decreed that American reporters couldn't ride into battle with ARVN troops aboard helicopters, even those piloted and crewed by Americans. On Thanksgiving Day, about forty-five Shawnee choppers lifted off and headed toward a jungled Viet Cong redoubt known as War Zone D, about thirty-five miles northwest of Saigon.

Each of the twin-rotor, banana-shaped Shawnees carried about a dozen government soldiers, more than five hundred in all. Every chopper also bore four Americans: two pilots and two gunners. Accompanying the ARVN troops were a number of American infantry advisers, meaning that roughly two hundred U.S. servicemen were involved altogether. That was news. Also, the mission was the largest heliborne assault in history, which made it bigger news. But no one had briefed Halberstam and his confreres in advance.

The flying armada's distinctive racket awakened Mert Perry, whose apartment sat directly atop Neil Sheehan's apartment-cum-office near the Saigon River. Perry rolled sleepily out of bed and made for his roof, which offered a panoramic view of the passing choppers. He began counting, and when the last one clattered overhead he raced downstairs to wake Sheehan. Lighting one cigarette after another, Sheehan made half a dozen calls to confirm the story and then banged it out for the UPI wire.

A few hours later, Halberstam stormed into the office of John Mecklin, chief press officer for the U.S. Mission, which comprised the embassy, MACV (Military Assistance Command, Vietnam), the CIA station, and civilian aid agencies. The *Times* reporter slammed down on Mecklin's desk a hastily written letter to Nolting, and sat "shaking with rage" while Mecklin read it.

Halberstam's letter began by announcing that official stonewalling had changed him "from a neutral bystander into an angry man." It continued:

> In my opinion the barring of reporters from the D zone operation is the most serious step taken yet by the [Saigon] government. . . . Two hundred Americans risked their lives. Yet we were not allowed to cover a story that would have been a fine opportunity to show Americans just what their fighting men were doing here, what our involvement is and why! And our people—from General Harkins on down—went along with this!
>
> The reason given is security. This is of course stupid, naive and indeed insulting to the patriotism and intelligence of every American newspaperman represented here. Let me point out that we, as our predecessors, in time of conflict have been, are fully prepared to observe the problems of security, to withhold printing of classified information; and that in this running conflict the government has never raised the charge of giving out military information. Many Vietnamese officers in the field, in fact, are rather naive about this sort of thing, and on several occasions reporters withheld information without being told to—simply because we know the rules of the game better than they do.
>
> Let me also point out that from the moment that fifty helicopters landed at a given point in Zone D certain aspects of the operation lost all classified status. You can bet the VC knew what was happening; you can bet Hanoi knew what was happening. Only American reporters and American readers were kept ignorant.

The dapper, Dartmouth-educated Mecklin was a veteran foreign correspondent who'd taken a leave from Time Inc. to join other newshounds eagerly flocking to new jobs as press agents for Kennedy's Camelot. During World War II, he'd crossed the Atlantic with troop convoys and covered Allied landings in Italy and fierce fighting in Normandy. Traveling through France with Patton's forces in 1944, he was briefly taken prisoner by the Germans and then spent a week with the French Resistance. As a *Time* correspondent based in Hong Kong, he witnessed the terminal stages of the French war with the Viet Minh, as well as Diem's struggle with the Binh Xuyen gangsters.

When Mecklin came to Saigon as mission press officer in May 1962, he was taken aback at the bitter standoff that had developed between American officials and journalists. Nolting and Harkins considered the reporters immature and irresponsible, and some of their articles as bordering on treasonous. The reporters in turn viewed U.S. Mission officials as a pack of stonewallers and Diem apologists too blinded by false optimism to see what was really going on in South Vietnam.

Mecklin was friends with some of the correspondents and respected their abilities, but he also felt they suffered from a persecution complex. They spent too much time together, nursing grievances and reinforcing each other's prejudices. "With one or two exceptions, they were so simon-pure that it was painful, always with basketball-size chips on their shoulders," he wrote in a 1965 memoir titled, tellingly, *Mission in Torment*. "Their solemn, self-righteous, unceasing complaints, however justified, became boring." They were often rude to U.S. officials and sometimes failed to show up for early-morning helicopter takeoffs, wasting a place on a combat mission.

Like many newsmen turned government press officers, Mecklin felt conflicted. He wanted Kennedy's Vietnam policy to succeed, but he also wanted the press to be able to do its job, delivering accurate, timely news to American audiences. A British journalist friend teased him, saying that as the U.S. spokesman, Mecklin was now a "poacher turned gamekeeper." Mecklin counted himself among the large number of Americans in Saigon who viewed the Diem regime as too unpopular and corrupt to beat the Viet Cong. Yet he felt compelled to keep trying to help Diem. There was no suitable alternative to the repressive leader, Mecklin believed; Washington would have to sink or swim with him, in Homer Bigart's barbed aphorism.

Well aware that unceasing press criticism could cripple Kennedy's policies in Vietnam, Mecklin's first priority was to get the embassy on a better footing with journalists. As he saw it, the root of what was known among U.S. officials as the "press problem" was the Kennedy administration's decision to defer to Diem's government when it came to releasing information to American reporters. The regime repeatedly promised to hold regular briefings, but never did. And on the rare occasions when it did put out a press statement, the information was too late, too vague, or just plain wrong.

A few days before his run-in with Halberstam, Mecklin had an unsettling conversation with Nhu, who appeared to be in charge of Saigon's media relations. Mecklin was certain that Diem's brother was using his power to harass and punish American reporters. Mecklin also was genuinely worried that Nhu might be "psychotic," since he'd argued during their talk in favor of an American nuclear attack on China.

In a memo to Nolting, Mecklin recommended what he called a "drastic shift" in U.S. press policy.

First, he said, Nhu should be kept as far away from American newsmen as possible. Second, MACV should quietly begin to brief reporters, on a background basis, whether Saigon liked it or not. And third, U.S. advisers in the field should insist that journalists be brought along on military operations. If the ARVN refused, U.S. support for that operation should be withheld.

In other words, as Mecklin put it, "no correspondents, no choppers."

ON THE LAST DAY of 1962, Harkins tried to extend an olive branch to Halberstam, Sheehan, and Browne. He called the newsmen to his spartan office at MACV headquarters near the cacophonous Saigon central market. All four men lit cigarettes, although Harkins smoked his through an ivory holder.

Gray-haired, hawk-nosed, athletically lean, and impeccably uniformed, the fifty-eight-year-old general had been in charge of U.S. forces in Vietnam for less than a year. Behind him was a long and distinguished Army career, including service in World War II and the Korean War. He'd visited Vietnam multiple times prior to his MACV assignment and commanded a five-thousand-man U.S. invasion force that was assembled but never sent to turbulent Laos in 1961.

But Harkins was a traditional military man to the tips of his well-buffed dress shoes. He had no experience fighting communist guerrillas and seemed to have scant understanding of Vietnamese history or the political dynamics that drove Viet Cong military actions. Indeed, he was baffled by the Vietnamese, telling an interviewer years later: "It's a funny thing, the Oriental mind and the Oriental ways and, well, we don't understand it, really."

The son of a Boston theater critic, Harkins played polo at West Point and graduated in the middle of his class in 1929. After World War II broke out, he served under Patton in North Africa and Sicily before becoming deputy chief of staff for Patton's Third Army as it raced across France into Germany. An operations planner, Harkins was nicknamed "Ramrod" for his determination to keep tanks, trucks, and troops moving. During the Korean War, he served as chief of staff of the U.S. Eighth Army, and later commanded the Twenty-Fourth and Fourty-Fifth Infantry Divisions.

Following a series of high-level Pentagon staff positions in the mid-1950s, Harkins was appointed commander of NATO troops in southeastern Europe in 1957. Three years later, he became deputy commander of U.S. Army forces in the Pacific. Kennedy named him chief of MACV in February 1962.

Like Nolting, Harkins liked and admired Diem, and thought the war could be won with him. The general grasped the political nature of the conflict to some degree, but seemed oblivious to the importance of symbolism and propaganda. He moved into a white mansion in Saigon's best neighborhood that was formerly occupied by the commander of the French army, not realizing or not caring about the unpleasant comparison between the Americans and the hated French that would arise in Vietnamese minds over his choice of quarters. He favored bombing with napalm because it "really put the fear of God into the VC," but showed little concern that exploding canisters of jellied gasoline also fell on innocent peasants, resulting in hideous deaths and injuries from burns and asphyxiation that made excellent grist for communist propagandists.

HARKINS'S BIGGEST BLIND SPOT, however, was his excessive optimism about how much time the ARVN needed to vanquish the Viet Cong.

He repeatedly told Diem, his Washington superiors, and the press that the war would be won in short order, although it had taken years for other national armies to beat back communist insurgencies, even under more favorable circumstances. (The British, for instance, had needed a dozen years and 350,000 men to defeat just 12,000 Malayan guerrillas. And that was with no enemy reinforcements infiltrating through adjacent countries.)

Shortly after taking over MACV, Harkins told Donald Gregg, chief of the CIA's Vietnam desk: "I don't care what you hear from other people, I tell you we will be out of here with a military victory in six months." When Defense Secretary Robert McNamara visited South Vietnam in May 1962, Harkins assured him the war would be "over by Christmas." Almost a year later, in April 1963, the general was predicting an end to the war by the next Christmas.

Worried that he was creating unrealistic expectations about the war's progress, the State Department tried to restrain Harkins. The general nevertheless refused to deviate from his self-appointed role as cheerleader for Diem and the ARVN. He believed they needed encouragement, not criticism, if they were to win, and that it was his job to be a bottomless well of boosterism. At conferences on the war and in written reports to Washington, he exuded nothing but confidence and insisted that his subordinates do the same. "I am an optimist," he told *Time* early in his tenure as MACV commander, "and I am not going to allow my staff to be pessimistic."

But Harkins's incessantly upbeat reports eventually undermined his credibility in Saigon and Washington. According to Mecklin, American military advisers mocked him with a ditty they sang to the tune of "Twinkle Twinkle Little Star":

We are winning, this we know.
General Harkins tells us so.
In the delta, things are rough.
In the mountains, mighty tough.
But we're winning, this we know.
General Harkins tells us so.

Harkins disliked and distrusted journalists (the AP's Peter Arnett thought the general viewed him and his colleagues as "dangerous imbeciles"), and was curiously ill-informed about how they operated.

Although the newsmen were intensely competitive, always trying to scoop one another on stories, Harkins thought Halberstam somehow had the power to dictate to his peers what to write. "If you ever look up the press reports in those days, you'll find Halberstam would write them and then hand out the circulars to all the other press guys and they'd actually put in the same thing, change a few words here and there," Harkins said after leaving Vietnam. "He handed out mimeographs, and sort of had the press eating out of his hand." None of that was true. The general also drew the mistaken (and arguably anti-Semitic) conclusion that the *Times* reporter's negative stories about Diem were motivated by religious resentment, since Halberstam was Jewish.

The journalists returned Harkins's scorn in full. One evening, Halberstam and Sheehan took a young State Department officer, a fellow Ivy Leaguer who'd just arrived in Vietnam, to dinner at one of Saigon's best French restaurants. After giving him some advice about the embassy and MACV ("Don't trust anything those bastards tell you"), the reporters spent most of the evening excoriating Harkins.

As wine flowed, they conducted a mock court-martial of the general for incompetence and dereliction of duty. After each "charge" was leveled against Harkins, Halberstam boomed: "Guilty!" Sheehan jumped up to carry out the "sentence," exuberantly pantomiming a firing squad against the back wall of the restaurant. The young diplomat—Richard Holbrooke, a future U.S. ambassador to the United Nations—looked around the room in panic, fearing that if anyone recognized him with these two maniacs his career would be over before it started.

Halberstam later described Harkins in a cable to a *Times* editor as "a particularly stupid and ill-informed man." Sheehan viewed Harkins as lazy and complacent, a congenital staff officer with no real intellectual curiosity about the nature of this very different war or how to fight it. The general had a propensity to observe the countryside from the air rather than tramp through it with his advisers and ARVN soldiers. He seldom appeared in public wearing anything other than his tan office uniform and shiny dress shoes, and carrying his swagger stick and cigarette holder. When Horst Faas, the AP photographer, asked to take a picture of Harkins clad in fatigues and combat boots with troops in the field, he refused, saying, "Forget that kind of picture. I'm not that kind of general."

Over time, Vietnam became a graveyard for the reputations of a number of high-ranking American government officials and military men, and Harkins was one of the first to fall into an open pit.

By the end of his tour in mid-1964, "to pull a Harkins" had become synonymous in Army circles with a major screwup, a particularly boneheaded move. His MACV successor, General William Westmoreland, recalled that when Harkins briefed him about what to expect, the outgoing general's optimism seemed to have deserted him as he wanly recited a poem by Rudyard Kipling:

And the end of the fight is a tombstone white
With the name of the late deceased.
And the epitaph drear: "A Fool lies here
Who tried to hustle the East."

AS HARKINS TALKED WITH Halberstam, Sheehan, and Browne on New Year's Eve 1962, his office grew hazy with cigarette smoke.

Sheehan was in a confrontational mood. For weeks U.S. Army investigators had been trying to find out who supposedly leaked information about the massive helicopter assault that Mert Perry had seen from his roof. Sheehan interpreted the inquiry as a flat-footed but deliberate campaign to silence his sources. He demanded to know why MACV was wasting army time and taxpayer money on it.

Harkins stared at the young newsman, less than half his age, over his cigarette holder. "I don't know anything about that," he said.

His reply only made Sheehan more agitated. Word of the MACV investigation was all over town. Mecklin even joked about it. Sheehan repeated his question.

"I'll look into it," said Harkins, an edge to his voice.

Browne said little; he'd been through these dog and pony shows before. Halberstam was uncharacteristically quiet. He didn't much care if Harkins was mad at him, or if Nolting was, or if anyone at the palace was. His instincts told him Vietnam was the story of a lifetime, and that he had it nailed.

He had good sources pointing him in the right directions. He was the de facto leader of a small but fierce tribe of truth seekers, all of them pursuing the news just as hard and enthusiastically as he was. Most of them were in their late twenties or early thirties. They often worked eighteen hours a day. Most had no wives, kids, mortgage payments, or anything else to distract them. "All we had was the story, a total belief in what we were doing, the excitement of it," Halberstam recalled. "We knew in a way we'd never have a shot at something like that again, that we were extraordinarily lucky as journalists to even have that one shot."

Covering the war was a noble endeavor, Halberstam felt. It was important, it was bigger than him and his colleagues. More and more, it was also becoming personal. The reporters often became friends with the American military men they met in the boonies: infantry officers, Green Berets, chopper pilots; guys their own age, guys they liked and respected. As time went on, some of these men were killed or wounded in action.

America needed to know what was happening to its sons in Vietnam, what this new kind of war was really like. And Halberstam and the other journalists were determined to tell the truth about the war, no matter how their stories were received at the embassy, the palace, or the White House.

CHAPTER 6

"A MISERABLE DAMN PERFORMANCE": THE BATTLE OF AP BAC

HARKINS AND OTHER senior American officers yearned for a battlefield showdown between the ARVN and the Viet Cong, a conventional slugfest in which the South Vietnamese would have a huge advantage in firepower and mobility over what the MACV brass derided as "raggedy-ass little bastards."

They got their wish at Bac, a hamlet in the upper Mekong Delta where 1,200 South Vietnamese troops closed in from three directions on a much smaller number of VC on January 2, 1963. But the battle didn't go as expected.

The operation had been planned by South Vietnamese and American officers attached to the Seventh Division. Their objective was to knock out a VC radio transmitter located near Bac, about thirty-five miles southwest of Saigon. (American news accounts called it the "Battle of Ap Bac," since the Vietnamese word for hamlet is *ap*.)

U.S. intelligence believed that no more than 120 VC were in the area of Bac and another hamlet just to the north, Tan Thoi. But in fact there were 350 guerrillas in two reinforced companies. They were part of two battalions, the 261st and the feared 514th, which had decimated the ARVN Ranger company in October. Many of the VC fighters lived in the area and were familiar with the terrain. Their intelligence network had reported that an attack was coming, although the exact target wasn't clear. Among the indicators was the recent arrival of seventy-one truckloads of ammunition and other supplies in the town of My Tho, near Seventh Division headquarters, which VC agents reported to their superiors.

The allied plan was to land a battalion of Seventh Division infantry north of Tan Thoi by helicopter and then attack that hamlet. Meanwhile, two battalions of Civil Guard provincial militia would march up from the south and attack Bac. Thirteen armored personnel carriers would sweep in from the west, overrunning Viet Cong positions from that direction. The idea was to force the guerrillas to flee into the flat, open rice fields and swamplands east of their positions, where Huey gunships and Skyraider fighter-bombers would slaughter them.

Peasants who lived in the two hamlets had already vanished in anticipation of the ARVN assault. The surrounding region was a checkerboard of rice paddies bordered by earthen dikes. The dikes were four feet thick at their narrowest and much thicker in other places; some were as high as levees on the Mississippi River.

The VC had dug foxholes in the dikes deep enough for a man to stand in. Camouflaged by banana and coconut trees and dense stands of bamboo and water palms that grew along the dikes, the holes were good protection from almost anything but a direct hit by a bomb or artillery shell. With the heavy foliage around them, VC fighters in the holes were almost impossible to see from across the rice paddies or from the air. They were deployed along the dikes so that they faced west and south from Bac, and north from Tan Thoi.

Thanks to weapons captured from Diem's U.S.-equipped forces, the guerrillas had better arms than ever: M1 semiautomatic rifles, Thompson submachine guns, Browning automatic rifles, and .30-caliber machine guns. They also had a 60-millimeter mortar and grenades that could be launched from rifles, vastly increasing their range.

The Seventh Division had badly mauled the VC several times during the summer and fall of 1962. With morale sagging, communist commanders needed a ringing victory to reassure their men. They also wanted to show peasants in the upper delta that they could still dominate Diem's troops regardless of how many new weapons the American imperialists showered on them.

Communist leaders had continued to refine their tactics for countering helicopters and M113 armored personnel carriers. Approaching helicopters could be heard from far away, and VC fighters learned to split up into small groups and calmly wait out the danger beneath the thick protective canopies of forests and jungles. If choppers used the same landing zones more than once or twice, the VC seeded them with sharpened bamboo stakes or set ambushes. They began limiting their attacks to fifteen minutes, withdrawing before even the swiftest airborne units could arrive.

VC machine gunners and riflemen were trained to aim ahead of choppers in flight, so that the "iron birds," as the communists called them, flew into their bullet streams. In hidden jungle clearings, trainers pulled small cardboard cutouts of Hueys and Shawnees along a string between two poles, to give troops a sense of how to lead them with their guns. VC soldiers were told to concentrate their fire when the choppers were most vulnerable, near or on the ground as troops jumped off.

Armored personnel carriers were harder to stop and therefore more terrifying, but VC riflemen were taught to aim for the men manning the .50-caliber machine guns atop the vehicles, since they lacked protective shields. The VC also learned to drop grenades into the vehicles' top hatches or the drivers' hatches in front. With larger, better trained units and more sophisticated weapons, VC leaders in the upper delta believed their men were ready to fight from fixed positions, a notable change in their usual hit-and-run tactics.

THE BATTLE OF AP BAC began at about 7:45 a.m. as one of the Civil Guard battalions approached the line of communist foxholes that faced south beneath a row of trees. The VC knew the troops were coming because they'd captured American radios tuned to the channel used by ARVN units, which didn't encode their transmissions.

The Civil Guard commander sent part of the battalion forward to reconnoiter; the rest of his men stayed behind the safety of a dike. The VC waited until the guardsmen were about thirty yards away in a paddy and opened fire. The guard leader and his executive officer were killed within seconds; the rest of the troops reeled backward through the water and muck. As they did so, the guardsmen behind the dike held up their rifles and fired over the top without looking, so that the retreating men were being shot at from behind as well as in front. Poorly directed ARVN artillery overshot the guerrillas, leaving them untouched. For the next two hours, the guardsmen attempted to outflank the communists in the tree line but failed.

Their commander was the local province chief, ARVN Major Lam Quang Tho. He didn't order his second battalion to attack in unison with the one under fire, nor did he correct his artillery fire even after an American adviser warned it was off target. Instead, he did what Diem's casualty-averse combat leaders often did when faced with strong enemy resistance: he called for someone else to do the fighting. Tho radioed a request to the Seventh Division commander, Colonel Bui Dinh Dam, to fly in two infantry companies being held in reserve and land them behind the guerrillas in the southern tree line.

But Tho didn't realize that the landing zone he had in mind was in another open paddy field directly in front of a different set of VC troops, dug into a tree line and facing west.

The Seventh Division's ranking U.S. adviser, Lieutenant Colonel John Paul Vann, was observing the fighting from an L-19 spotter plane. He'd watched ARVN infantrymen arrive outside Tan Thoi that morning only to find themselves pinned down by the VC there. Colonel Dam radioed that he wanted Vann to select a landing site for the two reserve companies near Bac. Vann was suspicious of the hamlet, thinking that it might harbor additional Viet Cong.

He ordered his pilot to swoop low over the tree lines around the hamlet, but even his experienced eye couldn't pick out the enemy soldiers beneath the dense green foliage. Nevertheless, he warned the helicopter pilots bringing in the reserve troops to stay at least three hundred yards away from the western tree line outside Bac, beyond the effective range of communist fire.

TEN SHAWNEE TROOP CARRIERS clattered in, escorted by five Huey gunships. But the lead Shawnee pilot ignored Vann's instructions, putting his ship down just two hundred yards from the west-facing VC, who had an unobstructed view of the ARVN soldiers leaping into knee-high water in the paddy.

As bullets cracked and zipped around them, the troopers ran to a low dike about fifteen yards in front of them and threw themselves into its muddy banks for protection. With nowhere else to hide and the communists firing down at them from their tall dikes, the government troops were trapped in a lethal shooting gallery. An American adviser with them, Sergeant Arnold Bowers, tried to rally them to charge VC positions, but the soldiers wouldn't move.

After disgorging their troops, nine choppers took off. The pilot of the tenth reported that his controls were shot away and he, his copilot, and two crewmen planned to abandon their crippled bird and join the soldiers in the paddy.

The helicopter crews felt deep loyalty to one another and under their informal code of chivalry downed airmen had to be picked up immediately, even if they were relatively safe with ARVN units. One of the departing Shawnees turned around and made a disastrous choice to land between the disabled chopper and the VC in the tree line. It, too, was quickly shot up and rendered unflyable. A third Shawnee was so damaged it had to land about a mile away, but its crew was picked up without incident.

The Hueys had been rocketing and machine-gunning the tree line, but with little effect, since they couldn't see the VC in their canopied foxholes. Now the commander of the Huey platoon decided to rescue the crews of the two downed Shawnees. He intended to set his bird down behind the damaged choppers, using them as shields. But as the Huey slowed and went into a hover, enemy rounds struck its main rotor blades. The helicopter crashed and flipped over on its right side, its driveshaft screaming as it spun at high speed with the blades stripped away.

Worried that the overheated engine would ignite the Huey's fuel tanks, Sergeant Bowers jumped up from behind the dike and ran toward the ruined chopper. One of the two pilots had escaped and was staggering toward a dike that offered some protection. Bowers managed to yank open a cockpit window and pull out the other pilot, dazed and bleeding from a leg wound. He helped the man hobble over to the dike and then rushed back for the door gunner, who, strapped in his seat, was hanging almost upside down.

Bowers kicked a hole in the Huey's Plexiglas windshield and crawled inside. He removed the gunner's helmet and discovered the man was dead, shot through the head. Bowers unbuckled his seat belt and dragged him out of the chopper anyway. The engine stopped, evidently burned out. Bowers began pulling the corpse toward the pilots behind the dike, but the man was heavy and the VC were firing rifle grenades and mortar shells at the downed helicopters. Bowers decided he couldn't do anything else for the gunner and was endangering himself for nothing. He left the body on a patch of dry ground and ran over to one of the Shawnees.

Bowers climbed inside the aluminum carcass and found the crew chief, who'd been shot through the shoulder. Bullets slapped into the fuselage, but the VC were aiming too high. Crawling along the floor to the crew chief, Bowers bandaged his wounds and got him to lie on his back to help stop his bleeding. He didn't seem badly hurt. Bowers lay next to him for a while, chatting about his wife and trying to keep him calm. After assuring the chief he'd come back to check on him, Bowers left to see if he could help the ARVN soldiers sheltering behind the dike.

The reserve companies had been under fire for about thirty minutes when a pair of Skyraider fighter-bombers appeared. They dropped napalm, but didn't hit any VC in the tree line and managed only to set some thatched-roofed houses on fire. The heat was so intense that Bowers could feel it out in the paddy. The planes began to dive-bomb the burning houses with conventional bombs. Some of the ARVN infantrymen, thinking the VC had been driven off, stood up to watch the spectacle, but two of them were immediately shot dead. The rest dove back into the dirt.

When Bowers returned to the wounded crew chief, he was dead, too.

WHEELING BACK AND FORTH above the battle in his little spotter plane, Vann was beside himself with frustration and anger.

He now had three helicopter crews on the ground—whether the men were dead or alive he didn't know—and two ARVN companies in danger of being overrun if the VC decided to charge out of their tree line. Earlier, Vann saw the thirteen dark green armored personnel carriers about a mile away and radioed two U.S. Army captains, James Scanlon and Robert Mays, serving as advisers to the armor unit. He ordered them to tell the ARVN captain in charge of the M113s, Ly Tong Ba, to get moving and relieve the infantrymen under siege in the paddy.

Scanlon came back on the radio after a few minutes with unwelcome news.

"I've got a problem, Topper Six," he said, using Vann's call sign. "My counterpart won't move."

"Goddammit, doesn't he understand that this is an emergency?" Vann demanded.

"I described the situation to him exactly as you told me, Topper Six, but he says, 'I don't take orders from Americans,'" Scanlon explained.

Vann signed off and called one of his fellow advisers at Seventh Division headquarters, telling him to get the division commander, Colonel Dam, to order Captain Ba and his M113s to head for Bac immediately. The adviser reported back that Dam agreed and was relaying the order through ARVN channels.

The M113s fired up their engines and began to roll. But almost immediately they ran into a canal with high banks. The heavy vehicles had a hard time climbing such slippery obstacles (reminding one journalist of rubber ducks trapped in a bathtub). Soldiers riding inside had to dismount, cut down trees and brush, and fill in the canals sufficiently for the machines to cross. About an hour was needed to get the M113s over this canal, and Captain Ba felt that was too long. He refused to go any farther. "Why don't they send the infantry?" he said, meaning the ARVN battalion bogged down outside Tan Thoi.

Scanlon was taken aback by the Vietnamese officer's hesitancy. The son of a prosperous delta landowner, Ba was usually aggressive in pursuing the enemy. He'd commanded a squadron of French armored cars against the Viet Minh and spent a year at the U.S. Army armor school at Fort Knox, Kentucky. But in December 1962, Diem reorganized his armor units, taking the M113s away from Colonel Dam's Seventh Division and putting them under a more politically reliable officer, Major Tho, the province chief. The personnel carriers weren't as potent as tanks, but they provided extra insurance against coup attempts.

Under Diem's ungainly, divided chains of command, designed as much as anything to stop his military from overthrowing him, province chiefs, not the ARVN, had command of Civil Guard and village-level militia forces. Diem personally appointed province chiefs and they had an open line of communication to the palace. ARVN commanders could request help from provincial troops, and province chiefs could go along or not, as they saw fit. Thus, Captain Ba could safely ignore Colonel Dam's orders. Until he got orders from Major Tho, his M113s weren't going anywhere.

Mays and Ba went on foot to look for another place to ford the canal and found a second high-banked irrigation channel beyond it. That reinforced Ba's unwillingness to move. It would take two hours for the M113s to cross both waterways; the infantry should go instead. Scanlon and Mays stood atop Ba's carrier, arguing with him. Soon all three men were yelling angrily.

Vann got on the radio to berate Scanlon and Mays. "I told you people to do something and you're not doing it," he raged. "Why can't you get the lead out of the son of a bitch's ass? He's got his order from the division commander."

Ba spoke English well and heard every word coming from the two-way radio. Vann was even more incensed because a few months earlier, he'd asked Harkins for portable bridging equipment for Ba's M113s to use in situations like this, but hadn't received it.

"Jesus Christ, this is intolerable," Vann spat over the radio. "That bastard has armored tracks and 50 cals and he's afraid of a bunch of VC with small arms. What's wrong with him?"

Vann flew off in his spotter plane to see if he could get the Civil Guards to attack the VC in the south-facing tree line. Cruising over the militia positions, he saw men lying on their backs behind the dike, where they'd taken refuge after their earlier VC contacts. Some were sleeping; no one was shooting. The guardsmen were in a position to attack the west-facing VC—the ones firing at the trapped reserve companies—from their flank. But when Colonel Dam called Major Tho at Vann's request and asked for the Civil Guards to launch an assault, Tho refused. He felt he'd already lost enough men that day.

Vann zoomed back over to the M113s. They hadn't moved an inch. It was 11:10 a.m., forty-five minutes after the Huey crashed. Vann had heard over the radio that two of the downed aviators were seriously injured. He saw Mays standing on top of Ba's carrier with the Vietnamese captain. Boiling with anger, Vann called Mays and asked if he could seize command of Ba's tracks and get them over the canals to Bac.

"Roger, Topper Six, I could do that," Mays answered carefully.

"Then shoot that rotten, cowardly son of a bitch right now and move out!" Vann screamed.

Mays knew Ba's men wouldn't act without orders from their own leader. The American and Vietnamese captains looked at each other. During four months in the field together, they'd become friends. Instead of drawing his pistol, Mays suggested that the carriers return to a place he'd seen earlier that day where the double canals merged into one. Ba agreed.

The M113s again switched on their engines and churned off.

IMPATIENT AND WORRIED ABOUT the chopper crewmen on the ground, Vann flew back to Seventh Division headquarters to refuel and organize an airborne rescue.

The firing from the western tree line had become sporadic and Vann thought the VC might be withdrawing, as they usually did in such circumstances. The Huey pilots agreed to go back and strafe the tree line while a Shawnee went in to pick up the injured airmen. A second Shawnee would circle nearby as an emergency backup.

Returning to the battlefield, Vann told his L-19 pilot to fly low over the downed helicopters and parallel to the VC in the foxholes, hoping to draw fire that would reveal their positions. But the guerrillas held back, waiting to see what the real game was. Vann turned and saw the rescue Shawnee lumbering in for a landing. At the same time, the Hueys began blasting the tree line with rockets and machine guns. But again, they scored few hits on the well-camouflaged enemy.

Bullets from enemy rifles, Browning automatic rifles, and .30-caliber machine guns began perforating the Shawnee. Almost as soon as he touched down, the pilot radioed that his controls were hit and he had to lift off without taking on any wounded. The bird staggered into the air, flew about three-quarters of a mile, and was forced to land again.

Captain Ba finally reached Major Tho on the radio at about 1 p.m.; Tho ordered Ba to proceed to Bac and attack. But Ba's men took their time; when they finally got within view of the ruined helicopters, the area was quiet. Scanlon figured the VC had already departed.

He was wrong. The VC commander had hoped that he and his men could slip away to the north, but the ARVN battalion in front of Tan Thoi effectively blocked that route. That meant the VC would have to stay in Tan Thoi and Bac until nightfall and exfiltrate to the east. Until then, they had to fend off heavily armed enemies on three sides.

It wasn't until 1:45 p.m. that the first two M113s reached the downed helicopters—three hours and twenty minutes after Vann had put out his emergency call to assist the surviving airmen. In that time, the armored tracks had traversed only a mile of terrain.

Captain Mays wanted to pick up the injured chopper crewmen right away and get them safely inside the mobile fortresses. Sergeant Bowers ran up to help and together they got the aviators into the rear hatch of Mays's carrier. The VC in the tree line opened up with a sustained fusillade, although most of the bullets bounced off the vehicle's aluminum-alloy skin, making a *bung-bung-bung* sound. At least one slug found its mark, however. When Mays climbed back into the vehicle, he discovered that the driver, sitting in the open front hatch, had been shot through the head.

Two other M113s trundled into action against the VC dug into the dike to the left of the helicopters. The dike jutted out into the paddy at that point, and the guerrillas had placed a .30-caliber machine gun there, so anyone approaching it would be caught in a cross fire with another machine gun on the right end of their line. The armored carriers stopped and dropped their rear doors; about a dozen infantrymen scrambled out of each one. The soldiers and M113s then began advancing together as trained.

Captain Scanlon was aboard one of the carriers and he jumped out, pistol in hand. He tried to spot the VC in the tree line ahead, but they were invisible in the green wall of trees and underbrush. Scanlon couldn't even see muzzle flashes from their guns. The American looked up at the M113 gunner blazing away with his .50-caliber gun. He should have been firing at the base of the tree line, where the guerrillas were dug in, but instead he was shooting high, chopping off the tops of banana trees with heavy slugs. The VC kept shooting back. An ARVN trooper a few steps away was hit and went down. A soldier with a Browning automatic rifle was wounded, too. Frightened, the M113 machine gunner ducked down into his hatch, but kept firing, his weapon pointed up at the clouds.

Realizing the entire squad was in danger of being cut down, Scanlon ordered the soldiers back inside their carriers. He'd never seen the VC react like this to M113s. The guerrillas had always cut and run when confronted by the armored monsters in the past. But today was different. The enemy wasn't panicking. And the ARVN wasn't performing well.

The .50-caliber gunner was still cowering inside his hatch. Like many U.S. advisers, Scanlon spoke little Vietnamese. He began screaming at the gunner to stand up and aim at the base of the tree line. Then he tried to shove the man up into position, pushing and struggling until he finally stood up and resumed firing in the general direction of the guerrillas.

The driver of the other M113 threw his machine into reverse. Scanlon saw a wounded soldier lying in the paddy. He yelled at his driver to stop, but no one got out to pick up the injured man. Scanlon jumped out, joined by an ARVN trooper with more nerve than his comrades. Together, they hauled the wounded soldier into the vehicle.

By then the M113 crews were too intimidated to reengage the VC. Both armored tracks backed up behind the Shawnee fuselages, seeking shelter from the ongoing enemy barrage. The VC ceased firing as soon as the machines retreated. Despite Scanlon's vocal protests, the two vehicles then fell back even farther, to the canal they'd crossed.

AT THAT POINT, CAPTAIN Ba arrived in his command carrier, accompanied by another M113. He drove toward two tracks ahead of him that were firing at VC on the right side of the tree line. Mays was in one of those carriers and saw Ba coming. The Vietnamese officer was sitting up against his open top hatch, where he had a clear view of the battlefield and could fire the machine gun. Mays wanted to call him on the radio to suggest that the M113s try a flanking maneuver, rather than a frontal assault, to take out the VC machine gun on the right. Mays wanted the carriers to roll up onto the dike and blast the enemy out of their foxholes, one by one.

As Ba's carrier drew close to Mays's, the Vietnamese captain lowered himself into the hatch, possibly to adjust his radio. The carrier hit a bump and the heavy machine gun swung around on its mount. Its barrel bashed Ba in the forehead, knocking him down into the vehicle's hull, dazed. Over the next twenty minutes, three or four more carriers pulled up. But Mays didn't speak Vietnamese well and couldn't communicate his flanking plan to Ba's second-in-command.

The carriers were supposed to attack as a group to maximize their firepower. Instead, they made individual forays against the tree line, and the VC repulsed each one. Enemy riflemen began picking off the machine gunners, silhouetted atop their vehicles with no shields. With Ba half-conscious, a sergeant took his place and ordered the driver to head for the VC machine-gun nest. But the sergeant soon fell back into the vehicle, dying of a bullet through the throat.

An M113 equipped with a flamethrower clanked to within a hundred yards of the tree line. At that range its burning jet of jellied gasoline could reach the men in the foxholes, setting the foliage around them ablaze and burning them to death or forcing them to run. The VC concentrated their guns on the fire-breathing behemoth, but their bullets only bounced off its armor.

The carrier swung its flamethrower nozzle from side to side menacingly. A dazzling tongue of flame shot out twenty or thirty yards, but evaporated in the air with "the force and effect of a Zippo lighter," in Scanlon's dejected words. The crew had failed to mix enough gelling agent into the gasoline to keep it blazing over longer distances.

Still stunned by the blow to his head, Captain Ba tried to organize a mass assault on the guerrillas' line. In his confusion he neglected to summon the four or five carriers still lingering at the canal to join him. Ba's group of four moved forward, but the drivers had trouble staying abreast of one another as they were supposed to.

Sergeant Bowers, lying in the paddy with the pinned-down reserve companies, watched with professional admiration as the VC opened fire at the advancing M113s. Instead of spraying all of them with bullets, they concentrated on the one closest to them. When it dropped back, the communists fired at the new lead vehicle, conserving their ammunition.

The VC used their machine guns to grip the lead M113 in a cross fire, blasting away until its exposed gunner had been killed or wounded. As more of their comrades were hit, one or two of the drivers began backing up.

Ba kept grinding forward until he was within twenty yards of the dike. It still seemed possible for the armored tracks to reach the VC foxholes. At that point the enemy's nerves would snap; they'd jump up and run away in panic. But that didn't happen.

Astonishingly, a VC squad leader jumped up and ran *toward* the M113s, hurling a grenade at one of them. It landed on top of the carrier and went off with a tremendous explosion. Other VC soldiers followed their leader, rushing out of their holes and throwing more grenades. From farther down the line, another VC fired rifle grenades. A couple of the explosives burst in the air, and several guerrillas were cut down either by their own shrapnel or ARVN bullets. But their unexpected and heroic charge against the machines had its effect. The earsplitting explosions shredded what was left of the M113 crews' courage.

The armored carriers backed away from the VC positions for the last time at about 2:30 p.m.

ORBITING OVERHEAD, VANN WATCHED the unfolding debacle in dismay.

Another U.S. adviser radioed him that Brigadier General Huynh Van Cao, commander of IV Corps, which included the Seventh Division, had requested that an airborne battalion be hurried in from Saigon. Vann wanted the fresh troops dropped east of Bac and Tan Thoi, closing the box around the VC and cutting off their only avenue of retreat. But he learned that Cao intended to drop the paratroopers west of the hamlets, behind the downed helicopters and trapped reserve companies.

The thirty-four-year-old Cao had carefully cultivated an image as one of the ARVN's most aggressive commanders. He converted the briefing room in his Saigon villa into a replica of Napoleon's map room and wrote an autobiographical novel, *He Grows Under Fire*, in which he promoted himself as a model military leader. Intelligent and glib, he liked to strut about carrying a polished swagger stick.

In reality, Cao was one of the most casualty-averse commanders in the ARVN. Despite his rapid career ascent, he'd seen relatively little combat and lacked the stomach of a good field leader. During one operation in which his artillery was firing in support of an ARVN unit battling the VC, Cao ran out of his command tent, threw up, and ordered the guns to stop shooting. The noise, he said, was too upsetting.

Cao's main qualification for command of IV Corps was his unswerving loyalty to Diem, to whom he referred as "my king." Like many high-ranking ARVN officers, Cao was a Catholic and a member of Nhu's Can Lao Party. He hailed from Hue, where his family knew Diem's. Prior to his elevation to corps commander, Cao was in charge of the Seventh Division, and Vann as division adviser had pushed him constantly to be more aggressive. But after a pair of firefights that cost the lives of thirty-eight soldiers and Civil Guardsmen, Diem summoned Cao to the palace one morning, made him wait all day in an anteroom, and then reprimanded him for permitting so many casualties.

Cao took his king's admonition to heart.

Vann quickly recognized Cao's intent in wanting to drop the parachute battalion to the west of the VC. He hoped to scare the enemy with a big show of force that would cause them to slip out of Bac and Tan Thoi toward the east, where his men wouldn't have to fight them.

Vann again flew to Seventh Division headquarters, where a nervous Cao had arrived after hearing news of the downed helicopters. Diem, Cao knew, would blame him for the fiasco. Vann marched into the command tent and told Cao he could still turn the situation around by blocking the VC on the east and destroying them with all the firepower at his disposal. Pointing out ARVN and VC positions on a large map, Vann jabbed at it so hard he almost knocked it off its easel.

Cao was unconvinced. "We must reinforce," he insisted, saying the airborne troops needed to join the M113s and trapped reserve companies west of Bac. Knowing the only thing the general's plan would reinforce was an ARVN defeat, Vann lost his temper.

"Goddammit, you want them to get away!" he shouted. "You're afraid to fight!" Cao pulled rank, saying he was the commanding general and his decision stood.

The paratroopers didn't begin to jump out of their aircraft until a few minutes past 6 p.m., not long before nightfall. Vann figured they'd just set up a defensive perimeter and start cooking dinner rather than go after the enemy in the dark. But many of the jumpers missed their mark, landing not near the M113s outside Bac but directly in front of VC riflemen at Tan Thoi. They came under heavy fire as they floated down in the gloaming and weren't able to organize a counterattack. Nineteen were killed and thirty-three wounded.

Vann wanted to give the ARVN one last crack at the enemy. He suggested that aircraft drop flares over their expected escape route that night. But General Cao refused.

The two VC companies began pulling out at about 10 p.m., moving east in a quiet column toward the safety of hidden base camps in the nearby Plain of Reeds. They'd scored a remarkable victory.

Instead of retreating as they usually did, the communists stood their ground against not only well-armed and more numerous infantry but the full panoply of U.S. weaponry: helicopters, armored personnel carriers, artillery, and planes dropping bombs and napalm.

They'd killed as many as eighty South Vietnamese soldiers and wounded more than one hundred. Three U.S. servicemen died and eight were wounded during the battle. Five helicopters had been knocked out in a single day—a record at that point in the war.

With Saigon troops blocking three sides of the battlefield, the enemy slipped away through the open side of the infamous "three-sided Vietnamese square." They suffered eighteen killed, thirty-nine wounded.

The communists had proven they could stand fast against anything the Saigon army and its American friends threw at them. They'd bucked up their own morale and showed delta peasants that even with all the new U.S. military aid, Diem's forces couldn't beat them.

The Battle of Ap Bac became a VC rallying cry. The hamlet's name appeared in gold letters on the 514th Battalion's battle flags. Four-color propaganda posters appeared across the delta, lionizing the brilliant and brave fighting men of Bac and Tan Thoi. Encouraged by the battle's outcome, Hanoi doubled the number of infiltrators it was sending south (to about 1,700 a month) and began smuggling heavy weapons (antiaircraft machine guns, 81-millimeter mortars, and recoilless cannons that could wreck M113s) to the VC in earnest.

AT SOME POINT DURING the battle, Nicholas Turner, Saigon bureau chief for the Reuters news service, got a tip that a big story was breaking at Bac. That night, he and Neil Sheehan hopped into Turner's car and zoomed off toward the delta at seventy miles per hour despite the threat of ambush.

The tip came from the witty VC spy, Pham Xuan An, then working as Turner's assistant. "He fed me the initial story and details that got me to write it," Turner remembered. "He told me some American helicopters had been shot down and that I should go to Ap Bac."

Turner and Sheehan pulled up at the Seventh Division airstrip. Sheehan spotted General Cao, pacing back and forth outside the command tent and nervously running his hands through his hair, over and over. He seemed incapable of talking coherently, but the two correspondents soon found Vann, who pulled them aside in the darkness and gave them details about the disastrous battle.

"They were brave men," he said of the VC. "They gave a good account of themselves today." Sheehan and Turner returned to Saigon and filed their initial dispatches. Then they ate dinner, showered, and drove back down to the airstrip that same night, so they could hitch a ride to Bac when the helicopters began lifting off again the next morning.

At daybreak on January 3, a Shawnee took them to the hamlet, where destroyed thatched houses were still smoking. The pilot cautiously set down far to the west. Sheehan could see the M113s parked nearby. He and Turner began walking along a dike toward the downed choppers. The ugly detritus of war lay all around. Sheehan counted twenty ARVN corpses laid out on another dike, their fatigues smeared with blood. The reporter did something he hadn't done in years: he made the Catholic sign of the cross.

Captain Scanlon appeared with two M113s to pick up bodies. There was no shooting and Scanlon said the VC were long gone. But the ARVN soldiers with him were badly demoralized and didn't want to touch their dead comrades.

Scanlon began yelling at them and yanking them off the vehicles. Sheehan and Turner helped load the corpses, including those of the two American helicopter crewmen. The M113s brought the bodies over to newly arrived choppers for evacuation, but the South Vietnamese didn't want to carry them into the birds, either. Scanlon again began shouting at and shoving them. Sheehan and Turner were appalled; they'd never seen an American officer and ARVN soldiers behave like this. Then the newsmen got mad and started bellowing at the soldiers, too.

After they finished with the bodies, Sheehan and Turner encountered Brigadier General Robert York, who'd flown down to examine the battlefield. A former West Point boxer and World War II combat commander, York headed a special detachment that was studying VC tactics. Of the dozen American generals then serving in Vietnam, York was the only one with enough curiosity about what had happened at Bac to actually go there and find out.

The general and an aide walked with the journalists along a dike where the VC had dug their foxholes. Sheehan was impressed by the clear field of fire they'd had from the dike at the helicopters and ARVN reserve companies as they landed in the open paddy to the west. The way the VC had positioned themselves and their weapons was a textbook example of how an outnumbered infantry unit could defend itself against a powerful attacker.

Sheehan asked York what he thought of the enemy's performance. "What the hell's it look like?" the Alabama native replied, a note of exasperation in his voice. "They got away—that's what happened."

The men stood on a dike watching fresh ARVN troops march into Bac. Suddenly, artillery began booming from the south. A shell cut through the air and exploded not far from the South Vietnamese, throwing up a column of mud and water. "Hey, that's pretty damned close!" York's aide yelled. More shells crashed beside a second line of soldiers on a dike about seventy-five yards away. The blast and flying debris knocked several of them off the dike; the rest leaped into the paddy, crying out in fear and confusion. "Let's get the hell out of here!" York shouted as additional rounds detonated about thirty yards away.

His group ran along the dike, desperately trying to get out of the kill zone. They'd sprinted only a short distance when another explosion nearly blew them off their feet. "Get down!" York yelled. The men threw themselves into the side of the dike, hoping they'd survive as shells continued to blow up around them. When the artillery paused for thirty seconds or so, York ordered everyone to get up and run farther down the dike. It was a fortunate decision, since the next two shells went off where the men had been lying.

By the time the bombardment ended, four ARVN troopers had been killed and twelve wounded. The fusillade of about fifty shells had been ordered by General Cao, who, Sheehan later wrote, "decided to fake an attack on Bac now that the Viet Cong were gone." The general sent the additional troops into the hamlet and then flew to Major Tho's headquarters and ordered the artillery barrage.

But neither Cao nor Tho had checked to make sure none of their men were in the target area. A South Vietnamese second lieutenant, serving as forward observer for the artillery, misread a map and reported that the troops were three-quarters of a mile outside Bac. But unlike Cao and Tho, he paid dearly for his sloppiness.

When the enraged commander of the troops who'd been shelled found out about the map-reading error, he pulled out his pistol and shot the forward observer in the head.

EARLY ON THE MORNING of January 3, Halberstam and Peter Arnett flew from Saigon to the Seventh Division airstrip and boarded a helicopter to Bac. Both had filed stories the previous evening based on interviews with angry helicopter pilots returning to Saigon.

The two reporters circled the hamlet for several minutes. Corpses sprawled in the paddies; parachutes lay crumpled on the ground like tiny handkerchiefs. Zigzag tread marks in the mud told of the futile attempts by the M113s to dislodge the VC.

The newsmen later returned to the airstrip, where a white-uniformed honor guard had been laid on for General Cao. Harkins was there, too, immaculately attired as always in his office uniform and polished black shoes, and carrying his swagger stick and ivory cigarette holder. He was preparing to fly back to Saigon when the reporters asked him what happened at Bac.

"We've got them in a trap and we're going to spring it in half an hour," Harkins replied.

Halberstam and Arnett looked at him, dumbfounded. As Halberstam later wrote: "The enemy was long gone, the Government troops were so completely disorganized that they would not even carry out their own dead, a province chief was shelling his own men—and a trap was about to be sprung? As on so many other occasions in Vietnam, we never knew whether Harkins believed what he was saying, or whether he felt that it should be said."

Harkins questioned York and then left for Saigon. Between the honor guard for Cao and Harkins's absurd comments, Sheehan felt himself recoiling.

"There was something obscene about all of this to me and the other reporters," he wrote. After Harkins left, Vann came over to apologize to Sheehan and Turner about the shelling. "It was a miserable damn performance," he said bitterly of the ARVN. "These people won't listen. They make the same goddamn mistakes over and over in the same way."

The news stories that Sheehan, Halberstam, and their colleagues wrote about Bac caused an uproar back home. The military battle was followed by a battle over the way the press covered it, with the resident reporters coming under fire from U.S. officials in Saigon and Washington.

The journalists realized that Bac was the most important story they'd encountered in Vietnam. All of them had written before about combat setbacks for the ARVN. But Bac encapsulated all of the problems that were hobbling Diem's armed forces: poor leadership, the divided chain of command, the unwillingness to take casualties, the refusal to listen to American advice.

U.S. newspapers gave prominent play to the stories coming out of Saigon. The Rochester, New York, *Democrat and Chronicle*, for example, ran Vann's "miserable damn performance" quote as a headline across the top of its front page. Halberstam's January 4 story in *The New York Times* portrayed Bac as "a major defeat" for the ARVN, noting that "Government troops got the sort of battle they wanted and they lost."

THE DRAMATIC DEFEAT SHOOK many Americans. With crises in Cuba, Berlin, Laos, and the Congo dominating recent headlines, news of Vietnam had been scant, and official optimism had tranquilized many people into thinking that the war was progressing nicely. After Bac, editorial writers vigorously attacked the Kennedy administration for trying to hide the realities of the war. A State Department analysis of media reaction across the country reported that "since Ap Bac the complaint has been increasingly heard that the American public is not 'getting the facts' on the situation in Viet-nam, even at this time when American casualties are mounting."

Two days after the battle, Admiral Harry Felt, the Honolulu-based commander in chief of all U.S. forces in the Pacific and Harkins's immediate superior, flew to Saigon on an inspection trip. Felt believed, oddly and without evidence, that unflattering news stories about Diem had been planted by a public relations agency hired by "someone either in South Vietnam or North Vietnam." Meeting Felt at the airport with other newsmen, Sheehan asked if he had any comment on Bac. "I'd like to say that I don't believe what I've been reading in the papers," Felt replied. "As I understand it, it was a Vietnamese victory—not a defeat, as the papers say." He turned to Harkins, who hastened to add: "Yes, that's right. It was a Vietnamese victory. It certainly was."

Harkins's comments left U.S. newsmen in disbelief and further undercut his credibility with them. They saw Bac not only as a loss for Diem's army but as evidence that it couldn't cope with the enemy, even with the advantages of U.S. technology, and that the American advisory program wasn't working.

In a cable to the State Department, Nolting attributed the "Ap Bac press eruption" to the Saigon journalists undergoing a "savagely emotional delayed reaction" to Diem's expulsion of the *Newsweek* and NBC reporters. The mutual dislike between the newsmen and the regime, he wrote, "verges on neurotic." The ambassador also charged that the reporters were too young and inexperienced to render a "balanced judgment on extraordinarily complex and mixed situation" in South Vietnam.

But Halberstam and his cohorts had their defenders within the government as well. One was William Jorden, a onetime *New York Times* diplomatic correspondent then working as a special assistant to Averell Harriman at the State Department. In a memo to Harriman, Jorden characterized the reporting from Vietnam as "exceedingly good." The Saigon journalists, he wrote, were pursuing their work "with energy and seriousness of purpose. They spend a considerable amount of time in the provinces and the villages and with the military forces in the field. They have both better information and a better feel for the situation than many military officers and officials in Saigon." Jorden also pointed out that some of the most critical reporting on the regime had come not from the younger newsmen but from older veterans like Keyes Beech of the *Chicago Daily News* and Robert Martin of *U.S. News & World Report*.

As the uproar over Bac continued, the U.S. Army chief of staff, General

Earle Wheeler, led a contingent of high-ranking officers to South Vietnam to assess the war effort. In his subsequent report to the Joint Chiefs of Staff, Wheeler wrote that U.S. press coverage had done "great harm" by leading Americans to believe that the war was "misguided" and by stirring doubts about "the courage, the training, the determination and dedication of the Vietnamese armed forces." Harkins made the same point in a January 10 statement that "anyone who criticizes the fighting qualities of the armed forces of the Republic of Viet Nam is doing a disservice to the thousands of gallant and courageous men who are fighting in defense of their country."

But other U.S. officials privately concluded that the Battle of Ap Bac had demonstrated the ARVN's weaknesses far more than its fighting prowess.

Roger Hilsman, head of the State Department's Bureau of Intelligence and Research, later described the battle as "a stunning defeat" and "a debacle." Many American combat advisers regarded it as dramatic substantiation of the warnings about the ARVN they'd been sending Harkins and other military higher-ups in Saigon for months. Major Robert Bayless, senior adviser to a South Vietnamese regiment in the Mekong Delta, later wrote that "every American who was in the IV Corps area realized that Ap Bac was a disaster."

Always looking for a foreign scapegoat on which to pin the Diem regime's troubles, government-influenced newspapers in Saigon went after Vann, saying he'd given unwise orders to ARVN units to attack, while swanning around in the safety of his spotter plane. (Vietnamese soldiers were praised for bravely staying put.) Diem-friendly papers also zeroed in on Sheehan, whose reporting on Bac had been particularly enterprising and pointed. One Saigon publication ran a photo of him in an army uniform, under the headline: "The American Adviser Sheehan: What Does He Really Want?" There was no news story, just the photo and incorrect headline. Halberstam and Sheehan's other friends turned it into a joke, repeatedly asking him, "What do you *really* want?"

AFTER BAC, HALBERSTAM JOINED forces with Sheehan, working out of the UPI man's makeshift office in his small apartment.

Halberstam liked Sheehan, a fellow Harvard grad, and admired his pluck and incredible appetite for work. Sheehan didn't just write a story, he attacked it, occasionally working all day and all night. His chronic lack of sleep led to raw nerves and emotional outbursts and, eventually, lifelong insomnia. Halberstam had to grin one morning when he found Sheehan sound asleep with his telephone still cradled against his ear. He'd nodded off in the midst of a conversation with a source.

The two reporters set up their typewriters on opposite sides of Sheehan's dining room table. They got together almost every day, comparing notes, trying to understand what was going on in the palace and the embassy. Because he had fewer deadlines and could travel more, Halberstam had better military sources. Sheehan had better CIA sources as well as a firmer grasp of the French war against the Viet Minh and Vietnamese history in general. The men talked about interviews they'd done, swapping information and trying to decipher ambiguous remarks they'd heard.

"We'd sit there every day as if we were putting a jigsaw puzzle together," recalled Halberstam. They became not only working partners but close friends.

It was a good arrangement for Sheehan, since it helped level the field with his more numerous competitors at the Associated Press. But it was also good for Halberstam, who didn't have a phone at his villa and disliked being alone. There was another bonus for the *Times* reporter. Sheehan was dating a lovely Vietnamese woman everyone called Blue Lotus, and she introduced Halberstam to a friend, an equally attractive schoolteacher. The four of them often double-dated. Halberstam kept going out with the teacher even though she was separated from her husband, a circumstance that the puritanical Madame Nhu might seize on as a pretext to kick the newsman out of the country.

One day in late February, he burst into Sheehan's office, loudly declaring, "Jesus Christ, have I got a hell of a story!" He'd just returned from another visit with Vann, who'd given him extensive details about how General Cao and his ARVN subordinates were deliberating avoiding combat in the delta.

Published on the front page of the *Times* on March 1, Halberstam's provocative story said that ever since Bac, the South Vietnamese had been using intelligence supplied by Americans to send their troops where enemy concentrations were minimal. In one such operation, two thousand ARVN soldiers managed to kill just one guerrilla, although air strikes left a woman and a child dead. Without naming Vann as a source, Halberstam summarized the concerns of U.S. advisers that the ARVN's lack of enthusiasm for fighting could have serious consequences in the delta as VC units grew in number and size. His piece also noted that high-ranking U.S. officials in Saigon—meaning Nolting and Harkins—refused to complain to Diem, since their policy was to get along with him no matter what.

HALBERSTAM RECEIVED PLENTY OF kudos for his coverage of the war, but some of his *Times* colleagues chided him for not writing more about political developments.

It was hard to find angles for such stories, however. The political situation hadn't changed much since Halberstam's arrival the previous year; South Vietnam was still an authoritarian state, ruled by a Catholic strongman. Most of Diem's noncommunist political foes were in prison, exiled, or afraid to speak out. No critics railed quotably about his excesses and errors from the floor of the tame National Assembly; no editorialists questioned his actions in the government-censored press.

Nevertheless, South Vietnam's political dynamics were changing in the wake of the Buddhist massacre in Hue.

On May 9, the day after the killings, Halberstam got a call from Diem's press director saying a news conference was to be held that afternoon. The government, he said, had evidence that the VC killed the Buddhists.

Like the rest of the Western journalists, Halberstam knew little about Buddhists or their beliefs. He'd never been inside a pagoda or had any contact with monks, other than seeing them moving quietly through the streets of Saigon in their saffron-colored robes. But he was suspicious of the motives behind the press conference; the regime was more likely to be trying to cover up something than revealing the truth of what happened in Hue.

In any event, Halberstam was scheduled to fly to Hong Kong that day to begin a two-week vacation. After eight months of running around the country and hammering out news stories nonstop, he was looking forward to the break. He skipped the news conference and headed for Tan Son Nhut.

But the Hue massacre and the Buddhists' reaction to it was slowly building into a political earthquake, with the potential to shake the regime apart. And Halberstam would soon be writing about little else.

CHAPTER 7

BEHOLD A BURNING MONK

ON THE MORNING of June 11, Malcolm Browne found himself inside a small Saigon pagoda amid hundreds of Buddhist monks and nuns, all of them chanting in unison.

The Buddhists murmured an ancient prayer of respect and devotion—"Na mo a di da phat"—over and over, their voices rising and falling in a faintly musical way. A monk with a loudspeaker led the chanting as a second monk kept time, beating rhythmically with a stick on a hollow gourd.

The air was stifling and scented with burning joss sticks. The Buddhists recited quietly at first, but their pace and volume gradually picked up. They seemed to be pouring their very souls into the prayer; Browne found the effect hypnotic.

When he first arrived, a nun in a white robe of mourning offered him tea in a glass cup, and he saw tears streaming down her face. A monk hurried over to tell him not to leave because "something very important" was about to happen.

For several weeks, the Buddhists had been organizing hunger strikes and marches in the monsoon-soaked streets to protest the killing of their fellow acolytes in Hue and pressure the government to meet their five demands. Western newsmen covered the protests at first, but lost interest as they took on a predictable sameness. The cops held back from interfering, knowing that any photos of them roughly breaking up peaceful Buddhist gatherings would only create more negative headlines for the regime. Instead, they merely shooed onlookers away.

The Buddhists saw international news coverage as their only real defense against a crackdown by Diem's secret police and soldiers. Since the government largely controlled the Saigon press, the Buddhists cultivated Western reporters, tipping them off in advance to their demonstrations and carrying protest signs in both Vietnamese and English. Without foreign media attention, Buddhist street actions were just trees falling in the forest.

The Buddhists needed to do something dramatic to rekindle interest in their cause. They passed word that two Buddhists would publicly commit suicide—one disemboweling himself, the other setting himself afire. Most journalists didn't take this seriously. But when a Buddhist tipster telephoned the Associated Press office to say that something big would happen on June 11, Browne decided to be there, and to bring his camera.

The chanting stopped at 9 a.m. Browne watched as the monks and nuns rapidly lined up in two columns—a drill they appeared to have practiced—in a muddy alleyway outside the pagoda and marched out to the street.

About 350 men and women made up the procession. Usually the Buddhists were on foot, but this group was accompanied by a small gray sedan bearing several monks. The regime had found out about the protest, and a white police jeep took up a position about a half block in front of the marchers, clearing the road ahead.

Shopkeepers and kids gawked as the Buddhists made their way along Phan Dinh Phung Street. They soon arrived at the intersection with Le Van Duyet Street, a major artery typically jammed with traffic. When the sedan reached the middle of the intersection, it stopped as if stalled. The marchers immediately formed a tight circle around it, about thirty feet in diameter and several people deep, blocking all traffic. They began to recite a Buddhist scripture in low, mournful tones.

Three monks got out of the car. Two were young, and they helped the third, a seventy-three-year-old schoolteacher named Quang Duc. One of the young monks laid a brown cushion on the street in the center of the human ring. Quang Duc sat down on it and arranged himself in the lotus position, legs folded and head bowed as if in meditation. Nuns began to weep.

The young monks exchanged a few quiet words with Quang Duc. Then they opened the front hood of their car and took out a five-gallon plastic jug filled with gasoline. One of the monks poured the pink fluid over Quang Duc's head and shoulders, thoroughly soaking his orange robes, and stepped back.

BUDDHIST MONKS IN SOUTH Vietnam generally led quiet lives of secluded asceticism. Also known as bonzes, monks often began their training as teenagers or even children. They spent their days chanting and meditating in pagodas, and begging for rice, bananas, and other alms in the streets.

Many of them were the barely literate sons of dirt-poor rural peasants. But some came to a pagoda as adults, abandoning careers as businessmen or white-collar professionals in search of enlightenment. Along with their shaven heads and displays of piety, these monks were well-educated and had some political awareness. Some had attended French or American universities; at least one Saigon bonze held a degree from Yale.

Buddhism encouraged letting go of the desire for material things, and monks' lives reflected that. They had few possessions and usually resided in austere cells in or around a pagoda. Many suffered from tuberculosis, a common disease of the poor. They were strict vegetarians and celibate.

The monks enjoyed great respect from ordinary Vietnamese, who addressed them by the title *thich*, meaning "the venerable" (and roughly equivalent to "reverend" for a Christian priest or minister). Monks presided at the most significant moments in the lives of many South Vietnamese—performing rituals at births, weddings, and funerals—and the countryside was dotted with Buddhist shrines, temples, and monasteries. Many families paid homage to the founder of Buddhism, Siddhārtha Gautama, also known as the Buddha, with altars and prayers in their homes.

From its origins in the Himalayan foothills of northern India in the sixth century BCE, Buddhism spread slowly throughout Asia over many centuries, carried by traders and itinerant monks along the Silk Road and sea routes. In Vietnam, Buddhism had been practiced for two thousand years. It was a code of ethics and behavior rather than a religion in the Western sense; the Buddha was considered a great philosopher and teacher, not a god. Buddhists believed that human life is endless, but marked by suffering, uncertainty, and impermanence. Humans were reincarnated over and over, doomed to suffer in each of their lives. But the cycle could be broken if a person achieved enlightenment—a state known as nirvana—by eliminating greed, hatred, and delusion from their thoughts and deeds, and living virtuously.

Buddhism enjoyed a long golden age in Vietnam under the Ly and Tran dynasties from the eleventh to the fifteenth century. Learned monks occupied honored positions in imperial courts, advising emperors on upright conduct in statecraft. With the rise of Confucianism in the fifteenth century, however, Vietnamese Buddhism fell into decline. Then, beginning in the early seventeenth century, came an influx of Jesuits and other Christian missionaries from Europe. They discovered fertile territory in Vietnam; by the mid-1700s, there were about 300,000 Vietnamese Catholics in the Red River Valley of northern Vietnam. But Western religion soon came into conflict with Asian beliefs. Catholics faced persecution from the beginning, as distrustful Vietnamese rulers killed missionaries and converts and burned their prayer books.

The persecution intensified in the early 1830s during the reign of the brilliant and ruthless Emperor Minh Mang, who despised Catholics and established Confucianism as the state religion. In 1833, he issued a decree banning the practice of Catholicism and proceeded to destroy churches and force believers to recant their faith.

Desperate Catholics joined an attempt to overthrow Minh Mang, but he brutally suppressed the rebellion. Twelve hundred captured insurgents—both men and women—were buried alive; dozens of European and Vietnamese missionaries implicated in the revolt were publicly executed. In a particularly grisly spectacle, a French priest, Father Joseph Marchand, was tied naked to a stake while soldiers with red-hot tongs ripped pieces of flesh from his body. State oppression of Catholics continued for decades, with an estimated fifty thousand believers perishing.

The pogroms led to military intervention by the French, who eventually occupied all of Vietnam. Under French colonial rule, Catholic fortunes rapidly improved, while Buddhists' suffered. The French gave tax breaks to commercial enterprises set up by Catholic parishes, and the Church acquired rubber plantations, timber concessions, and other properties. Catholics were favored in hiring for civil service jobs, and churches were constructed in prominent places in the major towns.

Buddhists, meanwhile, were required to get permission to build new pagodas and faced limits on the number of monks that could be assigned to each one. Buddhists observed bitterly that Vietnamese Catholics were "the claws by which the French crab has been able to crawl across and devour our land."

Within a few generations, the Catholic Church became one of Vietnam's most formidable institutions, with a well-educated, activist clergy; its own newspapers, universities, and high schools; and associations of militant laymen. Buddhism continued to wither until the 1920s, when Buddhist leaders began concerted efforts to revive it. Reform-minded bonzes established their own schools, youth groups, and a clerical association. They also allied themselves with Vietnamese nationalists, who were resisting French rule.

MANY VIETNAMESE CATHOLICS SAW Diem's ascension to power as a glorious victory for them.

His unsteady new government got a large infusion of political support with the influx of 650,000 Catholics who fled North Vietnam after the Geneva Conference. Some Buddhists worried that the new prime minister would turn South Vietnam into a Catholic republic, but he had no such intention. While he was a devout Catholic, he was also profoundly Confucian, reared in the Confucian tradition of devotion to family and service to the nation. South Vietnam, he told an American friend, was "not a Buddhist nor a Catholic country, but a Confucianist country," steeped in Confucian ethics of social harmony and justice.

Diem went out of his way to cultivate Buddhist support. He named a Buddhist, Nguyen Ngoc Tho, as his vice president, and appointed Buddhists to his cabinet (only two of his fourteen cabinet members in 1956 were Catholic) and top ARVN positions. Diem permitted the General Buddhist Association of Vietnam to hold its second national congress in Saigon, and his government contributed funds for the construction of the big Xa Loi Pagoda in a fashionable part of the city's downtown.

Diem often made the point in his speeches that he was the leader of all of South Vietnam, not just Catholic South Vietnam, and he attended holiday celebrations for Catholics and Buddhists alike. As the country's first constitution was being drafted in 1956, Diem refused to insert the word "God" in it, as Catholics demanded, but instead used the phrase "Most High," as Buddhists preferred.

Indeed, Buddhism in many ways thrived under Diem. By 1963, 1,275 new pagodas had been built, while another 1,295 had been renovated at government expense. Buddhist schools, libraries, and reading rooms proliferated. In March 1963, more than 25,000 South Vietnamese attended the dedication of a colossal image of Buddha in the old French beach resort of Cap St. Jacques, about thirty miles south of Saigon.

Yet many Buddhists still felt that the regime discriminated against them in a variety of ways and undermined their efforts to rebuild their faith.

Catholics held a disproportionate number of jobs in the civil and military bureaucracies, and defended their supremacy by arguing that, as products of Catholic schools, they were better educated—a rationale that couldn't fail to anger Buddhists, who'd long struggled to improve their own educational system. Many Buddhists believed the only way to move up on government or military career ladders was to become Catholic, and "rice-bowl conversions" became common. Buddhists also claimed that Catholic provincial officials were pressuring Buddhist peasants to convert, and that Catholic fanatics had attacked and, in some cases, murdered Buddhists who resisted.

Unlike Catholics, Buddhists had to get government permits to hold large gatherings. Many Buddhists were convinced that the government granted Catholics more land for their churches and schools. In 1957, when the regime unwisely ordered that Wesak Day—the annual observation of Buddha's birth, as important to Buddhists as Christmas is to Christians—be dropped from the list of national holidays, incensed Buddhists "held the greatest Wesak ever organized," forcing the government to back down.

With fewer than 2 million adherents in a population of 14 million, Catholics were a minority in South Vietnam. (About 70 percent of South Vietnamese considered themselves at least nominal Buddhists.) But, with one of their own as national leader, Catholics often engaged in unseemly triumphalism. In 1959, they organized a massive nighttime ceremony outside Saigon's Notre Dame Cathedral, witnessed by an estimated 250,000 people, during which South Vietnam was formally consecrated to the Virgin Mary. The event featured a procession by more than 1,000 Catholic archbishops, bishops, and priests from across Asia, and a Mass performed by a Vatican cardinal and attended by 20,000, including Diem and other top government officials. Big Catholic processions became a familiar sight in Saigon and other cities, tying up traffic on major thoroughfares.

The regime's official ideology, personalism, derived from Catholic doctrine; the ARVN had Catholic but not Buddhist chaplains; and Catholics formed the core of the covert Can Lao Party.

Even the influential Catholic journal, *Informations Catholiques Internationales*, warned of the government's pro-Catholic tilt, saying of the "much paraded fact" that only two of fourteen Diem cabinet ministers were Catholics: "The opinion of the people is not formed solely by an album of photographs of Ministers; it is more sensitive to the place of honour occupied by a bishop at a military parade, to the comings and goings of priests in the Ministries, to their power to intercede for the release of a suspect or for aid for a refugee." Catholic vainglory, the article went on, "does not fail to nourish a certain discontent among the non-Catholics" and "is easily observable in Saigon and in the most remote villages."

Diem's attempts to generate support among Buddhists were often undercut by members of his own family, especially his oldest surviving brother, Ngo Dinh Thuc, the strong-minded, self-righteous archbishop of Hue who seemed to go out of his way to entwine church and state.

Thuc's prominence and close relationship with the president inspired fear in many Buddhists, and derogatory stories circulated about the cherubic looking, cigar-smoking prelate's business dealings and acquisitiveness. (One Saigon businessman groused that Thuc's requests for donations to the Church read like tax notices.) Appointed in 1938 as the first Vietnamese bishop, at a time when the Church was still dominated by the French, Thuc ascended to archbishop in 1961.

In Hue, he'd formed a powerful duopoly with his younger brother Ngo Dinh Can, who controlled local government. While Can tried to downplay his Catholicism and cooperate with the Buddhist community, Thuc flaunted his ecclesiastical authority and initiated a highly visible program of church construction and renovation. When Buddhists hung a picture of Buddha on a bridge to celebrate Wesak Day, Thuc countered by covering it with a portrait of himself. Angry Buddhists refused to walk on the bridge, crossing the Perfume River in sampans instead. The archbishop's ceaseless aggrandizement of himself and the Church alienated many in Hue, the traditional stronghold of Vietnamese Buddhism.

The Nhus, too, became the focus of Buddhist suspicion and ire. Nhu was resented as the chief promoter of personalism and even for his birthday celebrations, which featured a Catholic prayer ceremony.

With her penchant for vitriol, Madame Nhu openly expressed contempt for Buddhism, telling a journalist a year before the Hue massacre: "Buddhism in Vietnam is weak and this might well become a Catholic country." And many Buddhists never forgot her sponsorship of the 1958 "family law" banning divorce, polygamy, and concubinage, which they viewed as an attempt to impose rigid Catholic morality on more tolerant Buddhists.

IN THE FIRST WEEK of May 1963, the Buddhists of Hue were preparing for the Wesak holiday, which that year marked Buddha's 2,507th birthday. Homes, businesses, and pagodas all over the city had sprouted the international Buddhist flag, with its bright vertical stripes of blue, yellow, white, red, and orange. Several weeks earlier, the city had been similarly festooned with gold-and-white Vatican flags to mark Archbishop Thuc's "silver jubilee," the twenty-fifth anniversary of his elevation to bishop.

Diem attended his older brother's gala, but had been upset by the glaring absence of the South Vietnamese flag. For years he'd tried to promote respect for the national standard as a symbol of national identity and unity, issuing a series of edicts that it must always be flown higher than religious banners in public places. He'd spoken to both Buddhist and Catholic leaders about giving prominence to the national flag, but they generally ignored him. (Buddhists argued that a country whose constitution guaranteed freedom of religion shouldn't restrict their emblems in any way.) In frustration Diem banned the public display of all religious flags, although the ban was rarely invoked.

On May 6, with Buddha's birthday just two days away, Diem sent an ill-timed order to his province chiefs to enforce the flag ban. Buddhists throughout South Vietnam saw the decree as a deliberate effort to disrupt Wesak celebrations. Police efforts to remove flags in Hue led to the May 8 radio station massacre—and catapulted Tri Quang into leadership of a burgeoning anti-Diem movement.

Lean, shaven-headed, and endowed with burning, deep-set eyes—"the eyes of the tiger," a colleague said—the forty-year-old monk was a Buddhist chauvinist and ardent Vietnamese nationalist. Born in a Central Vietnam village that later fell under communist control, he was one of three sons of a prominent landowner. At age eleven, he entered a Hue pagoda to train for monkhood. High-spirited and fond of practical jokes, he was kicked out, but later given a second chance.

Possessing nothing but his robes, a begging bowl, and a pair of rubber sandals, the young bonze went to Hanoi in 1946. There he was caught up in the feverish movement for freedom from French colonialism. French police jailed him for ten days on suspicion of being a communist, but Tri Quang consistently voiced only disdain for Ho Chi Minh's ideology. In a brief autobiography he provided to the U.S. embassy, he said his prosperous family was subjected to a Viet Minh "ostracism campaign" that eventually killed his mother. In the 1940s, he said, the Viet Minh forced him to serve as chairman of one of their front organizations near his home village until he was able to escape to Hue, where he claimed to have survived several communist assassination attempts.

Steeped in the dreams of the Buddhist Revival, he became a fervid advocate of strengthening Vietnamese Buddhism and returning monks to their former position as influential advisers to Vietnamese heads of state. He published numerous books and pamphlets about Buddhist philosophy and history, and regarded the Catholic Church as a powerful and dangerous rival. In 1951, he helped to set up the General Buddhist Association of Vietnam and became director of its six regional organizations throughout the country.

Seeing communism as antithetical to Buddhism, Tri Quang initially supported the strongly anti-communist Diem. But he later came to loathe the president and his family—especially his brothers Thuc and Can—and began searching for ways to build a popular movement to confront the regime over its treatment of Buddhists. Nhu characterized him, with a certain wary admiration, as "the perfect conspirator."

For years Tri Quang lived in a cramped cell at Tu Dam Pagoda in Hue. He wore robes of the cheapest cloth and cared nothing for food or physical comforts. (His only weakness seemed to be a fondness for candy, especially Hershey's chocolate kisses.) Although he understood French and English, he insisted on speaking only Vietnamese. He appeared uncomfortable at times with Americans, holding them at bay with opaque, Zen-like utterances. (When John Helble, the U.S. consul in Hue, asked him what his political objectives were, he stared out the window of his room and replied, "Well, the sky is blue, but the clouds are drifting by.") There was no doubting his intelligence, ambition, subtlety, or oratorical skill, however. As a CIA report put it: "He is one of that rare breed that all nations throw up occasionally but very infrequently—a natural political leader."

HAD DIEM PROMPTLY APOLOGIZED for the May 8 killings and punished the responsible officials, he might've been able to drain the energy out of the Buddhists' protests. Instead, his government reacted slowly and grudgingly to their demands, satisfying no one.

On June 1, Diem fired the province chief whose jurisdiction included

Hue and the chief's deputy for security matters, who'd commanded the government troops at the radio station. But the officials were dismissed on the grounds that they were "unable [to] prevent public disorder," not that they'd killed the demonstrators.

Resentment simmered in Saigon and Hue, and Buddhists embarked on hunger strikes, sit-ins, and street demonstrations. Armored personnel carriers and airborne troops were brought in to reinforce the Hue police.

The bitterness in Hue burst into the open on June 3, when about five hundred young people gathered outside a government office, facing off against three hundred soldiers. The protesters included Hue University students, high school kids, and Buddhist Boy and Girl Scouts. Accusations and insults flew back and forth between the crowd and the troops. A government loudspeaker car asked the youths to disperse, saying Viet Cong agents among them could start trouble. Protesters shouted back that the government "wished to kill them."

Some soldiers pointed their rifles at the crowd, but the protesters yelled mockingly, "Stupid killers!" and didn't budge. The troops then fixed bayonets, pulled on gas masks, and started marching toward the protesters. Some fled; others stood their ground and began praying. The soldiers threw tear gas, driving the crowd back several hundred yards, and then laid down another barrage of gas. The young people screamed curses at them.

Some demonstrators tried to retreat to Tu Dam Pagoda, but barbed-wire barricades erected by authorities blocked their way. They then sat down in the street and prayed. An inflammatory rumor circulated that Tri Quang had died while fasting. (In fact, he was alive, although in a dangerously weakened condition.) When soldiers ordered the youths to disperse, someone threw a rock. More gas-masked troops moved in, more tear gas clouds blossomed. The crowd kept growing until it reached about 1,500 people.

At about 6:30 p.m., the security forces again moved to break up the crowd. Soldiers walked up to some of the praying Buddhists, opened glass vials, and poured some kind of liquid over their heads. The doused protesters felt a burning sensation on their skin; sixty-seven of them wound up in the hospital in various states of distress.

At midnight, Helble telephoned the Saigon embassy to report that he'd gone to the hospital and seen people with blistered skin. Some were having respiratory difficulties; doctors said three might die (none did).

Martial law was imposed on Hue. An informant told the U.S. embassy that Diem's brother Can had said the government wouldn't compromise and was "prepared for military showdown" with dissidents.

American officials were alarmed that the protesters' symptoms suggested the possible use of mustard gas, a chemical weapon with ghastly effects. If the government had indeed exposed its own people to poison gas, the story would set off not only a wave of VC propaganda and damaging headlines in the United States but possible violence in Hue and Saigon. On June 4, the embassy urged Diem to investigate right away; within hours, he ordered three top officials to fly to Hue and look into the matter.

Two days later, the group reported that the chemical poured on the demonstrators' heads was a liquid form of tear gas, left over from French stocks; it became a gas when released into the air. U.S. Army chemists in Maryland confirmed that the tear gas was a type used by the French army in World War I.

MALCOLM BROWNE THOUGHT THE gasoline-drenched old monk looked strangely serene as he sat in the Saigon street intersection, encircled by chanting, wailing Buddhists. The sweetish smell of gas permeated the humid air. Quang Duc struck a match and dropped it in his lap.

A yellow fireball whooshed up his body and formed a pall of black smoke in the air. Some of the surrounding monks prostrated themselves on the pavement, moaning and crying. A momentary breeze pushed the flames away from Quang Duc's face; Browne could see that although his eyes were closed, his features were twisted with pain. The wire-service man reflexively began shooting photos.

Halberstam pushed his way into the crowd after running six blocks from his house. He was horrified by the spectacle—"too shocked to cry, too confused to take notes or ask questions, too bewildered even to think." The idea of trying to save the monk flashed through his mind, but he knew it was too late as the man's body shriveled, the skin on his shaven head turning black.

To Halberstam's astonishment, Quang Duc didn't move a muscle or utter a sound as the blaze consumed him. In the background, a monk with a bullhorn eerily repeated, in Vietnamese and English: "A Buddhist priest burns himself to death. A Buddhist priest becomes a martyr."

Some onlookers fell to their knees in prayer, rocking back and forth, sobbing and keening. Others, held spellbound by the dreadful sight, stared numbly at the figure in flames. A few Saigon cops, some in tears themselves, tried to keep spectators back. A fire truck arrived, but monks immobilized it, laying down in front of and behind its wheels as the frantic driver blasted his horn. Helmeted riot police ran up, but halted in confusion before the crowd.

Quang Duc sat in the lotus position, his flesh charring, for close to ten minutes. Finally, he toppled backward. His legs jerked convulsively for a minute or two and then he lay still, his remains smoking. A black delivery truck pulled up and monks unloaded a wooden coffin. They tried to lay Quang Duc in the box, but his roasted limbs were too rigid. The monks then took off their outer robes, fashioned a sling for the dead bonze, and marched off with him toward Xa Loi Pagoda, defiantly flying Buddhist flags as they went.

TRANSMITTED TO ASSOCIATED PRESS headquarters in New York, Browne's pictures of the burning monk were published in newspapers and magazines around the world. Nolting, still vacationing in the Aegean, saw one in a little newspaper on the Greek island of Mykonos.

Browne had shot a half dozen rolls of 35-millimeter film, but most publications ran an arresting image that showed Quang Duc's face, eyes closed, as flames streamed from his head like a gust of dragon's breath. The Buddhists turned the photo into a propaganda weapon, colorizing and enlarging it to make placards that then appeared at the forefront of their street processions. Postcards featuring the burning monk were soon being sold not only on the streets of Saigon but as far away as Lisbon and Dar es Salaam. China printed reams of Browne's photograph for distribution throughout Southeast Asia, with captions describing Quang Duc's self-immolation as the work of "the U.S. imperialist aggressors and their Diemist lackeys."

A rash of similar suicides was reported in other countries with large Buddhist populations, including Burma, Ceylon, India, Japan, and South Korea. Although Buddhists adhered to a code of nonviolence, self-immolation had precedents that went back centuries in the Mahayana strain of Buddhism, which was dominant in South Vietnam.

Vietnamese Buddhists viewed setting oneself afire not as self-destruction but as a supreme act of compassion for their suffering people, a way to focus public attention on the oppression of fellow adherents. Self-immolations weren't uncommon and Saigon newspapers matter-of-factly described such suicides in the 1920s and '30s. The French had tried to stamp out the practice with limited success. After they stopped one monk from torching himself, he fasted to death.

Quang Duc's fiery end shook some of the Western journalists in Saigon, none more so than Browne.

His images of Quang Duc helped make him one of the best-known war correspondents of the twentieth century, and they remain among the most famous news photographs ever taken.

Yet he was well aware that the Buddhists had staged the macabre event—he labeled it the "theater of the horrible"—to gin up publicity for their claims of persecution. He never forgot the monk's expression as the flames touched his face. Nor could he shake the feeling that his presence had contributed to the bizarre destruction of "a kind old man" who might not have lit himself on fire had Browne not been there with his camera.

"As shock photography goes, it was hard to beat," the newsman said laconically of his iconic photo many years later. "It's not something that I'm particularly proud of."

Sheehan was affected by the monk's death, too, but in a different way. Although he wasn't at the scene, he dashed off a story and cabled it to UPI's Asia news hub in Tokyo.

He apparently wasn't aware that another UPI reporter, Ray Herndon, a fun-loving Texan who'd recently come to Saigon from Hue, had written his own version of the monk's demise. When the two dispatches reached Tokyo, an editor, assuming Herndon had filed from Hue, combined them into a single account incorrectly reporting that two monks had incinerated themselves—one in Saigon, the other in Hue. (Herndon, who was staying at Halberstam's house, had sprinted to the scene with him and actually witnessed Quang Duc's burning.) UPI then distributed the erroneous story to clients across the globe.

On top of everything, Herndon had neglected to bring his camera, meaning UPI didn't have any pictures for its subscribers.

Sheehan happened to be in the U.S. Information Service office when the story of the two dead monks clacked out of the UPI teletype machine. Aghast, he fired off a cable telling the Tokyo office to issue a "mandatory kill" alert, warning editors not to publish the story. The kill signal arrived in newsrooms just fourteen minutes after the inaccurate story.

Diem's press allies nevertheless jumped on the opportunity to attack Sheehan's credibility. A Saigon newspaper, *Thu Do*, ran a front-page item clucking over UPI's "feat" of killing off a second bonze. The paper pointed out the errors in the story and sarcastically concluded: "No comment." (*Thu Do* failed to mention the quickly issued kill alert.) Sheehan wrote a letter to the paper's editor saying he was "profoundly disturbed" by its violation of "common standards of morality and ethics." He demanded a retraction and an apology.

Not only did *Thu Do* not apologize, it published a second assault on Sheehan the next day. The reporter urged his bosses to sue the paper for libel, but they declined, saying the matter wasn't serious enough.

WATCHING THESE EVENTS WITH interest was Mieczyslaw Maneli, chief Polish delegate to the International Control Commission, set up under the Geneva Accords to monitor violations of the 1954 ceasefire. (Communist Poland was a commission member along with India and Canada.)

During World War II, Maneli had been sent to Auschwitz, where he joined a communist cell and escaped to fight the Nazi occupation of Poland. After the war he became a law professor at the University of Warsaw. (Fired from his job in a 1968 communist purge of "liberals," Maneli wound up teaching political science at Queens College in New York.)

Maneli had been associated with the ICC since 1954 and was a keen observer of South Vietnamese politics and personalities. In a cable to his government, he described Quang Duc's theatrical death and its aftermath, pointing out that the self-immolation gave the Buddhists exactly what they needed: a high-visibility martyr.

In a subsequent cable, he concluded that the Buddhists also gained two important allies: Halberstam and Sheehan.

The two newsmen, Maneli wrote, were "decidedly on the side of the democratic demands of the Buddhist movement, and thus against the official line of the [U.S.] embassy. . . . The energy, speed, and accuracy with which they report on the demonstrations and political demands of the Buddhists indicate that they are emotionally and politically engaged and that the Buddhists are not entirely cut off from all American institutions."

CHAPTER 8

KENNEDY IN THE QUAGMIRE

JESUS CHRIST!" JOHN F. KENNEDY gasped into his bedside telephone.

The president had just gotten an eyeful of the burning monk on the front page of one of the multiple newspapers he read every day. On the other end of the line was his brother Robert Kennedy, the U.S. attorney general, who'd called before 8 a.m. to strategize about the administration's coming confrontation with Alabama Governor George Wallace. Despite a federal court order, Wallace was vowing to bodily block two African American students from enrolling at the University of Alabama.

JFK had paid only intermittent attention to Vietnam during the first two years of his presidency, as he faced one foreign policy crisis after another and tried to push back communist encroachments in Cuba, Berlin, and Laos. But as spring gave way to summer in Washington, it was clear that something had gone seriously wrong in Saigon.

Kennedy knew a good deal about Vietnam, dating back to a 1951 visit during which he dined with Bao Dai in his palace and met General Jean de Lattre de Tassigny, the brilliant, vain commander of French forces in Indochina. After he was elected to the Senate the following year, Kennedy became a persistent thorn in the side of the French, vocally criticizing their refusal to grant full independence to their onetime colony.

He strongly supported Diem, who he met in 1953 at a luncheon arranged by Supreme Court Justice William O. Douglas. JFK admired his fellow Catholic's courage in taking on the herculean task of leading his weak, nearly bankrupt country after almost a century of French subjugation. He called for more American aid for Diem's regime, describing it in a 1956 speech as "the finger in the dike" holding back "the Red Tide of Communism" in Southeast Asia. He agreed with Diem's decision not to participate in the reunification election that year, saying such a contest would be "obviously stacked and subverted in advance" by the communists.

But the Buddhist uprising had caught the White House completely off guard. "How could this have happened?" Kennedy demanded of an aide. "Who are these people? Why didn't we know about them before?"

The Saigon embassy wasn't much help. Nolting's contacts with anti-Diem dissidents apparently didn't extend to Buddhist leaders; embassy files on the Buddhists consisted of "two or three musty sheets of paper" on which Tri Quang's name didn't even appear. A State Department official recalled searching frantically for someone, anyone, who could explain the Buddhists and their newfound political muscle. He contacted academic experts, foreign service officers, and even an American Buddhist who worked for the U.S. Information Agency. But, the official said, "there wasn't anybody who really knew anything. Nobody."

The graphic images of Quang Duc's fiery self-destruction had shocked American newspaper and magazine readers. *Life* ran a particularly grisly series of photos, including one of the elderly monk's flesh blackening in the inferno and another of his smoking corpse lying on its back, arms stretched skyward almost beseechingly. To many Americans, Malcolm Browne's pictures seemed like indisputable proof that Diem was a monster. Why else would a fragile old man commit such an extreme act, setting himself on fire, if he and his fellow disciples weren't facing the most vicious, systematic persecution imaginable?

That wasn't the reality in South Vietnam, however. The Buddhists certainly had some legitimate grievances, but Diem wasn't Hitler or Nero. Government troops had killed a handful of them in Hue during a chaotic night, but Buddhists had never faced deliberate, state-sponsored persecution under Diem. Self-immolation was a form of political protest that had existed in Asia for centuries. Most Americans, however, were unaware of such distinctions. They'd never witnessed the spectacle of a man burning himself to death, and they found it revolting.

Quang Duc's burning had taken place far away, but it singed Kennedy nevertheless. Notoriously sensitive to press criticism, he found himself under attack in the media and in Congress, cast in the unenviable role of chief benefactor of a horrid dictator. Even his fellow Democrats and liberals were aghast.

As public opinion soured on Diem, many Americans questioned whether the onetime "tough miracle man" and heroic anti-communist deserved further U.S. aid despite his fight against the Viet Cong. In many media portrayals, Diem appeared to be the enemy of a cherished American ideal: freedom of religion. The burning monk forced Kennedy to pay much more attention to South Vietnam.

CHARMING, ELEGANT, WEALTHY, AND wryly detached, JFK was the most glamorous and talked-about man in America. A gifted speaker and early master of the new medium of television, he loved to banter with journalists at press conferences and drop last-minute witticisms into his speeches. Surveying a group of Nobel Prize winners at a White House dinner, Kennedy quipped: "This is the greatest assembly of talent and brains ever assembled in the White House, except perhaps when Thomas Jefferson dined here alone."

He savored gossip about fellow politicians and Hollywood stars, hated feeling bored, and was convinced he wouldn't live a long life, a premonition that proved to be cruelly true. His character had been profoundly shaped by his experiences as a torpedo boat skipper in the Pacific in World War II, and he still could curse like a sailor. He was surrounded in the White House by a tight group of adoring aides, operatives, and assorted liege men, who toiled diligently to protect and burnish the Camelot image that imbued his presidency.

Just forty-six years old in the summer of 1963, Kennedy was at the peak of his powers.

He was lionized for besting Nikita Khrushchev in the eyeball-to-eyeball confrontation the previous fall over the Soviet leader's attempt to install nuclear missiles in Cuba. ("The other guy blinked," as Secretary of State Dean Rusk put it.) As soldiers escorted two Black students into the University of Alabama on June 11, he made a televised speech on civil rights that Martin Luther King Jr. called "one of the most eloquent, profound, and unequivocal pleas for justice and freedom of all men ever made by any President." JFK initiated negotiations with Khrushchev that would soon produce a remarkable Cold War breakthrough: a treaty banning nuclear weapons tests in the atmosphere. And he was days away from embarking on a triumphal tour of Europe that would be marked by cheering crowds in West Berlin, London, Rome, and Ireland.

Elected by a minuscule margin over Richard Nixon in 1960, Kennedy had carefully stocked his administration with Republicans as well as Democrats, giving it a protectively bipartisan coloration in key policy areas. His much-admired defense secretary, Robert McNamara, was a Republican, as were CIA director John McCone and Treasury Secretary Douglas Dillon. McGeorge Bundy, his special assistant for national security, was a GOP member, too.

Kennedy looked forward to a relatively easy reelection victory in 1964. Long plagued by back pain and Addison's disease, the president was taking a new regimen of drugs and felt better than he had in years. And to top it all off, his wife, Jacqueline, was pregnant with their third child, due in August.

With its glittering promise and youthful vigor, the Kennedy administration had attracted into its ranks a flock of bright men, many with Ivy League degrees and wartime service, who embraced the tough, pragmatic rhetoric of JFK's "New Frontier." They regarded themselves as hard-nosed, action-oriented intellectuals: they wrote books, quoted poetry, stayed fit with handball and squash. Activist and internationalist in outlook, they believed they could change the world through unapologetic application of America's enormous military and economic power. Kennedy proudly declared that the torch had passed to a new generation, and he and his cavaliers were that generation, determined to pull the country out of what they viewed as the lethargy and stasis of the Eisenhower years.

McNamara epitomized the dynamism and self-assurance of the New Frontiersmen. A master of statistical analysis who JFK had lured away from the presidency of Ford Motor Company, he descended on the Pentagon like a scourge. He canceled expensive weapons systems he thought were outmoded and imposed stricter discipline on a sprawling, byzantine budget. He fired questions in all directions, making military bureaucrats look foolish as they fumbled for answers. Incisive, indefatigable, and supremely confident, he was an "IBM with legs," able to compute costs and untangle logistical problems faster than anyone else in the room. He was soon recognized as the star performer at meetings with the president, the cabinet, and on Capitol Hill.

But some older Democratic figures weren't so impressed with the young president's men.

His United Nations ambassador, Adlai Stevenson, a two-time Democratic presidential nominee, lamented "the damnedest bunch of boy commandos running around" the White House. When Lyndon Johnson, JFK's vice president, talked up what he called "the Harvards" to his old Texas friend Sam Rayburn, the longtime speaker of the House of Representatives, Rayburn said, "Well, Lyndon, you may be right and they may be every bit as intelligent as you say, but I'd feel a whole lot better about them if just one of them had run for sheriff just once." The administration's relentless activism in foreign affairs later caused Robert Kennedy to wonder whether he and his brother had paid "a very great price for being more energetic than wise about a lot of things."

When the president and his men gathered in the Oval Office or Cabinet Room to discuss policy and politics, the walls rang with witty repartee and comradely laughter. Eisenhower's White House staff meetings had been modeled along strictly hierarchical lines, reflecting Ike's military career, but

Kennedy's were more like graduate school seminars, with professors and students talking and arguing on a nearly equal footing.

JFK liked zestful discussion with a wide range of views, and he often invited lower-echelon desk officers and even men from the field to debate policy along with cabinet secretaries. "He'd get a lot of people in—people who had [policymaking] responsibility and people who had no responsibility—when any foreign policy matter came up," recalled U. Alexis Johnson, for years a high-ranking State Department official.

But these freewheeling discussions sometimes produced policy muddles. Difficult questions were assessed without sufficient time or evidence. Kennedy's top advisers were sometimes unsure what had been decided or whether the president had been told all he needed to know. And courses of action were occasionally set without adequate consideration of likely consequences.

IN HIS FIRST MONTHS as president, Kennedy faced a hair-raising series of foreign crises, one hard on the heels of the other.

In April 1961, his brand-new administration was humiliated when Fidel Castro's forces killed or captured 1,400 Cuban exiles, trained by the CIA, who landed at the Bay of Pigs in a doomed attempt to overthrow Cuba's communist government. At a June summit meeting in Vienna, Austria, Khrushchev badgered and bullied his younger adversary, crowing about communism's supposed superiority over capitalism. In August, the East Germans unexpectedly threw up a barrier of barbed wire and other obstacles between East and West Berlin, and then began pouring concrete for what became known as the Berlin Wall. With the communists threatening to swallow West Berlin, Kennedy sent a 1,500-man U.S. Army battle group on a perilous journey through East Germany to underscore the American commitment to preserve Western access to the city.

The Bay of Pigs debacle taught Kennedy to ask probing questions about proposed military ventures and view the advice of military men with a good deal of skepticism. The Laos crisis only heightened those instincts. The Pentagon tended to focus narrowly on purely military options, and shortsighted ones at that. The generals on the Joint Chiefs of Staff had recommended putting American troops into Laos without any real plan for them to win, or even survive, without a possible resort to nuclear weapons—an outcome that Kennedy deeply feared. Discussing the Joint Chiefs over dinner with his friend Ben Bradlee, Washington bureau chief for *Newsweek* (and later editor of *The Washington Post*), JFK said the most important advice he could give his successor was "to watch the generals and to avoid feeling that just because they were military men, their opinions on military matters were worth a damn."

His mistrust prompted the president to bring his own special military adviser into the White House: General Maxwell Taylor, an urbane former Army chief of staff and renowned World War II combat leader. Kennedy also asked his brother Robert—his most trusted political adviser and confidant—to begin attending high-level meetings involving foreign policy and national security matters.

SOUTH VIETNAM'S POSITION BECAME increasingly precarious as the Viet Cong ratcheted up their attacks. A State Department report in June 1961 indicated that an astonishing 43 percent of new ARVN recruits were being killed or wounded in combat. In September, three communist battalions struck Phuoc Vinh, a provincial capital about sixty miles north of Saigon, killing forty-two Civil Guards and publicly beheading the province chief. Two companies of ARVN Rangers were in the area, but fled into the jungle rather than try to rescue the guards. The VC freed 250 suspected communist prisoners and carried off one hundred captured rifles and six thousand rounds of ammunition.

In October, a wave of revulsion passed through Saigon when the mutilated body of ARVN colonel Hoang Thuy Nam was pulled from the Saigon River. Nam, South Vietnam's outspoken chief liaison officer to the International Control Commission, had been kidnapped, tortured, and killed by the Viet Cong. His brutal slaying seemed calculated to defy world opinion, since the ICC was the body that monitored compliance with the Geneva agreements, in which eight nations had taken part.

As Kennedy shied away from military confrontation in Laos, Republicans and conservatives clamored for toughness toward the communists. "What is crucial," wrote James Burnham in *National Review*, "is that we should *somewhere*, in *some* theater on *some* vital issue, make a stand of unconditional firmness: that we should strike a blow against the enemy." JFK knew he could sustain only so many high-profile foreign policy setbacks before his domestic political support suffered. After Khrushchev pushed him around in Vienna, a visibly shaken Kennedy told James Reston of *The New York Times* that he was now bound to demonstrate U.S. determination to resist communist imperialism, and "the place to do it . . . was Vietnam."

Even before Vienna, Khrushchev had issued what Kennedy interpreted as an epochal challenge to the West.

In a January 6, 1961, speech, the Soviet premier declared his support for "wars of national liberation" in South Vietnam, Algeria, and other fledgling states. By this, he meant revolutionary warfare carried out by communist guerrillas against colonial authorities or relatively new and unsteady noncommunist governments like Diem's.

Between the end of World War II and 1963, forty-three countries had become independent, many after splitting off from colonial empires. Mired in poverty and often deeply embittered toward their former European masters, the citizens of these newborn nations could be highly susceptible to communist blandishments.

Kennedy recognized wars of national liberation as a new form of aggression that had to be confronted with new tactics. With their large, well-equipped armies, the United States and USSR had every reason not to engage in a conventional war, and the leaders of both countries knew that pressing the nuclear button would be the act of a madman. But by backing guerrilla forces that might win control of a national government, the Soviets could expand their influence in the underdeveloped world while minimizing the risk of a head-to-head confrontation with the United States.

JFK thus became an impassioned proponent of counterinsurgency, the doctrine of suppressing revolutionary uprisings through a combination of military, political, economic, diplomatic, and psychological tactics.

He eagerly read the writings of Mao Zedong and Che Guevara, the South

American revolutionary, and ordered top U.S. Army officials to do the same. "Guerrillas must move among the people as fish swim in the sea," he said to his surprised wife, Jacqueline, quoting Mao's famous dictum as the couple lunched at their Virginia country house.

Under Eisenhower's doctrine of "massive retaliation," the U.S. military was geared toward an apocalyptic clash with the Soviet Union. Strategic Air Command bombers bearing atomic payloads were aloft around the clock, ready to incinerate Moscow, Leningrad, and other Soviet cities at a moment's notice. Submarines packed with nuclear missiles began prowling the world's oceans.

But Kennedy rejected such heavy reliance on nuclear weapons, preferring a strategy of "flexible response." He told the Pentagon to begin a major restructuring, placing the same emphasis on preparing to fight counterguerrilla wars as it did on conventional and nuclear wars.

WITH KENNEDY'S SUPPORT, THE Army's Special Warfare Center at Fort Bragg, North Carolina, converted itself into "a vigorous and ingenious seminary" in the new counterinsurgency methods. Kennedy had particular affection for the U.S. Special Forces, those tough, highly trained soldiers who could parachute into foreign conflict zones, kill enemies with a knife or their bare hands, bind up their own wounds, and live off the land for weeks at a time while fluently conversing with the natives in their own tongue.

Over the objections of Pentagon brass, the president decreed that Special Forces members be permitted to wear distinctive green berets. The White House press corps joined JFK on a trip to Fort Bragg for a special demonstration. A soldier with a rocket strapped to his back zoomed across a lake and touched down in front of the president. Frogmen swam ashore from a mock submarine.

There were demonstrations of ambushes and counter-ambushes, and of how to eat snake meat. From across the lake, a thousand men hiding in the brush suddenly jumped up, set off flares, and began yelling at the top of their lungs; they represented the number of indigenous guerrillas that could be trained by a twelve-man Special Forces "A" team. (After all the whizbang demonstrations ended, one of the participants, a sergeant, wrote: "Much of the equipment shown, including the rocket, had never been seen before and probably would never be seen again.")

Counterinsurgency became something of a fad among Washington's foreign policy intelligentsia. Kennedy's newfound enthusiasm for it, and the Pentagon's newfound need to understand it, unleashed a flood of special studies, think-tank analyses, doctoral dissertations, and memoirs about past guerrilla conflicts in Greece, the Philippines, Malaya, and elsewhere.

In January 1962, Kennedy created the Special Group (Counter-Insurgency), a secret committee chaired by Maxwell Taylor, that included top officials of the military, CIA, State Department, and U.S. Information Agency.

The group was tasked with riding herd on the Pentagon's efforts to expand its anti-guerrilla capabilities, while keeping an eye on counterinsurgency operations in South Vietnam, Thailand, and Burma. Its members included Robert Kennedy, who did nothing to hide his impatience with bureaucrats for not moving faster to enact his brother's agenda, often chastising them vocally. Robert seemed to have embraced idealized notions of rough-and-ready Green Berets fighting in exotic lands even more ardently than JFK. (He once invited the Green Berets to demonstrate their lethal skills at the Kennedy family compound in Hyannis Port, Massachusetts.)

Robert was particularly frustrated by the military's failure to develop, on a hurry-up schedule, a lightweight radio powerful enough to drive signals through thick jungle canopies. Pentagon men tried to explain, over the course of several Special Group meetings, the significant technical difficulties involved in producing such a device. At the conclusion of one unsatisfying update, the president's younger brother "blew up, just blew into fragments," recalled another group member. "He just went into orbit. He hated this."

The Pentagon, however, was in no rush to make the radical changes the president wanted.

The generals had invested their long, medal-draped careers in large bodies of men trained for conventional combat. Their job was to annihilate masses of enemy infantrymen with tanks and artillery on big, glorious battlefields, not creep around mangrove forests in bush hats and face paint trying to knock off a few little men in black pajamas.

The top brass had no interest in digging wells and building schools for peasants, and they thought the regular troops under their command could handle a few thousand ill-equipped guerrillas just fine. General Lyman Lemnitzer, who served as chairman of the Joint Chiefs from 1960 to 1962, carped that Kennedy was "oversold" on counterinsurgency.

Top officers dismissed it as a trendy distraction and saw little need to consider political factors in war fighting. A month after he became Army chief of staff in October 1962, General Earle Wheeler said: "It is fashionable in some quarters to say that the problems in Southeast Asia are primarily political and economic rather than military. I do not agree. The essence of the problem in Vietnam is military." Another U.S. officer went so far as to anonymously declare: "I'm not going to destroy the traditions and doctrine of the United States Army just to win this lousy war."

The foot-dragging was so blatant that Kennedy called Pentagon leaders to the Oval Office and told them bluntly: "I want you guys to get with it." He subsequently informed McNamara that he was unsatisfied with the Army's lethargic response. The Joint Chiefs did at least appoint a special assistant for counterinsurgency, Marine general Victor Krulak. But the armed services otherwise did little to adopt Kennedy's directives, watering them down or ignoring them altogether.

AS COMMUNIST ASSAULTS ESCALATED, Diem was forced to admit that VC strength had grown to the point that his government now faced "a real war waged by an enemy who attacks us with regular units fully and heavily equipped." At the end of September 1961, he surprised Nolting by requesting a mutual defense treaty with the United States.

Kennedy responded by dispatching Maxwell Taylor on a fact-finding mission to South Vietnam—the first of several such expeditions he ordered in a never-quite-successful effort to understand what was really happening there.

Cultured, suavely handsome, and renowned for his combat leadership in two wars, Taylor was the quintessence of a New Frontier military man. He taught French and Spanish at West Point (where he graduated fourth in his class in 1922), and his facility with languages landed him postings at U.S. embassies in Tokyo and Peking in the 1930s.

As American forces battled their way up the Italian peninsula in 1943, Taylor undertook a dangerous secret mission, slipping into Nazi-occupied Rome concealed in the back of an ambulance to assess whether U.S. airborne troops could be dropped near the city. (He decided it was too risky.)

He parachuted into Normandy on D-Day with the 101st Airborne Division (earning the nickname "Mr. Attack") and later commanded the division during the invasion of Holland and in other campaigns as Allied forces pushed toward Germany. After the war he served as superintendent of West Point and then as commander of the American military government in Berlin. He commanded the U.S. Eighth Army during the bitter last months of the Korean War in 1953.

Taylor was appointed Army chief of staff in 1955, but was uncomfortable with what he viewed as the Eisenhower administration's excessive dependence on the doctrine of massive nuclear retaliation. Resigning in 1959, he wrote a bestselling book, *The Uncertain Trumpet*, arguing that the Pentagon needed a more flexible response to future conflicts and should build up its conventional forces. The book secured Taylor a reputation as a military intellectual and influenced JFK, who used some of its arguments during his 1960 presidential campaign.

The following year Kennedy persuaded Taylor to leave a lucrative job as president of the Lincoln Center for the Performing Arts in New York City to head a special committee studying the causes of the Bay of Pigs disaster. Having lost patience with the Joint Chiefs and their single-minded military approach to politically complex world problems, Kennedy made Taylor his in-house military expert.

"Maxwell Taylor made such a big difference," recalled Robert Kennedy. "He had some sense. He could see the whole perspective. They [the Joint Chiefs] just wanted to go in and drop bombs on people."

Taylor entertained the brothers with tales of his Normandy exploits, beginning a long friendship with the Kennedy clan. JFK regarded him as "absolutely first class." Robert became especially enamored with the elegant general, who could quote Polybius as deftly as he could Clausewitz. (Robert even named one of his sons Maxwell Taylor Kennedy.)

TAYLOR FLEW INTO SAIGON on October 18, 1961, just after Colonel Nam's disfigured corpse had been dragged from the Saigon River.

The picture was grim. VC main-force strength had jumped to 17,000 from 10,000 earlier in the year, according to estimates, and the communists were active in the Mekong Delta, the Central Highlands, and central coast. Many South Vietnamese were watching events in Laos with dismay, believing their neighbors would soon fall under communist domination. In addition, the worst flood in decades hit the Mekong Delta, inundating huge swaths of rice lands and affecting a half-million peasants. Everywhere he turned, Taylor sensed "an oppressive feeling of hopelessness which seemed to permeate all ranks of Vietnamese society."

He was accompanied on his trip by Kennedy's deputy national security assistant, Walt Rostow, and a group of experts from the Pentagon, State Department, and CIA. Kennedy had asked Taylor and Rostow to determine "the courses of action which our Government might take at this juncture to avoid a further deterioration in the situation in South Vietnam." The retired general began his investigation by calling on Diem, who spoke to him for four hours.

Rostow set out to answer what he saw as the foremost question on Kennedy's mind: Did the South Vietnamese want an independent, noncommunist future, or did they prefer to be reunified with the north and under Hanoi's control? A former MIT professor of economic history, Rostow interviewed teachers, lawyers, labor leaders, soldiers, and bureaucrats, many of whom disliked Diem, and found them almost unanimously opposed to being under Hanoi's thumb. He talked with many villagers as well, learning that what they most wanted from the government was security, and after that better school and healthcare facilities.

But Rostow doubted that South Vietnam could be saved unless its long borders could be effectively sealed against communist infiltration. At the time, an estimated five hundred to seven hundred trained military and political cadres were slipping into the south each month. Even this relatively small inflow, he wrote, placed an enormous burden on the Saigon government, which would have to field as many as seven thousand new soldiers a month to maintain the ten-to-one ratio of government troops to guerrillas that counterinsurgency experts believed was needed to succeed. Rostow had previously recommended that North Vietnam be subjected to aerial bombing and occupied with ground troops as far north as Vinh in order to cut off the infiltration routes. But Kennedy rejected those ideas.

Taylor presented his report to the president on November 3, urging that the United States undertake a "massive joint program" with Diem to strengthen his armed forces and administrative apparatus. The situation was not hopeless, Taylor said, but Washington needed to act quickly.

He recommended that U.S. military personnel and equipment be shipped to South Vietnam on an emergency basis to perform air reconnaissance, air transport of troops, and other activities that were beyond the ARVN's capabilities. Patrol boats were needed to interdict VC smuggling of weapons and supplies along rivers and canals.

To free the ARVN from static guard duties, the United States should provide training and weapons for the Civil Guard and village militias. Diem's government ministries needed help from experienced American administrators, and his military intelligence system should be overhauled as well. (Taylor said the ARVN's intelligence gathering was so poor that it had been "fighting nearly blind for years.") Finally, Taylor recommended that U.S. troops be sent to help with flood relief efforts and logistics for the ARVN; the Pentagon later estimated that up to eight thousand soldiers were required.

Kennedy approved all of Taylor's suggestions except the troop deployment. He understood the dynamics of escalation, and he was serious about avoiding it. "They want a force of American troops," he told his special assistant and speechwriter, Arthur Schlesinger, a former Harvard history professor. "They say it is necessary to restore confidence and maintain morale. . . . The troops will march in; the bands will play; the crowds will cheer; and in four days everyone will have forgotten. Then we will be told we have to send in more troops. It's like taking a drink. The effect wears off, and you have to take another."

With Kennedy's go-ahead, the Pentagon began shipping advisers and equipment to South Vietnam under Operation Beef-Up. This large-scale introduction of foreign military men and matériel was a blatant violation of the 1954 Geneva Accords, which the United States hadn't signed, but promised to observe. Washington policymakers rationalized their decision by noting that Hanoi had been infiltrating men and combat gear into the south for some time.

But for all his military acuity, Taylor's proposals were strikingly conventional. He made no suggestions for reconfiguring the ARVN to better fight a counterguerrilla war, or for digging out the VC political and administrative infrastructure in the villages.

In exchange for its stepped-up assistance, Washington demanded the usual laundry list of political and social reforms from Diem; as usual, he promised to make changes, but took little action. But as eager as he was for U.S. help, he worried about the extra leverage the Americans would now have over him. He called Nolting in and asked whether the United States would use its aid to meddle in South Vietnam's internal affairs. Would it threaten or even get rid of his government if disagreements arose?

That "very disturbing question," Nolting later wrote, had never occurred to him. After consulting Washington, the ambassador assured Diem that the United States would never use its aid for such purposes.

The Taylor report was a milestone in America's fateful commitment of blood, treasure, and prestige in a noble but ultimately futile struggle to help a small, frail state preserve its independence. In a memo to Kennedy about Taylor's recommendations, McNamara said Washington should officially dedicate itself to preventing the fall of South Vietnam to communism, although as many as 205,000 U.S. troops might be needed to do that, especially if North Vietnam and China intervened.

But in a prescient secret report at about the same time, the U.S. intelligence community warned that any military escalation by the United States would trigger a similar increase in Hanoi's support for the Viet Cong.

IN FEBRUARY 1962, THE Pentagon announced the creation of the Military Assistance Command, Vietnam, to oversee the influx of American military advisers and equipment and get them into the war. Kennedy picked General Harkins to run MACV.

Considering the importance and complexity of the job, Harkins was a singularly poor choice. Roger Hilsman, chief of the State Department's intelligence bureau, later characterized JFK's failure to select a more imaginative military leader as "probably the biggest mistake Kennedy made about Vietnam."

But Harkins had a powerful patron: his old friend Max Taylor. When Taylor had been superintendent of West Point, Harkins was his commandant of cadets. When Taylor commanded the Eighth Army in Korea, Harkins was his chief of staff. Taylor strongly urged him on Kennedy for the MACV position. The Joint Chiefs backed Harkins, too.

While an imposing figure in the Army, Harkins was no one's idea of a strategist or innovator. He was a logistics guy, a staff planner, someone who kept ammunition, fuel, and food moving to frontline troops, and by all accounts was very good at it. He was also known as a silky military diplomat, able to get along well with almost anyone (except, as would soon become apparent, key South Vietnamese generals, American newsmen, and Nolting's successor as ambassador).

Harkins's views on warfare were strictly doctrinal, formed in World War II and Korea on battlefields dominated by phalanxes of infantry, tanks, and heavy artillery. He was no match for guerrilla commanders like General Le Quoc San, who led VC units west of Saigon and had patiently taught his demoralized soldiers to fight helicopters and armored personnel carriers, tactics that resulted in the stunning communist victory at Ap Bac. Not by training, experience, or temperament was Harkins equipped to defeat evanescent enemies like San's men, gliding quietly through elephant grass and groves of rubber trees, endeavoring more to win the allegiance of impoverished farmers than to take the lives of opposing soldiers who were, after all, fellow Vietnamese.

Both McNamara and McGeorge Bundy had qualms about Harkins. In a memo to JFK, Bundy noted that many in the military hoped the president would choose a younger, more forward-looking officer to run MACV, and warned that Harkins's nomination "moves in the opposite direction." Bundy urged Kennedy to "have a careful talk with Harkins" before appointing him. McNamara was impressed neither by Harkins's record nor his personality ("He just didn't think [Harkins] was strong enough," recalled a McNamara deputy), but went along with the appointment because Taylor, for whom the defense secretary had great respect, endorsed Harkins.

Hilsman and Michael Forrestal, the Vietnam specialist on Kennedy's National Security Council, actively tried to derail Harkins, imploring the president to pick someone with experience in guerrilla warfare. They suggested either Brigadier General William Yarborough, the "father of the Green Berets" who ran the Special Warfare Center at Fort Bragg, or Colonel William Peers, a big, cigar-chomping man who fought Japanese troops in Burma with the Office of Strategic Services, or OSS, and led Chinese Nationalist soldiers in covert operations against communist China during the Korean War.

Yarborough and Peers were experts in behind-the-lines, commando-style fighting, not communist revolutionary warfare, and there were big differences. Peers at least had experience in jungle fighting and dealing with Asian troops—which alone put him ahead of Harkins. But Kennedy sensed that reaching so far down the ranks for a MACV chief would alienate senior Pentagon generals and cost him politically.

"I can't do it. The military would crucify me," the president said, in Hilsman's recollection. "Don't try to push me."

Yet even with Harkins in charge of MACV, the war seemed to turn in South Vietnam's favor as U.S. advisers and military gear flowed in.

The ARVN added more soldiers and the Civil Guard and village militias received better weapons and training. Wilfred Burchett, a pro-communist Australian journalist, conceded that while 1961 had seen major gains for the Viet Cong, "1962 . . . must be largely credited to Saigon." McNamara assured Neil Sheehan: "Every quantitative measure we have shows we're winning this war." Returning to South Vietnam in 1962, about a year after his report to JFK, Taylor declared that he witnessed "a great national movement rising" to destroy the VC.

Mild optimism—if not a little euphoria—took hold in Washington, a sense that a new day had dawned, that the new U.S. advisory and assistance program was working.

THE OFFICIAL SANGUINITY RESTED partly on the apparent progress of the strategic hamlet program, which Diem and Nhu had launched on their own in 1962. They claimed that thousands of hamlets had been fortified against VC marauders as the inhabitants dug moats, threw up barbed-wire fences, and moved into houses within perimeters defended by local militiamen. Nhu poured his energies into getting the stockade communities up and running as fast as possible, before the VC had time to destroy them.

"Practically the first words out of his mouth anytime I saw him were 'hameaux strategiques,'" recalled Nolting.

Nhu was so enthused because he regarded the program as his brainchild. It had grown in part out of lengthy discussions between him and the CIA's cerebral Saigon station chief, William Colby. A graduate of Princeton and Columbia Law School, Colby fought with the OSS, forerunner of the CIA, against German troops in Norway and France during World War II and organized covert political actions against Italian communists in the late 1940s.

The two men spent many hours discussing the convoluted nature of the war and the need for a fundamental strategy to win it. They concluded that the key lay in South Vietnam's 16,000 hamlets, which were already the building blocks of the Viet Cong approach. Either by persuasion or force, VC organizers won over adherents in hamlets and obtained from them the recruits, food, money, and tactical intelligence they needed. The communists then gradually built their "people's army," expanding from local defense squads, to mobile guerrilla platoons, to main-force battalions.

In Mao's formulation, guerrillas swam among the people like fish in the sea. Nhu's idea was to use strategic hamlets to drain the sea, leaving the fish flopping helplessly. Colby viewed the concept as a potential game changer in the war, the basic counterinsurgency blueprint that South Vietnam lacked.

Hamlet populations ranged from a handful of people to thousands. The first step in fortifying one was for the ARVN to clear out any VC units in the area. Then government civic-action teams moved in, explaining the program to the inhabitants and helping them build physical defenses. People living outside the perimeter of a strategic hamlet were told to move their homes inside it, keeping defense lines as compact as possible. Defenses typically included a five-foot-wide moat, often lined with bamboo spikes, and fences made of bamboo or barbed wire in front of and behind the moat. Often there was a watchtower and a concrete storehouse for guns. Members of Nhu's Republican Youth were assigned to guard the hamlet along with local militiamen. If overwhelmed by VC attackers, they could summon help from the ARVN.

With physical security established, hamlet elections could be held (Diem had reversed himself on this policy), services provided, and nearby hamlets fortified as well. The idea was to keep expanding these cleared areas, like drops of oil spreading outward in water, pushing the VC away from their sources of sustenance as the oil spots began to merge with one another. Forced into smaller and smaller areas, the enemy would be easier to locate and kill. This "oil spot" strategy dated back to French general Louis-Hubert-Gonzalve Lyautey, who employed it against insurgent Algerian tribesmen early in the twentieth century.

Diem and Nhu, however, saw strategic hamlets as more than just a method for separating VC fish from peasants; they were also the vehicle for carrying out the personalist social revolution in the countryside.

By building fortifications and other community projects, the peasants would absorb the personalist ideal of working together for the collective good. Nhu explained to province chiefs that strategic hamlets would create "a new hierarchy" in rural communities "not based on wealth or position." Republican Youths would be elected to hamlet councils, replacing at least some of the wealthier farmers who traditionally dominated hamlet life.

The winners in this revolutionary reshuffling of classes would be "the model anti-communist fighters" in the villages; the losers would be the "notables and gentry," many of them "lackeys of the imperialists and colonialists," who could be "overthrown at once." (Though his rhetoric echoed Lenin, Nhu didn't address the contradiction inherent in dethroning the regime's strongest supporters in the countryside: landowners.)

WHILE SOME AMERICANS WERE miffed at the way the program was started, Nolting and Colby—and later Kennedy—embraced it, and U.S. aid began pouring into the hamlets.

MACV distributed strategic hamlet "kits" containing barbed wire, building materials, trip flares, light weapons, ammunition, and field telephones. The U.S. Operations Mission set up a new rural affairs branch, headed by Rufus Phillips, the ex–CIA officer. Under Phillips's energetic leadership, a corps of young Americans moved to the provinces full-time to help build schools, clinics, and wells, and distribute fertilizer and seeds.

As was so often the case, however, the Saigon government and the Americans were sharply at odds over how to accomplish their shared goal.

The Americans wanted to simply give the peasants construction materials, weapons, radios, and anything else they needed for their rural garrisons, and then help to construct them. But self-reliance and political struggle were central tenets for Diem and Nhu (as well as for Ho Chi Minh). Diem and Nhu wanted peasants to build strategic hamlets on their own, with little or no help from Saigon and especially not from foreigners, to avoid creating dependency among the rural population. Nhu didn't even want to arm the peasants, saying they should capture guns from the enemy, just as the Viet Cong did.

Under relentless pressure from Nhu, the province chiefs erected strategic hamlets at breakneck speed. By July 1962, about two thousand had been finished, with the government projecting that another five thousand would be done by the end of the year.

The armed hamlets soon created difficulties for the Viet Cong. Identification cards and curfews made it difficult for VC agitprop teams to move from place to place. In the Central Highlands, VC troops, cut off from the peasants, found themselves facing food and medicine shortages. The U.S. embassy estimated that their daily rice rations had dropped to half of their 1960 levels. Radio Hanoi reacted with a virulent propaganda campaign, calling the strategic hamlets "concentration camps" and urging residents to tear them down. But only a few scattered attacks on hamlets were reported, and the communists seemed unsure of how to cope with them.

As the construction program sped forward, however, problems emerged. Some farmers resented having to move inside a barricaded enclosure and then walk long distances to and from their fields each day. Others were made to labor without pay on earthworks and fences for days or weeks at a time, while their crops went untended. Obligatory unpaid work rekindled bad memories of the French, who made widespread use of so-called corvée labor.

Two researchers from the RAND Corporation, a California-based think tank under contract to the Pentagon, found that farmers in provinces near Saigon were required to work without pay for up to ninety days a year, and that some families who were promised subsidies for moving into a fortified hamlet never received them.

Peasants had no say in the siting of strategic hamlets or the pace at which they were built. "The present government position is unenlightened, to say the least," the researchers' report said. When one of them asked Nhu why the government didn't communicate better with people affected by the program, he said that would only cause peasants to demand more from the government.

"The only thing for the government to do," said Nhu, "is issue orders and back them up with force."

CHAPTER 9

"WE'RE GOING TO GET OUR ASSES THROWN OUT OF VIETNAM"

ON THE DAY after Christmas 1962, a speedboat raced toward JFK's presidential yacht, *Honey Fitz*, as it cruised the Inland Waterway near the Kennedy family's winter home in Palm Beach, Florida.

Aboard the vessel were Secret Service agents and U.S. Senator Mike Mansfield of Montana, who'd succeeded Lyndon Johnson as the Senate's Democratic majority leader. Mansfield and three other senators had recently visited South Vietnam during a fact-finding trip undertaken at Kennedy's request. Now Mansfield was headed toward *Honey Fitz* to discuss his findings in person—and to disabuse the president of any notion that things were going well in Vietnam.

A onetime copper mine mucker turned professor of East Asian history, Mansfield had been a steadfast supporter of Diem—who he regarded as "not only the savior of his country, but . . . the savior of Southeast Asia"—since meeting him in 1953. But the Montanan's recent three-day stay in Saigon left him with a very different perspective.

Mansfield had endured one of Diem's soporific monologues and attended a black-tie dinner with him before concluding that he was "a depressed man" burdened by "a feeling of lack of accomplishment." Diem had become "a recluse," while Nhu and his wife were apparently taking control of the government. "He wasn't the Diem I knew," Mansfield later said.

Mansfield also sat through an upbeat, four-hour briefing from Nolting and Harkins that the senator found unconvincing.

Nolting claimed he could "see the light at the end of the tunnel" in the war—a phrase Mansfield recalled hearing from a French general not long before Dien Bien Phu fell. Harkins argued that strategic hamlets represented the turning point in the struggle against the Viet Cong; as always, he predicted imminent victory. In a separate meeting, Nhu assured Mansfield that within a month, two-thirds of South Vietnam's 14 million people would be living in fortified hamlets, an assertion that to the senator sounded far-fetched.

Before leaving, Mansfield had a long lunch with Halberstam, Sheehan, Browne, and Arnett. The journalists recounted their difficulties with the U.S. embassy and Diem's government. Halberstam told Mansfield that the ARVN was losing ground and Diem's heavy-handed controls on his army weren't helping. The senator listened carefully and the reporters' doubts confirmed his own. At Tan Son Nhut airport, the embassy handed Mansfield an optimistic departure statement to read to the press, but he refused.

Clambering aboard *Honey Fitz*, Mansfield greeted JFK, casually clad in a blue sport shirt and white slacks, and the two men settled into comfortable deck chairs in the stern. The senator had written two reports: one for submission to the Senate Foreign Relations Committee, on which he sat, and a far more critical version for Kennedy's eyes only.

The private report said little had improved since Mansfield's previous visit to South Vietnam seven years earlier. Except for the major cities, the country remained insecure and was dominated, at least at night, by the Viet Cong. The peasants were mostly indifferent to Diem and his government. Present U.S. policies might succeed, Mansfield wrote, provided the situation didn't deteriorate significantly. If it did, he warned, Washington would have little choice except to make "a truly massive commitment of American military personnel and other resources" and launch an all-out war against the communists. The United States would then find itself in the same position as the French, enforcing "some sort of neo-colonial rule in South Vietnam."

As he read Mansfield's report, Kennedy's face reddened with anger. "This is not what my advisers are telling me," he snapped. But Mansfield pressed his case, urging the president to begin withdrawing U.S. military personnel. Otherwise, he said, Kennedy would face calls for more and more troops to reinforce the ones already there, a cycle that would take on a life of its own and lead to "a predominant American presence which would be counterproductive to this country's interests as well as Vietnam's."

JFK later told an aide that he "got angry at Mike for disagreeing with our policy so completely," and then got angry at himself "because I found myself agreeing with him."

BUT KENNEDY, WHO'D LONG portrayed himself as a stalwart cold warrior, wasn't ready to turn his back on Diem and South Vietnam. A few days after Mansfield's disconcerting visit, the president dispatched Roger Hilsman and Michael Forrestal to Saigon to see what more could be done to bolster the war effort.

A bright, abrasive West Point graduate, Hilsman fit in well with the bold young men of the New Frontier. With his horn-rimmed glasses and convivial smile, the forty-three-year-old Texan looked more like a mild-mannered academic than a battle-hardened jungle fighter. But during World War II he served with the storied Merrill's Marauders in Burma, commanding a battalion of Kachin and Karen tribesmen against Japanese troops.

Badly wounded by machine-gun fire, Hilsman recovered and later parachuted into Manchuria with an OSS squad tasked with liberating American prisoners of war. In one POW camp Hilsman came across his father, a U.S. Army colonel the Japanese had captured three years earlier in the Philippines. As they embraced, his emaciated dad asked Hilsman: "What took you so long?"

After the war Hilsman earned a PhD in international relations at Yale and went to work in the foreign affairs division of the Congressional Research

Service, getting to know Kennedy, then a U.S. senator and fellow veteran deeply interested in international issues.

In 1961, JFK appointed Hilsman to run the State Department's intelligence bureau. Chatty, ambitious, and cocksure, Hilsman turned the sleepy office into a powerhouse, churning out incisive, well-written papers on cutting-edge topics that he spread around Capitol Hill and the White House like party favors, giving the intelligence unit—and himself—higher visibility. He also allied himself with Averell Harriman, then assistant secretary of state for Far Eastern affairs, and Forrestal. The three men formed a powerful camarilla inside the administration, eventually becoming determined advocates of an anti-Diem coup.

In January 1962, Kennedy read a speech Hilsman gave about guerrilla warfare that was reprinted in the *Marine Corps Gazette*, and the two had a lengthy conversation about how to win such struggles. Impressed, the president sent Hilsman to South Vietnam to study the war and report back to him.

At Diem's invitation, Hilsman observed an ARVN attack, planned by a corps-level U.S. adviser, against a Viet Cong battalion in a village near the Cambodian border. The plan was for paratroopers to drop near the village and assault the VC while four infantry battalions, positioned the night before on boats in a nearby river, cut off a water escape. But the operation yielded little more than suffering and death for local peasants.

Because of a map-reading error, American-piloted B-26 bombers overshot the border and unloaded five-hundred-pound bombs on a Cambodian village, killing and wounding a number of civilians. B-26s and T-28 fighter-bombers then bombed, strafed, and rocketed the targeted Vietnamese village for forty-five minutes. When the smoke cleared, five peasants lay dead, including three children; eleven more had been wounded. Survivors said about two hundred communist troops camped near the village had cleared out an hour before the air strikes began; no contact was made with the VC that day. Hilsman regarded the operation as fruitless and likely to have generated more VC recruits.

Hilsman also spoke with Robert G. K. Thompson, a British counterinsurgency expert who was advising Diem. Astute and courageous, Thompson had participated in London's yearslong but ultimately successful effort to put down a communist rebellion in Malaya.

Thompson was a strong proponent of strategic hamlets, a version of which had worked well in Malaya. He told Hilsman the VC were spending most of their efforts not fighting the ARVN but trying to gain political and administrative control of the south's 16,000 hamlets. The government, he said, was wasting its time going after communist combat forces in the field. If the guerrillas took over the hamlets, they'd have a permanent source of recruits, food, local intelligence, and tax revenues. Thompson emphasized the need for trained civic-action teams to go in and set up basic services such as schools and clinics. Also vital were effective police squads that could root out VC agents who lived in the hamlets. Unless they were removed, it wouldn't be safe to hand out arms to local militiamen.

Hilsman enthusiastically embraced Thompson's ideas and presented them to Kennedy. The president in turn told him to brief Robert Kennedy and other prominent administration figures.

JFK even sent Hilsman back to Saigon to brief Harkins. But the general only seemed interested in discussing the need for bombing the Ho Chi Minh Trail to halt the infiltration of men and supplies from North Vietnam. Hilsman argued that based on his experience in Burma's jungles, bombing would never stop guerrillas from moving along remote trails and that in any case, the VC were drawing most of their recruits and supplies from South Vietnamese villages. U.S. strategy in the war, Hilsman said, required a fundamental rethinking and a new focus on protecting villagers and winning their allegiance. But, he later recounted, "it was as if I were talking to a brick wall."

Hilsman nevertheless had made himself a player in counterinsurgency circles. Upon his return to Washington, he began attending high-level administration meetings on both South Vietnam and Laos, growing impatient when Pentagon officials offered up what he considered painfully conventional options for dealing with communist insurgents.

He once went so far as to snatch a pointer out of the hand of an astonished

General Lemnitzer, the Joint Chiefs chairman, when Lemnitzer had trouble finding the Mekong River on a map. Hilsman's palpable lack of awe toward senior military officers tickled Kennedy, but rankled other government figures. McNamara stiffened at the mere mention of Hilsman's name, and even the imperturbable Dean Rusk couldn't conceal his distaste for his nervy subordinate. Hilsman was notorious within the State Department for his frequent recitation of self-glorifying anecdotes about his Burma days; colleagues usually just rolled their eyes.

For all his effrontery, Hilsman had as good a grasp of the fundamentals of communist revolutionary warfare as anyone in Washington. He viewed the Vietnam War as primarily a political rather than military struggle that couldn't be won with standard military tactics. Any successful counterinsurgency program, he believed, had to reliably protect the peasants from the VC and improve the material quality of their lives. Only then would they be motivated to actively support the government.

AS HIS INFLUENCE GREW, Hilsman conferred with his allies Harriman and Forrestal on a daily basis, often several times a day.

The thirty-six-year-old Forrestal was the son of James V. Forrestal, a driven Wall Street investment banker who became the first secretary of defense in 1947, but descended into depression and paranoia after President Harry Truman asked for his resignation two years later. The younger Forrestal, after graduating from Phillips Exeter Academy in 1945, obtained a commission as a naval officer at age seventeen (his father was then secretary of the navy) and worked in Moscow as an aide to Harriman, then ambassador to the Soviet Union and a family friend. When Harriman was appointed to oversee the Marshall Plan, he brought Forrestal to Paris as his assistant. Harriman and his wife essentially adopted Forrestal after his father committed suicide by hurling himself out of a sixteenth-floor window at Bethesda Naval Hospital.

Harriman remained close to Forrestal as he graduated from Princeton in 1949 and Harvard Law School in 1953. By the time Kennedy asked him to join his National Security Council staff in early 1962, Forrestal had made partner at his New York City law firm, Shearman & Sterling. He informed Kennedy that he'd never been to the Far East and knew nothing about it, but the president replied: "That's just what we want—somebody without preconceptions or prejudices." JFK's national security assistant, McGeorge Bundy, told Forrestal, only half in jest, that his job was to be "kind of an ambassador to that separate sovereignty known as Averell Harriman" at the State Department.

Like Kennedy an avid sailor, Forrestal became one of the president's favorite aides—as well as Harriman and Hilsman's conduit to the Oval Office. A large, bespectacled man with a wide circle of friends in Europe as well as America, Forrestal loved good food, fine wine, opera, and chocolates. Kennedy appreciated his irreverent intelligence and encouraged him to speak freely about foreign policy matters despite his junior status.

Forrestal soon concluded that the United States had identified itself much too closely with Diem. Washington needed to adopt a more independent posture, he felt, in part by listening more to South Vietnamese dissidents. Forrestal also believed that the administration must be more candid with the American press about what was happening in the war, even if that angered the Saigon regime.

Like Hilsman, Forrestal viewed the war as primarily a political contest. He saw large-scale ARVN sweep operations, "with one or two battalions and a lot of American-supplied equipment and advisers clanking over the countryside," as not only unproductive but counterproductive. Saigon's troops rarely made contact with the Viet Cong, but "almost always ran over a village and left that in flames," angering the surviving peasants.

Forrestal and Hilsman also objected to aerial spraying of American-made chemicals to defoliate forests and jungles, ostensibly denying the Viet Cong cover for ambushes.

Such herbicides, the precursors of Agent Orange, had undergone tests in South Vietnam beginning in August 1961. But their success was limited, since they stripped trees of leaves, but left trunks and limbs intact. American aircraft also dumped defoliants on fields where VC fighters were growing rice, manioc, and other food crops. The toxic mists, however, often drifted onto crops belonging to innocent farmers as well.

American officials claimed the chemicals were harmless weed killers, widely used in the United States, and the ARVN displayed soldiers who had been doused with them to demonstrate their purported safety. (Diem also donated sacrificial animals to Montagnards in order to "placate any spirits which might have been offended" by spraying.) But Radio Hanoi frequently broadcast charges that Diem was engaged in "chemical warfare" against his own people.

Despite its limited military usefulness and vulnerability to propaganda attacks, aerial spraying continued. Diem and Harkins supported it, as did Nolting, despite his qualms about the poisoning of rural fishponds and other ecological damage. Kennedy couldn't be persuaded to stop the program.

HILSMAN AND FORRESTAL ARRIVED in Saigon on New Year's Eve 1962, a couple of days before the Ap Bac debacle.

They toured a U.S. Special Forces camp in the Central Highlands that the VC had recently overrun, killing more than sixty Montagnard trainees. They also talked with U.S. diplomats, military men, and journalists, as well as Diem and Nhu.

Though Diem had come across as distraught, disorganized, and isolated from his people when Hilsman first met him, he seemed calmer and more self-possessed now. Nhu was another matter entirely. Though energetic and able, he radiated peculiarities that unnerved Hilsman: "a paranoiac suspiciousness . . . a grandiose, even apocalyptic view of himself and his family that hinted of madness." Over dinner Nhu told Hilsman he'd conceived of a grand strategy to destroy China by having the United States lure it into a war in Laos, which Nhu judged "an ideal" battleground. The very idea, Hilsman recalled, "made me shudder." He came away from the meal believing Nhu would someday lead Diem into an abyss.

Hilsman introduced Forrestal to Thompson, the British counterinsurgency expert, and the trio took a flight over the Mekong Delta to get a bird's-eye view of some strategic hamlets. Hopping from one small airstrip to the next, their plane flew low and slow over country roads and villages sprinkled amid green-and-brown swaths of rice paddies.

Thompson said the fortified hamlets were well defended and benefiting from the inflow of American fertilizer, cement for pigsties, construction materials for schools, poison to kill rats that ruined the rice crops, and other aid. Training programs for the Civil Guard and village militias were beginning to pay off. Bridges and roads destroyed by the VC had been repaired. Progress was visible, and Thompson expressed strong optimism that it would continue.

But Hilsman and Forrestal began to have doubts about the hamlets' effectiveness after inspecting more of them in the narrow coastal strip between Saigon and Hue. As Hilsman later wrote:

> Their defenses were a sham—a moat and a wall topped with barbed wire and bamboo spikes, meandering around fields and outlying houses for so many miles that a whole division would be needed to defend it. But the defenders were only a few old men, armed with swords, a flintlock, and half a dozen American carbines. One wondered where the young men were, and which of the many gaps in the wall they used when they came back at night to collect food and see their wives. . . . It seemed obvious that putting up defenses around a village would do no good if the defenses enclosed Viet Cong agents.

Hilsman worried that not enough police officers were being stationed in the hamlets to sniff out VC living inside them. Many hamlets, moreover, were being built with great haste in insecure areas, exposed to VC attacks and without sufficient ARVN protection. Hilsman heard of one hamlet that held off an assault for twenty-four hours, with ARVN troops arriving only after the communists had finally breached the walls, killed the defenders, scooped up their guns, and melted away.

Forrestal was appalled at the way the Saigon government was populating the fortified hamlets:

> They simply rounded up the peasants without any warning . . . burned their farms behind them so as to deny their houses to the Viet Cong, and forcibly

> incarcerated them—that is the only word you can use—into half-built villages. They weren't really even villages. They were just areas surrounded by barbed wire. . . . In addition to being pretty frightful by western standards, to do this sort of thing in Vietnam is foolish, because every Vietnamese peasant believes, as a matter of religious faith, that his ancestors live on the land which he has farmed.

IN SPITE OF THEIR misgivings about the conduct of the war, Hilsman and Forrestal delivered a carefully hedged report to JFK.

"We are probably winning, but certainly more slowly than we had hoped," they wrote, adding that the war "will last longer than we would like, cost more in terms of both lives and money than we anticipated, and prolong the period in which a sudden and dramatic event could upset the gains already made."

Their report noted a strange paradox: although the ARVN was killing large numbers of VC, enemy ranks kept growing. The Saigon government claimed 20,000 VC killed in 1962, yet intelligence sources said the number of communist regulars rose to 23,000 from 18,000 that year.

Part of the explanation, Hilsman and Forrestal wrote, was that some of the dead being counted as enemy soldiers were actually innocent peasants. But they also cited the VC's ongoing ability to recruit young men in the towns and villages of South Vietnam. Infiltration from the north amounted to only about four thousand men during the year, meaning that the war in the south was largely an indigenous affair. The strategic hamlet program was hurting the VC somewhat, restricting their freedom of movement and making food and medicine more difficult to obtain in some areas. But the enemy remained wily and potent, overrunning a fortified hamlet protected by a Civil Guard company in Phu Yen Province and escaping an "elaborate trap" laid for them in Tay Ninh Province.

In a secret annex to their report, Hilsman and Forrestal laid some of the blame for the war's difficulties at the feet of American officials in Saigon.

Even a year into Operation Beef-Up, they said, there was "still some confusion over the way to conduct a counter-guerilla war" among top American military and civilian officials in Saigon. Too much emphasis was still being placed on less-than-effective ARVN sweeps and air attacks that undoubtedly killed uninvolved peasants. In a thinly veiled swipe at Nolting, Hilsman and Forrestal criticized the lack of coordination among the multiple U.S. military and civilian agencies involved in the war effort. "No one man is in charge," they lamented, and American programs were "fragmented and duplicative" as a result.

As an example, they pointed to bureaucratic bottlenecks that slowed the transfer of U.S. weapons from Saigon warehouses to militiamen defending strategic hamlets. There also was the dispute between the U.S. Army and U.S. Air Force over who should fly to the aid of hamlets under attack. Although two thousand U.S. radios had been distributed to hamlet leaders, their calls for help often yielded slow or no assistance, either from ARVN ground units or American aircraft.

But perhaps Hilsman and Forrestal's most foreboding conclusion related to peasant attitudes toward the Saigon regime.

The central goal of any counterinsurgency effort was winning the people's hearts and minds—a phrase that would be repeated so often during the war it became a cliché. But with the United States committing itself more deeply every day, it still wasn't clear whose side the peasants were on. Some hamlet dwellers fought bravely to repel VC intruders, while others simply opened the gates and gave the communists food and money, without saying anything to the Saigon authorities.

"It is difficult, if not impossible, to assess how the villagers really feel," Hilsman and Forrestal wrote, "and the only straws in the wind point in different directions."

In coming months such reports—often inconclusive or contradictory—piled up on Kennedy's desk, making it hard to understand whether his policies were working in jungles and rice paddies nine thousand miles away.

Not long after Hilsman and Forrestal returned to Washington, General Earle Wheeler, the Army chief of staff, reported on his fact-finding mission to South Vietnam following the Battle of Ap Bac. Wheeler and his team found that the country had improved "from a circumstance of near desperation to a condition where victory is now a hopeful prospect," and that "there is no compelling reason to change" U.S. policies. (After Wheeler briefed Kennedy on his trip, Forrestal apologized to the president for wasting his time with such "rosy euphoria.")

Wheeler's assessment arrived at about the same time as a somber CIA estimate that characterized the war as "a slowly escalating stalemate."

But the direst warning of all had come from John Kenneth Galbraith, the Harvard professor serving as Kennedy's ambassador to India. Galbraith had seen cables about the Taylor-Rostow mission and adamantly opposed their recommendation to send U.S. troops to South Vietnam. He told Kennedy in late 1961 that South Vietnam's government and army were hopelessly ineffective, Diem would never reform, and Washington was "now married to failure." If JFK wanted to prevent the "bright promise" of his New Frontier from "being sunk under the rice fields," he needed to quietly withdraw American support for Diem. That action, Galbraith implied, was likely to trigger a military coup against him, paving the way for better leadership.

As Kennedy pondered the conflicting reports and advice, the Senate Foreign Relations Committee in March 1963 released the public version of Mike Mansfield's fact-finding report, generating political shock waves in Saigon.

Mansfield and the other senators who'd accompanied him to South Vietnam expressed "great admiration" for Diem, but deep concern about his lack of progress since the late 1950s. "Viet-Nam now appears to be, as it was then, only at the beginning of a beginning in coping with its grave inner problems," their report said. Diem's unpopular, narrowly based regime appeared unable to mobilize its people sufficiently to win the war. Even with substantial U.S. aid for many years, the senators wrote, Saigon could still lose to the communists.

The report stunned the South Vietnamese; rarely had powerful U.S. political figures chastised Diem so bluntly and openly. Many South Vietnamese interpreted the senators' comments as a prelude to a U.S. pullout. Nolting was appalled, seeing the report as encouragement both to the Viet Cong and

Diem's noncommunist domestic opponents. He knew it didn't represent a change in official U.S. policy toward Diem, but it did suggest a worrisome crack in the formerly solid American support for his friend.

Reflecting on the damaging report years later, Nolting called it "the first nail in Diem's coffin."

JFK HAD ENTERED THE White House on the wings of soaring rhetoric, pledging in his inaugural address to "pay any price, bear any burden, meet any hardship . . . to assure the survival and success of liberty" throughout the world. But there were distinct limits to the burdens the president was actually willing to bear, especially if it meant a resort to American combat forces.

While publicly he vowed no retreat from South Vietnam, privately he believed that the United States had overcommitted itself. He told Kenneth O'Donnell, his appointments secretary and close confidant, that he wanted to get out of Vietnam, but couldn't do so until after the 1964 election.

"In 1965, I'll become one of the most unpopular presidents in history," he said. "I'll be damned everywhere as a Communist appeaser. But I don't care. If I tried to pull out completely now from Vietnam, we would have another Joe McCarthy red scare on our hands, but I can do it after I'm reelected. So we had better make damned sure that I *am* reelected."

Kennedy was open to a negotiated settlement of the war. Indeed, in 1962 he'd quietly tried to lay the foundation for a Laos-style deal for South Vietnam. Shortly after Averell Harriman hammered out the final details of the Laos accord in Geneva, the president authorized him to secretly approach the North Vietnamese negotiators, who were also staying in the Swiss city.

Early one Sunday morning, hoping not to attract attention, Harriman and his aide William H. Sullivan slipped down an alley and stepped into a small hotel. They met in a private suite with Ho Chi Minh's foreign minister, Ung Van Khiem, but, as Sullivan recalled, Khiem was "brutally, arrogantly negative." The communist diplomat—Sullivan called him "an insulting little thug"—insisted that the north wasn't assisting the VC and began reciting a litany of complaints against Saigon. Before he could finish, Harriman stood up and stalked off.

In April 1963, Kennedy promoted both Harriman and Hilsman. Harriman became undersecretary of state for political affairs; Hilsman succeeded him as assistant secretary of state for Far Eastern affairs. The president summoned Hilsman to the Oval Office.

Sitting in his rocking chair, JFK said he wanted to do all he could to help South Vietnam, with military advisers and equipment, economic aid, and diplomatic support. But if Diem's government couldn't succeed with all that assistance, the United States needed to back out. Under no circumstances did Kennedy want American soldiers fighting in South Vietnam or American bombers attacking North Vietnam. Hilsman's job, JFK told him firmly, was to make sure his country didn't get dragged any deeper into the conflict.

The president was even more emphatic with his friend Charles Bartlett, a *Chicago Sun-Times* columnist (and the man who introduced JFK to his future wife, Jacqueline Bouvier).

At one point, Kennedy told Bartlett: "We've got to face the fact that the odds . . . are about a hundred to one that we're going to get our asses thrown out of Vietnam."

Such private frankness with a friendly newsman wasn't unusual for the president. Several journalists counted themselves among his intimates, including Ben Bradlee and Joseph Alsop, the influential Washington columnist. JFK liked reporters; he enjoyed exchanging raffish banter with them and gossiping about other journalists and politicians. (Briefly a newspaperman himself, Kennedy had covered the 1945 founding conference of the United Nations in San Francisco for the Hearst syndicate.) Bradlee, a frequent dinner and weekend companion of Kennedy and his wife, was fascinated by the president's seemingly bottomless appetite for juicy tidbits about newspaper people "and how clued in he was to their characters, their office politics, their petty rivalries."

A voracious newspaper reader, JFK was highly sensitive to unflattering portrayals of him and his administration. If he spotted a bad news story, he didn't hesitate to pick up the phone and deliver a tongue-lashing, often in a flare of blue language, to top officials of the department that had been skewered.

Dean Rusk got such an earful at seven thirty one morning. Irate about something he'd read on an inside page of *The Washington Post*, Kennedy ordered the secretary of state to "find out who leaked that story, and fire him." Hilsman and Forrestal both had been on the receiving end of media-induced tirades, and Hilsman thought JFK often overreacted to unfavorable stories. "Eisenhower had read the newspapers too little," Hilsman later wrote. "Kennedy was reading them too much."

But the president couldn't shake the bad press coming out of Vietnam. On April 29, he met in the Oval Office with John Mecklin, the Saigon embassy's chief press officer. Mecklin was having more trouble than ever with U.S. newsmen, some of whom had taken to calling him "Meck the Knife" after someone leaked part of a memo he wrote criticizing some published stories about Vietnam as "irresponsible, sensationalized, and astigmatic." (The unleaked portion of Mecklin's memo was actually a plea for more embassy cooperation with journalists.)

Kennedy asked how the coverage could be improved. Mecklin urged him to order everyone in Washington and Saigon to stop making overly optimistic statements about the war and complaining about negative stories. Instead, U.S. officials should take journalists into their confidence, giving them background information in hopes of at least obtaining a sympathetic hearing about what they were trying to accomplish.

The president was skeptical, but willing to try, and a State Department cable went to Saigon directing Nolting and other mission officials to cooperate more with the correspondents.

NOLTING WOULDN'T BE DEALING with them much longer in any event. His tour as ambassador ended in May, and he wanted to return to the States. Kennedy had no desire to reappoint Nolting; he respected his man in Saigon, but wasn't happy that he'd gone off on vacation just as the Buddhists were taking to the streets against Diem. As the president and his staff contemplated who to send next, Rusk surprised them by nominating a well-known Republican, Henry Cabot Lodge.

Lodge and Kennedy had a long history of political antagonism in their home state of Massachusetts, and the Irish-American Catholics in JFK's inner circle knew he harbored a certain distaste for the aloof Yankee blue blood. Lodge's family belonged to the wealthy Protestant class known as Brahmins that had dominated Boston's politics, business community, and celebrated universities for generations.

Kennedy had twice defeated Lodge: for a U.S. Senate seat in 1952 and again in 1960 when Lodge was Richard Nixon's running mate. Kennedy's youngest brother, Ted, beat Lodge's son, George, in a 1962 election for JFK's old Senate seat. (Political dueling between Kennedys and Lodges went back even further in Massachusetts, to a 1916 U.S. Senate race in which JFK's beloved grandfather, John "Honey Fitz" Fitzgerald, lost narrowly to Lodge's beloved grandfather, Henry Cabot Lodge Sr.)

A Harvard graduate and onetime newspaperman in Boston and New York, Lodge had been elected to the Senate in 1936, besting Boston's legendary Irish Catholic mayor, James Michael Curley. During the Depression, he often voted for New Deal legislation, gaining a reputation as a moderate-to-liberal Republican. In 1944, Lodge resigned his Senate seat and served as an Army reconnaissance officer in Italy and France, earning a Bronze Star for his forays into hazardous areas.

Reelected to the Senate in 1946, he became an outspoken advocate of the United Nations. In 1952, running for his fourth term, Lodge worked simultaneously as campaign manager for Dwight Eisenhower in his first bid for the presidency. Ike won his race, but Lodge lost his, having devoted insufficient time and energy to his reelection effort against JFK. Eisenhower rescued him from the political wilderness by naming him ambassador to the UN, a position he held throughout his patron's eight years in the White House.

At sixty-one, the tall, distinguished-looking Lodge was a figure of national prominence, a seasoned political hardball player regarded by some Republicans as a strong contender for the White House in 1964. Outwardly gracious and imbued with old-fashioned noblesse oblige, Lodge could also be cold, imperious, and condescending. He had a ruthless streak and was a deft manipulator of the press, never hesitating to torpedo an opponent with a well-timed leak of damaging information—a "very good switchblade fighter," in the words of an Australian diplomat who knew him at the UN.

A major general in the Army Reserve, Lodge became interested in Vietnam while serving a three-week tour of duty at the Pentagon and producing a paper on counterinsurgency theory. He still nurtured presidential ambitions, and the high-profile Saigon post would keep him in the limelight. And if by lucky chance he wound up presiding over a victorious end to the war—or something that even resembled a victory—it might help propel him into the White House.

Several of JFK's top aides opposed Lodge. When Theodore Sorensen, Kennedy's speechwriter and special counsel, learned of Lodge's possible dispatch to Vietnam, he asked sarcastically, "You mean, North Vietnam?" But no one was warier than Robert Kennedy. With Lodge's reputation for haughtily going his own way, Robert suspected that once ensconced in the Saigon embassy, the strong-willed Republican might prove difficult to control.

But there were significant advantages to enlisting Lodge. In their report on South Vietnam, Hilsman and Forrestal had urged Kennedy to appoint either "the right kind of general" or "a civilian public figure whose character and reputation would permit him to dominate" the heads of all of the U.S. agencies in Saigon. Lodge certainly met the latter criteria, and arguably the former as well.

In addition, his appearance in Saigon would put Diem on notice that a new, much tougher sheriff was in town. If South Vietnam deteriorated dramatically, Lodge's presence there would provide JFK with at least a partial shield against GOP attacks. And, according to Kenneth O'Donnell, Kennedy simply couldn't resist the delicious prospect of entangling his old political nemesis "in such a hopeless mess as the one in Vietnam."

IN JUNE, NOT LONG after the old monk set himself on fire in Saigon, Lodge met the president in the Oval Office.

"Cabot, I am beginning to spend more of my time on Vietnam than anything else," JFK said. He held up a copy of Malcolm Browne's photo of Quang Duc ablaze, saying the situation in South Vietnam was "extremely serious" and Diem's regime was entering "a terminal phase." An American failure in Vietnam, he said, "might have far-reaching repercussions." He hoped to persuade Lodge to accept the Saigon ambassadorship and take personal charge of the embassy's rocky press relations. Lodge wanted to consult with his wife about moving overseas, but soon accepted JFK's offer.

If Kennedy thought he was getting a good soldier in Lodge, one who'd follow his instructions as obediently and swiftly as a regular foreign service officer like Nolting, he was mistaken. Lodge was a former UN ambassador and U.S. senator, an Army Reserve general, and a man who still might someday sit in the Oval Office himself. Aristocratic and supremely self-confident, he was used to giving orders and getting his own way.

And that style wouldn't change an iota in South Vietnam.

CHAPTER 10

A SHARPENING OF KNIVES

AFTER NOLTING LEFT in May for his Aegean cruise, the running of the embassy fell to his deputy and good friend, William Trueheart.

On the day Quang Duc burned, Trueheart got word that two companies of Diem's feared Special Forces had moved into Saigon and an airborne battalion was placed on alert. Monks trying to enter the city from outlying provinces were turned back. Worried about possible clashes between security forces and Buddhist demonstrators, Trueheart ordered the closure of the American Community School, attended by the children of U.S. families living in Saigon. Embassy employees and their dependents were told to steer clear of street protests and any other large crowds of Vietnamese.

Trueheart believed that the old monk's fiery death, and the global outpouring of revulsion and outrage that followed, had drastically altered the situation facing Diem.

No longer would the president be able to make a few half-hearted concessions to the monks, deploy his police and soldiers to scatter Buddhist protesters, and easily tamp down the turmoil. Many Buddhists believed their grievances would never be resolved by the government as presently constituted; some began to talk about trying to overthrow Diem. If there was to be any chance of defusing the rising anger and frustration, Trueheart felt, Diem needed to make "an immediate, dramatic, and conciliatory move" toward the Buddhists.

Since coming to Saigon a few months after Nolting, Trueheart had labored in the shadow of his genial boss. Though somewhat stiff and socially awkward, Trueheart was a keenly intelligent man, with a mordant, even caustic sense of humor and a propensity for speaking his mind. After thirteen years as an intelligence officer for the U.S. Army and the State Department, he joined Nolting in Paris as a political counselor for the U.S. delegation to NATO. In 1959, he transferred to the U.S. embassy in London, where he worked with the British on bilateral nuclear issues.

Trueheart was aware that Washington was routinely violating the terms of the Geneva Accords with its military buildup. He was "disgusted," his son later wrote, by the Kennedy administration's hypocrisy in denying the violations to the press. He knew that under the secret "Farmgate" program, for example, American pilots were not merely training Vietnamese pilots but actually flying combat missions, strafing and bombing the VC. When two reporters showed up late one night at his home asking about Farmgate, Trueheart dutifully recited the company line, denying that U.S. pilots were anything more than instructors. But he pleaded with the State Department to be more forthcoming in its responses to "these insistent inquiries."

Trueheart's alarm at Diem's changed circumstances in the wake of the monk's immolation was shared by Harriman and Hilsman. For days Trueheart had been pushing Diem to grant the Buddhists at least some of what they wanted. But in a late-night cable to Saigon, Harriman and Hilsman went far beyond that position, instructing Trueheart to tell Diem that he must now "fully and unequivocally meet Buddhist demands" and do so in a "public and dramatic fashion." If he refused, the United States would publicly condemn his actions against the Buddhists—a move Hilsman knew could spawn a coup d'état.

Given his history of resisting American arm-twisting, Diem wasn't likely to cave in over the current brouhaha. When Trueheart on June 12 handed him a démarche stating Washington's latest demands, Diem read it in silence and passed it to an aide. He and the aide then discussed the memo in Vietnamese, and the assistant told Trueheart that any statement of disapproval from Washington would be "disastrous" for upcoming government talks with the Buddhists.

Trueheart promptly reported Diem's reaction to Washington, warning that it was "vital that there be no leaks about this." But the blunt U.S. threat to Diem leaked almost immediately, resulting in a front-page *New York Times* story by Max Frankel, the paper's State Department correspondent. John Mecklin, the embassy press officer, observed that the article was so accurate it was as if Frankel "had been shown the file of classified cables from Saigon."

Harriman and Hilsman both had good contacts in the Washington press corps, and neither of them was a stranger to tactical leaking. Frankel may have gotten his story from one or both of them, perhaps because they wanted to trumpet a Kennedy administration crackdown on Diem amid the Buddhist unrest.

Remarkably, the two State Department officials failed to obtain JFK's permission for their heavy-handed ultimatum to a key foreign ally, and the president wasn't pleased. Learning of it during his daily CIA briefing, Kennedy ordered that "no further threats are made and no formal [condemnation] is made without [my] own personal approval."

IN THE FOUR WEEKS that followed the Hue killings, Buddhists openly challenged the regime with street protests, hunger strikes, and memorial ceremonies in various parts of South Vietnam. Woefully ignorant about the Buddhist movement, Washington rushed to educate itself about its leaders, motives, and organizational structure.

CIA agents impersonating newsmen lurked outside Xa Loi Pagoda, trying to pick up any information they could. The State Department enlisted an American expert on Buddhism, Dr. Richard Gard, a vice president of the World Fellowship of Buddhists, to help produce a "crash study" on Buddhist grievances and how they might be resolved. But Gard seemed to know little about the political views or power relationships among South Vietnamese Buddhist leaders.

The Americans soon learned, however, that the Buddhists, loosely organized though they were, possessed an extraordinary ability to mobilize people throughout the country. South Vietnam had a number of Buddhist groups, but the largest and most important was the General Buddhist Association of Vietnam, founded in 1951 and headquartered at Xa Loi.

Rising behind yellow walls not far from Diem's palace, the ornate, three-story temple featured curled-up eaves, a large courtyard edged with banana and pine trees, and a one-hundred-foot-tall bell tower. From the main building jutted a broad deck from which Buddhist leaders addressed the faithful gathered in well-ordered rows in a plaza below. A shrine room big enough to hold hundreds was dominated by a huge image of Buddha, his face framed by a metallic disk representing the sun. Visitors said that upon entering the spotlessly clean pagoda, they immediately felt the heat-baked hubbub of Saigon's streets give way to a cool sensation of contemplation and spirituality and, as one American put it, "the stillness of eternity."

The General Buddhist Association of Vietnam claimed a membership of 3,000 monks, 600 nuns, and more than 3 million lay adherents, including as many as 90,000 in Buddhist youth groups. The association's clerical leader was Supreme Patriarch Thich Tinh Khiet, an eighty-year-old monk who lived at Tu Dam Pagoda in Hue. Until the Hue massacre, the GBAV had been mostly disengaged from public affairs but, as the State Department's hastily assembled study put it, with what turned out to be considerable understatement: "Buddhism is going to be significant in political terms from now on in Viet-Nam."

Diem and his family resented U.S. intervention in what was shaping up as a domestic crisis. They blamed American journalists for giving the Buddhists more momentum with frequent and generally sympathetic news coverage. But the Ngo family was sharply divided over what to do about the protest movement.

Brother Can, living in Hue, the Buddhist heartland, favored a peaceful settlement. Diem, who'd assisted the Buddhists in the past, seemed to veer between extending an olive branch to them and wanting to throw their leaders in prison. One day he delivered a conciliatory radio address to the Buddhists of Hue; the next day, a government plane dropped leaflets over the city attacking its top monks. The Nhus and Archbishop Thuc were adamant about not yielding any ground at all, fearing the regime would appear weak and any concessions to the Buddhists would only encourage more demands from them as well as other dissenters.

Madame Nhu regarded the Buddhists as "communists, crooks, and pimps" whose beliefs were little more than primitive superstitions. Her husband viewed them as an "infantile political movement" that had contributed nothing to building the nation. Both Nhus felt that if the Buddhists got much more out of hand, the army should crush them as it had the Binh Xuyen in 1955. But there were big differences between the two uprisings. For one thing, the gangsters had been armed and lacked popular support; the Buddhists were peaceful and had broad public sympathy. For another, a large majority of ARVN officers and enlisted men were Buddhists and might balk if ordered to use force against their brethren.

Nhu, however, told a regime official that he was "not deeply concerned" about the Buddhist revolt because he could stop it by the simple expedient of massacring "hundreds or thousands" of them in Saigon, just as French Catholic noblemen had slaughtered Protestant Huguenots in Paris and elsewhere on St. Bartholomew's Day in 1572.

UNDER PRESSURE FROM THE Americans, Diem's longtime vice president, Nguyen Ngoc Tho, a Buddhist, and two other top officials began face-to-face negotiations with a delegation of Buddhist leaders from Hue on June 14.

The talks went exceptionally well, with the parties reaching agreement within hours on two of the Buddhists' five demands. Supreme Patriarch Khiet sent an order to all Buddhists nationwide to avoid "all manifestations and incidents" in light of the progress being made; the regime removed barricades outside pagodas as a gesture of good faith.

Two days later, the negotiators released a joint communiqué announcing full agreement on the Buddhists' demands. Both sides had given up a little. Only the national flag could be flown on national holidays, but the

Buddhist flag could be flown in public on Buddhist holidays, alongside a bigger national flag. A French-era law that the Buddhists opposed, arguing that it restricted their ability to acquire land and other property, was to be amended in the National Assembly. Khiet and Diem signed the communiqué, but the president added a note saying the settlement had been "approved by me from the beginning," implying that he wasn't really conceding anything. The regime neither apologized nor acknowledged responsibility for the Hue massacre.

With tensions still high in Saigon, the Buddhists went along with a government request to postpone a funeral cortege for Quang Duc scheduled for June 16, the day the joint communiqué was released, even though thousands of people were already lining streets along the expected route. When the bonzes announced the delay, a crowd of people shouted that they were "traitors" and "sellouts to the government." About three hundred students charged toward police outside Xa Loi, where the dead monk lay in state.

In a swirling forty-five-minute melee, the youths threw bricks, rocks, bicycle chains, and shoes at cops, who responded with tear gas, clubs, and shots fired in the air. The Buddhists claimed a fifteen-year-old boy died of a gunshot to the head and one hundred demonstrators were arrested; the government denied there were any fatalities, but said thirty cops had been injured. Trueheart described the riot as "relatively minor," but the Associated Press reported it as "the most violent anti-Government outburst in South Viet-Nam in years."

That night, tanks and armored cars took up positions outside government buildings, while police and troops armed with machine guns and shotguns manned barbed-wire barricades at intersections throughout the city.

A brittle calm settled over Saigon. Trueheart believed that despite Diem's recent détente with the Buddhists, he'd suffered a severe loss of confidence in the eyes of his people as well as the Kennedy administration. He wanted Diem to use the June 16 peace agreement as a jumping-off point to make more concessions to the Buddhists and other groups. Hilsman agreed and told Trueheart to continue badgering the South Vietnamese president to meet American demands.

But Trueheart, working day and night seven days a week, was beginning to flag under the pressure. His wife, Phoebe, complained about their home phone "ringing all night long" and people showing up at the front door at 2 a.m. She'd throw on her nightgown, let the visitor in, make drinks for her husband and the new arrival, and wait outside his study with a book until they finished their business. "He is running on nerves," Phoebe wrote to his mother. "But don't worry. He really enjoys being in the thick of the fray."

QUANG DUC'S FUNERAL WAS finally held on June 19, with a motorcade from Xa Loi Pagoda to a Buddhist cemetery about nine miles south of Saigon amid a heavy police presence.

Thousands of people pressed against police barricades set up along the route in a deal between the government and Buddhists that mourners not be allowed to walk behind the motorcade for security reasons. Police in jeeps and on motorcycles kept watch.

The solemn procession passed slowly through the streets. The burned monk's remains reposed in a massive bier, decorated with flowers and the Buddhist swastika, an ancient symbol of Buddha's footprints, atop a flatbed truck. Old women knelt on sidewalks, praying as tears ran down their cheeks.

At the cemetery, women in white ao dais scattered flower petals before the casket, draped with a Buddhist flag, as it was borne on shoulder poles by monks. After the coffin was cremated, monks sifted through the smoking remains and collected ashes to be distributed to pagodas throughout South Vietnam. What was left of Quang Duc's robe was cut into tiny pieces said to have healing powers; the snippets were distributed to grateful Buddhist followers.

The Buddhists claimed that, miraculously, the monk's heart survived his incineration. The organ was placed in a small glass jar on an altar at Xa Loi, where it attracted throngs of pilgrims and tourists each day. (One American said the blackened, dried-up heart looked like overcooked liver.)

Wonderment spread through the land following the funeral; people insisted they could see the weeping face of Buddha in the clouds. Traffic jams formed at sunset as people jumped out of their cars and cyclo-pousses to search the reddening skies for the venerated image.

Buddhist leaders watched closely to see whether the regime would carry out the promises it made in the June 16 agreement. But the Nhus, furious about the peace deal, began an open campaign to wreck it.

Madame Nhu was particularly incensed. During a family lunch, she called Diem a "coward" and a "jellyfish" for negotiating with the Buddhists. "You defeated the Binh Xuyen, you defeated the Hoa Hao, you defeated the paratroopers, and now you have lost to a few miserable unnamed bonzes," she berated him. Diem responded: "You do not understand this affair. It has international implications. We had to settle it." At that, Madame angrily threw a tureen of chicken soup across the table.

She released a statement through her Women's Solidarity Movement effectively accusing the Buddhists of helping the communists, a charge that angered them deeply. And in remarks that made many Americans recoil, she described Quang Duc's self-immolation as a "barbeque," adding that if the Buddhists wanted to stage another such suicide, "I will be glad to supply the gasoline."

Her husband was equally irate. In a communiqué to his Republican Youth, Nhu charged that the June 16 agreement "creates privileges and monopolies to the benefit of one particular group" and "does not conform to the ideal of the Republican Youth." Meeting with the new CIA station chief, John Richardson, Nhu denounced Diem's modest concessions to the Buddhists, saying, "I don't give a damn about my brother. . . . If a government is incapable of applying the law, it should fall." Nhu went on to describe the regime as "mandarin," "feudal," and ineffectual, dismissing it in disgust as "a servile instrument under foreign domination."

Richardson, who'd taken over from William Colby the previous year, reported to his superiors that the political counselor seemed to be in "a dangerous frame of mind."

IN WASHINGTON, HILSMAN AND the other members of the administration's anti-Diem faction grew dismayed as the press and Democratic allies in Congress criticized Diem and, by extension, JFK's Vietnam policy.

Liberal journals like *The New York Times* and *The New Republic* hammered

Kennedy again and again, showcasing stories by Halberstam and other writers about the regime's missteps and friction with the U.S. embassy. The *Times* editorialized on June 17 that if Diem couldn't "genuinely represent a [Buddhist] majority," he wasn't fit to be president. Critics also were pushing the United Nations to publicly condemn the regime and its authoritarian practices.

Hilsman felt that not only was Diem alienating his own people, he was alienating his greatest ally, the U.S. government, from its people as well. As he later wrote: "The pictures in the press, the editorials, the grumblings on Capitol Hill, the polite but worried queries from allies, all began to mount." The situation in South Vietnam was so grave, he and his colleagues believed, that even one more monk suicide could tip the country into chaos—and trigger a backlash against the Kennedy administration. As Dean Rusk laconically put it: "We cannot stand any more burnings."

Groping for a way forward, Hilsman concluded that Diem could survive only by giving in completely to Buddhist demands. That was the reasoning behind his cable instructing Trueheart to pressure Diem until he "fully and unequivocally" acceded. By eliminating their grievances entirely, Hilsman believed, Diem could cut the political ground from beneath the Buddhists, making any further demands—especially if backed up with more burnings—seem unjustified. But that strategy had little chance of success when applied to a proud, stubborn nationalist who'd based much of his political career on resisting foreign pressure.

As he discussed the problem with Harriman, Forrestal, and Under Secretary of State for Economic Affairs George Ball (who considered Diem a "weak, third-rate bigot"), Hilsman also considered squeezing Diem to get rid of the Nhus. One possibility was to ship them to diplomatic posts abroad. But again, Hilsman overestimated Washington's power to influence the South Vietnamese president.

Diem held loyalty to family as a supremely important value and had promised his dying father that he'd always take care of Nhu. The president's power, moreover, rested in no small part on the mass political organizations controlled by his brother and sister-in-law: Nhu's Republican Youth and Madame's two women's groups. Diem could hardly afford to lose that support now. As the CIA pointed out in a June 28 analysis, Diem was unlikely to jettison the Nhus under any circumstances.

In his 1967 memoir, *To Move a Nation*, Hilsman stated that "the facts of whether or not there had been religious persecution in Vietnam instantly became irrelevant" when Quang Duc set himself afire. That was so, Hilsman argued, because Browne's photos of the monk's spectacular suicide had convinced the world that such oppression must be rampant in Diem's domain.

But facts are never irrelevant, and the fact was that systematic, state-directed punishment and harassment of Buddhists—genuine religious persecution—had never existed under Diem. On the contrary, he often helped the Buddhists. But he failed to allay their long-simmering fears about his and his family's flamboyant embrace of Catholicism. He failed to give them the greater role in civic life they craved. He tried to enforce a flag ban that even Nhu regarded as foolish. And when the Hue massacre erupted, he failed to take responsibility and apologize.

Given the Buddhists' strong public support, Diem couldn't resort to his usual methods of suppression. But he feared what would happen if he granted too many concessions. On the night of Quang Duc's death, he'd gone on the radio to express his sadness and remind his countrymen that freedom of religion was guaranteed under South Vietnam's constitution, "of which I personally am the guardian." Later he told Trueheart he was completely committed to honoring the June 16 agreement.

A FEW DAYS AFTER the settlement, Trueheart informed Diem that Henry Cabot Lodge would arrive soon as the new U.S. ambassador.

Diem gave his assent, but his old mistrust of American motives began creeping back. Did Lodge's appointment signal a change in U.S. policy? Were the Americans trying to maneuver him into a position where he could be unseated? "They can send ten Lodges," Diem vented to an aide, "but I will not permit myself or my country to be humiliated, not if they train their artillery on this palace."

His compromises had already outraged the Nhus and their followers, but the Americans still weren't happy. "If we make [another] concession now, the

United States will ask for more," Diem told Father Luan, the prank-loving rector of Hue University and a family friend. "How many concessions do we have to make to satisfy them?"

Hilsman and his clique did indeed want more.

In a July 2 cable, they told Trueheart to demand that Diem make a "dramatic speech" intended to "bridge the gap of misunderstanding" with Buddhists and restore public confidence in the regime. Discussing with a Diem aide the president's apparent refusal to bend any further, Trueheart confessed that he was "beginning to feel helpless in this affair." But he did as ordered, urging Diem to deliver a major speech, meet with Buddhist leaders again, and take personal charge of his government's handling of the crisis, rather than delegate it to Vice President Tho.

Diem promised to consider Trueheart's suggestions. He added that he understood the Kennedy administration had a problem with domestic public opinion, but that it stemmed from inaccurate and exaggerated news coverage of the Buddhists. The U.S. government, he said, should "set the record straight." Diem ended the meeting after less than thirty minutes and ushered Trueheart out "with great, but perhaps forced, politeness." He didn't make the requested speech.

Vaguely written, difficult to enforce, and freighted with mutual suspicion, the June 16 peace agreement began to unravel less than two weeks after it was signed.

Thich Tinh Khiet, the octogenarian Buddhist leader, charged in a letter to Diem that local government officials were still arresting and intimidating Buddhists in various parts of the country. Monks were being denied entry to Saigon, and police were writing down license plate numbers of Buddhists visiting Xa Loi and other Saigon temples.

Rumors were afoot, Khiet wrote, that the regime planned a "pitiless repression" that included kidnapping and assassinating Buddhist leaders. Vice President Tho denied the allegations a few days later, calling on Khiet to scotch anti-regime chatter and restrain his followers from "sowing disunity."

AS BATTLE LINES WERE slowly redrawn, Trueheart threw a Fourth of July party at the spacious U.S. ambassador's residence, stylishly redecorated by Nolting's wife.

Despite Nolting's absence and rising tensions between Buddhists and the regime, it was a large and vibrant gathering. (Phoebe Trueheart rented five hundred champagne glasses for the occasion.) Nhu was there, along with most of Diem's cabinet ministers and fifteen foreign ambassadors. Also on hand were embassy employees, U.S. and South Vietnamese military officers, CIA operatives, and—given JFK's directive to make nice with them—newsmen. Vietnamese servers circulated with food and drink, and a team of embassy wives helped Mrs. Trueheart to greet guests, who then circulated through the magnificent dining room and intimate courtyard out back.

Among the invitees was David Halberstam, making little effort to conceal his anger over the "lying machine." He was beginning to view the war as unwinnable, a waste of Vietnamese and American lives. Nolting and Harkins's incessant optimism disgusted him. "To David, they were not just fools and liars," Sheehan recalled. "They were criminal fools and liars."

The correspondent contemptuously refused to shake Harkins's hand at the party and got into a row with the wife of another general. When Trueheart and other diplomats raised their champagne glasses to Diem, a traditional toast to the leader of a host government, Halberstam clutched his glass to his chest and loudly proclaimed, "I'd never drink to that son of a bitch!"

A much-less-abrasive guest was the smoothly handsome, French-educated ARVN major general Tran Van Don.

Suave and aristocratic, Don loved the company of beautiful women and the pleasures of Saigon's high society. He was even said to have had an affair with Madame Nhu. Don had risen to the ARVN's top ranks despite the gossip and Nhu's suspicion that he was involved in the 1960 paratrooper revolt. (He wasn't.)

Don commanded the ARVN's I Corps in the northern provinces from 1957 to 1962, leading fifty thousand troops responsible for blocking an invasion by Ho Chi Minh's army. But in December 1962, Diem reorganized the ARVN and Don was made "army commander," a grand-sounding title for a powerless position that left him in charge of only a few dozen soldiers on a Saigon headquarters staff.

At the embassy bash, Don spotted an old friend, a tough, swaggeringly irreverent CIA agent named Lucien Conein.

Conein had known many South Vietnamese military men since World War II, when he led Allied commandos fighting Japanese troops in French Indochina. Back then, the Vietnamese were enlisted men and junior officers in the French colonial army; now they ran the ARVN. (Conein had a dim view of the military talents of some top ARVN officers, describing them as "corporals with stars on their shoulders" who weren't capable of leading "a two-car funeral.") After the party, Conein joined Don and other senior officers for drinks in the packed basement nightclub at the Caravelle Hotel.

Conein was one of the few Americans Don trusted, and amid the noise and smoke of the nightclub the general revealed a jaw-dropping secret: he and other ARVN commanders were plotting Diem's overthrow.

Don had been thinking of a coup for several years. He was convinced that Diem would never stop mucking around in military matters and that the war couldn't be won with him in charge. Over the next four months, Don's faith in Conein would give the CIA agent a central role in covert exchanges between the U.S. government and a cast of Vietnamese conspirators bent on upending one of Washington's most important anti-communist allies.

A FREQUENT PATRON OF Saigon's watering holes, rarely without a Gauloises cigarette dangling from his lips, forty-three-year-old "Lou" Conein was one of the city's most memorable characters. A high school dropout, he'd fought in both the French and American armies during World War II, retired from the U.S. Army with the rank of lieutenant colonel, and become a full-time CIA operative. The muscular, beetle-browed former paratrooper was well known for his creative cursing and penchant for embroidering his considerable exploits.

He called the CIA "the cookie factory," described black operations as "playing cowboys and Indians," and impishly cautioned acquaintances: "Don't believe anything I tell you; I'm an expert liar." As an OSS guerrilla leader in 1945, Conein met Ho Chi Minh in Hanoi and later joked that Ho was so persuasive that he was tempted to join the Viet Minh himself.

Born in Paris, Conein was shipped off to America at age five by his penniless mother after his father, a veteran of France's famed Zouave infantry, died in a car crash. He was raised in Kansas City, Kansas, by a maternal aunt, a French war bride who'd moved there with her disabled American husband. After quitting high school in 1936, he worked as a typesetter and printer before joining the French army in 1939. German tanks demolished his unit on the Belgian front early in World War II. He enlisted in the American Army in 1941 and was trained in behind-the-lines fighting by the OSS.

Conein parachuted into Nazi-occupied France in 1944 with one of the small commando teams known as Jedburghs, whose mission was to arm and fight alongside French resistance forces, an often-quarrelsome amalgam of communists, socialists, and supporters of Charles de Gaulle's Free French.

His four-man unit joined local maquis groups in a night attack against a three-hundred-man German garrison in L'Isle-Jourdain, a village about twenty miles west of Toulouse. But, as Conein noted with a touch of humor in his after-action report, it was an odd operation, with the resistance fighters and Germans negotiating a lengthy ceasefire in the middle of the battle and maquis reinforcements failing to show up because their commander was too busy "celebrating . . . and looting the tobacco stores" in a nearby village. The attackers nonetheless managed to kill sixty-two Germans and wound forty-six. An OSS evaluator wrote admiringly that Conein "enjoys fighting" and was "an excellent conversationalist" to boot.

After the liberation of France, the OSS transferred Conein to China and put him in charge of a group of American, French, and Chinese irregulars operating over the border against the Japanese in northern Indochina. In a July 1945 mission that earned him a Bronze Star, he led an assault on the headquarters of the Japanese Twenty-Second Division.

He later helped to infiltrate saboteurs into Eastern Europe and train paramilitary forces in Iran. Conein returned to Vietnam in the watershed year of 1954, attached to the CIA's Saigon Military Mission headed by Edward Lansdale. The unit was under orders to help strengthen Diem's fledgling government, while undermining Ho's. Conein was dispatched to Hanoi to organize stay-behind agents and conduct sabotage before the Viet Minh established full control. In one operation, he and a confederate poured chemical contaminants into the fuel tanks of a Hanoi bus company; the fumes briefly knocked both saboteurs out cold.

Conein was at his swashbuckling zenith. Meeting him for the first time, Rufus Phillips, then a young CIA officer under Lansdale, sensed "a dangerous man, a kind of John Dillinger on our side. There was a hint of barely restrained violence about him that his alert blue eyes under bushy eyebrows, as well as his abrupt, blustery manner and short temper, did nothing to belie."

With tensions at a flashpoint between the confident, incoming Americans and the demoralized, departing French in the mid-1950s, a number of cars belonging to Americans were blown up in Saigon, ostensibly by communist terrorists. Lansdale, however, suspected the French and told his team the bombings would be stopped.

Phillips showed up one night at the house Lansdale used as his headquarters to find Conein in the kitchen, sticking fuses in chunks of plastic explosive. As he worked he angrily muttered curses in French and English: "salauds, espéces de con, bastards, goddam sons of bitches, assholes."

Conein got in his car after midnight with his fiancée, who cradled the explosives in her lap. He drove past the homes of various French officials and, touching his cigarette lighter to fuses, tossed his homemade bombs over the walls enclosing their yards. One bomb went into an army colonel's yard. The last one plopped onto the grounds of the French ambassador's residence. No more American vehicles were targeted after that.

Lansdale, who usually praised Conein in official performance reviews, privately referred to him as "the thug."

BY RELIEVING HIGH-RANKING ARVN officers like General Don of their field commands and relegating them to make-work desk jobs, Diem had made a serious error. The embittered generals had plenty of time on their hands to plan a revolt against their commander in chief.

After Don was given the hollow title of army commander, he began visiting ARVN posts throughout the country, talking to officers, enlisted men, and local peasants. Part of his purpose was to sound out field commanders about their willingness to turn their men and weapons against Diem. The general also wanted a close-up look at how the army was faring in the countryside.

The situation was worse than he thought. Many officers were more upset than ever that promotions continued to be based more on affiliation with the Can Lao Party or the Catholic Church than on genuine ability. With the army's low pay for enlisted men and junior officers, their families often lived in misery. Villagers still complained of mistreatment by corrupt local officials. But when Don reported all this to Diem, proposing that incompetent officers be fired and crooked government subordinates punished, "my pleas fell on deaf ears."

In June 1963, Don went to Thailand to observe maneuvers by multinational military forces under SEATO, the Southeast Asia Treaty Organization. He was accompanied by Major General Duong Van Minh, a highly popular ARVN officer nicknamed "Big Minh" because, at six feet and two hundred pounds, he was significantly taller and heavier than most Vietnamese. In Thailand, the two generals had a chance to talk with foreigners and read foreign newspapers. To their surprise, they discovered that Diem's reputation was even more tattered abroad than in South Vietnam.

Returning to Saigon at the end of the month, they found that relations between the regime and the Buddhists had fragmented even more, creating, in Don's words, "a boiling atmosphere with people furious all over." Unrest had spread from Saigon to other cities and towns, and the government seemed paralyzed. The two generals sensed that the Viet Cong were making political gains every day.

Like Don, the forty-seven-year-old Big Minh had been sidelined by Diem, although for much longer. A Buddhist and native of Long An Province, adjacent to Saigon, he'd joined the French colonial army and been seized during World War II by the dreaded Japanese military police, the Kempeitai, who broke two of his front teeth while torturing him. Minh never got the teeth fixed, proudly displaying them as emblems of his toughness and endurance.

As a colonel in Diem's army in 1955, Minh was in charge of troops that drove the Binh Xuyen gangsters out of Saigon and pursued the sect armies. Calling him the "best and most loyal" soldier he had, Diem embraced Minh and kissed him on both cheeks during a celebratory parade in the capital. But as Minh's fame and popularity rose, he fell out of favor with Nhu, who distrusted generals and especially the lionized ones, who might become political rivals to his brother.

When Minh returned from a training program in the United States in 1957, he was put in charge of the ARVN's new "field command," a position in which he was reduced to inspecting soldiers commanded by others.

Minh had ample time to pursue his hobbies: tennis, the cultivation of orchids, and adding to his collection of Japanese dolls, which he enjoyed showing off at his home. He became an open critic of Diem, for his military meddling, and the Nhus, whom he regarded as evil and a huge liability to the president. Minh complained about Diem and the Nhus so often and so vocally that Nolting and Harkins dubbed him "General Bellyache."

During the 1962 ARVN shake-up, Diem diluted Minh's job even further, appointing him as his personal military adviser, but rarely listening to his advice. Yet for all of Minh's blatant insubordination, Diem didn't fire him. That may have been because of his popularity with the officer corps—or because the ever-wary president took to heart the old adage to always hold your enemies close.

Minh, Don, and a third conspirator—General Le Van Kim, Don's brother-in-law and former chief of the South Vietnamese military academy at Dalat—began detailed planning for a coup in mid-July.

Their biggest problem was that none of them commanded combat troops. So, they each began contacting other generals and colonels to test the level of military enthusiasm for a takeover. One of their goals was to minimize bloodshed when they made their move against Diem and Nhu. Another was to keep the Americans in the dark as much as possible. Although Don had confidence in Conein, the Vietnamese generals viewed Nolting, Harkins, and John Richardson, the CIA station chief, as too close to the palace to be trusted with their dangerous secret.

TAKING QUIET SOUNDINGS AMONG dissidents, the CIA discovered that another coup group was being organized by Dr. Tran Kim Tuyen, the smiling, diminutive former head of Nhu's secret police.

Tuyen's influence at the palace had been in decline since he joined like-minded regime officials in writing a lengthy report about the underlying causes of the 1960 paratrooper rebellion. Twenty pages were devoted to problems created by Madame Nhu.

As Tuyen feared, the Dragon Lady was incensed. The secret police chief nonetheless stayed on friendly terms with Nhu until early in 1963, when Nhu bugged the tables at La Cigale, a popular Saigon nightspot frequented by Tuyen and his associates. The listening devices established that the man who knew many of the regime's most sensitive secrets was engaged not in foiling coups, but in plotting one himself.

Tuyen was relieved of nearly all of his duties and tagged for exile abroad in a minor diplomatic role—South Vietnam's consul general in Cairo—a common fate for regime officials who fell from grace with Diem. A CIA report said he'd meanwhile recruited a number of prominent military and civilian figures into his anti-Diem group (including, perhaps implausibly, the Catholic archbishop of Saigon).

The U.S. embassy, too, was preparing for a possible coup.

A secret memo circulated among embassy officials said the putsch would begin with no advance warning, and that the VC "will seek to exploit confusion by sabotage, incitement of mob violence, [and] probable attacks on Americans." "Refugees, sympathy seekers, spies" were expected to swamp the ambassador's residence; government troops or coup forces were likely to cordon off the embassy and MACV headquarters.

"Coordinated action will be essential if the Americans are not to lose more face, both here and abroad," the memo said. "We must secure a position of influence with the group taking power, without compromising ourselves either for or against it." An emergency operations group should be set up immediately, the memo recommended, with a "pre-arranged code word" to alert all U.S. agencies when the coup started.

But speculation about a possible uprising wasn't limited to the embassy and a gaggle of disaffected Diemists. It seemed to be the most popular guessing game in town.

"Everyone in Saigon is talking about it: shopkeepers, cab drivers, intellectuals, and the whole diplomatic corps," Mieczyslaw Maneli, the sharp-eyed Polish observer, cabled his government. "No one doubts that the situation between the Diem family and Washington is tense."

PRESIDENT KENNEDY PLANNED TO spend the long Independence Day weekend on Cape Cod with his family and do some sailing. But he'd set aside time on the morning of July 4 for an urgent meeting with his Vietnam team on the burgeoning Buddhist crisis.

The core members of the anti-Diem coterie were present: Harriman, Hilsman, and Forrestal. Hilsman began the briefing by saying that Saigon was filled with talk that the regime wouldn't carry out the peace agreement with the Buddhists in good faith. He cited a recent article in *The Times of Vietnam* that suggested that Quang Duc had been drugged and all but dared the Buddhists to incinerate more monks. (Though it had only a few thousand readers in Saigon, the English-language *Times of Vietnam* was widely regarded as a mouthpiece for the regime. The newspaper was published by an American couple, Gene and Ann Gregory, who were close to Diem and his family, and Madame Nhu wrote some of its articles.)

Kennedy asked whether the drugging story was true, and Hilsman replied that "religious fervor was an adequate explanation" for the monk's suicide. He said Trueheart had put "extremely heavy pressure" on Diem to make a dramatic speech about the Buddhists, but that he'd agreed only to think about it. Hilsman again argued that Diem should be publicly condemned if he failed to do what Washington wanted. But no matter what he did, a coup attempt was likely in the next four months, Hilsman said. He added that Nolting believed civil war would break out if Diem was killed in a takeover, although Hilsman didn't think that would necessarily happen.

American presidents rarely take action in foreign affairs without considering the domestic implications. The men in the room with Kennedy were moderate-to-liberal Democrats who wanted to see him reelected in 1964, and they knew that events in South Vietnam could affect his chances. As the Buddhist struggle dragged on, the crescendo of criticism from Congress and the press over the administration's support of Diem had only intensified. In a July 3 article in *The New York Times*, Max Frankel summed up JFK's dilemma. Vietnam, he wrote, was "a politically embarrassing war in which the United States finds itself allied with the authoritarian South Vietnamese regime, whose methods it doubts and whose popularity it questions."

Hilsman's proposal that the administration publicly "dissociate" itself from Diem in the event of more burnings was a way to protect Kennedy's political flanks. While such a statement might deflect some domestic criticism from JFK, it could also prove fatal to Diem if his political enemies took it as a sign that American military and economic support was waning. Such an interpretation could easily set off a coup by Saigon's military.

The conversation turned to filling the ambassadorial vacancy in Saigon. Forrestal thought Trueheart had done "a grand job" in Nolting's absence, but that it was unwise not to have a full-time ambassador in place during such a tumultuous period. Nolting was finally back in the United States after his vacation, and Kennedy wanted him sent to Saigon straightaway. Lodge was scheduled to replace him in September, but the president wanted his new envoy in Saigon sooner.

Unlike some in the room, JFK thought Nolting had done outstanding work in Saigon. Kennedy remarked that it was "almost miraculous" how the ambassador had succeeded in "turning the war around from the disastrously low point in relations between Diem and ourselves" two years earlier. Kennedy said he hoped Nolting could be publicly commended and that "an appropriate position could be found for him in Washington so that he could give his children a suitable home in the years immediately ahead."

Before the meeting broke up, Forrestal mentioned that General Victor Krulak, the counterinsurgency expert for the Joint Chiefs of Staff, had recently visited South Vietnam and found that, for all the political waves it had made, the Buddhist tempest hadn't affected the ARVN's performance against the Viet Cong. In his written report, Krulak gave a couple of examples of recent ARVN successes and concluded that "we are indeed winning the war, that our present course is sound and that, resolutely pursued, it will see the job done."

It was a buoyant note on which to start the holiday weekend.

LIKE THE REST OF the Western journalists in Saigon, Peter Arnett had been covering Buddhist street demonstrations for weeks.

The twenty-eight-year-old Associated Press reporter had become familiar with Xa Loi Pagoda, the Buddhists' nerve center, where young monks and college kids operated mimeograph machines that ran off thousands of leaflets and statements to be distributed to the press and Buddhists throughout the country. Journalists flocked through the pagoda's iron gates for news briefings delivered by a frail-looking, twenty-four-year-old monk named Duc Nghiep, who announced himself as "chairman of the propaganda committee" and served visitors delicate Chinese tea and snacks in his office.

Buddhist leaders told the foreign reporters they were their only hope of getting their message to the outside world. Indeed, ordinary Vietnamese had begun to treat them as heroes. Horst Faas, the AP photographer, had to move off a balcony from which he was shooting street demonstrators below when they began cheering wildly whenever he clicked his shutter. Shopping at a grocery store after one protest march, Arnett found store clerks hailing him as the owner patted him on the back.

On the morning of July 7, Arnett joined Halberstam, Sheehan, and half a dozen other reporters and photographers as they gathered outside a small pagoda in anticipation of the day's street action. About twenty plainclothes police were also there, along with uniformed riot police.

The newsmen watched as about three hundred monks and nuns filed along a narrow alley from the pagoda toward the street. Security men tried to block them and Arnett and other newsmen began taking pictures. Suddenly, two plainclothes cops punched Arnett in the face, knocking him to the ground. Several cops then started kicking him with their sharp-toed boots and grinding his camera to pieces.

Bellowing in anger, Halberstam charged into the fray like a bull elephant, shoving the cops away from Arnett. "Get back, get back, you sons of bitches, or I'll beat the shit out of you!" he screamed, fists balled. As other reporters pulled Arnett to his feet, Browne snapped a photo of the bloodied journalist standing behind Halberstam for protection, just before a cop smashed Browne's camera with a brick. The plainclothesmen broke off the attack and disappeared in the crowd. Uniformed cops nearby didn't lift a finger to help the foreigners.

Browne's camera was ruined, but his film was intact, and he needed to get it to an AP bureau outside South Vietnam as fast as possible. Censors at the government telegraph office had been holding up transmission of stories and pictures by foreign correspondents, so they began turning to "pigeons"—friendly pilots, stewardesses, and GIs on outbound airline flights—to get their work to the outside world.

Browne got lucky when he ran into Chester Bowles, Kennedy's new ambassador to India, who was passing through Saigon on his way to New Delhi. Bowles agreed to smuggle out Browne's pictures, and images of the police attack were widely printed in U.S. and foreign newspapers.

Their run-in with the undercover cops convinced the journalists that the regime was trying to scare them away from covering the Buddhists, and they were livid. In a stormy session at the embassy, they demanded that Trueheart file a formal protest with Diem's government. But Trueheart declined, saying he didn't have enough information about what happened. That only made the reporters—who were, after all, professional witnesses—madder.

When Trueheart later expressed "concern" to the Vietnamese, they claimed the newsmen provoked the skirmish by objecting when cops stopped the Buddhists, and that one journalist struck a cop first. Trueheart cabled Washington: "Given extreme emotional involvement of correspondents these days—amounting regrettably to intense hatred of all things GVN [Government of Vietnam], in certain cases—I would not feel sure about refuting police."

Drained and on edge after many days and nights of nonstop, high-pressure work, the reporters felt the embassy was abandoning them, refusing to defend them against a hostile government hell-bent on silencing them one way or another.

For months they'd endured verbal attacks from the regime; now they faced physical assaults as well. Halberstam, Sheehan, Browne, and Peter Kalischer of CBS News fired off a telegram to Kennedy, alleging that Diem had inaugurated a "campaign of open physical intimidation to prevent the covering of news which we feel Americans have a right to know." They asked the president to personally protest the police attack and "obtain assurances that [it] will not be repeated."

The day after the attack on Arnett, he and Browne were interrogated for four hours at Saigon's central police station about whether *they* beat the *cops* outside the pagoda. It looked as if the two AP reporters might actually be arrested and prosecuted. That was too much for their comrades. Eight of them angrily crowded into John Mecklin's office that night, clamoring to know what the embassy was doing to protect Browne and Arnett.

On Trueheart's orders, Mecklin said he couldn't discuss the matter, whereupon the newsmen "exploded in such a tumult of four-letter invective on the theme of American 'gutlessness'" that another embassy employee next door came in to see if Mecklin was all right.

Three days later, Trueheart cabled Washington that "resident correspondents have become so embittered towards [the government] that they are saying quite openly to anyone who will listen that they would like to see regime overthrown." Diem, he added, was convinced that "correspondents have been actively encouraging Buddhists."

AS DIEM TRIED TO simultaneously fend off agitated Buddhists, angry Nhus, and demanding Americans, a new anti-regime martyr was created.

Nguyen Tuong Tam was one of South Vietnam's best-known literary figures. A poet and novelist, he'd been a leader of the Vietnamese intellectuals who tried with their underground writings to incite popular uprisings against the French in the 1930s. His themes often touched on Vietnamese nationalism and resistance to colonial rule, and his books were widely studied in South Vietnam's colleges and secondary schools.

The fifty-eight-year-old Tam was among more than fifty civilians and military men facing possible death sentences after the regime charged them with treason in connection with the 1960 paratrooper rebellion. Many Vietnamese saw their upcoming trial before a military tribunal as a warning from Diem to the current crop of conspirators about the consequences of rising against him. At the time of the 1960 revolt, Tam's name appeared on a declaration of support for the mutineers by nationalist politicians and other civilians. But it wasn't clear whether he actually signed the broadside or someone forged his name to give it more gravitas. Tam had been under police surveillance ever since.

Two days before Tam's trial was to begin, he called his sons to his home to drink whiskey with him. "I feel very happy tonight," he said. "I am going to die very soon." He then collapsed and was rushed to a hospital; he died the next day. It turned out that he'd put cyanide in his drink and left a suicide note attacking Diem's government.

"The arrest and trial of all nationalist opponents of the regime is a crime that will force the nation into the hands of the Communists," Tam wrote. "I oppose this crime, and I kill myself as a warning to those people who are trampling on our freedoms."

A wave of emotion coursed through Saigon's student population, and a struggle began over how Tam was to be buried. Young people asked his family for permission to hold a public funeral procession, which the government opposed. It soon relented, however, and on July 13 about 1,500 people shuffled silently through the streets behind a hearse carrying the writer's body from the hospital to Xa Loi Pagoda. Some 1,000 police lined the route, with soldiers and armored cars tucked into nearby courtyards. But there were no clashes as the cortege made its way past throngs of onlookers.

Hoping to dampen the possibility of street violence over Tam's death, the government acquitted him posthumously. But the CIA, watching closely as always, reported that "we are more uneasy than ever about the situation in Saigon."

"The various opposition groups are sharpening their knives, but seem not yet to have the unity and determination to act against Diem and the Nhus," the agency said in a report that went to JFK. "All elements seem to be waiting for something. In such an atmosphere, a minor incident could cause the opposition to coalesce overnight."

If the CIA was apprehensive over the recent uproar and unrest, Trueheart was simply bewildered.

Meeting with Nguyen Dinh Thuan, Diem's capable chief of staff, Trueheart confessed that he didn't understand the regime's seemingly contradictory actions.

On one hand, Diem's vice president had sent conciliatory letters to the Buddhists; on the other, the Diem-influenced *Times of Vietnam* insulted and attacked them. Nhu first denounced the peace agreement with the Buddhists to his Republican Youth minions, then reversed course and called on them to support it. Diem's interior minister recently told Trueheart the president would after all make the dramatic speech that Washington so badly wanted. At the same time, the government prosecutor in the treason trial revived the falsehood that the Americans had sided with the 1960 rebels against Diem.

"What the hell is going on?" Trueheart implored.

"C'est un panier de crabes," Thuan said with a shrug. After all these years, Saigon was still a basket of crabs.

CHAPTER 11

CITY ON THE BRINK

NOLTING FINALLY FLEW back to Saigon on July 11, a brutally hot, humid day. He was appalled by what had happened in the six weeks since his departure and furious at his old friend Trueheart, who he blamed along with Hilsman and Harriman for taking advantage of his absence to undermine Diem.

Two years of painstaking work with the touchy South Vietnamese president lay in ruins. Relations between Saigon and Washington were near a complete breakdown. As an added humiliation, Nolting had learned of Lodge's appointment to succeed him not from the State Department but from a radio news program on a New York–bound ocean liner as he and his family crossed the Atlantic at the end of their vacation.

By coincidence, the ambassador arrived at Tan Son Nhut at the same time as Diem, returning from Hue. The president's ministers were there to greet him, but only one of them bothered to say hello to Nolting, emphasizing the awkwardness of his position as a diplomatic lame duck. The ambassador walked to a cramped waiting room, where two dozen American and Vietnamese newsmen awaited his homecoming speech amid billows of cigarette smoke.

Dripping sweat in the heat and the glare of TV lights, Nolting read a statement gently conveying Washington's dissatisfaction with Diem's handling of the Buddhists, but concluding that victory wasn't far off as long as

South Vietnamese unity and determination weren't "weakened by internal dissension." The reporters pounced immediately. With all that had happened in recent weeks, they demanded, did Nolting still believe the Vietnamese people should stop criticizing Diem and simply get on with the war? The ambassador managed to duck most of the questions and get away from the airport.

Saigon was visibly tense. Police and barbed-wire barriers walled off Gia Long Palace, where Diem and the Nhus had moved after Independence Palace was bombed the previous year. Whenever the Buddhists threatened another street action, the security zone around the palace was enlarged and more streets were closed, creating monstrous jams of overheated vehicles and sweltering, fuming people in the city center. Buddhist picketers appeared in front of Nolting's residence; large crowds outside Xa Loi forced him to detour around the pagoda when driving to the embassy.

Before coming back to Saigon, Nolting had stopped off in Washington, encountering what he described as "great agitation and confusion." The official optimism over South Vietnam in recent months had been replaced by sharp opposition to the get-along-with-Diem policy. The ambassador met with a testy, tight-lipped Harriman, who said that if he had his way, Nolting wouldn't be going back to Saigon at all.

Alarmed at the frosty new attitude toward Diem, Nolting tried to convince policymakers to give the president some slack. He warned George Ball, the undersecretary of state for economic affairs, that if the United States publicly repudiated Diem, his government would fall. Diem had promised to carry out the June 16 peace agreement, Nolting said, and he always kept his word. The South Vietnamese leader would deal with the crisis in his own way; he'd get through it if left to his own devices.

Nolting also testified behind closed doors to the Senate Foreign Relations Committee, assuring its members that South Vietnam was still making progress, albeit slowly and at times painfully.

While the regime had made a "series of bonehead plays" in the aftermath of the Hue massacre, he told the committee, the press was often unfair to Diem, criticizing him for the wrong reasons. The ambassador couldn't resist a swipe at his nemesis Halberstam, saying he sometimes became "very emotional" and "is not as accurate and objective in his reporting as he ought to be" (but providing no examples of the newsman's alleged transgressions).

Nolting had a brief audience with President Kennedy, who was considerably more cordial than Harriman. Although Nolting's two-year tour in Saigon was technically over, JFK instructed him to go back and do his best "to help restore confidence and trust" until Lodge relieved him.

ALMOST AS SOON AS he reached Saigon, Nolting got a call from Diem asking him to come to the palace.

Nolting found the president tense and exhausted, torn by conflicting advice, mistrustful of U.S. intentions, and, as always, indignant at "calumnies" in the foreign press. Nolting got the impression that Diem had both lost some control of his government and was in "a martyr's mood."

Diem worried that Lodge's appointment signaled the Kennedy administration's adoption of a new, harsher attitude toward his government. Nolting said Washington had assured him that wasn't the case. To prove his point, he cabled the State Department and was informed by return telegram that "highest authority"—meaning JFK—wasn't changing course. When the ambassador later read the telegram aloud to him, Diem said: "I believe you, but not that telegram."

Meanwhile, Nolting found the U.S. Mission more divided than ever.

Some top officials, including Harkins and John Richardson, the CIA station chief, still strongly backed Diem. But some younger ones felt it was time to part company with him. His government was too disorganized to ever win the war, they felt, and his performance in the Buddhist crisis only underlined his ineptitude. Some embassy officers had even formed an informal network, passing information back and forth among themselves about what they thought was really going on in the war. They were no longer listening to the effervescent optimism of Nolting and Harkins and began to believe instead "that the only ones telling the truth were the press," recalled John T. Bennett, a thirty-four-year-old embassy economic specialist.

What upset Nolting most was that although he'd instructed both Trueheart and the State Department to contact him about any big developments during his vacation, no one told him about the Buddhist blowup. The reason, he concluded, was that the anti-Diem faction in Washington wanted to keep him away from Vietnam, depriving Diem of his counsel and increasing the chances that the president would overreact in some way and fatally wound himself and his government.

The ambassador was particularly irate at Trueheart, with whom he had "a very straight talk." (Trueheart's son, Charles, later described the exchange as an "angry confrontation.") While Nolting's deputy had once shared his positivity about Diem and South Vietnam, the ambassador believed Trueheart had "shifted with the winds blowing from Washington" and sided with the anti-Diem cabal. Diem's chief of staff, Thuan, told Nolting he'd twice tried to get the embassy to send him a telegram while he was overseas, pleading for him to cut short his trip and rush back to Saigon. But the ambassador only learned of the request in a short letter from Trueheart that wasn't delivered to him until his ship docked in New York.

Nolting had never seen evidence that Buddhists were being persecuted and came to believe that their protests were a "contrived, cold-blooded political move" to topple Diem's government, abetted by gullible American diplomats and journalists. By carrying out Washington's poorly conceived instructions "with a vengeance," Trueheart had overlooked the Buddhists' true motives and the questionable merits of their case, the ambassador felt. He later criticized his friend in a job-performance report, saying he "failed . . . in keeping with the responsibilities and loyalties" of a deputy to his ambassador.

Trueheart had different views. His close-up experience of Diem during the Buddhist uproar left him deeply pessimistic about South Vietnam's chances of beating the Viet Cong: "I had concluded this long before Nolting came back. . . . I don't have any guarantee that anybody else will do better, but we can be sure that this man will lose. . . . And if it's not going to work, you don't start putting more money on the table."

Trueheart also had newfound respect for Halberstam, Sheehan, and other

American journalists, whose news stories, he thought, were "on the whole more accurate than what we were reporting from the embassy." He hadn't notified Nolting of the emergency while he was on vacation, he said, because he was so busy and the situation changed so rapidly that it was impossible to summarize at any given moment.

And while Nolting felt his number two should have been loyal to him, Trueheart believed he owed a greater allegiance to the U.S. government and carrying out its orders. But there was no question that his run-in with Nolting had reduced their long, warm friendship to ashes, an outcome that Trueheart described years later as "a very painful thing."

WITH TIME RUNNING OUT on his ambassadorship, Nolting tried to patch up Washington's relations with Diem, laboring up to fourteen hours a day, seven days a week.

Several subordinates told him he should never have left and that Trueheart's high-pressure tactics had created an impasse that made it impossible to do business with their regime counterparts. "It looks like the State Department thinks Diem is the enemy, rather than the Viet Cong," Harkins remarked. Garbage had been thrown into some embassy employees' yards; the suspected culprits were Nhu's men. Maneli, the Polish diplomat, cabled his superiors: "Mr. Nhu's secret police spend more time shadowing the mistresses of American officers than Communists. . . . The Viet Cong are practically forgotten."

Nolting's problems multiplied when the Buddhists, having lost all faith that the government intended to abide by the June 16 agreement, decided to revive their protest campaign.

In a letter to Diem, the patriarch of the General Buddhist Association of Vietnam, Thich Tinh Khiet, cited "acts of a terrorist nature" aimed at Buddhists by local government officials in various parts of the country. Those acts purportedly included volleys of gunfire at a Buddhist monastery, narrowly missing the monks inside, and repeated bombings of a pagoda in the Camau Peninsula. A monk had disappeared; a missing nun had been dumped outside a pagoda, bound hand and foot with wire. Khiet further complained that many of those arrested during previous anti-government marches still hadn't been released.

He instructed all monks, nuns, and laypeople to resume mass marches and hunger strikes. If police stopped them on the street, he wrote, "have everyone sit down and chant 100 Buddhist prayers." If soldiers surrounded their pagodas, the faithful were to "pray calmly until death comes."

On July 16, about 150 bonzes began a two-day hunger strike at Xa Loi, watched carefully by riot police and undercover men. Three fire trucks parked nearby, ready to hose down anyone who tried to set themselves on fire. On the same day, another hundred monks showed up outside Nolting's residence, along with a larger number of cops, reporters, and spectators. Speaking in English through a bullhorn, Duc Nghiep, the Buddhists' self-proclaimed chief propagandist, pleaded for American help in ending the crisis and threatened that more Buddhists would burn themselves if their demands weren't met. Fearing that an immolation was about to happen right then, Nolting placed an urgent phone call to Diem. But the demonstration ended without incident.

The next day, about one thousand Buddhists came under police attack as they tried to march from Giac Minh Pagoda in Cholon to Xa Loi.

The demonstrators, including many women and children, had gathered in secret at the pagoda the night before. When police the next morning got wind of the march, they threw up a barbed-wire barricade in the street to stop it.

Led by monks, the Buddhists began tearing at the barbed wire with their bare hands as combat police, trained by the CIA to fight Viet Cong attackers in the streets, and plainclothesmen tried to hold them back. The protesters then sat down in the street as cops unspooled more barbed wire across the road behind them and called for reinforcements.

Some of the Buddhists began making speeches as several truckloads of white-uniformed police and four fire engines rolled up. Saigon's police director appeared with about fifty officers brandishing submachine guns and tear gas launchers. Through a loudspeaker, the police chief told the marchers they were to be transported to Xa Loi in government vehicles. The barbed-wire barricades were opened and five stake-bed trucks backed toward the seated Buddhists.

The police went after the monks first, picking them up by their arms and legs and heaving them into the trucks. The Buddhists offered no resistance, but the cops hit them with nightsticks and rifle butts, kicked them, and slammed their heads down on the metal truck beds. Several monks were knocked to the ground, kicked, and beaten. Others were punched in the head while they lay in the trucks. Laypeople were treated with the same unnecessary violence.

"The policemen grabbed priests as they knelt and clubbed them," Halberstam reported from the scene. "They grabbed seated old women and smashed down with clubs. In one alley, several policemen grabbed an old woman and beat her." A cop told one Western newsman: "That's what happens when there is too much liberty."

One of the trucks kept backing into the crowd, knocking down several people and running over one. As a woman voluntarily climbed into a truck, a police officer "proceeded to give her a very forcible kick in the buttocks, projecting her into the truck," according to a U.S. embassy observer. Scuffles broke out when cops tried to seize cameras from newsmen. About fifty people were hurt, some badly. They included monks who tried to jump out of trucks as they were taken away.

Police then went down an alleyway to Giac Minh Pagoda and dragged out more people to be arrested. They tried to enter the building, but were forced to retreat under a hail of rocks thrown by people inside. The cops tore down the pagoda's flagpole and public-address system and strung barbed wire across the entrance. They announced that the temple was closed and no one could enter or leave. In all, 263 people were arrested.

Security forces barricaded and sealed off the rest of Saigon's pagodas. Nolting cabled Washington that a "heavy concentration" of combat police and soldiers was guarding Gia Long Palace; police had automatic weapons and troops were in full battle gear. Machine guns were set up around the building. The National Assembly was cordoned off as well. Halberstam reported that the capital was "extremely tense."

After Nolting left on vacation, U.S. intelligence agents had swarmed Xa Loi and other pagodas, calling on the monks repeatedly in an effort to learn more about their leaders and plans. (At one point, ten or so officers from the CIA, MACV, embassy security office, and other intelligence units were visiting Xa Loi each week.) When the ambassador returned, he promptly stopped the visits lest they give the regime a pretext to charge the Americans with encouraging rebellion.

But the CIA's inquisitiveness had uncovered a foreboding shift in the Buddhist leadership. As dissatisfaction and anger rose over the government's supposed failure to carry out the June 16 agreement, militants were replacing moderates in the topmost ranks.

The chief militant was Tri Quang, the master provocateur from Hue, who'd openly stated his goal of pressuring the government until it collapsed. The monk was prepared to call for more burnings, and among the purported volunteers was Dieu Hue, a Buddhist nun and mother of Dr. Buu Hoi, a nationally respected figure who was head of South Vietnam's atomic energy program as well as Diem's ambassador to six African nations. *The Times of Vietnam* reported that Dieu Hue had come from Hue to Saigon to prepare for another self-immolation spectacle.

THE LIKELIHOOD THAT MORE street actions would lead to more violence weighed on Nolting, who kept "urging, encouraging, warning" Diem to move in a constructive direction with the Buddhists.

The president took to the radio again on July 18, affirming his support for the June peace pact and announcing that the government was willing to undertake joint investigations of alleged violations of it in conjunction with the Buddhists. Nolting praised the brief address as forthright and statesmanlike, but Hilsman thought it was "inadequate and accomplished nothing."

Privately, however, Diem was seething. He vented his feelings in a meeting with his old friend Rufus Phillips, the ex–CIA agent who now ran the U.S. rural affairs program, working closely with Nhu's strategic hamlets.

Diem denounced the Buddhist insurrection as the "ultimate in ingratitude," pointing out his record of financial support for Xa Loi and other temples. The Buddhists, he said, were clearly trying to subvert his government and he resented American pressure to appease them. His police and army had "acted with the greatest of restraint," even though the Buddhists employed "hooligans" disguised as monks to stir up trouble in the streets. Diem also blamed "distorted" U.S. news coverage of the protests for generating international pressures that weakened his hand in dealing with the Buddhists.

Taken aback by Diem's remarks, Phillips summarized them in a memo to Nolting, concluding that "it was most depressing to find [Diem] with his mind so closed, and so convinced that he was being unfairly treated."

At the same time, the president's ever-watchful brother, perhaps sensing a coup in the works, was playing cat and mouse with the generals.

Nhu called together more than a dozen of them on July 11 in what may have been an attempt to smoke out traitors. Many generals despised Nhu and his wife, but the political counselor was friendly and flattering as he spoke to them at Joint General Staff headquarters near the airport. Within days, four generals separately reported Nhu's comments to the CIA, producing a *Rashomon*-like tangle of conflicting interpretations.

The informants agreed that Nhu had criticized his brother's handling of the Buddhist crisis, but also appealed for their loyalty and support in resolving it. One general said he believed Nhu was sincere in his plea and that most of those present would back him; another said the majority of generals had "reacted negatively" to what Nhu said. The most remarkable report was that Nhu told the group that if they were thinking of launching an anti-Diem coup, he didn't blame them and indeed "would be with them."

Several days later, Richardson, the CIA station chief, asked Nhu about the meeting.

Describing ARVN leaders as confused and agitated by the Buddhist unrest, Nhu explained that he'd used the session as a "kind of 'psychoanalytic' procedure . . . to try to surface some of the problems they had been brooding about inwardly." Coup d'états, Nhu said, were mentioned only in the context of how they often erupted in underdeveloped countries like South Vietnam. Richardson accepted Nhu's explanation at face value. But

Nolting and others at the embassy believed the president's cunning brother knew a coup was in the making and was testing the generals' fealty.

In Washington, coups and conspiracies were much on Hilsman's mind as well.

In a July 23 cable to Nolting, the assistant secretary of state said that given the regime's intransigence, Buddhist protests were likely to escalate, complete with more burnings. The disorder and disaffection in Saigon would spread to rural areas, damaging the war effort. Hilsman speculated that a coup attempt was coming in the "next few months, if not weeks," and was likely to succeed.

In these circumstances, the Kennedy administration had several options, he wrote. It could issue statements of support for Diem and hope that would help him to weather the Buddhist storm. Or it could publicly chastise him, possibly setting off a coup, or even secretly encourage his military leaders to overthrow him. Hilsman concluded that the wisest course was simply to watch and wait, since bolder action "runs obvious risk of putting us in position of having backed loser."

Nolting waited two days before politely rejecting Hilsman's central premise in a follow-up telegram. He felt that the "heat is slowly going out of this crisis" and that Diem was likely to survive it.

The present government, the ambassador wrote, stood the best chance of successfully carrying out the counterinsurgency program, and Washington should try to keep Diem in power. The atmosphere in Saigon had "perceptibly calmed" in recent days; Diem seemed to have seized the political initiative from the Buddhists by repledging his support for the June 16 agreement in his recent radio address. If the government stuck to that position, said Nolting, agitation by the more radical monks would stop. What Washington needed to do now was to publicly praise any conciliatory steps taken by either side.

STRUGGLING TO KEEP UP with the geyser of news in Saigon, Halberstam, Sheehan, and the other reporters shifted into overdrive, cranking out story after story about the protests. "Halberstam and I and the other correspondents had seized on the Buddhist crisis as we had on Ap Bac," Sheehan later wrote. "We had been holding it up as proof that the regime was as bankrupt politically as it was militarily."

The police were getting in the correspondents' way less, but the Nhus had found new ways to bedevil them.

Madame Nhu dropped another of her verbal bombs, telling a British journalist that "Halberstam should be barbecued, and I would be glad to supply the fluid and the match." In late July, a plainclothes policeman approached a Vietnamese cameraman who worked for Sheehan, urging him "to tell your boss to be careful when he goes out at night" because the cops might get orders to kill him and make it look like a VC attack.

The correspondents tried to shrug off the menacing words. But warnings kept coming from police sources, some of whom seemed as alienated as many ARVN officers over what was happening to Buddhists in the streets. A cop told a Vietnamese journalist who worked for UPI that the Nhus had drawn up a list of enemies to be assassinated. Halberstam and Sheehan were on it, along with some high-ranking ARVN officers and civilians suspected of coup plotting. The Nhus were serious, the source said, adding that the reporters should take precautions.

If Nhu's thugs came for him, Sheehan's office-apartment would provide little protection. Lobbing a grenade through the front window or shooting the place up with a submachine gun would be easy. Though it might not be of much use in such an attack, Sheehan bought himself a .38-caliber revolver. Every night he loaded the gun and placed it carefully on his nightstand. Every morning, he unloaded it and put it away in a closet. Without the comforting nightly ritual, he was unable to sleep.

Halberstam seemed immune to the dark whispers as he churned out articles. Even amid the turbulence in Saigon, he kept his eye on the war in the countryside. On July 21, he and other journalists were informed of a "great government victory" near the delta town of My Tho, where the ARVN had supposedly killed three hundred guerrillas from the Viet Cong's 514th Battalion, the heroes of Ap Bac.

Eager to publicize its triumph, the Saigon government invited newsmen to fly to the area the next day. Halberstam and others choppered down to find that only fifty-eight VC, not three hundred, had been killed. (Eighteen ARVN soldiers were killed, most of them while trying to cross an open rice paddy in the face of communist fire.)

Disgusted by the exaggeration, the reporters flew back to Saigon. Harkins's command wanly reported to its superiors in Honolulu that it could offer "no sound explanation of wide disparity between initial report and final [body] count."

AFTER THE SAIGON CORRESPONDENTS complained to JFK about Diem's cops beating up Peter Arnett, the State Department's top public relations official was dispatched to Saigon to try to make Diem understand the pitfalls of bullying the press.

Gregarious and witty, Robert Manning was a former writer, editor, and London bureau chief for *Time* magazine who joined the State Department in 1961 as assistant secretary for public affairs. Asked by Rusk if he was "willing to lie for your country," Manning icily replied, "No." Despite his proclivity for candor in an administration that often preferred secrecy and press manipulation, he spent two and a half years in the department's upper echelons.

Unsurprisingly, Manning got an earful from Diem and Nhu. Diem argued that American and other foreign journalists were "consistently irresponsible and unfair" in their criticism of his government and "insulting" to his army. Nhu, moaning that "all the forces of hell are leagued against us," claimed that Halberstam and his young colleagues were engaged in the "stimulating pastime" of trying to overthrow his brother. By painting his family as "monsters," Nhu said, the press had turned American public opinion against South Vietnam's government. He insisted it was the newsmen who were oppressing the regime, not the other way around.

Manning agreed that some of Diem's and Nhu's grievances were justified. But he strongly emphasized that harassing and expelling journalists would backfire badly. They were an essential part of the American political system, Manning said, comparable to building inspectors who ensured that construction projects are well-built and safe. Preventing them from doing their jobs would pose an "extreme danger" to President Kennedy's ability to maintain U.S. support for South Vietnam.

He insisted that despite the negative news coverage coming out of Saigon, the American public was solidly behind Kennedy's efforts and the U.S. government was convinced it had "a winning program in Vietnam." He even talked Diem into letting James Robinson, the NBC News correspondent kicked out in 1962, back into the country.

Manning also spoke with Halberstam and other correspondents, listening to their gripes as well. At the end of his four-day visit, he wrote a blistering report that spared neither the newsmen nor the Kennedy administration.

The root of the problem, he pointed out, was "the long-standing desire of the United States government to see the American involvement in Viet-Nam minimized, even represented as something less than in reality it is." The restrictive press policies that grew out of that desire had caused "serious deterioration in the credibility" of U.S. authorities in Saigon and Washington.

Manning faulted Nolting and Harkins for their artless handling of the Saigon newsmen. Although they and other senior officials spent a great deal of time on press matters, their disdainful view of the reporters as "young, immature, and irresponsible" and "sometimes rude, insulting, and insufferable"—while justified in some cases—served only to widen the gulf between the two groups. Manning chided Nolting and Harkins for not speaking candidly to reporters on a background basis. By putting too rosy a spin on almost every development in the war, the ambassador and MACV chief instead gave correspondents the impression they were being fed nothing but bunkum.

The end result, the State Department PR executive wrote, was "the complete destruction of the Embassy's credibility."

Manning didn't let Halberstam and his colleagues off the hook either, writing that they suffered from "localitis," which he defined as a journalistic affliction caused by being stationed in one place for too long. Its symptoms, he said, included a loss of perspective combined with an excessive focus on one's own "irritations, adventures and opinions." The correspondents also had developed a "unanimous bitterness toward, and contempt for" the Diem regime and believed to a man that the war effort couldn't succeed as long as the Ngo family remained in power. That conviction, Manning said, became the implicit premise of every news story and analysis piece they wrote.

There were "no journalistic giants" among the Saigon reporters, Manning went on, although one he didn't name was "very promising" and several others were "obviously bright men." As a group, they were exceptionally hardworking, unafraid to face danger, and doing a good job of staying on top of the news under very difficult circumstances. Manning depicted them as "decent, patriotic Americans" who still backed Washington's commitment to defend South Vietnam.

Manning concluded that it was imperative for the embassy and MACV to recognize the press for what it was: an independent oversight body that could affect not only the political situation in Vietnam but also domestic American support for the war. Part of the hostility between the press and U.S. officials in Saigon arose from the newsmen's "wounded egos" and "highly developed sense of importance," Manning wrote. Given their maturity and diplomatic skills, Nolting and other U.S. officials might still be able to mend the relationships. In any event, they needed to start treating the correspondents as influential actors and potential allies in the war effort, rather than as "socially objectionable and professionally incompetent young cubs."

It was a perceptive dissection of the so-called "press mess," and White House aides placed a copy of Manning's report in Kennedy's weekend reading file.

AS SUMMER WORE ON and Diem's struggle to survive became a bigger and more dramatic story, a new face appeared in the ranks of the Saigon reporters: Marguerite Higgins, a Pulitzer Prize–winning correspondent for the *New York Herald Tribune*, a vibrant, direct competitor with Halberstam's *Times*.

Born in Hong Kong in 1920, "Maggie" Higgins was educated at Berkeley and Columbia University's journalism school before landing at the *Herald Tribune*. In 1944, the paper sent her to cover the Allied armies as they charged across France and the Low Countries toward Berlin. Higgins accompanied U.S. troops when they liberated the Nazi death camp at Dachau and captured Hitler's mountaintop aerie at Berchtesgaden.

Her cyclonic energy and almost pathological competitiveness made her a legend at the *Herald Tribune* in an era when women reporters were usually relegated to the society pages. At twenty-five, she was named chief of the *Herald Tribune*'s Berlin bureau. She wrote about the Nuremberg war crimes trials and the Berlin Airlift, which doomed the Soviet attempt to blockade the city and drive out the Western allies.

In 1950, Higgins was assigned to Tokyo as the paper's Far East correspondent not long before North Korea invaded South Korea. She jumped aboard the last American plane to Seoul as communist soldiers poured across the 38th parallel. General Walton Walker, commander of the U.S. Eighth Army, ordered her out of the war zone, but Higgins appealed to General Douglas MacArthur, who let her stay.

She covered the daring amphibious landing at Inchon, riding an assault boat packed with Marines to "Red Beach" in the fifth wave of the attack. *Life* magazine burnished her fame with a 1951 feature story on the "Girl War Correspondent"; in one photo Higgins wore GI fatigues and a winsome grin, her blond curls poking out from a battered army cap and a notebook jutting out of her shirt pocket. That same year, she shared the Pulitzer Prize for international reporting with five male Korean War correspondents. With more than a touch of condescension in that prefeminist time, the prize judges declared that Higgins was "entitled to special consideration by reason of being a woman, since she had to work under unusual dangers."

While in Berlin, she'd fallen in love with Air Force Major General William Hall, who had a wife and four children back in the States. They married in 1952. She covered the fall of Dien Bien Phu two years later and traveled throughout the Soviet Union in 1954 to '55, producing a book, *Red Plush and Black Bread*. Joining the *Herald Tribune*'s Washington bureau in 1956 as a diplomatic correspondent, she accompanied Vice President Richard Nixon to the USSR in 1959 and President Kennedy to Europe in 1961. Over the years her writing grew more stridently anti-communist in tone, perhaps not surprising for someone who had firsthand experience with the Berlin blockade, the Korean War, and Ho Chi Minh's proletarian army, and was married to a Cold War general.

AFTER CHECKING IN AT the Caravelle Hotel in Saigon, Higgins spent a hectic month traveling widely and interviewing people everywhere she went. She then produced six lengthy articles that flatly contradicted much of what Halberstam and the other Saigon-based newsmen had been reporting.

She portrayed Tri Quang and other Buddhist leaders not as righteous victims of religious persecution but as cynical manipulators bent on using a Western press predisposed to scorn Diem to induce the collapse of his government. (She later described Tri Quang as "Machiavelli with incense.") American pressure to mollify the Buddhists, she believed, had tied Diem's hands as he tried to suppress a dangerous internal rebellion amid a desperate war. She also upheld Nolting's and Harkins's claims that the war was being won, and that the Buddhist clamor in the cities had affected neither ARVN morale nor peasant attitudes.

One of Higgins's first reporting stops was Xa Loi, where messengers scurried in and out and senior monks barked orders at their juniors, reminding her of wartime military command posts she'd visited.

When she arrived at the big pagoda, a monk with a loudspeaker was haranguing a crowd of several thousand young people, cyclo-pousse drivers, and street beggars. He was standing atop Xa Loi's souvenir shop, which was doing a brisk business in postcards depicting Quang Duc's fiery death. Egged on by the monk, the crowd enthusiastically shouted slogans: "Buddhism forever!" "Down with Madame Nhu!"

Higgins was astonished by the Buddhists' astuteness in public relations. She watched as Duc Nghiep, the poised young propagandist, descended a staircase into a clutch of waiting journalists, amiably addressing each one by name and handing out mimeographed menus of new allegations of government repression and abuse.

"Ah, Miss Higgins, you are from New York," Duc Nghiep greeted her. "What is the play?"

Confused at first, the journalist thought he was referring to a stage play. Then she realized he was asking how news about the Buddhist uprising was "playing" in New York newspapers—how prominently it was featured. The monk's question indicated a sophisticated knowledge of American media that she hadn't expected. Higgins assured him the Buddhists were front-page news in New York.

When Duc Nghiep learned she was staying in Vietnam only a few weeks, he insisted she was making a great mistake. The new U.S. ambassador, Lodge, was expected to arrive in late August, and when he did, the monk said, "There will be many demonstrations that will make what went before look like nothing. And there will be many more self-immolations . . . 10, 15, maybe even 50." His icily detached prediction of more horrifying suicides made Higgins wonder whether the Buddhists' campaign contained an element of madness.

She also discovered that the monks weren't averse to exaggerating or spreading falsehoods about their suffering at Diem's hands.

Duc Nghiep told journalists one day, for example, that Diem's police had arrested 365 Buddhists in predawn raids in a Saigon suburb "because they were Buddhists." The dramatic tale made headlines in U.S. newspapers. Higgins decided to investigate the monk's claim, interviewing people through an interpreter as they emerged from a police station.

She talked to twenty Vietnamese—Catholics, Caodaists, ancestor worshippers, and others—before she came across her first Buddhist. Everyone she spoke to described the incident as a routine identity check in a district through which Viet Cong agents often passed. (All but sixteen unregistered people had been released by that afternoon, according to a U.S. embassy cable.) When Higgins asked the local police chief why the arrests came at night, he said it was because "the Communists do not sit around and wait for us to come and get them in daylight hours." Such intrusions into people's homes were unquestionably a harsh, disruptive, police-state tactic. But they didn't constitute government persecution or targeting of Buddhists.

Another Xa Loi monk made the breathtaking allegation that a Catholic province chief had staged public burnings of Buddhists who refused to convert to Catholicism. But when Higgins traveled to Quang Ngai Province, on the central coast south of Danang, to look into the claim, local monks she spoke with "acted as if they thought I had lost my mind." Higgins didn't question the Xa Loi bonze's sincerity. He really did seem to believe that the government was inflicting such torments on his distant compatriots. Higgins concluded that militant Buddhist leaders like Tri Quang were taking advantage of lower-ranking monks' credulity and respect for superiors, feeding them phony atrocity stories in order to whip them into an antigovernment lather.

From her interviews it was clear to Higgins that the Buddhists had expanded their campaign far beyond their original five demands: their goal now was to overthrow Diem. Tri Quang and others calculated that Washington would restrain Diem from cracking down on them too harshly. In the meantime, they'd keep sending their followers into ever-larger street demonstrations and sacrificing monks and nuns in grotesque immolations until the Americans became so embarrassed by their association with Diem that they withdrew all support for him. The regime would then disintegrate and the Buddhists would be seen as kingmakers, their power correspondingly enhanced with any new government that took Diem's place.

The monks, Higgins told her readers, "were going for [Diem's] political jugular," and Washington's demands for conciliation "were only making them more thirsty for his political blood."

As more of Higgins's stories appeared in the *Herald Tribune*, Halberstam's editors in New York peppered him with cables implying that her information might be more accurate than his. Halberstam was both angry and disheartened that his bosses didn't trust him after all this time. He cabled one: "if you mention that woman's name to me one more time I will resign repeat resign and I mean it repeat mean it."

POLICE TOOK DOWN THE barricades outside the pagodas and released scores of bonzes, nuns, and laypeople arrested during the July 17 roundups. Five days later, about two thousand of the faithful crowded happily into Xa Loi for prayers.

But the Buddhists were still on edge. They continued to claim that the regime wasn't honoring the June agreement, and pointedly failed to respond to Diem's offer to set up a joint commission to investigate alleged violations of it. (Tri Quang later charged implausibly that the government planned to assassinate Buddhist leaders if they went on field inspections with the joint commission.)

On July 23, the nun Dieu Hue held a macabre press conference at Xa Loi—open only to foreign newsmen—to announce that she planned to burn herself.

The tiny sixty-nine-year-old woman had a shaved head and sunken cheeks and seemed nervous before the reporters and their popping flashbulbs. She sat silently, her hands pressed together prayerfully, while Duc Nghiep read a statement from her in English. Disturbed by the ghoulishness of the proceedings, the newsmen questioned him sharply: Is the nun doing this of her own free will? Doesn't suicide violate Buddhist proscriptions against violence? Hasn't the government tried to conciliate? What will be achieved by her death? Duc Nghiep's answers were vague.

As the press conference went on, a commotion arose outside the temple as hundreds of ARVN veterans noisily tried to push their way inside and monks slammed the gates shut.

Many of the ex-soldiers had lost arms or legs; some wore head bandages or used crutches. They were accompanied by war widows and their children, and militiamen in black uniforms. The counterprotesters carried signs denouncing the Buddhists for not contributing to the war effort and shouted: "Why don't Buddhists pray for those killed in the fighting against the communists?" Word spread that Nhu had organized the demonstration, but a palace spokesman denied that, even though government sound trucks were used. Nolting later cabled Washington that embassy observers had noted the "obvious close cooperation between police and demonstrators."

Three months on, the crisis and its crushing pressures seemed to be taking a toll on Diem and Nhu. An American journalist visiting Diem described "an unhealthy plumpness and pinkness about him in his white-sharkskin suit." Nhu, too, appeared to be buckling. One evening in late July, the political counselor dined with Nolting, Mecklin, and several senior officials. Nhu droned on at his tablemates for five hours, meandering from topic to topic after downing one or two brandies too many.

"There was a trace of thickness in his speech," Mecklin recorded, "and he joked wryly several times about 'in vino veritas' as he launched into new tangents."

By the end of the evening, Mecklin realized that Nhu's monologue had been so rambling and fuzzy that it was impossible to summarize for his superiors. But some of his remarks stood out sharply in Mecklin's mind. So disgusted was he with his brother's weakness in dealing with the Buddhists, Nhu said, that he'd submitted his resignation. The Buddhists were supposedly conspiring with Cambodia's leader, Norodom Sihanouk, a longtime antagonist of Diem and Nhu. Police excesses against the monks were attributable to the cops' tiredness and resentment at being "separated from their families."

Long after midnight, as Nhu was leaving the dinner, he fell back on what was apparently becoming a family catchphrase to express his anger at his robed adversaries: "If the Buddhists wish to have another barbeque, I will be glad to supply the gasoline and a match."

IN A LAST-DITCH EFFORT to get himself right with newsmen, Nolting began setting up individual interviews with them. He also wanted to mitigate some of the damage that ongoing news coverage of the Buddhists was wreaking on Diem's relationship with Washington. But in the superheated atmosphere of the moment, Nolting's comments to UPI reporter Don Becker backfired. (Normally stationed in Singapore, Becker had been brought in to help Sheehan.)

The ambassador bemoaned that the Buddhist crisis had diverted attention from the genuine progress Diem was making in the war. "The trouble with this damn thing, if I may speak frankly," he told Becker, "is that everybody focuses on a tiny aspect of it. I myself—I say this very frankly, after almost two and a half years here—have never seen any evidence of religious persecution." The interview was published in *The Times of Vietnam* as well as in U.S. papers.

The Buddhists reacted swiftly and skillfully, with a spokesman decrying the ambassador's sentiments as a "parting gift" to Diem. At a quickly arranged press conference, Buddhist leaders said they hoped Nolting's words didn't reflect the official U.S. position on their grievances; the Buddhist leader, Thich Tinh Khiet, sent President Kennedy a wire deploring his envoy's views.

Incensed, Harriman telephoned Hilsman and declared that Nolting ought to be "recalled at once" from Saigon.

The Buddhists further charged that the ambassador knew nothing of their struggles because he'd never been inside a pagoda. When an American reporter called Mecklin and asked if Nolting had ever set foot in one, the embassy spokesman said he didn't think it was relevant.

But the journalist, his "voice taut with emotion," persisted, saying: "This is a formal demand for an official statement. Has or has not the American ambassador ever been inside a pagoda?" The reporter's aggressiveness was a striking indicator of how completely the Buddhists had thrown the embassy on the defensive with the press; his tone reminded Mecklin of McCarthy-era congressmen grilling witnesses about whether they were now, or ever had been, members of the Communist Party.

Mecklin solemnly declared that yes, the ambassador had ventured into a pagoda in the past.

Nolting had spoken truthfully about the absence of systematic government persecution. But his comments came less than two weeks after photos of Diem's police brutalizing monks and nuns in the streets had been flashed around the world. The U.S. press hammered him for his tone deafness, and the State Department made no effort to defend him. The blowup evidently left Nolting somewhat shaken. A few days later, he let a CBS News camera crew into his office for an interview. Before it started, the ambassador asked an aide to switch a portrait of Thomas Jefferson on the wall behind his desk with one of George Washington, saying the latter was "less controversial."

But Nolting didn't pause in his frenetic efforts to defuse the antipathy between Diem and the Buddhists. He implored the president to personally ask Khiet to meet with him. Diem couldn't bring himself to go that far, offering only to receive Khiet if he so requested. Nolting also urged Diem's foreign minister to get Dr. Buu Hoi, son of the nun threatening to burn herself, to come to Saigon from his laboratory near Paris and talk his mother out of her plans. (Told that the scientist had a heart condition that made travel difficult, the ambassador snapped that "he'd have worse than that if he didn't come back soon.")

Nolting finally got some encouraging news from Diem's interior minister, who said the government had decided to no longer use force to break up Buddhist demonstrations. Most South Vietnamese, said the minister, "were bored with Buddhist agitation" and convinced that government proposals to end the strife were "just and sincere."

There was more good news when a call by Buddhist leaders for the faithful to walk off their jobs and join a major demonstration on July 30—an action that would amount to a general strike in Saigon—went largely unheeded.

Outside Xa Loi that morning, a festive atmosphere prevailed as street vendors hawked their wares near the temple's front gate.

One man offered fresh coconut milk, whacking open the green-shelled fruit with a machete as customers reached for their piastres. Others sold peanuts, oranges, jellied coconut, and purple mangosteen fruit. The air was filled with the rhythmic, lulling words of a Buddhist scripture, read by someone inside the pagoda and amplified into the street over a loudspeaker. Hanging from Xa Loi's yellow walls and bell tower were brightly painted signs, in Vietnamese and English, proclaiming "The Free World Is Expected to Do Everything Possible for the Buddhists" and "Religious Persecution Is an Act of the Middle Ages."

About three thousand people showed up, most of them older women and men. Half of the crowd was jammed into the pagoda's main courtyard, while the rest spilled into the street. Buddhist Boy Scouts in their blue-and-gray uniforms brought offerings of fruit, long-stemmed lotus flowers, and gladiolas. As people came through the front gate, they were handed a mimeographed proclamation from Khiet saying that although Buddhist demands had been settled on paper, "in practice no concrete realization has been possible to appease the ever-lasting suffering of all Vietnamese Buddhists."

Ranking monks exhorted the crowd to keep up their struggle for government compliance with the five demands and reminded them of Quang Duc's fiery sacrifice. Plainclothes police slipped among the people, but the day was peaceful. Some businesses opened later than usual, but few stayed closed for the whole day. The leader of South Vietnam's biggest labor union, an old ally of Nhu's, told his members to go to work as usual.

From Hue, John Helble reported that 15,000 Buddhists paraded peacefully from Tu Dam to the city's other major pagoda, Dieu De. Police lined the route, but didn't interfere with the procession. Unlike in Saigon, most shops in the Buddhist heartland were shut up tight.

CHAPTER 12

A WILD ALARM IN THE HOT NIGHT

NOLTING'S LAST DAYS as ambassador were marked by frustration and embarrassment. It seemed, noted Hilsman, as if "all the fates of Asia were conspiring against him."

Diem and Nhu made it known in early August that they wanted to honor Nolting by naming a strategic hamlet after him. It was a well-intentioned gesture, but a singularly bad idea; the Viet Cong could be expected to work zealously to destroy any rural outpost named for a prominent American. Nolting tried to get out of the ceremony, claiming he was too busy. The palace insisted, however, and he finally gave in.

The ambassador wanted the visit kept secret, but it leaked to the press and things began to go wrong. The day before the event, an American helicopter accidentally machine-gunned the chosen hamlet, wounding six peasants. That evening, an ARVN jeep struck and injured a small boy in the hamlet. To top off the debacle, the Associated Press reported erroneously that it was the ambassador's jeep that hit the boy, and that he died.

Such setbacks aside, Nolting remained convinced that the Buddhists were losing momentum and Diem was gradually overcoming the crisis. The turmoil in Saigon, he cabled Washington, "should not repeat not throw us off the course here." But even as he worked on Diem to reach a durable rapprochement with the Buddhists, the Nhus redoubled their efforts to derail any further compromises.

Madame Nhu went out of her way to attack and denigrate Buddhists. "What have the Buddhist leaders done, comparatively?" she asked in her imperfect English during a CBS News interview that American viewers saw on August 1. "The only thing they have done, they have barbecued one of their monks, whom they have intoxicated, whom they have abused the confidence. Even that barbecuing was done not even with self-sufficient means, because they used imported gasoline." She followed up that malicious performance two days later with a bitter speech to hundreds of her paramilitary women outside Saigon city hall, labeling the Buddhists murderers, traitors, and "so-called holy men" with no compunctions about using communist political tactics.

In an interview a few days later with Halberstam, Madame again failed to restrain her spite, saying the regime would celebrate more self-immolations. "If they burn 30 women we shall go ahead and clap our hands," she said. "We cannot be responsible for their madness."

Not to be outdone, her husband told Nicholas Turner, the Reuters correspondent, that if the conflict wasn't resolved soon, it would set off a coup d'état and usher in a new government that would crush the Buddhists and turn against the Americans. He didn't specify who would foment such a rebellion, and laughed when Turner asked if he was aware of a rumored plot to depose Diem and install him, Nhu, in power. "Why overthrow my brother?" Nhu replied. "That would lead to anarchy."

Sinister tales oozed through the agitated capital. Madame, it was said, had put her brother in charge of a secret police squad that was making surreptitious arrests. The regime was planning to demolish Xa Loi Pagoda and "eliminate" Buddhist leaders.

Feeling increasingly under siege, Buddhists complained of ongoing assaults and arrests of the faithful, and tight police controls on the movements of monks and nuns. They peppered Diem and Vice President Tho with letters reporting "wicked conspiracies" against them. Khiet, the Buddhist patriarch, claimed that unnamed blackguards planned to steal Quang

Duc's preserved heart from Xa Loi and plant documents implicating prominent Buddhists in illegal acts. Khiet said the monks discovered the conspiracy, code-named Operation Flood, when someone put a written description of it in Xa Loi's mailbox.

The Buddhists kept up their campaign to turn international opinion against Diem, sending a "memorandum of grievances" to the United Nations that made a number of over-the-top charges against the regime. Diem, they alleged, was engaged in "open warfare" against Buddhists as part of a concerted drive to replace their belief system with Catholicism. They also claimed—without providing names or evidence—that some of their leaders had been assassinated and others "disappeared" while imprisoned.

Yet the Buddhists hadn't deployed their most potent political weapon—public burnings—in nearly two months. When an Australian journalist, Denis Warner, visited Xa Loi, the militant leader, Tri Quang, told him that as many as five of his brethren were prepared to immolate themselves despite the Buddhist hierarchy's efforts to restrain them.

Just then, as if to underscore his words, another monk hurried past carrying a gasoline can. Warner asked whether Tri Quang had heard yet another rumor that Diem planned to attack Xa Loi with his Special Forces.

The monk smiled and gave a disturbing reply: "Don't you think it will help our cause if some of us are killed?"

Then the burnings began again.

IN THE FIRST HALF of August, three monks and a nun set themselves afire.

The first to die was a twenty-year-old novice bonze who burned himself on August 4 in Phan Thiet, a provincial capital on the South China Sea about a hundred miles east of Saigon. On August 13, a seventeen-year-old monk was consumed by flames at 2 a.m. outside a pagoda a few miles west of Hue.

Helble, the Hue consul, reported that a thousand people soon gathered at the scene, with more on their way from the city despite police efforts to stop them. The following day, the Buddhists organized a memorial service outside the pagoda. About 250 bonzes and laypeople attended. A company of ARVN soldiers suddenly descended on the mourners, beating them with fists and steel helmets and badly injuring five people. The soldiers then loaded the monk's casket into a truck and drove off.

A nun torched herself on August 15 in the central coast town of Ninh Hoa. Local Buddhists demanded her body from provincial officials, and about a hundred monks made speeches outside the province chief's house until they were driven off with water hoses. Flying in to cover the story, Peter Arnett discovered that authorities had seized the nun's corpse and "given it a pauper's burial." He called his boss, Malcolm Browne, who said demonstrations had broken out in Saigon, Hue, and Danang.

"The whole place is going sky high!" Browne exclaimed.

The next death came on August 16, when a seventy-one-year-old monk burned in a courtyard at Tu Dam Pagoda. Hue officials declared martial law. Soldiers ringed the temple and residents were ordered off the streets; the province chief told Helble he'd received "numerous reports" that further suicides were in the offing.

Even Buddhist leaders now seemed afraid of the furies they'd unleashed. Thich Tinh Khiet issued an order for his followers to "limit" immolations. The dreadful burnings sent shudders throughout South Vietnam. Saigon, wrote John Mecklin, "was like a mental institution." No one, Vietnamese or American, seemed to understand what was happening, what to do about it, or even what to say.

Americans made bad jokes about "hot cross bonzes" and "Buddhist cookouts." The atmosphere was mesmerizing, if not tinged with lunacy. One day the young son of an embassy officer poured gasoline on his clothes, lit a match, and was badly burned before the blaze could be put out.

Asked why he did it, the boy said simply: "I wanted to see what it was like."

FROM HIS STATE DEPARTMENT perch in Foggy Bottom, Hilsman assessed the situation in South Vietnam as "tense, volatile, and potentially explosive." Buddhist leaders, he believed, intended to prolong their protests until Diem's government fell apart.

The assistant secretary of state calculated the chances of a coup attempt in the next few months at fifty-fifty. A successful one, Hilsman thought, would probably lead to a military junta, perhaps with Vice President Tho as a figurehead president. But it also might open the door to a power grab by Nhu or even civil war between noncommunist factions.

In a memo to George Ball, Hilsman said he'd prepared a contingency plan for the U.S. government to "throw all our influence behind Tho and the military" if Diem was overthrown. The embassy, Hilsman said, was "urgently seeking further but discreet contact" with anti-Diem dissidents "in order to give us a better chance to manipulate the outcome of coup attempt." He recommended that Washington not encourage or discourage the plotters. "We do not know whether or not Diem can survive," Hilsman wrote. "With all that is at stake in Viet-Nam, we obviously cannot afford to back a loser but we are not yet in a position to pick a winner with any confidence."

The CIA warned Kennedy about the increasingly dangerous struggle between Diem and the Buddhists. It reported on August 3 that a "Conservative Buddhist leader" had expressed concern that control of the protest movement "may be slipping into the hands of extremist bonzes"—a clear reference to Tri Quang. Michael Forrestal informed JFK that he'd asked the Pentagon to draw up plans to protect U.S. citizens in South Vietnam, and to evacuate them if things turned ugly.

The American press, meanwhile, began to focus on the political power of the Nhus and their vocal efforts to disrupt any peace settlement with the Buddhists. *The Washington Post* suggested in an editorial that the couple might try to shove Diem aside, take over the government, and put their anti-Buddhist views into action. If that happened, the paper said, the United States, as South Vietnam's main patron, would find itself facing "a moral Dien Bien Phu of tragic dimensions." A *Time* cover story on Madame Nhu depicted her mocking Diem's efforts to mollify the Buddhists. The president, she said scornfully, only wanted to "conciliate as the Americans desire, smooth, no bloodshed, everyone shaking hands."

For Hilsman, Madame Nhu's insulting statements were the last straw. He cabled Nolting that Diem couldn't afford to ignore such comments, since they had the effect "of undercutting his authority and creating image abroad that he being led around by apron strings." The best thing for Diem to do now was to get his irksome sister-in-law out of the country. Hilsman also directed the ambassador to pressure Diem to publicly state his policy of conciliation "without any equivocation."

Nolting replied wearily that "Madame Nhu is out of control of everybody—her father, mother, husband, and brother-in-law." He said he'd had an audience with Diem, but when he asked that the Dragon Lady be sent away, the president replied only that he thought she "ought to take a rest," and wouldn't budge beyond that. When the State Department inquired, somewhat plaintively, whether Diem might be persuaded to go on "vacation" with the Nhus, while other regime officials tried to settle matters with the Buddhists, Nolting said there was no chance of that.

The ambassador requested permission to stay on in Saigon a while longer, in hopes of reducing tensions between Diem and the Buddhists. But he was turned down and told to pack his bags before his replacement, Henry Cabot Lodge, arrived.

Nolting did, however, score one small victory before departing. At a farewell dinner for him at Gia Long Palace, Diem pledged to publicly reaffirm his intention to cooperate with the Buddhists. There would be no high-profile speeches or radio addresses, however. Diem made his declaration in his own low-key way, during an interview with Marguerite Higgins, the *New York Herald Tribune* correspondent. In a sit-down arranged by Nolting, Diem told Higgins that his government's policy of "utter conciliation" was "irreversible." Besides the New York newspaper, his terse statement was published in several pro-government papers in Saigon and broadcast on local radio.

Nhu privately assured Nolting that he fully supported conciliation with the Buddhists and "did not favor" crushing them. Nolting replied skeptically that if Nhu was telling the truth, he was "a most misunderstood man."

On the morning of August 14, the day before he was to leave South Vietnam, the ambassador made a final call on his friend at the palace.

Nolting felt that the embassy had helped to calm things down in recent weeks, but that the mutual trust between his government and Diem's had been shattered. In their last conversation, Diem complained that the American government and press didn't understand the complexities of the Buddhist problem. Nor did the Americans grasp the lasting contributions to South Vietnamese independence made by members of his family—especially the "absolute selflessness" of his brother Nhu.

The president nevertheless warmly told Nolting that he considered the ambassador's tenure in Saigon "one of the best souvenirs of his life" and asked him to thank President Kennedy for all he'd done for South Vietnam. Diem's chief of staff, Thuan, later confided to Nolting that his boss had privately asked the Australian ambassador to extend an invitation for Madame Nhu to visit Australia and New Zealand for several months—a significant diplomatic win, if it ever came to pass.

Nolting gave a farewell statement at the airport the next day, stoutly maintaining that South Vietnam had "a winning program." When a reporter asked if he thought the press had contributed to his departure, Nolting suppressed his real feelings and made an uncomfortable joke about being "dis-Lodged" from Saigon. Then he sadly shook hands with his staff and waved goodbye.

Halberstam thought he looked lonely as he disappeared into a Pan American jetliner. Except for a chance encounter a few years later in Washington, Nolting never spoke to his old friend Trueheart again.

AS THE BURNINGS AND street protests continued, Nhu tried to defuse the Buddhist movement through a back-channel emissary: Dr. Buu Hoi, the nuclear scientist and Diem's African ambassador. Hoi secretly met several times with Tri Quang, urging him to call off the demonstrations and "simply accept [the] situation."

Hoi said Nhu wanted to set up a private meeting with Tri Quang during a dinner arranged by the chairman of the International Control Commission. But the monk rejected the offer, believing Nhu was only trying to "buy him off," while continuing to oppress Buddhists.

When Tri Quang asked what he thought of the regime, Hoi replied that it was "so rotten it was not even worth overthrowing." The monk said that while Diem was acceptable to the Buddhists, the "rest of the family had to go." But Hoi warned that removing Nhu would require a "very bloody process."

Although he carried messages from Nhu, the scientist seemed sympathetic to the Buddhists, offering advice about how they could advance their cause. He stressed the importance of cultivating the U.S. press, noting that Halberstam was the "most truthful" of the correspondents. He also urged Tri Quang to prepare a dossier for the incoming ambassador, Lodge, summarizing how the regime "had wronged Buddhism."

At one meeting, Tri Quang suggested that Hoi quit his ambassadorial posts and take his mother, the nun Dieu Hue, away before she burned herself as planned. But Hoi said he'd resign only if he was convinced the regime was about to collapse. When the monk questioned Dieu Hue about her son's motives, she said he cooperated with the government because it gave him money, which allowed him "to keep several women."

Diem's opponents gained another avenue of attack on him when he fired Father Luan, the popular Catholic rector of Hue University.

The holder of a doctorate in philosophy from the Sorbonne, Luan was a respected academician whose prestige had attracted French, British, and West German professors to teach at the three-thousand-student university, regarded as South Vietnam's most progressive. He was also a longtime friend of Diem and his family, and a member of the Can Lao Party. According to Nhu, however, Luan had turned against the president, encouraging students to strike and claiming "that the Diem administration was finished and its days numbered."

Fifty professors—almost the entire faculty—swiftly resigned over Luan's removal and the government's failure to resolve the Buddhist crisis after more than three months. At a ceremony to "welcome" Luan's replacement, a number of deans and faculty members stood up, one by one, and announced they were quitting, leaving the new rector "green with anger." More than a dozen professors were later arrested in early-morning raids; Luan was placed under house arrest. Hundreds of students vowed to boycott their classes, and demonstrations erupted in Hue and Saigon.

Hue smoldered with discontent. Even some ARVN soldiers began wearing yellow patches on their uniforms to show solidarity with the Buddhists. An American historian visiting the city, Ellen Hammer, found young men standing guard at Tu Dam Pagoda against a "surprise attack" by security forces. Among them was an elderly man who said he'd fight government troops to the death if they dared to invade the holy place.

Many local Buddhists were deeply offended by Madame Nhu's hard-edged comments about them; her words were even cruder in Vietnamese than translated English and made her sound, the locals said, like a common fishwife. Some residents believed that Archbishop Thuc intended to convert the whole city to Catholicism, by force if necessary. "Believe lid is off the kettle in Hue," Helble cabled.

In Saigon, monks began "fortifying" Xa Loi. Duc Nghiep, the propaganda monk, called in newsmen for a look at how the pagoda's inhabitants intended to defend themselves if the police tried to barge in. Six young bonzes lined up before the cameras to demonstrate their "weapons"—cans of bug spray. Sheehan reported that the monks also had fashioned "grenades of salt and pepper wrapped in papers, pans of chili sauce, and cans filled with lemon juice, red peppers and curry powder."

At first blush, it was a faintly ridiculous photo op: monks armed only with spray cans and condiments wouldn't be able to hold off invading security forces for long. But the image was another example of the Buddhists' media savvy, for it also conveyed to the watching world that while monks and nuns might be largely defenseless, they were filled with steely determination.

On August 18, the Buddhists staged one of their most impressive demonstrations yet as more than 15,000 enthusiastic supporters flocked to Xa Loi. It was a joyful, enthusiastic crowd, assembled as if to show off Buddhist political muscle for the benefit of the incoming ambassador, Lodge.

Streets around the pagoda were jammed, and when it began to rain the people stayed put. For several hours, monks denounced the regime for its purported tyranny and openly called for Diem's overthrow. The speeches were mixed with prayers, and occasionally a monk told a scurrilous joke about Madame Nhu, eliciting gales of laughter from his listeners.

Watching the scene, Halberstam sensed that if the monks suddenly ordered their followers to march on Gia Long, the huge crowd would immediately head for the palace.

HALBERSTAM OFTEN BANGED OUT three thousand to four thousand words a day on his well-worn Olivetti typewriter as the Buddhist imbroglio heated up, and his articles continued to grate on the Kennedy administration.

In a front-page story published on August 15, he reported that the Viet Cong were mounting a "sizable military offensive" in the Mekong Delta despite the U.S. buildup. VC units were growing larger and better armed—mostly with captured American-made weapons. Two new enemy battalions had appeared in the past year, bringing the total to twenty-one. Instead of limiting their attacks to isolated, lightly defended militia outposts, the guerrillas were now taking on regular ARVN formations.

"They are almost cocky about it," one U.S. adviser told Halberstam.

The article said advisers were "extremely worried" about the strategic hamlet program in the delta. Not only were the hamlets not stopping the VC in some areas, they seemed to be backfiring, since the enemy was now able to move more easily through territory cleared of its usual inhabitants.

Harkins's staff countered with a lengthy, classified memo noting that delta roads were open, rice shipments were reaching Saigon, and the percentage of the population under government control was rising. But the analysis—which Forrestal showed to JFK—failed to contradict Halberstam's central point that Saigon's military position in the delta was deteriorating.

At the same time, "a veritable flood" of U.S. intelligence reports warned that the Saigon government was "near collapse" and the war effort was bogging down as a result. "Vouchers were not being signed to get food and materials out to the front," Forrestal recounted. "Munitions were being held up. Civil servants were going on vacation, or at least refusing to turn up at the office. And we began for the first time to get reports from the field, not so much that there was political disaffection, but that the war was grinding to a halt."

THE MAKESHIFT LITTLE OFFICE Halberstam shared with Sheehan was an oven in the summer heat. Shirtless, the two men faced each other across Sheehan's dining room table, sweat dripping down their chests as they worked punishingly long hours. Halberstam urged his New York editors to publish every word of every story he sent. Something big was about to happen, he insisted; the indications were everywhere.

A few weeks earlier, an important Vietnamese who Halberstam trusted had taken him to meet another Vietnamese in Cholon. The men made the reporter an intriguing offer: they were involved with some military officers who were organizing a coup, and they wanted Halberstam to cover it from the inside. If the coup failed, they told Halberstam, they couldn't guarantee his safety, or even his survival.

After talking it over with Sheehan, Halberstam replied that he wanted in. The plotters gave him a military radio and his own call sign. The plan was to "kidnap" him and a *Saturday Evening Post* photographer and take them to coup headquarters. That way, the two Americans would have a measure of deniability if the takeover fizzled. Over the ensuing weeks, Halberstam and the photographer were alerted several times, but the promised coup never materialized.

Amid rumors that Nhu was planning his own putsch, Halberstam learned that the political counselor had brought more Special Forces troops into Saigon. Selected for their size and strength, the elite soldiers were trained, armed, and bankrolled by the CIA. They were supposed to be deployed in counterguerrilla operations, but Nhu had made them his family's private army, and they rarely fought the VC. Their commander was Colonel Le Quang Tung, a Catholic from Central Vietnam and one of Diem's most fiercely loyal officers. Regular ARVN officers hated and feared the bespectacled, mild-mannered Tung, who worked for Diem's family as a servant before the president gave him a commission.

Another of Halberstam's Vietnamese sources called him on August 19, but didn't want to say much on the phone. The two men later went for a walk beside the Saigon River. The source told Halberstam that Nhu intended to raid the pagodas, using Colonel Tung's troops. The same day, Halberstam found out that Nhu had met with his generals and berated them for not taking better precautions against a coup. Nhu said a revolt was inevitable and when it broke out, the Ngo family planned to flee to an "underground hide-out" in mountains north of Saigon. The generals were then to raze the capital with artillery rather than battle the mutineers at close quarters. Halberstam hurried back to his office and pounded out a story.

By then, the reporters were exhausted. For the past five days, Halberstam, Sheehan, and Nicholas Turner had stayed up all night, ready to alert the other newspeople if anything broke. They were edgy and irritable, and repeated tales that Nhu's secret police were targeting them didn't help.

On the afternoon of August 20, Halberstam and Sheehan went to a seedy bar on Rue Catinat to have a drink with a palace source: Dang Duc Khoi, deputy director of the government press office. A notorious womanizer, Khoi was also a regime intelligence operative who liked to hang out in nightclubs favored by Saigon gangsters. But he'd fallen into disfavor with Madame Nhu, having tried to block publication of an inflammatory anti-Buddhist article she wrote for *The Times of Vietnam*.

Khoi had two messages for the newsmen. The first was that Nhu intended to hit the pagodas full-blast with military forces that night or the next. The second was that Khoi's gangster buddies had thoughtfully mentioned that the Nhus gave them a list of people they might want killed. Khoi was on the list, and his criminal associates recommended that he get out of town as soon as possible; after all, they didn't want to have to gun down a pal in some dark alley.

Halberstam's and Sheehan's names were on the hit list, too. "They're going to plastique your office," Khoi warned, meaning that plastic explosives would be used to make the attack look like VC handiwork. Khoi said he was taking the gangsters' advice and leaving the country.

About two weeks later, he slipped down to the riverfront, boarded a freighter loaded with fertilizer, and sailed away to Japan.

AT ABOUT THE TIME Khoi was drinking with Halberstam and Sheehan, Diem met with several of his top generals.

The military leaders were alarmed at the ongoing unrest in Saigon and elsewhere, fearing it could eventually undermine national security. Most of their troops were Buddhist, and morale was beginning to suffer. ARVN officers and enlisted men were showing up, sometimes uniformed, in street demonstrations, and the generals worried that troops might desert. In Danang, an ARVN captain and two soldiers had tried to stop a Buddhist march involving about four thousand people. A soldier fired at the crowd, wounding two Buddhists. In response the marchers threw rocks at the soldier, hitting him in the head. They also wrestled a carbine and pistol away from the captain and set his jeep on fire.

The generals couldn't abide such "insults" to the armed forces and asked Diem to impose martial law, giving them a free hand to get the country back under control. Their delegation was led by Tran Van Don, the polished, French-trained army commander who was one of the key coup plotters. Don was concerned about the growing size of Buddhist crowds; if a mob of thousands decided to march on Gia Long Palace, the army might not be able to stop it.

He and the other generals proposed breaking up the Buddhist protests by "moving" monks who'd come to Saigon from other places back to their home pagodas. Although they didn't specify how this was to be done, any such effort was likely to result in some bloodshed and another uproar.

Diem, too, believed the disorder was spinning out of control. He told the generals he'd approve their martial law recommendation, but only on the condition that no monks were hurt in the process of taking them out of Saigon.

He added that a martial law declaration wouldn't change his policy of trying to achieve peace with the Buddhists "on the basis of justice." To carry out the martial law edict he chose Don, elevating him to chief of the Joint General Staff, the ARVN's highest rank.

ON THE EVENING OF August 20, Halberstam and Sheehan sat down to dinner with some other correspondents.

Sheehan was sure Khoi's tip about imminent raids on pagodas was good, and he wanted to be prepared if the story broke. After UPI failed to get a photo of the first burning monk in June, some client newspapers threatened to drop the wire service, and Sheehan had taken a considerable amount of heat from his bosses. ("This is a helluva costly mistake," noted one in a letter, pointedly advising Sheehan to "be ready" when the next big story loomed.) Sheehan could afford no further lapses.

Finishing supper, he and Halberstam found a taxi and began a tour of the city's pagodas to see if anything might happen that night.

Xa Loi was cheerfully illuminated, with colored lights strung along a stone archway and a large swastika, the ancient symbol of Buddha, outlined in blue neon atop the main temple. The pagoda's great iron gate was closed behind a police barricade of barbed wire; surrounding streets were empty. The early-rising monks were asleep, but the two reporters woke up the propaganda bonze, Duc Nghiep. He told them that yes, the temple's inhabitants were aware a raid was coming, and calmly went back to bed.

With the city apparently quiet, Sheehan and Halberstam split up and headed home. Sheehan's cab putt-putted past the midnight crowds on Rue Catinat before stopping outside his apartment near the river. As he was getting out, Mert Perry, the *Time* magazine freelancer who lived above him, leaned his hefty body out a window.

"Now! Now! They're going in now!" Perry shouted excitedly. He'd just gotten off the phone with a tipster; the regime was indeed making its move against the Buddhists that night.

Sheehan jumped back into the cab and headed for Halberstam's villa. The rattletrap little car zoomed up Rue Catinat and past the towering Catholic cathedral in the middle of town. Speeding along, Sheehan noticed that the 3rd arrondissement police station was brilliantly lit by floodlights. The compound was jammed with two-and-half-ton trucks—more largesse from

America—and combat police and troops in battle gear were climbing into them.

Moments later, Halberstam dashed out of his villa and piled into the taxi. Heading for Xa Loi, the reporters suddenly found themselves behind a troop convoy. Sheehan screamed at the cabdriver: "Di di!" (Go! Go!) "Di di mao!" (Go fast!) Sheehan wanted him to speed up and wedge his car into the column of trucks so the journalists wouldn't be cut off if police blocked streets after the convoy passed. As Sheehan shouted and cursed in French and pidgin Vietnamese, the terrified driver squeezed in among the military vehicles.

The convoy barreled up to the pagoda's front gate. The newsmen threw piastre notes at the cabbie and jumped out as soldiers and police vaulted from their trucks and massed for an assault. To Halberstam there seemed to be thousands of them, their officers shouting orders to form up. Wide-awake monks and nuns were making an enormous racket, yelling at the top of their lungs and banging on pots, pans, gongs, and drums.

Atop the pagoda's high tower someone struck the heavy copper bell over and over, a wild alarm in the hot night.

Police battered open the entrance gate and well-disciplined squads of Colonel Tung's men—smartly clad in red berets and camouflage fatigues, holding submachine guns at port arms—strutted forward to lead the charge inside. They were followed by heavily armed combat police and helmeted regular police in white uniforms. Halberstam was amazed that such a force had been assembled to subdue the temple denizens; to him, it was like siccing Green Berets on peaceful civil rights demonstrators in the States.

Streetlamps and truck headlights cast enough light for the reporters to see the soldiers' shoulder patches. The men were clearly Tung's Special Forces, not regular ARVN units.

The elite troops poured through the bashed-in gate, followed by police. The night exploded with the sounds of gunfire, screams, breaking glass, and splintering wood.

Monks and nuns had barricaded themselves in their rooms, but the soldiers and cops broke open the doors with axes and boots. The Buddhists tried to defend themselves by throwing "rocks, flower pots, everything" at their pursuers. Behind the pagoda, soldiers fired automatic rifles in the air to discourage anyone from trying to scale the back wall and escape.

Hundreds of bonzes and nuns were shoved, dragged, or carried through the courtyard and forced into trucks. Some were beaten with rifle butts; some were bleeding. Watching the pandemonium from the street, Halberstam felt more and more uneasy. He knew he was somewhere he wasn't wanted, seeing things he wasn't supposed to see; Tung's men could turn on him at any moment.

The frenzy lasted around two hours, ending at about 2:30 a.m. on August 21. Halberstam and Sheehan regrouped afterward at Sheehan's apartment. They'd learned that troops and police crashed into pagodas all over Saigon, arresting everyone inside. Their problem now was how to get their stories out.

The regime had shut down its cable office and cut local phone lines, trying to sever Saigon from the rest of the world during the raids. (Browne was "met with bayonets" when he tried to file a story at the cable office.) Anticipating such moves, Sheehan had previously gotten Ivan Slavich, the friendly helicopter pilot, to teach him how to navigate a special U.S. Army telephone system. Using that network, Sheehan managed to get a dramatic, 150-word bulletin on the raids—complete with gunshots and screams—to the UPI office in Manila, giving him a huge scoop over his archrivals at the Associated Press.

SHEEHAN AND HALBERSTAM SHOWED up at 4 a.m. at the U.S. embassy, which was in an uproar. Its phones, too, had been shut off, and its officers were frantically trying to find out what had happened during the raids. "Why didn't you tell us?" one high-ranking diplomat implored Halberstam, who was so taken back by the man's befuddlement that he didn't know what to say. Could the embassy, with its large staff and numerous regime contacts, really not have known that the pagodas were going to be stormed?

With the cable office closed, Trueheart agreed to transmit several journalists' stories to the State Department over the embassy's internal communication system. From there they could be forwarded to the reporters' Washington offices. But, without informing the newsmen, Kennedy administration officials sat on the stories, although Forrestal made sure JFK saw the information they contained.

Rattled and exhausted, Halberstam and Sheehan sought out Mecklin and asked if they could stay at his house for a while. They were afraid to go back to their own quarters, with good reason. A regime insider had said they were marked for assassination, as was Mecklin. Sheehan, so tired from lack of sleep that he'd developed a stutter, thought Nhu had "gone bananas, just simply completely bananas." It'd be child's play for his goons to put a bullet in the hated newsmen's heads on a crowded street, or toss a grenade into their unprotected homes.

Mecklin's house was guarded around the clock. But the reporters' plea to stay there created a prickly dilemma for him. As a former foreign correspondent, he knew Halberstam and Sheehan were in a precarious position. A friend of his, a United Press reporter named Gene Symonds, had been beaten to death by a mob in Singapore in 1955. On the other hand, Mecklin was now a government gamekeeper who was supposed to keep journalistic poachers at bay. He felt as if Sheehan and Halberstam, in appealing for sanctuary, were almost daring him to take sides. Did his true loyalties lie with his old colleagues of the press or with his current government employers, even though they were enabling a repressive regime?

Mecklin knew some of his superiors would be angry if he opened his home to the reporters, so much so that his government career could be jeopardized. "They were the two most controversial newsmen in town, whose hostile but competent reporting had harassed both the regime and the [U.S.] Mission to distraction," he later wrote. "They must have known that it would hurt my own relations with almost everyone to take them in."

After consulting Trueheart, who was once again the acting ambassador, Mecklin told the bone-tired, anxiety-ridden reporters they were welcome to stay with him.

THE PEOPLE OF SAIGON awoke that morning to find themselves under martial law.

Soldiers patrolled the streets in jeeps mounted with machine guns. Tan

Son Nhut airport was closed to commercial flights. Under a 9 p.m. to 5 a.m. curfew, soldiers had orders to shoot anyone caught on the streets during those hours if they tried to run. Military censors told newspapers what they could and couldn't print. The capital was controlled by a newly appointed military governor: Brigadier General Ton That Dinh, a young, erratic, whiskey-loving ex-paratrooper said to be intensely loyal to Diem.

The raids the night before had decapitated the Buddhist movement in a single stroke. More than 1,400 monks, nuns, and laypeople—including key leaders—had been arrested at pagodas in Saigon, Hue, Danang, and elsewhere. Thich Tinh Khiet, the octogenarian supreme bonze, was under guard in a military hospital after "falling" during the seizure of Xa Loi. Grisly stories of monks being thrown from balconies and otherwise killed made their way into the foreign press. An ABC News journalist reported that "ambulances removed many dead [and] wounded" from Xa Loi. *Newsweek* reported that "at least" thirty Buddhists were killed in Hue.

But such tales, like so many in South Vietnam, were hard to verify. The regime insisted that no deaths occurred during the incursions. The embassy informed Washington that it couldn't "affirm or contradict" the claim that no one died in the Saigon raids. A U.S. Army report said no one was killed at Xa Loi. The ARVN commander in Hue insisted no loss of life had occurred there. But John Helble, the Hue consul, cabled that some people had died, and thirty was "probably reasonable estimate."

Helble had heard gunfire on the night of the raids and drove around Hue the next morning in his official car, a Nash Rambler. Hue, too, was under martial law and the streets were empty. He believed his phones were tapped and he was now under twenty-four-hour surveillance; everywhere he went he saw a black Citroën in his rearview mirror. A Citroën was parked outside his house at all times, "and not very discreetly."

Helble crossed the Perfume River bridge into the old part of Hue. The bridge was under heavy police guard, but Helble, with his consular license plates, was allowed to pass. Spotting armored personnel carriers at key locations around the city, he grew angry that American military equipment was being used to repress South Vietnamese civilians rather than fight the VC.

Helble learned that there had been some violence at Tu Dam Pagoda, resulting in injuries to monks and their supporters, who'd camped on the pagoda grounds for weeks. Many people had been arrested. He reported to the embassy that combat police from Saigon "largely destroyed" the interiors of Tu Dam and Hue's other main pagoda while arresting people inside.

A few days later, a young man Helble knew, a dissident, appeared at his house. He wanted to talk about recent events and told Helble he feared for his safety. "Can you give me something that I can send back to you in the event I am arrested, something that you will recognize?" he asked. Helble gave him a paperback book, Dostoyevsky's *Crime and Punishment*. The next day, the man's wife called and said he hadn't come home. When Helble asked his gate guard if he'd seen anything unusual when the young dissident left, he said yes: the man had been forced into the black Citroën parked outside the house.

THE PAGODA ASSAULTS CAUGHT the embassy completely unawares. Apparently trying to forestall any American attempt to intervene on the Buddhists' behalf, the regime had disconnected not only embassy phones but the home phones of top U.S. officials as well. The CIA hadn't known in advance of the raids despite its close relationship with Nhu. Harkins's command, too, had been bamboozled. When U.S. advisers asked why so many of Colonel Tung's Special Forces troops were assembling in Saigon before the raids, they were told it was because VC guerrillas were preparing to attack the city.

Madame Nhu was overjoyed by the pagoda sweeps. She and her husband had watched from the open hatch of a tank, not far from Halberstam, as troops and police smashed their way into Xa Loi. As far as the Nhus were concerned, the Buddhists finally were quashed. There'd be no more humiliating negotiations and compromises. It was a victory as clear-cut and resounding as the destruction of the Binh Xuyen gangsters in 1955. A correspondent described the Dragon Lady as being in a "state of euphoria, chattering like a schoolgirl after a prom." The action against the "Communist Buddhists," she said, marked her "happiest day in eight years."

Diem called a meeting of his "furious and depressed" cabinet ministers at 5:30 a.m., telling them he'd declared martial law on an emergency basis, without consulting them, because "Communists were infiltrating the outskirts of the city." Then he went on the radio and read his martial law proclamation, which gave the military the power to search houses, arrest anyone considered "harmful to public security," and exercise "full control of all media," including movie theaters. Public gatherings were banned.

The regime claimed it found weapons in the pagodas and that the Buddhists were planning a coup. General Dinh, the military governor, blocked off large parts of Saigon with troops and cops, creating even bigger traffic jams than usual. The embassy reported that Saigon residents were "too stunned to react" to the raids, although a CBS News crew filmed troops pushing back angry civilians trying to enter Xa Loi.

At least some regime officials were holding their breath to see how the public responded once the full scope of the raids was understood. A Saigon military source predicted to a U.S. attaché that Buddhists would protest with more hunger strikes and suicides, and that the VC would step up their attacks in the provinces. "Source fears that if pandemonium develops, the troops may well join with the populace in a massive revolt against the governmental policy," the attaché reported to Washington. "Source stated that if it appears that the situation is getting out of control, Gen. Don may seize control of the government."

AMERICAN OFFICIALS THOUGHT DIEM and Nhu had gone crazy, but their actions were rooted in a certain logic as well as in their past experiences with Washington.

The brothers believed that their strategic hamlets and other nation-building policies were working, and they were winning the war. It was imperative to neutralize the Buddhists before they damaged the war effort and upended the government; trying to appease them had only fed their demands and stiffened their resistance. Diem probably concluded, Truehart cabled Washington, that "this policy had become a one-way street to catastrophe for him, his family, and his Government."

The Americans always counseled peaceful compromise; back in 1955, they urged the brothers to placate the Binh Xuyen and the religious sects. When Diem and Nhu instead went to war against their foes, the Americans got behind them and even increased their aid. The brothers may have anticipated a similar reaction from Washington after they put down the Buddhists. Not only would they weather the storm, they'd emerge stronger in its wake.

If that was their thinking, they had miscalculated. Much of the world was shocked and disgusted by the pagoda raids, and Diem and Nhu were engulfed by the political furor that followed.

South Vietnam's longtime ambassador to Washington, Tran Van Chuong, who was also Madame Nhu's father, resigned and publicly called for Diem's ouster. All but one member of his embassy staff followed him out the door. Chuong's wife quit her position as South Vietnam's United Nations observer. (Once a wealthy landowner in Vietnam, Chuong had never forgiven Diem for taking away some of his rice-growing acreage under his land reform program in the 1950s, and both Chuongs were estranged from their daughter.) Diem's foreign minister, a devout Buddhist named Vu Van Mau, resigned, shaved his head in solidarity with arrested monks and nuns, and asked permission to go on a pilgrimage to India. Diem and Nhu were vilified around the world; heavily Buddhist Cambodia severed diplomatic relations with South Vietnam.

Overnight, it became deeply problematic for the Kennedy administration to do business as usual with the Saigon government; the policy of unswerving support for Diem had been severely, if not fatally, wounded. The State Department released a public statement condemning the raids as a "direct violation by the Vietnamese Government of assurances that it was pursuing a policy of reconciliation with the Buddhists."

Nolting contemplated these developments in sadness and anger. After leaving Saigon, he'd flown to Honolulu to consult with Hilsman and Lodge. (Lodge dismissively waved off a briefing by his predecessor because "he had nothing to learn from him.") The three men watched as a wire-service ticker spat out news of the raids. Someone cursed softly; Nolting looked stricken. To Hilsman, the action was a deliberate affront to the Americans, a calculated effort to present them with a fait accompli prior to Lodge's arrival as the new ambassador. Worse, Diem and Nhu had done it with arrogance and contempt and no attempt to salvage Washington's dignity, confident, as Hilsman put it, that "we would swallow this just as we had swallowed so much in the past."

For Nolting, it was more personal. He'd worked long and hard to help Diem, jeopardizing his career in the bargain. But in the end his friend betrayed him, first promising to make peace with the Buddhists and then beating and arresting them in their shrines. Nolting dejectedly wired Diem: "This is the first time that you've ever gone back on your word to me."

No reply came from the palace.

HALBERSTAM AND SHEEHAN SPENT most of August 21 trying to figure out who ordered the raids. It was no easy task. Many of their usual Vietnamese sources were too scared to talk. And the curfew made it dangerous to move around on the tense, troop-filled streets after dark.

Trueheart reported to Washington that the generals were the likely culprits. "Expertness, speed, and coordination with which operations carried out against Buddhists in widely separated cities," he wrote, "indicate that careful and detailed prior planning must have been carried out on contingency basis before final decision to move taken."

Halberstam suspected Nhu. After all, the raids had unfolded exactly the way the palace tipster, Khoi, said they would, and the action was largely carried out by the Special Forces, long associated with Nhu. Halberstam did hear from one Vietnamese source that some Special Forces troopers had worn ARVN uniforms in an effort to disguise themselves. To Halberstam, the reason was obvious. Nhu wanted it to look like the army conducted the crackdown, creating the impression that it had broader support within the government than it actually did.

The next day, Halberstam went to see John Richardson, the CIA station chief, who looked tired and shaken. A rumor was circulating that his agency had known about the raids in advance and had even approved them.

But Richardson admitted that he'd been just as surprised as everybody else in the embassy. "We just didn't know," he told Halberstam. "We just didn't *know*, I can assure you." It was an embarrassing disclosure from a man who not only had close personal connections to the palace but was in charge of more than two hundred professional spies and support personnel. Another U.S. intelligence agent, however, insisted that Nhu and Colonel Tung were responsible for the raids, telling the newsman: "It didn't have a damn thing to do with the army."

Halberstam and Sheehan compared notes and began knocking out their stories. They still faced another difficult hurdle: all news materials—print articles, film, and still photos—had to undergo censorship before Diem's cable office would transmit them to New York or anywhere else.

The censors were ARVN officers assigned to the psychological warfare branch, and they were so heavy-handed it was almost humorous. News articles had to go through at least three of them, sitting at a long table. Each officer made his cuts, rubber-stamped the story, and passed it to the next officer for more cuts. The general in charge of the censoring said the main goal was to block all references to "the past," which he defined as the Buddhist turmoil. A more candid censor said the policy was simply "to cut out anything they don't like."

All references to gunfire and screams at Xa Loi were excised. The word *raided* was replaced by *searched*. In a Halberstam story that referred to "this troubled country," *troubled* was dropped. Sheehan's three-page story summarizing events at Xa Loi was thrown out in its entirety.

Joseph Fried of the New York *Daily News* managed to score an interview with the always-quotable Madame Nhu. But the Dragon Lady had one condition: that she be allowed to personally edit Fried's story. When she was done, Fried saw that her revisions mostly involved inserting the adjectives *despicable* and *miserable* in front of every reference to Buddhists.

Even stories that made it through the censorial meat grinder piled up at the government telegraph office, unsent. So newsmen resorted to Browne's ruse of smuggling out stories and film with sympathetic pigeons at Tan Son Nhut.

In the days following the pagoda raids, dozens of foreign journalists poured into Saigon. On particularly hot stories, one of them would buy a plane ticket and fly out, his suitcase stuffed with dispatches from his colleagues. Mecklin recalled that one correspondent arrived at the airport just as a jet was taxiing away from the terminal. The man ran onto the tarmac, waving his arms wildly. Realizing what he wanted, the pilot cut his engines, opened his window, caught the packet of news stories tossed up to him, waved goodbye, and took off. According to Mecklin, the censors' biggest impact was to delay outgoing news stories by a few hours.

Halberstam got out a long article that fingered Nhu as having planned and executed the pagoda attacks without the army's knowledge. His story was packaged on the front page of *The New York Times* with a second story, written by one of the paper's Washington correspondents, that said ARVN commanders had persuaded Diem to suppress the Buddhists and declare martial law. In a short explanatory note, *Times* editors described the two stories as "conflicting," but evidently they were both accurate, describing different sides of the same coin.

The generals had indeed sought a state of siege declaration, partly, as Halberstam later learned, as a pretext to bring additional troops into Saigon for a coup. According to General Don, before he and his colleagues could act on their plan to remove monks to their home pagodas, Nhu got the jump on them, sending in Special Forces troops and police for the mass roundup. (The CIA reported Nhu's contrary claim that he had no involvement in the action, although he agreed with it.)

In any event, the regime, in one fell swoop, had jailed most of the protest leaders, destroyed any remaining hopes for amity with the Buddhists, and, for good measure, stuck its thumb squarely in Washington's eye.

HENRY CABOT LODGE LANDED at Tan Son Nhut on the rainy, oppressively hot night of August 22.

Lanky and craggily good-looking, his thick salt-and-pepper hair neatly parted to one side, the new ambassador stepped off his plane wearing a dark suit and holding a straw hat, looking for all the world like a proper Bostonian on a business trip in the tropics. He'd radioed ahead that he didn't want to speak to the press, but nonetheless found himself facing about forty reporters who'd come to the airport in special buses escorted by armed police jeeps, since it was past curfew.

Flashbulbs popped and TV cameras whirred; the arrival of Nolting's replacement was big news in Saigon. Rather than get off to a bad start with the reporters by hurrying wordlessly past them, Lodge stood at the microphones and made a short speech, saying nothing of substance about U.S.–South Vietnam relations, but talking about the importance of a free press in a democracy, and promising to help the newsmen. It was the opening move of a masterful campaign to win over a group of people whose goodwill and indulgence Lodge knew he needed.

Many Americans as well as South Vietnamese assumed Lodge's presence signaled a much tougher, less tolerant U.S. policy toward Diem. If Nolting had been the good cop, Lodge was to be the bad cop. "They have sent us a proconsul," Madame Nhu sniffed at news of Lodge's appointment, adding that he was "on probation" with the regime. Americans in Saigon began sharing a witticism that played on the ages and patrician pedigrees of both the new ambassador and Diem: "Our old mandarin can lick your old mandarin."

A week before he landed in South Vietnam, Lodge visited the Oval Office for a conversation with Kennedy in which the president suggested that the United States might have to get rid of Diem. Much of the exchange was picked up by a hidden taping system the Secret Service had installed so JFK could secretly record his talks with advisers and visitors. From his rocking chair he could reach the taping switch concealed in a bookend on a side table.

"The time may come when we're gonna have to try to do something about Diem, and I think that's going to be an awfully critical period," Kennedy said.

"Oh, yes," Lodge replied.

Kennedy continued: "I don't know how well you're prepared for that out there, or who we would sort of support. . . . I think that's going to be one of your key problems this year. . . . It may be that they ought to go, and it's just a question of how skillfully that's done, and if we get the right fellow."

JFK noted that Diem had resisted both the French and the communists, and "that's a pretty good record." But it might no longer be possible to save him or his government. The president mentioned that he'd asked Forrestal to prepare a report on the extent to which the Buddhist movement was purely religious as opposed to subversively political. Lodge said he thought the Buddhists had experienced discrimination at the regime's hands, but not systematic persecution—much the same sentiments that Nolting had voiced to UPI.

Kennedy warned that "we do have a problem" with American newsmen in Saigon, and Lodge could expect a hard time developing a favorable relationship with them. "The press out there—you know how they can get in those places," the president said. "They feel they're trying to do a job because they're trying to get rid of, they're carrying out a political action to get rid of Diem, because they would argue that's the only way they can win."

He mentioned Halberstam's story in that morning's *Times* saying the war in the delta wasn't going well. Most reporters, Kennedy said, were liberal-minded and instinctively opposed to authoritarians like Diem. But he didn't want U.S. policy toward South Vietnam being "made for us by a couple of smart, young reporters." Lodge assured him that he had a plan for winning over the newsmen.

Kennedy didn't want to move against Diem until he could be "sure that there is somebody who would be better than [him]." He also told Lodge: "I think we have to leave it almost completely in your hands and your judgment. I don't know whether we'd be better off, if the alternative would be better. Maybe it will be. If so, maybe we have to move in that direction. But I think I'd take a good look at it before I'd come to that conclusion. . . . I just figure we don't want to get carried away until you've had a good chance to look at it."

While he admired Diem to some extent, Kennedy couldn't contain his dislike for "this bitch" Madame Nhu. "Is she a lesbian or what?" he demanded of Lodge. “She seems awfully masculine.” Lodge averred that she probably was gay.

Lodge had recently discussed Madame with her parents, the Chuongs, who said their daughter had “always been violent” and “not stupid, but crazy.” Nhu and Diem let her speak her mind, no matter who she offended, because they agreed with her views, the Chuongs asserted. They added that their daughter, her husband, and Diem were dangerously out of touch with the real situation in their country. If they didn’t leave South Vietnam soon, the Chuongs said, there was “no power on earth” that could prevent them from being assassinated, given all the arbitrary arrests, imprisonments, and executions they’d inflicted on their countrymen.

They urged Lodge to persuade their daughter to get out while she still could.

LODGE TURNED HIS FIRST full day in Saigon into an unmistakable show of support for the Buddhists.

Security forces had seized Quang Duc’s iconic heart during the raid on Xa Loi. But two monks carrying some of his ashes in a small urn managed to scamper over a back wall, landing outside a building that housed the U.S. economic aid agency. They requested and were granted asylum. The regime wanted the fugitives turned over to police, but the embassy refused. In a deliberate slap at Diem and Nhu, Lodge paid an ostentatious visit to the two monks, asking how they were and if they had enough to eat.

The new ambassador wasted little time in wooing the journalists he regarded as the most important in Vietnam: Halberstam, Sheehan, and Browne.

Within a week, he’d invited each of them to lunch with him and his lively wife, Emily, at the ambassadorial residence. He flattered the newsmen by seeking their advice on how to handle Diem and Nhu, and seemed to share their distaste for the regime.

Browne liked him right away. “Unlike his predecessors and most of the other Americans guiding Viet Nam policy, Lodge spoke bluntly and honestly, and newsmen rarely if ever felt they were being misled by him,” the

AP bureau chief later wrote. Lodge passed on the pleasing tidbit that JFK had a copy of Browne's photo of the burning monk on his Oval Office desk. (He subsequently did Browne a valuable favor, writing a preface for his 1965 Vietnam book, *The New Face of War.*)

Halberstam liked Lodge's newsman-like skepticism, writing approvingly that he "didn't believe anything that the [South Vietnamese] government said, nor much of what the U.S. military said."

With his many years of experience in big-city journalism as well as big-league politics, Lodge knew all the tricks of petting the press.

He was always available to talk. While he had a reputation for haughtiness and rudeness, he never acted that way toward journalists. He solicited their ideas, fed them newsy morsels, and treated them as equals. Unlike Nolting, he never lectured or argued with them. By insisting they had better sources than he did, he made them purr. "The ambassador's on our side," a top AP executive gushed to Arnett after Lodge obligingly let the executive and three other newsmen hitch a ride on his government plane from Tokyo to Saigon, the last leg of his flight from the United States to his new job.

Mecklin said admiringly that Lodge converted newsmen into his "disciples." Another American official, a Nolting fan, put it differently, labeling them Lodge's patsies. In any event, the new envoy began to receive much better treatment from the press than the old.

THERE'S A HOARY AXIOM in American politics and government: Never waste a good crisis. Almost as soon as news of the pagoda blitz broke, Hilsman, Harriman, and Forrestal set out to take advantage of the ensuing political tumult.

The day he returned to Washington from Honolulu, Hilsman convened a meeting with Forrestal; William Colby, who'd risen to become the CIA's Far East division chief; and General Victor Krulak, the Joint Chiefs of Staff's counterinsurgency specialist, asking them "how we might exploit the situation." At that point, who was running the South Vietnamese government was an open question. Was Diem still in charge, or had the military seized power under the cloak of martial law? Had Nhu somehow taken over?

No one knew for sure. Krulak said it was imperative to find out and also to get Madame Nhu out of the country. Hilsman agreed and told Colby to "bend every effort" to determine Nhu's power position as well as Diem's relationship with the military.

In Saigon, CIA agents, embassy political officers, and U.S. military men reached out to their contacts. Information flooded in, much of it contradictory. Some sources said Diem was still firmly in charge; others claimed Nhu had pushed his brother aside. Posters of Nhu appeared on walls and in government offices; radio broadcasts referred to him as a "beloved" leader. But there was no clear consensus, and the CIA informed Kennedy on August 24: "We cannot determine as yet who is calling the shots in Saigon—Diem or the Nhus."

There were other questions as well. Who exactly ordered the raids, and who carried them out? Initial broadcasts on the government-funded Voice of America radio network said the operation was carried out by the ARVN. But that wasn't the case, as the CIA learned from General Don.

Don told his old friend Lucien Conein that the ARVN hadn't been aware of the pagoda invasions until after the Special Forces and police launched them. He himself hadn't known until a call came over his command radio that the Xa Loi roundup was underway. The generals, he explained, asked Diem to declare martial law and proposed removing visiting monks from Saigon. But within hours, Nhu's shock troops hit the pagodas, employing iron-fist tactics that made even army commanders recoil.

Many South Vietnamese were furious about the incursions; Don was upset that the ARVN was being blamed for them. He cited the Voice of America broadcasts and said the radio network should make it clear that Nhu's legions were the responsible party, not the army.

Don didn't say who'd ordered the onslaught, but he noted that the Special Forces were under the joint control of Diem and Nhu. There was speculation in Washington that the brothers timed the move to take place during the changeover of U.S. ambassadors, the better to crush the Buddhists without interference from the Americans. It was also suggested that the palace wanted to pin the operation on the ARVN in order to taint it in Washington's eyes. That way, if the Americans ever began to think seriously about overthrowing Diem, the generals would be politically less attractive as allies.

But it was Nhu who was really in Hilsman's crosshairs. He'd long been a source of irritation and embarrassment to the U.S. government, and Hilsman wanted him gone.

Shortly after the pagoda raids, Hilsman met with his staff and announced confidently that Nhu had organized them, adding: "We just can't stand for this." When a subordinate pointed out that it wasn't clear at that point who the culprit was, Hilsman replied, with a "shit-eating smile" on his face, "If it isn't true, then let's make it true."

With Nhu in power, South Vietnam was doomed, Hilsman believed. Nhu's proclivity for repression would eventually turn the people against the government, dragging it into "ignominy and disaster" along with its ally, the United States. Diem's aide, Thuan, told an American official that Nhu had tricked the generals, who didn't know about the pagoda strikes in advance, but were taking the fall for them. Nhu was now in "a dangerously triumphant mood" and "contemptuous of the Americans," believing himself "in full control of the situation."

Whatever they did, Thuan warned, the Americans mustn't acquiesce in Nhu's actions.

Hilsman received a phone call after the raids from Admiral Harry Felt, commander in chief of U.S. forces in the Pacific and Harkins's direct superior. Felt told Hilsman: "Roger, I hope you do what is necessary. We've got to stop this thing. You've got to persuade people in Washington to effect a change in government out there."

Hilsman also claimed that two unnamed Vietnamese generals contacted the embassy, saying they believed Nhu planned to kill them and "make a deal with Hanoi and sell out the whole country." If the generals moved first against Nhu, what would the U.S. government's attitude be? They wanted an answer right away. Hilsman decided to act.

ON SATURDAY, AUGUST 24, in his office at the State Department, Hilsman drafted one of the most fateful directives of the Vietnam War, a message to Lodge that came to be known as "the green light cable."

"US government cannot tolerate situation in which power lies in Nhu's hands," Hilsman wrote. "Diem must be given chance to rid himself of Nhu and his coterie and replace them with best military and political personalities available." The embassy was to inform South Vietnamese military and civilian leaders that if Nhu and his wife weren't axed, Washington "would find it impossible" to extend further military and economic support to South Vietnam.

Diem should be given a "reasonable opportunity to remove Nhus," Hilsman went on, but if he refused, "we are prepared to accept the obvious implication that we can no longer support Diem." The cable also instructed Lodge to tell Diem's generals that Washington would give them "direct support in any interim period of breakdown" of Diem's government.

The new ambassador—in Saigon barely two days—was further told to "urgently examine all possible alternative leadership and make detailed plans as to how we might bring about Diem's replacement if this should become necessary." Lodge should work with Harkins to protect American citizens during "this operation." Hilsman closed by assuring Lodge that "we will back you to the hilt on actions you take to achieve our objectives."

Thus, with a single telegram, Hilsman laid the groundwork for a complete reversal of nearly a decade of American policy toward Vietnam. On the strength of no authority but his own, he moved to pull the rug out from under a longtime anti-communist ally during wartime.

Worse, he did so in pursuit of a chimera. U.S. diplomats had been telling Washington for years that as corrosive as Nhu's presence was, he and his brother were Siamese twins who could never be separated. Nolting's predecessor, Elbridge Durbrow, urged Diem in 1960 to appoint Nhu as an ambassador and send him into comfortable, semipermanent exile abroad. Diem ignored him. He and his brother were bonded not only by blood, but by past triumphs and a shared vision for the future of their country.

Nhu was Diem's right-hand man, the cutthroat executor of his policies. He headed the crucial strategic hamlet program, ran the secret police, and oversaw the Republican Youth, all key pillars of strength for the regime. Nhu functioned as his brother's big thinker, writing his speeches and coming up with personalism as the regime's official ideology.

To Diem, resisting foreign pressure was an art form. Getting him to ship his indispensable brother out of South Vietnam had as much chance of success as persuading JFK to send his brother and right-hand man, Robert, to the moon. (Recognizing this sibling parallel, some Americans called Nhu "Bobby Nhu.")

The green light cable didn't directly order Lodge to foment a coup. But by imposing an unattainable condition on Diem, and encouraging his generals to turn against him when he failed to meet it, Hilsman's instruction set in motion a series of events that culminated in the president's overthrow and brutal murder nine weeks later.

AS SOON AS THE green light cable was drafted, Hilsman and his bureaucratic allies set out to ram it through the government's interdepartmental clearance process without nearly as much top-level scrutiny as it needed.

On that late-summer weekend, much of official Washington was on vacation or otherwise out of town. Kennedy was with his family in Hyannis Port, mourning his prematurely born son Patrick, who'd died at a Boston hospital on August 9, after less than two days of life. Secretary of Defense Robert McNamara was climbing the Grand Teton mountains in Wyoming. Secretary of State Dean Rusk was in New York meeting with UN officials and taking in a Yankees game. CIA director John McCone was yachting in Puget Sound. McGeorge Bundy, JFK's national security assistant, was at his vacation home in Manchester-by-the-Sea, Massachusetts.

Hilsman took the draft telegram to Harriman, his immediate superior, for approval, and they brought it to Forrestal. Forrestal telephoned George Ball, the acting secretary of state in Rusk's absence, and relayed the message to him. Then Forrestal sent a copy over the secure White House communications system to JFK in Hyannis Port.

In a memo earlier that day, Forrestal told the president "it is now quite certain" that Nhu is "calling the shots"—even though the CIA was reporting that it was unclear who was in charge in Saigon. Forrestal added: "Averell and Roger now agree that we must move before the situation in Saigon freezes." When Forrestal later sent Kennedy the text of the green light cable, he again nudged the president to act quickly, writing in a cover memo: "Since the situation in Saigon may not remain fluid for long, [the State] Department believes desirable transmit this message tonight."

Forrestal next called Roswell Gilpatric, McNamara's second-in-command, at his farm on Maryland's Eastern Shore. Immediately suspicious of how the cable was being handled, Gilpatric had Forrestal read it to him twice. He realized the message was "highly controversial" and figured the anti-Diem clique was trying to rush it through at a time when top officials who might object were gone.

"I frankly thought it was an end run," Gilpatric recalled. "I didn't see why it had to be done Saturday night with the president away, with Rusk away, with McNamara away, Bundy away." But Gilpatric raised no show-stopper objections to the cable, seeing it as a political matter more in the State Department's bailiwick than the Pentagon's.

Forrestal then turned to Krulak, who was in Forrestal's White House office as he made the clearance calls. Forrestal asked him to deliver a copy of the cable to General Maxwell Taylor, who JFK had made chairman of the Joint Chiefs of Staff in October 1962. Krulak hurried away.

Kennedy called Forrestal, saying, "I want to talk to George Ball and Harriman about this telegram. Where are they?" Forrestal said he'd find them. Ball, it turned out, was playing golf in Potomac, Maryland. As he finished up the ninth hole, Harriman and Hilsman "appeared in a great sweat" and drove Ball to his home, where he got on the phone with the president to go over the cable.

"He asked me what I really thought," Ball remembered. "I had told him that Averell and Hilsman very much wanted to do this. I had made some changes in the telegram; I had watered it down myself, actually, over their earlier version. I read him the critical paragraphs. I told him that this would certainly be taken as encouragement by the generals to [mount] a coup. But I said I thought that, in my judgment, the situation with Diem was becoming an enormous humiliation to the United States, that we were supporting a regime which was behaving in the most unconscionable and cruel, uncivilized way toward a significant minority of the population. Madame Nhu was making the most outrageous statements, and Nhu was a very devious and unreliable fellow. I thought to send this telegram to Lodge, who'd just arrived there, was probably all right. So [Kennedy] approved it."

At about 7 p.m., Forrestal got in touch again with Krulak, asking him if he'd shown the cable to Taylor. Forrestal recalled Krulak replying that Taylor had reviewed the text and "it's all right with him if everybody else is in agreement." Forrestal checked again with Kennedy, who gave his final sign-off.

The cable was transmitted to Saigon at 8:11 p.m.

But Krulak gave a different account, saying he wasn't able to show the message to Taylor until about 9:45 p.m., after it had already been sent to Lodge. Taylor, who opposed ousting Diem, read the text and commented to Krulak that it reflected "the well-known compulsion of Hilsman and Forrestal to depose Diem."

Taylor added that he was glad he wasn't on the receiving end of the instruction, since it was so vague, and more thought should have been put into drafting it. He later complained that Hilsman, Harriman, and Forrestal had executed "an egregious end run" around the usual vetting process.

Hilsman subsequently insisted that the green light cable was properly cleared with Kennedy and other Washington principals. But some top officials said they'd been hustled rather than consulted. After Hilsman asserted that he'd discussed the message with Marshall Carter, the CIA's acting director in McCone's absence, Carter "took angry exception," saying he never saw the text before it was sent to Saigon. In a 1967 memorandum, Carter branded the message "ill-conceived, ill-timed, and inadequately coordinated."

Nevertheless, in a matter of hours, the Kennedy administration had made a decision, after years of full-throated U.S. support for Diem, that could trigger a revolt against him. Kennedy and his men had given little if any consideration to important questions raised by the green light cable. If Diem were deposed, who or what would replace him? Would the new government be an improvement over the present one? Would it have the support of the people and the ability to prosecute the war any more effectively?

IN SAIGON, TROOPS, ARMORED vehicles, machine guns, and bayonets were in evidence everywhere, especially along the approaches to Gia Long Palace. Government radio blared that the Viet Cong were preparing to infiltrate marches and demonstrations and instigate violence. Soldiers put up posters urging the public to support the army and the regime. Nhu's blue-suited Republican Youths paraded through slum neighborhoods, warning that anyone participating in anti-government activities faced arrest.

Some citizens expressed their rancor anyway, tearing down pro-regime posters. On August 24, about a thousand students at the University of Saigon law school gave thunderous applause to Diem's foreign minister, Vu Van Mau, who'd quit following the pagoda raids. Furious students ejected plainclothes police who tried to photograph a protest meeting at the university's medical school. When the cops arrested three U.S. newsmen covering the students, Lodge, without waiting to hear details of the incident, went to the Foreign Ministry and complained to the highest official he could find.

But Diem and Nhu still held powerful levers of repression and control.

General Dinh, Saigon's strutting military governor, promptly closed the university and all secondary schools in the city following the student mass meetings. On Sunday, August 25, police, paratroopers, and marines swarmed into the university neighborhood and arrested more than one thousand students, knocking some off their bicycles as they pedaled by.

Those arrested were shoved into trucks marked with the distinctive handshake emblem of the U.S. aid program. Male arrestees' records were checked to see if they were eligible for the draft. Some students later rushed into a public square near the central market and unfurled anti-government banners. Police closed in and began fighting with them as cars, scooters, and cyclo-pousses whizzed by. Shots were fired and a young woman, a third-year pharmacy student, was killed. Several hundred people were arrested.

In Hue, police went door-to-door that day, ordering residents to show up for a rally staged by the regime's mass political party, the National Revolutionary Movement. Some thirty thousand people dutifully trudged to an assembly area on the banks of the Perfume River. Attendance was mandatory, with police checking people's names off a list. Pro-Diem speakers claimed that the pagodas were entered because Buddhist leaders were being "used by [the] VC." Consul Helble reported that the crowd remained impassive throughout the event, as four armored personnel carriers stood watch nearby.

But the student outbursts were a threatening omen for the regime. Traditionally, South Vietnam's college and secondary school pupils were quiescent and apolitical, concerned mostly with getting good grades and graduating. Now they were fighting cops in the streets and vowing to take up leadership of the Buddhist movement on behalf of jailed monks and nuns.

Hammering on his typewriter after the mass arrests, Halberstam produced yet another page one story for the next day's *Times*. "It is clear," he wrote, "that the Government has lost the youth of the country." Such sweeping pronunciamentos were one of the brash young journalist's trademarks, but this one seemed close to the mark.

HILSMAN HAD ONE MORE piece of unfinished business that climactic weekend.

He was anxious to convince South Vietnamese as well as Americans that it was Nhu's minions—Special Forces and police—that carried out the devastating pagoda raids, not the ARVN. Since Nhu had disguised some of his men as regular soldiers, and Voice of America initially pinned the raids on the army, many Vietnamese associated the ARVN with the brutal takedown of the monks and nuns. If the generals were now to execute a coup and take over the government, they needed public support. And for that, they clearly needed an image cleanup.

Hoping to plant a useful news story, Hilsman called UPI's State Department reporter, Stewart Hensley, at home. The U.S. government, Hilsman said, was convinced that Nhu, not the generals, was responsible for storming the pagodas. Hilsman's game plan was to instruct Voice of America editors to pick up Hensley's story when it hit the wire and broadcast it in South Vietnam, where VOA had a large listenership as one of the few credible sources of news in the country.

As any good journalist would, Hensley pushed Hilsman to say what next steps the Kennedy administration might take in South Vietnam. For instance, would it reduce U.S. aid as an expression of its strong disapproval of the pagoda forays? Hilsman said no such decision had been made, and it would be better if Hensley didn't speculate in his article. But Hensley argued that he had a responsibility to lay out Washington's possible courses of action in such an important foreign policy matter, and Hilsman had to agree.

The assistant secretary of state hoped to avoid any problems by telling Voice of America editors to make sure only the portion of Hensley's story that exonerated the ARVN reached South Vietnamese ears. Any speculation about possible aid cuts was absolutely *not* to be aired.

But, as Hilsman ruefully acknowledged later, "something went wrong."

CHAPTER 13

"WE HAVE TO MAKE THIS WORK"

AS HE ATE breakfast on Monday, August 26, John Mecklin, the embassy press officer, listened to the English-language Voice of America newscast. For the next few minutes, he was transfixed. When the program ended, he grabbed the phone to call a member of his staff.

"Did you hear that?" Mecklin blurted. He told his subordinate to get hold of a transcript of the broadcast and meet him at Lodge's residence.

Lodge was scheduled to present his ambassadorial credentials to Diem later that morning. Gathered at his home were eight or nine U.S. officials who were going with him to Gia Long Palace, including Trueheart, Harkins, and Richardson. The civilians were dressed in white protocolaire suits for the ceremonial occasion; Harkins wore a dazzling white dress uniform. The VOA transcript arrived as the men sat around a coffee table.

Lodge began reading it, becoming upset as his eyes moved down the page.

Most of the broadcast presented no problems. The VOA news anchor had said that Special Forces and secret police carried out the pagoda raids, not the ARVN. The army had "agreed to the imposition of martial law" in hopes of ending the Buddhist turmoil. (The broadcast didn't mention that the generals had *proposed* martial law and had their own plan to eject dissident monks from Saigon.) Nhu had disguised some of his men as ARVN soldiers, VOA said, while others wore the blue uniforms of the Republican Youth. Near the end was the line that had alarmed Mecklin:

"American officials indicated the U.S. may sharply reduce its aid to Vietnam unless President Diem gets rid of secret police officials responsible for the attacks."

This was precisely the speculation that Hilsman told VOA not to put on the air. Lodge clearly hadn't known of it in advance. Now, just hours before he was to meet Diem for the first time, the new ambassador's government had publicly slapped the South Vietnamese leader with an ultimatum: cast out your brother or face possible loss of the American aid that largely holds your country together. It wouldn't be hard for Diem's domestic enemies to read between the lines that Washington was finally ready to toss him overboard. And such a reading could touch off a revolt and a great deal of bloodshed.

Lodge tossed the transcript on the table. The newscast couldn't have come at a more awkward moment. "Jack Kennedy would never approve of doing things this way," he said. "This certainly isn't his way of running a government."

Besides complicating his job, Lodge was concerned that the VOA report could put him in physical danger as well. Diem might simply cancel the palace ceremony in a fit of pique. But what if Diem and Nhu did something crazy, like grabbing the Americans as hostages? That scenario was highly unlikely, but Lodge was prepared to believe almost anything about Diem. He turned to Harkins.

"Paul, perhaps you better not come," he said. "If they try any funny business, it might be better if one of us were on the outside."

Hilsman was horrified that VOA had failed to follow his instructions. Dean Rusk quickly cabled Lodge an apology, pledging that Washington wouldn't do or say anything else "which would catch you by surprise or make your formidable task more difficult."

Despite the radio broadcast, the traditional diplomatic ritual went off smoothly at Gia Long. Lodge presented a letter of introduction signed by Kennedy and chatted amiably with Diem for about fifteen minutes.

WITHIN HOURS OF SHAKING Diem's hand, however, Lodge and his new subordinates were discussing how to execute the green light cable.

Although the message didn't explicitly mention a coup, the ambassador interpreted it as "an order to overthrow the government," according to Richardson. JFK had warned Lodge that Washington might decide to move against Diem, and the green light cable seemed to be the next step. It was certainly a momentous step for someone who was brand-new to South Vietnam. Yet Lodge didn't ask his more experienced Saigon colleagues whether they thought driving Diem out of the palace was a good idea or a bad idea, and what consequences might flow from it.

The green light cable directed that Diem be given a "reasonable opportunity" to unload the Nhus, but Lodge didn't want to do that. Demanding their banishment yet again was futile, he believed, and might even alert Diem and Nhu that an uprising against them was afoot. Instead, the ambassador wanted to bypass the president and go directly to the generals, who the green light cable all but invited to carry out a coup. When he asked the State Department for permission to skip Diem, it was promptly granted in a return cable from Hilsman, Harriman, and Ball. No one bothered to consult Kennedy about this abrupt change of plan, which made a coup more likely to happen sooner rather than later.

Lodge also decided that the Americans' "official hands should not show" as they reached out to the generals. Rather than have Harkins or Richardson make the contacts, Lodge assigned the job to CIA agents Lucien Conein, a familiar face to ARVN brass, and Alfonso Spera, known for his skill at tapping telephones.

The Americans couldn't be sure which generals might be receptive and which wouldn't. Attempting to overthrow Diem was, of course, a delicate and dangerous business. Anyone who tried and failed could easily find himself in a torture room at the Saigon Zoo or with a bullet in the back of his head. With Nhu's spies seeded throughout the South Vietnamese military, an incautious American feeler could be hazardous to a general's health.

William Colby, the CIA's Far East director, told the Saigon station the agency's leadership hadn't been consulted about the green light cable before it was sent. Nonetheless, he advised Richardson that the CIA "must fully accept directives of policy makers and seek ways [to] accomplish objectives they seek," even though the cable "appears be throwing away bird in hand before we have adequately identified birds in bush, or songs they may sing." That was his oblique way of criticizing the shortsightedness of pushing Diem overboard before an acceptable replacement had been found.

Richardson suggested two generals to be contacted initially. One was Nguyen Khanh, who commanded the ARVN's II Corps and its four infantry divisions in the Central Highlands. A bantam figure with darting eyes who sported a goatee and a paratrooper's red beret, the thirty-six-year-old Khanh was regarded by many Americans as the best of South Vietnam's nineteen generals; some of his ARVN peers considered him a mercurial opportunist.

Richardson's other pick was Tran Thien Khiem, a silent, humorless man—"an inscrutable sort of a fellow," as John McCone described him—who served as General Don's deputy on the ARVN's Joint General Staff. A Catholic and Can Lao Party member, Khiem also was Diem's godson. As a colonel during the 1960 paratrooper revolt, he rushed tanks and troops from the Mekong Delta into Saigon to rescue Diem. But he'd developed a deep antipathy toward Nhu. Although the thirty-seven-year-old Khiem had no troops under his command, he was well situated in the ARVN hierarchy to coordinate action against Diem with other high-ranking officers.

CONEIN SWIFTLY PAID A visit to Khiem. The embassy had drawn up a list of conditions the generals had to adhere to if they wanted U.S. support, and Conein conveyed them to Khiem. First and foremost, the Nhus had to go, although it was up to the generals whether they wanted to keep Diem in some sort of figurehead role after they took over the government. Arrested monks and other protesters must be promptly released, and the generals must fully implement the June peace agreement with the Buddhists. If the Nhus remained in power and the Buddhist situation was not redressed as Washington wanted, American military and economic aid would end.

The generals would be on their own when they went up against Diem and his loyal troops; the Americans wouldn't bail them out if they seemed to be losing. Bloodshed was to be kept to an "absolute minimum" and, after the coup, the generals must work closely with Americans to prosecute the war.

Khiem replied that the generals agreed to the conditions. He warned Conein against approaching General Don, since Nhu agents were embedded in his staff. Khiem also told Conein that a jeep would pick him up shortly and take him to see General Duong Van Minh—Big Minh—who was soon to emerge as the coup leader.

Minh had disturbing news for Conein: Nhu planned to take over the government in the "next three days." He was forcing Diem's cabinet members to resign and had gotten his other brother, Ngo Dinh Can, "under control." (Can was later reported to be under house arrest in Hue.) Nhu's actions, said Minh, were likely to trigger a popular rebellion against the government.

Meanwhile, Spera flew to the Central Highlands to speak with General Khanh at his field headquarters in Pleiku.

Khanh was less than enthusiastic about a coup. Referring to the bungled VOA broadcast, he said he hoped the United States halted its aid and Diem was forced to dump Nhu, eliminating the need for a military takeover. "My impression [is] he much prefers it that way," Spera reported. Khanh also asked whether Washington would guarantee the generals' families a safe haven and financial support if an anti-Diem revolt failed. Khanh had a wife and four children, "no money stashed away," and wanted an immediate reply to his questions. To Spera, the general seemed "caught off base by our timing" and unsure what to do.

Conein saw Khiem again the next day. Khiem had important information: a committee of generals had met and decided to stage a coup within a week.

As one of their first acts, they planned to kill Colonel Tung, the Special Forces commander, and "destroy . . . his entire encampment" at the Long Thanh training center outside Saigon. Conein promised to give Khiem a list of all the weapons available to Tung's men at the camp. Khiem and his fellow rebels also planned to "neutralize" two other Diem loyalists: General Dinh, Saigon's military governor, and General Huynh Van Cao, the IV Corps commander who presided over the Ap Bac debacle.

The rebel generals planned to install as their new head of state Diem's vice president, Tho, who knew of the coup plan and favored it. Khiem warned Conein not to contact Big Minh again, explaining that his position was too precarious.

ON THE SAME DAY that Lodge met Diem, a procession of cars departed from the South Vietnamese Foreign Ministry, escorted by police and bound for the airport.

In one car sat Vu Van Mau, Diem's foreign minister, who'd embarrassed the regime by resigning and shaving his head, monk-style, as a protest against the pagoda raids. Trailing his vehicle were cars bearing other Foreign Ministry officials. Mau was scheduled to fly to India, where he planned to go on a pilgrimage. Western diplomats and newsmen were at Tan Son Nhut to see him off.

But the officials following Mau's car were unable to keep pace with it, and Mau disappeared in traffic. He didn't arrive at the airport and police removed his luggage from the airliner.

Some of his well-wishers assumed the worst. "Hitlerian gangsterism," a waiting diplomat remarked in disgust to a journalist.

IN WASHINGTON, ELEVEN HOURS behind Saigon, the members of Kennedy's National Security Council gathered at the White House on August 26 to review the weekend's chaotic events. With the generals supposedly poised to move, the noon meeting in the Cabinet Room marked the start of a series of daily emergency sessions on Vietnam that resembled the tense, top-level conferences held during the Cuban Missile Crisis the previous year.

While the president had signed off on the green light cable, he knew it was drafted and sent precipitously; he was upset that he'd been pushed too hard and too fast by his subordinates.

"He passed it off too quickly over a weekend at the Cape," Robert Kennedy recalled. "He had thought it was cleared by McNamara and Taylor and everyone at State. In fact, it was Harriman, Hilsman, and Forrestal at the White House, and they were the ones who were strongly for a coup." The president admitted that the message to Lodge "was a major mistake on his part," his brother said.

Prior to the meeting, JFK had discussed the cable with Robert, who in turn discussed it with McNamara and Taylor, who both expressed disapproval of the way it was handled. Despite his qualms, the president didn't cancel it.

Like the Oval Office, the Cabinet Room was wired to secretly record conversations. The switch for the taping system was underneath the long conference table, directly in front of JFK's chair. The president flipped it on as Hilsman delivered an update on the CIA's initial contacts with the generals and predicted "some snowballing" of public anger against Diem as a result of the mass arrests of university students.

Kennedy told his men he didn't want his support for the insurgent generals to look like capitulation to media pressure. He claimed that Halberstam was "running almost a political campaign" to bring down Diem with critical news articles. Halberstam's coverage, he said, reminded him of another *New York Times* reporter, Herbert L. Matthews, who helped to undermine Cuban dictator Fulgencio Batista with his fawning coverage of Fidel Castro in the 1950s.

"When we move to eliminate a government, we want to be sure we're not doing it because *The New York Times* is excited about it," JFK said.

"We're not, sir. We're not, sir," Hilsman assured him.

"They're just not right very often," Kennedy groused.

"And they've been wrong in this situation continuously," replied Hilsman.

Taylor said the generals would have trouble pulling off a coup, partly because Diem and Nhu had divided authority over combat troops in the Saigon area among several of them. But Hilsman pressed for a military takeover without delay.

He related the phone call he'd gotten from Admiral Felt, the U.S. Pacific forces commander. Felt believed that unless the Nhus were removed, many mid-level ARVN officers and noncommissioned officers "would just lay down their arms and go home," Hilsman said. Felt realized a coup was dangerous, but thought delaying it was even more dangerous.

When Kennedy asked Taylor, based on his Pentagon experience, what chance the rebel generals had of prevailing, the Joint Chiefs chairman replied that "in Washington we would not turn over the problem of choosing a head of state to the military"—a remark that set off guffaws from other men in the room. Hilsman told the president that the embassy was making "every effort" to learn more about the generals' plans.

THE DISCUSSION MOVED ON to who might replace Diem as South Vietnam's leader. The State Department was examining various alternatives but, Hilsman said, "they're not pretty." One possibility was that the generals would boot the Nhus but keep Diem. Another was that the military would set up a junta and name Vice President Tho as head of state. (Under South Vietnam's constitution Tho was next in the line of succession after Diem.) In that scenario, Tho would serve as a constitutional fig leaf—"a front man," as Hilsman put it—for the generals, who'd hold the real power.

McNamara objected sharply to Tho, who he described as "completely unacceptable" as the post-coup president. "We have our prestige, we have our troops committed there, and it seems to me we ought to have some voice in the man to replace Diem," said the defense chief. "We put a weak man in there, and we'd be in real trouble. And Tho . . . from what little I know, is really quite unacceptable because he's too weak, he has no political base, no power to control anything." Moreover, McNamara said, a government run by generals who'd never governed before was likely to engender serious criticism in the United States, especially among liberals in Congress and the press.

When JFK asked what would happen if the coup failed and Washington still had to deal with Diem and Nhu, Hilsman replied: "It's pretty horrible to contemplate, sir. Nhu is basically anti-American. There's an element of emotional unstability here." But Rusk insisted that if the regime's repressiveness was allowed to continue, "we're on the road to disaster." At some point, he said, Washington would face two unappealing choices: either withdraw from Vietnam or commit "such forces as would involve our taking over the country."

Hilsman made one last emotional pitch for action against the Ngos. Without it, he said, the South Vietnamese people would turn against the United States: "Now this is what you get everywhere from the people in the streets. The [arrested] students in the trucks were yelling at the Americans, 'It's up to you now. We've done our part. It's up to you.'" Monks, nuns, and students kept coming into the embassy, risking arrest as they pleaded for American help, Hilsman said. "The only blame that's attached to the United States, so far and throughout, is, when are you going to make up your minds? They expect us to correct the situation. . . . If we fail to act, then we'll get blame."

Kennedy directed the State Department to prepare biographies on the coup generals and other key personalities in Saigon. He wanted to meet again the next day for further discussions, and asked that Nolting be present to answer his questions.

Acutely aware of Nolting's avid support for Diem, Hilsman tried to undercut the ex-ambassador, asserting that he was "very deeply involved, emotionally" and "deeply shocked over the past few days because he felt that Diem has doubled crossed him." Kennedy wanted Nolting in the room nevertheless.

JFK didn't lose his usual composure as the ill-conceived green light cable was discussed. But, watching the meeting unfold, McNamara's deputy, Roswell Gilpatric, sensed the president's annoyance.

In pushing through the message to Lodge, a handful of underlings had effectively hijacked his Vietnam policy, steering it in a direction fraught with uncertainty and, as would soon become apparent, creating volatile divisions in the top ranks of his administration. The cable also limited Kennedy's ability to back away from a coup, since if he now broke the U.S. pledge to help the generals, they'd never again trust Washington, making collaboration with them in the war more difficult.

"It was perfectly evident to us as we left the meeting," Gilpatric recalled, "that he was not pleased with this particular performance of his advisers in State, Defense, and on his own staff."

Gilpatric was right. "This shit has got to stop!" Kennedy exploded privately at Forrestal, who he blamed for overreaching his authority and creating the weekend mess. Distraught, Forrestal went to Harriman, his mentor, and said he thought he should resign. But Harriman told him to "quit being a god-damned fool" and "get back to work." When Forrestal nonetheless told Kennedy he was prepared to leave, the president snapped: "You're not worth firing. You owe me something, so stick around."

Robert Kennedy thought McGeorge Bundy bore some of the fault as well, saying the national security assistant "wasn't particularly helpful." Bundy later noted dryly the lesson he learned: "Never do business on the weekend."

FEARING THAT JFK MIGHT ultimately turn against a coup, Hilsman telephoned Harriman on August 27 to talk strategy before that day's White House conference got underway.

Harriman asked if some of the president's advisers "were getting cold feet." Hilsman said he thought he could "bring Nolting around," but that he was "afraid of Max Taylor." Urging Harriman to attend the upcoming meeting with the president, Hilsman anxiously insisted: "We have to make this work."

But Nolting remained firmly in Diem's corner despite the pagoda raids and their fallout.

On his first day back at the State Department after returning from Saigon, he found a letter from Kennedy praising his "significant contribution for strengthening the relations between the Governments and peoples of the United States and Viet-Nam." Shortly after reading it, he got a call from a White House press aide, who asked him not to release the letter publicly. The aide explained: "The president would find it awkward and embarrassing because of his references to the close relations you established between the Government of South Vietnam and the United States."

That same day, visiting Hilsman, Nolting read the green light cable for the first time and interpreted it as "a plot . . . to overthrow the constitutional government of President Diem." When he stopped in at Harriman's office to say hello, the Crocodile yelled: "Get out!"

Meeting with Kennedy and his advisers in the Cabinet Room on August 27, Nolting declared his profound misgivings about a coup. In his slow, stentorian, southern-gentleman voice, he said none of the rebel generals possessed "the guts or the sangfroid or the drive of either Diem or Nhu." Moreover, he said, the generals were divided and lacked sufficient forces to knock over the regime.

JFK asked whether the South Vietnamese president had ever explained why he broke his promise to make peace with the Buddhists. Nolting replied that he regarded Diem as a man of integrity who kept, or at least tried to keep, his promises. He pointed out that Diem had tried to abide by Washington's wishes to uproot Madame Nhu, appealing to the Australian ambassador to invite her for an extended stay in his country.

But with monks burning, street demonstrations multiplying, and military leaders pleading for a crackdown, Diem apparently decided that conciliation wasn't working and force had to be used. When Kennedy wanted to know why the regime had acted with such harshness toward the Buddhists, Nolting speculated that Nhu ordered the raids, but not the brutality; the Special Forces and police got "jittery and smash[ed] things up."

JFK peppered Nolting with questions about the Nhus. Why, the president inquired, with all the trouble Madame stirred up, had there been "no effort to take control of her?" Nolting said multiple attempts had been made, the most recent being Diem's initiative to ship her to Australia. But, he added, "she's a strong-willed woman" who was not "under anyone's domination." (Nolting evidently didn't know that a few days earlier Diem had finally ordered her "to make no public statements and give no press conferences," according to his chief of staff, Thuan.)

Kennedy asked whether Nhu was "anti-American," as Hilsman claimed, but Nolting said he viewed him as "pro-Vietnamese." The ex-ambassador summed up Nhu as a "schizophrenic personality" who wasn't a liar but who "rationalizes changes to the point that he can't tell the difference." While Nolting didn't want Nhu to acquire any more power, neither did he believe the political counselor was trying to take over the government. The brothers would never abandon one another, he said. If the generals went after Nhu, Diem "would go down with him."

The president also wanted Nolting's views on whether the momentum of the war effort could be kept up under Diem and Nhu. Nolting replied that Washington should go "slow and easy" for a few weeks and see what developed. It was quite possible, he said, that Nhu's "brutal surgical operation" on the Buddhist leadership would succeed in cooling things down, and the counterinsurgency could go on without pause. If domestic protests and ARVN disaffection grew to the point that the war effort faltered, then the United States would face an entirely different problem.

Nolting noted that if Washington now chose to pull back from the generals, "we've either lost some friends, or lost some necks among some friends." But he again counseled patience: "My instinct is, since we don't have a good place to jump to, not to jump right now. Wait a little more."

His remarks seemed to give the president pause about the wisdom of a coup. Rusk still wanted Diem and Nhu removed, arguing that they were impeding progress against the communists. But Kennedy ordered that a telegram be dispatched to Lodge and Harkins, soliciting their views on the prospects for a successful coup. Did they think Washington should keep working with the generals, or hang back for a while, as Nolting suggested?

WHEN JFK CONVENED HIS advisers again on August 28, Harriman was in attendance and primed for a counterattack against Nolting. So was George Ball, the other undersecretary of state. (Ball specialized in economic affairs; Harriman handled political affairs.)

Taylor began by noting that the balance of forces in and around Saigon seemed to be stacked against the coup generals, with rebel units outnumbered two to one by those loyal to Diem. In the rest of the country, pro-coup forces appeared to be dominant. He added, however, that successful revolts are usually carried out by small, determined forces, so the larger number of Diem's troops in Saigon wouldn't necessarily be decisive.

Nolting resumed his defense of Diem, pointing out that the U.S. government had pledged not to interfere in South Vietnam's domestic politics when it agreed in 1961 to dramatically boost military and economic aid. Diem had insisted on such a promise because he foresaw the temptation for his powerful ally to use its aid to force changes in his government that he didn't want.

"I have very grave reservations in my own mind, based on personal commitments . . . which in turn were based on government instructions, about putting ourselves in a position of engineering a coup d'état, for the purpose of establishing a government with which we can deal more effectively," said Nolting. "In my mind, this is a bad principle and a bad precedent."

Ball countered that the actions of Diem and the Nhus—raiding the pagodas, making numerous anti-American statements—invalidated any promises Washington made in the past. The war, he said, couldn't be won with Diem and Nhu in charge. "This is an impossible situation," said Ball. "American prestige is being damaged every day that this situation persists," especially in other Buddhist nations in Asia. Since the coup was already in motion, he believed, Washington should mobilize all of its resources and make sure it succeeded.

Harriman agreed, arguing that without a coup, South Vietnam would be lost to the communists. Diem's troublesome brother should have been "eliminated" long ago, Harriman said, but the Kennedy administration stuck with him because he ran the vital strategic hamlet program. However, Diem and Nhu had betrayed the United States. And they were so unpopular that the South Vietnamese people could easily be rallied against them.

Hilsman sided with his two superiors, noting that the CIA was making plans to bribe additional generals to turn against the regime. He warned that Diem and Nhu were "perfectly aware" of the plot and American support for it.

"The generals are committed, sir," Hilsman told Kennedy. "In my opinion, they are either going to make it, or they're going to die." He added pointedly, "I don't think you can stop it now."

Robert Kennedy raised the question of what countermoves Diem and Nhu might make to break up the coup. Had they placed suspected mutineers under surveillance? Were they planning to swoop in and arrest the rebel generals? And if they did neutralize them, what would the United States do in response? No one in the room offered any answers.

The president didn't think the chances of pulling off a coup were favorable. "Maybe [Diem and Nhu] know about it, maybe the generals are going to have to run out of the country, maybe we're going to have to help them get out. That still is not a good enough reason to go ahead if we don't think the prospects are good enough," he said. "I don't think we're in that deep, and I am not sure the generals are. They've been probably bellyaching for months."

If the generals did overthrow the regime, Kennedy wanted Diem and Nhu sent into exile rather than imprisoned or killed. When Hilsman said he had no information on the generals' intentions regarding the brothers, Kennedy said, "I think it'd be important that nothing would happen to them."

Nolting made a final plea on Diem's behalf, insisting that he was the only leader who could hold his fragmented nation together. The former ambassador thought he should be approached, and that it was "quite likely" he could be persuaded to usher Madame Nhu out of the country. Getting rid of Nhu would be harder, but not impossible, he said.

But Harriman had had enough. "Shut up! We've heard you before!" he shouted from across the table. Nolting, he charged, had "been profoundly wrong all along in his advice to 'go along' with Diem."

The Crocodile's outburst stunned the others in the room. "It was almost, you know, insulting, and the only time I remember in the presence of a president where anybody took the tongue-lashing that Nolting did from Harriman," recalled Gilpatric. "I don't think from anybody else it would have been tolerated by the president."

Kennedy, who respected Nolting, intervened to say he wanted to hear his ex-envoy's advice. But an ugly split was developing among his most trusted counselors, and he wasn't happy about it.

He wanted his top men united over Vietnam policy, not fighting among themselves and maybe leaking to the press to promote their own viewpoints. After the president found out that Taylor had privately wired Harkins, saying "Authorities are now having second thoughts" about a coup, he took the dignified, much older general into the Oval Office and "read the riot act to him."

At 6 p.m., the president rejoined his Vietnam advisers for a second meeting. They decided to send Lodge and Harkins another cable, asking whether Diem should be pressured one last time to cashier the Nhus.

Kennedy also wanted their views on the "latest point" at which the coup could be called off, and what the consequences would be.

APPREHENSIVE ABOUT KNOWING SO little about the generals' machinations, the U.S. government had begun secretly eavesdropping on ARVN communications shortly after the pagoda invasions.

The surveillance was carried out by the Army Security Agency, a military arm of the National Security Agency, the enigmatic U.S. government organization, based at Fort George Meade, Maryland, that listened in on phone calls and radio transmissions worldwide. The NSA had been operating in South Vietnam for several years, intercepting and decoding radio messages from North Vietnam to the Viet Cong, and among VC field units. (By 1963, nearly twenty radio intercept and direction-finding sites throughout Southeast Asia were feeding intelligence to MACV.)

As coup rumors intensified, the NSA demanded reports from its listening stations every six hours. With their manpower stretched, the eavesdroppers stopped listening to the VC in order to concentrate on the South Vietnamese generals. Another dozen Vietnamese-speaking translators were rushed to Saigon.

The NSA was also tapping diplomatic cables between the Diem government and its embassies in Washington, Paris, Bangkok, and elsewhere.

When Saigon's ex-ambassador to the United States, Tran Van Chuong, bluntly informed Diem that most Americans believed his government couldn't win the war and urged him to "renounce the absolute and arbitrary power" of his brothers Nhu and Can, the NSA intercepted the message. The agency also picked up a poignant plea from Chuong's wife to Madame Nhu, their estranged daughter. Madame Chuong believed that angry South Vietnamese would eventually slaughter the entire Ngo clan. She urged her daughter to flee to America with her four children while there still was time.

The message ended, "Love, Mamma."

WHILE KENNEDY TRIED TO weigh the generals' odds of success, he also was concerned about the safety of the 3,600 American civilians in South Vietnam.

They were the spouses and children of military personnel, State Department employees and their families, businessmen, tourists, and others. What would happen to them if the generals rose up but were defeated? Would Diem's loyal troops turn on their erstwhile allies, especially if a lot of Vietnamese blood was spilled in an uprising those allies had abetted? In a disturbing August 28 report, George Carver, a senior CIA analyst who'd served in Vietnam, wrote that Nhu "is perfectly capable of ordering his forces to massacre every American they can reach."

The president and his advisers discussed the possible need for an emergency evacuation, and the Seventh Fleet began moving ships toward South Vietnam. A Navy amphibious group—consisting of the helicopter carrier USS *Princeton*, two destroyers, and two transport vessels bearing a Marine landing battalion—positioned itself in the South China Sea about seventy miles east of Saigon. Farther out was a second task force, made up of the aircraft carrier USS *Hancock* and three destroyers. Attack aircraft from the *Hancock* would provide air cover for an evacuation.

Most of the 15,000 U.S. military personnel in South Vietnam were staff officers and support workers; only about 3,000 were combat advisers in the field with the ARVN. As Hilsman pointed out, the ability of Harkins's MACV to defend itself was "not great." If serious trouble broke out, heavily armed Marines aboard the *Princeton*'s helicopters could begin landing at Tan Son Nhut in two hours. Civilians could be flown out on those choppers to the amphibious group, or to Bangkok or the Philippines aboard C-123 and C-47 transport planes already in South Vietnam.

But in an eyes-only telegram to Harriman, Lodge pointed out that a single Marine battalion might not be enough to protect so many American civilians if widespread fighting erupted in Saigon.

"Prudence demands that we assume some bloodshed," he wrote. "If the

Nhus see defeat staring them in the face, their Gotterdammerung complex is such that they would gladly see Saigon in flames before they perished." The Pentagon alerted two more Marine battalions on Okinawa to prepare for airlift to South Vietnam. Another carrier task force was dispatched to the South China Sea.

AS JFK'S MEN ARGUED the pros and cons of a coup, the CIA station chief, John Richardson, fired off a feverish cable on the night of August 28, warning that the generals were set to move and Diem was ready for them:

"Situation here has reached point of no return. Saigon is armed camp. Current indications are that Ngo family have dug in for last ditch battle. It is our considered estimate that general officers cannot retreat now."

He continued that the "overwhelming majority of general officers . . . are united, have conducted prior planning, realize that they must proceed quickly, and understand that they have no alternative but to go forward. Unless the generals are neutralized before being able to launch their operation, we believe they will act and that they have good chance to win. . . . We all understand that the effort must succeed and that whatever needs to be done on our part must be done."

With his horn-rimmed glasses, thick lips, and balding, beach-ball head, the forty-nine-year-old Richardson exuded the air of a scholarly bullfrog. Bookish and outdoorsy, he'd vowed as a young man not to lead an ordinary life and had succeeded magnificently.

His intelligence career began in 1943, when the wartime draft pulled him out of the University of Chicago as he studied for a PhD in sociology. Assigned to the Army's Counter-Intelligence Corps, a brainy outfit that counted Henry Kissinger and J. D. Salinger among its recruits, Richardson found himself hunting German spies behind the lines in Italy. He and his unit trailed American troops as they slugged their way north up the Italian boot, arresting stay-behind saboteurs and clandestine radio operators.

After the war, Richardson took part in the Allied effort to denazify Austria, nabbing Hitler's minions who'd fled ruined Germany. He switched to the Central Intelligence Agency at its creation in 1947, serving as Vienna station chief and evolving into a passionate anti-communist as the Cold War enveloped Europe.

A rising star in the CIA, he was given the prestigious job of southeastern Europe division chief, based in Washington. But he grew restless after a few years and sought a return to the field. In 1955 he was made chief of the agency's Athens station, which organized covert operations behind the Iron Curtain in Yugoslavia, Bulgaria, Hungary, and Albania.

Listed on U.S. embassy rosters as a diplomat, Richardson made frequent appearances at state dinners and parties, charming the women and showing off his considerable skills as a dancer. He loved to smoke, drink martinis, play poker, hike mountains, and engage in deep, all-night conversations with friends. He also proved adept at court politics, getting to know the Greek royal family and once taking Queen Frederica on a fly-fishing expedition.

At his core, however, Richardson was a quiet, reserved man, unfailingly polite and almost painfully modest. (His son called him "the humble warrior.") His nightstand usually held a copy of the *Meditations* of Marcus Aurelius, the ancient Roman emperor and Stoic philosopher. He rarely raised his voice or pounded the table, preferring low-key persuasion to get things done.

Richardson took over as Saigon station chief in May 1962. He lived with his wife and two children in a large, luxurious villa near downtown. Vietnamese servants initially refused to work in the house because it had once been used to interrogate VC suspects, a number of whom died in the process. Buddhist monks had to exorcise their ghosts before any domestics would enter the place.

The Saigon station was a big one, with more than two hundred officers and support employees running various paramilitary and political-action programs. They worked with Green Beret teams that trained Montagnards and other rural people to defend themselves against VC marauders. They trained South Vietnamese saboteurs and parachuted them into North Vietnam (although communist security forces arrested most of the infiltrators). Richardson's people even tried to turn Diem's sycophantic National Assembly deputies into American-style populists, prodding them to develop closer ties to their constituents through personal visits and small favors.

Like Nolting and Harkins, Richardson believed the South Vietnamese were making headway in the war. Part of his job was to work closely with Nhu, who the CIA man admired as shrewd, realistic, and a keen counterinsurgency theorist. "He finds particular pleasure in analyzing the subtleties and intricacies of the problems of war and of the political chess game," Richardson wrote. He was intrigued by Nhu's esoteric doctrine of personalism and agreed that the strategic hamlet program was working.

Unlike other Americans, Richardson seemed to understand what Nhu was trying to say and do. The political counselor was struggling to establish a modus vivendi with Washington, while limiting what he saw as its increasingly pernicious leverage over the Saigon government. Richardson viewed Diem as the more forceful and dominant of the two brothers, but he believed Nhu was maneuvering to expand his power and at some point would try to assume the presidency.

For most of his tenure in Saigon, the station chief had wanted the Ngo brothers to prevail. Buddhist claims of persecution, which he regarded as untrue, upset him so much that he had trouble sleeping. But his attitude changed after the pagoda raids.

When the green light cable arrived from Washington, Richardson worried that the coup generals might at some point turn on each other, producing deadly street fighting in Saigon and endangering American lives. He didn't want his agents serving as messengers to the generals, fearing the CIA's role might be exposed. But he agreed with Lodge that the generals should be encouraged to revolt.

BY AUGUST 29, THE day after Richardson's "point of no return" telegram, Lodge could barely restrain his enthusiasm for a coup.

"We are launched on a course from which there is no respectable turning back: the overthrow of the Diem government," he cabled the State Department. Diem, he wrote, had forfeited public support in both South Vietnam and the United States, couldn't regain it, and wouldn't win the war without it. To encourage the rebel generals, Lodge recommended that Harkins be ordered to personally reiterate U.S. support for them and that Washington publicly announce an aid cutoff.

Richardson started that day by meeting with his two liaison agents, Conein and Spera, at 7:15 a.m.

The two were scheduled in just half an hour to meet Big Minh and Khiem for further talks about a coup. But a MACV officer showed Richardson the telegram from Taylor—the one JFK reprimanded him for—indicating that Washington might be getting cold feet. After a hurried discussion about whether to cancel the parley with the two generals, Richardson told his operatives to go as planned, but merely hear the South Vietnamese out and make no promises.

Big Minh and Khiem, however, seemed suddenly wary of Conein and Spera, apparently thinking they might be trying to trap them on behalf of the regime.

The ARVN officers distrusted the CIA because of its long-standing closeness to Nhu and Colonel Tung. The flubbed VOA broadcast about a possible aid cutoff was the only indication they had that the U.S. government might be ready to pull the plug on its support for the palace.

Big Minh told his CIA visitors that he and his fellow generals wanted Washington to follow through and actually halt its aid. That action, he said, might induce Diem and Nhu to open ceasefire negotiations with Hanoi, since South Vietnam would have a hard time fighting without U.S. help. Such talks would give the strongly anti-communist generals the political cover they needed to move against the brothers. Nhu, said Big Minh, already knew that the Americans were reaching out to him; Colonel Tung had stationed a company of his soldiers threateningly near the general's house.

When Lodge learned what had happened, he exploded at Richardson, angrily asserting that he'd "destroyed" any chance for a coup by instructing Conein and Spera to make no firm U.S. commitments to the nervous generals. The genteel Richardson "expressed a firm dissenting opinion."

So far, the coup generals had revealed few details of their plans. But the embassy got some unsettling insights into their thinking from ARVN Lieutenant Colonel Pham Ngoc Thao, a congenital conspirator with a beguiling personality and a personal history as tangled and violent as his nation's.

Thao was a character out of an André Malraux novel. He'd been born in 1922 into a large family that, like many in Vietnam, later split between those loyal to the communist north and those who adhered to the noncommunist south. (One of Thao's brothers became Hanoi's ambassador to East Germany.) In 1947, shortly after war with France broke out, he left a job as an elementary schoolteacher and joined the Viet Minh.

Posing as the leader of a student association, Thao was soon running the insurgents' spy network in Saigon. He reported on French shipping schedules and troop movements, and later participated in ambushes and assassinations. (He claimed to have personally liquidated a French colonel.) A dynamic, intelligent leader, Thao was promoted to colonel and put in charge of a Viet Minh battalion in the delta.

By 1955, claiming to have left the Viet Minh, Thao was teaching at a Catholic school in Vinh Long Province, where he became a protégé of Diem's brother, then-Bishop Ngo Dinh Thuc. He joined the Can Lao Party and became an ARVN captain in 1957. Three years later, he was named chief of Kien Hoa Province, a fecund, river-laced coastal area south of Saigon where VC fighters hid in coconut plantations. He gained the peasants' confidence by organizing effective local defenses and economic aid projects. Touring Thao's watery domain with him by motorboat, William Colby was impressed that Thao traveled without bodyguards and was greeted as a familiar face by many villagers. In August 1962, Thao was elevated to inspector general of the strategic hamlet program.

Short and slight, Thao was a witty, articulate man who spoke excellent French and English and usually dressed in green-and-black jungle fatigues. He had a walleye that, according to Malcolm Browne, "always seemed to be watching for enemies while the other [eye] twinkled right at you." Thao loved to reminisce and his colorful storytelling attracted a string of Western reporters. Seemingly an independent man of strong judgments, he openly criticized the regime to Americans and acted as a CIA informant. He eventually fell out of favor with Diem and Nhu, and was demoted to advising the government on canal construction.

In 1963, Thao joined the coup group assembled by Dr. Tran Kim Tuyen, the ex–secret police chief who'd also plummeted from grace at the palace. A CIA dossier described Thao as "a complex figure of considerable energy, no discretion, shady background, and mixed motives very difficult for U.S. observers to diagnose." In fact, Thao was a VC agent, tasked with fomenting as much trouble for the Saigon government as possible—an assignment he performed brilliantly.

On August 29, Thao dined with three of the coup generals: Big Minh, Khiem, and Khanh. As he later told the CIA, they seemed reluctant to organize a takeover on their own; Khiem said they had too much to lose. They were willing to jump in "if someone else takes [the] initiative." The generals said that if Diem was killed at the start of an uprising, they'd openly support it.

Thao's information cast considerable doubt on the notion that the generals were on the verge of acting against Diem, although it's unclear whether Lodge was told about it.

AS THAO ATE AND drank with the generals that night, the CIA station received a tip that Diem and Nhu planned to start arresting suspected traitors within hours. The news touched off a frantic effort to warn the would-be mutineers.

The CIA quickly got in touch with Ralph Newman, a U.S. Air Force colonel who was an adviser to Big Minh and lived next door to one of Minh's aides. But no one answered the door at the aide's house and Newman wasn't able to reach him by phone.

Newman also knew another one of the plotters, General Le Van Kim. The CIA told Newman to call Kim with a phony story that a Vietnamese friend's son had been arrested during the student roundups a few days earlier, and that Newman needed Kim's help in getting the boy released.

Newman called Kim's home, but sensed that his phone was bugged. Someone imitating Kim's voice came on the line and repeatedly asked where Newman was calling from. The American then asked to speak with Kim's wife, and recognized the voice that came on as that of the real Mrs. Kim. Newman told her the fictitious tale about the jailed boy and asked to come to the Kims' house, but the line went dead.

Soon afterward, one of General Kim's aides showed up at Newman's door and took him and a CIA agent to Kim's residence. The Americans told Kim about the impending arrests; he promised to warn Big Minh right away. Kim added that it was very dangerous for Newman to come to his house and asked him not to do it again. Kim's assistant then led the two Americans "away from the house over a back road and through gates apparently very seldom used," according to a CIA report to Washington about the incident.

The report added that it was "puzzling" that the regime hadn't already squelched the coup by arresting four or five of the main plotters.

FOR ALL THEIR TALK, the generals still hadn't made any move, prompting Lodge to complain of their "inertia."

"The days come and go and nothing happens," he impatiently cabled Rusk, just a day after declaring that the embassy was "launched" toward a coup. He likened his attempts to prod the generals into action to "pushing a piece of spaghetti."

The plotting seemed to be an open secret in Saigon. When Lodge, on August 30, paid a call on the French ambassador, Roger Lalouette, an urbane and gifted diplomat who'd been in Vietnam for five years, the Frenchman strongly advised against a coup, despite the French government's past hostility toward Diem.

With his steadfastness and determination, Diem was in many ways the best chief of state in Southeast Asia, Lalouette insisted. He'd never be a popular leader, given his inability to make inspiring speeches or cultivate the press. But his brother Nhu was intelligent and efficient, and Diem was much better off with him than without him. Lalouette was confident that together, the brothers could win the war.

The current unrest, the Frenchman continued, was "largely the work of the press, helped greatly by Vietnamese ineptness." In the days of French colonialism, he said, Buddhist immolations were common and had no effect whatsoever on the public; the recent burnings had stirred far more outrage abroad than in South Vietnam. Things now were quieting down. Arrested Buddhists were being released and damaged pagodas were undergoing repairs at government expense. There was still a chance of a violent popular uprising, but it was lessening.

Lalouette asked what the regime could do to please Washington, to which Lodge replied: get rid of the Nhus. That was impossible, the Frenchman said. But he suggested that Nhu's influence could be watered down if someone else was installed under Diem as prime minister, to carry out day-to-day government business.

He was hearing reports that the VC were very demoralized and predicted they might give up in a year or two. South Vietnam would then be in a strong position to work out some sort of rapprochement with the north. As Lodge departed, Lalouette said he wanted to make two final points:

"First, try to calm American opinion," he advised. "And second, no coups."

JOINING HIS ADVISERS FOR the fourth straight day, Kennedy wanted to know whether they were still on board with a coup. Did anyone, he asked, think the United States shouldn't get behind the insurgent generals?

McNamara didn't see any adequate substitute for Diem and wanted him to have one last chance to fire Nhu. The generals, he warned, were "not capable of running the government for long." But if an ultimatum was to be presented to Diem, McNamara wanted to wait a few more days, until the generals were ready to move immediately if he rejected it.

Hilsman suggested that MACV supply the rebels with helicopters, under the guise of using them against the VC. McNamara objected, saying Washington needed to know more about the generals' plans before "making any commitments whatsoever for the participation of U.S. forces in any way."

Still uneasy about the fate of U.S. civilians if fighting broke out, JFK again asked if the military's evacuation preparations were sufficient. Taylor replied: "It's very hard to say, sir. When you consider there's 35,000 [South Vietnamese soldiers] in the Saigon area, anything we could put in is insufficient." The Joint Chiefs chairman also worried that Washington was on the verge of committing itself "to a coup run by people we don't know for objectives which we don't know."

McGeorge Bundy, Kennedy's national security assistant, had a different concern: keeping his boss's involvement with the generals' conspiracy secret. He suggested that the president and his inner circle cover their tracks by calling back all previous cables that mentioned a potential putsch. From now on, he said, everyone present should write coup-related messages in such a way that they couldn't be tied to the White House.

"This is not . . . going to be a matter of public record at any point, to the degree we can prevent it," Bundy said. "And in drafting cables from now on, we ought to try to draft them so that they do not indicate where the basic decisions and impetus for this enterprise have come from."

Later that day, with a smaller group of senior counselors, JFK mused about growing public and congressional sensitivity to American casualties in Vietnam, which then included about one hundred deaths. If the communists won the war, Kennedy knew he'd face political attacks from Republicans and other critics. Yet even holding the line in South Vietnam would inevitably cost more American lives and treasure. "I know that everybody's mad at this situation," he said. "But I know they'll be madder if South Vietnam goes down the drain."

Rusk again argued that Diem would never discard Nhu, but Kennedy reminded him that Nolting still thought there was a chance to separate the two. Like Hilsman, Rusk tried to disparage the former ambassador, saying he was still "in a little bit of a mild state of shock." But the president brushed aside the amateur psychoanalysis, pointing out that simply because Nolting disagreed with dumping Diem didn't mean he was mentally impaired.

Before Kennedy departed for the long Labor Day weekend on Cape Cod, he approved a cable instructing Harkins to personally reassure the generals that the United States backed the coup. But the president still had doubts. From his summer home, he telephoned Bundy and later dispatched an "entirely private" cable to Lodge that reflected a key lesson he'd absorbed from the Bay of Pigs:

> Until the very moment of the go signal for the operation by the Generals, I must reserve a contingent right to change course and reverse previous

> instructions. While fully aware of your assessment of the consequences of such a reversal, I know from experience that failure is more destructive than an appearance of indecision.
>
> I would, of course, accept full responsibility for any such change. . . . When we go, we must go to win, but it will be better to change our minds than fail. And if our national interest should require a change of mind, we must not be afraid of it.

Lodge wrote back that he respected the president's right to change direction at any time. But Kennedy's old political adversary had a more realistic understanding of Washington's limited power to stop the generals once their tanks were fueled, their troops were briefed, and they were set to lunge at Diem's jugular.

"To be successful, this operation must be essentially a Vietnamese affair with a momentum of its own," Lodge said. "Should this happen you may not be able to control it, i.e., the 'go signal' may be given by the Generals."

WHEN KENNEDY'S ADVISERS ASSEMBLED without him in Dean Rusk's spacious State Department office on August 30, they'd already seen the disquieting CIA report on Colonel Thao's dinner with the generals.

Rusk found the recent cable traffic from Saigon "highly confusing." He wasn't sure who the Americans were dealing with and felt as if they were "operating in a jungle." He suggested that the generals' talk of upending Diem might be nothing but "an exercise in frustration and gossip," and that Washington should get them back to fighting the war.

Echoing what the French ambassador told Lodge, Marshall Carter, the CIA's deputy director, said the regime appeared to be making changes to mollify Washington and reduce the pressures for a coup.

He listed several indicators: arrested students and monks were being let go; Madame Nhu hadn't shot off her mouth in a while; some Buddhist organizations were issuing obsequious statements of support for the government. Vu Van Mau, the foreign minister who vanished on his way to the airport, had been allowed to fly off to his Indian pilgrimage after all. (A Vietnamese official later reported that Mau had been permitted to leave only after Vice President Tho phoned Diem and threatened to resign.)

Carter figured the generals were backing down and his intuition was correct. Before dawn the next day, another cable from Richardson arrived in Washington: Harkins had met with Khiem, who informed him that coup planning had been called off. The generals weren't able to line up sufficient forces to bring down their president, Khiem said.

"This particular coup," Richardson declared, "is finished."

Lodge chimed in with a self-protective message, insisting that the embassy "used every asset that we had" to stimulate a coup and that "our record has been thoroughly respectable throughout."

Taylor was more blunt about the outcome of the abortive coup. "I was sure," he wrote in a 1972 memoir, "that our bungling had deprived us of most of our remaining leverage on the Diem government."

CHAPTER 14

VISIONS, PROPHESIES, AND CELESTIAL PORTENTS

ON THE EVENING of September 1, a trio of nervous monks walked past the U.S. embassy. Then they turned and sprinted toward the front door.

Two Marine guards tried to stop them, but one Buddhist squeezed past and into the building. The other two pleaded to be admitted, saying, "Let me in! Help me!" A Saigon cop rushed up and tried to seize the bonzes, but the Marines let them into the embassy, blocked the cop, and locked the gate.

One of the monks turned out to be Tri Quang, the Buddhist leader who'd been arrested during the raid on Xa Loi Pagoda eleven days before. But he'd disguised himself, shaving his eyebrows and adopting the identity of a lowly novice bonze, and the authorities failed to recognize him. Released from custody earlier on September 1, he went to a different pagoda, but found it watched by police. Fearing he'd be rearrested or killed, Tri Quang caught a taxi to the embassy and, along with his two companions, requested asylum.

Washington instructed Lodge to protect the monks. The Saigon government demanded that Tri Quang be handed over, but the embassy refused, granting him asylum and housing and feeding him in the building. Thus did two wartime allies find themselves locked in an extraordinary standoff, one nation giving sanctuary to a high-profile fugitive that the other regarded as public enemy number one.

With Tri Quang marooned in the embassy and other Buddhist leaders jailed, hospitalized, or in hiding, Diem and Nhu turned their attention to crushing the students who'd vowed to take the Buddhists' place in the protest movement. Having already rounded up many university students, the regime went after secondary school pupils.

On September 7, combat police and Special Forces soldiers surrounded Saigon high schools whose students were shouting anti-Diem slogans. When the youths began throwing rocks, about eight hundred of them were arrested, including six hundred girls. Many of the detainees were between thirteen and fifteen years old. As they were forced into trucks, some of the kids shouted to American reporters: "Tell President Kennedy students do not like Diem! The United States government helps Diem! Do not help Diem!"

Two days later, another demonstration broke out at a boys' high school in Cholon. When a government sound truck urged calm, the students pelted it with rocks and bricks and barricaded the school's front gate. One boy ran around the courtyard waving a Buddhist flag as others cheered and chased after him. Then they tore down the national flag flying over the school and raised the Buddhist flag.

Police and soldiers tried to force their way through the gate, but the kids repelled them. More troops arrived, and the combined force succeeded in busting into the courtyard. The students responded by hurling desks down at them. The cops and soldiers beat some kids and threw them headfirst into trucks. By the time the melee was over, more than one thousand students had been arrested. Halberstam's vivid story about the clash appeared the next day on page one of *The New York Times*.

By mid-September, the regime had arrested about eight thousand students, although most of them were soon released to their parents in exchange for a pledge to abstain from protests.

Many of those rounded up were the offspring of civil servants and military officers. In Saigon, police stations filled up with anxious fathers in army uniforms and office attire searching for kids who hadn't come home. Stories circulated of beatings and torture of the arrestees, leaving Saigon's middle and upper classes—the people who ran Diem's government, army, and economy—boiling with anger at the regime. A girl who emerged from jail with a broken shoulder told of seeing electroshocks applied to the vaginas of other female captives to induce them to divulge protest leaders' names.

Walking around the city, Peter Arnett came across hundreds of bicycles abandoned on the side of a road. They belonged to students at a private girls' school, Marie Curie High School, whose entire student body had been arrested. Neighbors told him the girls were stopped on their way to classes and taken away in trucks bearing the now-ironic handshake insignia of the U.S. aid program.

"By late afternoon, desperate parents were searching for their daughters' bicycles and swapping terrifying stories of alleged torture and other atrocities," Arnett recalled. "I wondered at the stupidity of this crude attempt at intimidation by the regime."

With their kids getting arrested and abused by U.S.-trained police and soldiers and carried off to jail in U.S.-supplied trucks, parents began venting their anger at Washington as well. One asked a newsman: "How can you Americans support a government that arrests children?"

DIEM AND NHU DIDN'T stop at rounding up students. Reports poured into the embassy of predawn arrests of lawyers, teachers, and others suspected of disloyalty or simply being too friendly with Americans.

An embassy officer whose wife recently delivered a baby learned that her obstetrician, who also served as Diem's health minister, had been placed under house arrest for supposed opposition to the president. A prominent lawyer had some teeth knocked out while in detention. On September 4, General Dinh, Saigon's military governor, arrested the editor of *Tu Do*, the city's leading newspaper, and shut it down as a "security measure." (The paper's title meant "freedom.") Saigon's Catholic archbishop released a message from Pope Paul VI expressing his "apprehension and anguish" over the unrest in South Vietnam.

Having neutered the Buddhist leadership, Diem and Nhu set about constructing a new, tamer version.

Jailed bonzes were required to declare their loyalty to the regime before they were released. Buddhist factions in Danang and elsewhere promised to stay out of politics and concentrate on "pure religion." Still in a military hospital, Buddhist patriarch Thich Tinh Khiet abruptly reversed his opposition to the regime and called on his brethren to "remove themselves from politics." He handed over leadership of the General Buddhist Association of Vietnam to a Nhu-approved monk, Thich Thien Hoa. In conversations with embassy officers, Tri Quang described Hoa's organization, the Union Committee for the Defense of Pure Buddhism, as a "bunch of lackeys . . . completely under the control of the government." Wags dubbed a government minister who was purportedly stocking pagodas with more pliable monks as "the pope of the false bonzes."

Mass arrests had cowed the student movement as well. Riddled with police agents, it lacked effective leaders and allies among labor, the military, or what was left of the anti-Diem political parties. Though bitter at the regime, most students came from cautious, conservative families; few were willing to risk their necks in serious fighting against Diem's security forces or by joining the VC.

With Saigon still under martial law, armored personnel carriers rattled through the streets. Marines and paratroopers with Browning automatic rifles stood behind barbed wire at checkpoints. Antiaircraft artillery ringed Gia Long Palace, protecting it from renegade pilots. Diem and Nhu declared that the Buddhist crisis was over. The British ambassador, Gordon Etherington-Smith, agreed, telling U.S. diplomats that the brothers were "strongly in the saddle." Like his French counterpart, Etherington-Smith warned against a coup, saying it was unlikely to succeed despite the resentment of the middle and upper classes toward Diem and the Nhus.

The regime tried to demonstrate that it enjoyed public support by organizing a huge gathering outside the U.S. Information Agency. More than 75,000 people waved banners and shouted, "Long live President Diem!" But in some ways the government seemed oddly paralyzed. Diem's chief of staff,

Thuan, told Rufus Phillips that virtually all work had stopped in the ministries. Thuan recounted a recent visit from the national economy minister, who was clutching a detective novel. When Thuan asked why he had the book, the man replied: "All we, or anybody else, do in the office is to read these. We are waiting."

Nhu was now in effective control of the country, Thuan claimed. Diem trusted no one else and had "mentally abdicated" to his younger brother. At most meetings, Nhu spoke for Diem and the president gave his assent; in some cases, Diem simply repeated what Nhu told him to say.

Thuan was obviously terrified of Nhu. Fluent in English and impish in manner, he'd long been a favorite of U.S. diplomats, who regarded him as their best ally, the most pro-American official in Diem's inner circle (and one of the most talkative). But now he feared that Nhu would have him killed if he tried to resign.

Golfing one day with Harkins, Thuan confided that he was being watched and bemoaned that "things were going so well and all of a sudden everything seemed to disintegrate." (Harkins replied characteristically that things weren't as bad as Thuan thought.) When Thuan heard that the Italian ambassador had suggested that he'd make a fine prime minister—a job Nhu was already effectively doing—Thuan remarked: "Does he want to get me assassinated?"

Also living in fear was Dr. Tuyen, the ousted secret police chief. Although he'd been assigned months earlier to a diplomatic post in Cairo, he'd managed to linger in Saigon. Diem finally ordered him to leave for Egypt on September 12. Tuyen lived in a walled villa across the street from William Trueheart, and he asked the embassy's second-in-command to help his wife and five children in the event that "civil disorder" broke out.

Trueheart said he'd do what he could, but he wouldn't be able to protect Tuyen's family if Diem's police came for them.

While Trueheart was at work one day, a prominent Saigon businesswoman came to his house to plead with his wife, Phoebe, for sanctuary. A widow, she was known to be anti-Diem and wanted to be flown to Cambodia on a U.S. plane.

Phoebe already was rattled by the tension and anxiety gripping the city. Her husband had become a pariah in the Ngos' eyes over his tough demands regarding the Buddhists, and Phoebe believed their phone was bugged. They played loud music whenever they had a visitor, American or Vietnamese. The only time she was able to sleep, she wrote to stateside friends, was "when I've had lots to drink or taken Seconal." Horrible dreams about "blood, soldiers, and little children torn apart" plagued her.

She wound up talking to the frightened businesswoman for two hours and tried to enlist the help of a Canadian general who had his own plane. But she had two young sons to think about and didn't want "police beating down my doors." Her husband eventually came home, listened to the businesswoman's story, and "showed her nicely and firmly to the door." Before departing, she turned to him and said "it would be on his conscience when she was tortured."

MANY REGIME OFFICIALS SHARED Thuan's belief that Nhu was running the show, but felt powerless about the situation. The CIA reported that disaffection had spread from government executives to "practically all leading elements of the population." The agency predicted, however, that few South Vietnamese would rise up against Diem "unless strong leadership should emerge from some quarter."

Yet the soft, monsoon-laden air was infused with a feeling of impending upheaval. Everywhere there was a sense of anticipation and suppressed excitement. It seemed to be common knowledge that the United States had tried to take down Diem and Nhu in August, and many Vietnamese were waiting to see what their powerful patron did next. Mecklin compared the atmosphere in Saigon to a "deathly still summer night with heat lightning flickering on the horizon."

With their predilection for the supernatural, ordinary Vietnamese sought comfort in visions, prophesies, and celestial portents.

For several days crowds gathered on Saigon street corners, faces upturned, after a soothsayer predicted a Buddhist miracle: that the sun would be shaken out of its usual arc in the sky. "Even the heavens are protesting the miserable fate of Vietnamese Buddhists," one spectator told a newsman. Troops assigned to break up public assemblies kept trying to disperse the sun watchers, but sometimes couldn't resist squinting skyward themselves.

A rumor ricocheted around the city that a statue of Buddha in one of the pagodas was seen to shed tears. (The Saigon press tried to squelch the tale by pointing out that heavy rains had leaked through the roof.) Thousands of people were said to have climbed a mountain in the Central Highlands where a bonzess was performing amazing cures.

Then there was the very large carp, swimming in a pond near Danang, which local Buddhists believed was a reincarnated disciple of the Buddha. As more and more Buddhist pilgrims arrived at the pond, the district chief, a Catholic, became alarmed, interpreting their enthrallment as an "act of opposition." He called in Colonel Tung's Special Forces to destroy the fish.

Tung's men riddled the pond with automatic-weapons fire, but the creature escaped. Then they put mines in the water; the explosions killed almost everything in the pond except the big fish. Finally, the soldiers tossed in pieces of bread, to lure the fish to the surface, and threw in grenades. The carp swam on, convincing Buddhists it really was a supernatural being and attracting even bigger throngs of worshippers. Buddhists carried away "magical" water from the pond by the bucketful; helicopters began landing so soldiers could fill their canteens.

Despite the regime's efforts to quash opponents, there were flickers of resistance.

An underground group circulated leaflets calling on college students to be ready "to give the final hammer blow to the head of the Ngo Dinh Diem clique." On September 12, a bonzess burned herself to death outside Nha Trang. Sitting in the embassy, Tri Quang felt that even though the Buddhist movement had been hobbled by the arrests of so many of its leaders, it succeeded because it "had aroused great forces" against Diem and Nhu.

Someone gave Mecklin an advance copy of a *Times of Vietnam* story about an amusingly subversive incident at the central market. The story reported that shoppers had fled in shrieking panic after pranksters released eleven monkeys wearing Diem name tags into their midst.

The paper never published it.

ON THE DAY TRI QUANG scampered into the embassy, Diem and the Nhus received a visit from Archbishop Salvatore Asta, the pope's special emissary to South Vietnam.

A bright and bustling man, the young papal delegate had become fast friends with Lodge, who was looking for reliable sources of information in his first days as ambassador and had decided, in his brusque way, that the embassy staff was insufficiently knowledgeable. Lodge turned instead to the affable Asta, seeing him as a "very wise man with great gifts of leadership and courage," as well as a close relationship with Vietnamese Catholics.

Asta's deep involvement in South Vietnamese affairs grew out of Vatican fears that Diem's suppression of the Buddhists might generate a backlash against Catholics that could spiral into bloodshed. As the representative of America's first Catholic president, Lodge was quite sensitive to the Church's desires and later declared that "everything we did [in South Vietnam] had the approval of Archbishop Asta."

Like many American officials, Asta felt that the Nhus' departure from South Vietnam would help matters a great deal, and he entreated the couple to go. Perhaps because he was the pope's personal envoy, and the Ngos were devout Catholics, Asta achieved what at first looked like a major diplomatic breakthrough: Madame Nhu agreed to leave the country on an extended trip. While Nhu insisted on staying, he pledged to withdraw from public life as a gesture toward restoring trust between his brother and the United States.

The next day, September 2, Asta brought along Lodge as well as the Italian ambassador, Giovanni D'Orlandi, to follow up with Nhu. The political counselor now promised to permanently leave his brother's government and move to Dalat. His resignation would be portrayed, he said, as a sign that the war was going so well his services were no longer needed. He couldn't leave the country because of his contacts with the Viet Cong who, Nhu claimed, were "extremely discouraged" and ready to give up.

Nhu added that he was willing to consider broadening Diem's cabinet—for years one of Washington's highest priorities—and push for the appointment of a prime minister, who could unburden Diem of his less important work. Nhu pledged to retire after martial law was lifted and "certain U.S. agents" who were promoting the ouster of his family left the country.

Shortly afterward, Asta arranged to have Archbishop Thuc, who was as vocally anti-Buddhist as the Nhus, sent to Rome for an upcoming meeting of the Vatican's Ecumenical Council. Thuc arrived in Rome on September 6, under Vatican orders not to discuss the political situation in South Vietnam. Three days later, Madame Nhu flew off to Belgrade, Yugoslavia, where she planned to attend a conference before traveling on to Rome and Paris.

But Nhu's attitude of pained acquiescence didn't last long.

Meeting again with Asta and d'Orlandi on September 6, he launched into a long tirade, pacing up and down the room. He accused his two visitors of pushing him to commit "political suicide" and insisted that if he left his position the armed forces would take over the government and CIA "schemers" would sabotage the war effort.

"I'm the winning horse; they should bet on me. Why do they want to finish me?" Nhu ranted.

He didn't quit or move to Dalat, as promised. Instead, the regime initiated an unnerving campaign of harassment and intimidation against American diplomats and newsmen that included police surveillance, phone taps, and assassination threats.

PLAINCLOTHESMEN WATCHED THE Associated Press office. Reporters were tailed and their phones monitored. Some Vietnamese who called the AP office subsequently received sinister threats from the government. Those who visited in person were sometimes seized by police as soon as they left. The embassy received word that Diem and Nhu planned to use force to extract Tri Quang.

Halberstam wrote that Saigon was full of frightened people in the wake of "what was in effect a palace coup" by Nhu. He and Sheehan were still staying at Mecklin's villa, where they'd jury-rigged trip wires to alert them if regime agents tried to creep inside. Outside, the neighborhood swarmed with security men. At night, Nhu's secret police sat in taxis or on cyclo-pousses, watching the homes of various Americans.

The stress and tension were starting to get even to Halberstam. "Sure, we were paranoid," he recalled. "But people *were* trying to get us. They had been scraping layers of skin off us for weeks. Our nerves were rubbed raw." The correspondents were exhausted; their editors, worried that they would become erratic, began pressuring them to take vacations. Halberstam's bosses pushed him to take some time off; Sheehan and Browne got similar hints from their home offices.

But the newsmen sensed that the Vietnam story was nearing a climax, and no one wanted to be away when it happened. Besides being arm-twisted into taking vacations by their editors, they worried about being expelled. Many of them had Vietnamese girlfriends and under Madame Nhu's blue laws, they could easily become ensnared in a "morals scandal" and get thrown out of the country.

Nicholas Turner of Reuters reluctantly broke up with his girlfriend; other correspondents were reevaluating their relationships as well. Halberstam parted ways with his girlfriend, Ricki, after her angry husband burst in on him one night with a pistol. Ricki happened to be translating for Halberstam as he typed up a story. True to form, Halberstam turned the tables on the irate spouse, chasing him around the room and yelling, "How dare you come in here and interrupt me while I'm working!"

Assassination rumors multiplied. Denis Warner, the Australian correspondent, had an alarming conversation with Tran Van Khiem, Madame Nhu's eccentric brother. Khiem claimed he was setting up his own secret police force, with money from his sister, and expected to take over security duties in Saigon once martial law ended. Astonishingly, he then scribbled on a piece of paper his "secret" list of Americans to be murdered. The names included Richardson, Mecklin, and Conein.

Warner was appalled. He warned Khiem that if any Americans were killed, the U.S. Marines would descend on Saigon. As a World War II correspondent, Warner had seen Marines in action in the Pacific; he told Khiem they were the most ferocious fighters in the world. Within three hours, he said, they'd wipe out every Vietnamese soldier in the city.

Taken aback, Khiem nevertheless went on to describe his brother-in-law, Nhu, as the "greatest evil in Vietnam." Nhu had to be eliminated somehow, Khiem said, so that he and his sister could run the government. He claimed the regime had planted documents at Xa Loi to make it look like the Americans were in cahoots with the Buddhists.

One of those documents was a draft magazine article that Warner himself had written while staying at Mecklin's house. Highly critical of the Ngos, the piece had mysteriously disappeared from Warner's desk. Khiem said it wound up in his sister's hands and she wanted the Australian newsman to explain why he'd written it; if he refused, he'd be arrested. Warner had no intention of explaining anything to Madame Nhu. His intention was to get out of South Vietnam right away, which he did.

Predictably, *The Times of Vietnam* joined the anti-American onslaught as well. On September 2, it ran a sensational story under the banner headline "CIA Financing Planned Coup d'Etat." The paper claimed that U.S. spies had passed out as much as $24 million in bribes in an effort to overthrow Diem. Military attachés from three unnamed foreign embassies, the story said, had helped organize the attempt, which had been scheduled for August 28, but was called off when the regime caught wind of it.

While exaggerated and wrong about key details, the article bore some resemblance to the truth of the aborted coup Lodge had pushed for. The State Department flatly denied the newspaper's account, calling it "ridiculous." But it was picked up by the New York *Daily News*, *Chicago Tribune*, *Baltimore Sun*, and other prominent stateside papers.

Nhu told the CIA he had nothing to do with the story and would never "hide himself behind the backsides of a woman," an apparent reference to *The Times of Vietnam*'s American editor, Ann Gregory. But a reporter for the German magazine *Der Spiegel* said Madame Nhu admitted to him that she'd written most of the article. (Gregory later said she felt it was her duty as an American to publish it in order to expose "a Nazi-like band of cynical young men who nourish their egos on their abilities to overturn friendly governments.")

MECKLIN'S NAME CAME UP in almost every assassination rumor, perhaps because Nhu believed, as he told an American visitor, that the embassy press officer was plotting a coup. It got so bad that Lodge called him in and asked if he'd like a transfer. Mecklin said no, that would only give Nhu what he wanted. Besides, he didn't regard the threats as serious, unless the Nhus were convinced they could get away with making his killing look like the work of the VC.

Mecklin did take some precautions, however. He told the guards at his house not to let in anyone without his specific permission. He also bought a pistol, secreting it in a pocket of his jacket. But the thing was so heavy and made such a conspicuous bulge that he stopped carrying it.

Yet the daily nuttiness worked on his nerves. One night he dreamed of watching a play about a U.S. diplomatic mission that gradually discovers it's been negotiating over the years with a government of madmen. Nothing the foreign officials promised would happen ever happened; their words were meaningless. The embassy nevertheless was forced to continue to deal with the crazy government forever; there were no realistic alternatives to it.

Mecklin had known Madame Nhu's brother, Khiem, fairly well since 1955, when he'd covered Vietnam as a journalist and Khiem was Diem's press secretary. Not long after learning that Khiem had threatened to kill him, Mecklin got a phone call from him.

"John," said Khiem, "have you heard that story about how I'm supposed to be head of an assassination squad?" Mecklin said he had. "And how I'm going to assassinate you?" Mecklin had heard that, too. "John," Khiem continued, "please don't believe stories like that. You and I are old friends. I would never assassinate you." Mecklin said he was glad to know that, and thanked Khiem for calling.

"Let's have a drink sometime," Khiem offered. Mecklin agreed that was a fine idea.

ANOTHER ODD AND ERRATIC character with a hand in threatening Americans was General Dinh, Saigon's military governor.

Dinh commanded thousands of troops in the capital area—troops that could provide the margin of victory or defeat in the event of a coup. Usually accompanied by a tall, silent Cambodian bodyguard, Dinh favored sunglasses, a red beret worn at a jaunty angle, and a tight-fitting paratrooper's uniform. He was given to fierce statements about how he'd deal with regime "enemies" and was roundly laughed at by Western newsmen when he grandiosely described himself at a press conference as South Vietnam's "savior."

Dinh had known Conein for years and anointed the CIA agent as his personal nuncio to the embassy. Dinh installed a red phone in Conein's home that gave the general a direct line to him. He periodically called up Conein to say he was coming over, then roared up to his house with a motorcycle escort. Dinh swaggered inside, sat down at the bar surrounded by armed guards, and asked for whiskey. He and Conein drank and bantered back and forth until Dinh and his men got up and roared away.

Conein met Dinh under far less convivial circumstances on September 4, when soldiers forcibly took him to the general's headquarters. There Conein found Dinh's men aiming submachine guns at him and the general himself in an "exultant, ranting, raving mood." Dinh crowed that he had the power to kidnap or kill anyone in Saigon, including Diem, and that he, not the president, was "the man of the hour who would save Vietnam from Communism." He angrily accused Mecklin of being a communist and rushed around the room, gesticulating at wall maps and exclaiming that Saigon was surrounded by VC.

Dinh's men shoved the CIA officer against a wall as the general demanded to know whether he was intriguing against Diem. Conein denied such activity, an untruth that may have saved his life. The general's mood then veered in another direction. He grabbed a phone, called Conein's wife, and congratulated her on her good luck at having a chance to speak with Saigon's vaunted military governor. Hanging up, Dinh ordered a bouquet of flowers rushed to her at home.

Throughout this manic, four-hour performance, Dinh's guards kept their guns pointed at Conein, even during a break for lunch. Conein later told his bosses the general's words and actions had been even more disjointed and incoherent than his written report indicated. It would take little, if any, provocation for Dinh to try to seize more power, Conein said.

Another ARVN general later told the CIA that Dinh had been acting under Nhu's orders to intimidate Conein.

LODGE, TOO, HAD SOME unsettling moments. About two weeks after he arrived in Saigon, a naval attaché rushed into his office to report that a mob was surging toward his residence, two miles away. Lodge's wife, Emily, was there by herself and the house had virtually no protection—"a retired Vietnamese policeman, perhaps, pulling guard duty at night or something, and a gardener during the day," as one aide put it.

Lodge ran into the adjacent office of his special assistant, Freddy Flott, a former World War II Army officer. The ambassador told Flott to come with him to his house, asking, "How do we hit this kind of thing?" The two men would drive as close as possible to the front door, Flott replied, and then get out of the car. Flott would head into the crowd, with Lodge right behind him.

Take off your tie, Flott instructed, so there's nothing for people to grab on to. Don't make eye contact with anyone. "Use your elbows," he told the ambassador, "and just steamroller right through to the door."

But when they arrived at the residence, no one was there. The mob report was false. Lodge fired the excitable attaché.

Given the residence's poor security, Flott and another aide took turns guarding Lodge and his wife at night. Armed with a Schmeisser submachine gun and an M1 carbine supplied by Conein, Flott and the other man alternated four-hour shifts outside the couple's bedroom for several nights until better protection could be arranged.

Security was hardly Lodge's only problem. The embassy staff was as bitterly divided as it had been in Nolting's last days, if not more so.

When Washington requested an overall assessment of conditions in South Vietnam, the "country team"—made up of the heads of the various U.S. agencies in Saigon—couldn't even agree on a summary. "We seem to have reached the point in official American community that, if you think we can win with present government, you are simply not running in right direction with the majority," complained Richardson, who was back in Diem's camp as the Buddhist unrest subsided, to his headquarters.

From his first hours in Saigon, Lodge made it clear that he and he alone was running the show. He was President Kennedy's man in Saigon and would brook no opposition. He instructed subordinates not to talk to regime officials they'd dealt with, in some cases, for years. He later stopped showing Harkins and Richardson cables from Washington, leaving them in the dark about important policy issues.

Suspicious and secretive, Lodge was a canny bureaucratic player who kept his cards close to his vest. He imported two aides to handle his confidential business: Flott and John Michael Dunn, a U.S. Army lieutenant colonel he'd met at the Pentagon during a reserve mobilization exercise. ("Lodge has never been betrayed," one of them told Mecklin. "He seldom confides in enough people to be betrayed.") Lodge regarded "Mike" Dunn, a Harvard graduate who also held a PhD in political science from Princeton, as "energetic and brilliant," but some in the embassy came to see him as the ambassador's hatchet man.

Some subordinates, including Trueheart, were greatly impressed with Lodge and his self-assured takeover of the troubled embassy. Others found him a poor substitute for his treasured predecessor, Fritz Nolting. "We all loved [Nolting]," said his staff assistant, Kenneth N. Rogers. "We got in his place a distant, rather arrogant, cold, famous person." Mecklin, who Lodge later fired, said the new boss "disrupted the morale of some of us to a degree that even Madame Nhu had failed to achieve."

LODGE EVENTUALLY BEGAN TO place more trust in the rest of his embassy staff. But he soured entirely on John Richardson.

Even before coming to Vietnam, Lodge became convinced that the CIA had too much power and autonomy. In a note to himself, he wrote that the Saigon station "has more money; bigger houses than diplomats; bigger salaries; more weapons; more modern equipment."

Not long after arriving in Saigon, he sent a laundry list of grievances about the CIA station to the U.S. Office of Management and Budget, which oversaw the performance of federal agencies. Richardson's outfit, he complained, was acting on its own initiative without any control from either him or Washington; dealing "improperly" with Nhu; and dragging its feet after being directed to turn over to MACV its paramilitary operations with the Montagnards. Also, the station was "too large and too visible" in Saigon.

Lodge grumbled that Richardson lived "in a palatial mansion and entertained government officials there," and that the pagoda raids had caught his agents by surprise. The OMB director, Kenneth Hansen, later told Lodge that his "charges were erroneous" (although the ambassador was at least right about the CIA getting caught flat-footed by the pagoda onslaught).

The ambassador disapproved of the CIA's habit of holding background briefings for reporters as well as its efforts to build up a Vietnamese central intelligence organization. Nor had he forgotten his recent clash with Richardson, when Lodge angrily claimed that the station chief had ruined the chance for an August coup.

Lodge's animosity meant Richardson's days in Vietnam were numbered. The first indication came when Mike Dunn told Conein, at a September 6 dinner party at the latter's house, that Lodge had "chewed out" the station chief for "disobeying orders" and planned to get rid of him. A week later, Lodge wrote privately to Dean Rusk, requesting that Richardson be replaced "at once" by Edward Lansdale, the crafty former CIA operative who'd helped Diem defeat the Binh Xuyen and sect armies in 1955.

Still eager to see Diem overthrown, Lodge embraced an inflated image of Lansdale as "a sort of Lawrence of Arabia" who could "take charge, under my supervision, of all U.S. relationships with a change of government here." A vocal "Lansdale mafia," led by Rufus Phillips, an admirer since working under him in the 1950s, was lobbying for his return to South Vietnam, arguing that he was the one American who might be able to persuade Diem to change his ways. (Phillips didn't hold Richardson in the same esteem, mocking him in a letter to an associate as "our tranquilized friend.") But CIA director John McCone was implacably opposed to Lansdale running the station, and the dispute wound up in President Kennedy's lap.

On September 9, Lodge took yet another crack at peeling Nhu away from his brother, urging Diem to send the political counselor on a four-month sojourn abroad. But the president, Lodge reported, "looked at me aghast." It was out of the question for his brother to be gone for so long, he said; Nhu was critical to the ongoing success of the strategic hamlets.

Diem denied that Nhu organized the pagoda raids, adding that of the country's 4,700 temples, only 20 to 30 had been searched. The chaste bachelor president then seemed to go off the deep end, insisting that the Buddhists had turned their sacred places of worship "into bordellos," and that his police found "a great deal of female underwear, love letters, and obscene photographs" inside them. Virgins were "being despoiled" in the pagodas, Diem said; one particularly wanton bonze "had despoiled 13 virgins."

Such peculiar fantasies aside, Diem wanted to demonstrate that the Buddhist crisis was over and resume normal relations with Washington. In mid-September, he lifted martial law, ended press censorship, and announced that National Assembly elections, postponed after the pagoda raids, would be held on September 27.

BY THEN LODGE HAD concluded that Diem and the Nhus were incapable of governing, and had lost all patience with them.

"They are essentially a medieval, Oriental despotism of the classic family type, who understand few, if any, of the arts of popular government," he cabled Washington. "They cannot talk to the people; they cannot cultivate the press; they cannot delegate authority or inspire trust; they cannot comprehend the idea of government as the servant of the people. They are interested in physical security and survival against any threat whatsoever—Communist or non-Communist." Diem's government was in a death spiral, Lodge said; it would fall to the communists within a month.

On September 11, the ambassador urged the Kennedy administration to impose economic sanctions sufficiently harsh "to bring about the fall of the existing government." Before Washington even had a chance to reply, Lodge was discussing with his Saigon staff how to set another coup in motion—despite admonishments not to do so from the British and French ambassadors.

Huntington Sheldon, the CIA's assistant deputy director for intelligence, discovered Lodge's actions while on a fact-finding tour of Vietnam undertaken at McCone's request. Trueheart told the visiting CIA executive that Lodge was thinking about instructing MACV to contact Diem's generals again and "stimulate early coup action with appropriate U.S. assurances." When Sheldon asked if the ambassador had sought permission from his superiors, Trueheart said such a move was "within Lodge's authority."

Sheldon wanted to know whether the embassy had considered the possibilities that the generals would inform Nhu of any new American approach, or that another coup attempt might fizzle. Trueheart acknowledged that a second unsuccessful stab at overthrowing Diem might result in the United States "being invited out" of South Vietnam.

Like Lodge, Trueheart was convinced the war couldn't be won with Diem. But Sheldon emphasized in his report to McCone that "we are at present in no position to proceed" with a coup. The failed August attempt, he wrote, was "based on hope rather than reality," since the conspirators lacked the military muscle to throw out the regime. In the interim, Nhu had had time to reposition and strengthen loyalist forces in Saigon. Attacks by *The Times of Vietnam* had left the CIA station in a defensive crouch, unable to ascertain whether commanders of key South Vietnamese units, such as the marines and the armored brigade, supported another coup effort.

"At this time," concluded Sheldon, "we know too little about where they would line up at moment of decision to base new coup plans on them with any great confidence."

WHILE TRI QUANG HAD been standoffish when John Helble spoke with him in Hue, he proved to be a gusher of information when U.S. officers questioned him after he took refuge in the embassy.

The monk was comfortably ensconced in an embassy conference room, where he became fond of the Marine guards who brought him food every day.

He told his interviewers that he'd long planned an anti-Diem campaign and seized on the May 8 killings in Hue to stage a showdown with the government. He denied instigating the violence, as the regime claimed, and insisted the Buddhists wouldn't have tried to bring down Diem if he'd moved quickly to ameliorate their grievances in May.

Additional U.S. action to get rid of the Ngos, he said, "would please people immensely." On the other hand, all of the Kennedy administration's good works in South Vietnam "will be dissipated" if it continued to support an oppressive government.

The reason Saigon was so calm now, Tri Quang added, was that the regime had spread word that if street demonstrations and burnings didn't stop, "Buddhist leaders would be killed."

CHAPTER 15

"YOU BOTH WENT TO THE SAME COUNTRY?"

FOR KENNEDY, SOUTH Vietnam was becoming a bigger political headache with each passing day.

Congress was growing restless about sacrificing American lives and treasure on behalf of an authoritarian regime that beat up and jailed Buddhist dissidents, while harassing Americans. The press speculated about whether the administration was trying to organize a coup against its wartime partner. (*Newsweek* said Washington was "plainly hoping" to engineer Diem's overthrow, but warned there was no guarantee that a new government would prosecute the war with the same determination and vigor as the Ngos.) At the United Nations, a group of member states led by heavily Buddhist Ceylon was calling for an investigation of human rights abuses in South Vietnam, a move that could lead to an embarrassing public censure by the global peacekeeping body.

On Labor Day, Kennedy settled into a wicker chair on the lawn outside his rented summer home on Squaw Island, not far from his family compound in Hyannis Port, for an interview with Walter Cronkite of the *CBS Evening News*.

Putting aside the carefully modulated talking points prepared by his staff, the president unambiguously tightened the screws on Diem. He called the regime's anti-Buddhist moves "very unwise" and faulted Diem for losing touch with his people. Without popular support, he said, the Saigon government couldn't defeat the communists. When Cronkite asked whether Diem could regain his people's favor, Kennedy said he could, but that doing so would require "changes in policy and perhaps with personnel"—a not-so-subtle swipe at the Nhus.

JFK's words undoubtedly pleased Hilsman, Harriman, Forrestal, and Lodge. But some in the U.S. press rebuked the president for his foray into "TV diplomacy." *Time* magazine labeled it a "lamentable failure" that served only to increase "tensions and animosities between two governments that must continue working together for their mutual security." James Reston, *The New York Times*'s Washington bureau chief, used his influential column to argue that Kennedy stepped on his own message by first warning Diem to reform and then, later in the interview, declaring that the United States shouldn't withdraw from Vietnam. Kennedy thus communicated to Diem that Washington would stick with him whether he changed his ways or not, Reston wrote.

But to the coup plotters in Saigon, the president's words were an unmistakable signal. General Don, one of the main planners, interpreted them to mean that America's powerful leader "would support any change" in the Diem government.

JFK convened his Vietnam advisers again on September 6. Amid a discussion that Hilsman described as "meandering," Robert Kennedy asked a bracingly direct question: Could the war be won with Diem and Nhu?

Rusk replied that if the Nhus continued to hold power and stayed on the same disastrous course, the answer was no. Robert then asked a logical follow-up question: If it was a foregone conclusion that Diem would lose, "why do we not grasp the nettle now" and pull U.S. forces out of Vietnam? As JFK's special assistant and speechwriter, Arthur Schlesinger, recalled, the forthright question "hovered for a moment, then died away, a hopelessly alien thought in a field of unexamined assumptions and entrenched convictions."

Nine and a half years later, an exhausted United States would withdraw the last of its 500,000 troops from Vietnam. But in the summer of 1963, retreat in the face of communist aggression was, if not unthinkable, at least highly unpalatable politically. Rusk hastened to reply that if the Americans left and the Viet Cong took over, "we are in real trouble." When Robert asked what Washington should do if Diem couldn't beat the VC, McNamara said his question was unanswerable because "we have insufficient information in Washington."

The defense secretary then proposed a fact-finding mission to Vietnam led by Victor Krulak, the counterinsurgency specialist for the Joint Chiefs of Staff. It was no secret that Krulak, a Marine major general, was a strong supporter of Diem and MACV. Evidently worried that Krulak's report to JFK would be another bucket of upbeat military bilge, Hilsman requested that a State Department official go along with him, to make sure that the less sanguine views of American and Vietnamese civilians reached JFK as well.

The president asked Krulak how soon he could leave. Right away, the general replied. "I'll give you 48 hours in Vietnam, then come back," JFK said. Although it was questionable how much useful new information a pair of Washington bureaucrats could glean by flying nine thousand miles to rush around Vietnam for two days and then rush back, the matter was settled.

Less than two hours later, Krulak was aboard a helicopter as it lifted off from the Pentagon and headed for Andrews Air Force Base.

A HIGHLY DECORATED VETERAN of World War II and Korea, Krulak was widely regarded as a brilliant, even visionary officer. He was instrumental in developing the "Higgins boat," a landing craft with a bow that dropped down to become a ramp for rapid off-loading of troops and vehicles on invasion beaches.

After World War II, he championed the battlefield use of helicopters, realizing that even though they were then considered little more than underpowered gadgets, they'd become larger and more powerful over time. In 1948, he staged a pathbreaking demonstration of how the machines could quickly take Marines to a beach from an aircraft carrier stationed off Camp

Lejeune, North Carolina. During the Korean War, he advised General Douglas MacArthur on the amphibious assault at Inchon, a strategic masterstroke that forced the invading North Korean army to retreat in disarray up the Korean peninsula.

Charming and sophisticated, Krulak was well liked at the White House as well as the Pentagon. He played golf with McCone and picked up Robert Kennedy on his way to White House meetings. His nickname was "Brute," a jesting reference to his diminutive size—he stood five feet, five inches tall—acquired in his days at the Naval Academy.

Krulak also had a unique personal history with his commander in chief. In 1943, Krulak led a Marine battalion in a diversionary attack that helped a larger Marine force capture Bougainville Island from the Japanese. As Krulak's Marines withdrew under fire, one of their landing craft snagged on a reef and began to sink. A Navy torpedo boat skippered by Lieutenant John F. Kennedy rescued some of Krulak's men.

The Marine leader promised Kennedy a bottle of whiskey to thank him, but wasn't able to deliver it as the war rolled on. When JFK was elected president, Krulak left a bottle at the White House with a note reminding him of their South Pacific adventure. Delighted, Kennedy invited Krulak for a celebratory drink and some reminiscing.

The State Department official Hilsman chose to go with Krulak was Joseph Mendenhall, an experienced Vietnam hand who'd served as Nolting's political counselor, but had turned against Diem.

A White House jet awaited the pair at Andrews Air Force Base. It refueled in Nebraska and zoomed on to Travis Air Force Base in California. There the men hustled up the stairs into a KC-135 Stratotanker, two of its four engines already running. "I am told that you want to go to Saigon as fast as you can," the pilot said. "Well, we have 192,000 pounds of fuel, and we're going to try and go nonstop. It's never been done before."

With Saigon under martial-law curfew, the Air Force jet had to land in Okinawa for the night. Krulak and Mendenhall went to the Saturday dance at an officers' club, caught some sleep, and arrived at Tan Son Nhut at six o'clock the next morning.

The two men split up to pursue their different itineraries. Traveling in a military plane laid on by Harkins, Krulak made a whirlwind tour of all four ARVN corps zones, talking to more than a hundred American and Vietnamese army officers. Mendenhall took off in a small plane provided by Lodge, spending time in Hue and Danang before returning to Saigon to talk with Vietnamese friends whose judgment he trusted. Then the quick-turnaround fact finders got back on their jet and headed home.

KRULAK FINISHED HIS REPORT to Kennedy while still aboard the KC-135. Unsurprisingly, he concluded that the war was going well and that Diem and Nhu could still triumph, despite their "grave defects." Most Vietnamese military officers were fully aware of the Buddhist crisis, but hadn't let it impede their operations in any significant way. Many of these men would be happy to see the Nhus depart, Krulak wrote, "but few officers would extend their necks to bring it about." He'd witnessed a government attack in the delta involving ground as well as air and riverine units, and he declared that American forces "could not have executed the complex operation any better."

While Krulak was encouraged by the determination and efficiency of the Vietnamese military, Mendenhall was concerned about a restless, resentful civilian populace living in "a police state atmosphere."

"I have been struck by fear which pervades Saigon, Hue, and Danang," he wrote in his report. "These cities have been living under reign of terror which continues." On the day he and Krulak left Saigon, hundreds of students were arrested there. Most government and military officials in the three cities had felt the regime's "oppressive hands on their children," producing a great deal of anti-government anger.

"These are also cities of hate directed mainly at Nhus," wrote Mendenhall, "but President Diem himself is increasingly identified with Nhus as sharing responsibility."

THE BIG JET'S LANDING wheels hit the runway at Andrews at about 6 a.m. on September 10. Within four hours, Krulak and Mendenhall were at the White House to deliver their diametrically opposed reports to Kennedy and his National Security Council. When they'd both finished, the president asked pointedly: "You both went to the same country?"

Nervous laughter filled the room. Krulak tried to explain that he'd given a "national viewpoint," while Mendenhall provided a "metropolitan viewpoint," focused on the attitudes of city dwellers. But the general's explanation underscored the military tendency to pay attention solely to military factors in a conflict that required an unwavering focus on political factors, too.

Besides Krulak and Mendenhall, the KC-135 had carried two other passengers: John Mecklin and Rufus Phillips. They'd been invited to brief Kennedy based on their specialized knowledge of conditions in Saigon and the provinces.

When Krulak finished speaking, Phillips was invited to give his views. He'd first come to Vietnam in 1954 and knew Diem, Nhu, and many ARVN commanders well. Through his work delivering American supplies to strategic hamlets, he was familiar with rural conditions and attitudes. Most Vietnamese military officers and civil servants, he said, had lost confidence in and respect for Nhu and wanted him out of the government.

The Vietnamese, he continued, were watching to see whether Washington would back up its strong disapproval of the Nhus with concrete action. Phillips recommended a U.S. campaign of political and psychological warfare to "isolate" the couple and shred their image as untouchable, all-powerful figures. The objective was to pressure Diem to get rid of Nhu and his wife, and for the military to do it if Diem refused. And Phillips knew just the right man to run such a campaign: his old CIA mentor, Ed Lansdale.

Sharply contradicting Krulak, Phillips drew a pessimistic picture of the war's progress. While the ARVN seemed to have the upper hand in northern and central Vietnam, he said, it was losing badly in the delta. Strategic hamlets there were being "chewed to pieces" by the Viet Cong. Sixty percent of the fortified hamlets in Long An Province, which bordered Saigon, had been overrun. Phillips added that VC advances in the delta had nothing to do with the Buddhist crisis.

When Kennedy asked Krulak what he thought of Phillips's comments, the Marine general said with a mild note of irritation that Harkins and the U.S. advisers under him were convinced that the South Vietnamese were winning. Phillips was "putting his judgment against General Harkins's judgment," Krulak said tartly, adding that he gave far greater weight to Harkins.

Phillips replied that the struggle in Vietnam was not a conventional military clash, but "essentially a political war . . . for men's minds." Since MACV had instructed American advisers in the field not to discuss politics with their Vietnamese counterparts, he noted, they were in no position to render judgments about the all-important political dimensions of the war. (When word of Phillips's critique got back to Saigon, Harkins pledged to "get that goddamn Rufus Phillips.")

Kennedy wanted to know what specific actions Phillips thought the United States ought to take now, and the rural aid official recommended cutting off funding for Colonel Tung's Special Forces to show Washington's distaste for "Tung and Nhu and what they stood for."

The previous day, Halberstam and Sheehan had again embarrassed the White House by revealing that the CIA continued to bankroll Tung's men after the pagoda raids. Halberstam's front-page story said the CIA was giving $3 million a year to the Special Forces, and had made its regular monthly payment of $250,000 in September over the objections of many agency staffers in Saigon.

Sheehan's story ran in the *New York Herald Tribune* and other prominent U.S. newspapers. Afterward, working late at night and alone, the UPI reporter got a phone call.

"You are in very big trouble," said a voice he didn't recognize.

THE CIA-TUNG EXPOSÉ GAVE more fodder to those in Congress who wanted to end American aid. "It is shocking that we are giving support to a regime so dictatorial and tyrannical as the Diem regime," declared Senator Wayne Morse, an Oregon Democrat who was emerging as a leading critic of the war. "I consider such support to be a misuse of the American taxpayers' dollars." But during a September 9 interview with NBC News, JFK reiterated that he opposed halting U.S. assistance since such a move might cause Diem's government to collapse.

While publicly frowning on a total cutoff, however, Kennedy was quietly considering selective aid cuts to put more pressure on Diem.

He instructed Hilsman to look into reductions that would scare Diem without degrading the war effort. The regime was deeply dependent on U.S. assistance, which was then running at about $500 million a year. American tax dollars subsidized not only weapons, military vehicles, and uniforms, but cars, refrigerators, air conditioners, Scotch whiskey, and other goods coveted by middle- and upper-class Vietnamese. The U.S. government also financed a variety of agricultural and industrial products, including wheat flour, tobacco, cotton, iron, cement, and chemicals. And Washington had granted millions of dollars in loans to construct a water treatment plant for Saigon and Cholon, and a transmission line to bring electricity from a hydroelectric power plant to the capital's homes and businesses.

The centerpiece of the American economic aid effort was the Commercial Import Program, designed to hold down inflation in the anemic Vietnamese economy as hundreds of millions of dollars were pumped into it.

Under the program, Washington gave dollars to the Saigon government, which sold them to licensed Vietnamese importers at less than the official exchange rate. Piastres from those sales went into a special counterpart fund that largely paid for Diem's army, police, and government ministries. The importers then purchased American goods with the discounted dollars and sold them locally. Since the government-issued import licenses generated windfall profits, businessmen who were able to acquire them—sometimes by bribery—were among Diem's most fervent supporters.

The idea of reducing U.S. assistance touched off a fierce debate within the administration. Joseph Brent, who headed U.S. aid operations in South Vietnam, said he knew of no cuts that "would not adversely affect this country's closely balanced economy or the war effort." For example, piastres from the counterpart fund paid for 70 percent of ARVN salaries. Even selective cuts, he said, posed "extremely complex problems" and could create shortages that would drive up prices for ordinary Vietnamese. Advocates, however, argued that substantial reductions were the only way to get Diem's attention and convey the message that Washington was finally serious about bringing him into line.

But unbeknownst to Kennedy, bureaucrats at the U.S. Agency for International Development had, on their own initiative, already temporarily halted the Commercial Import Program. "The cutting off of aid, as nearly as I can determine looking back on it, was an accident," Forrestal recalled years later. "It was not something that was the subject of [a presidential] decision." AID officials had suspended the program in mid-August, apparently fearing an outcry in Congress if they continued "nonessential" aid amid all the turmoil in South Vietnam. They also felt that so many American products were already in Vietnamese warehouses or the supply pipeline that the import program could be safely paused for a few weeks until the Buddhist crisis blew over.

What the officials apparently overlooked was that the aid spigots couldn't be turned back on without sending the wrong message to Diem that all was forgiven. "Well, there's no point in arguing it now," Kennedy remarked. "It can't be undone. We're stuck with that whether we like it or not." But the secret cutoff wouldn't stay secret for long.

Kennedy was well aware of the domestic political risks of reducing or terminating U.S. help to a friendly nation locked in a life-or-death struggle with communists. As a young congressman, he'd witnessed the uproar that ensued when the Truman administration began holding back U.S. military aid to Chiang Kai-shek's shaky and corrupt Nationalist government in the late 1940s. Mao's armies defeated the Nationalists and President Truman was vilified by Republicans for "losing" China. (Indeed, Representative Kennedy had been a singer in the anti-Truman chorus.) He was certain to be subjected to similar attacks if he curtailed American help to Diem and South Vietnam went under.

Yet some in Congress were ready to cut Diem off cold. On September 12, Senator Frank Church, an Idaho Democrat, introduced a resolution demanding discontinuation of all U.S. assistance, military and economic, unless the regime "abandons policies of repression against its own people and makes a determined and effective effort to regain their support." Church reiterated American revulsion at the monk burnings, asserting, with a touch of old-fashioned senatorial hyperbole, that "such grisly scenes have not been witnessed since the Christian martyrs marched hand in hand into the Roman arenas."

The White House quietly gave its blessing to Church's resolution, and twenty-two other senators signed on to it. Kennedy hoped the measure could be used as another lever to squeeze Diem, and Hilsman worked with Church on its wording. But the resolution also ran the risk of backfiring if enough senators concerned about weakening South Vietnam voted against it. Such a defeat would be a strong indication to Diem that his American support was, as always, bulletproof.

A SURE SIGN THAT a presidential administration is in the throes of bureaucratic infighting is a wave of leaks to the press. Leaks can be used to advance a policy agenda, bash a political foe, or burnish the leaker's public image—with little risk of the leaker's identity or motives becoming known. In the fall of 1963, the Kennedy administration was shot through with leaks.

The nonstop whispering made JFK's government look disorganized and uncertain, and it drove him to distraction. On September 5, the eagle-eyed president called Hilsman to complain about a story, based on anonymous sources and headlined "Washington Officials Accuse Nhu of Blackmail," on page five of *The New York Times*. "We can't have people saying that U.S. officials are saying these kinds of things," he snapped. "If somebody is, we've got to put a stop to it."

Kennedy knew the profusion of news stories based on unnamed sources reflected the increasingly rancorous struggle between the pro- and anti-Diem factions in his administration. He admonished his advisers about dishing to the media, saying he wanted their disagreements "resolved in the privacy of the White House and not in the press." It was clear that some leaks were emanating from Saigon; the president was particularly irked by an article that said a U.S. officer had urged a news photographer to take a picture of a U.S.-supplied truck carrying off arrested students "so that it could be seen in Washington."

Shortly after Lodge's arrival in Saigon, Mecklin noticed a surge of news articles that flattered the new ambassador. The stories emphasized that strong leadership was needed to ride herd on the unruly embassy and that Lodge was the man to provide it. He'd been feeding reporters off-the-record information for twenty-five years, as a senator and UN ambassador, and he made no bones about his fondness for leaking.

"The leak is the prerogative of the ambassador," he told Mecklin. "It is one of my weapons for doing this job."

Lodge was a past master of using leaks to strangle political opponents without leaving any marks on their throats. In 1954, he throttled one of President Eisenhower's most powerful critics, Senator Joseph McCarthy, by facilitating the leak of a U.S. Army report that charged McCarthy with applying undue pressure to obtain an officer's commission for an aide, G. David Schine, who'd been drafted. The leak came on the eve of the televised Army-McCarthy hearings that sent the Red-baiting McCarthy's political career into a terminal tailspin.

Despite JFK's scolding, the September 11 edition of Washington's *Evening Star* carried a banner headline reading: "Lodge Requests Ouster of Nhu." The story, datelined Saigon and written by an Associated Press reporter, was based on Lodge's private meeting with Diem two days earlier, and it wasn't difficult to guess the name of the "high official source" who planted it.

The article wasn't merely another annoying example of an underling's agenda-advancing leak. The bigger problem, from JFK's perspective, was that it set up his administration to look foolish and weak once again when Diem inevitably ignored Lodge's entreaty. Hilsman cabled Lodge in exasperation: "This is further cause why we must again request you hold tightest hand on press leaks."

Lodge's hardball tactics and resistance to instructions were starting to cause twinges of discomfort, if not alarm, in Washington. On his own initiative he adopted what he called his "correct but cool" policy toward Diem, refusing to talk to him until he promised to make reforms in exchange for a resumption of U.S. aid. When Rusk cabled Lodge that Kennedy wanted him to keep talking with the South Vietnamese leader, no matter how frustrating it was, Lodge replied offhandedly that he didn't see any point in doing so.

"Visiting Diem," he wrote back, "is an extremely time-consuming procedure, and it seems to me there are many better ways in which I can use my waking hours."

Although Diem steadfastly refused to discard his brother, he acceded to other American demands, weakening the case for removing him. For instance, he agreed to shift the ARVN Ninth Division from the Central Highlands to the delta, a move long sought by MACV in order to bring more firepower to bear against the VC there.

In a September 17 telegram, Kennedy pointedly told Lodge that he saw "no good opportunity for action to remove present government in immediate future." But the president's words seemed to have little impact on his headstrong ambassador, who continued to lobby for putting Diem under the guillotine.

Lodge peppered Washington with dire-sounding reports conveying the impression that Diem and Nhu were lunatics about to implode. Diem, said Lodge in one dispatch, was "cut off from reality and very slow and dull in his reactions." The ambassador also repeated a claim by a Vietnamese labor leader (who even Lodge regarded as "a thorough-going scoundrel") that Nhu was smoking opium, was "off in the clouds," and was indifferent to a purported longtime affair between his wife and General Don "because opium amuses him more."

On the same day Lodge reported Nhu's alleged opium use, David R. Smith, the CIA's deputy Saigon station chief, who was then in Washington, brushed off the story in a meeting with JFK's advisers. The opium rumor had been circulating since 1954, he said, and he didn't believe it.

LODGE HAD EVEN MORE ammunition to work with when rumors bubbled up in Saigon diplomatic circles that Nhu was secretly negotiating some sort of deal with Hanoi, possibly involving a ceasefire with the VC.

The stories intensified after French President Charles de Gaulle issued a statement on August 29 that peace would return to Vietnam only when the north and south were reunited under a government immune to foreign influence. France, he said, stood ready to help the Vietnamese move in that direction.

Kennedy and his advisers dismissed de Gaulle's proposal as a meddlesome intrusion into U.S. policy (McGeorge Bundy referred to de Gaulle as "Nosy Charlie") and a transparent French attempt to regain influence in Vietnam. In White House eyes, de Gaulle seemed to be calling for a neutralist government, and *neutralism* was a dirty word in Washington. Hanoi and the National Liberation Front had repeatedly called for a neutral or coalition government—one that included both communists and noncommunists—in Saigon. But American policymakers saw that as the first step on the road to a North Vietnamese takeover of the south.

Although Kennedy had secretly tried to feel out Hanoi on a possible neutralization deal in 1962, he concluded by the fall of 1963 that neutralization hadn't worked in Laos and wouldn't work in Vietnam. But after years of death and destruction, neutralization appealed strongly to some South Vietnamese who yearned for peace at almost any price. (In his 1995 memoir, *In Retrospect*, McNamara admitted that Washington had erred by not seriously exploring de Gaulle's ideas, which, nebulous though they were, might have paved the way to a negotiated U.S. exit from Vietnam.)

Even before de Gaulle's announcement, the French ambassador to South Vietnam, Roger Lalouette, had quietly reached out to Hanoi, using as his intermediary the Polish diplomat Mieczyslaw Maneli. Lalouette's plan was to lay the groundwork for serious peace talks with a series of token trade and cultural exchanges between Hanoi and Saigon. (Despite past tensions between France and Diem, Lalouette believed that only Diem could carry off a reunification plan and viewed his removal in a coup as a calamity that would destroy any chance for peace.)

In private discussions, Maneli found Ho Chi Minh and other northern leaders open to the idea of cross-border trade (the north wanted to swap its coal for southern rice), postal service, and joint publication of books. Such activities were intended to build trust and lead to political talks about a coalition government in Saigon. Hanoi wanted such an arrangement to be accompanied by a complete withdrawal of American forces. The North Vietnamese pledged not to push too fast for reunification and even to permit Diem to continue as chief of state in the south.

At Nhu's request, Maneli met him on September 2 in his palace office. The political counselor promptly launched into a rambling monologue on the war, Marxism, spirituality, Hegelian dialectics, and other topics. He wasn't opposed to "negotiations and cooperation" with the north, he said, adding: "Even during the most ferocious battle, the Vietnamese never forget who is a Vietnamese and who is a foreigner." But he told Maneli he didn't see any prospects for direct talks with Hanoi in the near future.

As Saigon buzzed with rumors of a supposed north-south rapprochement, Joseph Alsop, a prominent syndicated columnist who counted JFK among his most attentive readers, revealed Nhu's secret get-together with the communist diplomat in a September 18 *Washington Post* piece headlined "Very Ugly Stuff."

Alsop wrote that Nhu, who he'd interviewed on a recent Saigon visit, claimed that Hanoi, through Maneli, had "begged" him to open negotiations for a ceasefire. Though Nhu characterized the northern proposal as "almost an attractive offer," he rejected it, he told Alsop, because he "could not open negotiations behind the backs of the Americans." (Maneli later denied to Western reporters that he'd conveyed any proposals from Hanoi to Nhu.) Alsop's article also noted Lalouette's role in the affair, prompting the French to recall their Saigon ambassador in an evident gesture of propitiation to an irritated Washington.

Nhu sometimes met clandestinely with individual VC field commanders in an effort to persuade them to defect. He saw them in his palace office and, it was said, in remote forest or jungle clearings during his tiger hunts. But negotiations with Hanoi over a ceasefire and possible neutralization were a very different matter, a dangerous gambit that could trigger a revolt by staunchly anti-communist ARVN commanders if they found out.

AS SUMMER TURNED INTO autumn, the reports that trickled into the U.S. embassy were fragmentary and far from conclusive. A CIA informant claimed that Nhu had told a group of generals about his contacts with Maneli and Hanoi's desire for trade talks, and promised to keep his commanders informed about any future moves. Dang Duc Khoi, the regime PR man who warned Halberstam and Sheehan they might be murdered and then fled the country, resurfaced in Washington, naming a South Vietnamese diplomat, Tran Van Dinh, as Nhu's go-between in talks with the communists.

Some U.S. officials, however, doubted Nhu was in touch with the enemy. Trueheart, for one, regarded the idea as "a lot of horseshit, frankly." He doubted that Nhu would even try to contact the other side, since the VC wouldn't "have given him the time of day." McNamara felt that any substantive peace deal with Hanoi was unlikely since Diem's generals would probably respond to it with an immediate coup. There was speculation that Nhu was trying to frighten Washington into easing up on its pressure on him and Diem, for fear of driving them into Hanoi's arms. Even Maneli wasn't sure what Nhu was up to, writing later that he and his brother were "carrying on such a complicated and many-sided game that one could not be certain about the direction in which they were heading."

But the State Department's anti-Diem claque pounced on the purported talks as another reason for a coup.

Lodge pointedly asked the State Department to study "what our response should be" if Nhu suddenly demanded, as part of a pact with Ho Chi Minh, that all U.S. forces leave the south. "This is obviously the only trump card he has got," Lodge cabled, "and it is obviously of the highest importance." Hilsman, who figured Nhu was trying to blackmail Washington into lifting its economic sanctions, suggested a surreptitious counterattack that could easily get Nhu killed: "appropriately timed" leaks of Nhu's supposed contacts with Hanoi "to effect that Nhu is selling out to Communists."

At one point Hilsman met privately in a Georgetown apartment with Lansdale. Worried that a coup was being engineered against his old friend, Lansdale proposed several possible ways to separate Diem and Nhu. One was to install Nhu at South Vietnam's London embassy. Another was to establish an academic position for him at Harvard, an approach that might appeal to Nhu's intellectual pretensions.

Hilsman said the administration was more concerned about "a report that Nhu was trying to arrange a deal with NVN [North Vietnam] whereby Nhu would assume power and form a coalition with the North." According to Lansdale, Hilsman was less interested in his ideas for removing Nhu nonviolently than "in asking about Australian beaches, etc., since he was preparing for an Asian trip."

On September 18, at the height of the Nhu-Hanoi controversy, Lodge and his wife attended a small dinner party whose guests included Nhu. The political counselor was his usual garrulous self, arguing that Buddhist monks who burned themselves were victims of murder rather than suicide, and boasting that he'd pushed the strategic hamlet program forward despite American skepticism. In a vividly written cable to the State Department the next day, Lodge portrayed Nhu as a doomed and pathetic character out of a Shakespearean tragedy:

"He has a handsome, cruel face and is obviously very intelligent. His talk last night was like a phonograph record and, in spite of his obvious ruthlessness and cruelty, one feels sorry for him. He is wound up as tight as a wire. He appears to be a lost soul, a haunted man who is caught in a vicious circle. The Furies are after him."

JFK SAT THROUGH ONE unproductive meeting after another as September wore on and the pro- and anti-Diem factions continued to argue. "This is impossible," he said in disgust after yet another inconclusive arm wrestle among his advisers. "We can't run a policy when there are such divergent views on the same set of facts."

His CIA director, John McCone, had the uncomfortable feeling that the anti-Diem activists were deliberately trying to undermine those who opposed a coup, including himself and John Richardson. He started to discuss his qualms in back-channel get-togethers with fellow coup skeptics.

A small-framed man with white hair and steel-rimmed spectacles, the sixty-one-year-old McCone was quite capable of engaging in bureaucratic slugfests. Born in San Francisco, he was a conservative Republican who grew wealthy as a cofounder of what became the Bechtel Corp., an international engineering and heavy construction firm. He served as undersecretary of the Air Force in the Truman administration and chairman of the Atomic Energy Commission under Eisenhower, with whom he formed a close bond.

In 1961, Kennedy appointed him to replace the legendary spymaster Allen Dulles as head of the CIA in the aftermath of the Bay of Pigs. Keenly intelligent and demanding of subordinates, McCone shifted the agency's emphasis away from its traditional covert derring-do to better intelligence gathering and analysis. Some at the agency worried that his militant anti-communism would distort CIA reporting, but instead found McCone to be open-minded and reasonable in his judgments. In 1962, his stock rose at the White House after the CIA discovered evidence that the Soviets were installing offensive missiles in Cuba, giving Kennedy precious time to prepare for the coming confrontation over the weapons with Khrushchev.

A late and devout convert to Catholicism, McCone became close to Robert Kennedy and his wife, Ethel, who spent time consoling McCone after his wife died. JFK liked him as well, and McCone didn't hesitate to make his way into the Oval Office when he felt the need to emphatically state the CIA's case. Hilsman described him as "very ambitious but disarmingly candid about it."

McCone invited Rusk to lunch at his six-bedroom home in Washington's elegant Embassy Row neighborhood and learned that the secretary of state felt Lodge "had probably gone too far too fast." Often sphinxlike in White House meetings, Rusk was frank in the privacy of the intelligence chief's house. He "appeared critical of Hilsman and somewhat critical of Harriman," McCone wrote in a memo to himself, adding that his guest "agreed with me that we should go slowly; that there was no apparent acceptable successor to Diem."

McCone also met quietly with McNamara and his number two, Roswell Gilpatric. They believed Kennedy "had been poorly advised" on Vietnam and that State Department cables to Lodge—many of which were Hilsman products—didn't reflect the president's true intentions as expressed in White House meetings. The Pentagon men also thought State was leaking to the press, particularly *The New York Times*. (Lodge admitted in a memoir that he'd been giving tips to Joseph Alsop since the 1952 presidential campaign.)

McCone sat down as well with Diem's chief defender, Nolting. Hilsman and Harriman had hoped that the ex-ambassador would "disengage" from the Vietnam dispute at some point. In a September 3 phone call with Harriman, Hilsman said Nolting was "behaving well" lately.

Nolting hadn't pulled back from the fray, however. When JFK drew him aside after one White House session and asked what needed to be done to get back on track with Diem, Nolting recommended replacing both Harriman and Lodge. "You don't expect me to do that, do you?" the incredulous president replied.

Nolting thought there was still time for Washington to reverse course and get behind Diem. All that was necessary was for the Kennedy administration to admit it had misunderstood the Buddhist issue, acknowledging that the claim of religious persecution was a red herring and that the monks were the spearhead of a broader political movement to unseat Diem.

As Nolting told McCone over lunch at the CIA's new headquarters in Langley, Virginia, on September 4: "We ought to come very clean on that and come out and say, after looking at this thing and being horribly confused, and dreadfully depressed by the burnings, and dreadfully thrown off course by Madame Nhu's intemperate statements on the burnings and similar matters, we have nonetheless reached the conclusion that this movement . . . was used from the beginning to rally politically dissident elements under a religious flag, and had very little if anything to do with religious persecution or even discrimination.

"Now, this is going to take quite a bit of courage on our part to face up to that and so move," Nolting added. "We did get snowed on this. It's not what we thought it was originally. It's going to take a lot of talking to *The New York Times* editorial board, the *Washington Post*, and a lot of other people who have been snowed. . . . We ought to get our facts and then meet this one head on, and take our lumps as necessary but clear that misunderstanding away, if we can." McCone generally agreed.

But JFK was as unlikely to admit he was "snowed" by faraway little men in colored robes as he was to dump Harriman and Lodge, and Nolting apparently didn't propose his come-clean idea to the White House.

Never one for subtlety, Harriman—the Crocodile—again displayed his contempt for Nolting one day after he and Rusk climbed into the back of a chauffeured State Department limousine to go to the White House. When Nolting got in the front seat, next to the driver, he heard the glass partition slide firmly shut behind him.

BY MID-SEPTEMBER, THE WHITE House had arrived at what Forrestal dejectedly described as "a position of stall" on Vietnam.

JFK's foreign policy and national defense experts were deadlocked. Harriman, Lodge, Hilsman, and Forrestal were adamant that a coup was necessary; McNamara, Rusk, McCone, Taylor, and Nolting believed that, with no viable alternative to Diem, a coup was unwise.

Forrestal pleaded with McGeorge Bundy for "Presidential guidance" to break the logjam, adding in a September 16 memo: "The longer we continue in an attitude of semipublic fluidity, the worse the leak problem becomes." Mike Mansfield warned on the Senate floor that the United States would be "face-to-face with a disaster" unless the internal rift was healed and U.S. government agencies began working together. The press, too, took notice of the administration's uncertainty. *Newsweek* told of a "crisis of indecision" in the White House and ran a cartoon of an aggrieved-looking Kennedy in a Hawaiian shirt pulling Madame Nhu in a rickshaw, her ao dai festooned with dollar signs and her hand clutching a bloody scimitar.

Kennedy appeared to have little appetite for another coup attempt, which might lead to some very unpleasant outcomes, including ugly, three-way fighting among pro- and anti-Diem ARVN factions and the Viet Cong. JFK's position, as Bundy summarized it, was "one in which we must express our reservations as to the mistakes and misdeeds of Diem, but not be in a position where we cannot deal with him further."

At a National Security Council meeting on September 17, Kennedy concluded he still didn't have enough information to understand what was going on in South Vietnam and ordered yet another fact-finding mission, this one to be headed by McNamara and Taylor, two of Diem's most influential and vocal supporters.

The anti-Diem group was aghast. Hilsman was so upset that he got up from the conference table and trailed the president into the Oval Office, arguing against the mission. Harriman telephoned Forrestal, saying it would be "a disaster" to send "two men opposed to our policy" of getting rid of Diem. Lodge cabled the president, warning that Diem would interpret the arrival of two high-ranking Americans as "the end of our period of disapproval of the oppressive measures which have been taken here since last May."

Kennedy, however, had internal political factors to consider as well. McNamara and Taylor had largely bought Harkins's excessively rosy reports on the war, and the Pentagon had a strong institutional imperative to defeat the communists. The military didn't want any steps taken to undermine Diem as long as he appeared to be winning.

JFK looked at the problem differently. He was under pressure from Congress and the press to wring reforms out of Diem and prevent him from committing more authoritarian abuses that made Americans' skin crawl. Perhaps if McNamara and Taylor saw firsthand how Diem's political support was eroding, and how that could eventually impede the war effort, they'd understand the need to squeeze him harder to institute changes.

But Hilsman thought it was a mistake to send such prominent figures to South Vietnam; doing so would reinforce the view that the stakes there were high, something the administration wanted to avoid.

As Hilsman continued to fuss in the Oval Office, Kennedy turned on him impatiently, "as if he were dealing with some unruly child," Hilsman recalled.

"Look, Roger," the president snapped, "I know that. I know that it's costly and bad to send McNamara out there. But the only way that we can keep the [Joint Chiefs of Staff] on board is to keep McNamara on board, and the only way we can keep McNamara on board is to let him go see for himself. Now that's the price we have to pay."

KENNEDY'S INSTRUCTIONS TO MCNAMARA and Taylor were to evaluate the effectiveness of South Vietnam's fight against the Viet Cong and its prospects for success. If the prognosis was poor, they were to find out what changes needed to be made, and how to persuade Diem to make them. Talking to the two Pentagon officials in person just before they left for Saigon, JFK said he wanted to "come to some final conclusion as to whether . . . [Diem and Nhu] are going to be in power for some time . . . and whether there is anything we can do to influence them, or do we stop talking about that."

McNamara and Taylor took off from Andrews Air Force Base on September 23, bundled into a KC-135 along with a number of high-level helpers. General Krulak was to set up meetings with U.S. military advisers, including many he'd talked to little more than two weeks before. Forrestal was to interview CIA officials and American and French businessmen. William Bundy, assistant secretary of defense for international security affairs (and McGeorge's older brother), would help McNamara write the mission's report and recommendations. The CIA's William Colby was to pick the brains of his old Vietnamese contacts.

Hilsman had been excluded from the trip; instead, State was represented solely by William H. Sullivan, Harriman's special assistant. JFK was none too impressed by State's performance in August, telling George Ball: "The fact of the matter is that Averell was wrong on the [abandoned] coup. We fucked that up."

Undeterred, Hilsman gave Forrestal a letter to hand-deliver to Lodge. "I have the feeling that more and more of the town is coming around to our view," it read, "and that if you in Saigon and we in the Department stick to our guns the rest will also come around. As Mike will tell you, a determined group here will back you all the way."

By the time the Washington visitors touched down at Tan Son Nhut, Lodge was primed and ready.

As McNamara strode toward a throng of waiting American officials, two of Lodge's "muscular embassy men" physically blocked Harkins so Lodge could be the first to greet the defense secretary—an eye-popping maneuver that didn't go unnoticed by newsmen. Lodge had already persuaded McNamara to stay at the ambassadorial residence, the better to bend his ear about the depredations and shortcomings of Diem and Nhu.

Lodge also ordered Colby not to have any contact with the palace. Colby—who'd conferred weekly with Nhu during his time as Saigon station chief—was furious, even though he knew Lodge was trying to maintain his "correct but cool" stance toward Diem.

McNamara and his entourage soon fanned out from Saigon. He, Taylor, and Harkins flew about the country in a C-54 aircraft protected by fighter planes and helicopter gunships. Lodge warned McNamara that lower-ranking U.S. military officers weren't likely to be very forthcoming in Harkins's presence. But at least one conference with young combat advisers, in the delta town of Can Tho, erupted into a round-robin of painful truth-telling.

Taylor asked a major how the war was progressing. "Lousy, General," the officer replied. When Taylor asked what he meant, the major began laying out all the problems in his province in a very convincing manner. That encouraged other advisers in the room to speak up, and "all hell broke loose," recalled Forrestal. "There was a very pessimistic appraisal from the whole group." Elsewhere, however, briefers put a happier spin on what they told Taylor.

THE CIVILIANS MCNAMARA SPOKE with painted a uniformly dire picture. Lodge arranged for the defense secretary to meet privately with Professor Patrick J. Honey, a Vietnam scholar on sabbatical from the University of London.

Honey had first visited Vietnam in 1945 as a lieutenant with the small British army contingent that briefly occupied Saigon after the Japanese surrender. Fluent in Vietnamese, he was personally acquainted with leaders in both North and South Vietnam and had once thought Diem could win the war. But he no longer believed that, he told McNamara. The president had "aged terribly" and become "slow mentally" since Honey had last seen him in 1960. He'd never democratize his regime and Washington would never be able to force him to.

Honey believed that a small group of "fanatically ambitious" monks had exploited the Hue killings and the credulity of foreign newsmen to generate opposition to the regime, and that Diem and Nhu lost their usual cool and overreacted. Nonetheless, Vietnamese of all creeds and social classes were disgusted by the regime's treatment of the Buddhists and shocked that government troops had violated the sanctity of the pagodas. Instead of whispering their criticisms as in the past, people were now openly saying that Diem had lost the mandate of heaven to govern.

If Diem couldn't prevail, Honey went on, the question was how to replace him, and with whom. Any move to depose him was risky, and neither the students nor the Buddhists were strong enough to do it. Only an assassination or a military coup would be effective, and one or the other would take place soon. The chances that South Vietnam would end up with a better government were only fifty-fifty, the Briton predicted.

McNamara also quietly conferred with Diem's aide, Thuan, who described the situation as "really desperate," and Vice President Tho, who made the astounding statement that while Nhu claimed to have built thousands of strategic hamlets, no more than thirty of them were properly defended. Archbishop Asta, the papal delegate, told McNamara the regime was engaged in "widespread torture" and that if Nhu gained power, he'd demand that the United States withdraw its forces and then "cut a deal with the Communists."

McNamara and Taylor went to the Saigon officers' club for a few rounds of tennis on September 29. Taylor loved tennis, but the games were actually cover for a hide-in-plain-sight meeting with Big Minh, an accomplished player and frequent presence on Saigon's courts. The Americans had been told the South Vietnamese general had "an important message" for them, possibly about a new coup attempt. Since Nhu's agents watched Minh closely, the tennis courts provided an innocuous-looking venue for him to talk to the Pentagon men.

McNamara sat on the sidelines, sweltering in the heat, as Taylor and Minh swatted balls back and forth. During breaks, Taylor dropped "broad hints" of his interest in discussing non-tennis topics, but Minh said nothing of significance. Puzzled, Taylor assigned a U.S. Army colonel to find out what went wrong.

The colonel reported back that Minh had been "confused yesterday as to what was taking place" and had no message to convey. As far as Minh knew, "the occasion was simply a game of tennis." Taylor concluded that another coup "did not seem to be in the offing."

After the unenlightening tennis game, McNamara, Taylor, Lodge, and Harkins went to Gia Long Palace to talk with Diem. South Vietnam's chief of state hated when Americans tried to browbeat him, and he wasn't about to let this latest delegation, as high-powered as it was, push him around. Chain-smoking as always and "purring French in somnolent tones," he defended his policies in a monologue that stretched on for two and a half hours. He touted Saigon's progress in the war, frequently springing to his feet to point out various places on maps.

Disconcerted by Diem's "serene self-assurance," McNamara finally broke in to press Washington's points. He bore down on the contrast between battlefield progress and the regime's political problems, emphasizing that further repression could imperil public support for the war in both South Vietnam and the United States.

Diem rebutted him point by point. He blamed "vicious press attacks" for Americans' "misunderstanding" of the real situation in South Vietnam. He'd been "too kind" to the Buddhists, and blamed the recent wave of arrests on "immature, untrained, and irresponsible" students.

McNamara also raised the subject of Madame Nhu, saying the regime's difficulties with the United States grew in no small part out of her bridge-burning comments. From his pocket he drew a newspaper clipping about her latest outburst, in which she complained that junior American military officers in South Vietnam were "acting like little soldiers of fortune." Americans found such remarks deeply offensive, McNamara said. Although Diem's facial expression suggested he understood the point, he once again defended Madame's freedom to speak her mind.

Taylor subsequently wrote that he left the palace depressed by "the refusal of this stalwart, stubborn patriot to recognize the realities which threatened to overwhelm him, his family, and his country." Diem evidently felt differently, displaying the attitude "of a man who had patiently explained a great deal and who hoped he had thus corrected a number of misapprehensions," according to the U.S. embassy note-taker at the meeting.

More than thirty years later, McNamara admitted that he never really understood the South Vietnamese leader: "Diem was an enigma to me, and, indeed, to virtually every American who met him."

SETTLED INTO THE KC-135 for the long flight home, McNamara and his party pondered their recent conversations and experiences.

The defense secretary regarded his talks with Honey and Thuan as "particularly illuminating and disturbing." Taylor confirmed his suspicion that Lodge was barely speaking to Harkins, even about military matters. Pro- and anti-Diem cliques in the embassy were leaking furiously.

Colby, however, was convinced that Diem and Nhu might have succeeded in breaking up the Buddhist rebellion. If Washington restrained itself from overreacting, the brothers could refocus on expanding the strategic hamlet program and prosecuting the war.

But Colby was dismayed by the political and bureaucratic dynamics driving U.S. policy on South Vietnam. Lodge, he later wrote, "was beyond control by the Democratic administration as he continued his lone-wolf vendetta against the Diem regime, communicating with it, and Washington, largely by leaks to journalists who shared his distaste" for Diem.

As the Stratotanker roared back over the Pacific, McNamara and Taylor worked on their official report, assisted by William Bundy. After talking to dozens of people, Bundy was impressed by the difficulty of accurately interpreting what was going on in the war. "It was just too diffuse, and too much that was critical took place below the surface," he later wrote. But an unreconstructed Diem, Bundy felt, stood little chance of beating the VC.

He and McNamara kept editing and rewriting, passing their draft back and forth. "He finished off all the gin on the plane and I finished off all the whiskey," Bundy recounted. By the time the KC-135 rolled to a stop at Andrews at about 6 a.m. on October 2, the report was nearly ready.

McNamara and Taylor presented their conclusions and recommendations to Kennedy a few hours later. Their report said that despite the regime's growing unpopularity, "the military campaign has made great progress and continues to progress," although that momentum could be slowed by future acts of repression.

The latest presidential fact finders said Lodge should maintain his correct but cool stance toward Diem, and Washington should stop bankrolling Colonel Tung's Special Forces unless they were brought under ARVN control. Although the practical effect would "probably be small," since Diem could pay for Tung's men from his own budget, an end to American financing would at least "remove one target of (U.S.) press criticism" and probably be welcomed by regular South Vietnamese military officers.

McNamara and Taylor further urged that the unauthorized suspension of the Commercial Import Program be extended, and that U.S. loans for the water treatment plant and hydroelectric power line be canceled. The fact finders detected "no solid evidence of the possibility of a successful coup," although they noted that "assassination of Diem or Nhu is always a possibility." They recommended that Washington make no efforts to stimulate a coup, adding that Diem's generals "appear to have little stomach" for it.

But Bundy later acknowledged the "clear internal inconsistency" between the report's military analysis—that the war was going well and was winnable as long as government reforms were made—and its political analysis that such reforms were unlikely under Diem. He'd gotten just two hours of sleep on the boozy flight from Saigon, and he noted ruefully that "neither draftsmanship nor judgment is likely to be at its best under such working conditions."

McNamara and Taylor advised that the unapproved aid suspension would have little immediate impact on the war, since so much U.S. matériel was already in the pipeline. But within a few months, South Vietnam's anemic economy would start to suffer, their report warned. Hoarding, speculation, and inflation would rise as consumers and businessmen realized that imported goods were drying up. Once inflation began, it would be hard to stop and "could have a serious effect on [the government's] budget and the conduct of the war." And regardless of how hard Washington squeezed Diem economically, he was unlikely to unload Nhu.

McNamara and Taylor also encouraged Kennedy to publicly state that he'd pull a thousand U.S. advisers out of South Vietnam by the end of the year, and that "the bulk of U.S. personnel" could probably be withdrawn by 1965. Other White House counselors thought such a declaration was imprudent. What if the war went badly, especially in light of South Vietnam's political troubles, and the advisers had to stay longer? What if more were needed to help battle the VC?

Kennedy himself was reluctant, saying the proposed statement was "overly optimistic" and didn't have much value. McNamara, however, insisted it would show congressional critics that the administration had a plan for reducing American combat casualties. Kennedy ultimately agreed to issue a press release along the lines his defense secretary wanted.

But the president's instincts were right; he was quickly attacked in the press. *The Washington Post*, for example, lambasted the prediction of a 1965 pullout as "groundless prophecy" and an affront to the "maturity and intelligence" of the American public.

BY LATE SEPTEMBER, MCCONE had become convinced that the administration's anti-Diem posse was using leaks in a deliberate attempt to damage the CIA in general and Richardson in particular. That belief left him, as he put it, "possessed of a cold anger."

To McCone, it was no coincidence that CIA activities in Vietnam had received almost no press coverage prior to Lodge's arrival, but had since become the subject of dozens of news articles, editorials, and radio and TV commentaries, many of them critical. McCone believed that Lodge and other State Department officials who wanted to ditch Diem were angry at the CIA for urging caution about a coup, and "are now carrying on a campaign" against the agency and its Saigon station.

The CIA had been taking a beating in the press since early September, when Hilsman told Marguerite Higgins and two other prominent Washington journalists over lunch that the agency "did not have the skill, the eptness, or the perceptiveness" to bring off a coup.

Soon afterward, a *San Francisco Chronicle* editorial called for abolition of "this organization of international wrong-wirepullers." Syndicated columnist Max Freedman bashed the agency for its "incredible and garish blunders committed in a sickening sequence"—without citing any examples—while praising Lodge for "doing a first-rate job in very hard conditions." The *St.*

Louis Post-Dispatch reported that younger CIA agents in Saigon were "going outside agency channels in a desperate effort" to stop Richardson from giving further support to Nhu. *The Times of Vietnam* gleefully jumped into the fray with a story mockingly headlined: "Pardon CIA, Your Split Is Showing."

The anti-CIA stories erupted at about the time Lodge began to push for Richardson's removal, and some of them were aimed squarely at the station chief. There were allegations that Richardson had gone rogue, refusing to obey orders and carrying out his own policies, and that the station was out of control. Mecklin, for one, knew none of that was true. He'd once seen Lodge give Richardson an order with which Mecklin knew he disagreed. The station chief's reply was a simple "Yes, sir." Mecklin figured the leaks were just a way to shove Richardson out the door faster.

When Lodge formally asked that Richardson be replaced, Kennedy decided to honor his request, but left it to him and McCone to work out the details. In a letter to Lodge, McCone indicated he was willing to install a new station chief, but that Lodge's preferred candidate—the swashbuckling Edward Lansdale—"would not be acceptable to the organization or to me personally." CIA officers had lost confidence in Lansdale, McCone indicated, based on his involvement in Operation Mongoose, the Kennedy administration's unsuccessful covert program to destabilize Cuba's communist government and overthrow Fidel Castro.

The leaks didn't abate, reinforcing the impression of disarray and infighting within the administration. On September 20, Hilsman warned Lodge a second time, instructing him to give a "stern lecture" to anyone in the embassy who might be talking to the press without authorization.

In a reply that fairly reeked with disingenuousness, Lodge blamed much of the problem on American *wives* in Saigon, saying they were "often the most prolific leakers." (He didn't explain how wives, or most of their husbands for that matter, would have access to closely held secrets about CIA operations and personnel.) The ambassador also pointed a finger at U.S. officials who blabbed to newsmen at Saigon parties, "where much talking is done after the fourth cocktail."

McCone tried to turn the tables on Lodge, privately criticizing him to

Kennedy in the same terms that were being used against the CIA and Richardson. He claimed that during Lodge's tenure at the United Nations, he "was inclined to make policy rather than follow instructions . . . , to be reckless in his criticism of Washington in his discussions with representatives of other foreign countries . . . , [and had] an amazing desire for nearness and closeness to the press." The ambassador's "complete lack of consciousness of security," McCone said, made it risky to inform him about covert operations.

Indeed, McCone went so far as to order his subordinates not to discuss sensitive operations with Lodge, who, the CIA director said, "has no concept of security, and has long used the press as an instrument of power."

Lodge, meanwhile, ordered Richardson and his agents to have no contact with Nhu, evidently to reinforce his policy of silence toward the palace and put additional pressure on Nhu to leave.

THE CIA WAS HIT by yet another media torpedo on October 2, when the *Washington Daily News* published a venomous story that characterized the agency's record in South Vietnam as "a dismal chronicle of bureaucratic arrogance, obstinate disregard of orders, and unrestrained thirst for power."

Written by a reporter named Richard Starnes, the article was a flagrant hatchet job laden with unfounded allegations leveled by unnamed sources. For example, it falsely charged that the Saigon station refused to carry out an "action plan" that Lodge supposedly had brought with him from Washington (no such plan existed, according to Rusk). Starnes twisted the knife by claiming that one American official in Saigon—"a man who has spent much of his life in the service of democracy"—had compared the CIA to "a malignancy" that even the White House might not be able to excise.

The most damaging aspect of Starnes's piece was that it named Richardson as the station chief, burning his cover as a diplomat. (Robert Kennedy later insisted it was Lodge who fed Richardson's name to the press; Starnes denied getting his name from Lodge.)

The day after Starnes's article appeared, an irate McCone asked Frank Wisner, a retired CIA deputy director, to hunt down whoever was passing information to Starnes and other newsmen. Wisner soon reported that the CIA "has been attacked with deliberate and calculated design" by Lodge, Harriman, Hilsman, and Lodge's aide, Mike Dunn.

McCone sent off an acerbic cable to Lodge, asking whether he agreed with the "incredible charges" in the Starnes article and whether he still wanted Richardson to leave. The CIA director emphasized that he had "great confidence" in his station chief.

Discussing McCone's message face-to-face with Richardson, Lodge said that as a personal matter, he'd be happy to have him stay. But, he added, Richardson's close association with Nhu created "atmospheric disadvantages," since Nhu had become "the worldwide personal devil and one-man symbol of all that is wrong in South Vietnam"—an image that Lodge had done a good deal to create. But it was clear that Lodge wanted Richardson gone. McNamara drove another nail into his coffin, telling McCone upon his return from Saigon that the station chief "had been too visible to the people in Saigon."

Richardson left South Vietnam on October 5. Not long afterward, Lodge took over the large, luxurious villa he vacated, redecorated it, and moved in. But the ambassador's cutoff of CIA contacts with Nhu and his own refusal to talk to Diem left the embassy with a significantly smaller window into what the brothers were thinking and doing.

AFTER A BRIEF PERIOD of silence, Madame Nhu energetically resumed her role as anti-Washington bomb thrower not long after she arrived in Belgrade, the elegant old capital of Yugoslavia and the start of her European tour.

Even before Madame left Saigon on September 9, JFK told his advisers that "he did not want her to come to the U.S., and above all, did not want her to make a speech in Washington." The president worried that another verbal grenade or two from the woman a French magazine labeled *l'irritante petite indochinoise* might cause Congress to abruptly terminate aid to South Vietnam. He considered asking Diem in a personal letter to keep his sister-in-law away, but held back out of fear that the missive—like almost every other move the White House made these days—would leak. The simple but ham-handed expedient of denying her a visa would only cause a press uproar.

If U.S. officials hoped that getting the Dragon Lady out of South Vietnam would keep her quiet, they must have been disappointed. Journalists mobbed her in every foreign capital she visited, hanging on her every word and giving her at least as much, if not more publicity than she attracted at home.

In Belgrade, she made news as soon as she stepped off her plane, opining to reporters in her unpolished English that Kennedy "is a politician and when he hears a loud opinion speaking, he tries to appease it somehow." The next day, U.S. newspapers headlined that she'd called the president an "appeaser," a politically loaded term that conjured memories of Neville Chamberlain's craven deal with Hitler at Munich—and probably wasn't at all what Madame Nhu intended.

She followed up with a blistering speech before hundreds of delegates at a conference of the Inter-Parliamentary Union, an organization created to promote democratic governance worldwide. In a ten-minute torrent of French, she claimed that South Vietnam was the victim of "an international campaign of blackmail and terror," earning a thundering ovation from the audience. At a news conference, she blasted journalists covering the war, calling them "spoiled children," "horrible," and "terrible."

"I am a good girl," she exploded, pounding the table with a white-gloved fist. "I do not know why the press is so horrible to me."

By chance, she was seated next to Senator Ted Kennedy, the president's youngest brother, at a luncheon for U.S. Congress members attending the conference. A UPI photographer got a shot of the thirty-one-year-old senator listening intently to something she was saying to him. After JFK expressed his pique at the encounter, Harriman phoned a State Department subordinate, telling him: "The president wants it discreetly found out, without anybody else knowing about it, how this happened. The president wants her to have a cold shoulder from the Democrats."

It turned out that Madame had been gabbing animatedly in a hotel lobby with a female member of Congress as other members gathered around; the congresswoman eventually invited everyone to lunch, including Ted Kennedy and his wife. When he called JFK to explain, less than a minute before he was to make a televised speech on tax cuts, the exasperated president chided him: "This woman kicks me in the nuts, and the next day you have lunch with her." A few days later, the South Vietnamese first lady erupted again, proclaiming that she did "not feel terribly safe" with the Kennedy administration.

Madame Nhu moved on to Rome, where she set off another media firestorm by comparing junior American military officers in South Vietnam to "little soldiers of fortune." Lodge publicly rebuked her, saying U.S. military men were risking their lives and dying next to their ARVN comrades and "should be thanked, not insulted."

In Paris, she claimed in an ABC News interview that the "so-called Buddhists" were led by communists trying to overthrow the government and that Americans were their "instruments." She added that "Americans don't take seriously enough their role as an ally" and instead acted like they "consider themselves just spectators to a show." When she visited the South Vietnamese embassy in the French capital, angry Vietnamese students pelted her limousine with eggs and paint.

In spite of JFK's wishes that she stay away, it became clear she intended to come to the United States, although her arrival date was unknown. The notion that she could be kept under wraps by getting her out of South Vietnam had backfired; once she hit American soil she'd have a bigger media megaphone than ever.

No one knew what she'd say. Would she continue her waspish ways, alienating Americans with offensive remarks and further weakening support for the war? Or would she pour on the charm and whip up enthusiasm for her struggling government? That's what the lovely Madame Chiang had done on her U.S. tour in 1943 when her husband, Chiang Kai-shek, was desperately in need of American arms and cash to fight both Japanese invaders and Mao's communists.

Harriman wanted to be prepared. He phoned Hilsman on September 23 and emphasized "the need to do something" about press coverage of

Madame Nhu's visit. He also called Raymond Lisle of the State Department's press office:

"H[arriman] asked L[isle] what they were doing about Madame Nhu & asked when she was arriving. L replied they weren't doing anything about it, did not know when she was arriving. H said they had better start as she would be a headache to them from the day she arrived. L said he would ask his news people about it and prepare for it."

Harriman phoned Forrestal the same day to say he'd heard Madame Nhu on the radio that morning, "got the flavor of the lady," and was worried. It was important, Harriman said, "that no one official see her." The undersecretary also called Alfred Friendly, managing editor of *The Washington Post*. In the late 1940s, Friendly had worked as a press aide to Harriman when he supervised the Marshall Plan. Harriman wanted Friendly's advice on how to handle the Dragon Lady. She was "cruel and calculating," Harriman said, and was doing exactly what he was afraid she'd do: flattering Americans that they were "dear friends" of her country. If he had his way, he'd cancel her visa.

Friendly said "they would try and do what they could on the paper" to give people "the proper perspective." He recommended that someone from the administration talk to members of the Senate Foreign Relations Committee "before they get taken." One theme that would resonate was "the lust for personal power that this woman has." Friendly closed by saying that Americans needed to be "preconditioned as to what this woman is after. People on the inside know she is a thief."

The *Post* later savaged Madame Nhu in an editorial that compared her to the beautiful woman in a Nathaniel Hawthorne short story, "Rappaccini's Daughter," who tends an experimental garden of toxic plants and poisons everyone who comes near her.

IN ROME, MEANWHILE, ARCHBISHOP Thuc was generating almost as many headlines as his sister-in-law.

He claimed to Italian newsmen that Washington had spent $20 million trying to overthrow Diem, and that "many communists" infiltrated the Buddhist monkhood simply by donning robes. His statements drew a warning from the Vatican to make no further political remarks while he was outside his own archdiocese; his scheduled audience with the pope was abruptly canceled.

Undaunted, Thuc flew to New York to make arrangements for Madame Nhu's forthcoming visit. McGeorge Bundy heard the news at a White House staff meeting, where he already was "visibly disturbed" at the way things were going in South Vietnam. When a staffer brought in a wire-service story announcing that Thuc had left Rome for New York, "this was close to the last blow for Bundy." This was the first time, he gravely told others in the room, that "the world had been faced with collective madness in a ruling family since the days of the czars."

On October 2, the National Security Agency intercepted a message to Saigon from the South Vietnamese embassy in Washington that laid out the full details of Madame Nhu's itinerary in America.

The three-week trip, to begin in a few days, was packed with media interviews and speeches at prestigious universities and foreign affairs organizations. She'd be interviewed on NBC's *Today* show, CBS's *Face the Nation*, and David Susskind's *Open End* television program. Reporters from *Time* magazine and the Knight newspaper chain would meet with her. She was to speak at the Overseas Press Club in New York and—despite JFK's wishes—the Women's National Press Club in Washington. Appearances were scheduled at Columbia University, Princeton, Radcliffe, Fordham, Sarah Lawrence, Howard University, North Carolina State, the University of Texas, and Berkeley. She'd dine at Harvard and Yale law schools and meet with members of the Phoenix Press Club, Los Angeles World Affairs Council, and San Francisco's august Commonwealth Club.

In all, she'd visit twelve cities, appear on seventeen national and local TV and radio programs, and be the guest of honor at fifteen luncheons and dinners.

It was an extraordinary, high-profile itinerary, not unlike the campaign schedule of a serious candidate for the U.S. presidency. For the expectant media, Madame Nhu's tour would yield a bumper crop of controversy. For JFK, it meant only more political heartburn.

CHAPTER 16

"ARROGANT UPSTARTS" VERSUS THE "SPECIALS"

THREE DAYS AFTER Madame Nhu's itinerary was intercepted, Saigon cops again attacked Halberstam and other newsmen as they tried to cover a story.

A woman had phoned reporters that morning, saying "something will happen at the central market today." Arnett walked over to the market while keeping an eye out for "anti-suicide squads"—jeeps carrying soldiers and fire extinguishers—that roamed the city looking for monks about to torch themselves. John Sharkey, an NBC News freelance reporter, was already at the market, trying to look inconspicuous. Halberstam showed up with Grant Wolfkill, an NBC cameraman with whom he was friends. The monk burnings had stopped weeks earlier; Halberstam didn't expect another one that day.

Standing at a traffic roundabout outside the market, Arnett barely noticed the taxi that pulled up and disgorged a robed young man clutching a rubber bag. The man immediately took a small jerrican from the bag, sat down with his legs crossed, and doused his lap with gasoline. Staring into the middle distance, he struck a match. Though engulfed in flames, he stayed in the lotus position and made no sound or movement.

Arnett clicked a few pictures with his camera and tried to write in his notebook, but his hands were shaking badly.

A collective moan rose from the gathering crowd of onlookers. A woman with tears running down her face grabbed Arnett by the shirt and opened her mouth, but no words came out. She kept tugging at his shirt and pointing at the monk as flames crackled over his body. A mother with a crying baby in her arms couldn't take her eyes off the burning figure. Another woman began to laugh hysterically. A man pushed at Arnett, saying: "You take pictures, you write story. You must tell Mr. Kennedy what is going on in this country."

A cop grabbed a conical straw hat off a street vendor's head and tried to fan the flames away, but only made them worse. He staggered backward from the heat as what sounded like a low growl came from the crowd, punctuated by cries and wails. A fire engine pulled up, sirens screaming, and firemen hosed down the monk. Paramedics then bundled the seared body in a sack, heaved it unceremoniously into their ambulance, and drove off.

All that was left was a charred circle on the sidewalk.

About two dozen plainclothes cops surrounded Wolfkill as he finished filming with his handheld Bolex camera. A tall ex-Marine, Wolfkill was the first TV journalist to record a burning and he wasn't about to let go of his footage without a fight. While on assignment in Laos, he'd been captured by communist guerrillas and held in horrific conditions for fifteen months, often in a lightless cell with crude wooden stocks clamped around his ankles. Worried that Wolfkill might be in for a serious beating, Halberstam rushed over to help him. Sharkey joined them.

The three men formed a defensive triangle—Wolfkill and Sharkey in front and Halberstam right behind them, walking backward—and headed for the Caravelle Hotel, which, though six blocks away, was filled with Americans and other Westerners and might offer some sanctuary. The police encircled the journalists and then, according to Halberstam, "they went at us like a wolfpack."

One cop who seemed to be the leader waved a .38-caliber revolver in Wolfkill's face; others lunged for his Bolex. Moving along the street, the newsmen kept the camera out of the cops' hands by lateraling it back and forth like a football.

Halberstam tried to shield it as he was kicked, punched, and "got a couple sharp cracks over [the] head." The cops dragged him to the ground; Halberstam looked up to see one of them jump off a car onto him. Sharkey thought Halberstam lost consciousness for a moment as he was beaten. When Sharkey bent over to help Halberstam to his feet, someone bashed him in the head with a wooden barstool from a sidewalk café; he began to bleed badly.

One of the plainclothesmen grabbed the Bolex and ran off. Halberstam called out to nearby uniformed cops for help, but they did nothing.

The rest of the undercover men walked away, and the Americans stumbled the remaining distance to the Caravelle. They later went to the newly opened U.S. naval hospital, where Sharkey got six stitches in his scalp and a cast on his right hand to protect a broken knuckle. Wolfkill had been clubbed on the back and kicked in the groin; Halberstam was bruised, but suffered no serious injuries. On Sharkey's cast he playfully wrote: "Personalism Forever"—a mocking reference to the regime's official philosophy.

The government closed its telegraph office, but a pigeon took Arnett's photos of the dying monk and smuggled them to Hong Kong for transmission to New York.

THE SAIGON REPORTERS FACED a more insidious assault from a completely different direction: their own journalistic brethren.

Covering the Vietnam War was extraordinarily difficult for American newsmen in the early 1960s. They were up against a regime that tried to impede their work at every turn. Most of them didn't speak or read Vietnamese and knew little, at least when they started their exotic new beat, about the war's complex history. Unlike World War II, battlefield progress couldn't be measured in terms of how many miles Allied forces traveled in a day or the number of towns they liberated along the way, as was the case when Patton's tanks rolled across Europe. Both the ARVN and the Viet Cong exaggerated combat victories and tried to conceal losses. And the VC's all-important political maneuverings were largely hidden from view.

The resident Saigon reporters didn't want to see South Vietnam fall to communism; they wanted the ARVN, with American help, to succeed. But they couldn't ignore the evidence of their own eyes and ears.

The correspondents traveled widely, interviewing numerous U.S. and South Vietnamese military men, diplomats, civilian experts, and ordinary people. They knew VC units with inferior weapons were able to hold off larger, better armed ARVN units, which had all the advantages of artillery, armored vehicles, helicopters, and bombers. They saw Diem's maladroit response to a local religious disturbance set off a nationwide rebellion that threatened to bring down his government. They read each other's work and compared notes about the latest military and political developments. Over time, their reporting grew more skeptical, if not openly critical of Diem, his government, and his army.

Just as a split developed in the Kennedy administration over whether the war could be won with Diem, the U.S. press divided along similar lines. And just as the anti-Diem faction in the U.S. government attacked the pro-Diem faction, Diem skeptics in the press came under fire from his journalistic supporters.

Most of the pro-Diem journalists were so-called specials, who visited South Vietnam only occasionally and for limited periods. One of the most prominent of the specials was Marguerite Higgins, whose six-part "Vietnam—Fact and Fiction" series in the *New York Herald Tribune*, published in August, hewed closely to Nolting and Harkins's optimistic line. She bluntly told Malcolm Browne that she viewed him and the other resident reporters as "arrogant upstarts." Over dinner with Charles Mohr, *Time* magazine's Southeast Asia bureau chief, Higgins went even further, claiming that the residents "would like to see us lose the war to prove they're right." (Higgins later denied making that comment.)

Other U.S.-based journalists piled on. Frank Conniff, a columnist for the conservative Hearst newspapers, labeled Halberstam's work a "political time bomb" that could mislead Kennedy and unravel the war effort. But the sharpest attack came from *Time*, one of the most influential magazines in America, with a nationwide circulation in 1963 of nearly 3 million copies a week.

The magazine accused the Saigon press corps of "helping to compound the very confusion [about the war] that it should be untangling for its readers at home." The reason, said *Time*, was that the correspondents—who "pool their convictions, information, misinformation, and grievances" over drinks at the Caravelle Hotel bar—were mired in groupthink and no longer able to see the Vietnam story from any angle but their own. They routinely blasted Diem and his family, while uncritically presenting the Buddhists as purehearted avatars of truth and justice. The reporters downplayed ARVN victories, according to *Time*, because giving them "splash treatment" undermined their argument that defeat was inevitable under Diem. But when South Vietnam's forces lost, the headlines were big and "the color is rich and flowing."

The September 20 article caused an uproar among the Saigon newsmen. Mohr and Mert Perry, the *Time* stringer who alerted Sheehan to the pagoda raids, both quit over their employer's maligning of their colleagues. But the critics weren't finished.

Three days after *Time*'s broadside, the Saigon reporters came in for a beating from Joseph Alsop, the widely read syndicated columnist who'd made hay over Nhu's talk with Maneli, the Polish diplomat.

Alsop had devoted decades to cultivating sources among Washington's most powerful figures, often over dinner at his art-filled Georgetown home. He'd been an early backer of Kennedy's presidential campaign, and the young president-elect capped his inaugural festivities with a stop at the columnist's home, talking with him long into the night over turtle soup.

Strongly anti-communist, Alsop viewed Diem as flawed, but far less objectionable than Ho Chi Minh. He felt the American newspapermen in Saigon were deliberately vilifying Diem, and accused them of "carrying on another of these egregious crusades" comparable to the criticisms leveled against Chiang Kai-shek by some U.S. correspondents in China during World War II. "It is easy enough," he wrote, "to paint a dark, indignant picture, without departing from the facts, if you ignore the majority of Americans who admire the Vietnamese as fighters and seek out the one U.S. officer in ten who inevitably thinks all foreigners fight badly."

Alsop assailed the Saigon newsmen for helping to transform Diem "from a courageous, quite viable national leader into a man afflicted with a galloping persecution mania, seeing plots around every corner, and therefore misjudging everything." (Alsop nevertheless told Kennedy privately that Diem had "lost his ability to govern," a conclusion with which many Saigon reporters fully agreed.)

THE SAIGON RESIDENTS WEREN'T without their spirited defenders, however.

James Reston praised Halberstam as "brilliant" and insisted he and his colleagues were doing a superb job under difficult, often dangerous conditions. Louis Lyons, curator of Harvard's coveted Nieman Fellowships for journalists, described Halberstam as "absolutely prophetic." Never shy about flattering those who wrote flatteringly about him, Lodge characterized the Saigon newsmen as "appealing, brave, tremendously hard working."

But *Time* wasn't done with the faraway correspondents. In its October 11 edition the magazine questioned whether they were giving their readers "an unduly pessimistic view of the progress of the war and the quality of the Diem government." It noted that some publications were sending other writers, like Higgins and Alsop, to Vietnam for "a fresh look," since the residents were "severely critical of practically everything" and made no apologies for "their total dislike of the Diem government."

The criticism didn't always come in the pages of competing publications. Sometimes it was bitterly, painfully face-to-face.

Halberstam had the opportunity to accompany one of his heroes, the veteran war correspondent Richard Tregaskis, on a reporting trip to the Mekong Delta. As a boy, Halberstam had read and greatly admired Tregaskis's 1943 bestseller, *Guadalcanal Diary*, about the bloody struggle by U.S. Marines to take Guadalcanal, one of the Solomon Islands northeast of Australia, from the Japanese. When he met Halberstam, Tregaskis was finishing a similar book, *Vietnam Diary*.

The two journalists spent what Halberstam called an "entirely pleasant" two days in the field as he introduced Tregaskis to some of his most valued sources. Driving back to Saigon, Tregaskis turned to his companion and said softly: "If I were doing what you are doing, I would be ashamed of myself." Halberstam—who was particularly proud of his military reporting—was stunned and upset at such harsh words from a man he held in high esteem. They rode the rest of the way to Saigon in stony silence. (When he returned home, Tregaskis wrote that the ARVN was fighting well, Diem was expanding the territory under his control, and "we're winning, not losing, in Viet Nam.")

Halberstam had a much more vocal confrontation with Krulak after learning that he was spreading a story that Halberstam burst into tears when he saw some photos of dead Viet Cong. The tale originated with Higgins, who supposedly showed Halberstam the pictures at the Caravelle Hotel. She told Krulak, who relayed the anecdote to editors at *Time*. The editors told Charles Mohr, who told Halberstam, who became enraged at this "penultimate assault on my manhood."

When Krulak later flew into Tan Son Nhut, Halberstam was waiting for him—not in the terminal building, but right on the tarmac as the Marine general alighted from his plane.

"My name is David Halberstam and I hear you've been telling people I was crying on the roof of the Caravelle Hotel," the reporter began, loudly enough to be heard over the jet engines. Krulak acknowledged that he had, but said he'd been quoting Higgins.

"I want to tell you that the story is a bunch of shit!" exclaimed Halberstam, towering over his much shorter antagonist. "It is not true and no one ever showed me pictures like that and I did not break into tears and I just want you to fucking know it. And don't *ever* put shit out like that again!" (Higgins denied telling the crying story.)

THE DAY BEFORE *TIME* published its second broadside against the resident newsmen, John Buquoi, a twenty-two-year-old Army enlistee from Louisiana, arrived in Saigon. He was a well-trained Vietnamese translator with a top secret job: eavesdropping on ARVN generals' phone calls for hints of coup planning.

Buquoi worked for the Army Security Agency and lived with other ASA linguists in a guarded compound at Tan Son Nhut. The men worked at a secret installation bulldozed out of the rice paddies about eight miles west of Saigon, near the village of Phu Lam.

There the Americans had set up a state-of-the-art communications system that bounced radio signals off the troposphere using two large antennas about the size and shape of drive-in movie screens. This "troposcatter" system allowed military and civilian officials to make fast, reliable telephone calls throughout South Vietnam.

In a corner of the Phu Lam base were two trailers in which the ASA specialists worked around the clock. Buquoi stood twelve-hour shifts, noon to midnight, jammed in with six or eight other eavesdroppers. He sat before a switchboard wearing headphones and when a circuit lit up on the board, he plugged into it and listened.

The ASA had been monitoring the generals since August 26, just before they abandoned their first attempted coup. Buquoi and his comrades taped the Vietnamese officers' conversations and wrote summaries of anything that seemed relevant. The tapes were then packed in empty ammunition boxes along with incendiary grenades.

At midnight, a U.S. Army lieutenant drove out to the ASA trailers in a jeep. Buquoi and other men ending their shift got in with the ammo boxes for the return trip to Tan Son Nhut. If the jeep was stopped for any reason by Vietnamese police or soldiers, the lieutenant was under orders to pull a lanyard that would ignite the incendiaries and destroy the tapes. In all likelihood the jeep would catch fire, too, forcing the linguists to jump out and run for their lives.

The rides home through the darkness, Buquoi recalled, weren't comfortable experiences.

Sitting in their air-conditioned trailers day after day, the eavesdroppers picked up little of value. The generals talked about military operations, passed on rumors, and gossiped about each other's sex lives. There were occasional cryptic comments that might or might not be related to a coup, such as "So-and-so decided to come to the party with us," or "You need to talk to so-and-so because he's nervous about the wedding." But nothing definite, and nothing that really helped Washington understand the subterranean vortex of Saigon maneuverings.

BUQUOI AND HIS ASA colleagues may not have been the only secret listeners in Saigon that autumn. Visiting the French embassy, Maneli was told: "All of your conversations, especially over the telephone, are listened in on from three sides: the Saigon government, the Americans, and the Viet Cong."

In such an environment, conspirators who wanted to keep drawing breath communicated face-to-face. When General Don ran into Conein by chance at the airport on October 2, he said Big Minh wanted to speak with him—in person.

Shortly after the collapse of the August coup, Don and General Dinh, Saigon's military governor, petitioned Diem to put ARVN commanders in charge of key government ministries including defense and interior. They also wanted control of the Saigon police and a permanent military governorship for the capital. It was an assertive set of demands—the generals were effectively asking Diem to turn over much of his government to them—and may have been intended to reduce pressure within the ARVN for a coup.

When Dinh went to the palace again a few days later seeking a response, Diem told him, "You generals are too greedy!" ARVN leaders became convinced Diem would never make significant concessions to them.

As a result, coup planning was back on, Big Minh informed Conein on October 5.

Minh said he needed to know Washington's current position on a coup "within the very near future." The war would be lost unless action was taken soon, he said. The generals didn't need material support, but they did want a U.S. pledge of noninterference. Minh knew that some lower-ranking troop commanders were champing at the bit for a takeover, and he wanted to get the jump on them. A premature move against Diem, Minh felt, could be catastrophic.

Minh named other generals he was working with and said they'd developed three possible action plans. The first was to assassinate Nhu and his brother Can, but allow Diem to remain in office. The other two plans involved combat between rebel troops and regime loyalists in the streets of Saigon. Minh thought Diem could mobilize about 5,500 men to fight for him in the capital. The "easiest plan to accomplish," said Minh, was simply to kill Nhu.

Conein reported the conversation to Lodge, who requested State Department guidance on how to respond. While he and Harkins didn't "have great faith in Big Minh," Lodge thought the best course was for Conein to tell the general that the embassy wouldn't impede a revolt and offer to review his tactical plans "other than assassination plans."

But David Smith, who'd become acting station chief following Richardson's removal, urged Lodge to reconsider. He suggested that "we do not set ourselves irrevocably against the assassination plot," since the other two schemes could lead to a bloodbath in Saigon or a protracted internecine struggle that might shatter the ARVN.

Smith's advice brought a quick reproach from McCone, who cabled that the United States couldn't be in the position of endorsing an assassination and "engaging our responsibility therefor." He ordered Smith to withdraw his recommendation to Lodge. When Smith did so, the ambassador commented that he "shares McCone's opinion."

MEANWHILE, REPORTS OF PLOTTING by other groups filtered into the embassy. Saigon seemed awash in conspiracies cooked up not just by military men but by lawyers, students, National Assembly members, civil servants, teachers, and alienated former Diem adherents. Two or three people a day contacted the CIA station to discuss their ideas for purging the palace of the Ngos.

It turned out that Dr. Tuyen, the former secret police chief, had never gone to Cairo as ordered. He surfaced instead in Hong Kong, still trying to organize an uprising.

His original scheme was for some ARVN battalion and company commanders he'd enlisted to seize key facilities in Saigon while a small group armed with automatic weapons stormed the palace. The plan later changed to blowing up Nhu with the help of a palace staff member, who "has demolition equipment."

Tuyen's agents tried to kill Nhu during a September 13 meeting with Colonel Tung and several cabinet ministers. But the plastic explosive failed to go off due to a defective detonator, according to an account given to the CIA by the chief of the political bureau for Diem's security service. (A different source said the attack was postponed because Nhu didn't attend the meeting as scheduled.)

The CIA also received updates on the activities of Colonel Thao, the VC agent who was plotting his own coup. Thao claimed to have the support of four ARVN generals as well as a unit commander in the Presidential Guard. He wanted to attack the palace with three battalions, hoping that more generals with more troops would join him.

Thao had an alternative plan to ambush Nhu and his wife as they drove to the palace from the airport following her overseas trip. Thao's group acquired a house along the route and was negotiating for an apartment across the street from it, apparently so snipers could catch the Nhus in a fatal cross fire.

The most powerful of the would-be insurrectionists were, of course, the generals. But there was more than a little mistrust not only between the generals and some lower-ranking rebel officers but among the generals themselves. They circled one another as warily as alley cats. Who among them was a committed insurgent? Who might be a palace snitch?

Both Big Minh and Don regarded the mirthless General Khiem with suspicion. Minh thought Khiem might have played some sort of double role during the abortive August coup; Don was in a ticklish position because Khiem was his chief of staff. Prior to the August attempt, Conein had given Khiem the layout of Colonel Tung's Special Forces garrison outside Saigon. Tung's compound was high on the list of targets the generals wanted to neutralize rapidly when they made their move. Now Minh asked Conein to give him the same diagrams, so he could compare them with what Khiem showed him in August.

Nor did the generals place much trust in the Americans. They'd long felt that anything they told Nolting or Harkins soon made its way to the palace. They were especially skeptical of Richardson, believing that he'd passed information about coup activities to Nhu. There's no evidence that Richardson did so, but the generals were delighted when the CIA station chief disappeared from Saigon.

NOT LONG AFTER RICHARDSON'S departure, fear gripped the embassy when CIA informants reported that Nhu had targeted Lodge for assassination.

The notion that Nhu might murder the American ambassador seemed crazy on its face. Besides a monumental uproar in Congress and the press, such an action could lead to a severing of U.S. diplomatic relations with Saigon and an American pullout from South Vietnam. For the rest of his life Nhu would have to look over his shoulder for possible American retaliation. The CIA cautioned that the assassination reports were murkily sourced and should be "viewed with skepticism." But Lodge found them credible, partly because he believed that Nhu was irrational from smoking opium.

The story was that Nhu planned to give official permission for a student demonstration outside the embassy and then seed it with a hundred undercover agents, who'd force their way into the building, kill Lodge and other U.S. officials, and set the place on fire.

Lodge cabled the State Department on October 10 that if a crowd began to gather, his plan was to lock the embassy's steel gates and have Marine guards set off tear gas against anyone trying to force their way in. The ambassador also instructed Smith, the acting station chief, to pass the word to the CIA's sources that if he were killed, "American retaliation will be prompt and awful beyond description," with U.S. forces delivering "a horrible and crushing blow" to Diem and Nhu.

In his inimitable fashion Lodge saw a silver lining if he actually was killed: Washington then would have a good pretext to carry out the coup he yearned for, using any violent means it wanted. "If I am assassinated," he cabled, "a new situation would be created which might give us a chance to move effectively for a change of government using methods which would now be rejected by U.S. and world opinion, but which would then become acceptable. There should be State-Defense planning on this."

In Washington, McCone remarked to Harriman that Lodge's cables "seemed rather hysterical." Harriman agreed that the idea of a regime attack on the embassy was far-fetched.

Others, however, shared Lodge's concern about the embassy's vulnerability. Its only on-duty protection was two Marine guards, although another sixteen off-duty Marines could be summoned to back them up. In addition, civilian embassy officers had access to .45-caliber pistols.

While a Marine guard station behind a concrete wall protected the chancery's front doors, the building was alarmingly open in the rear, where a courtyard faced a two-story private home owned by a Chinese merchant. Lodge worried about attackers crashing through that house and storming the embassy from behind. State Department security officers agreed, concluding that the building was "indefensible and wide open to determined attack."

The CIA's informants claimed that the purported invaders also wanted to kill Tri Quang, who was still under embassy protection. The State Department suggested striking a surreptitious deal with the palace to let the monk quietly slip out of the country, eliminating the ongoing standoff over him between Saigon and Washington. But Lodge didn't think that would work.

Hilsman cabled that U.S. naval forces could be moved closer to Saigon if Lodge thought that was prudent. Harkins noted that 150 military police officers could be rushed in to protect the embassy, along with a "provisional battalion" slapped together from clerks and other support personnel. He also promised a helicopter to rescue Lodge from the embassy roof—a scheme that prefigured one of the most iconic scenes of the Vietnam War when Saigon fell to the North Vietnamese army in 1975.

THE COUP GENERALS LOOKED to Big Minh, the ARVN's most popular officer, as their leader. But Minh was concerned that he and his co-conspirators might not be able to muster enough troops to overcome Diem's defenders or that an informer might sell them out before they were ready to act.

In mid-October, Minh decided to exercise his "easiest" option—killing Nhu—rather than trying to take over the government. He assigned a squad of army sharpshooters to assassinate the political counselor as he drove through a busy intersection about a mile from Gia Long Palace. The plan was so closely held that even General Don didn't know about it.

On the day the attack was to take place, Nhu presided at one of his weekly meetings with the generals at Joint General Staff headquarters near the airport. When it was over, he asked Don to return with him to his palace office. As Don was stepping into Nhu's black Mercedes, Minh tried to wave him away. But he got in anyway and the car moved off.

The snipers had to be hastily ordered to stand down for fear that Don, too, would die in the ambush. Minh later upbraided his ARVN collaborator for inadvertently saving Nhu's life.

ON THE MORNING OF October 5, Kennedy met with a handful of his closest counselors to discuss the touchy issue of the economic sanctions imposed on Diem's government without JFK's knowledge or approval.

The press and public still didn't know that Washington had suspended the Commercial Import Program about six weeks earlier. McCone and David Bell, who headed the U.S. Agency for International Development, both told the president they were unhappy with the freeze. McCone argued that holding up subsidized imports was more likely to pitch South Vietnam into an economic crisis than scare Diem into compliance with U.S. demands.

Kennedy ordered that the suspension be continued, but monitored "very, very carefully" in case it began to boomerang in undesirable directions. He also wanted financial support for Colonel Tung's forces stopped until they were removed from Nhu's control and placed under the ARVN.

A cable sent to Lodge the same day explained that Kennedy's decisions were designed to "create significant uncertainty" in South Vietnamese minds about Washington's intentions. Diem wasn't to be formally notified in the hope that he'd come to Lodge for an explanation.

When that happened, Lodge was to give him a list of actions he should take to boost popular support for his government, including the release of jailed bonzes and students and an end to "night-time arrests, brutal interrogation (including women) and other police-terrorist methods." Significantly, JFK and his advisers backed away from their previous insistence that Nhu and his wife be banished from the government, indicating that they'd settle for "some feasible reduction in influence of Nhus."

McGeorge Bundy followed up with a telegram to Lodge indicating that the White House was "making every possible effort to limit public knowledge" about what it wanted from Diem, and that the ambassador shouldn't tell newsmen anything. "Nothing could be more dangerous," wrote Bundy, than for the press to get the impression that the Kennedy administration had presented yet another set of demands that Diem shrugged off. Bundy further instructed Lodge not to encourage any coup activity, but to undertake an "urgent covert effort" to identify possible alternatives to Diem.

Two days after the White House meeting, *The Times of Vietnam* revealed the aid suspension in a front-page story that quoted one Vietnamese asking, "Who is the U.S. fighting—us or the communists?" Halberstam relayed the news to American readers with a much more detailed story in *The New York Times*, noting that the aid holdup could cause serious disruptions in South Vietnam's economy within a few months.

Although it wasn't Kennedy's intention, the aid moratorium greatly encouraged the rebel generals. Indeed, Big Minh had specifically asked for such action as a signal of continued U.S. support for a coup. And the generals later cited it as one of the main reasons they moved forward with their revolt.

ON THE EVENING OF October 6, Bundy got into a series of heated discussions at a dinner party at the home of Frank Wisner, the retired CIA deputy director who'd tracked down anti-agency leakers at McCone's behest.

Chatting with a small circle of fellow guests, Bundy remarked that he "wished very much" that all participants in the Vietnam policy debates would keep their mouths shut, since "further recriminations would do no one any good and since it was already a matter of acute embarrassment." He then turned to Wisner, a mercurial man who supervised CIA clandestine operations in the 1950s, including the 1954 coup against Guatemala's president. Bundy told him that CIA people in particular should stop complaining publicly and privately.

Wisner rejoined that while the CIA had been the victim of "a considerable campaign of abuse and vilification," he knew of no one in the agency who griped to the press. Bundy didn't like that. He snapped that Wisner's comment was childish, "just like one six-year-old saying that the other had started the fight."

Wisner cornered Bundy later in the evening, arguing that certain members of the press had been crucifying the CIA for weeks even though it had done nothing wrong. High-level authorities had approved all of its actions in Vietnam, yet no administration official had spoken out in its defense. Did Bundy seriously believe, Wisner asked, that the agency had no right to defend itself against attacks that were damaging its reputation and its employees' morale? Bundy replied that he was hearing the same grumbles from State Department and Pentagon people, who claimed their departments were under similar attacks.

Wisner then demanded to know if Bundy thought Richardson was guilty of insubordination and operating at cross-purposes with national policy, as some in the press claimed. No, Bundy said, he didn't believe that. He described Richardson as "an absolutely outstanding example of a fine civil servant" who deserved some expression of gratitude, such as a medal, when he got home.

Bundy went on to say that "contrary to what appeared in the press," the real reason Richardson was pulled out of Saigon was "the unfortunate . . . clash of personalities" between him and Lodge. McNamara and Taylor discovered on their recent visit that the ambassador and the station chief had "reached the point where anything done or said by one was absolute anathema to the other." Under such circumstances, said Bundy, Kennedy had no choice but to permit the relief of the lower-ranking man.

Wisner's guests included Harriman, who "sounded off from the other end of the room" that while other officials seemed to be blabbing to the media quite a bit, he "wanted it clearly understood by all concerned that he personally was not." But Harriman may have protested too much. His wife, Marie, promptly contradicted his claim of innocence, remarking "that that was not the way she had heard it."

Harriman tried again later to deflect the leaker label, maintaining "with some show of acerbity" that he was happy to leave the whispering to Bundy "and others in that entourage." Bundy "sought to turn this pointed statement aside with numerous observations to the effect that, as is well known, the ship of state leaks mainly from the top"—an apparent reference to JFK.

Despite Bundy's efforts to close bureaucratic mouths, the divisions and animosity within the administration kept spilling into the press.

Someone at the Pentagon leaked details of the green light cable to the *New York Herald Tribune*, touching off a new round of controversy. *Time* picked up the story and gave Hilsman, the telegram's instigator, a severe drubbing.

The magazine said he belonged to a "small but determined core of State Department liberals, known around Washington as the 'Gung Ho Boys,' who sometimes seem more interested in overthrowing the heavy-handed Diem regime than in pushing the war against the Viet Cong."

Hilsman was known derisively at the Pentagon as "the field marshal," the magazine continued, by critics who faulted him for trying "to run the whole military-political war in Viet Nam" himself. *Time* took a potshot at Harriman, too, saying that while he was an acknowledged expert on the Soviet Union, some career State Department officials regarded him as "a rank amateur on the subject of Southeast Asia."

RICHARDSON DIDN'T GET A medal when he came home, at least not right away. He went into hiding instead. The CIA stashed him at a friend's house to keep newspeople away from him.

Always fascinated by the inner workings of America's spy agency, the media persisted in asking why Richardson was recalled from Saigon. At a White House news conference on October 9, Kennedy vigorously defended the CIA and its former Saigon boss, saying it was "wholly untrue" that the agency was pursuing its own agenda in Vietnam.

"I know that the transfer of Mr. John Richardson, who is a very dedicated public servant, has led to surmises," the president said, "but I can just assure you flatly that the CIA has not carried out independent activities, but has operated under close control of the director of central intelligence . . . with the cooperation of the National Security Council and under my instructions."

Kennedy was asked if disputes and backbiting among U.S. officials involved with Vietnam were the result of "a lack of a clear-cut operational policy in Washington." He denied that, too, saying: "As you know, we are faced with a very difficult problem in South Vietnam . . . both in the military and the political sides. Men have different views about what actions we should take, and they talk to members of the press—to all of you—in Saigon, here in Washington.

"But I must say that as of today—and I think this is particularly true since General Taylor and Secretary McNamara came back—I know of no disagreement between the State Department at the top, the CIA at the top, Defense at the top, the White House, and Ambassador Lodge on what our basic policies will be and what steps we will take to implement them."

That, of course, wasn't true. There were furious disagreements at the top over whether or not Diem should be overthrown. The bickering was so intense that JFK privately exclaimed to his friend Charles Bartlett, the *Chicago Sun-Times* columnist: "My god, the government is coming apart!"

McCone continued to express his objections to a coup, both in the Oval Office and on Capitol Hill. On the day of JFK's press conference, the CIA director told the Senate Foreign Relations Committee behind closed doors that the war was going reasonably well. Peasant militiamen were being trained and armed, and strategic hamlets were proving to be effective, McCone said. Political upheaval hadn't yet damaged the war effort, although over time it would if left uncorrected. While the regime was certainly repressive, it wasn't guilty of "large-scale corruption." And he saw no alternative to Diem as national leader.

McCone attended more than three dozen Vietnam meetings at the White House and CIA headquarters that autumn—more than on any other global trouble spot. But he found the extended discussions among JFK and his advisers "confusing and disorganized." He wondered what Kennedy's real position was. Did he want to preserve Diem or did he want him removed? Was he trying, in his haphazard, college-faculty-debate way, to bring his quarreling subordinates together by letting them talk themselves out in meeting after meeting? Did he hope one faction would eventually out-argue and persuade the other? McCone sensed that the president was uncertain about how to proceed.

McCone was sure of one thing: Richardson had been treated disgracefully. At one point, the intelligence chief sat outside the Oval Office for three hours, waiting for a chance to speak with Kennedy about his former station chief. When he finally got in, McCone described Richardson as a very good CIA officer and a patriot. He'd come home under a cloud, but he deserved a commendation.

Kennedy evidently agreed. Later, in a secret ceremony at CIA headquarters, Richardson was awarded the Distinguished Intelligence Medal "for performance of outstanding services or for achievement of a distinctly exceptional nature in a duty of responsibility."

MCCONE WAS FOLLOWED TO the Senate Foreign Relations Committee by McNamara and Taylor, who also testified in private. And behind closed doors they did what the Kennedy administration was unwilling to do in public, mounting a strong, pragmatic defense of Diem in spite of his authoritarianism.

McNamara told the senators that Diem had done an extraordinary job of holding his country together for nine years under very difficult conditions. It was "only realistic," he said, to expect some degree of repression from a government fighting for its life against determined aggressors. The defense secretary acknowledged that South Vietnam was a "near feudal state" that was "singularly awkward and clumsy" in conducting its affairs. He noted that a "very primitive form of democracy" was emerging in strategic hamlets, whose inhabitants were now able to elect their own village chiefs. But it was unfair and unrealistic, he said, to expect the besieged Diem regime to adhere to standards of democracy that the United States had been refining since the eighteenth century.

Taylor went further. "We need a strong man running this country," he said. "We need a dictator in time of war and we have got one." He noted that even Abraham Lincoln suspended habeas corpus—a cornerstone of constitutional governance—at the start of the Civil War to prevent Confederate sympathizers in Maryland from blocking Union troop trains.

Americans generally dislike dictators and authoritarian leaders, but there was ample precedent for JFK to vocally back Diem. During World War II, President Franklin Roosevelt publicly embraced Joseph Stalin, the murderous Soviet autocrat, calling him "Uncle Joe" and prodding Hollywood producer Jack Warner to make a propaganda movie, *Mission to Moscow*, that portrayed Stalin as a courageous, pipe-smoking defender of the Russian people. FDR shipped huge amounts of war matériel to Stalin under the Lend-Lease program, confiding to an associate that he was prepared to "hold hands with the devil" if doing so would help to defeat Hitler. JFK could have made the same sort of realpolitik argument on Diem's behalf.

Instead, in less than two years, Kennedy veered from backing Diem to the hilt to continually undercutting him—largely because of negative press and public reaction to Diem's handling of an internal political-religious ruckus whose true nature and convoluted history few Americans understood. Kennedy regarded defending Southeast Asia against communist aggression as a central goal of U.S. foreign policy. But rather than shield Diem from critics, JFK and his administration put intense pressure on him to take actions he viewed as inimical to his political survival.

AS OCTOBER WORE ON, news articles and analysis pieces highlighting Diem's military and political difficulties practically flew out of Halberstam's typewriter. He produced eighteen bylined stories that month, seven of which landed on page one. And he refused to buckle to official pressure to tone it down.

When a major battle erupted in the delta, he and Sheehan tried to hitch a ride to the scene on a helicopter, but were denied. They made "a bunch of phone calls" to Lodge and Harkins, hoping the higher-ups would let them make the trip. No luck.

MACV held a press conference later that day. About a dozen correspondents showed up, but Halberstam noticed something unusual: the room was packed with generals and colonels. The usual lower-ranking briefer had been replaced by Major General Richard Stilwell, MACV's assistant chief of staff for operations and, according to Halberstam, "their brightest and their best spin guy." The reporter interpreted the large presence of heavyweight brass as "a clear attempt to intimidate us."

Stilwell promptly went after Halberstam and Sheehan. "Now, today's battle, there were two young men, Mr. Halberstam and Mr. Sheehan, who bothered Ambassador Lodge and General Harkins about trying to get down there," Stilwell said. "Gentlemen, Ambassador Lodge and General Harkins are very busy men. They do not need you to call them. You will come here for your briefings."

Stilwell's imperious and condescending words brought Halberstam's hackles to full attention. His heart was pounding as he stood up to speak.

"General Stilwell, we are not your sergeants and your corporals and your PFCs," he began, with barely suppressed anger. "We are here for *The New York Times*, the United Press, AP, *Time* magazine. . . . Americans are dying here. It is our job to report. We will keep calling, we will keep trying to go, we will do everything we can.

"We will call General Harkins if need be; we will call Ambassador Lodge. If you think we are too aggressive, you may write our publishers and tell them you think we are pushing too hard to go into battle. And perhaps they'll send someone else. But until then, we will keep doing this."

EVEN AS THEY STRUGGLED to cover the news, the Saigon reporters kept getting dragged into the news themselves.

In a *Newsweek* interview, Halberstam denied that he and his colleagues were misleading their readers by exaggerating the regime's deficiencies. Nor did he think they'd emphasized religious aspects of the Buddhist uprising at the expense of its political dimensions.

"What's been exaggerated?" he huffed. "It's all been proven. We've been accused of being a bunch of liberals, but even that's not true. I suppose I'm a Democrat, but Sheehan is a Taft Republican, and Perry [the *Time* freelancer who'd recently quit] speaks highly of Goldwater." (Arizona Senator Barry Goldwater, a hard-right conservative, was widely considered a strong contender to become the Republican nominee for president in 1964.)

But nearly two years in Vietnam had radicalized Malcolm Browne, the straight-down-the-middle AP man. He'd come to view the journalists' endless struggles to pry information out of hostile and uncooperative officials as a Manichaean battle between good and evil. "The world," he told *Newsweek*, "is divided into two classes: journalists and fact suppressors."

Predictably, the American reporters faced sniping and harassment from the Saigon press. Parroting Joseph Alsop, *The Times of Vietnam* labeled them "crusaders" whose only interest was advancing their careers. The paper also took an anti-Semitic swipe at Halberstam, suggesting in an editorial that he add "Jewish" to his byline so readers could judge whether his "anti-Catholic reports" were based on religious prejudice. The editorialist argued that Halberstam often pointed out Diem and Nhu's Catholicism in order to bolster "trumped-up accusations" that the brothers persecuted Buddhists—a line that echoed Harkins's conviction that Halberstam wrote critical stories about Diem and Nhu because he was a Jew.

In any event, it looked like Halberstam's tour in Vietnam might soon be at an end. His visa was set to expire on October 15, and palace sources told him it probably wouldn't be extended. Nicholas Turner of Reuters had applied for a renewal at the same time as Halberstam and had been approved two weeks earlier. But Halberstam heard that Nhu was very angry over his reporting and wanted him out of the country.

WRAPPED IN A MINK stole over a silken, scoop-neck ao dai, Madame Nhu stepped out of a Pan American jet into the glare of TV lights at New York's Idlewild Airport just after 8 p.m. on October 7.

A CBS correspondent who'd flown with her from Paris said she giggled and "fluttered a little, like a butterfly in trouble," but was otherwise composed as she headed across the Atlantic toward what she called "a cage of lions." The cage door swung open at Idlewild, with more than a hundred reporters and photographers roaring questions at her. Her purpose in coming to America, she said, was to "try to understand why we can't get along better." Asked if she wanted to meet President Kennedy, she said diplomatically that she didn't want to bother any government officials.

Other than the media horde, her reception was a distinctly cold one. No representatives of the city, state, or federal governments greeted her. Her parents, who lived in Washington, were nowhere to be seen. She departed for her Manhattan hotel in a rented Cadillac limousine without even a police escort.

The stakes were high for her three-week, coast-to-coast tour of America. She was the one South Vietnamese figure who might be able to generate a groundswell of public sympathy and support for her embattled brother-in-law and his government. There was tremendous public interest in her: not just what she had to say about Diem, the Buddhists, and the war, but in her bouffant hairdo, inch-long fingernails, elegant outfits, and exotic beauty. By the time she reached San Francisco, the local press reported that no foreign visitor had drawn so many cops, journalists, protesters, and lookie-loos since Nikita Khrushchev's U.S. tour in 1959.

From Saigon, Mecklin and others at the embassy followed her east-to-west pilgrimage with what he described as "bug-eyed fixation." So did the CIA, compiling confidential summaries of her speeches and activities each day.

Some members of Congress couldn't restrain their hostility, labeling her variously as "this shrew," an "evil woman," and a "comic strip Dragon Lady." Senator Stephen Young, a bombastic Ohio Democrat, characterized her "vaudeville tour" as "an affront to all Americans" and urged the Kennedy administration to kick her out of the country. Columnist Charles Bartlett, JFK's friend, wrote that her visit ran the risk of damaging the president's ability to "maintain a consensus that the military effort in South Viet Nam be pursued in spite of the Nhus."

Above: John Helble, the American consul in Hue, investigated the May 8, 1963, massacre of Buddhist protesters in the city and warned the State Department that angry Buddhists were headed for a showdown with South Vietnam's leader, Ngo Dinh Diem. (*Courtesy of Joan Helble*)

Right: Ambassador Frederick Nolting (*right*) brought his close friend William Trueheart to the Saigon embassy as his chief deputy. But the two diplomats' long friendship was shattered when the Kennedy administration turned against Diem. (*Courtesy of Charles Trueheart*)

Left: Nolting's most formidable Washington antagonist was Undersecretary of State Averell Harriman (*left, with arms outstretched*). Here Harriman greets Soviet premier Nikita Khrushchev amid U.S.-Soviet negotiations over a partial nuclear testing ban. (*Alamy*)

Above: Communist-led Viet Minh guerillas seized the remote French army base at Dien Bien Phu in 1954, capturing ten thousand legionnaires and other soldiers. The defeat knocked an exhausted France out of the war, and Diem became South Vietnam's prime minister. (*Alamy*)

Below left: The 1954 Geneva Accords split Vietnam into two states, prompting about 900,000 people to flee from communist North Vietnam to noncommunist South Vietnam. Many departed aboard U.S. Navy ships in what was known as Operation Passage to Freedom. In this photo, refugees wait to board the USS *Montague* in Haiphong harbor for the voyage south. (*Naval History and Heritage Command*)

Below right: CIA operative Edward Lansdale used black propaganda to scare people into leaving North Vietnam and helped Diem to drive a gangster army out of Saigon. He is shown here, in his uniform as a U.S. Air Force major general, in 1963. (*Alamy*)

Above: Though an ardent Catholic, Diem sought to establish good relations with South Vietnam's large Buddhist population. Here he chats with Buddhist monks in 1955. (*Naval History and Heritage Command*)

Left: Ngo Dinh Nhu, Diem's younger brother and closest adviser, was a Machiavellian intriguer who controlled the secret police, South Vietnam's feared Special Forces, and the clandestine Can Lao political party. (*Shutterstock*)

Above: Nhu's wife, Madame Nhu (*aiming pistol*), was a powerful figure in her own right. A member of the National Assembly, the Dragon Lady, as she was often called, also headed her own army, the Women's Paramilitary Corps. (*Alamy*)

Right: President Eisenhower (*left*) greets Diem at the start of his triumphant U.S. tour in 1957. (*Alamy*)

Journalists David Halberstam (*left*), Malcolm Browne (*middle*), and Neil Sheehan wrote news stories that depicted the harsh realities of the faraway war, often contradicting official optimism in the process. (*Associated Press*)

Above: Diem and Nhu herded rural people into thousands of hastily built "strategic hamlets," believing the fortified communities would protect them from Viet Cong marauders. This aerial view shows a small hamlet enclosed by multiple barricades. (*Alamy*)

Below: U.S. combat advisers look on as South Vietnamese troops board American-supplied H-21 "Shawnee" helicopters. The aircraft gave the Saigon army great mobility but were vulnerable to communist ground fire. Four Shawnees and a UH-1B "Huey" helicopter were shot down during the Battle of Ap Bac in January 1963, a record number at that point in the war. (*Alamy*)

Right: General Paul Harkins (left), the ever-optimistic commander of U.S. forces in South Vietnam, declared victory in the Battle of Ap Bac, leaving journalists in disbelief. (*Naval History and Heritage Command*)

Left: Tri Quang, the charismatic monk from Hue, helped to lead the Buddhist uprising against Diem. (*Getty*)

Right: Lieutenant Colonel John Paul Vann was furious over the hesitancy of South Vietnamese commanders to engage the enemy during the Battle of Ap Bac and gave newsmen details of the debacle. He resigned from the Army and returned to Vietnam as a civilian adviser. Here he relaxes in his Saigon office. (*Alamy*)

Left: Strong-willed and self-righteous, Archbishop Ngo Dinh Thuc, Diem's older brother, moved forcefully to raise the Catholic Church's profile in Hue and often antagonized Buddhists. (*Alamy*)

Below: Buddhist grievances against Diem received worldwide publicity in June 1963 when an elderly monk burned himself to death at a Saigon intersection to protest alleged government persecution of his brethren. (*Alamy*)

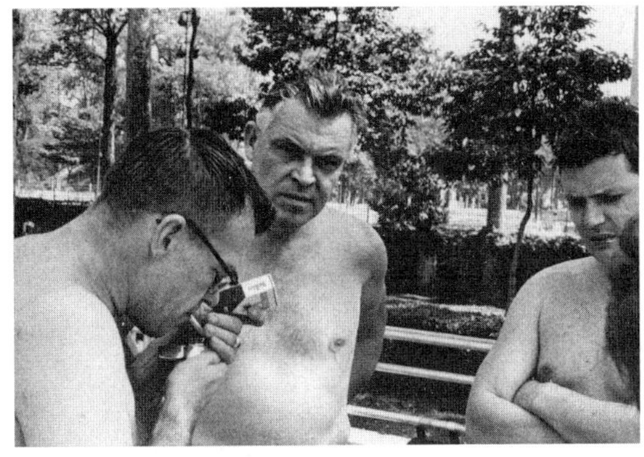

Right: Kennedy advisers Roger Hilsman (*left*) and Michael Forrestal (*right*) speak with Ambassador Nolting at Saigon's Cercle Sportif country club in 1962. Hilsman's "green light" cable the following year offered secret U.S. support to anti-Diem generals. (*Courtesy of Charles Trueheart*)

Left: JFK surprised his inner circle by picking Henry Cabot Lodge (*right*), a prominent Republican and longtime political rival, to succeed Nolting as U.S. ambassador to South Vietnam. Lodge had been Richard Nixon's running mate in the 1960 presidential election. (*Alamy*)

Below: Furious Buddhists try to tear down a barbed-wire barricade outside Giac Minh Pagoda on July 17, 1963, as anti-Diem street protests multiply. (*Associated Press*)

Above: South Vietnamese generals (*left to right*) Duong Van "Big" Minh, Le Van Kim, and Tran Van Don were key organizers of the coup against Diem. An unidentified officer stands behind Don. (*Alamy*)

Below left: CIA agent Lucien Conein was the main liaison between the plotting South Vietnamese generals and the U.S. government. During World War II, Conein fought behind the lines in France and Indochina as a member of the famed Office of Strategic Services. He is shown here as an OSS captain. (*National Archives*)

Below right: Marguerite Higgins, a prominent *New York Herald Tribune* correspondent, wrote news stories sympathetic to Nolting and Harkins, breaking ranks with other American reporters who often criticized them. (*Shutterstock*)

Left: JFK met Lodge in the Oval Office on August 15, 1963, telling his new Saigon envoy that Washington might need to "do something" about Diem. (*Kennedy Library*)

Below: South Vietnamese soldiers and police invaded Xa Loi Pagoda and other Buddhist temples on the night of August 20–21, 1963, arresting hundreds of monks and nuns and triggering a political crisis for Diem. Prior to the raids, monks at Xa Loi displayed protest signs in Vietnamese and English. (*Bettman*)

Right: Marine general Victor Krulak (*third from left*) and a State Department counterpart returned from a fact-finding trip to South Vietnam with separate reports that were so divergent, JFK asked them, "You both went to the same country?" (*Alamy*)

Left: McGeorge Bundy, Kennedy's national security assistant, urged the president's advisers to draft coup-related memos and cables in such a way that they couldn't be tied to JFK. (*Kennedy Library*)

Below: Defense Secretary Robert McNamara (*middle*) and Joint Chiefs of Staff chairman General Maxwell Taylor (*left*) concluded after visiting South Vietnam that the war was going well but that more repressive acts by Diem could jeopardize further progress. Here they discuss their findings with Kennedy on October 2, 1963. (*Kennedy Library*)

Top left: After clashing with Lodge, John Richardson, the CIA's Saigon station chief, became the target of damaging press leaks and was pulled out of South Vietnam. (*Courtesy of John H. Richardson*)

Top right: CIA director John McCone (*left*) commissioned a secret probe into who was leaking against Richardson. Prime suspects included Lodge, Hilsman, and Harriman. In this photo, McCone arrives at the White House during the Cuban Missile Crisis of 1962. (*Library of Congress*)

Below: Rebel soldiers murdered Diem (*pictured*) and Nhu inside a U.S.-made armored personnel carrier on November 2, 1963. Later testimony indicated that the order came from General Big Minh. (*Alamy*)

Above: Joyful Saigonese hail coup troops in the wake of Diem's overthrow and death. (*Alamy*)

Left: Less than three months after the anti-Diem putsch, the generals who overthrew him were themselves ousted by General Nguyen Khanh. For the next year and a half, South Vietnam was wracked by political instability and religious violence. (*Alamy*)

Right: Lodge became a serious contender for the 1964 Republican presidential nomination following his surprise win as a write-in candidate in the New Hampshire primary. *Life* magazine put him on its March 20, 1964, cover, striding out of the U.S. embassy flanked by two young Marines. (*Shutterstock*)

Above: On instructions from President Johnson, McNamara (*left*) and Taylor (*wearing cap*) appeared with Khanh at public rallies, emphasizing Washington's faith in South Vietnam's latest strongman. (*Shutterstock*)

Below: Supporters mobbed LBJ, the self-proclaimed peace candidate, in Manchester, New Hampshire, as he cruised toward a landslide victory over Republican Barry Goldwater. On the day he was elected, Johnson secretly convened an interagency group to look into ways to attack North Vietnam. (*Johnson Library*)

Above: An A-4 Skyhawk jet is cleared for takeoff from the USS *Coral Sea* as part of Operation Rolling Thunder, under which U.S. aircraft began sustained bombing of North Vietnam on March 2, 1965. (*Naval History and Heritage Command*)

Below: A Viet Cong car bomb exploded next to the U.S. embassy on March 29, 1965, killing and wounding Americans inside the building and leaving the streets outside strewn with dead and injured Vietnamese. The attack reinforced the Johnson administration's determination to put more military pressure on Hanoi. (*Associated Press*)

A State Department spokesman criticized newspaper editors and broadcasters for giving her a "triumphal reception," but the media couldn't get enough of her, especially in New York City, where she and her eighteen-year-old daughter, Le Thuy, took a suite at the Barclay Hotel on East Forty-Eighth Street. She spent her first day secluded in the hotel, going over her schedule of public appearances as about fifty reporters and TV cameramen waited in the lobby for any stirrings from her rooms.

HER FIRST SPEECH WAS before the Overseas Press Club at the Waldorf Astoria Hotel, where about a thousand people crowded into the hotel's Grand Ballroom to see her. Clad in turquoise silk brocade, she was barely visible behind the four-foot-high lectern. Someone brought over a barstool and lifted her onto it, but after a moment she asked to have it removed; she was more comfortable standing.

She spoke briefly and answered questions, although many of the mink-draped women in the audience seemed most interested in the thirty-nine-year-old first lady's youthful appearance and long fingernails. ("You don't have nails like that and do much around the house," sniffed one.)

Madame Nhu denied that the Diem government persecuted Buddhists and claimed that American reporters were distorting the news about her country—themes she was to repeat again and again during her trip. She suggested that the United States was less skilled at fighting counterguerrilla wars than conventional ones, and asserted that the communists knew they were headed for defeat. But her imperfect English was on full display as the audience laughed at some of her comments about South Vietnamese customs, probably not the reaction she wanted.

Four photographers trying to take her picture as she emerged from a TV studio that day claimed they were punched in the face by New York cops, prompting a CIA report writer to note puckishly that Madame "may have felt she never left home."

The following day, October 10, a crowd of three hundred people watched as she arrived under heavy police escort at the Time-Life Building in Midtown Manhattan for a lunch with magazine editors. She later spoke at Sarah

Lawrence College, repeating the regime line that a VC bomb, rather than government troops, had been responsible for the May 8 deaths in Hue. But the pace of her travels was wearing her down. Her voice quavered, her small body shook, and it looked like she might collapse onstage. She gulped some pills and later summoned a doctor to her hotel suite to treat her for exhaustion.

She was back in action the next day, reveling in an exuberant welcome from more than four thousand students at Fordham University, a Catholic institution.

The youths gave her a standing ovation as she entered the packed gymnasium and interrupted her speech repeatedly with vigorous applause. Twice she blew kisses at the audience. She voiced no criticisms of JFK and said of her country's attitude toward the United States: "We are very proud people but never ungrateful people—never."

On October 13, she went to NBC Studios to appear on *Meet the Press.* Before the broadcast, she encountered John Sharkey, his head still bandaged from his run-in with Saigon cops eight days earlier. Sharkey was one of the panelists who would question her. When she asked what happened to him, Sharkey said: "I was beaten up by your secret police." Madame Nhu politely replied that she was very sorry and hoped he recovered soon.

There was no mention of the police attack during the program. She nevertheless made news by accusing the U.S. government of being softer on communism than the Saigon regime.

"It appears," she said, "that it is only because we still are too much anti-Communist that there is misunderstanding; that if we change more, if we become soft anti-Communists, it will be better." She also charged that the U.S. Information Service in Saigon was trying to overthrow Diem—a remark that sounded nutty, but wasn't far from the truth, given the embassy's most recent clandestine contacts with the generals.

She then flew to Boston to speak at Harvard and Radcliffe. She charmed more than two hundred Radcliffe students packed into a dormitory lounge by relating her efforts to emancipate Vietnamese women, who she described as the "real power" in South Vietnam.

Returning to Manhattan, she met in her hotel suite with the parents of a U.S. Army lieutenant who'd been captured and executed by the Viet Cong. She spent thirty minutes talking with the couple and expressing her condolences.

KENNEDY FOLLOWED MADAME'S HIGH-PROFILE visit and vitriolic attacks on his Vietnam policy with "great annoyance," according to his speechwriter, Theodore Sorensen.

When someone asked how "so feminine a female" could be so harsh, the president speculated that she "resented getting her power through men." (He overlooked the power she held in her own right as a National Assembly member and leader of two large women's groups, one of them armed.) But there was little Kennedy could say or do that wouldn't bring her even more attention. In a memo to Hilsman, a State Department colleague suggested that journalists be reminded that Madame Nhu wasn't an official of the South Vietnamese government, but acknowledged that she was highly quotable and "unfortunately too beautiful to ignore."

When she traveled to Washington for another round of speeches, no government protocol officer or ranking elected official showed up to welcome her—an uncommon snub of an important representative of a wartime ally.

On October 16, she addressed the Women's National Press Club, explaining to a packed house of eight hundred that she learned the word *barbeque* from her teenage daughter, who overheard Americans using it at a Saigon snack bar. When Buddhists began incinerating themselves, she came up with her "monk barbeques" line in the hope of stopping the burnings by mocking them.

"I thought that ridicule was the best weapon," she said. "It was not cruelty." But her widely publicized derision came up over and over during her visit; it was impossible for her to shake the callousness of her words.

That night, Madame Nhu created a plaintive spectacle as she chased about the capital looking for her parents, who lived there but were estranged from her. With newsmen trailing her, she dashed from her hotel to her parents' modest home and to the South Vietnamese embassy.

Her parents had no desire to see her. Her mother referred to her as a "monster" and urged anti-Diem Vietnamese living in the United States to "run her over with a car" during her visit.

Her father, who'd quit as Diem's U.S. ambassador after the pagoda raids, launched his own speaking tour, following in his daughter's wake and denouncing her, her husband, and Diem at every stop. (Back in Saigon, Nhu returned the animus in full, telling an Italian journalist: "I will have his head cut off. I will hang him in the center of a square and let him dangle there. My wife will make the knot on the rope because she is proud of being a Vietnamese and she is a good patriot.")

The next morning's newspapers carried a photo of Madame Nhu standing disconsolately outside her parents' house, hands on hips, as her daughter knocked on the door but got no answer.

She again made headlines during an October 18 speech before the National Press Club, accusing "a handful of people" in the Kennedy administration of treason for "childishly" reducing aid to her government. Though she didn't name anyone, she said some JFK subordinates were "angry because they wanted to topple the Vietnamese government but couldn't." She agreed with McNamara's prediction that the war could be won by 1965, but said a handful of State Department officials were doing "their best to make McNamara a poor prophet."

There were more speeches, and more large audiences, in Los Angeles, San Francisco, and other cities. There were gossipy news stories about her daughter dancing with a young man at a Manhattan nightspot, and dining with another young man in San Francisco's Chinatown. (Asked at a press conference if romance might be in the air, Le Thuy, a member of her mother's paramilitary corps, replied: "What I really love is shooting guns: pistols, carbines, machine guns, rifles, bazookas, everything.")

If Madame Nhu's goal was to generate a surge of empathy and enthusiasm for her government, she failed. Former President Harry Truman declared that she "has made a fool of herself." *Time* magazine observed that she'd received the "worst press notices since Tokyo Rose," and many Americans remained skeptical of her and her family. “I had my doubts but she won me over completely—but I still have my doubts,” said a Fordham student, summing up the ambivalence felt by many.

By the time her junket ended in late October, polls indicated her favorability rating among Americans had dropped to 8 percent.

CHAPTER 17

KENNEDY'S BIG SQUEEZE

STATE DEPARTMENT WITS like to describe the gradual cutting off of U.S. assistance to a client nation as "salami-slicing." But Washington's abrupt aid suspension cut into South Vietnam's feeble economy like a chain saw.

With the flow of imports drastically curtailed, prices increased sharply for certain foods, consumer goods, and construction materials. By mid-October, the cost of wheat flour was up 30 percent. Cement jumped 30 percent; sweetened condensed milk rose 10 percent. Prices for soap, charcoal for cooking, and nuoc mam, the pungent, fish-based sauce used in virtually every Vietnamese kitchen, were up an average of 20 percent.

The value of the piastre dropped, with the black-market exchange rate for dollars spurting to 180 to one, the highest ever. The price of gold soared; people began to hoard so much that dentists found it hard to obtain. There were reports of bank runs in Cholon, Saigon's Chinese community. Speculators snapped up canned milk and flour, creating artificial shortages.

A pro-regime newspaper, *Tieng Doi*, branded the American aid reduction as "a criminal action" and "a betrayal of the ideal of freedom." Diem told a CBS News interviewer that he'd keep up the fight against the communists with or without U.S. help, and the regime dug in for a prolonged period of austerity. Government workers were told they might face pay cuts; Diem set aside foreign currency reserves to pay for imports of necessities such as chemicals, wood pulp, and coke, used to make iron.

Despite his outward bravado, Diem was in trouble. Thuan, his chief of staff, told Lodge his boss had ordered "elaborate studies" of whether the South Vietnamese could tighten their belts and go it alone economically; the conclusion was they couldn't. The CIA reported that the aid cutoff was beginning to hinder the war effort; Saigon couldn't pay its share of costs for the allies' joint counterinsurgency program.

Though it was clear that inflation was already destabilizing South Vietnam's economy, Lodge—who hadn't spoken to Diem in weeks—wanted the choke hold tightened. "Pressures should be continued," he cabled Washington, "until point where they likely result in severe economic dislocation."

Diem and Nhu openly expressed their anger at the Kennedy administration to journalists and third-country diplomats. Speaking to reporters in his cluttered palace office on October 17, Nhu said South Vietnamese had lost confidence in the U.S. government, and that the aid suspension had "initiated a process of disintegration in Vietnam." Yet the brothers gave no sign of being ready to undertake the reforms Washington wanted in exchange for the aid faucet being turned on again.

In an interview with the Australian novelist Morris West, Nhu—who'd said in May that he wanted U.S. forces in his country cut by half—now declared that *all* American advisers and helicopter pilots should leave. Nhu claimed it was him who planned ARVN operations, but he couldn't do so without first asking MACV for helicopter support. Americans, he complained, didn't understand VC-style warfare. "Without the Americans, we could win the war in two or three years," Nhu asserted. "With the Americans here, who knows?" Washington, he said, should give South Vietnam military and economic assistance with no strings attached.

West, whose books often focused on the abuse of power and the role of Catholicism in politics, passed on Nhu's words to the embassy, describing them as "the most blatant anti-American tirade I have heard." So provocative was the political counselor's diatribe that Kennedy and Bundy discussed "how to make use of the story," but took no apparent action. (In 1965, West published *The Ambassador*, a fictional account of an American diplomat who helps to stir up a military coup against an unpopular South Vietnamese Catholic ruler.)

Meanwhile, *The Times of Vietnam* and other pro-government newspapers kept up their strident attacks on the embassy, the U.S. Information Service, and American journalists, accusing the latter of "subversive activities." Vietnamese employees of U.S. government agencies were harassed, as were Vietnamese whose only offense was having American friends. The regime again demanded that Tri Quang be handed over; the embassy again refused. Lodge thought it was still possible that Nhu agents would try to invade the embassy and forcibly remove the monk; the ambassador kept a loaded .38-caliber pistol in his desk.

JOHN MECKLIN FIGURED NHU had launched another war of nerves against the Americans. There was a new wave of assassination threats and near-daily rumors of "spontaneous" mob attacks on the embassy, U.S. Information Service headquarters, and the AP and UPI offices. Mecklin believed Nhu was behind them all.

One persistent rumor was that regime hooligans planned to attack the U.S. Information Service building seeking evidence that U.S. officials had egged on the Buddhists and plotted to overthrow Diem. With 20 American and 150 Vietnamese employees under him, Mecklin couldn't ignore the multiplying threats. He and his staff made plans to close the steel gates that sealed off the building's upper floors and dusted off barrels of special chemicals used to destroy classified documents in an emergency. They studied possible escape routes in case attackers managed to break through the gates.

The USIS people depended for protection on the small, overextended U.S. Marine detachment that guarded the embassy, located in a different building. As threats intensified, the Marines repeatedly stood thirty-six-hour watches, without a break and without complaint. Their leader was Gunnery Sergeant Leroy Westrom, a soft-spoken, six-foot-six combat veteran who looked, according to Mecklin, "as though he could handle any ordinary mob single-handedly."

Westrom and his men stashed tear gas grenades, gas masks, pistols, and a submachine gun in various places around the USIS building. Whenever word spread of a coming attack, two or three Marines would appear to defend the place. Mecklin's third-floor office, which had good views of the street approaches to the building, was their command post. Besides the Marines, the alerts attracted an expectant knot of reporters and TV cameramen.

The morning of October 22 brought yet another report of a supposed assault, a massive one to be carried out by four thousand secret police and troops in civilian clothes. They were expected to hit the offices of USIS, UPI, and AP, and possibly the embassy as well. At about 11:30 a.m., Mecklin received another, more emphatic report that the attack was "imminent." Westrom and his men began lining up tear gas shells on Mecklin's desk. At 12:10 p.m., security officers at the embassy called to warn that an assault on Mecklin's building was coming "now."

It was the worst scare yet and it sounded all too real. Many employees were frightened and wanted to evacuate the building right away. But there was no sign of an advancing horde in the streets outside, only normal traffic thinning out as the lunchtime siesta began. The staff was scheduled to go home for lunch at 12:30 p.m. If they panicked and ran out of the building now, Nhu would win. Yet if a real attack occurred, and employees were injured or killed, it would be Mecklin's fault for disregarding an urgent notification.

At 12:15, the streets were still quiet. Mecklin felt that a large mob couldn't simply appear out of nowhere; surely there'd at least be a few minutes' warning before they reached the front door.

Partly due to instinct and partly because he was tired of being jerked around by Nhu, Mecklin decided to wait. The next fifteen minutes seemed like an eternity, but nothing happened. At 12:30, his staff left for lunch at the usual time.

American newsmen, too, tried to maintain their work routines in the face of more threats.

Browne thought the AP office and his apartment were under continual surveillance by plainclothes agents. Fearing they might burglarize his office, he moved some files to the embassy for safekeeping. AP reporters began hearing telltale pings when they answered their phones. When they heard that Vietnamese sources who called them were being arrested, they started answering with a warning: "Associated Press. This line is being monitored by public officials. Go ahead, please."

Unlike some of the journalists, who abruptly dumped girlfriends to avoid possible expulsion, Browne refused to abandon his fiancée, Le Lieu. They met when she worked at Diem's information ministry. But she quit her job and joined the USIS, one of the Nhus' primary bugbears.

One night at about 2 a.m., someone began pounding on the door of Browne's apartment. Through the frosted glass he saw two white-uniformed cops. When he opened the door, the newsman was armed with a Schmeisser submachine gun. The cops, hands on pistols as they nervously eyed Browne's more powerful weapon, demanded to search the apartment for Le Lieu. Browne told them no one else was there and "it would be better for all of us not to insist on a search."

After a whispered exchange, the cops turned and disappeared into the night.

AT A PARTY HOSTED by a British military attaché on October 22, Harkins made an unsettling blunder.

General Don was there, too. Harkins drew him aside and said he had reports that a colonel on Don's staff was planning a coup in the next several days. It was the wrong time for a coup, Harkins insisted. The war was going well, and Don should instruct his colonel to knock it off.

Don didn't trust Harkins, given his closeness to Diem, and said little in response. But the contradictory signals he'd received from Harkins and Conein left him confused and upset. While Conein had told the generals they'd have post-coup support from Washington, here was the top American military officer in Vietnam trying to discourage a mutiny.

Don summoned Conein to Joint General Staff headquarters the next morning. The generals' coup committee, he confided, planned to launch a revolt within a week, taking advantage of National Day, October 26, when many military field units would again gather in Saigon. But word of the ARVN colonel's activities had reached not only Harkins but the palace as well, and Diem ordered two nearby ARVN divisions on which the rebels were depending to go on extended operations in the countryside.

Don demanded to know what Washington's real position was. Conein replied as instructed: the Americans would neither thwart a change of government nor deny military and economic assistance to any new government that could generate popular support, improve relations with Washington, and increase the effectiveness of the war effort.

The CIA operative in turn challenged Don to prove that a coup committee even existed or had any real plans to unseat Diem. Both Lodge and the CIA suspected that the generals' second stab at an uprising might be more talk than action; Lodge doubted whether Don had "enough iron in his soul," as he told Washington, to pull off such a risky operation. Don insisted that the generals' plans were well advanced and promised to ask his fellow conspirators to show Lodge their blueprint for a new government the next day. He also said "appropriate disciplinary action" would be taken against the loose-lipped colonel.

That afternoon Lodge admonished Harkins over his exchange with Don, explaining that administration policy was not to stimulate a coup, but not to discourage one, either. According to Lodge, Harkins said he'd "misunderstood" and thought that Washington opposed a revolt. He also "expressed regret if he had inadvertently upset any delicate arrangements in progress" and promised to assure Don his remarks didn't reflect U.S. policy. Conein angrily summed up Harkins's faux pas in a conversation with a friend: "That stupid Harkins almost blew it."

The next night, Harkins met Don again and retracted his previous comments. But, according to Lodge's report on the incident, the MACV commander committed another serious indiscretion, telling Don his remarks opposing a coup were "contrary to a presidential directive" that U.S. officials were not to stymie one. Don also met Conein that night. The CIA agent confirmed that Harkins's anti-coup comments were inadvertent and "contrary to a presidential guidance from Washington"—thus making the same mistake as Harkins.

The encounters with Don set off alarms in Washington, especially at the CIA. McCone worried that Don might be a double agent, secretly working on Nhu's behalf to entrap Americans and link them to the generals' conspiracy. If that was the case, Harkins's and Conein's careless words had directly tied Kennedy to the plot. (Harkins later denied saying anything about presidential instructions to Don.)

"We here are concerned at possibilities of Don leading Conein (and thru him U.S.) down garden path to control our efforts at least, to entrap Conein at most," McCone cabled Saigon. He urged the CIA station to secretly tape conversations with Don and deploy countersurveillance agents to make sure Nhu's people weren't watching when he met with Conein. McCone also wanted a cover story developed so that if Conein was arrested, Lodge and Harkins would have "some degree of deniability."

Bundy fired off his own telegram to Lodge, questioning whether Conein should remain the sole conduit to the generals.

But Don insisted on communicating with the Americans through Conein and only Conein. When Lodge heard about Harkins's second gaffe, he cut him out of all further coup discussions, an action that would cause complications in the future. And the ambassador made it clear to Conein that if the operation blew up in their faces, and the embassy's surreptitious contacts with the generals became public, Lodge would deny that Conein even existed.

ON OCTOBER 24, HALBERSTAM was lunching at a Chinese restaurant near Gia Long Palace with Ray Herndon, the UPI reporter from Texas, and Seth King, a fellow *Times* correspondent sent in to backstop him on the burgeoning Vietnam story. Halberstam had a tip that a group of younger ARVN officers, led by Colonel Thao, the VC agent, was to launch a revolt that day. Every five minutes or so, one of the newsmen got up from the table and walked around the block, looking for telltale troop movements.

The CIA station had reached the same conclusion, telling Washington in a top-priority message that a coup was at hand.

According to a CIA source, Thao was to lead five ARVN battalions in an attack on the palace. If it failed, South Vietnamese air force planes would bomb the building and a second ground assault would follow. Meanwhile, 500 students were to seize the Saigon radio station. Altogether, Thao had about 2,500 troops, some armored vehicles, and a handful of air force pilots behind him. The CIA thought that although his forces weren't strong enough to succeed, Thao's onslaught might prompt other ARVN commanders to join him.

In any event, the purported rebellion seemed to be off to a shaky start. The source reported that Thao's troops, unable to line up transportation, were commandeering civilian buses and trucks. They also lacked enough ammunition. The CIA discovered that the Vietnamese air force officer who was to direct the palace bombing spent the afternoon drinking beer with American buddies. When CIA officers finally reached Thao himself, he denied any intention to act soon. It turned out that the generals had foiled his plans by withholding trucks and moving a key armor unit out of town for the day.

That night, General Don met Conein again, this time at a downtown dentist's office. Conein knew the secret police were on to him; they parked outside his house and followed him on his drives to the embassy. The dentist's office, he felt, gave him some cover if Nhu's men were watching. Don arrived first, then Conein. The CIA agent sat in the chair while the dentist tied a bib around his neck and performed some pro forma ministrations on his teeth before discreetly bowing out.

Don told Conein the generals had decided for "reasons of security" not to show Lodge their military and political plans now, but to do so two days prior to the coup, rescheduled for no later than November 2. Conein replied that the United States could make no firm commitments without seeing the generals' plans in advance.

When Conein asked which generals sat on the coup committee, Don named himself, Big Minh, and two others. Nguyen Khanh, the commander of the ARVN's II Corps in the Central Highlands, wasn't a member, but would take orders "like everybody else." Don added that General Dinh, the

Saigon military governor and presumed Diem loyalist, didn't pose an obstacle. He was surrounded by coup supporters and "will either cooperate or be crushed."

The post-coup government, said Don, would be made up of civilians; no member of the coup committee would have a senior position in it. Noncommunist political prisoners would be freed, opposition parties were to be permitted, and honest elections held. No religious group would enjoy favoritism or face discrimination. South Vietnam was to remain pro-Western, but not a "vassal" of the United States. The war effort would intensify.

When the coup began, Don went on, the generals would communicate with Lodge through Conein. Don also warned that "it would do no good to send anyone around to attempt to stop" the rebellion.

The ARVN general then slipped out a back door. CIA countersurveillance agents watching the dentist's office reported no "unusual activity" on the streets outside.

IN MID-OCTOBER, JOHN HELBLE, the U.S. consul in Hue, went on vacation with his family in the lovely Philippine resort city of Baguio, nestled in the cool mountains north of Manila.

Helble, his wife, Joan, and their young son rented a bungalow at the Baguio Country Club. By coincidence, William Trueheart, Lodge's deputy, was also there on vacation. One day when Joan wasn't around, Trueheart asked Helble when he was returning to Hue. October 28, Helble replied.

"When you get back," Trueheart said, "I want you to pack one bag containing what you would need immediately for you and your family. Not more than one bag. We have intelligence reports that the Vietnamese government is going to issue a massive white paper about the whole Buddhist episode. The blame is going to be placed very directly on the United States. Specifically, it's going to fall on you as the consul in Hue, whom they will accuse of having created the problem, agitating about it, exacerbating it, and directing it."

Helble was stunned. "I couldn't direct something like that in my wildest dreams," he protested.

Trueheart said he knew Helble had nothing to do with the unrest in Hue. But the regime was looking for a scapegoat, and he was it. When the incendiary white paper came out, Trueheart continued, "you and your family are going to be in serious danger up there." He promised to send a plane to evacuate them. The white paper probably would be issued, he said, when Madame Nhu returned to Saigon from her U.S. trip.

HALBERSTAM'S VISA EXPIRED IN mid-October, and he expected to be booted out of South Vietnam at any moment. Nevertheless, he was determined to do good, hard-charging reporting as long as he could. When MACV secretly informed Colonel Tung that U.S. subsidies would stop unless all of his Special Forces soldiers were committed to regular combat, Halberstam sniffed out the story the same day, filing an account that ran on page one.

But, as he told his old mentor John Paul Vann in a letter, he took "damn little joy" in covering the regime's heavy-handed struggle to fend off both its U.S. ally and its own people. On the other hand, he was impressed with Lodge's "near perfect" performance. "He's tough and intelligent and he has few illusions about the situation; he doesn't intend to see the U.S. kicked around . . . and he doesn't think this Ngo outfit is worth a tinker's damn," wrote the journalist.

Sheehan may not have been quite so enamored with Lodge. He was piecing together a blockbuster story: that the U.S. government was intent on seeing the troublesome Diem deposed in a coup d'état helped along by its wily Yankee ambassador. If Sheehan could write it in time, he'd have the biggest foreign news scoop since *The New York Times* exposed plans for the ill-fated Bay of Pigs invasion in 1961.

But Sheehan's Irish luck deserted him when his flinty, Tokyo-based boss, Earnie Hoberecht, not only killed the story but ordered Sheehan to come to Japan for "a rest." It was the last week of October, and Sheehan was terrified the coup would go off without him. Despite his fears that his phone was tapped, Sheehan placed a call to Hoberecht.

"This is the wrong time," Sheehan pleaded. "It's boiling over down here. I know more than I can tell you on the phone."

Hoberecht was adamant. Confronted with the prospect of losing his job if he disobeyed, Sheehan flew to Tokyo—but not before setting up what he hoped was a fail-safe system to warn him when rebel tanks were ready to roll. He contacted a favorite source, ARVN Colonel Pham Van Dong, who promised to try and alert him before the coup began. The go signal was: *Please buy me one bottle of whisky at the PX.* Dong agreed to notify Halberstam or Ray Herndon, Sheehan's UPI colleague, and no one else. They in turn would cable a coded message to Sheehan in Tokyo: *Please buy Blue Lotus two geisha dolls, Kyoto style.* Blue Lotus was the nickname of Sheehan's Vietnamese ex-girlfriend.

Landing in Tokyo, Sheehan tried again to persuade Hoberecht. "Earnie, I'm going to miss the coup," he said in despair.

"Take your rest, Neil," his boss repeated. "You're all going off your rockers with your coups and your plots. You, Halberstam, Browne, the bunch of you."

"Earnie! The reporters are not plotting the overthrow of the regime!" Sheehan blurted. "*Henry Cabot Lodge* is! *The U.S. government* is trying to get rid of these people!"

On his first day in the Tokyo office, Sheehan begged other reporters, rewrite men, and executives alike to be on the lookout for the "Blue Lotus" message. Call me any time, day or night, he told them, posting his hotel and room number in a dozen places around the newsroom. Somehow, some way, he had to get back to Saigon in time.

Then, nerves quivering, he waited.

ON THE WARM AFTERNOON of Saturday, October 19, President Kennedy sat amid a crowd of football fans at Harvard Stadium, watching his alma mater grind out a 3–3 draw against Columbia while curious undergraduates and alumni kept sneaking glances at him.

Toward the end of the first half, his aides noticed that Kennedy was unusually quiet, as if his mind was far away. He turned to his appointments secretary and longtime confidant, Kenneth O'Donnell.

"I want to go to Patrick's grave," he said, referring to his newborn son who'd died two months earlier. "And I want to go there alone, with nobody from the newspapers following me."

After the game, Kennedy and his entourage made their way to their cars as a gaggle of reporters hurried to their own vehicles to tail him. O'Donnell said a few words to a Secret Service agent, who said a few words to the Boston Irish cop manning the parking lot. The cop made sure the journalists stayed bottled up in the lot until the president was safely away.

At the cemetery in nearby Brookline, the president's birthplace, the headstone above Patrick's grave was inscribed simply "Kennedy." "He seems so lonely here," JFK said to O'Donnell. After the visit, the president headed to a favorite spot, Schrafft's restaurant in Boston's Back Bay neighborhood, where he downed a butterscotch sundae at the lunch counter and autographed napkins for well-wishers. Then he strolled along Boylston Street toward his hotel; motorists tried to keep from plowing into each other as they rubbernecked at the unexpected sight of their glamorous leader on foot.

That evening, Kennedy and his brother Ted joined nearly eight thousand local Democrats at the Commonwealth Armory in Boston for a fundraiser that netted $750,000 for the 1964 campaign. He drew laughs from the crowd with a joke about Ted, who had won a U.S. Senate seat in Massachusetts the previous fall. Complaining that he was being accused of trading on the family name, JFK's youngest brother supposedly asked whether he could change it to Roosevelt.

The president was in good shape for reelection. The Senate had recently ratified his partial nuclear test ban treaty with the Soviets and the British, an achievement that gave him the most personal satisfaction of his three years in the White House. In September, he'd toured eleven Western states under the guise of promoting conservation, but really to strengthen himself politically in areas he'd lost to Nixon in 1960. When he found that his audiences were more interested in his plans to ease Cold War tensions than to protect natural resources, he switched speeches and happily discussed his ideas for keeping the peace in the nuclear age.

With many Southern whites angry over his efforts to advance civil rights, Kennedy's approval ratings had been slipping steadily since the start of 1963.

But they still hovered just below 60 percent that autumn, a level that future presidents would envy. Kennedy looked forward to campaigning against the man he regarded as the likely Republican presidential nominee, Arizona Senator Barry Goldwater, whose saber-rattling comments about nuclear war with the communist bloc scared many voters. Kennedy was confident he'd beat Goldwater by a large margin.

Kennedy took a helicopter to Hyannis Port on October 20 to visit his ailing seventy-five-year-old father for what turned out to be the last time. Sitting in a wheelchair on his front porch, paralyzed and unable to speak, Joseph Kennedy enjoyed seeing his son land on the big front lawn, where the Kennedy brood played touch football. The president took his father for a gentle ride in a powerboat. In the afternoon, he walked across the street to visit a neighbor, Larry Newman, and talked about his plans for Vietnam.

He told Newman that both General MacArthur and President de Gaulle had warned him not to commit ground troops in Asia. "The first thing I do when I'm reelected, I'm going to get the Americans out of Vietnam," Kennedy said as Newman's young daughter crawled into his lap. "Exactly how I'm going to do it, right now I don't know, but that is my number one priority—get out of Southeast Asia. . . . We are not going to have men ground up in this fashion, this far away from home. I'm going to get those guys out because we're not going to find ourselves in a war it's impossible to win."

Back in the White House, the president met on October 22 with Arthur O. Sulzberger, the newly appointed, thirty-seven-year-old publisher of *The New York Times*. Sulzberger had come to the White House to pay a courtesy call, but JFK glimpsed a possible solution to his problems with Halberstam, whose critical stories appeared with exasperating regularity.

Sulzberger expected his first meeting with the president to be purely social, but almost immediately Kennedy began criticizing the paper's coverage of Vietnam. "He was relentless," Sulzberger recalled. The conversation made Sulzberger more and more uncomfortable. After several minutes he realized the president was asking him, in all seriousness, to pull Halberstam out of Saigon.

The young publisher had no intention of doing that. Halberstam was scheduled to take a two-week vacation, but the paper canceled his holiday rather than give even the appearance of caving in to White House pressure on such an important story.

IN THE HEART OF the southern Mekong Delta, amid the coconut groves and muddy waterways of Chuong Thien Province, two ARVN battalions were preparing to overrun the dug-in Viet Cong 1096th Battalion from three directions.

The October 19 operation began with air strikes to soften up VC defenses. Then Shawnee transport helicopters, accompanied by Huey gunships, whirled in and deposited ARVN squads near enemy positions. Although the VC were outside artillery range, B-26s and other aircraft bombed and strafed them throughout the day. But the communists had learned the lessons of Ap Bac well, and again applied them with lethal effectiveness against a bigger force.

The first wave of 150 ARVN soldiers jumped out of their choppers about a third of a mile from the objective, a village in a dense grove of coconut trees. They'd crossed three hundred feet of flat rice paddies when the VC opened up with heavy automatic-weapons fire. Within minutes, thirty ARVN men had been hit. The second, third, and fourth ARVN waves ran into the same buzz saw.

Ground fire forced one of the Shawnees down, injuring the American pilot, copilot, and crew chief. They were evacuated and friendly forces stripped and destroyed their crippled craft. Five of the seven Hueys were also hit and temporarily knocked out of action. Repeated air strikes failed to neutralize the strong defenses and the VC kept blasting American aircrews. A B-26 with its rudder controls shot away ran off the runway as it returned to base.

The battle stretched into the night. Flare ships lit up enemy positions and bombers hammered them some more. At some point during the night, the VC climbed out of their firing holes, boarded sampans, and slipped away along the canals. Helicopter sweeps the next day found no trace of them. The

ARVN suffered forty-four dead, eighty-three wounded. In addition, twelve American airmen were wounded, two seriously, along with an infantry adviser. Thirty enemy corpses were found, although others may have been carried away.

The ARVN occupied the village, which the Viet Cong had turned into "an impressive fortified base, developed with skill and patience." MACV concluded that despite some "tactical deficiencies" and "bad breaks," the ARVN had conducted itself well under difficult circumstances. The CIA, however, discerned a deeper meaning in the battle, noting in a report to Kennedy that, as at Ap Bac, "the Communists made good use of carefully prepared defenses to hold off a superior force."

A FEW DAYS LATER, the Pentagon and State Department engaged in their own bureaucratic firefight over whether the war effort was making headway or sliding backward.

It began when State's intelligence bureau circulated a paper saying recent statistics indicated that South Vietnam's military position "may have been set back to the point it occupied six months to a year ago." Since July, the paper said, the number of VC attacks and other incidents had risen, while the number of enemy casualties, weapons losses, and defections dropped.

Saigon's weakening military position coincided "with the sharp deterioration of the political situation." But even if the Buddhist crisis hadn't arisen, the ARVN might have lost ground "in the face of the accelerated Viet Cong effort." The State Department analyst who wrote the paper, Louis Sarris, had relied on Pentagon statistics, although he noted that those numbers were "neither thoroughly trustworthy nor entirely satisfactory as criteria" for measuring progress in the war. (Sarris also reported that ARVN morale had deteriorated, and that the deputy commander of III Corps had recently told a U.S. military official that he feared mass desertions "possibly as high as 80%.")

Sarris's findings contradicted McNamara and Taylor's relatively optimistic report to Kennedy after their recent Vietnam tour. But McNamara and

Taylor were upset not by his findings, but because State hadn't sought Pentagon input before releasing its paper.

In a note to Rusk, McNamara wrote: "If you were to tell me that it is not the policy of the State Department to issue military appraisals without seeking the views of the Defense Department, the matter will die."

Two days later, Rusk wrote back: "It is not the policy of the State Department to issue military appraisals without seeking the views of the Defense Department. I have requested that any memoranda given interdepartmental circulation which include military appraisals be coordinated with your Department."

The Joint Chiefs produced their own paper arguing that Sarris overlooked a number of positive factors, including a drop in the estimated number of VC fighters to 93,000 from 123,000 a year earlier. The number of people resettled in strategic hamlets had nearly quintupled, to nearly 10 million, in the past year, and many of the fortified communities now had radios to call for help. In addition, more militiamen had been trained and equipped, and the ARVN's "confidence and fighting efficiency" had risen.

"Overall," the chiefs wrote, "the military campaign is still progressing favorably."

Harkins—who'd had a recent scare when his plane belly-landed because the pilot forgot to lower the landing gear—concurred, saying the Saigon government was "way ahead" in central and northern parts of the country and "making progress" in the delta.

Diem, too, firmly believed the war was being won. "We are now in a position to go over to the offensive on all fronts," he proclaimed in an address to the National Assembly. "It has become obvious—all observers admit—that the war has taken a major turning towards an undoubted and significant victory."

People living in strategic hamlets enjoyed "a reasonable degree of security," he said, and nearly all of the 11,864 planned hamlets would be built by the end of the year. Gradually freed from static defense duties, the ARVN was relentlessly harrying "roving bands" of VC "operating without a base."

More than ten thousand enemy fighters had surrendered under the Open Arms amnesty program in the past seven months.

A fresh CIA analysis, however, largely confirmed the State Department's pessimism. It pointed out that ARVN weapons losses had risen sharply and since July exceeded VC weapons losses by two to one—enough arms to equip as many as five enemy battalions. VC defections had declined over the summer, while the number of government troops captured or missing in action quadrupled. Government casualties, too, were running higher. From a ratio of two VC casualties for every one ARVN casualty in 1962, the ratio was now almost even—seven to six—over the past three months.

The Viet Cong appeared to have recovered from their initial shock and uncertainty over the introduction of U.S. weaponry, and were conducting small-scale attacks aimed at disrupting and defeating the strategic hamlets, the CIA said. By improving their defensive tactics and striking more often at softer targets such as the hamlets, they'd reduced casualties and bolstered morale. In a separate report, Chester Cooper, a CIA Vietnam expert detailed to the National Security Council, concluded that the VC could be ground down enough to safely withdraw U.S. forces "only with a substantially increased US commitment over a considerable period of time (well beyond present US military schedules and domestic expectations)."

Thus, as the anti-Diem conspiracy careened toward its denouement, the U.S. government was still arguing with itself over whether, in Homer Bigart's barbed adage, it was sinking or swimming with Ngo Dinh Diem.

KENNEDY SUMMONED A HANDFUL of his core advisers to the White House on October 25: his brother Robert, McNamara, Bundy, and McCone. They were concerned about Harkins's and Conein's latest interactions with General Don.

McCone told of his suspicion that Don might be working for the palace and trying to implicate U.S. officials in the coup plot. He read aloud from an embassy cable that described Harkins admitting to Don that he'd "misunderstood a presidential directive." Harkins's thoughtless words, said

McCone, left Washington with "absolutely no plausible denial" to the charge that Kennedy was directly involved in the conspiracy.

McNamara vociferously agreed. "We're like a bunch of amateurs. I hate to be associated with this effort, dealing with Conein. He's an unstable person; none of the messages are evaluated. . . . We're dealing through a press-minded ambassador and an unstable, French, five-times-divorced . . . ," he said, his voice trailing off on Kennedy's hidden tape machine.

"This is what we have to stop. I don't think we can mastermind this coup contact from here. . . . I sure would like to be dealing through some experienced men of sound judgment. And I don't think we are."

(The defense secretary misstated Conein's citizenship—he was a naturalized American—and exaggerated his marital partings; he was only on his third wife, Elyette. Born in Vietnam to French parents, she'd acquired U.S. citizenship in 1959. A CIA memo prepared for McCone stated that "she is *not* Vietnamese" and noted that Conein already had been "fully investigated" for potential security problems.)

JFK asked if Conein worked for the CIA; McCone confirmed that he did. The group then discussed bringing in different, more experienced agents to deal with Don and the other generals. McCone suggested William Colby, the astute head of the CIA's Far East division. Robert Kennedy suggested that maybe someone from a third country, such as France or Britain, could be the go-between. But the president noted that the generals insisted on dealing exclusively with Conein.

JFK said he sensed that McCone wasn't on board with the policy of not frustrating the generals' plans, and he was right. McCone replied that the ARVN commanders weren't capable of governing South Vietnam. He predicted that the most likely result of a coup would be a period of political upheaval followed by a second coup. During this tumultuous interregnum, he believed, the war might be lost.

There were civilians, McCone said, both inside and outside South Vietnam, who were more capable of running the government than military officers. Washington should either pursue a coup more professionally and forcefully, or work out a détente with Diem. He preferred the latter option.

There was palpable irritation with Lodge in the room. McCone complained that the ambassador's "cool correctness" policy prevented the CIA station from collecting intelligence about Diem's and Nhu's likely next moves. He quoted from one of Lodge's cables in which the ambassador said he personally approved all of Conein's contacts with Don and that the CIA agent had been "punctilious" in carrying out his instructions.

That brought a sarcastic comment from Bundy: "Lodge is his own press relations officer, he's his own [CIA] case officer. He's quite an economical investment that we've had." The other men laughed. Someone chimed in: "You get what you pay for!"

But cool correctness was about to end. Despite their standoff, Diem had invited Lodge and his wife to spend the upcoming Sunday with him at one of his villas in Dalat. Lodge accepted. McCone was optimistic about the get-together, saying he hoped it would lead to an understanding that "would permit us to go forward with this government."

JFK agreed. He instructed that a cable be sent to Lodge asking him again whether the coup generals were strong enough to win. Kennedy knew Diem had made some of the military changes that Washington wanted, such as shifting the Ninth Division to the delta. He wanted to explore what political reforms Diem might now be willing to make.

"Let's see where [Lodge] can get with him this weekend," said the president. "In other words, Lodge ought to try, it seems to me, to get along with Diem this weekend. And explain what our policy is."

The president also directed McCone to prepare a plan for continued monitoring of the coup plotters "in a way that would be non-attributable and therefore deniable."

But Kennedy had lingering concerns about his ability to control his Republican envoy. Earlier that month, Lodge asked to speak with Bundy face-to-face, saying he had some "new ideas . . . which might just change the situation here." A military jet was scheduled to deliver Lodge to Washington on November 3, and Kennedy planned to see him then.

"I think there's more or less unanimity that there's some reservation about Lodge's conduct since he's there," JFK told his advisers. "But he's there, we can't fire him, so we're going to have to give him some direction when he comes back to us. So we ought to make sure that we've given as much thought as we can to how we're going to handle Lodge. . . . We got to get him to end up where we want to go, and not end up where he wants us to go."

Yet Kennedy himself seemed not to know where he wanted to go, although it was clear he wanted to keep his options open. On one hand, he wanted a fresh assessment of whether the generals could subdue Diem. On the other hand, he wanted Lodge to reach some sort of understanding with Diem that would allow the two allies to keep working together. But he couldn't have it both ways, and his choices were narrowing much faster than he seemed to realize.

OCTOBER 26 WAS NATIONAL DAY in Saigon. Diem reviewed the troops as he always did, although the embassy, in a further sign of its pique, refused to provide the customary U.S. planes and ships for the annual cavalcade.

For two hours, ARVN paratroopers, Civil Guards, and hamlet militiamen paraded past the reviewing stand. Harkins sat watching with Big Minh and Don, but neither of them breathed a word about their momentous plans for the following week.

Don did drop one hint: he was transferring some of Colonel Tung's Special Forces companies to the ARVN's two northernmost corps zones, far from Saigon.

THE NEXT DAY, LODGE clambered into a helicopter with Diem for the flight to Dalat.

They stopped for lunch at a plantation and then roared over Quang Duc Province. With engine noise drowning out their voices, Diem scribbled notes to Lodge about what they were seeing on the ground.

"Diem was at his best, describing the public improvements that he had put into effect," Lodge later wrote. "He is very likeable."

Prior to his departure, Lodge received a telegram from Bundy indicating that he and JFK were "particularly concerned" about the possibility of a failed coup, the responsibility for which would be laid squarely at the White House's door. Bundy urged Lodge to provide advance warning of any coup plan "with poor prospects of success."

In his reply, Lodge agreed that blame for an unsuccessful putsch would fall on the administration. But, he added, "I believe that if we cover up our tracks, as I think we are doing and will do, that we can enter a very vigorous denial and effectively challenge those who criticize us to produce proof." In any event, once the coup got underway, he wrote, Washington wouldn't be able to stop it. He pledged, however, to do all he could to ensure that Kennedy "has influence on the situation right up to the last minute."

At Diem's villa Lodge enjoyed a sumptuous dinner with his host. If the ambassador felt any awkwardness about breaking bread with a man he knew might soon be killed in a revolt encouraged by the U.S. government, he gave no sign of it. After the meal the two men warmed themselves before a crackling fireplace. In a "casual, rather supercilious tone," as Lodge described it, Diem asked when Washington intended to resume the Commercial Import Program. "He said it as though it were a matter of indifference to him," reported Lodge, who told Diem he didn't know.

Lodge asked Diem what he was willing to do for Washington if the program was restarted. Would he reopen schools, release dissidents from detention, and repeal the law that Buddhist leaders claimed made it harder for them to acquire property? Diem insisted that schools had gradually reopened, protesters were being let go, and revising the law was a matter for the National Assembly, not him.

He then rehashed old grievances about the CIA and U.S. Information Service allegedly inciting the Buddhists, and the American press supposedly lying about his government. He complained about Washington letting his former ambassador, Tran Van Chuong, publicly criticize the regime and Madame Nhu. Then he sailed off on one of his odd sexual digressions, claiming that Chuong's other daughter, Madame Nhu's sister, was "acting like a prostitute," and had "scandalized Georgetown" and "even jumped on priests."

Lodge emphasized the importance of public opinion in the United States and said it wasn't smart for the regime to be "beating up newspapermen." The only way to stop Madame Nhu from generating bad headlines, he said, was to stop her from talking.

Near the end of the conversation, Lodge said with some exasperation: "Mr. President, every single specific suggestion which I have made, you have rejected." Wasn't there even one action Diem could take to improve his government's image? But the South Vietnamese leader, Lodge reported, "gave me a blank look and changed the subject." While Lodge was disappointed with the weekend, Diem was pleased, telling his secretary that his relations with Washington had finally taken a turn for the better.

DIEM IN THE MEANTIME had taken another big political gamble, inviting a seven-man United Nations team to South Vietnam to investigate whether the regime was violating Buddhists' human rights.

The UN delegates ensconced themselves at the Majestic Hotel near the Saigon River. They represented seven UN members: Afghanistan, Brazil, Ceylon, Costa Rica, Dahomey, Morocco, and Nepal. Their chairman was Abdul Rahman Pazhwak, a former Kabul newspaper editor with a reputation for studiously avoiding taking sides in big-power conflicts. He vowed to keep an open mind and listen to anyone who cared, or dared, to testify.

Diem pledged that the UN investigators could freely interview monks and students, including those in prison. It was a dicey move, since a negative report by the UN mission could bring down even more international opprobrium on his government. Lodge found it hard to believe that the UN team would be accorded much latitude, telling Washington that student leaders were being arrested to forestall demonstrations during the visit.

"All evidence to date points to concentrated GVN [Government of Vietnam] attempt to cow potential adverse witnesses and prevent their appearing before the delegation and to keep delegation busy on a cook's tour," he wrote.

At first, it looked as if Lodge was right. Armed troops were stationed at the Majestic Hotel's entrance, and police and soldiers patrolled its hallways, common areas, and bar. People entering the hotel were stopped and questioned about why they were there. Police arrested three Vietnamese drivers hired by Western journalists to help them keep up with the UN fact finders as they moved around town.

The regime had prepared an itinerary for the UN men, and initially they followed it. On October 25, they visited Xa Loi Pagoda, once the bustling nerve center of the Buddhist protest movement. A crowd of newsmen awaited, but there were no monks or laymen in sight. The investigators waited ten minutes until an elderly monk in a brown robe appeared along with a younger bonze. Despite assurances that their statements would remain anonymous, the Buddhists refused to give their names and said little.

Soon after that, the UN inspectors announced they'd go their own way and set off to interview people of their own choosing. They spoke with monks in prison and students at a youth detention facility. Arrested in various demonstrations, the young people were required to attend lectures on the dangers of communism and the government's efforts to improve "the well-being of the people." Most were released to their parents after about fifteen days.

Diem was as good as his word, allowing the fact finders to speak with almost anyone they wanted, including high-ranking Buddhist detainees. Government officials were barred from the interviews.

Even Lodge seemed surprised. The regime, he reported, "appears to be off to a good start with the U.N. mission. So far they have allowed them to meet everyone, including imprisoned Buddhists." The one person the UN team was not permitted to see was Tri Quang, still under U.S. embassy protection.

The Buddhist leader nevertheless wrote a letter to the United Nations, making the utterly unfounded allegation that Diem was trying to "annihilate" Buddhism. But other monks told the fact finders that Diem's government wasn't persecuting them. Instead, they described harassment and abuse—what one witness described as "oppressive acts, vexations, and ill-treatment"—at the hands of province- and village-level officials who were often Catholic. Such vexations included Catholics throwing dirt at a statue of Buddha during a Buddhist procession and a Catholic police chief fining a Buddhist villager a few piastres for saying a prayer aloud.

More serious charges were leveled at officials of three central Vietnam provinces who allegedly tried to force Buddhists to convert to Catholicism. "Some Buddhists who resisted these attempts were forced to surrender their identity cards to the authorities, and some were ordered to migrate to other regions," according to a summary of written testimony the UN team received from Buddhists. "Others were kidnapped, arrested, and tortured, and one, in Quang-Ngai province, was said to have been buried alive. After their arrests some Buddhist leaders were not heard of any more. One bonze, who had strongly protested against such persecution, in Phu-Yen province, had allegedly been murdered."

Buddhists said they complained to local authorities, the National Assembly, and Diem himself, but nothing was done. One witness said he pleaded with Diem in 1961 to intervene, warning the president he'd be blamed if the national government didn't rein in oppressive local functionaries.

Before coming to Saigon, the UN inspectors had asked the Vietnamese public not to engage in any protest demonstrations during their visit. The regime claimed that ten monks had planned to immolate themselves while the delegates were there, but police scooped up five of them before they could douse themselves with gasoline.

The investigators asked to speak with the arrested monks and the regime produced a nineteen-year-old who testified that he came within a day of killing himself based on atrocity stories that turned out to be false. The tales he heard included government agents breaking monks' and nuns' hands, drowning them, setting them on fire, and ripping open their stomachs.

The young bonze said he met two men who asked if he was willing to burn himself at the National Day celebration, where the UN delegates were supposed to be in attendance. Angry at purported government barbarities, he agreed. The two men, he said, were "very happy" he was prepared to die for the Buddhist cause. They gave him a gas-soaked yellow robe and pills "so that I wouldn't feel the pain." A car with a special sticker would drive him past security guards and into the parade area. Once there, he was to torch himself. He signed pre-written letters, including one to Diem and one to the UN examiners, explaining why he'd committed suicide.

The day before National Day, however, the police, apparently tipped by an acquaintance, picked him up. The bonze realized he'd been misled when the cops explained that "no monk had been killed by the authorities, that no atrocities had been perpetrated, and that the whole story had been invented."

Another monk, however, eluded police and, on October 27, became the seventh Buddhist to die in flames. He chose a highly symbolic place and time: near Saigon's Catholic cathedral as parishioners arrived for a Sunday morning service.

The man, about thirty-five years old, rode up on the back of a motorbike, already drenched in gas. He assumed the lotus position and went up in a geyser of fire. Dozens of people gathered around him, praying and weeping. Police rushed toward the burning figure, but some of the onlookers cursed them and shoved them away. When firemen came to put out the flames, the crowd jeered.

An NBC cameraman filmed the suicide and the Associated Press took pictures and sent out a story. It landed on the front page of *The New York Times.*

CHAPTER 18

"WE'RE WORKING PRETTY MUCH IN THE DARK"

THE EMBASSY STILL knew alarmingly little about the plotters' designs as October drew to a close.

When Lodge ran into General Don at the airport on October 28, he demanded, "Let me see your plans." Don was noncommittal, saying the generals weren't ready to move yet and the Americans should keep their distance.

But he warned darkly that the ARVN "has lost its drive. We must win before you Americans leave. We cannot do it with this government." The general also wanted to know if Conein spoke for Lodge; the ambassador assured him that he did.

Don again met with Conein at the dentist's office that evening. The CIA go-between reiterated that the embassy wanted to see the coup plan; Lodge needed "a complete grasp" of it before he left for Washington on October 31. Don, however, reneged on his commitment to provide the blueprint two days in advance; the Americans still might get a look, he said, but no more than four hours before the revolt began. Don questioned Conein closely about the exact time of Lodge's departure, urging that he not change it for fear of tipping off the palace.

Don said he wasn't involved in military planning for the coup, but gave Conein a sketchy rundown of which units he expected to side with the rebels. The Fifth Division, based at Bien Hoa, was committed; the attitude of the Seventh Division wasn't known. The commandant of the Vietnamese Marine Corps wanted to throw all of his men against Diem, but was afraid of what might happen to his family if he were killed and the coup collapsed. With the exception of its commander, the air force was committed to the coup.

Don also disclosed that the mutiny would be directed from Joint General Staff headquarters. When it started, phone lines throughout Saigon would be cut and the cable office closed. The generals were aware, he said, that Diem and Nhu might try to escape through two underground tunnels that led away from the palace. One ended at the zoo, the other in a cemetery.

Don was headed north the following morning, under the guise of handing out medals, to "perfect the planning" with the commanding generals of I and II Corps. He pleaded with Conein not to tell the American community to stockpile food; the palace would read that as a sure sign that an uprising was coming.

Conein persuaded Don to stop meeting in person or talking on the phone; it was too dangerous. From now on, they'd communicate through "cutouts," or trusted intermediaries. A personal aide was designated as Don's cutout; Conein's was a junior CIA officer who lived near him but knew nothing about the coup operation. If a face-to-face meeting was unavoidable, Conein was to "confirm his safety and continued security of the operation" to the CIA station with a series of code words within an hour of leaving Don. If he failed to do so, the station would assume he'd been arrested and was under Nhu's control.

Before they parted, the ARVN chief assured Conein that nothing would happen in the next forty-eight hours, but warned him not to leave his house from the night of October 30 on.

Once again, CIA watchers outside the dentist's office detected no Nhu spies in the area.

THE EMBASSY'S INABILITY TO come up with better information about the generals' game plan was producing a good deal of anxiety at the White House.

Kennedy convened his advisers yet again on October 29. But before the meeting got underway in the Cabinet Room, a verbal skirmish broke out during a preliminary session among several officials gathered in the Situation Room in the basement.

Taylor argued that the coup would have "disastrous results" even if the generals succeeded in knocking over Diem. Bundy countered that "we cannot reconsider our position" of covert support for the coup. The only option, he said, was to ask the embassy for another assessment of the generals' chances.

That ticked off McCone. He found Bundy's statement "extremely disturbing" in light of the serious reservations expressed by the Joint Chiefs of Staff chairman, who, after all, bore responsibility for ensuring the success of American military actions in the war. In fact, even Bundy had his doubts. "Should we cool off the whole enterprise?" he jotted on a background paper prepared for the upcoming meeting with the president.

Unsettled, the men moved upstairs to the Cabinet Room, where JFK again switched on his hidden recorder.

Colby gave a briefing on the relative strength of the pro- and anti-Diem forces. Pointing to a color-coded order of battle chart, the CIA executive said the two groups were roughly even, with about 9,800 troops on each side. Another 18,000 forces in the Saigon area appeared to be neutral.

In response to Kennedy's question, Colby said the most potent units known to be loyal to Diem were the Presidential Guard, Colonel Tung's Special Forces, and a tank battalion stationed outside Saigon.

The rebellion could begin in as little as twenty-four hours, Colby said. Yet Kennedy and his team could only guess at whether Diem or the generals were more likely to come out on top. What little they knew came from a single source, General Don, who might be a double agent for the palace. And the generals' refusal to share their plans more than a few hours in advance dashed any chance for a meaningful U.S. review of the operation before it got underway.

The White House was even more in the dark about what sort of new government the generals envisioned, who'd run it, and whether it was likely to be an improvement over Diem's.

Don had promised that the post-coup government would be composed of civilians. But did the generals really intend to step aside after they took over, or would they keep power in their own hands? Military rule could prove even more repressive than Diem's reign. Would a junta, for instance, abolish the National Assembly? Would it dismantle the network of powerful province chiefs, all handpicked by Diem? And most importantly from Washington's viewpoint, would the new government, military or civilian, be any better at overcoming the VC than the present one?

THE KENNEDY ADMINISTRATION HAD received warnings, from both its own experts and knowledgeable Vietnamese, that the generals weren't capable of running the country. Back in August, even Don admitted to Lodge that no one in the military could replace Diem and described himself, much too modestly, as unambitious and "not smart."

But JFK didn't seem particularly concerned with the future government's effectiveness. Undoubtedly worried about a repeat of the Bay of Pigs calamity, when Castro slaughtered CIA-trained invasion forces on Cuban beaches, the president focused on whether the generals were strong enough to overcome Diem's loyalists. As he'd emphasized before, nothing was worse than failure.

Kennedy didn't like the rebels' chances. If it was true that their forces were no more than equal to Diem's, he told his men, "then of course it doesn't make any sense to have a coup" and "we should discourage it at this time." On the other hand, he was skeptical that the generals would rise up at all.

Robert Kennedy was taken aback by the paucity of available information, given the enormity of the stakes.

"I may be the minority but I just don't see this makes any sense on the face of it, Mr. President," he said. "I mean, it's different from a coup in Iraq or a South American country. We are so intimately involved in this. . . . We're putting the whole future of [South Vietnam] and, really, Southeast Asia in the hands of somebody that we don't know very well, that one official of the United States government has had contact with."

"We risk a hell of a lot" if the coup failed, Robert warned. The war was going reasonably well, but the United States was gambling its position on the basis of "these rather flimsy reports" from Lodge. With so much on the line, Washington was entitled to know how and why the generals' plan would work, and "not just hope that the coup's going to go through."

"We're going to be involved; everybody's going to say that we did it," the younger Kennedy went on. "Then if we think that's the right thing, I think we should play a major role. I don't think that we can go halfway on it, because we're going to get the blame for it. If it's a failure, I would think Diem's going to tell us to get the hell out of the country. He's going to have enough, with his intelligence, to know that there's been these contacts and these conversations. He's going to capture these people; they're going to say the United States is behind it. I would think that we're just going down the road to disaster."

No one in the room reacted to his nebulous suggestion that the U.S. government get even more deeply enmeshed in the coup.

Rusk cautioned that no Vietnamese should be trusted, including Don. He agreed with Robert that "we're working pretty much in the dark in the present situation." Lodge, he said, should be instructed to tell the generals that Washington wanted quick, decisive action, not prolonged fighting and a bloodbath in the streets of Saigon.

McCone repeated his warning that the coup could trigger a lengthy period of political disarray and work to the VC's advantage. Taylor elaborated on his earlier point that even a successful coup would represent a setback in the war, for two reasons. First, he said, "because you'd have a completely inexperienced government." And second, because the generals were likely to replace all of Diem's province chiefs, disrupting military operations.

Lodge's impending departure posed another problem. He planned to leave Saigon aboard a Pan American jet in two days, on October 31, and arrive in Washington on November 3. The president wanted him to stick to his timetable, reasoning that if he stayed longer in Saigon, and the coup erupted, the delay would imply Lodge had known of it beforehand. If the generals made their move after he left, Harkins should take over for him, JFK said, adding: "I think we've all got confidence in [Harkins]."

But McNamara complained that Lodge had kept the MACV commander in the dark about the latest coup developments, making it harder for him to step in when the ambassador left. "This is going to be a problem for [Harkins] because I don't believe they've been talking," McNamara said.

KENNEDY REGROUPED WITH HIS advisers at 6 p.m. that day to finalize new instructions to Lodge. The stark warnings from his brother, McCone, and Taylor seemed to have increased his misgivings. Unless the generals could demonstrate conclusively that they'd triumph, the president declared, Lodge should tell them that "in our opinion, it would be a mistake to proceed."

"We can discourage a coup in ways other than telling Diem of the rebel generals' plans," JFK said. "What we say to the coup generals can be crucial, short of revealing their plans to Diem. . . . If we miscalculated, we could lose our entire position in Southeast Asia overnight."

Bundy conveyed JFK's directive in an eyes-only telegram to Lodge shortly after the meeting. Since extended fighting or a rebel defeat "could be serious or even disastrous for U.S. interests," Bundy wrote, "we must have assurance balance of forces clearly favorable." He directed that Conein be sent to tell Don that Washington did "not find presently revealed plans give clear prospect of quick results."*

Bundy further instructed the ambassador to bring Harkins up to speed about all recent coup contacts. The president wanted it "clearly understood" that Harkins would take charge of the U.S. Mission if Lodge flew off and a coup broke out.

Lodge was to use McNamara's personal, berth-equipped military plane,

* The author knows of no evidence that Lodge relayed the message to Don through Conein or any other channel.

which had been placed on alert for him, Bundy said, rather than fly commercial, as he originally planned. McNamara's jet could deliver Lodge to Washington on November 3 even if he left Saigon as late as the afternoon of the previous day.

Finally, wrote Bundy, the White House was again ordering the Marine landing battalion into waters off South Vietnam to provide protection for U.S. civilians. A second Marine battalion could be flown to Tan Son Nhut from Okinawa within twenty-four hours.

Lodge, who was now using the CIA's communications channel rather than the regular embassy system, registered his objections in a bristling return cable.

The United States, he insisted, didn't "have the power to delay or discourage a coup," since it was "essentially a Vietnamese affair." Even if the generals could be talked into canceling the operation, Lodge continued, lower ranking officers—colonels and majors—would try to take down Diem, possibly creating a chaotic situation "ideally suited to VC objectives."

The coup leaders' reluctance to share their plans was understandable given their fears, justified or not, that the Americans would leak them to Diem, Lodge said. South Vietnam's "best generals" were planning the coup and probably had calibrated their chances very carefully, figuring that uncommitted commanders would jump in when rebel soldiers began swarming toward the palace.

Lodge said he didn't know what guarantee of success the generals could offer other than that they "are obviously prepared to risk their lives and that they want nothing for themselves." (This was a questionable assumption; Lodge had no way of knowing whether or not Big Minh and his co-conspirators would stick to their promise to stay out of the new government.) If the rebels asked for money to buy off fence-sitting commanders, Lodge wanted Washington to give it to them, provided the cash could be "passed discreetly."

Lodge also protested having Harkins, rather than Trueheart, the ambassador's deputy, take charge if a coup broke out.

While Harkins was "a splendid general" and "an old friend of mine to whom I would gladly entrust anything I have," he wrote, "it does not seem sensible to have the military in charge of a matter which is so profoundly political as a change of government." Lodge said he was aware that a failed coup would undermine the U.S. position in Southeast Asia, but added: "We also run tremendous risks by doing nothing." He pledged to do everything he could to stop any revolt that appeared to be doomed—contradicting his assertion that the coup was unstoppable.

At the end of his cable, the ambassador attached a tart footnote:

"Gen Harkins has read this and does not concur."

THERE WAS ANOTHER IMPORTANT gap in the White House's knowledge: What exactly would the generals do if they captured Diem? Put him on trial? Banish him from South Vietnam? Kill him?

An all-out attack on the palace obviously would jeopardize Diem's life. If, however, he survived and slipped out of Saigon, there was a chance that he'd be able to rally loyalist forces for a counterattack. For the coup commanders, the safer course might be simply to liquidate him.

Kennedy didn't want Diem to die, as he told his advisers during the run-up to the abortive August coup. He had a good deal of respect for the stouthearted South Vietnamese leader despite his authoritarian excesses and resistance to American demands. He'd pulled an independent nation together under extraordinarily difficult circumstances, kicked out the French, and fought the communists for years. He was, moreover, a Catholic head of state, like the American president.

Kennedy was warned repeatedly that a coup could put Diem in a great deal of danger. In July, Forrestal gave him a CIA report indicating that Dr. Tuyen's coup group planned to assassinate the Nhus and "eliminate" Diem. On September 18, JFK's daily intelligence brief, prepared by the CIA, indicated that "an opposition group . . . has plans to assassinate Diem, Nhu and several associated generals."

At some point that autumn, Kennedy secretly dispatched a trusted friend, Torbert Macdonald, a Democratic congressman from Massachusetts and JFK's Harvard roommate, to personally inform Diem that a coup was coming and his life was in jeopardy.

After Forrestal briefed Macdonald, the congressman flew to Tan Son Nhut on a military plane to maintain secrecy. He bluntly told Diem: "They're going to kill you. You've got to get out of there temporarily to seek sanctuary in the American embassy." He also urged Diem to "get rid of" the Nhus. But as Macdonald later reported to Kennedy: "He just won't do it. He's too stubborn; just refuses to."

As obvious and acute as the threat to Diem's life was, the Kennedy administration made little, if any, additional effort to protect its longtime ally.

Lodge suggested that the embassy evacuate "key personalities" by helicopter if fighting broke out but ended with a truce. Those evacuated, he cabled, could be taken to Saipan, more than 2,600 miles away in the Northern Mariana Islands, "where the absence of press, communications, etc., would allow us some leeway to make a further decision as to their ultimate disposition." If senior Vietnamese figures and their families showed up at the embassy requesting asylum amid a coup, the ambassador added, "we would probably have to grant it."

But Lodge had another tool at his disposal: McNamara's aircraft, which was to whisk him to Washington. There was no reason Diem couldn't be aboard, too, if he chose to flee—and if anyone offered him a seat.

GETTING TOGETHER CAUTIOUSLY, NEVER committing their plans to paper, constantly watching for Nhu's spies, the generals continued their preparations. After months of quiet organizing, the key to their success or failure came down to the volatile General Dinh, who commanded the troops in and around Saigon.

Most soldiers in the ARVN's I, II, and IV Corps areas were too far away to respond quickly to an emergency in the capital. Dinh was in charge of III Corps, which surrounded Saigon and comprised three infantry divisions. If Dinh sided with them, the rebels would be able to attack the palace guards and Special Forces units without encountering much other serious resistance. But if the thousands of troops under Dinh fought to protect their commander in chief, the result could be a block-by-block struggle costing many lives, or even a rebel defeat. With both sides bloodied and weakened, the VC might then try to seize the capital.

Although widely regarded as intensely loyal, Dinh had long harbored doubts about the regime. In 1962, he told a CIA agent that the South Vietnamese people had lost confidence in Diem and Nhu because of their "continued toleration of corruption in high places." Like many other ARVN leaders, he resented palace interference in military operations. "I did not like being told how to fight the Viet Cong," he said.

Dinh and Don went to the palace together in early September to ask Diem to appoint several generals to cabinet posts and send the Nhus away. When the two generals returned a few days later, Diem said he refused to entertain their proposals and denounced them as "men of ambition." Annoyed, Dinh went back the next day and again was rebuffed. He was so upset at Diem's reaction that he retreated to Dalat on the pretext of being sick.

Don and other coup generals knew they needed Dinh and were determined to seduce him into their ranks. They flattered him as a "great hero" admired by all South Vietnamese. Diem and Nhu didn't appreciate him, they said; he deserved a prominent place in the government. The other generals convinced him to demand that he be elevated to minister of the interior, calculating that Diem would not only reject Dinh but humiliate him in the process.

The gambit worked splendidly. Always sensitive about his Interior Ministry, which controlled much of his police apparatus, Diem angrily turned Dinh down and lectured him to "stay out of politics and leave them to me." When Dinh related what happened, the coup generals oozed sympathy, saying he was being badly treated and it was all Nhu's fault. They kept stroking his ego, reiterating how much the country needed him. They even paid a fortune teller to predict a long career in politics for him.

Alarmed at Dinh's sudden burst of political ambition, Diem and Nhu assigned security agents to keep an eye on him. In the gossipy hothouse of Saigon, Dinh soon found out about the surveillance, accelerating his slide toward sedition. Still, his enticers didn't fully trust him, as evidenced by

Don's remark to Conein that Dinh would be killed if he tried to stand in the plotters' way.

BESIDES DINH, DON HAD been trying for months to enlist other high-level troop commanders in the insurrection. He needed to line up as many as possible, both to be able to overpower palace defenders and block reinforcements from outside Saigon. Don's rank and position allowed him to travel freely, and by the last days of October he'd also brought aboard the heads of the Dalat military academy and the military intelligence service.

One top officer whose allegiance remained unclear was General Khanh, the II Corps commander who helped rescue Diem three years earlier.

Don had known Khanh for years and regarded him as a talented soldier of high intelligence, but also as an unpredictable, deceitful opportunist, ready to side with whomever appeared strongest at a given moment. Don made sure Khanh had no involvement in the current planning.

Don also was hesitant to disclose the coup to General Do Cao Tri, the hard-bitten commander of I Corps. Although Don considered Tri a friend, he was wary of the northernmost corps commander, whose harsh repression of Buddhists and students in Hue had earned him much esteem at the palace.

Don finally decided to take a chance on Tri and flew up to Hue to talk to him. Two hours after Don boarded his return flight, another plane landed in Hue bearing Tri's father, who carried a handwritten letter from Diem. The missive instructed General Tri to arrest anyone who came to him to discuss a coup.

Because of his friendship with Don, Tri reported nothing to Saigon.

DIEM'S LETTER LEFT NO doubt that the palace knew a coup was in the works and was taking steps to block it. "Coups are like eggs," Nhu told an aide, "and they must be smashed before they are hatched." With his cunning and talent for subterfuge, Nhu had come up with an elaborate plan to break the coup egg: a fake rebellion intended to liquidate the real plotters and scare the Americans at the same time.

Nhu called it "Operation Bravo One" and scheduled it for early November.

Under his scheme, Saigon radio would falsely announce that a "neutralist coup" had put a coalition government in power. As its first act, the new government was to demand that all U.S. forces leave South Vietnam. Diem and Nhu were to "flee" to a prepared retreat in Cap St. Jacques, the nearby coastal resort. In the confusion, Colonel Tung's men and Nhu's hired gangsters would hunt down and murder Big Minh, Don, and other pro-coup officers; presumed civilian allies, such as Vice President Tho; and some Americans, possibly including Conein and Mecklin.

Diem and Nhu then would order loyal troops into Saigon to "crush" the imaginary rebels. The brothers planned to return in triumph, blaming the killings on "neutralist and pro-communist elements." They figured the properly chastened Americans would hurriedly reaffirm their support for the brothers, realizing they were the only real bulwark against a neutralist regime that would be easy prey for the communists.

The deadly chess game went on in silence as each side tried to figure out the other's next moves.

The generals caught a break when Diem approved a shift in ARVN operating zones that placed the Seventh Division under General Dinh's control. The Seventh was important because it was based forty miles south of Saigon along a well-paved highway. Thus, its tanks and trucks could move rapidly into the capital either to support or beat back a coup attempt. If the division joined the rebels, it also could be used to bottleneck two other divisions, the Ninth and the Twenty-First, deployed farther south in the Mekong Delta, if they tried to save Diem. Both of those divisions remained under the control of General Huynh Van Cao, the "victor" of Ap Bac and arguably the president's most reliable votary.

By the end of October, Dinh had joined the conspirators. On October 29, he dispatched a deputy, Colonel Nguyen Huu Co, to speak with several top Seventh Division officers whom the coup leaders thought could be won over. Co told them it was the ARVN's duty to overthrow Diem because he'd lost popular support and could no longer govern. To protect his boss, Co said every general in the army was participating in the putsch except Dinh.

The local province chief, a loyalist, attended the meeting and reported Co's words to Diem the next day. No longer fully trusting Dinh, Diem and Nhu summoned him to the palace. When Diem read an account of his colonel's damning incitement, Dinh responded with an inspired bit of playacting.

Boiling with affected rage, Dinh yelled: "That louse Co! So, Co's a dirty little traitor! I'll cut off the bastard's head!" Nhu calmly said no; it was better to secretly investigate Co and arrest anyone working with him. But Dinh's outburst seemingly restored his credibility in the brothers' eyes. Nhu put him in charge of the phony coup, Operation Bravo One. When Don and his co-conspirators found out, they gave their real coup a tongue-in-cheek code name: Operation Bravo Two.

WITH TIME RUNNING OUT and the generals offering up only crumbs of information about their plans, the CIA station reached out to anti-Diem politicians, some of whom were already in covert talks with General Le Van Kim, Don's brother-in-law, about the shape and composition of a post-Diem government.

One longtime dissident reported that the generals apparently planned the "complete removal of the Ngo family." Tran Quoc Buu, president of South Vietnam's largest labor organization, the General Confederation of Vietnamese Labor, volunteered that his countrymen would support a military government, even one tougher than the Diem regime, "as long as it proved itself honest and capable of pursuing a sound policy." But the civilians seemed to know as little as the embassy.

The station did learn that Big Minh and his colleagues were far from the only people conspiring against Diem: at least nine other groups were bent on his overthrow.

The most significant ring, aside from Big Minh's, was led by Colonel Thao, the VC agent whose planned October 24 revolt the generals had stymied. Thao's followers were mostly middle-rank army officers. He'd also forged an alliance with another faction made up of alienated politicians and government bureaucrats headed by Saigon University economics professor Huynh Van Lang. (Lang served as head of the regime's foreign exchange office until Diem ousted him for alleged "financial speculation.") After Dr. Tuyen finally left Saigon, his group, too, joined Thao's.

Lodge believed that most of the pro-coup forces were coalescing around the generals, who were doing their level best to hamstring Thao, putting trucks and armored vehicles beyond his reach. (The CIA helped by foiling Thao's attempt to enlist an armored squadron.)

But the enigmatic officer remained a wild card. If he moved before the generals, he might force them to act before they were ready. Thao and the generals were vying for support from many of the same ARVN units, and the question was which group would emerge as the unchallenged leader of the coup forces. As fragmented and uncoordinated factions, they might not have sufficient strength to defeat the palace.

Discreetly clad in civilian clothes, the principal conspirators—including Big Minh, Don, Dinh, and Khiem, Don's chief of staff—slipped into a Cholon restaurant on the evening of October 30 to finalize their plans. Some of Dinh's soldiers stood guard outside as the generals ate, drank, and had some laughs.

Their plan was to hit Gia Long Palace with heavy concentrations of armor and infantry on November 1. Dinh insisted that the lives of Diem and Nhu be spared, and Don and Khiem strongly agreed. Following the meal, the army leaders retired to Dinh's headquarters to go over operational details one last time.

ON THE DAY THE generals met, JFK and a half dozen top advisers got together to discuss how to reply to Lodge's peremptory insistence that Washington was helpless to influence events in Saigon.

JFK refused to accept that the Americans lacked the power to delay or discourage the coup. If the uprising looked like a loser, he wanted Lodge to put the brakes on it. "I think we ought to give him one last rocket," said Kennedy, meaning a swift and emphatic order, "that the burden of proof ought to be on the coup people. Otherwise, it's a mistake to proceed."

Lodge, the president added, "knows that we've been rather negative about a coup. . . . He's strong for a coup, for what he thinks are very good reasons.

I'd say he's much stronger for it than we are here. I admire his nerve, if not his prudence."

Brandishing cables from Harkins that had arrived that morning, McNamara again complained that Lodge was freezing the general out. Harkins claimed Lodge hadn't shown him several important messages from Washington and failed to inform him of Conein's latest contacts with Don. On top of that, Lodge had been making his own military judgments, with little input from the MACV commander, in his private weekly reports to Kennedy. Harkins took particular umbrage at the ambassador's conclusion that the South Vietnamese and Americans were "just holding our own" in the war.

Harkins also reiterated his opposition to a coup, saying none of the rebel generals had Diem's strength of character or were qualified to take over from him.

"Rightly or wrongly, we have backed Diem for eight long hard years," he wrote. "To me it seems incongruous now to get him down, kick him around, and get rid of him. The US has been his mother superior and father confessor since he's been in office and he has leaned on us heavily." Leaders of other underdeveloped nations, Harkins warned, would hesitate to take American aid if they thought the same fate awaited them for crossing Washington.

McNamara also urged Kennedy to shake up the embassy staff. "We just have to strengthen that country team out there," he said. "We must get a man in there of Colby's type as [station] chief. Because I think none of us have the feeling that Conein has been instructed by anyone other than Lodge. And we don't have confidence in Lodge's instructions to Conein to carry out the daily contacts. I personally doubt that Trueheart is strong enough for this situation."

Harriman defended Trueheart, saying he handled the early stages of the Buddhist crisis "extraordinarily well" during Nolting's absence. But McNamara countered: "The problem is that there is not an exchange of views there between Lodge and Harkins. It's not a tightly-run organization. And we're in a very difficult situation."

A few hours later, Bundy fired off the rocket to Lodge, telling him in no uncertain terms that "we do not accept as a basis for U.S. policy that we have no power to delay or discourage a coup." Lodge was instructed to block any uprising that, in his judgment, "does not clearly give high prospect of success." The White House, Bundy said, rejected its stubborn ambassador's position that he should only intervene if the coup appeared to be headed for certain failure.

Bundy declared flatly that Harkins was to be in charge of the U.S. Mission if the rebellion started after Lodge departed for Washington. U.S. military assets were not to be committed to either side during the fighting. But, Bundy added, once the takeover began, "it is in the interest of the U.S. Government that it should succeed." The embassy was authorized to offer the generals asylum if their coup collapsed.

Lodge's acknowledgment dripped with barely suppressed Brahmin ire. "Thanks your sagacious instruction," he cabled back. "Will carry out to best of my ability."

"I told you he was going to be trouble," Robert Kennedy observed when he had a few moments alone with his brother in the Oval Office.

"You know what's terrific about you? You always remember when you're right," JFK retorted.

The president evidently thought that by threatening to cancel U.S. aid unless the generals stood down, he could stop the coup. Earlier in the year, such a threat might well have worked. But by the time of their dinner in Cholon, the generals had amassed their forces and were just two days away from giving the go signal. They were gambling their lives, and possibly those of their families, on toppling Diem. At that point they probably would have gone ahead despite a stand-down demand from Washington, betting that the Americans inevitably would get behind them if they took power.

Kennedy had failed to scotch the green light cable when he had the chance in August. He opted instead to step up political and economic pressure on Diem, criticizing him on TV and going along with the unapproved U.S. aid suspension. But those hardball tactics had unintended consequences. Many South Vietnamese interpreted them as a clear-cut repudiation of the regime; the generals took them as an open invitation to revolt.

While the generals revved up their plotting in October, JFK drifted along, buffeted by the pro- and anti-Diem cliques in his administration and unwilling or unable to take a firm position on the coup. Even now he was leaving it to Lodge's judgment about whether or not to intervene. By his indecisiveness, Kennedy relinquished whatever leverage the United States might have had either to stop the coup or influence the generals' decisions about the makeup of the post-coup government and what to do with Diem.

By the end of October, JFK had effectively boxed himself in; the rebellion stood a good chance of hurting American interests regardless of how it turned out. If it failed, the United States would be blamed for playing footsie with the insurrectionists and might get kicked out of South Vietnam. If it succeeded, it might lead to a period of political disorder that could help the VC.

And even if the generals won, there was no guarantee that their new government would do a better job of running the war than Diem's.

ALL OF SAIGON SEEMED on edge, waiting to see what Diem, the generals, or the Americans would do next. David Elliott, a young Vietnamese linguist with the Army Security Agency, watched as a crowd of people outside his Vietnamese fiancée's house gestured agitatedly at the sky.

"The sun is spinning!" some cried.

Elliott, the son of a Harvard professor, looked up and to his amazement saw what appeared to be a black corona rotating around the sun.

His fiancée, Mai, a graduate of Georgetown University's School of Foreign Service, saw it, too. Elliott was baffled; he wondered if they were all falling victim to mass hysteria. But the neighbors saw the dark ring as an undeniable portent: Diem was about to lose the mandate of heaven, his divinely granted right to rule. Natural disasters or strange phenomena always prefigured the loss of the mandate. An earthquake might strike or roosters might lay eggs. Or a black halo might circle the sun.

The neighbors had no doubt: Diem was finished.

ON THE SAME EVENING the generals met for dinner in Cholon, Ray Herndon, the UPI reporter, ambled along Rue Catinat toward his own supper.

A boy he didn't know stopped him. The kid handed Herndon a folded piece of paper and skittered away. Perplexed, Herndon opened the note and read:

Please buy me one bottle of whisky at the PX.

It was the coup-is-nigh signal from Sheehan's source, Colonel Dong. The boy, as Herndon learned much later, was the ARVN officer's fourteen-year-old son. Dong had kept his promise to alert Sheehan, even though he was then confined to his barracks by the generals.

Herndon went to the government cable office and sent an urgent message to Sheehan in Tokyo:

Please buy Blue Lotus two geisha dolls, Kyoto style.

Now it was up to Sheehan to get back to Saigon in time.

EARLIER THAT DAY, RUFUS Phillips, the outspoken head of the U.S. rural aid program, went to Gia Long Palace to visit Diem.

Phillips wasn't on official business. He'd known Diem for years and was on warm personal terms with him. But on this occasion Phillips had a bone to pick.

Three weeks before, *The Times of Vietnam* had falsely named Phillips as the "number two man" at the CIA station and claimed he was behind the "purge" of John Richardson. The story appeared just before Phillips had hurriedly flown out of Saigon to attend his father's funeral in the States. Infuriated, he wrote a letter to Diem, demanding a retraction.

As soon as he arrived at the palace, Phillips was ushered in to see Diem. The president expressed condolences for his loss and apologized for the newspaper article, saying he hadn't known about it in advance. He asked if Phillips had seen their mutual friend, Edward Lansdale, in Washington. Phillips said he'd talked to Lansdale on the phone, but was too busy with family matters to see him. He added that despite his best efforts, he'd failed to persuade the Kennedy administration to send Lansdale to help Diem. The president sighed.

Diem displayed none of the agitation that Phillips had seen during the worst days of the Buddhist turmoil. Instead, he seemed in a philosophical mood, resigned to whatever fate might have in store for him. After a while, he cast his eyes down, puffing on his omnipresent cigarette.

"Do you think there will be a coup?" he asked quietly.

Phillips stared at his old friend. He felt like crying. "I'm afraid so, Mr. President," he replied. He wanted to take Diem out of the room, in case it was bugged, and plead with him to make some sort of deal with Lodge. But he caught himself. He'd already said too much; anything more might endanger Conein, a personal friend, or the generals.

Sensing Phillips's emotion, Diem touched his arm, trying to comfort him. He stood up, grasped the American's hand, and again said he was sorry about his father. Then he bid his visitor au revoir.

CHAPTER 19

DAY OF THE DEAD

AFTER A SLEEPLESS night, General Don arrived at Joint General Staff headquarters at 7:30 a.m. on November 1.

There was much to do before the coup began in six hours. The night before, he'd been with General Dinh, looking on as armored cars drove into Dinh's command compound. Now Don instructed an aide to stockpile several days of extra food at JGS in case the revolt dragged on longer than expected. He also added more bodyguards to his personal security detail.

Rebel troops were already in stealthy motion. Elements of the Fifth Division had pulled out of their base at Bien Hoa the previous day, ostensibly headed east to the coast. ARVN commanders told their American advisers to stay behind. Once on the road, the soldiers turned south, toward Saigon, where they were to spearhead the attack on Gia Long Palace.

Even at this late stage, the coup leaders didn't fully trust one another. General Khiem had laid a trap for Dinh just that morning. Khiem rubbed an irritating ointment into his eyes to make it look as if he'd been crying. Then he tested Dinh by saying the coup should be called off, since Diem might get hurt. To Khiem's relief, Dinh insisted on going forward as planned. Both men then separately reported the encounter to Don.

Don left his headquarters for a 9:15 a.m. appointment at MACV with Harkins and Admiral Harry Felt, the Honolulu-based commander in chief of U.S. Pacific forces. Felt had unexpectedly flown into Saigon the day before and asked to see Don. Sensing a way to use the admiral in his plot, Don quickly agreed. He was afraid Diem might leave Saigon on November 1 for some reason and persuaded him to spend some time at the palace that day with Felt.

Don made small talk with Harkins and Felt, but said nothing about the impending revolt. Indeed, he lied to them, saying he was shifting two airborne battalions to Tay Ninh, a provincial capital about sixty-five miles northwest of Saigon. In fact, Don had ordered those units to Saigon.

But the coup got off to a premature start when rebels went after the pro-Diem commander of South Vietnam's small navy, made up mostly of patrol boats.

Suspicious of the unexplained troop movements around Saigon, Captain Ho Tan Quyen had driven off to consult another officer outside the city. Rebel marines gave chase, eventually using their jeep to stop Quyen's car. Quyen tried to run away across an open field, but stumbled and fell. The marines caught up with him. One of them drew his pistol and shot Quyen in the head.

Learning of the unplanned incident, Big Minh ordered the coup timetable moved up.

Felt went to Gia Long Palace at 10 a.m. accompanied by Lodge and an embassy interpreter. Despite Conein's report that the generals would act no later than November 2, some at the embassy remained skeptical.

The day before the coup, Lodge insisted to Felt: "There is no general with hair enough on his chest to pull one off." Early on November 1, MACV's General Richard Stilwell urged David Smith, the acting CIA station chief, to spare himself further embarrassment and stop making coup predictions; Stilwell was confident no uprising would take place in the foreseeable future.

Lodge and Felt sat down with Diem in brocade armchairs in the ornate palace salon. Diem launched into a monologue that repeated much of what he'd told McNamara and Taylor in September. He then made several new points, claiming that "junior CIA officers" were spreading coup rumors and that the VC were certain to take advantage of any attempt to overthrow him. He complained that the ongoing aid suspension would hurt the war effort, inflicting special hardships on the ARVN and militiamen guarding strategic hamlets.

Felt got ready to leave and Diem pulled Lodge aside for a fifteen-minute private conversation.

He encouraged Lodge, when he went to Washington, to get in touch with Nolting and Colby. They'd confirm, he said, how valuable Nhu was to him and his government. Indeed, it was Colby who'd talked Nhu into not "living in an ivory tower" and adopting a more public profile. No sooner had Nhu begun following Colby's advice, Diem said ruefully, than critics started carping that he was trying to usurp his brother's power. Diem also explained that some Saigon schools were still closed because of reports that the communists were trying to get students to lob plastic explosives while the UN investigators were in town. Once they left, he said, the schools would reopen "little by little."

As Lodge stood up to go, Diem implored him: "Please tell President Kennedy that I am a good and a frank ally, that I would rather be frank and settle questions now than talk about them after we have lost everything."

Lodge replied that he'd admired Diem's courage long before coming to South Vietnam and had since "formed sentiments of friendship for him." He thanked Diem "for being so extremely nice to my wife and me." A few hours later, he relayed Diem's words to the State Department, concluding that it might now be possible to strike some sort of "package deal" with him.

But that last-minute note of optimism came too late, buried under a pile of more urgent telegrams reporting the opening stages of the coup.

Before taking off for Hong Kong, Felt held a press conference at the airport. Harkins and Don stood nearby. The coup was supposed to begin in just two hours; Don kept glancing nervously at his watch and chewing gum with a vengeance. Halberstam, who knew the insurrection was near, watched him closely, trying to restrain a devilish impulse to keep asking questions simply to prolong the conference.

When it finally ended, Harkins invited Don to lunch. But the ARVN commander begged off, saying he needed to hurry to work.

BY THE TIME DON got back to the Joint General Staff compound, Conein was there.

One of Don's aides had shown up earlier at the CIA operative's house, saying the coup was underway and Don wanted him at JGS. Conein radioed a special code to the CIA station—nine-nine, nine-nine, nine-nine—signaling the start of the uprising.

Since he didn't want to be seen at ARVN headquarters in civilian clothes, he put on his army uniform and his U.S. Special Forces green beret. Then, carrying two radios and a .38-caliber revolver, he jumped into a jeep driven by an ARVN sergeant. One radio was to communicate with the embassy; the other was for Conein to stay in touch with the twelve-man Green Beret combat team he'd arranged to guard his family while he was gone.

When he arrived at JGS, Big Minh belligerently demanded: "What are you doing here?" Conein replied that he was told to come. The coup leader then said that if the generals lost the upcoming battle and had to go on the run, "you're going with us." The generals hoped to escape to Cambodia—the border was just forty miles west of Saigon—in a convoy of nine armored cars loaded with extra gasoline. If they were cornered by Diem's forces, Conein might be a useful bargaining chip.

The CIA man was useful another way as well. Don's aide had asked him to bring as much cash as he could lay his hands on, and Conein carried a diplomatic pouch stuffed with 3 million piastres, about $42,000 at the official exchange rate, much more on the black market. Don used the money to induce Diem loyalists to switch sides.

To secure the allegiance of any commanders still on the fence, the coup ringleaders concocted a ruthless setup. By midday, generals and other top officers had gathered for their regular Friday lunch at the JGS officers' club. As dessert was served, a brace of military policemen with submachine guns burst into the room and surrounded the diners.

Big Minh stood up and announced that the military was taking over the government. All those who supported the insurrection were invited to stand. Those who stayed in their seats were arrested. A tape recorder was brought into the room and Minh read a declaration setting out the reasons for the revolt. He highlighted Diem's dictatorial actions and promised a more effective war effort. Minh asked everyone to sign the proclamation and voice their support for it into the recorder. The tape was to be broadcast over the radio later in the day; copies were made as insurance that no one tried to disavow their anti-Diem position later.

The rebels soon arrested Colonel Tung, whose troops at Special Forces headquarters, adjacent to JGS, were already fighting anti-Diem soldiers. With a pistol to his head, Tung was told to telephone his men and order them to cease firing. Terrified, he did so.

He was held captive at JGS along with two other Diem devotees: the commanders of the airborne infantry brigade and the air force. The air force chief was stripped of his rank and allowed to go home. The airborne leader "broke down completely," refusing to abandon Diem and offering to resign or be executed. Moved by his sincerity, Big Minh merely detained him until the coup was over.

Tung wouldn't be so lucky. Minh's bodyguard took him to another room in the JGS building while troops hunted for his brother, the Special Forces' chief of staff, who was still at large.

AT 1:45 P.M., DON telephoned General Stilwell, who'd just admonished the acting CIA station chief about forecasting coups, and officially informed him that the coup was underway.

The generals had chosen the date and time carefully. Not only was it All Saints' Day—a holiday for Catholics—but the daily siesta had just begun. Most Saigonese were having lunch or a nap at home, and the boulevards were conveniently uncluttered with civilian traffic and open to military movements.

Three battalions of rebel marines, red bandannas tied around their necks for identification, raced into the capital. Facing little resistance, they seized the airport, defense ministry, and government cable office. They surrounded national police headquarters, denying Diem's forces access to a large arms cache there and holding on despite a determined counterattack by presidential guardsmen in armored cars. Loyal troops also put up a strong fight at the radio station, which abruptly went off the air at 2 p.m. But the rebels soon won control of it.

Meanwhile, the commander of the Seventh Division—a mutineer—ordered ferryboats moved to the north bank of the Mekong River, ensuring that ARVN units based farther south couldn't cross. That meant that General Cao, the Diem ultra-loyalist who commanded IV Corps in the delta, wouldn't be able to get armor and troops up to Saigon to protect the president.

Heavy fire from artillery, machine guns, and rifles erupted across the city. A CIA officer making his way through the streets reported a "strong fire fight" outside the palace. From his vantage point inside the generals' command post, Conein radioed a stream of detailed updates to the embassy, which forwarded them as top-priority cables—designated CRITIC—that jumped ahead of other traffic to the White House, State Department, and CIA headquarters.

Diem had turned his sprawling palace into a fortress, its grounds defended by pillboxes, dug-in tanks, and half-tracks mounted with 20-millimeter cannons. His Presidential Guard consisted of an estimated 2,500 men backed with about eighteen American-made M24 light tanks and eight armored personnel carriers. The guardsmen were a formidable force, but they lacked the combat experience of the marines and other coup troops.

As insurgent soldiers and armored vehicles moved through the streets, Diem and Nhu retreated to an air-conditioned bunker beneath a palace courtyard, seemingly confident that Nhu's Operation Bravo One—the fake coup—was unfolding as planned.

Diem calmly drank tea and smoked. When a loyal general called prior to the Joint General Staff lunch, saying there was something fishy about it, Nhu told him not to worry; everything was under control. But as the afternoon wore on, it became clear that things weren't as they seemed. Another loyalist, Saigon's deputy mayor, surveyed his contacts around the city and learned that something was very wrong. For one thing, police headquarters was under siege by the military.

When the deputy mayor phoned his news to the palace, Nhu angrily blurted: "Dinh has betrayed us!"

At about 3 p.m., Diem and Nhu began radioing for help from outside the city. Their first broadcast ordered corps and division commanders and province chiefs throughout the country to send men to Saigon. Field commanders were told to acknowledge receipt of the message, but no one did. By then, eighteen of Diem's nineteen generals had joined the coup. The lone holdout was General Cao of IV Corps. Diem ordered him to rush four battalions from the delta to Saigon. But Cao discovered that wasn't possible: the ferries his tanks, trucks, and infantry needed to cross the Mekong River had been moved out of reach.

The military's abandonment of Diem was stunning in its completeness.

Listening on their earphones, American eavesdroppers picked up a "desperate call" from Nhu to his wife, who was in Los Angeles at the end of her U.S. tour. Nhu warned her: Don't come back to Saigon.

INSURGENT TROOPS SURROUNDED THE palace and moved into position to attack the nearby Presidential Guard barracks. Evidently realizing the seriousness of his predicament, Diem telephoned General Don at JGS.

Don reminded him of his rejection of the generals' reform requests in September; Diem claimed he was now willing to restructure his government along lines the military wanted. "Why didn't you tell me that yesterday?" Don asked. "It is too late now. All the troops are moving on the capital." Big Minh took the phone, berating Diem for the "agonies the people had suffered because of the corrupt government" and for losing ground to the Viet Cong.

The generals nevertheless told Diem that if he surrendered, they'd protect him and "allow him to escape from the country."

Diem next called Lodge. When shooting broke out, the ambassador had been lunching at his residence with his aide, Mike Dunn, and Dunn's wife and two sons, who'd arrived in Saigon that day. The home's windows were sandbagged and it was guarded by a dozen U.S. military police—"the biggest men I've ever seen," Lodge said—armed with riot guns and tear gas. Dunn bundled his family in flak jackets and put them in a bathroom.

Lodge got on the line with the embattled Diem at 4:30 p.m.

Diem: Some units have made a rebellion and I want to know: What is the attitude of [the] U.S.?

Lodge: I do not feel well enough informed to be able to tell you. I have heard the shooting, but am not acquainted with all the facts. Also, it is 4:30 a.m. in Washington and [the] U.S. government cannot possibly have a view.

Diem: But you must have some general ideas. After all, I am a chief of state. I have tried to do my duty. I want to do now what duty and good sense require. I believe in duty above all.

Lodge: You have certainly done your duty. As I told you only this morning, I admire your courage and your great contributions to your country. No one can take away from you the credit for all you have done. Now I am worried about your physical safety. I have a report that those in charge of the current activity offer you and your brother safe conduct out of the country if you resign. Had you heard this?

Diem: No. [*Pause.*] You have my telephone number.

Lodge: Yes. If I can do anything for your physical safety, please call me.

Diem: I am trying to re-establish order.

Lodge's comments were disingenuous at best. He knew full well what Washington's attitude toward the coup was, regardless of any time difference. Diem may have been trying, with his vague first words, to secure U.S. intervention to stop the insurrection. But with his government, and very possibly his life, hanging by a thread, the top envoy of his strongest ally offered no assistance. Instead, Lodge suggested that Diem quit his presidency and run.

Lodge called Trueheart at the embassy and dictated his exchange with Diem for relay to Washington. The ambassador later claimed that he, not "those in charge of the current activity," offered Diem safe passage out of South Vietnam aboard a U.S. aircraft. His assertion was backed up by his two closest aides, Dunn and Freddy Flott. (Flott, who sat next to Lodge and overheard the call, later said the ambassador was prepared to send him to the palace in the embassy limousine to pick up Diem and get him out of Saigon "on my jet aircraft.")

Trueheart, however, contradicted Lodge's account. "Lodge expressed concern for Diem's safety," he told an interviewer years later, "but he definitely did not say we will help get you out of the country." And Lodge's own account of his exchange with Diem contains no explicit offer of safe conduct or asylum.

In an interview for a 1991 book, *Facing the Phoenix*, Dunn claimed that Lodge offered Diem asylum in a phone call around 7 a.m. the next day. However, the author knows of no written record or any other corroboration of the supposed second call. Lodge himself never asserted that he spoke twice to Diem during the coup. Moreover, the authors of *The Pentagon Papers* state that Lodge's conversation with Diem on the afternoon of November 1 was "the last that any American had with Diem."

FLYING BACK TO SAIGON from a reporting expedition in Laos, Arnett felt his airliner suddenly wheel around in midair and beeline away from South Vietnam.

Arnett guessed that the Vietnamese pilot had just learned that the coup had begun and it was unsafe to land. He jumped up from his seat and began pounding on the cockpit door. When it opened, his fear was confirmed: the pilot was talking to an air traffic controller who said Tan Son Nhut was closed due to the revolt.

Horrified at the prospect of missing the biggest story of his young life, Arnett begged the pilot to go there anyway, arguing that his family might be in danger and need his help. To Arnett's astonishment, the pilot agreed and swung the plane back toward Saigon.

Twenty minutes later, the jet touched down at the airport, ringed by rebel tanks and armored cars. Ground crews had fled and taxi stands were empty. Smoke plumed above downtown Saigon three miles away; Arnett could hear the boom of cannons and the crackle of small arms.

He found a bus whose nervous driver dropped him near the three-story Associated Press complex on Rue Pasteur close to the besieged palace. The building contained the wire service's newsroom as well as apartments for employees. Rebel troops had turned it into a forward attack post, firing from behind sandbags in the parking lot and the balcony outside Arnett's first-floor unit.

Arnett dodged down the street amid gunfire and ricochets, using tamarind trees for protection. He burst into the office to find a lone newsman, Ed White, calmly puffing on a pipe and tapping on his typewriter. "The others are at the Caravelle," White said, "and I'm holding the fort." The phones were dead, but the news agency had managed to get off several dispatches on the coup through the U.S. and South Korean embassies.

Arnett made his way to the Caravelle Hotel and found his boss, Browne, on an upper floor, surveying the firefights around the palace and Presidential Guard barracks. The guard compound was ablaze after its ammunition bunker had been hit.

He watched the fighting for a while, smoking a cigarette and sipping scotch, before going back into the streets, where life went on more or less normally.

Two GIs stopped him on Rue Catinat to ask where the nearest bar was. A young mother played with her little son in the grassy center of a traffic circle, in full view of a nearby tank.

Arnett walked over to the Rex Hotel, crowded with American military men. Ordered to stay off the streets, they passed the time shooting dice and playing slot machines.

WITH THE RADIO STATION in their hands, the generals began broadcasting bulletins every five minutes.

One announced that the ARVN was doing away with Diem's "cruel family dictatorship" and called on citizens to "cooperate and maintain order." Another, addressed to "fellow soldiers," acknowledged that "the army was used in cruel acts against the people. Who knows how many students and people have been arrested? We felt bitter over being used against the people. . . . Never could we tolerate this, so we established a revolution to save the people." That message was followed by the taped voices of Big Minh and other generals, all committing themselves to Diem's overthrow.

As the afternoon wore on, politicians began showing up at JGS to discuss the composition of the new government. Conein informed the embassy of the generals' pledge that leaders of the post-Diem government would be exclusively "anti-communist, pro-western" civilians. The embassy in turn flashed an optimistic message to Washington: "There will be no military personalities in high positions in the new government. Military hopes to turn over government to the civilians within two to three days."

The generals kept trying to get Diem to surrender in order to minimize bloodshed. Around 5 p.m., Big Minh telephoned Nhu and warned that if he and his brother didn't give up within five minutes, Gia Long Palace would come under massive air attack. To underscore the hopelessness of the brothers' position, all of the field commanders present got on the phone and repeated the message. Nhu seemed unmoved.

Forced to the phone at gunpoint, Colonel Tung confirmed he was under arrest and that the rebels held most of the city's main military and civilian facilities. By then, Tung's brother had been seized and brought to the generals' headquarters. A short time later, both men were shoved into a jeep with their hands tied behind their backs. Big Minh's bodyguard drove them to another part of the JGS compound where two graves had been dug, and shot them dead.

After talking to Nhu, Big Minh called Diem, but the president contemptuously hung up on him. Enraged, the coup leader ordered the air force to bomb the palace, but the attack was inconclusive.

Despite his anger, Minh seemed reluctant to mount an all-out assault on the palace. Some of the generals told Conein their attack had bogged down because a crucial unit still wasn't in position. Conein urged them to charge ahead without pause. "Once you are into the attack, you must continue," he stressed. "If you hesitate, you're going to be lost."

The generals got a welcome morale boost when about 140 students, newly liberated from jail by rebel troops, were brought in. As the coup leaders walked into a courtyard to meet them, the students fell to their knees in gratitude. Most of the generals, Don recalled, "were moved to tears."

"In front of us were the emaciated young people in their dirty clothes but, at that moment, happiness clearly showed on their faces because their hopes had finally been fulfilled," Don later wrote. "Big Minh told the students the coup forces were making progress and advised them to devote themselves to building a strong and democratic country." The students applauded and "vowed absolutely" to support a new government.

While the palace was subjected to harassing fire for most of the afternoon, the heaviest fighting took place around the Presidential Guard barracks.

Lined up side by side, rebel tanks fired earsplitting volleys at the guard quarters. The cannon blasts shook nearby buildings and shattered windows, sending spectators on scooters and bicycles diving to the ground. But the guards refused to buckle, and two T-28 planes began strafing and rocketing their barracks.

At about 7 p.m., Big Minh called the palace with a final warning: surrender or be "blasted off the surface of the earth." Diem still refused to speak with him.

A gray drizzle began to fall as night enfolded the city. Diem's voice blared from loudspeakers on the palace grounds: "We shall not give in!" Then martial music played defiantly across the huge estate, bordered by seven-foot fences topped with barbed wire.

LIEUTENANT COMMANDER BOBBI HOVIS, head nurse at the U.S. Navy's brand-new hundred-bed hospital in Saigon, finished her shift and returned to her apartment building, five blocks from the palace.

A few hours earlier, as she watched from the hospital's fifth-floor balcony, swarms of bullets flew past from a nearby machine-gun nest. Tree limbs snapped off; slugs ricocheted off the hospital and other buildings. One round struck the waist-high balustrade just inches from Hovis, spraying her with stucco fragments. The hospital's Vietnamese police guard stripped off his uniform and ran away.

From her apartment balcony, Hovis spotted a small black Peugeot navigating slowly along the street below. Suddenly, the rear window shattered and the windshield blew out in the same split second. The car rolled to a stop and the driver stumbled out, his shirt splotched with blood. Two men ran out from a doorway and dragged him out of sight.

Gunfire peppered vehicles, buildings, and people. Thunderous booms rolled across the city.

By 8 p.m., fuel farms along the Saigon River were burning fiercely, bathing everything around them in deep orange. Most of the rest of the city was pitch-black. U.S. Armed Forces Radio aired Top 40 music and news from seemingly every other world capital except Saigon.

Hovis heard the telltale grind and clank of steel treads coming from the street around the corner from her building. A tank coughed out a round that blew up something in the distance. *My God*, she thought, *is there going to be a tank fight in the middle of downtown Saigon?* Shells began exploding all around, apparently coming from 105-millimeter howitzers on the edge of the city and aimed at the palace.

Large, smoking holes opened in the roofs of nearby buildings. Flying glass, bits of broken tile, and other shrapnel rained down. More shells whistled in; waves of concussion compressed the air around Hovis. The streets and tall buildings seemed to funnel the battle sounds upward; the noise on her balcony was deafening. The night was streaked red from tracer bullets.

The furious barrage of artillery and 81-millimeter mortar shells on the palace stopped as Big Minh ordered a ground assault. An infantry battalion backed by tanks began the attack at about 9 p.m.

Browne saw big slabs of white masonry blown off the handsome old palace. He figured everyone inside must be dead. A tank battle erupted on Rue Pasteur; a rocket hit a U.S.-made M48 tank, which burst into flames outside the evacuated AP office. "The crew tried to escape," Browne recorded, "but was cut down by blistering machine gun fire." Flames ignited the tank's ammunition with "a horrifying explosion."

THE FIRST REPORTS OF the coup reached the White House Situation Room at about 2 a.m. on November 1.

Forrestal got there as quickly as he could. He was amazed at how fast CRITIC cables were pouring in from Saigon, but skeptical that a revolt was really happening. But when he got a phone call through to the embassy, Trueheart confirmed: "This coup is real. It is not more of our scare reporting."

Forrestal woke up Kennedy, who joined him in the Situation Room. From there the news spread rapidly; McNamara, Rusk, Taylor, and Bundy were alerted, too.

Hilsman rushed to the State Department and got in touch with Bundy. Together they drafted a cable to Lodge. "If coup succeeds," it read, "acceptance and understanding of its purpose here will be greatly increased if Generals and their civilian associates continue to develop strongly and publicly the conclusion reported in one of their broadcasts that Nhu was dickering with Communists to betray anti-Communist cause. High value of this argument should be emphasized to them at earliest opportunity."

Although Nhu had met with a Hanoi intermediary, exactly what was discussed wasn't known. The generals' propaganda broadcast hardly constituted firm evidence that he was "dickering" to "betray the anti-Communist cause." Yet Hilsman and Bundy were comfortable exploiting that flimsy allegation to make a violent military takeover of a civilian government more politically palatable to Americans.

Less than two hours later Lodge replied: "Point has been made to Generals."

At about 10 a.m., JFK walked into the Cabinet Room to go over the night's events with his National Security Council. There were about twenty men in the room, many of whom had been up most of the night.

Colby brought everyone up to date on the tactical situation, noting that the rebels had neutralized some of Diem's forces by arresting or executing their leaders.

"The last report we have was that some tanks—real tanks, not just armored cars—were moving in, the artillery had been lifted, and that General Minh had ordered an infantry attack on the palace," Colby reported. "He ordered a battalion in there. A rough estimate of what is in the palace now would not be more than a couple hundred men, at the most."

The president wanted to know the whereabouts of the U.S. warships sailing toward South Vietnam. Taylor said the seaborne Marine battalion and its helicopters were scheduled to arrive near the mouth of the Saigon River that evening. Two Navy battle groups, led respectively by the aircraft carriers *Hancock* and *Oriskany*, were also en route, one from Okinawa, the other from Hong Kong. Both were expected to be in position the next day.

With the revolt seemingly going well for the generals, Kennedy knew he might soon be faced with the question of U.S. diplomatic recognition for a new Saigon government. It was a sticky issue because if the generals succeeded in taking power, they'd have done so by upending a constitutionally elected, albeit unpopular, government. Washington had recently condemned two such military power grabs, in Honduras and the Dominican Republic, refusing to recognize the new ruling juntas in both countries. If the administration now did an about-face and gave its blessing to Big Minh and his fellow military "revolutionaries," critics in Congress and the press would have a field day with the inconsistency.

"How do we square that?" JFK asked the others in the room.

Rusk replied that the dictatorial nature of the Diem regime justified both its overthrow and U.S. recognition of the overthrowers. Not all civilian heads of state were good, he suggested, and not all military men were bad as civil government leaders. "Stalin was a civilian and Eisenhower was a soldier," the secretary of state noted.

Rusk pointed out another problem: the inevitable press and public speculation over the degree of Washington's involvement with the generals. "We need to get that straightened out," he said. "The fact is we were not privy to these plans . . . in the sense that we didn't really know what they were going to do, when, and the fact that the coup was [often] reported as rumor. . . . But I think it would be to our interest to indicate that this was Vietnamese, that we were not participants in the coup, that Americans were not involved in the fighting."

By framing the issue in such narrow terms, Rusk evidently hoped to provide the administration with a way to divert public attention from the abundant measure of U.S. culpability for the coup.

While it was true that Americans had no role in planning or carrying out the plot, the Kennedy administration had richly fertilized the soil in which it grew. Hilsman's green light cable gave ARVN commanders a huge incentive to revolt. Kennedy criticized Diem's "policies and personnel" on national television, and Washington imposed sanctions that were damaging South Vietnam's economy as well as the war effort. Lodge further undercut Diem by ostentatiously refusing to speak with him for weeks.

As Mecklin scathingly noted, to claim that Washington was blameless for the coup was "a bit like claiming innocence for a night watchman at a bank who tells a known safecracker that he is going out for a beer."

JFK stepped out of the Cabinet Room for about thirty-five minutes to attend Mass, but came back while the meeting was still in progress. He agreed with Rusk about how to respond to questions from the press and Congress about U.S. involvement.

"For many of these conversations," he said, "I think we have to make it clear that this is not an American coup."

IN SAIGON, THE GROUND assault on the palace had failed.

Troops and armor from the Fifth Division tried to storm the shell-pocked building, but its defenders repulsed them. By attacking the Presidential Guard barracks, the generals had pinned down many of Diem's men. But perhaps four hundred of them, supported by tanks, were at the palace, holding off a much larger number of insurgents.

Mortar shells continued to crash into the building; tanks and armored personnel carriers blasted away as they moved closer. Rebel-controlled radio announced that the palace was surrounded and assured citizens that the fighting would be over by morning. At about 10 p.m., palace loudspeakers barked out a statement from Diem calling on the armed forces to remain loyal and falsely claiming that reinforcements were coming from the provinces. The message was repeated for a half hour until the loudspeakers went dead.

Some of the generals wanted to hit Gia Long with more air strikes. But Big Minh overruled them in order to give the defenders more time to surrender. Despite his fury at the president, he didn't want to kill any more of his fellow Vietnamese than necessary.

The shelling of the palace and Presidential Guard barracks fell off at about 11 p.m. Two infantry battalions and fifteen armored personnel carriers from the Seventh Division arrived; strong reinforcements from the Fifth Division were en route. Brilliant white magnesium flares floated down from the sky on parachutes, turning night to day until they burned out.

A clutch of Americans watched the battle from the embassy roof. Some of the artillery rounds aimed at the Presidential Guard compound passed directly over their heads; one American compared the sound the shells made to an express train rushing through the sky. Once in a while the zing of a ricochet caused everybody to duck behind the parapets. Cigarettes were smoked and bottles passed. As the rebels closed in on the palace, someone cracked: "I wish they would fight like this against the VC."

When the shooting started, the embassy had locked its gates and employees began to monitor the radio and transcribe Conein's reports for transmission to Washington. Lodge called in from his residence to say he was going to bed at 9:30 p.m., as was his custom; Trueheart told him there was "no change" and to go ahead. A staffer went to tell Tri Quang that the coup was on.

"Do you think I am deaf?" the monk snapped.

The Americans heard a radio announcement instructing members of the Diem government to turn themselves in to the generals before 11 p.m. Those who did so would receive clemency; the rest would be considered enemies of the new state.

Not long before the deadline, Diem's chief of staff, Thuan, called the embassy and asked what he should do. Several hours earlier, he and two other regime officials had shown up at the Italian embassy, suitcases in hand, requesting asylum. But now Thuan said he was calling from a private home. Should he give himself up? Could the generals be trusted?

Trueheart took the phone and gestured to the others for quiet. Thuan was not only the embassy's best friend at the palace, he was Trueheart's closest Vietnamese friend. But his call posed a dilemma. It implied that Thuan thought the Americans were mixed up in the coup and had special knowledge of the generals' intentions. If the coup failed, an influential figure like Thuan, who was also a cabinet minister, might use whatever the embassy told him now to embarrass the United States later. In any event, the embassy had no way of knowing how the generals would treat regime stalwarts who surrendered.

"Mr. Minister, we know only what we have heard on the radio," Trueheart said. Thuan apparently pleaded for more guidance than that. Gripping the phone, Trueheart said: "We know only what we have heard on the radio." Thuan persisted, but the American repeated the same answer several times, with increasing embarrassment. Finally, he said, "Good night, Mr. Minister," and hung up.

Trueheart looked around the room and took a swig of bourbon from a paper cup. No one said a word. The embassy had given no help at all to its desperate friend.

THE MISTY RAIN KEPT falling. Rebel troops and armor continued to accumulate in the dark streets around the palace.

After doggedly trying to reach General Dinh all day, Diem and Nhu finally got him on the phone around midnight at JGS. With other generals listening, Dinh was anxious to demonstrate where his allegiance now lay.

"I've saved you motherfuckers many times," he yelled at the brothers. "But not now, you bastards. You shits are finished. It's all over."

The generals were planning a final blitz on the palace, but no one was especially eager to lead it. Diem was still a figure of considerable respect and no ARVN commander wanted to be burdened with killing him, if it came to that. The generals finally settled on Colonel Nguyen Van Thieu, commander of the Fifth Division.

Thieu's men had carried out the attacks on the Presidential Guard barracks, whose exhausted defenders finally surrendered at midnight after ten M24 tanks, firing en masse, blew out the middle of the rambling, six-story structure. During the Buddhist uproar, Thieu, a Catholic, was presumed to be a Diem acolyte. But now he had the opportunity to demonstrate his fealty to the generals by taking the palace. And if a Catholic president had to die in the process, so much the better if a Catholic officer did the killing.

AS REBEL COMMANDERS MADE last-minute arrangements, Halberstam was at his villa, trying to catch some sleep before the final assault, which he learned was to commence at 3 a.m.

He'd spent the day trying to figure out which troops were Diem's and which belonged to the generals. It wasn't easy because many of them were wearing the same uniforms. At about 5 p.m., he jumped into a cab for a tour of the city. The driver, apparently guessing his purpose, grinned and made a slashing gesture across his throat, saying, "Tong Thong [President Diem] fini."

On one boulevard Halberstam saw long columns of paratroopers marching toward the palace, accompanied by about twenty armored cars. In the center of the city one of Diem's armored cars prowled around, firing at anything that moved. Children ran behind it, scooping up expended bullet casings made of valuable brass.

Most adults seemed impassive; they'd seen armed mutineers in the streets before. They calmly waited to see which side would win this time.

COMMANDER HOVIS, THE NAVY head nurse, peered down into the streets below her apartment again in the early hours of November 2. It was now All Souls' Day, the day of the dead, a time for Catholics to pray for departed souls marooned in purgatory.

The moon had risen, a gorgeous tropical moon, orange and huge.

Hovis saw a spectral procession in the pale moonlight: more than two dozen tanks and armored personnel carriers, slowly moving forward with about two hundred soldiers behind them. A star shell exploded, bathing her apartment in white light. She and three other Navy nurses who lived in her building had packed their bags, but it was too dangerous to leave. The women held their breath as the flare burned out and darkness again engulfed them.

Shortly after 3 a.m., artillery, tanks, machine guns, mortars, and rifles began firing, blending into a continuous roar. Attackers fired from several side streets at the palace and its protective walls.

From the defenders came a murderous counterfire, their tanks spitting long, jagged tongues of yellow and blue. Close-range tank duels reminded one observer of two heavyweight boxers slugging it out in a closet. A palace tank caught fire and exploded in a tower of flames and smoke. Two rebel tanks were destroyed. Nearby buildings hit by stray gunfire became infernos.

Rebel soldiers darted from doorway to doorway, drawing closer to the palace.

The sudden cacophony jolted Halberstam awake. He and Ray Herndon took a carefully circuitous route to the palace area, where it was clear that the generals had amassed superior forces. The newsmen watched as several of Diem's tanks were demolished and a platoon of armored vehicles surrendered.

The two Americans crept along with some Vietnamese marines until, at about 5 a.m., they were only a block from Gia Long.

"It was still very dark," Halberstam recorded, "and the night was filled with the noise of heavy tank and antitank guns; the only light came from two burning tanks." A tremendous explosion went off close to them. Halberstam was terrified; a source once told him that Nhu had booby-trapped streets around the palace with deadly claymore mines that could be detonated remotely. Halberstam told Herndon about the alleged mines and they decided to back away from the palace a bit.

The tempo of the battle increased at first light. Clad in jungle fatigues and camouflaged helmets, more marines filtered in, armed with bazookas and 57-millimeter recoilless rifles. To an American observer, they looked "sinister and somehow relentless in the wan light." A civilian rushed across a boulevard and presented them with an armload of baguettes.

Shells blasted out windows, shattered doors, and blew more chunks off the palace walls. Big holes opened up in the perimeter fence. Rebel riflemen, lying flat on the ground, sniped at Diem's last-ditch protectors. The end seemed near. After a day and a night of close combat and heavy bombardment, the palace guards were exhausted and demoralized by the lack of reinforcements.

A white flag appeared from a window. Thinking it signaled surrender, the assault troops began advancing in the open until a burst of automatic-weapons fire cut down a rebel captain. The rest of the attackers angrily rushed the palace.

Halberstam and Herndon ran across the lawn behind some marines. A few defenders were still shooting, and the journalists hit the dirt until the gunfire subsided. Then they entered the building, where victorious insurgents were happily looting everything from Madame Nhu's negligees to her husband's whiskey.

The soldiers ran from room to room, finding all sorts of interesting artifacts: an expensive Austrian hunting rifle; piles of American adventure magazines in Diem's bedroom; a memoir by Robert G. K. Thompson, the British guerrilla fighter, titled *Shoot to Kill*, on Nhu's desk. They grabbed pieces of china and tore down curtains for souvenirs.

The troops weren't alone in their looting. Halberstam swiped an ornate Laotian sword, probably from Nhu's collection, which he later gave to Mecklin. Flott, Lodge's aide, pocketed a few "souvenir" ashtrays.

But the biggest prizes of all—Diem and Nhu—had vanished.

AS FIGHTING RAGED THE night before, the brothers slipped out of Gia Long at about 8 p.m. Some newspapers reported that they escaped through a secret tunnel. But, according to Don, they simply walked out of the palace and past the hostile troops around it, got into a car, and drove off.

To avoid detection, they traveled not in the presidential limousine but in a Citroën deux chevaux, a small, four-door car seen everywhere on Saigon's streets. Diem's aide-de-camp, an ARVN captain, talked the president into wearing a pair of mirrored sunglasses to further conceal himself.

With a jeep full of bodyguards trailing it, the Citroën took the brothers to Cholon. They stopped at a government youth center, where they were met by Saigon's deputy mayor and some Republican Youth officers. The group then proceeded to the home of Ma Tuyen, a prominent Chinese merchant who'd worked closely with Diem since 1954 to root out communists among Cholon's 700,000 ethnic Chinese residents.

Diem told the others to go home. Nhu took the deputy mayor aside and asked if he could drive them to the Central Highlands. The man agreed to do so, but Diem angrily objected. "If you want to go, you can go," he told his brother. "I'm going to the JGS headquarters to talk to the generals. Presidents don't run away."

The brothers spent the night at Ma Tuyen's house. Nervous and exhausted, Diem paced and chain-smoked. He was too upset to eat, so Ma Tuyen served tea. Possibly as part of Nhu's fake coup scheme, a special phone relay had been rigged up so Diem could make calls from Ma Tuyen's house that appeared to originate from the palace. Diem stayed in his room all night, making numerous calls and not sleeping.

By morning, he'd given up hope of defeating the coup. He telephoned Don at about 6:20 a.m., saying he knew he must surrender, but wanted to do so with "military honors." Don told him about the palace guards' treachery with the white flag, and said the generals were in no mood to "render any kind of honors to him." Don advised his former boss to surrender unconditionally and promised to get him and Nhu safely out of South Vietnam.

Diem called JGS again at 6:45 a.m. and spoke with General Khiem. The president was ready to give up. He gave his location as a Catholic church in Cholon.

DON WAS TO CLAIM years later that he asked Lodge on November 1 to arrange for a plane to take Diem and Nhu into foreign exile, and "everything was ready."

In fact, nothing was ready. Neither the generals nor anyone at the embassy or in Washington had arranged for an aircraft to be on the tarmac at Tan Son Nhut, fueled and ready to whisk the brothers away when the palace fell.

This oversight was perplexing, since Hilsman had raised the issue of flying Nhu out of South Vietnam when the generals were planning their

August coup. Hilsman feared that if the wily political counselor survived an ARVN takeover, he'd find a base somewhere else in Southeast Asia and relentlessly plot a return to power.

In a memo to Rusk in late August, Hilsman wrote that the generals should "destroy the Palace if necessary to gain victory." If Nhu somehow emerged from the rubble alive, an American plane should be available to take him into permanent exile in France or any other European nation willing to accept him. Diem, wrote Hilsman, "should be treated as the generals wish."

With no aircraft earmarked for Diem and Nhu on November 2, the generals turned to Conein for last-minute help.

At 6 a.m., the CIA agent called his boss, David Smith, and requested a plane. Smith thought France was the country most likely to grant the Ngo brothers asylum. He told Conein the nearest aircraft that could fly them to Paris without stopping to refuel, a KC-135, was in Okinawa. It would take twenty-four hours for the plane to get to Saigon.

As Conein noted pointedly in a subsequent report, while the KC-135 was too far away to be of immediate help, Harkins's personal C-54 could have saved Diem and Nhu. "This aircraft was available," Conein wrote, "as were other commercial planes arriving and departing Saigon."

With its 4,200-mile range, a C-54 couldn't get to Paris without landing and gassing up along the way. But it could easily fly nonstop to Manila, Tokyo, Guam, or Australia. There was another alternative as well: Diem and Nhu could have been evacuated aboard the U.S. Air Force jet—McNamara's plane—that was standing by to fly Lodge to Washington.

When Conein told Big Minh he'd have to wait a day for a KC-135, the coup leader replied ominously: "We can't hold them that long."

NOT LONG AFTER THE rebels made their move, John Buquoi, the Army eavesdropper from Louisiana, was ordered out to the U.S. listening station near the village of Phu Lam. Throughout that day and into the next, he monitored the conversations of Big Minh and two other rebel generals.

He listened as they discussed which ARVN units had joined them, and which were still holdouts. He followed the bloody struggle at the Presidential

Guard barracks. And he heard the generals' trepidation upon learning that Diem and Nhu had somehow escaped from the battered palace.

"There was just a manic, frenetic pace going on, trying to find out where Diem and Nhu were off to," he recalled. "The generals were obviously terrified that they'd gotten away."

As soon as Big Minh found out the brothers had surfaced at the church, he called the other generals together to decide what to do with them.

Conein later claimed that the coup leaders took a "blood oath" never to discuss with outsiders their lengthy arguments over the brothers' fate. But in a 2008 memoir, Don wrote that he spoke first at the meeting, urging that Diem and Nhu be detained temporarily and then sent into exile abroad.

Other generals favored subjecting Nhu, and possibly Diem as well, to a court-martial. Still others wanted them liquidated. "To kill weeds, you must pull them up by the roots," one general argued. But Don said that forcing the brothers out of the country was sufficient, and he believed that most of the others agreed. He left to prepare holding rooms for the Ngos when they arrived at the generals' headquarters.

At about 7:30 a.m., a small convoy drove out of the Joint General Staff compound to pick up the brothers. It was commanded by General Mai Huu Xuan, who headed Diem's military security service in the 1950s and detested the president for later relegating him to a lesser job. The convoy consisted of jeeps and an M113 armored personnel carrier. Among its officers was Captain Nguyen Van Nhung, Big Minh's bodyguard, who'd killed Colonel Tung and his brother the previous day.

The convoy pulled up outside St. Francis Xavier Church, a small, lemon-colored structure attended by Chinese Catholics in Cholon. Diem and Nhu were already there, having arrived in Ma Tuyen's car. Both wore gray suits.

The church's stocky, goateed priest, Father Fernand Billaud, didn't believe it was the president until a former palace servant who attended Mass that morning ran up to Diem, embraced him, and exclaimed: "I want to live or die with you." Diem replied merely, "Have courage; we face difficulties."

Two ARVN officers got out of their vehicles and saluted the president. Father Billaud remembered Diem climbing into the M113 without a word.

The convoy headed back toward JGS. It stopped at a railroad crossing to let a train pass.

When the rear hatch of the armored vehicle opened at JGS, Diem and Nhu were lying on the floor, bloodied and dead.

BOTH MEN'S HANDS WERE tied behind their backs. Diem had been shot once or twice in the back of the head. Nhu hadn't just been killed; he'd been horribly butchered, bayoneted more than thirty times. According to a CIA report, Big Minh's bodyguard, Captain Nhung, "leaped from the M113 with the bayonet in hand and proudly displayed it to all observers. His arms were soaked with blood."

Don began to worry when the convoy pulled into JGS and he didn't see any passenger cars, only military vehicles. Two other generals informed him that Diem and Nhu had been slain.

Don went to Big Minh and demanded: "Why are they dead?"

"What does it matter that they are dead?" the coup leader replied, a note of pride in his voice. Moments later, General Xuan, the convoy commander, burst into the room. Apparently unaware of Don's presence, he uttered two words in French to Big Minh: "Mission accomplie."

Perhaps better than his colleagues, Big Minh understood that the brothers might be able to rally Catholics and other supporters against the generals and their new regime. Minh certainly didn't want to wind up fighting not only the VC but a guerrilla army organized by Diem and Nhu as well. Nor did he want to bear sole responsibility for ordering the assassination of his country's longtime nationalist leader. Hence his consultations with the other rebel generals, which if nothing else diffused blame for the killings.

Prior to the convoy's departure from JGS, Big Minh spoke with his bodyguard, Nhung.

"I will give you publicly an order to go and fetch Diem and Nhu," the general said. "At that moment, look at my hand. If you see only one finger raised, you will kill Nhu only. But if you see two fingers raised, you will kill both." When Big Minh ordered Nhung at the last minute to join the convoy, another officer noticed the general discreetly lift his right hand to the level of his belt, with two fingers extended. (In testimony to a U.S. Senate committee in 1975, Conein confirmed that Minh ordered Nhung to kill the brothers.)

At St. Francis Xavier Church, the brothers approached the M113, where Captain Nhung and an ARVN major stood. Apparently expecting to be treated with more dignity, they were taken aback to see only military vehicles.

"Where is the car for us?" asked Nhu. The major pointed to the armored personnel carrier and said: "Here it is." Nhu angrily replied: "You use such a vehicle to drive the president?" The major answered coldly: "There is no more president." He added: "We soldiers of the armored corps always use this kind of vehicle; it is perhaps time for you to taste it." Nhu seemed to calm down, asking how to enter the carrier. The major showed the brothers the back hatch and they climbed in.

Nhung and some other soldiers clambered onto the carrier and dropped inside through its top hatch. The convoy began to roll. The soldiers tied Diem's and Nhu's hands. Nhu argued, but Diem convinced him to quiet down. Then the president began to pray.

According to a CIA account, Nhu taunted an unnamed officer whose wife had been tortured by the secret police. The officer grabbed a bayonet and stabbed Nhu over and over. Diem tried to intercede, but the officer shot him in the head with his pistol. Captain Nhung later confessed to the double assassination, saying that Big Minh gave the order.

THE GENERALS SOON BEGAN to tell various lies about what happened to Diem and Nhu.

The ARVN-controlled radio station declared at about 10:30 a.m. on November 2 that the brothers had committed suicide by taking poison. Don instructed another officer to tell the press the deaths were attributable to "accidental causes." Big Minh told Diem's former aide, Thuan, that the brothers killed themselves with a gun left by mistake in the M113.

Conein had left JGS headquarters after the long night and gone home to shower and eat something. Despite Big Minh's comment about not being able to detain Diem and Nhu very long, Conein had departed under the impression that the generals were getting ready to house them at JGS "under proper security" until the KC-135 arrived.

But as news of the brothers' deaths spread, the embassy received orders from Washington to "urgently ascertain" exactly how they died. Conein was instructed to go back to JGS and find out. (He later told the U.S. Senate committee that the order came from JFK.)

Big Minh tried to feed Conein the falsehood that Diem and Nhu "had committed suicide in the church." A Catholic himself, Conein called that explanation "ridiculous." No one would believe that two devout Catholics like Diem and Nhu had taken their own lives—a mortal sin, the gravest type a Catholic can commit—much less that they'd done so within the sacred confines of a church. Conein told the coup leader "he would be well-advised to change his story."

Minh then made the CIA operative a macabre offer: Would he like to see the bodies, lying in a basement room at JGS? Conein reflexively declined, saying he couldn't take part in any identification of Diem and Nhu. His real concern was that if he saw the brothers' wounds, he'd probably be able to tell whether they'd been murdered. And if he was the only Westerner who knew that dangerous secret, he might become a target for murder himself.

In any event, Conein didn't need to see their corpses to guess what had befallen Diem and Nhu. He again went home, where his friend Rufus Phillips had spent the night with the Green Berets guarding Conein's home.

Conein's face was ashen; he was in a rage. "Goddamn bastards," he spat. "They killed Diem; they murdered him and Nhu." He repeated Big Minh's spurious story about suicide in the church, saying it was "the stupidest thing he had ever heard."

Phillips was shocked and flooded with grief. He, too, had thought Diem was going to be put on a plane and taken to safety.

SHEEHAN RACED DOWN THE gangway of the noon flight from Tokyo. The "Blue Lotus" alert had reached the UPI bureau there prior to the coup, but no one told him about it. He learned the generals were on the move from reports coming out of Seoul, based on information from the South Korean embassy in Saigon.

Back in his apartment-office, he scrambled to put together a news story on the sensational demise of the South Vietnamese president and his brother.

Quoting "highly reliable sources," his dispatch reported that Diem and Nhu had been assassinated and gave other details of the fatal convoy. Halberstam's story noted that while military radio had characterized the deaths as suicides, "extremely reliable private military sources said both men were assassinated."

Browne and his AP colleagues were trying to confirm the assassination angle when Captain Nhung, the killer, walked into their office and offered to sell a photograph of Diem's blood-smeared corpse inside the armored personnel carrier. Browne said he rejected it as "carrion." He also wasn't sure it was authentic.

Arnett told a different story. He said Nhung wanted $2,000 for the image. But while the Saigon AP office haggled over the phone with its New York headquarters about how much to pay, Nhung left and sold the picture to UPI.

HILSMAN'S SUBORDINATES KNEW THEY were never to disturb their boss at home before 7 a.m. So, the State Department watch officer on duty November 2 waited until shortly after that time to telephone him with news of the purported suicides in Saigon.

"Goddamn it," Hilsman said, and hung up.

Hilsman had already been awakened by a 2 a.m. call from Marguerite Higgins, the journalist, whose first words were: "Congratulations, Roger. How does it feel to have blood on your hands?"

"Oh, come on now, Maggie," he responded. "Revolutions are rough. People get hurt."

His offhandedness reflected the Kennedy administration's chilling lack of concern for the life of its longtime ally Diem. It was Hilsman's zealotry that had helped to breathe life into the coup, but now his moment of triumph was permanently stained.

He was too intelligent not to grasp the negative political implications of

Diem's death, especially with the press calling it an assassination. For one thing, the generals would now be subjected to worldwide condemnation for the cold-blooded murder of their commander in chief. For egging them on, the Kennedy administration would face a good deal of vilification, too. (The conservative *New York Journal-American*, for example, soon accused JFK of "murder most foul.")

Kennedy learned of Diem's brutal demise when Forrestal hurried in with a telegram during the National Security Council meeting later that morning. The president was horrified. "Kennedy leaped to his feet and rushed from the room with a look of shock and dismay on his face which I had never seen before," Taylor remembered.

The Joint Chiefs of Staff chairman was less surprised by the coup's vicious denouement. After the president left the room, Taylor remarked: "What did he expect?" Although JFK wanted Diem to suffer no more than exile, the president "had been led to believe or had persuaded himself that a change in government could be carried out without bloodshed," Taylor later wrote.

Kennedy seemed to recover rapidly from his consternation, huddling with his advisers at least three times that day to discuss how to cope with the political fallout from Diem's liquidation. The president and his men were quick to absolve themselves of responsibility, pinning the blame for Diem's death on him instead.

"I think the suggestion is that the United States made the coup inevitable by applying pressures which developed the atmosphere," JFK said at one point. "I think that certainly in September, after the conclusion of the McNamara-Taylor visit, our intention was to apply pressure to persuade Diem to modify his course of action. That time we were not pushing a coup. Now . . . he didn't give at all and a coup developed. I would say that that was our policy. And we ought to stick with it."

Bundy agreed, saying: "In other words, he had an honorable chance to come to terms with us, which he didn't take."

At another meeting that afternoon, the men debated how deeply to delve into the question of whether Diem committed suicide or was assassinated. Kennedy didn't believe the suicide story, given Diem's fervent Catholicism.

McCone announced that he'd just received a wire from Saigon indicating that Conein declined Big Minh's invitation to inspect the bodies.

"I interpret that as the suicide story is out and Conein is pretty conscious of the fact that it was an assassination and doesn't want to get involved in it," said McCone. "I would suggest that we not get into this story. I don't see that knowing it is going to do us any good. They have put out the suicide story. That's their story."

Hilsman noted that the Saigon newsmen were already digging into the matter: "It's going to come out via Halberstam and company anyway. They're already on the wires with it, with different versions. I think we ought to stay out of it." He recommended that Washington tell Big Minh "not to try to sell a false suicide story."

"If they were indeed assassinated, it's better for him to come out and say so—in the heat of battle, and so on and so forth—and regret it publicly than to leave it a mystery or try to palm off this suicide story," Hilsman said.

The brothers hadn't died "in the heat of battle," of course. They'd been tied up and slaughtered in cold blood after surrendering.

Kennedy wanted to know who was responsible for the murders. "Did Big Minh order the execution?" he asked the room. "Do we know that?"

"Some think he did," answered Hilsman.

No one needed to point out the problem if Big Minh and his co-conspirators had indeed killed Diem and Nhu in such a brutish manner: any new government they formed would be seen as having blood on its hands. The butchery would be denounced in Congress and the U.S. press, further dampening enthusiasm for aid to South Vietnam.

Kennedy clearly understood the issue. "What are we going to say about the death of Diem and Nhu?" he asked. "If we were going to say anything about that, I would think it would be better to indicate our feeling that this is an . . . unfortunate event. Nonetheless, it would be regrettable if it were ascribed—unless the evidence is clear—if it were ascribed to Big Minh or the responsible council of the generals."

Bundy then cabled Lodge to advise the generals to come clean:

"Deaths of Diem and Nhu, whatever their failings, has caused shock here and there is danger that standing and reputation of incoming government may be significantly damaged if conviction spreads of their assassination at direction of one or more senior members of incoming regime," Bundy wrote.

"Evidence available here is thin and conflicting, but simple assertion of suicide obviously will not end the matter. We believe that it is deeply in the interest of the regime to make prompt and full explanation, and if the deaths not by suicide, to emphasize with clear evidence all mitigating circumstances. They should not be left under illusion that political assassination is easily accepted here. Across the months of repression and increasing ineffectiveness, American people and government remember great services to freedom rendered by Diem over many years."

Kennedy knew that the generals' violent takeover would be a source of embarrassment to his administration, although he thought it could be overcome. But he was nonplussed that Diem had been murdered. "I didn't think there was that much hatred for him," he said at one point. At another: "I don't know why they did that."

JFK may not have been caught entirely off guard by Diem's death, however. He subsequently told Cardinal Spellman of New York he knew Diem might be killed, but that he couldn't control the generals.

He also decided to hold his most annoying antagonist, Madame Nhu, responsible for the whole dismal affair.

"That goddamn bitch," he told his old Navy buddy Paul Fay. "She's responsible for the death of that kind man. You know, it's so totally unnecessary to have that kind man die because that bitch stuck her nose in and boiled up the whole situation down there."

ON THE EVENING OF November 2, as news of the murders circulated in Washington, Nolting, Colby, Richardson, and their wives got together at Colby's house for dinner and what he called "probably the only American wake over the deaths of Diem and Nhu."

Nolting had absorbed the unfolding reports from Saigon with "disbelief, then horror, then anger." He felt America "had betrayed an honest ally and that we would suffer the consequences in one way or another." No one with any realistic understanding of South Vietnam, he thought, could have imagined that the coup would be bloodless.

He resigned from the State Department less than four months later. In 1988, Nolting summed up his Saigon experiences in a memoir, whose title neatly encapsulated the disastrous arc of Kennedy's relationship with Diem: *From Trust to Tragedy.*

"In twenty-two years of public service, I never saw anything resembling the confusion, vacillation, and lack of coordination in the U.S. Government," he wrote of the Kennedy administration's policy deliberations on Vietnam in the summer and fall of 1963. "While I had sympathy for President Kennedy in his dilemma, one cannot admire his failure to take control. The Harriman-Lodge axis seemed too strong for him."

Colby, too, admired the Ngo brothers and was stung by their deaths. Over dinner, he, Nolting, and Richardson discussed the problems South Vietnam faced and whether they'd ever be resolved without Diem's strength and leadership. They marveled at the U.S. government's shortsightedness in abetting his overthrow and killing.

The communists felt much the same. They were surprised that Washington would be so foolish as to help facilitate the demise of South Vietnam's toughest, most experienced leader. Indeed, the chief of the Viet Cong's front organization, the National Liberation Front, called Diem's removal a "gift from Heaven for us."

CHAPTER 20

THE GENERALS TAKE OVER

SOON AFTER THE shooting stopped at Gia Long, curious civilians began edging their way toward the shattered palace to see what had happened.

Burned-out tanks and jeeps littered the well-kept grounds and adjacent streets. White sheets covered corpses and captured presidential guardsmen were being tied up. The walls of the palace bore thousands of holes and pockmarks from shells and bullets.

Jubilant citizens poured into the streets as it became known that Diem and Nhu had been driven from power. They cheered rebel soldiers, heaped flowers on their armored vehicles, and plied them with fruit, candy, and bread. People paraded around in happy throngs, blocking traffic. Victorious troops fired their rifles exuberantly into the sky; warplanes did barrel rolls above the rooftops.

Young people waving flags jumped onto tanks and rode triumphantly. Chubby Checker sang on the radio; people twisted and tangoed in the streets to their heart's content. There was tremendous excitement and a feeling of liberation, as if Mardi Gras had broken out across the city.

"Every Vietnamese has a grin on his face today," Lodge gleefully cabled Washington

People waved and applauded when the ambassador rode by, small American flags fluttering from the front of his limousine. Some were overheard saying that if he ran for president of their country, he'd win. Tri Quang walked out of the embassy, a free man after two months of precarious sanctuary. He thanked Lodge and pledged to forgo politics and concentrate on religious matters.

By afternoon, the streets were still crowded, with military police interacting with the public in a friendly, relaxed manner. Big Minh and Don moved easily among the people, shaking hands and receiving congratulations. That night, some of the generals hit the nightclub circuit, partying with grateful Saigonese. Arnett joined Minh and Don at the popular La Cigale nightclub.

The collective joy was mixed with deep anger at the defeated regime. People destroyed any and all symbols of Diemism they could get their hands on. They set fire to the headquarters of Madame Nhu's Women's Solidarity Movement and wrecked the offices of *The Times of Vietnam*. (The paper's frightened editor, Ann Gregory, who'd published so many attacks on Americans and American policy, fled to the U.S. embassy for protection.)

Young men with acetylene torches and steel cables pulled down the infamous statue of the Trung sisters, wrought in the images of Madame Nhu and her daughter; children threw rocks at the broken figures as they lay on the ground. The homes of some high-ranking Diem officials were sacked.

In Hue, furious citizens "desecrated . . . in an unspeakably obscene manner" a large villa where Diem had planned to retire, according to a State Department memo.

Within hours of Diem's murder, Don and Le Van Kim arrived at the embassy to consult with Lodge, apparently oblivious to the bad optics. As TV cameras rolled, Conein hopped out of the front seat of the generals' car, opened the back door, and saluted as Don and Kim emerged. Watching the scene, James Rosenthal, a young embassy officer, was taken aback at how the generals' prompt report to Lodge reinforced the impression of U.S. collusion in the putsch.

"Here were the guys who had just carried out a coup, killed the chief of state, and then they walk up to the embassy, as if to say, 'Hey, boss, we did a good job, didn't we?'" Rosenthal said. Don recalled that Lodge was "extremely enthusiastic and congratulatory about our achievement."

THE BRUTAL SLAYINGS OF Diem and Nhu weren't the only public relations mess the generals and their American sponsors faced. There was also the matter of Nhu's three youngest children: two boys, ages fifteen and eleven, and a four-year-old girl. Where were they and what had happened to them? Had Big Minh snuffed them along with their father and uncle?

Madame Nhu was still in Los Angeles with her oldest daughter. Distraught that her other children might have perished in the attack on the palace, she left an urgent message for Marguerite Higgins. Late that night, after returning from a party, the journalist called her back.

"Do you really believe they are dead?" Madame Nhu asked, referring to her husband and brother-in-law. Higgins said she was afraid they were. "I could spit upon the world," Madame said bitterly. After a pause, she asked, "Are they going to kill my children, too?"

That prospect horrified Higgins. "It's the last thing President Kennedy would want," she replied, although she could imagine agitated South Vietnamese taking vengeance on even the littlest members of the hated Nhu clan.

"Then why doesn't the United States government do something to help me get them out?" Madame Nhu implored, sobbing.

That was when Higgins phoned Hilsman, waking him at 2 a.m. and accusing him of having blood on his hands. She demanded to know whether the Nhu children would be hurt.

Hilsman promised that if Madame Nhu found out where they were, the U.S. government would get them out of South Vietnam and fly them anywhere in the world to rejoin her. "The president is deeply shocked over the death of Diem and Nhu," he said. "He will do anything he can to safeguard Madame Nhu's children."

It turned out that the kids had left the palace before the coup and gone to Dalat. The boys were on a school vacation and had begged their father to let them go hunting. Nhu sent them north accompanied by fifteen presidential guardsmen. When the revolt broke out, the children, surrounded by armed men, but not knowing who to trust, fled into the woods behind their house and spent the night in a cold rain. They walked all the next day to a mountain village, where sympathetic Montagnards fed them rice and ground meat.

The children eventually surfaced and General Khanh, the II Corps commander, picked them up in his personal plane and flew them back to Saigon.

While Harkins's C-54 aircraft wasn't enlisted to evacuate Diem and Nhu, Taylor ordered that it be made available to get the three youngsters out. The State Department emphasized in a wire to Lodge that "prompt and chivalrous treatment of children will be particularly helpful here in context of death of father."

But the kids weren't to be flown to their mother in Los Angeles. In an effort to lure the nettlesome Madame Nhu out of the United States, her offspring were to be sent to Rome and handed over to Archbishop Thuc, who was attending a Vatican conference. Because they lacked passports, Lodge gave them "travel documents" forged by his staff and festooned with official-looking eagles, stars, and scrolls. Lodge assigned his aide, Freddy Flott, to chaperone the children on the long flight to Rome.

Flott rushed out to Tan Son Nhut on the night of November 4. The children were already aboard the C-54, along with a CIA secretary who was also a nurse. The group flew to Bangkok, where they switched to a commercial jet.

Thuc met the plane at the Rome airport, trailed by a horde of about 150 newspeople. The Nhu boys stepped off the jet dressed neatly in jackets and ties; the fifteen-year-old carried his little sister in his arms. The archbishop refused to speak or shake hands with Flott, who was miffed. "Total ice treatment," he complained. "Packed [the children] into the car, not a word of thanks, nothing." It evidently didn't occur to Flott that he might be met with something other than gushing gratitude by someone whose brothers had just been shot and stabbed to death during an American-enabled coup.

Hilsman and Lodge were soon trying to manipulate the children's presence in Rome to "draw the mother out of Los Angeles," as Flott put it.

It was apparent that Madame Nhu could become a problem for the

Kennedy administration if she stayed in the United States. Although her recent speaking tour had damaged her public image, she was now a more sympathetic figure: a bereft widow, the mother of four fatherless children, the whole family stateless as a result of the coup.

She was still a media magnet with a razor-sharp tongue. "Whoever has the Americans as allies does not need any enemies," she snapped at a press conference, accusing Washington of responsibility for the assassinations. In the days after the coup she spoke with two powerful Republicans, Richard Nixon and Clare Boothe Luce, a former congresswoman and ambassador to Italy who was married to *Time* magazine publisher Henry Luce. With the 1964 presidential campaign getting underway, Madame Nhu could easily continue in her role as a high-profile critic of JFK's Vietnam policy, attracting press coverage wherever she went.

From her Beverly Hills hotel suite, Madame announced that she couldn't endure a trip to Italy and wanted her children brought to the United States. The next day, Hilsman released a cable to the American embassy in Rome: "Until further instructed do not give visas to children if requested. Stall but do not refuse." Lodge chimed in, suggesting that the South Vietnamese embassy in Rome be asked not to issue passports to the kids. "They now have none," Lodge noted. "This might make visa stall easier and assist in getting Madame Nhu out of the United States."

But JFK overruled his devious subordinates. A handwritten note on Hilsman's telegram said: "Pres[ident] does not want to hold up children's visas if they clearly wish come U.S."

Madame Nhu nevertheless left Los Angeles for Rome on November 13.

WITH THE KIDS SAFE, the generals tried to figure out what to do with the torn bodies of their father and uncle.

The coup leaders again changed their story about Diem and Nhu's demise, claiming they were killed when Nhu lunged for an officer's pistol as the brothers entered the armored personnel carrier. (The generals' press spokesman characterized the supposed incident as an "accidental suicide.")

The Ngos' remains had been moved from the Joint General Staff compound to the Clinique St. Paul, a small, private hospital formerly staffed by French doctors. On November 3, Big Minh and Don paid a call on Diem's niece and her husband, Tran Trung Dung, the dead president's onetime assistant defense minister.

"We are not here to present our condolences to you," Minh coldly informed the couple. "We hope you will understand that their deaths occurred as an unfortunate incident during the coup d'etat." The generals asked the niece to accept the bodies and arrange the funerals, but she became "hysterical" and refused.

On their way back to their headquarters, Minh and Don saw a large crowd gathered outside the hospital. Civilians were angrily demanding that the cadavers be turned over to them. If that happened, the ugly desecrations that would inevitably follow would be photographed and publicized around the world, giving the generals another black eye. Minh and Don posted soldiers around the hospital to keep the citizenry out.

Minh and Don didn't want the bodies buried in the municipal graveyard, where they could be dug up and defiled. That night, they were brought back to JGS and locked in a basement. Diem and Nhu were eventually interred in a vacant field within the JGS complex. Don ordered the graves cemented over as, he explained, "a kind of last tribute to them as the onetime leaders of our nation."

Three other Ngo brothers remained alive. Archbishop Thuc was unlikely to return to Vietnam any time soon. Ngo Dinh Luyen, Diem's ambassador to Britain, resigned with an angry blast at the generals for committing "murder camouflaged as suicide."

Ngo Dinh Can, the onetime Hue strongman, disappeared.

The collapse of Diem's government left Can in serious trouble, isolated in his residence with his sickly, nonagenarian mother as rumors burned through the city of past cruelties he'd allegedly inflicted on the populace. He slipped out of his house at night and went into hiding.

Thousands of people flooded into his neighborhood on November 3 when word spread that his property contained "mass burial sites." John Helble reported that as many as 180 bodies had supposedly been found, although he couldn't confirm their existence. However, many Hue residents believed the story, and there was angry talk of attacking Can's residence. The local ARVN commander cordoned it off with concertina wire, troops, and armored personnel carriers. (When Harkins asked Don about the purported graves, the ARVN general, who'd once commanded troops around the city, smiled and said they had nothing to do with Can; people in Hue had been burying family members in the area long before Can moved into his house.)

The next day, agitated crowds looted and wrecked the elaborate country estate (one observer called it "a kind of Xanadu") Can was building about two miles south of Hue. On that property the marauders discovered something that made them even madder: a filthy secret prison. Its cramped cells had been fashioned from old French ammunition bunkers dug into a hillside. About three and a half feet high and five or six feet long, the barred cells lacked beds and were filled with trash and human excrement. Some appeared to have been occupied recently. Helble described them as "rather horrific."

Facing a possible lynching, Can sent an emissary to ask whether Helble would give him asylum in the U.S. consulate. Helble refused, saying he and his small staff couldn't protect Can from an angry mob that might tear the consulate apart to get at him, injuring or killing Americans in the process.

But Washington was concerned about more international censure of Big Minh and his colleagues if another member of the Ngo clan was slain. To Helble's amazement, the State Department ordered him to grant Can asylum. Hilsman approved a cable directing Helble to remind the Hue authorities that the United States had taken similar action to protect Tri Quang and "can do no less in Can's case."

The White House agreed, instructing Lodge in a separate message to "make every effort to get him and his mother, if necessary, out of country soonest" and to ensure their protection in the meantime.

ON NOVEMBER 5, A black Citroën sedan driven by a Catholic priest pulled up outside the consulate. (Can reportedly had been hiding in a Catholic Redemptorist seminary.) The priest stepped out and opened the back door, revealing a man in peasant garb lying face down on the floor: Hue's former political boss, disguised and frightened.

"I was now meeting the man who would never previously see me, who . . . had terrorized Hue and environs for years," Helble recalled. "Now I was his last hope."

Helble shook Can's hand and escorted him into the consulate, trying to conceal his identity from his two Vietnamese employees. Can said he wanted to go to Tokyo.

General Do Cao Tri, the tough I Corps commander, showed up at the consulate next. He said he knew Helble had Can, and he wanted him. Helble boldly replied that "whether I had Ngo Dinh Can or not was a matter of my concern and not his." Tri tried to frighten him, saying that if angry local people found out he was sheltering Can, the general "could not assure the security of the consulate or of the American community in Hue in general." Helble responded that it was Tri's duty to protect American lives and property, and demanded his promise to do so, adding that he'd report Tri's answer to the embassy. But the general gave no assurances and left empty-handed.

Helble phoned the embassy and gave a coded message: "The bird is in the cage." The embassy replied that a CIA aircraft would land in two hours to bring Can to Saigon.

Working with U.S. military advisers in Hue, Helble assembled a three-vehicle convoy to take Can to the airport. At the front and rear were jeeps, each carrying an American officer and an enlisted man. In the middle was Helble's Rambler. An army man drove the Rambler, with Jerry Greiner, the rugged CIA agent who played bridge with Helble, riding shotgun. Helble and a U.S. Army lieutenant colonel sat in the back, on either side of Can.

No one was armed; Helble knew that if an ARVN detachment stopped them, gunplay would be a very bad idea.

The convoy made it to Phu Bai airfield, about nine miles southeast of Hue, without incident. Can boarded the CIA aircraft, a C-46 cargo plane, along with Greiner, the lieutenant colonel, and a pair of military policemen. Helble instructed Greiner that upon landing, he was to turn Can over only to someone from the State Department—no one else.

When the C-46 rolled to a stop at Tan Son Nhut, Greiner realized it was parked in the airport's military zone and surrounded by ARVN soldiers. A couple of two-and-half-ton trucks were nearby. Greiner was greeted by the ubiquitous Lucien Conein.

"All right, Jerry," he said. "I will take it from here."

Greiner protested that he'd been told to deliver Can to the State Department, not the CIA. "Well, have it your way, but here's your transportation," Conein replied, indicating the trucks. Greiner and Can climbed into the back of one and a canvas flap was pulled down behind them.

The truck rumbled into Saigon. When it stopped and the canvas was raised, Greiner saw that they were in an ARVN compound, again surrounded by troops. Conein reappeared and said, "This is the end of the road." Greiner had no choice but to let soldiers take Can, in a "state of emotional shock," away.

Lodge, it developed, had made a deal with the generals, who refused to permit Can to be flown out of South Vietnam. So Lodge settled for a personal guarantee from General Don to protect Can and ensure he'd be "dealt with 'legally and juridically.'"

"Giving him asylum, as I understand it, was to protect him from being lynched and to provide him with physical safety," Lodge explained in a cable to Rusk. "As government gives assurances his personal safety and that he will be dealt with by legal process, it seems to me that our reason for giving him asylum therefore no longer exists.

"I also consider that we would be subject to justified criticism if we attempted to obstruct the course of justice here, particularly as Can is undoubtedly a reprehensible figure who deserves all the loathing which he now receives."

It was an interesting rationale, especially in light of how Lodge handled Tri Quang's asylum plea. The Buddhist leader had been taken into the embassy and protected by Marine guards for two tense months as Lodge resolutely rejected demands from Diem's government to turn him over.

Can, by contrast, was granted asylum, but handed over to the generals the same day. (Six months later, as Can was about to be executed, Lodge denied in an Associated Press interview that he'd turned him over to the military.)

Lodge gave up Can despite White House instructions to get him safely out of the country. The CIA aircraft that landed in Hue presented a golden opportunity to fly him straight to, say, Manila, less than nine hundred miles away. (The C-46's range was 2,300 miles.) Alternatively, Lodge could have kept Can in the embassy indefinitely. There was little chance the generals would risk forcibly removing him, no matter how loudly the South Vietnamese public clamored for his blood.

But the political calculus had changed for Lodge. Tri Quang was the enemy of a regime Lodge wanted to undermine; therefore, he was defiantly sheltered. Can was the enemy of a new regime Lodge wanted to succor; he was thrown to the wolves. Can was certainly an unsavory character. But through Helble, the United States had promised him sanctuary. Lodge then broke that promise and delivered him into the hands of his pursuers.

The whole episode disgusted Helble. "I knew I had been double-crossed by my own authorities—in Washington, Saigon, or both," he wrote later. "There were no 'asylum' intentions. In Hue we were all put at risk."

THE PEOPLE OF SAIGON were still celebrating Diem's downfall. Dancing returned to nightclubs. Multiple newspapers sprang up, with citizens eagerly crowding outside their offices as they awaited the latest editions. For the first time in two years, police barricades came down around Gia Long Palace, easing traffic congestion.

"In the towns and cities," commented Mecklin, "there was a feeling everywhere of a fresh breeze in a musty room."

The generals decreed an end to arbitrary arrests and confinement. They ordered the release of anti-Diem political prisoners and "people sort of came up out of the ground," as Trueheart put it, with sickening stories of torture and abuse.

One of the pilots who'd bombed the palace in 1962 emerged from a dungeon beneath the Saigon Zoo with both hands chopped off. A twenty-nine-year-old woman, an ardent Buddhist, told Browne she'd been stripped, tied to a bench, and waterboarded "until I lost consciousness" on the day the coup began. A young girl told of enduring electric shocks to her breasts from an army field generator. Others said they had fingers cut off or were forced to drink soapy water, resulting in internal bleeding. Browne reported that some prisoners were blinded and one student died after his liver was ruptured by truncheon blows.

Freed prisoners came home from Poulo Condor, the penal island in the South China Sea. A boat bearing thirty-three of them—all sentenced in connection with the 1960 paratrooper uprising—docked in Saigon to the cheers of some ten thousand well-wishers. Those waiting on the dock placed garlands of flowers around the released men's necks, hoisted them to their shoulders, and carried them joyously off. People shouted and wept with happiness.

"Just for this fleeting, golden moment," wrote a British journalist, "it seemed as if we had reached a happy ending. Vietnam had been exorcised."

The happy ending, however, proved to be short-lived.

The generals appeared at first to be a determined group of liberal reformers. They proclaimed their commitment to freedom of expression and religion. They banished corvée labor in the provinces. Martial law was lifted six days after the coup, and curfews were shortened. When a spokesman announced at a news conference that the coup principals hoped to establish "new principles" for press relations, journalists cheered.

But the generals were fundamentally authoritarian souls. While they'd promised to stay out of the new government, they soon backpedaled, forming a junta and saying they'd turn power over to civilians only at some unspecified date in the future.

Calling themselves the Military Revolutionary Council, the generals suspended the constitution and abolished the National Assembly. "Demonstrations in any form" were prohibited. Anyone handing out pro-communist leaflets would be shot on the spot. Movie houses and theaters were ordered to play the national anthem at the start of each performance; spectators were required to stand at attention. Political parties were allowed to operate, but only "within the limits required by national defense security."

"The army advocates the necessity of applying democracy under the conditions of a country at war—that is, on the basis of discipline," warned a broadcast on the military-controlled radio.

It became clear that democracy was on as short a leash under the generals as it had been under Diem.

Censorship was imposed, with white spaces appearing in newspapers in place of stories about the deaths of Diem and Nhu and the disposition of their remains. It was lifted after a few days, but publishers were ordered to print "nothing contrary to the spirit of the revolution" and "nothing contrary to good morals." The new information minister, General Tran Tu Oai, formerly in charge of mosquito eradication, warned that newspapers that "repeatedly print false or harmful stories" would be shut down.

Big Minh became chief of state. Exercising power through a twelve-man executive committee, the generals appointed Diem's vice president, Tho, as prime minister. Tho in turn named a fifteen-man cabinet to oversee day-to-day government affairs. But the generals had final approval over cabinet appointments and installed military men to run key ministries, including defense. An ungainly "council of notables," composed of up to eighty civilian political figures, was created to draft a new constitution and oversee elections, when and if they were held.

"The military holds the reins of the new provisional government," the CIA reported to Kennedy. "Executive and legislative powers are centered in the [generals' committee.]"

SUPREME POWER IN SOUTH Vietnam now lay in the hands of Big Minh, the plainspoken, unpretentious career soldier who loved to play tennis and grow orchids.

For a long time, Minh had felt that his country was in a nosedive, and he wasn't sure if it could pull out in time. He'd hoped that a coup could be avoided, but now that it had come to pass, he found himself in a role he never wanted: head of state in a new government that had inherited all the old problems.

Minh believed that changes were needed almost everywhere: in the army, the strategic hamlet program, the manner in which regime bureaucrats treated the people. Rampant government corruption had to be stamped out. The VC support system in the delta had to be uprooted. Unlike Diem and Nhu, who more often than not kept Washington at arm's length, Minh eagerly sought American help.

Kennedy's people were impressed. "He appears more politically sophisticated than some of us thought," Forrestal commented to Bundy after reading a French newspaper article in which the new Vietnamese leader said he opposed neutralism, but had no objection to rice sales and cultural exchanges with Hanoi, as long as it stopped helping the Viet Cong.

Minh and the other generals placed great importance on winning the allegiance of the armed religious sects, the Hoa Hao and the Cao Dai. The groups had strong influence in their home areas, and long experience fighting both the communists and Diem's regime.

Although Minh had led government troops that pursued Hoa Hao fighters in the mid-1950s, he wanted to incorporate them into the ARVN. Less than a month after the coup, he traveled to the heart of Hoa Hao country—An Giang Province, about eighty miles west of Saigon—where his request for help in battling the VC was met with cheers from sect followers. Several companies of Hoa Hao soldiers sided with his new government, as did some Cao Dai troops.

Minh thought the strategic hamlet program was basically sound, but had been badly run by Nhu and exploited for his personal political advantage. Like many U.S. advisers, Minh wanted to consolidate existing hamlets, making them more defensible, before the program was expanded any further. He was an enthusiastic supporter of the "oil spot" strategy of pacifying one small area and then expanding it gradually until it blended with others, squeezing out the VC.

A native of the delta province of Long An, Minh knew the hamlet-building program had been pushed too far and too fast in the delta. In areas where mass relocations had been imposed, he wanted to give resentful peasants a choice between remaining in the hamlets or going back to their old homes. And in parts of the delta where homes were widely dispersed, he thought fortified hamlets should be abandoned in favor of continuous patrols by small ARVN units and local militiamen.

Minh viewed the primary job of South Vietnam's military as pacification, not large-scale combat operations. The VC, he believed, were less afraid of ARVN sweeps than small military patrols and effective civic-action teams that could break up their support networks in the villages.

One of Minh's biggest problems was finding enough qualified people to serve as government administrators in the countryside. But he and the other generals were caught in a paradox that often plagues successful revolts: as they energetically purged despised "Diemist elements" from their government and army, they were sacking the very people—experienced bureaucrats—needed to run those organizations.

Less than two months after the coup, nearly half of the forty-one Diem-appointed province chiefs had been fired, with more to go. U.S. experts had set up a special school in Saigon to train government administrators, but Minh needed more of them, and fast. (He explained that his goal with all the turnover was to install officials who were natives of the areas they administered. That way, local peasants would be more likely to know and trust them, and provide the government with information on VC movements.)

Another millstone around the junta's neck was corruption among rural officials. Practically everybody under Diem had been involved, Minh said in a lengthy conversation with Rufus Phillips. The Americans, Minh said, had no idea of the extent of the corruption or the damage it did to the morale of people in the countryside.

For example, some province chiefs sold barbed wire to peasants, who knew very well the United States had given it for free. It was critical to put an end to such profiteering, and the new regime planned to publicly execute the first few chiefs caught stealing. The peasants, said Minh, weren't fools: they knew when they were being robbed, and they knew the difference between good and bad government.

Speaking with Lodge, Minh said he hoped that Washington would provide a "brain trust" of American experts to assist his fledgling regime; he particularly wanted to improve South Vietnamese intelligence-gathering abilities.

BESIDES COLONEL TUNG, THE generals had killed about ten members of Diem's government and military during the coup. Now came the arrests.

Dr. Tuyen, the former secret police chief who'd abandoned the safety of Hong Kong, was seized at his home in the middle of an interview with journalist Stanley Karnow. (He was later charged with extorting money from Chinese businessmen in exchange for licenses to cut timber in the Central Highlands.) Thuan, Diem's chief of staff, was picked up as well. Madame Nhu's feckless brother, Tran Van Khiem, who supposedly was going to run his own secret police force, was arrested and shipped to Poulo Condor, despite his mother's protests that he was "only a stupid boy."

So many Diem subordinates were arrested that the generals began to get a reputation for arbitrary arrests as bad as Diem's. According to one estimate, about five hundred people had been jailed within a month or so of the coup.

Particularly baffling was the arrest of Tran Quoc Buu, South Vietnam's preeminent labor leader.

Buu's detention on November 3 triggered alarm in Washington, which feared a backlash from American as well as foreign labor organizations. Lodge met with Big Minh and Don, who, after scouring police stations and "interrogating" other generals, claimed the military didn't have Buu. They later insisted that Dr. Tuyen's coup group kidnapped Buu to embarrass the new regime.

Released at 2 a.m. on November 5, Buu said he'd been held at a villa by General Oai, the information minister. A source later told the CIA that Big Minh "exploded in anger and vented his wrath for fully five minutes" over what he regarded as U.S. interference in the Buu case. The embassy never got to the bottom of what really happened or why.

Only a few days into his reign as chief of state Minh looked "tired and frazzled," according to Lodge, and it was no wonder. Conflicts and power plays were already breaking out between the generals and civilian politicians, and among the generals themselves.

Le Van Kim, the most politically astute junta member, complained to the CIA's David Smith that he had the hardest job in the new government because, unlike the other generals, who only had to fight the VC, "he had to argue with the politicians, which he was not trained to do and for which task he evidently had very little taste."

Friction also was developing between the generals and Prime Minister Tho, who, according to Don, lacked the "speed and revolutionary zeal required to be a truly effective premier." Proposals requiring quick attention, Don complained, instead disappeared into the black hole of the Saigon bureaucracy, just as in the days of Diem.

Another problematic figure was General Dinh, who the other generals viewed as "opportunistic and perhaps insane," according to a CIA report given to JFK.

The junta principals had put him in charge of internal security, giving him control of the powerful national police force. But his wary colleagues tried to limit his other powers, shifting the strategic hamlet program out of his office and assigning his vital III Corps to another general. As of late November, however, Dinh still hadn't relinquished command of III Corps troops around Saigon. He was also making campaign-style visits to the provinces, telling people the coup was largely his doing; the CIA concluded he was trying to build an independent power base.

Perhaps the generals' biggest burden was the original sin they'd never be able to expiate: they'd murdered their way to power.

Killing Diem and Nhu sapped the junta's political and moral legitimacy from the beginning. Even South Vietnamese who detested Diem's autocratic methods were upset at the squalid manner in which he died. His slaying created deep and lasting antagonism toward the junta among many of the government fonctionnaires who'd served him. It also exacerbated religious tensions, since many Catholics were angry over the murder of two Catholic leaders at the hands of rebels who were largely Buddhist.

"To have compelled Diem to abdicate might have opened the way for constitutional changes and reforms," wrote the Australian journalist Denis Warner. "But the moment orders were given for the assassination, constitutional methods were forgotten and jungle law prevailed."

SEVERAL PROMINENT VIETNAMESE PLEADED with the Americans to step in, advise the generals how to set up and run an effective government, and make sure they followed the advice.

Father Luan, who, to the delight of his students, had been restored to his position at Hue University, told Lodge the United States should use its influence "because this is our last chance." Tran Van Chuong, who'd quit as Diem's ambassador to Washington, urged the Americans to set firm conditions before granting the junta diplomatic recognition and restarting aid programs. But the Kennedy administration quietly extended recognition and resumed assistance without imposing any hard-and-fast requirements on the generals.

Seemingly intent on avoiding accusations of "neocolonial" intervention, Lodge took a hands-off approach toward the shaky new government. (There was irony aplenty in that posture, given his energetic promotion of the ultimate neocolonial intervention: a coup.) Lodge did advise the generals to improve their press relations, and warned against arbitrary arrests and "anti-Christian actions," which would further damage their international reputation.

Big Minh and the others liked and respected Lodge and were grateful for his advocacy during the run-up to the coup. In mid-November, the ambassador hosted a black-tie dinner for the leading junta members, complete with "small talk, champagne and cigars, as though we had all been working together for years," Mecklin remembered.

Lodge sometimes accompanied junta members into the countryside, where they were received with great enthusiasm. He tried to give tips to Big Minh on increasing his popular appeal, such as shaking hands with people, signing autographs, and taking off his army hat during public appearances so people could see his face better. But he was informed that Minh "did not like doing that kind of thing."

While he was happy to dispense American-style campaign advice, Lodge wasn't much interested in the nuts-and-bolts details of standing up a new government. He made little if any effort to help accelerate the training of government administrators so desperately needed in the countryside.

Although the generals twice asked for CIA help in assembling a post-coup government, Lodge enjoined the agency from providing it.

Lodge's "curiously detached attitude" made an impression on William Colby when, at JFK's request, he visited Saigon to assess the post-coup situation. Colby renewed his old acquaintances with the generals and concluded that they were overwhelmed by the simultaneous tasks of running the country and getting the war effort back on track.

"They looked anxiously to the Americans to show them how to do one and the other and even to do both for them—in the best French colonial manner under which they had grown up," Colby later wrote. "'Big' Minh showed no inclination to take charge and provide the necessary leadership, much preferring to consult with his fellow generals in a series of briefings and discussions that led to no decisions." As the junta dithered, Lodge remained "remote from the mere details of getting an American mission to pull together a strategy and a structure to carry it out."

Colby cabled his findings home, and McCone passed a copy to Bundy, who said he "understood the problem."

AFTER FOURTEEN MONTHS OF front-page stories and trenchant observations that made him a star among foreign correspondents, Halberstam was now a short-timer in Saigon, soon to head to a new assignment in New York City.

But his notebooks held plenty of material for more articles. In an all-out, two-day effort, he hammered out a detailed, five-thousand-word reconstruction of how the generals organized their takeover, focusing on their clever enticement of General Dinh. The story ran on page one on November 6.

That same day, the *New York Post* published a column by its editor, James Wechsler, arguing that the generals' revolt had "dramatically vindicated" Halberstam, Sheehan, and the other Saigon-based reporters from the criticisms of older colleagues such as Marguerite Higgins and Joseph Alsop.

The gaiety in Saigon that followed Diem's death, Wechsler wrote, proved the Saigon correspondents' case that his popular support had largely evaporated. And the coup made a mockery of Harkins's insistence that the war was being won since, as Wechsler tartly observed, military leaders who are winning a war don't normally take time out to overthrow their government.

Higgins and company, he went on, owed the Saigon journalists an apology: "They chose to report what they saw as the truth rather than play it safe. They risked their necks and, in some cases, their jobs. To Halberstam . . . and the others, I respectfully tip my hat." Coming from the editor of a rival newspaper, it was a noteworthy tribute.

Halberstam, meanwhile, began putting together a devastating, post-coup appraisal of his bête noire, Harkins.

His story noted that the reasons ARVN leaders gave for staging the coup were sharply at odds with much of what Harkins had been telling Washington. Big Minh and his colleagues insisted that the war couldn't be won under Diem's leadership, that politically motivated restraints hobbled their operations against the VC, and that military morale was deteriorating as a result of the Buddhist unrest. The junta members, wrote Halberstam, regarded Harkins as "a symbol of the old order" and kept him in the dark about their planning because they feared he'd tip off the palace.

The article went on to say that on the day of the coup, while the embassy and CIA station informed Washington in a joint message that the uprising was coming, "the military command said it would not happen." (The newsman mischaracterized the MACV message to a degree. What Harkins's command actually reported to Washington, just thirty minutes before the first shots rang out, was that it lacked "clear evidence of an impending coup." But Halberstam's essential point that Harkins was poorly informed about the revolt was correct.)

When the *Times* published the story on its November 13 front page, under the headline "Saigon Coup Hurts Position of Harkins," it caused a stir at the White House.

During the National Security Council's daily staff meeting, Bundy and Forrestal denounced the article as "very unfortunate" and "everyone seemed pleased that Halberstam would be leaving Saigon soon for another post." Forrestal phoned Robert Kleiman, a *Times* editorial writer who specialized in foreign affairs, and complained that the story was "irresponsible and mostly reflected a personal animus against General Harkins instead of accurate news reporting."

Rusk complained to Lodge for the umpteenth time about loose tongues at the embassy; Lodge again asserted that no leaks came from his shop and suggested that someone in Washington fed anti-Harkins material to the *Times*'s Washington bureau, which forwarded it to Halberstam. A more likely explanation is that Halberstam assembled his story with the help of his extensive network of sources in Saigon. (Sheehan wrote a similar piece about Harkins, but it was spiked for unknown reasons at UPI headquarters in New York, according to a message from Harkins to Taylor.)

Halberstam was certainly right that the generals weren't fans of Harkins. On the day Halberstam's story was published, General Kim had a conversation with Rufus Phillips. The ARVN was losing the war, Kim said, and needed to make many changes in order to win. But Harkins opposed the changes "because he told so many lies, which he cannot now retract, about how the war was being won."

ARVN leaders, Kim added, had "tried to tell him many times what the true situation was but he would never listen." Kim and his fellow commanders worried that needed reforms would never be made because MACV wouldn't permit them.

Phillips reported the conversation to Lodge.

Three days later, the CIA station informed its headquarters that Lodge wanted Harkins replaced. The station also confirmed most of the points in Halberstam's story.

BUT IT WAS LODGE, not Harkins, whose head was on the chopping block in Washington.

Irritated by the criticism of his Vietnam commander, Kennedy told a press conference he had "great confidence" in Harkins and extended his two-year term as MACV chief for several months beyond its scheduled end in February 1964.

JFK had a very different attitude toward his obstreperous ambassador, who he felt had forced his hand on the coup, according to Robert Kennedy.

Lodge had given unsatisfactory answers to Washington's questions about the generals' plans and hadn't communicated with Diem or Harkins. The Kennedys abhorred his habitual press leaking and divisive impact on the administration. "He was very difficult to deal with and heartily disliked by McNamara, by McCone, by Maxwell Taylor," Robert said.

The president and his brother began to discuss getting rid of Lodge, who'd been rescheduled to meet with JFK in Washington on November 24. It was a politically sensitive issue because Lodge was being talked up in some quarters as a Republican candidate for president in 1964. Easing him out of Saigon without appearing to be trying to damage a potential election rival would be tricky.

Meanwhile, JFK's remorse over the deaths of Diem and Nhu hadn't left him. Arthur Schlesinger, the president's special assistant and speechwriter, hadn't seen him so depressed since the Bay of Pigs. His appointments secretary, Kenneth O'Donnell, said the president's shock over the killings made him all the more "resolved to withdraw from further entanglement in the Vietnam war."

Alone in the Oval Office on November 4, Kennedy turned on a Dictabelt machine and began recording his thoughts, apparently for a future memoir:

> Over the weekend the coup in Saigon took place. It culminated three months of conversation about a coup, conversation which divided the government here and in Saigon. Opposed to a coup was General Taylor, the attorney general, Secretary McNamara, [and] to a somewhat lesser degree, John McCone, partly because of an old hostility to Lodge which causes him to lack confidence in Lodge's judgment, partly as a result of a new hostility because Lodge shifted his station chief. In favor of the coup was State, led by Averell Harriman, George Ball, Roger Hilsman, supported by Mike Forrestal at the White House.
>
> I feel that we must bear a good deal of responsibility for it, beginning with our cable of early [*sic*] August in which we suggested the coup. In my judgment that wire was badly drafted. It should never have been sent on a Saturday. I should not have given my consent to it without a roundtable con-

> ference in which McNamara and Taylor could have presented their views. While we did redress that balance in later wires, that first wire encouraged Lodge along a course to which he was in any case inclined.
>
> Harkins continued to oppose the coup on the ground that the military effort was doing well. There was a sharp split between Saigon and the rest of the country. Politically, the situation was deteriorating. Militarily, [the deterioration] had not had its effect. There was a feeling, however, that it would. For this reason, Secretary McNamara and General Taylor supported applying additional pressures to Diem and Nhu in order to move them.

After playing briefly with his three-year-old son, John Jr., the president returned to his dictation.

> I was shocked by the death of Diem and Nhu. I'd met Diem with Justice [William O.] Douglas many years ago. He was an extraordinary character. While he became increasingly difficult in the last months, nevertheless over a ten-year period he'd held his country together, maintained its independence under very adverse conditions. The way he was killed made it particularly abhorrent.
>
> The question now is whether the generals can stay together and build a stable government, or whether . . . public opinion in Saigon, the intellectuals, students, etcetera, will turn on this government as repressive and undemocratic in the not-too-distant future.

Two days later, Lodge sent Kennedy a private message, declaring that the military "revolution" had led to a closer relationship between the new government and the people and increased the prospects for victory, "provided the Generals stay united."

JFK replied that because the United States had encouraged the generals, it bore a special responsibility to help their government "in every way that we can." He noted that the biggest opportunity for Washington to assist was during the first few weeks after the coup. But it was an opportunity that Lodge largely squandered.

WITH THE 1964 ELECTION only a year away, Kennedy was already planning his campaign. On November 12, he met in the Cabinet Room for three hours with Robert Kennedy; Theodore Sorensen, his speechwriter; John Bailey, chairman of the Democratic National Committee; and several other political advisers to go over his upcoming run and how to frame the Democrats' pitch to voters. The economy and civil rights clearly would be hot-button topics.

"What is it that we can [do to] make them decide that they want to vote for us, Democrats and Kennedy?" JFK asked. "What is it we have to sell them? We hope we have to sell them prosperity but for the average guy, the prosperity is nil. He's not unprosperous but he's not very prosperous; he's not going [to] make out well off. And the people who really are well off hate our guts. So that, what is it—there's a lot of Negroes. We're the ones that are shoving the Negroes down his throat. What is it he's got, though? We've got peace, you know what I mean? We say we hope the country's prosperous. I'm trying to think of what else."

Vietnam, too, loomed as a campaign issue, and the White House worried that Madame Nhu might resurface and make potent attacks on both Kennedy and the junta. Forrestal instructed Colby, still in Saigon, to dig up some usable dirt on her.

"It may thus become necessary to make clear the exact quality of her own performance and that of her husband and his brothers and to show both evidence of and reasons for her and their intense unpopularity among Vietnamese people," Forrestal cabled the CIA executive. "You should stimulate fullest analysis and reporting on this topic. We are interested in hard facts."

Diem's elimination and the advent of a new government also gave Kennedy an opening to reassess and perhaps revamp his uncertain policy toward South Vietnam. The president dispatched McNamara, Rusk, McCone, Bundy, and other senior Washington officials to Honolulu to put their heads together with Lodge, Harkins, and their Saigon staffs. The purpose of the November 20 conference, JFK told the press, was "to attempt to assess the situation, what American policy should be, what our aid policy should be, how we can intensify the struggle, how we can bring Americans out of there."

As Forrestal was getting ready for his flight to Hawaii, Kennedy called him aside. "He said, 'When you come back . . . I want to start a complete and very profound review of how we got into this country, what we thought we were doing, and what we now think we can do,'" Forrestal remembered. Kennedy added: "I even want to think about whether or not we should be there."

The Honolulu briefings unfolded in a predictable manner—Lodge and Harkins made generally optimistic noises—until McNamara zeroed in on South Vietnam's anemic economy, plagued by perilously large budget deficits. The defense secretary warned that the revenue shortfalls left the generals "sitting on top of a keg of political dynamite" and "right on the ragged edge of running out of money needed to win the war."

Some in the Washington delegation flew home distinctly unimpressed with the performances of both Lodge and Harkins. McCone returned "more discouraged about South Vietnam than ever in the past." He believed that McNamara and Bundy felt the same way.

Bundy told his White House staff that Lodge wasn't up to the changed circumstances of his job. As a strong-willed, lone-wolf type, he'd been the right man to spur on the coup generals. Now, however, what the embassy needed was a skilled, hard-driving manager to lead a large team of people in carrying out a multitude of complex civilian and military programs. Lodge, said Bundy, "apparently has neither the inclination for, nor the interest in this type of management task."

Bundy further noted that Harkins was convinced he'd lost Lodge's confidence, and that the ongoing alienation between the two men was affecting U.S. operations. Colby told McCone that he, too, thought Harkins should be removed.

In Honolulu, McCone and Lodge had dined privately and discussed Lodge's political prospects. The CIA director certainly wasn't a fan of Lodge, but both men were experienced, high-profile Republicans and McCone may have felt compelled to do what he could to help if Lodge decided to enter the presidential race. McCone offered his opinion that the ambassador would emerge from his stint in Saigon "either as a political giant 14 feet tall or as a thoroughly washed-up government official." But, as the intelligence chief wrote later, Lodge "did not care much for this frank view."

ON NOVEMBER 21, KENNEDY and his wife, Jacqueline, boarded Air Force One for a two-day, five-city tour of Texas. He spent part of that morning reading an article in *The New Republic* about South Vietnam's new leaders.

Prior to leaving, the president told Kenneth O'Donnell that he wanted to run up a landslide reelection victory in 1964. A big win, he believed, would give him the political cover necessary to pull U.S. troops out of the war, a move that wouldn't be popular. But he felt that American involvement would only grow deeper and more costly over time, without doing much to contain communist expansion in Southeast Asia.

The trip to Texas was a political one, aimed at raising campaign money and trying to woo more of the oil executives, businessmen, and well-off suburbanites who made up the conservative wing of the Texas Democratic Party. The Kennedys spent their first night at a Fort Worth hotel. On the morning of November 22, standing hatless in light rain outside the hotel, JFK spoke briefly to a friendly crowd of several thousand. Then he flew on to Dallas.

Lee Harvey Oswald shot and fatally wounded the president at about 12:30 p.m. that afternoon as he rode in an open convertible to the Dallas Trade Mart for a lunch speech. He was pronounced dead at 1 p.m. at Parkland Memorial Hospital after a priest gave him last rites.

His assassination came just twenty days after Diem's.

Early the next morning in Tay Ninh, Samuel Thomsen, a U.S. civilian adviser, was walking to the province chief's house to officially inform him of JFK's death. It was a beautiful autumn day.

A little boy approached Thomsen. He was about eight or nine years old and he was crying. He was so sorry, he said in Vietnamese, that the American president, who'd done so much for his country, was gone.

CHAPTER 21

"LET US CONTINUE"

LODGE PACKED HIS bags after the Honolulu conference and headed for Washington.

He was staying at the elegant old St. Francis Hotel in San Francisco when Kennedy was shot. The ambassador was supposed to have lunch with JFK two days later at his new Virginia country house. He phoned McGeorge Bundy to see whether he was still needed in Washington. Bundy told him to come ahead; the new president needed his counsel more than the old one.

Lodge reached the capital on Saturday, November 23. A steady rain was falling and the White House was draped in black. He joined the throngs of people filing past JFK's casket as his remains lay in state in the East Room; many of the mourners were weeping.

The following afternoon Lodge met Lyndon Johnson in his former vice presidential office, a roomy, high-ceilinged suite in the Executive Office Building, adjacent to the White House. Johnson had just come from the Capitol, where he placed a wreath on JFK's bier in the Rotunda. His eyes brimmed with tears, and his long, deeply lined Texas hound-dog face was drawn.

LBJ had met Diem during a whirlwind, campaign-style visit to South Vietnam in May 1961, overpraising him as "the Churchill of Southeast Asia." He liked the Vietnamese leader enough to display an autographed photo of him in his office. Johnson thought the coup was a bad idea, though he hadn't vocally opposed it in the few Vietnam meetings he attended. Like JFK, he was repulsed by Diem's murder. As he later lamented to Democratic Senator Eugene McCarthy: "We killed him. We all got together and got a goddamn bunch of thugs and we went in and assassinated him."

Oswald's bullets made Johnson the "accidental president," and few men ever entered the Oval Office on shakier political legs. Though a towering figure in the Senate, the fifty-five-year-old LBJ wasn't a skilled orator or the leader of a powerful political bloc. Liberals were uncomfortable with him as a Southerner, and the Eastern media often caricatured his countrified speech and mannerisms. Kennedy and his inner circle never fully accepted him and he was locked in an increasingly bitter feud with Robert Kennedy, who regarded him as "mean, bitter, vicious—an animal in many ways."

Johnson wanted to drape himself with JFK's mantle as quickly as possible. Returning from Dallas on Air Force One after the assassination, he silently vowed to carry out his predecessor's programs and commitments, including in Vietnam. When he landed at Andrews Air Force Base, he was met by McNamara, Bundy, and George Ball, who flew in the helicopter with him to the White House. Johnson told Kennedy's advisers they were the best men around, he needed them, and he wanted them all to stay in their jobs. He later asked every member of JFK's cabinet and White House staff to stick with him; most did.

For LBJ, an exodus of Kennedy people from the White House would have meant an exodus of Democratic Party confidence in him. As he later told his biographer Doris Kearns: "I needed that White House staff. Without them I would have lost my link to John Kennedy, and without that I would have had absolutely no chance of gaining the support of the media or the Easterners or the intellectuals. And without that support I would have had absolutely no chance of governing the country."

Both Eisenhower and LBJ's longtime friend, Democratic Senator Richard Russell of Georgia, chairman of the Senate Armed Services Committee, urged him to clean house and bring in his own people. But there was no time to hire an entirely new staff. More important, Johnson wanted to make it clear that he was but a loyal trustee who could be depended on to carry forward Kennedy's domestic and foreign policies.

As he declared before a joint session of Congress on November 27: "Let us continue."

KENNEDY'S STAFF ALSO HELPED Johnson paper over one of his greatest deficits: a conspicuous lack of experience in foreign affairs. "Johnson came in and didn't know up from down on foreign policy; that was his Achilles' heel," said David Bell, who headed the U.S. Agency for International Development under both Kennedy and Johnson.

LBJ knew enough, however, to recognize that South Vietnam was a political tar pit. As a U.S. senator, he'd been one of the most vocal congressional opponents of using American forces to help the French break the siege of Dien Bien Phu. He and Russell agreed that one of the central lessons of the Korean War was that the United States should never again mire itself in an Asian land war.

After his 1961 visit, Johnson told Kennedy that the United States should make clear to Diem that, short of an invasion by Hanoi, it wouldn't commit combat troops to defend South Vietnam "or [use] even naval or air-support which is but the first step in that direction." The vice president noted France's inability to pacify the country with several hundred thousand soldiers and warned against sending U.S. troops to die in Vietnamese jungles and rice paddies while "our principal enemies China and the Soviet Union stand outside the fray and husband their strength." But Johnson would gradually abandon his own advice as South Vietnam unraveled in the months ahead.

LBJ put great stock in some of JFK's men, particularly McNamara, who he revered as "the ablest man I ever met." McNamara, for his part, barely knew Johnson when he assumed the presidency. But he came to view him as "one of the most complex, intelligent and hardworking individuals I have ever known," with a multifaceted personality that was by turns open and devious, gentle and tough, compassionate and cruel.

Johnson largely delegated running the U.S. war effort to McNamara. A master of domestic politics, he feared making a serious mistake in the realm of foreign affairs. He believed that if men with foreign policy expertise approved his actions, he was protected from accidentally plunging the country into a crisis or making himself look incompetent or foolish. Ironically, it was McNamara and other Kennedy advisers—brought to the White House by a president deeply wary of military entanglements abroad—who nudged and cajoled LBJ ever further down the path toward the Americanization of the war that proved so tragic.

LODGE TOOK A SEAT in LBJ's vice presidential office, joining McNamara, Bundy, Rusk, Ball, and McCone.

The ambassador's first report to his new boss was predictably bullish. The junta, he said, was a distinct improvement over Diem, and the generals were expected to show marked progress in the war in the next few months. Lodge insisted that Americans were "in no way responsible" for the deaths of Diem and Nhu, and that if the brothers had only followed his advice, they'd still be alive. He showed photos of festive, post-coup crowds in Saigon, saying South Vietnamese were very happy with Diem's downfall. He also claimed to have saved the life of Diem's brother Ngo Dinh Can.

But Lodge, usually the embodiment of patrician aplomb, seemed nervous and "didn't distinguish himself" in his initial audience with the new president, according to Bundy. He speculated to Harriman that the ambassador "may know that [LBJ] never thought much of him." Indeed, Johnson later told Bundy he'd always regarded Lodge, his vice presidential opponent in 1960, as a "headline-hunting phony."

Worried that LBJ would get the wrong impression from Lodge's rosy summation, McCone said the CIA's estimate of the situation in South Vietnam was "somewhat more serious."

The VC had intensified their attacks since the coup, he told the president, and heavy traffic on their radio networks might indicate preparations for a new offensive. The generals were having trouble organizing their government and were getting little help from civilian political leaders, who seemed willing, as usual, to do nothing more than carp from the sidelines. McCone saw little reason for optimism.

LBJ bluntly told Lodge he'd never been happy with the U.S. operation in Vietnam. He noted that critics were raising questions about the degree to which Washington had supported the coup, and that some in Congress were calling for a U.S. pullout. Lodge, he said, needed to clean up the embassy: no more bickering, no more leaking. Anyone who didn't comply was to be fired. Johnson would hold Lodge personally responsible.

Too often, the president continued, U.S. foreign aid efforts seemed intended to remake the target country in America's image. That was a mistake, he said. He wanted U.S. officials in Vietnam to concentrate more on winning the war, and less on "so-called social reforms." "I am not going to lose Vietnam," LBJ declared. "I am not going to be the president who saw Southeast Asia go the way China went." He faced his advisers and demanded: "Win the war!"

Relaxing after Lodge and the others had departed that Sunday afternoon, LBJ tilted back in his big chair and swirled the ice cubes in his glass. His young special assistant, Bill Moyers, was the only other person in the room.

Moyers asked how the meeting with Lodge had gone. Johnson gave him a rundown, adding that he planned to stand by the generals, but wanted them to "get off their butts and get out in those jungles and whip hell out of some communists." Then he wanted to put Vietnam aside because "I've got some bigger things to do right here at home."

Moyers said he hoped the president got his wish. LBJ was quiet for a while, swiveling back and forth in his chair and staring at the high ceiling. He hoped he got his wish, too. But at that moment, he said, his predicament in Vietnam made him feel like a Texas catfish that had just swallowed a juicy worm "with a right sharp hook in the middle of it."

AS BIG MINH AND the other generals struggled to establish themselves, the VC launched a wave of military and terrorist strikes intended to demonstrate that the new government wasn't able to protect its people.

Communist activity—military attacks, harassing fire, terrorist incidents, and propaganda activities—doubled in the weeks after the coup. Their weapons, tactics, and communications had improved. They'd learned how to jam ARVN radio calls for artillery support and use hamlet frequencies to lure militiamen into ambushes. Their combat units were equipped with Chinese-supplied 75-millimeter recoilless rifles and 60-millimeter mortars. Since May, they'd captured 2,700 weapons more than they lost—enough to arm seven guerrilla battalions.

By conservative estimate, Viet Cong strength was now 80,000 to 100,000 fighters, including at least 21,000 to 23,000 well-trained regulars. The South Vietnamese had increased their armed forces to a half million, including 215,000 regular troops, 83,000 in the Civil Guard, and 200,000 in paramilitary groups such as the Self-Defense Corps and hamlet militias.

Even before the coup, the VC had regained much of the momentum they lost during the early stages of the U.S. buildup. They tightened their grip in provinces immediately south and north of Saigon, building up strong bases in areas where the ARVN seldom penetrated. Food was plentiful and VC units could easily slip over the Cambodian border to rest and refit.

The communists' campaign against strategic hamlets was made easier by the junta's wholesale switching of province chiefs, which nearly paralyzed the government apparatus in much of the countryside. "The political impetus had gone out of every program there was, including the strategic hamlet program," recalled James Rosenthal, an embassy officer who often visited the delta. "Because there was so much turmoil in Saigon, the people in the field didn't know who was in charge, who to report to, who to be loyal to, what program was the one they were supposed to carry out."

The hamlet program had stalled during the summer and fall as Diem and Nhu became distracted by street protests, coup rumors, and escalating pressure from the Americans. The ARVN had never been closely involved with the program, and the coup generals, trying to distance themselves from anything associated with Nhu, made little effort to reinvigorate it, despite Big Minh's embrace of the oil spot strategy.

The South Vietnamese increased the tempo of their operations and emphasized new tactics such as night patrols and ambushes. They boosted their psychological warfare activities, with emphasis on the Open Arms program, which sought to encourage VC defections. The junta leaders recognized that the war was going poorly in the delta and put some of their top commanders there. But the communists were deeply entrenched in many areas and didn't pause in their long-running efforts to win peasant hearts and minds.

Traveling agitprop troupes entertained the inhabitants of remote villages with songs, dances, and plays larded with anti-government propaganda—to which rural audiences often responded with enthusiasm.

The VC operated their own schools almost side by side with government schools. A radio broadcast by the National Liberation Front on November 19 claimed the communists had some one thousand schools with 2 million pupils in "freed areas" of South Vietnam. Though probably inflated, the figures suggested "a fairly extensive Communist educational effort," according to the CIA.

Speaking with Rufus Phillips, Prime Minister Tho said the South Vietnamese government had been losing popular support in the delta for a long time and was losing the war there as a consequence. One only needed to look at the statistics for VC strength in the region, which was higher than it was two years ago, even though some twenty thousand enemy fighters had been killed during that period.

One big reason for the government's waning support, Tho said, was its insistence on using forced labor to build strategic hamlets. In his home province, An Giang, on the Cambodian border west of Saigon, peasants had to work on government projects without pay for up to a hundred days a year. That cost them as much as one thousand piastres, either because they couldn't do their own work during that time or had to hire someone to take their place in a construction gang. Many peasants broke down and cried when describing the situation to Tho. The VC, meanwhile, collected only fifty to a hundred piastres in taxes, causing many peasants to side with them. Tho wanted to build more strategic hamlets, but some way had to be found, he said, to pay people for their labor.

By early December, the pace of enemy attacks had slowed, but remained well above normal levels. The intensified activity, the CIA reported, appeared to be aimed as much at testing the new military government and making a psychological impact on its citizens as at gaining any battlefield advantage. "The Communists," wrote Chester Cooper, the CIA Vietnam expert on the National Security Council, "apparently hope to encourage internal strains in the new regime until its leadership bogs down and the war-weary South Vietnamese and US public become receptive to a negotiated solution."

TWO WEEKS AFTER THE coup, Halberstam took a lengthy reporting trip to the delta to see how things were shaping up under the junta. What he saw and heard saddened him.

There was noticeable deterioration since his first foray there in the fall of 1962, when the government seemingly had a decent chance of prevailing. Now VC sniper fire met planes as they landed at government airstrips. In villages once controlled by Saigon, children looked away when ARVN soldiers marched through. Touring one village with an American officer, Halberstam spotted a VC flag flying from the roof of a small Catholic church. The officer asked the young priest to explain.

"It is very simple, Captain," the priest replied. "You and the government come here once every three or four months and you have tea with me and then you leave. But the Viet Cong are here every night, and this is the price they exact for the survival of my church. They are very clever, I think."

Halberstam spent most of his time, as he often had in the past, in areas patrolled by the Seventh Division. With the recent addition of another ARVN division to the delta, the Seventh's jurisdiction had shifted. It was now responsible for four provinces, including Long An and Dinh Tuong. About 1.5 million people lived in Long An and Dinh Tuong.

Halberstam's findings appeared on the front page of *The New York Times*. He wrote that VC forces had "seized the initiative" and were threatening government control of Long An and Dinh Tuong. One U.S. adviser told him the situation was "desperate." The Seventh Division was being "extremely cautious" about getting into firefights with VC regulars, effectively ceding territory to the enemy.

Of the more than four hundred strategic hamlets in the two provinces, no more than 20 percent were militarily viable, Halberstam wrote. "Our side got the people into these strategic hamlets and then we weren't able to protect them," a U.S. embassy officer told him. VC squads used many hamlets as way stations, stopping at night for food and sleep before moving on. They often forced residents to tear down the hamlet's barbed-wire barriers and take the roofs off their own houses as gestures of submission.

Halberstam's time in South Vietnam was nearly over. On his last day, December 9, his journalist buddies organized a boisterous send-off for him at Tan Son Nhut. Arnett described it as "a victory party."

After all, Halberstam's stories had repeatedly contradicted the saccharine appraisals of the war by MACV and the embassy. His reporting had both angered Washington policymakers and made them think twice about what they were doing in South Vietnam. In the years to come, as the war grew bigger and uglier, Halberstam's coverage would serve as a model for other reporters who came to Vietnam. Bear-hugging his colleagues goodbye, he expressed his only regret: exiting Saigon before Harkins.

IT WAS BECOMING CLEAR that Big Minh and the coup generals weren't up to running the government. Other than flushing Diemists out of the army and civil bureaucracy, they seemed to have no coherent vision for the future. The citizenry that once cheered them as liberators and heroes now began to regard them with disappointment and distrust.

The junta, the CIA's Colby concluded, "proved weak, indecisive, and incapable of governing, demonstrating the folly of our having concentrated wholly on the weaknesses and evils of the Diem regime to the exclusion of any serious discussion on what would replace it."

Though popular, Big Minh turned out to be an indolent and ineffective chief of state. He skipped meetings at the U.S. embassy and seemed content to drift. Lodge asked General Don several times to get Minh moving, but "my lazy friend," as Don called him, wouldn't budge. His "only decisive act," Colby noted sarcastically, was killing Diem and Nhu.

Prime Minister Tho was another problem. Short, balding, and often smiling cheerfully, the fifty-five-year-old Tho had served as a province chief under the French and as interior minister in Diem's first cabinet. He subsequently was appointed ambassador to Japan and economy minister before being named vice president in 1958. An economist by profession and a Buddhist, Tho worked with American experts in 1961 to overhaul South Vietnam's antiquated and inefficient tax system.

But like Diem, Tho was detail-oriented and slow to make decisions. Job hunters and favor-seekers laid siege to his office. He seemed overwhelmed by his new duties and became a symbol of the junta's irresolution. After Tho engaged in a heated confrontation with Vietnamese journalists during a press conference, the CIA predicted that he'd "increasingly be a center of controversy and a political liability for General Minh."

Jean Lacouture, the French journalist, labeled the generals "invisible men" who'd retreated behind the well-guarded walls of their headquarters, cutting off contact with the public and communicating their ideas and intentions only through statements to the press. They seemed to have no plan for land reform or any other programs to help the poor and dispossessed of South Vietnam. And as their popularity declined, political unrest resurfaced.

In Hue, ten thousand students protested because the generals hadn't fired several pro-Diem professors at the university. Buddhists, too, were restless over the continued—and, as they saw it, pernicious—presence of old Diemists such as Tho in the new government.

Faced with such pressures, the generals accelerated their expulsion of Diem associates. Province chiefs, military commanders, and department heads considered too close to the old regime got the boot. The generals were well on their way to replacing all of the 41 province chiefs and most of the 253 district chiefs. In some provinces, the chiefs turned over five or six times in the junta's first few months. In all, about 7,500 civil servants throughout the country were abruptly dismissed.

At the same time, General Dinh, Saigon's military governor, continued to make a spectacle of himself, while inducing spasms of unease in his fellow junta members.

Western photographers talked him into going to a nightclub and doing the twist, apparently to show how modern and in tune with the public he was. When Marguerite Higgins interviewed him, she was startled by Dinh's hints that not only was Big Minh guilty of Diem's murder, he was an incompetent chief of state. Dinh even suggested it might become necessary for him to oust the junta leader at some point. Higgins was astonished that Dinh would make such comments to a journalist; it didn't bode well for the generals' chances to stay unified.

Higgins also asked the coup leaders, in separate interviews, which U.S. actions had prompted them to move against Diem.

They cited JFK's "changes in policy and perhaps with personnel" comment as well as his announcement that a thousand U.S. advisers would be withdrawn by the end of 1963, and most of the rest by 1965. "That convinced us that unless we got rid of Diem, you would abandon us," said one general.

The most decisive goad was the suspension of economic aid, which convinced the generals that Washington was finally ready to let go of Diem. They wanted to win the war, and they knew that was impossible without American dollars. "In cutting economic aid, the United States was forcing us to choose between your country's help in the war and Diem," said one plotter. "So, we chose the United States."

Yet despite the resumption of U.S. aid, the military government was so dysfunctional by December that nine worried province chiefs wired Big Minh: "Please send us orders." The Viet Cong made more gains. On top of everything came a poor rice harvest and a cholera epidemic.

THROUGH IT ALL, LODGE seemed "surprised and puzzled," according to Mecklin.

Arguably, no U.S. ambassador ever had or ever would have a better opportunity to work with Saigon leaders to bring together South Vietnam's diverse people behind a new, popularly accepted government. But Lodge was unprepared or unwilling to use his influence and U.S. power for such a project.

He resisted digging into the junta's problems. His approach seemed based instead on the gossamer hope that the lackluster Big Minh would somehow metamorphose into a skilled and inspiring leader. He didn't discuss the structure or functioning of Minh's government with him. Nor did he encourage him to bring Buddhist clergy or laymen into his inner circle in order to cement Buddhist support. Instead, Lodge seemed increasingly distracted by the multiplying reports from home that he had a chance to win the Republican presidential nomination. (*The New York Times*, for instance, reported on December 8 that Eisenhower had urged Lodge to jump into the GOP primary race against Goldwater.)

Lodge did find time, however, to try to bury the ninety-page report issued by the United Nations investigators who looked into charges that Diem's government violated Buddhist rights.

The UN published the report in early December, but it contained no findings and received little attention in the press, except for Catholic media. A reporter for a Catholic news service contacted one of the investigators, Fernando Volio Jiménez, Costa Rica's ambassador to the UN. Volio Jiménez stated that his team's numerous interviews in South Vietnam uncovered no evidence of a deliberate Diem policy to persecute or discriminate against Buddhists.

"When a witness tried to give some concrete proof to the [UN] mission, the incident he cited came down to individual or personal actions," Volio Jiménez said. "On the basis of the evidence, there was not a governmental policy against the Buddhists on religious grounds." He explained that the UN team decided not to publish any findings or conclusions because the Diem regime no longer existed.

The UN inquiry had been undertaken at the request of Ceylon, a majority Buddhist nation whose politicians and newspapers had vociferously criticized Diem. Ceylon was represented at the UN by Sir Senerat Gunewardene, a lawyer, diplomat, and former president of the All-Ceylon Buddhist Congress. Gunewardene had worked with Lodge when he was U.S. ambassador to the UN and considered him a personal friend.

When the UN delegation was in Saigon, Gunewardene paid a call on Lodge, and the two men met again in Washington just before the Buddhist report was to come up for discussion in the UN General Assembly. Since the persecution charge was a central element of the Kennedy administration's casus belli against Diem, the absence of evidence to sustain it wouldn't reflect well on the administration and its fallen leader.

A UN debate on the report was likely to result in coverage by the world press. Lodge asked Gunewardene to discourage any such airing, and the Ceylonese envoy agreed to do so as a personal favor. On December 13, the General Assembly closed the investigation with no public discussion of what its investigators had found.

The handling of the report so incensed Senator Thomas Dodd, a Connecticut Democrat, that he called Volio Jiménez, who confirmed that the UN team uncovered no Diem-sanctioned oppression. In a subsequent letter to a U.S. Senate subcommittee, Dodd said his reading of the report led him to conclude that news accounts of "massive persecution of the Buddhist religion were, at the best, vastly exaggerated, at the worst, a sordid propaganda fraud.

"What this adds up to, in my opinion," Dodd continued, "is that the American people have once again been grievously misinformed by some of their newspapers on a foreign situation that vitally concerns them. We were told that the Diem government was guilty of such brutal religious persecution that innocent Buddhist monks had been driven to commit suicide in protest. Now it turns out that the persecution was either nonexistent or vastly exaggerated, and that the agitation was essentially political."

Time magazine wrote that Dodd's letter revived the bitter controversy over whether Halberstam and other Saigon journalists "may have distorted the news and helped shape Washington's Viet Nam policy." Conservative columnist William F. Buckley labeled as "fishy" the UN decision not to publish any findings. The Senate published the report in its entirety, but Lodge's efforts had helped to smother public awareness of it.

IN MID-DECEMBER, EVERETT BUMGARDNER, the Vietnamese-speaking chief of field operations for the U.S. Information Service, interviewed about three hundred secondary school students in Long An Province. Bumgardner wanted to find out why the Viet Cong were making so much headway in Long An. What the kids had to say was deeply revealing.

Bumgardner began his interviews at a school in the provincial capital of Tan An. Most of the students were from families living in strategic hamlets, and the idea was to give them a chance to talk freely, away from their parents and possible VC agents. Bumgardner spoke with the youngsters under a large shade tree, and more and more of them showed up as the discussion went on.

The students saw themselves as mere bystanders in the war between the Saigon government and the communists. Their primary concern was to keep clear of the fighting and stay alive. They said bluntly that they didn't care who won—an opinion that under South Vietnamese law constituted sedition—and would be fine with either a communist or noncommunist government, if only the death and destruction would stop.

Besides being able to live in peace and safety, the teens wanted to be allowed to move back to their old homes. Houses in the strategic hamlets, they said, were too small and too close together, and required them to walk long distances to get to their fields. Moreover, the government had never made the promised payments to those who relocated.

While the students respected ARVN soldiers, they complained bitterly about Self-Defense Corps militiamen who mistreated them, stole their chickens, and refused to go out and fight. The VC, they said, laughed at the Self-Defense Corps and the Civil Guard, but were afraid of the ARVN.

Bumgardner also interviewed students in the Can Duc district, considered the most VC-infested part of the province. Their responses were similar to those of the first group, especially their yearning to live in peace and their intense dislike of the Self-Defense Corps.

Both groups of youngsters had loathed the Diem government. Their ire was directed not at the president but at his local representatives, such as the police, hamlet construction bosses, and militiamen. When Bumgardner asked the kids where VC recruits came from, they candidly said "from us." The communists, they said, told them they'd eventually have to join either the ARVN or the guerrillas. If they sided with the communists, they'd at least be allowed to fight in their home areas and stay with their families. The ARVN would send them far away to fight and die. As a result, many teens joined the VC.

The students had a favorable impression of the new military government, noting that many of its members were southerners, and expressed a willingness to give it a chance. But their naive disinterest in which side ultimately won the war was alarming. Reading Bumgardner's survey results, another U.S. official in Saigon wrote: "It appears that we have failed completely to explain either the faults of a Communist system or the benefits of freedom to these students."

Another unnerving report came from David Smith, the acting CIA station chief.

In a December 17 memo to McCone, Smith predicted a possible counter-coup against the junta unless Big Minh took a stronger leadership role. Calling him the "reluctant dragon," Smith wrote that not only was Minh failing to correct the mistakes and abuses of the Diem era, he was dragging his feet on enacting sensible programs his fellow generals were proposing. "The problem to be resolved," Smith wrote, "is to pressure Minh into accepting a role to which he does not aspire." While the bluff general enjoyed personal prestige and popularity, he lacked the driving ambition and opportunistic instincts required to become what South Vietnam needed, a "benevolent strongman."

Minh also was being tarred by his association with the increasingly unpopular Tho, who'd become a lightning rod for dissatisfaction among Buddhists and students, Smith indicated. Many older nationalist politicians simply refused to work with Tho. The primary rationale for installing him as premier—preserving the constitutional line of succession—became moot when the generals tossed out the constitution. Describing Tho as a millstone around Minh's neck, Smith wrote that "his early departure would be desirable."

As a result of Big Minh's inertia, a power vacuum was forming that could easily be "filled by less palatable individuals," Smith continued. He named General Dinh as well as General Nguyen Khanh, recently reassigned to command I Corps, the ARVN's northernmost army group. Khanh was becoming a vocal critic of the junta's lack of progress, and some suspected he'd been shipped farther north to keep him as far from the Saigon political scene as possible.

Minh was the only figure who could regain the momentum the junta had lost since the coup, Smith wrote. He needed to be pushed to make a clear statement about when the country could expect a new constitution, elections, and democratic reforms. "Without clean lines of advice and guidance from top U.S. levels," Smith went on, the military government would continue to meander, opening the door to another coup.

It was a warning that soon proved prescient.

IN WASHINGTON, LBJ AND his team began to realize that South Vietnam was in far worse shape than they'd realized—a "god-awful mess," as McNamara put it. With Diem gone, the country now struggled under an ineffectual military government, a weak economy, serious religious divisions, corruption, and, worst of all, a widening guerrilla insurgency that was making significant gains in the wake of the coup.

The nonstop optimism that had radiated from the embassy and MACV was exposed as wishful thinking; the recent euphoria of the dump-Diem partisans gave way to a sense of foreboding.

LBJ called in McNamara and gave him "quite a lecture" on Vietnam, expressing his concern "that we as a government were not doing everything we should." The president told him to make another inspection trip soon. McNamara did so, arriving in Saigon on December 19 and characteristically plunging into meeting after meeting with American and South Vietnamese officials.

The briefings were a highly unpleasant wake-up call. The defense secretary discovered that many of the reports he received from Saigon indicating progress in the war were based on inflated statistics and false information. His neck reddened as he listened to one MACV briefer after another repeat Harkins's mantra that a military victory was just six months away.

"I'm totally dissatisfied with this reporting," McNamara snapped at one point. "It is unsatisfactory to have all of you say the same thing."

By contrast with the confidence at headquarters, U.S. field advisers delivered "uniformly discouraging" updates on the state of the war in six important provinces around Saigon and in the delta. Long An, Big Minh's home province, was in particularly bad shape. Remarkably, the VC had more soldiers there than the ARVN—about 7,900 versus 5,900.

The VC controlled large swaths of two other provinces, Kien Hoa and Binh Duong. In the latter, one adviser said, "the people are not afraid of the Viet Cong but go to them with their administrative problems" and pay taxes to them as well. The ARVN's Ninth Division, recently shifted from the Central Highlands to the delta, had engaged in few operations so far, partly because its troops had to be taught how to swim in delta waterways.

Those waterways—4,700 miles of rivers and canals along which the VC moved fighters and supplies—posed a major problem. MACV presented a plan to create a system of barriers, checkpoints, patrols, and curfews intended to restrict VC movements. But William H. Sullivan, who attended the briefing in his role as Harriman's special assistant, criticized the plan as "not very useful," since it didn't address the smuggling of heavy weapons and ammunition down the Mekong and other rivers from Cambodia.

Meeting with Big Minh, his top generals, and Premier Tho, McNamara irritably demanded: "Who is the boss here?" Big Minh looked at his colleagues and said nothing; they responded only with "courteous smiles." Later Minh insisted he was in charge. McNamara argued that the generals were each trying to do too much; Don, for instance, served as both defense minister and chief of the Joint General Staff. The generals insisted such dual roles were only temporary, but "could not convince the hostile secretary."

McNamara then "brought up the question of General Minh's acting like a chief of state and making some speeches to the people which would give them hope and faith in the future." Minh countered that he and Tho had just held two press conferences and asked, somewhat meekly, "Wasn't that enough?" The generals tried to explain that South Vietnam wasn't like Western democracies. The Vietnamese people were "extremely difficult," and if the junta members gave too many speeches, people would label them dictators.

MCCONE, TOO, HAD COME to Saigon, both to attend the briefings and introduce his new station chief, Peer de Silva.

The balding, forty-six-year-old de Silva was a West Point graduate who, toward the end of World War II, had become chief of security for the Manhattan Project, the top secret U.S. effort to build an atomic bomb. Despite this background, he had an "almost pathological distrust of the military," according to Halberstam, and resigned from the Army to join the CIA in 1953. Prior to Saigon, he ran CIA stations in Hong Kong, South Korea, and Austria.

Lodge had wanted the station chief job to go to David Smith, perhaps because he figured the younger man would be easier to control. But LBJ instructed the ambassador to work closely and cooperatively with de Silva without any more backbiting or muttering to the press.

"I cannot overemphasize the importance which I personally attach to correcting the situation which has existed in Saigon in the past," the president wrote to Lodge.

McCone, Colby, de Silva, and Smith had a strained lunch with the ambassador at his residence on December 18.

The CIA chief had warned de Silva that Lodge could be cold-blooded and abrupt, and the ambassador didn't take long to prove the point. Gesturing in de Silva's direction, Lodge emphasized that he neither wanted or needed a new station chief. While he knew and liked Smith, he continued, de Silva was an unknown quantity and could "only be a bother."

De Silva and Smith studied the ceiling in embarrassment as they were discussed "like competitors at a dog show," de Silva recalled. McCone, "wearing a tight little smile," said that unless Lodge had some material reason for rejecting de Silva, he as CIA director had to insist that the new man be accepted as station chief. (When Smith assured Lodge that he always expected to be replaced by a more senior CIA officer, the ambassador snapped: "Do you think I give a damn about you?")

McCone also implored Lodge to refrain from mentioning de Silva's name to the press, noting that Richardson's usefulness as station chief ended when his name was leaked. Lodge protested that he "had no control over the press," but McCone insisted there was "ample evidence that Richardson's name had been discussed freely with press," and he didn't want the same thing to happen to de Silva.

After McCone dismissed his CIA subordinates, he and Lodge had another tête-à-tête about the ambassador's prospects for winning the Republican presidential nomination.

Lodge claimed he "had no ambitions," but was being deluged with requests to enter the upcoming New Hampshire primary election; he wanted McCone's advice on what to do. The CIA chief observed that Lodge had a vital job in Vietnam, and that "the greatest harm that could come to him would be to walk away from this job." Lodge was in "a very delicate situation," McCone said, and shouldn't do any campaigning or permit his name to appear on any primary ballots as long as he was ambassador.

McCone also met that day with Harkins, who confidently declared: "This operation will be reduced to a police action after the middle of 1964."

CONFRONTED WITH A QUICKSILVER war with no clear-cut battle lines, McNamara relied on numbers to measure progress: numbers of VC killed, of weapons seized, of strategic hamlets completed. A onetime Price, Waterhouse accountant and assistant business professor at Harvard, he spent World War II teaching U.S. Army Air Corps officers to perform statistical analyses to determine how many bombers were available to fly each day. He saw numbers as a way of comprehending the world, once describing mathematics as "a language in which to express much, but certainly not all, of human activity."

Most numbers about the war were supplied by the Diem government. But the coup revealed that much of that data was fictitious. The problem was particularly egregious with the strategic hamlets, many of which now looked more like Potemkin villages. Of the 8,600 hamlets reported as finished and properly defended, only 20 percent actually were secure. Although the Diem regime claimed there were 219 fortified hamlets in Long An Province, for instance, just 45 could be identified in the wake of the coup.

In his memoir, Hilsman told a revealing anecdote about Saigon's massaging of numbers. "Ah, les statistiques!" an ARVN general exclaimed to an American friend. "Your secretary of defense loves statistics. We Vietnamese can give him all he wants. If you want them to go up, they will go up. If you want them to go down, they will go down."

Such deceptiveness was nothing new. As early as March 1962, Army intelligence analysts in Hawaii warned that the ARVN's psychological warfare chief "has ordered government casualty figures to be slashed by 30 percent and enemy losses augmented by the same amount."

According to Mecklin, government statistics on the number of VC killed in action were "a joke around Saigon." The Diem regime frequently pumped up KIA figures by counting innocent civilian victims of artillery fire and air strikes as enemy casualties. It was often difficult to distinguish peasants from VC, and unless a corpse could be positively identified as a civilian, it was counted as a combatant.

Not only were the statistics unreliable, they were often open to interpretation. When the number of attacks on a defended hamlet dropped to zero, did that mean the VC had given up and moved on, or that they'd successfully infiltrated and taken over that hamlet? Even Lodge complained of "the multiplicity of often contradictory military, political, social and economic 'facts'—any one of which can be used to prove almost anything."

Halberstam recalled an argument between Sheehan and a high-ranking U.S. officer over the meaning of the ARVN's kill statistics. The officer claimed that a high number meant the army was destroying the enemy and winning the war. But Sheehan countered that if the ARVN was winning, it should be killing fewer and fewer VC as the insurgency weakened and enemy ranks thinned—a point with which many counterinsurgency experts agreed. Instead, the ranks of main-force VC units expanded even as their casualty figures rose.

Even accurate data had limited value when applied to revolutionary warfare. Numbers could take you only so far in understanding the shape and nature of such a conflict. Certain measurements could be useful, such as how many soldiers deserted and how many weapons were lost to the enemy. But numbers couldn't express the communists' progress in extending their political and administrative control in the countryside. Nor could they measure the VC's ability to learn from mistakes and adapt to changing battlefield conditions.

In spite of the post-coup revelations, McNamara's faith in statistics wasn't completely shaken, according to de Silva. The new CIA station chief remembered the defense secretary scribbling on a yellow legal pad as various MACV briefers tossed out numbers on newly built strategic hamlets, terrorist acts, and VC versus ARVN losses. McNamara listened intently and then began bombarding the briefers with questions, mostly about logistics. How many strategic hamlets had been erected since his last visit? How many yards of barbed wire were distributed? Did the ARVN have sufficient fuel and oil? Did it have enough tires?

"I sat there amazed, and thought to myself, what in the world is this man thinking about?" de Silva later wrote. "This is not a problem of logistics and, in any event, there are plenty of people here at MACV fully competent to handle the matériel side of the war. This is a war that needs discussion of strategic purpose and of strategy itself. What is he talking about?"

THE SOUTH VIETNAMESE WEREN'T the only sources of misleading and dishonest information. It emanated from MACV, too.

As a self-described cheerleader for the Saigon army as well as the U.S. advisers under him, Harkins sent his superiors weekly updates called "headway reports," which by their very name implied that allied forces were marching steadily toward victory.

The reports, however, were carefully edited by Harkins's operations chief so that any developments that might reflect adversely on the image of relentless progress were reworded, discounted, or simply deleted, according to George Allen, a veteran intelligence analyst for the U.S. Army, Defense Intelligence Agency, and CIA. "Thus, Washington was consistently fed a somewhat distorted view of the situation," Allen wrote.

He noted that the Diem government supplied MACV with statistics on the strategic hamlets that, by their nature, indicated nothing *but* progress: miles of barbed-wire fences erected, number of corrugated-metal house roofs distributed, number of medical dispensaries set up, and so on.

But such data didn't reflect the impact of VC actions like disemboweling a hamlet chief or tossing a grenade over a fence into a strategic hamlet to terrorize the inhabitants. Nor did they reflect the attitudes of the people penned up in the fortified encampments. Did those people feel safe at night or when working in their fields during the day? Were they convinced that the ARVN would respond swiftly if they came under attack at three o'clock in the morning? Did they feel the government was giving them a real shot at a better future?

Besides selective editing of "headway reports," Allen witnessed Harkins and his staff manipulating information in other ways as well.

In the spring of 1962, Allen helped MACV prepare for a visit by McNamara, Admiral Felt, and General Lyman Lemnitzer, then chairman of the Joint Chiefs of Staff. Allen and his team assembled a map with colored overlays showing the relative degree of control of different parts of South Vietnam by government forces versus the VC. Blue signified areas where government control was strong; red indicated areas of communist dominance.

On the eve of the conference, Allen's group previewed the map for Harkins and his aides. But they expressed "great dismay," saying there was altogether too much red and too little blue. Harkins's intelligence chief, Colonel James Winterbottom, then "began stripping off areas of the red acetate overlay, converting 'Viet Cong control' to 'status unknown,'" Allen recounted.

The next day, Harkins presented the watered-down map to McNamara and his entourage, with the caveat that "it was overly generous to the enemy." Given more time to toss out overlays, Allen noted sarcastically, Winterbottom might have been able to win the war single-handedly—on paper, at least.

After leaving Vietnam, Halberstam wrote an article for *Esquire* magazine that showed MACV simply deep-sixing a negative report. Its author was Colonel Daniel Boone Porter, the ranking U.S. adviser to IV Corps. A professorial-looking man with a briefcase usually tucked under his arm, Porter was reputed to be one of the U.S. Army's top experts in small-unit infantry tactics.

Porter drafted his twenty-five-page report just before the end of his tour. It was sharply critical of ARVN officers, citing their lack of skill in executing battle plans, refusal to care properly for their wounded, and resistance to American advice. Porter's Army peers counseled him to tone it down, but he'd checked with his subordinate advisers and they agreed with his conclusions.

The report, predictably, angered MACV brass. Harkins wanted to know how many copies had been produced, and they were collected. After that, Halberstam wrote, "the report was never seen again."

Were Harkins's actions the product of self-delusion or a deliberate attempt to deceive the Kennedy administration and American public about the state of the war? Some U.S. officials in Saigon concluded the latter. "He was quite notorious for cooking the numbers," remembered Erland Heginbotham, an embassy economic officer.

In the final analysis, Harkins's motives were less important than his deeds. His suppressions and manipulations obscured serious flaws in the war effort that cried out for amelioration. Instead, his trickery and unwarranted optimism misled many Americans, including Vietnam policymakers, into believing that victory was always just another Christmas away.

AFTER A WHIRLWIND THIRTY-SIX hours in Saigon, McNamara was back in Washington, putting on a false front about his findings. "We reviewed the plans of the South Vietnamese," he told the press, "and we have every reason to believe they will be successful."

In truth, the defense secretary had grave doubts about the new government's ability even to survive much longer. "The situation is very disturbing," he wrote in a secret report to President Johnson on December 21, warning of the possibility of a communist takeover within three months.

The generals were "indecisive and drifting"; McNamara wasn't even sure who was in charge. "There is no clear concept," he continued, "on how to re-shape or conduct the strategic hamlet program; the Province Chiefs, most of whom are new and inexperienced, are receiving little or no direction; military operations, too, are not being effectively directed because the generals are so preoccupied with essentially political affairs."

Another overarching problem, McNamara reported, was the American team in Saigon under Lodge: "It lacks leadership, has been poorly informed, and is not working to a common plan." Lodge still was barely communicating with Harkins. The ambassador "sends [Washington] reports with major military implications without showing them to Harkins, and does not show

Harkins important incoming traffic," McNamara went on. "My impression is that Lodge simply does not know how to conduct a coordinated administration. . . . I do not think he is consciously rejecting our advice; he has just operated as a loner all his life and cannot readily change now."

Although there had been serious deterioration in the countryside since July, the Americans were largely blind to it "because of our undue dependence on distorted Vietnamese reporting," McNamara wrote, adding that communist progress since the coup "has been great."

The Viet Cong, he continued, "now control very high proportions of the people in certain key provinces, particularly those directly south and west of Saigon. The Strategic Hamlet Program was seriously over-extended in these provinces, and the Viet Cong has been able to destroy many hamlets, while others have been abandoned or in some cases betrayed or pillaged by the government's own Self Defense Corps. In these key provinces, the Viet Cong have destroyed almost all major roads, and are collecting taxes at will."

The Pentagon and CIA, McNamara said, were "acting vigorously" to improve "the grave reporting weakness." But MACV's plans for interdicting the VC on delta waterways were "unsatisfactory" and a special naval team from Honolulu was being sent to see what else could be done.

More artillery was being shipped to the ARVN and the Self-Defense Corps would get new uniforms to boost its sagging morale, McNamara told Johnson. However, "we should watch the situation very carefully, running scared, hoping for the best, but preparing for more forceful moves if the situation does not show early signs of improvement."

The ARVN continued to stumble, however. On December 31, a Vietnamese Ranger battalion found itself pinned down by two VC battalions. For some reason, an ARVN division commander in III Corps refused to send reinforcements, which the U.S. embassy described as an act of "almost criminal negligence."

WITH MORE THAN 16,000 military personnel in South Vietnam as 1963 ended, the United States found itself in a quagmire. The strategic hamlets were coming apart, the generals weren't running an effective government, and the communists appeared to be stronger than ever.

In addition, neutralist sentiment, though hard to gauge, appeared to be spreading in South Vietnam and internationally as the war dragged on. But President Johnson and almost all of his advisers adamantly opposed neutralization, seeing it as surrender "on the installment plan," as Bundy put it.

The notion of a political settlement of the war again became a focus of debate after Cambodia's prime minister, Norodom Sihanouk, proposed an international conference to discuss ways in which the big powers could guarantee his country's independence and neutrality. The conferees would include the United States, Soviet Union, China, Britain, and France, as well as Laos, Cambodia, and both Vietnams.

Neutralization was gaining traction among some influential Americans, including Walter Lippmann, a widely respected syndicated columnist who often wrote about foreign affairs, and editorial writers at *The New York Times*. The newspaper declared in a December 8 editorial that Sihanouk's proposal "deserves serious consideration," and that a big-power conference should seek the removal of both American and communist forces from South Vietnam.

Another prominent voice calling for a negotiated settlement was Senate Majority Leader Mike Mansfield, who warned LBJ in a December 7 memo that the war might eventually involve U.S. combat forces and spill over into the rest of Southeast Asia and even China. "What national interests in Asia," he asked, "would steel the American people for the massive costs of ever-deepening involvement of that kind?"

Mansfield suggested that the United States should push to expand South Vietnam's control of its territory and then pursue a truce and a coalition government, using France as mediator. Such a formula would reduce the political influence of both Washington and Beijing in Southeast Asia, Mansfield argued, citing neutral Cambodia as the prototype for an eventual peace settlement.

But when Johnson sought the opinions of his three top advisers—McNamara, Rusk, and Bundy—about Mansfield's ideas, they stood shoulder to shoulder in rejecting them.

Bundy invoked the domino theory, saying neutralization would lead not only to a communist seizure of South Vietnam, but a collapse of anti-communist forces in Laos as well. Thailand would move toward neutrality, with China and North Vietnam gaining sway there, and Malaysia would find itself under heavy communist pressure. Even close U.S. allies like Japan and the Philippines would edge toward nonalignment.

What was needed instead, Bundy added, was "a wholly rejuvenated military command and a rapidly stepped-up political effort" in the war. McNamara and Rusk delivered similar memos, with McNamara arguing that the risks to U.S. global interests of losing in South Vietnam were so high that "we must go on bending every effort to win."

De Gaulle triggered a tectonic shift in Cold War diplomacy on January 27, 1964, when France granted diplomatic recognition to communist China, rattling both Washington and Saigon. The following day, an essay carried by Agence France-Presse, the state-owned news agency, suggested the move was part of de Gaulle's plan to neutralize France's former Indochinese colonies.

At the end of World War II, de Gaulle had backed the costly French drive to regain control of those colonies, but eventually concluded that the Viet Minh couldn't be vanquished militarily. In 1962, he'd signed a peace agreement that ended a long, bloody insurgency in Algeria, another one-time colony, even though 500,000 French troops had fought rebel forces to a standstill. He thought the United States should withdraw from South Vietnam, but that China, as Asia's most important power, had to be part of any settlement of the struggle between Saigon and the communists.

De Gaulle tried and failed to interest Kennedy in his ideas and kept talking them up after his assassination. He wanted Washington to pull its forces out as a precondition for peace talks that adhered to principles established by the 1954 Geneva agreement: a commitment by both South and North Vietnam not to enter into military alliances or accept military aid from foreign nations. The eventual goal was reunification of north and south, envisioned but never achieved under the Geneva deal. The great powers, de Gaulle hoped, would enforce the terms of a new agreement.

French officials argued that the North Vietnamese were willing to wait as long as ten years after hostilities ended to achieve their central goal of national reunification, and would accept a neutralized Saigon regime in the meantime. De Gaulle hoped for a new international conference that would lead to eventual neutralization of Vietnam.

The New York Times thought de Gaulle's approach was worth a try, saying in an editorial that "it would be wise for the United States now to welcome rather than to resent General de Gaulle's renewed interest in the Vietnamese problem." Mansfield agreed, urging LBJ in a February 1 memo to encourage the French president, since his idea "offers a faint glimmer of hope of a way to solution at a cost to us commensurate with our national interests." (While the president treated Mansfield with the utmost respect in person, in a private conversation with Bundy he denigrated the majority leader—who enlisted in the Navy at fourteen during World War I and later served in the Army and Marines—as having "no spine at all.")

De Gaulle's and Sihanouk's ideas might have ended the war with a multinational agreement, just as the Geneva conference led to the 1954 ceasefire. More than thirty years later, McNamara admitted that "we erred seriously in not even exploring the neutralization option." If France had concluded that a neutral Vietnam wouldn't present a security threat to the West, he wrote, "then we should, at a minimum, have fully debated the issue. We did not."

Instead, Washington latched on to the questionable idea that victory was possible in South Vietnam if enough military pressure could be brought to bear on North Vietnam.

BY JANUARY 1964, SAIGON was again in turmoil. A cholera epidemic had killed dozens of people, and two thousand women workers were on strike at three textile factories. After police failed to restore order at one plant, troops were brought in.

Big Minh and his colleagues were running out of time to get their government moving. Public disaffection was growing, with Tho a prime target.

And rumors were rife that "French agents" were plotting a coup to install a pro-neutrality government.

While some South Vietnamese viewed neutralism as a panacea to end the conflict that was killing so many of their countrymen, the generals, along with many businessmen, Catholics, and intellectuals, vehemently opposed it. They viewed neutralism the same way LBJ and his advisers did: as a slippery slope to communist domination. Big Minh and other generals repeatedly denounced a neutralist solution as unacceptable.

Rumors of a possible neutralist coup were fed not only by de Gaulle's pronouncements but also by the return of Lieutenant Colonel Tran Dinh Lan, a shadowy figure long suspected of being a French intelligence operative. A steady stream of exiles, from France and elsewhere, was flowing into Saigon, and Lan was among them. He went to work for General Mai Huu Xuan, who'd commanded the military convoy in which Diem and Nhu were murdered. Following the coup Xuan had become mayor of Saigon and director of the national police. Widely considered a French agent himself, Xuan added to the speculation about a neutralist conspiracy by freeing a few prominent VC prisoners.

The most significant upshot of the supposed French scheming, however, was to provide a pretext for General Nguyen Khanh, the opportunistic commander of I Corps, to launch a coup against Big Minh.

Khanh, who'd joined the anti-Diem uprising only on condition that the president's life be spared, was outraged when he was assassinated. He'd since fallen into an apparent depression, holing up in his quarters and seeing only close associates.

In late January, he told Harkins he was growing a goatee and wouldn't shave it off "until I've taken over." Harkins said in a 1974 interview that he told Khanh he didn't mind him initiating a coup because "I think you are a very fine general." The MACV commander didn't bother to inform Big Minh, who he disliked, that he was in danger. (In 1981, Harkins changed his story, telling another interviewer that his response to Khanh was "Oh, General Khanh, we don't want another coup.")

On the night of January 28, Khanh summoned his U.S. adviser, Colonel Jasper Wilson, and said he was very disturbed by allegations of French machinations and was going to Saigon the next day to investigate. Wilson reported the story to Lodge's assistant, Mike Dunn, who immediately went to the ambassador's residence and roused him from bed with the news.

Once in the capital, Khanh got in touch with General Khiem, who'd finally taken over III Corps from General Dinh. During the November coup, Khiem had been the liaison with younger officers who commanded the troops that stormed Gia Long Palace. Some of those officers were now disgusted with Big Minh and other junta members and concerned about talk of French plotting. Khiem agreed to help Khanh.

Lodge met with top embassy and MACV officers, including Wilson, to discuss the highly unappetizing prospect of a second putsch in less than three months. According to Dunn, the consensus was "that there would be no coup, that Khanh was loyal, supportive of the regime."

The consensus was wrong. At 4 a.m. on January 30, troops surrounded the homes of Big Minh, Don, Kim, Dinh, and Xuan. Big Minh was detained at home, while the others were arrested and taken to Joint General Staff headquarters.

By 7 a.m., the latest power play was over, with virtually no shots fired. There was only one fatality: Big Minh's bodyguard, Captain Nhung, who'd murdered Diem and Nhu. Nhung was arrested on Khanh's orders and, depending on which story you believe, hung himself in jail, shot himself at home, or was executed by a general who'd returned from foreign exile.

Khanh declared himself prime minister and chairman of the Military Revolutionary Council and requested a prompt sit-down with Lodge. Dunn suggested that, for purposes of secrecy, the general and the ambassador get together at Dunn's apartment; his wife and several servants rushed around preparing breakfast.

The general was in no mood to hide his triumph, however. He arrived in a convoy of jeeps and police motorcycles, lights flashing and sirens blaring. Dunn noticed that balconies in nearby apartment buildings were filled with applauding people.

Khanh came up to Dunn's apartment, strode to the balcony, and began bowing grandly.

CHAPTER 22

SOUTH VIETNAM IN FREE FALL

THOUGH ONLY THIRTY-SIX, Khanh was widely considered one of South Vietnam's best generals. A Buddhist, he was born in a small Mekong Delta town, Tra Vinh, near the Cambodian border. His father was a wealthy landlord who lived there with his mistress, a performer in folk operas. His mother ran a bar in Dalat that catered to rowdy French soldiers.

Like many Vietnamese of his era, Khanh had fought with the Viet Minh before switching to the French. He graduated from the Dalat Military Academy as a second lieutenant in 1947 and trained in France as a paratrooper. In the early 1950s he rose rapidly through company and battalion commands to the rank of lieutenant colonel. In the last days of the French war he commanded Groupement Mobile 11, a regimental task force battling guerrillas in the Central Highlands.

In October 1960, as a brigadier general, he was named chief of staff of the Joint General Staff. During the paratrooper rebellion the following month, Khanh played a role in saving Diem. Hearing gunfire near his quarters in downtown Saigon, he raced to the besieged palace, climbed over a wall, and helped to rally the president's defenders.

By 1962, however, Diem suspected that Khanh was turning against him.

When the president shook up ARVN commands that year, Khanh was moved out of Saigon and put in charge of II Corps in the Central Highlands.

Jauntily outfitted in aviator sunglasses, a red beret, and a silk scarf, the pudgy, pint-size Khanh had considerable personal magnetism and a flair for showmanship. Forceful and intelligent, he was a beguiling speaker in French or English. He was acutely aware of South Vietnam's dependence on American support and got along well with U.S. military men. His admirers included Colby, who regarded him as a "perceptive, courageous leader with the potential to control the military and run the country."

Others, including many Vietnamese, had a less flattering view. They saw Khanh as mercurial, power-hungry, egotistical, and prone to dark episodes of paralyzing despair. Conein, who knew Khanh better than most Americans, considered him manipulative and a habitual liar. Even Madame Nhu, a friend who spent time with him when she lived in Dalat, characterized him as "a conniver."

Khanh's unexpected seizure of power was a stark reminder to U.S. policymakers that they were still largely in the dark about the byzantine Saigon political scene and the personalities and baroque motives that animated it. The second coup in three months also demolished any notion that Diem's fall might usher in a beatific period of political stability.

In any event, Khanh was South Vietnam's new leader, and Washington had to deal with him as best it could. Lodge, who evidently never met Khanh prior to his takeover, had to ask Harkins who he was. In a cable to the State Department, the ambassador acknowledged that the latest coup was "obviously extremely disconcerting," but added that what South Vietnam needed was "a tough and ruthless commander. Perhaps Khanh is it."

LYNDON BAINES JOHNSON STRODE down the center aisle of the U.S. House of Representatives on January 8, 1964, amid a standing ovation that rang throughout the ornate old chamber.

A wild "yahoo!" erupted from one of the hundreds of senators and representatives applauding the new president as he took the podium. Donning his reading glasses and speaking in his low-pitched drawl, LBJ proceeded to announce the most ambitious agenda for reforming American society since the New Deal, instituted three decades earlier by his hero Franklin Roosevelt.

Johnson's sweeping array of government programs to end poverty, dismantle racial segregation, protect the environment, improve public education, extend health insurance to the elderly and poor, and elevate the arts would come to be known as the Great Society. Kennedy had tried to push some of the same legislation through Congress, but failed. In the aftermath of the young president's death, Johnson—who vowed to finish what Kennedy started—found himself riding a wave of public sympathy and approval that translated into a great deal of political capital. Such goodwill was an evanescent commodity, as LBJ knew from long experience. He was determined not to waste it.

White House lights burned late into the night as Johnson, with his volcanic energy and iron will, drove his staff and an army of federal bureaucrats to turn his ideas into government action. As a boy growing up in the parched Hill Country of south-central Texas, he'd seen firsthand the ravages of poverty and racial discrimination, and he grew into manhood as a populist passionately committed to eradicating social inequality. Now, after twenty-six years in public office, he held in his hands the unrivaled powers of the presidency, and was eager to use them to materially improve the lives of those on the margins of America's unprecedented affluence.

Over the next three years, LBJ would sign into law Medicare, Medicaid, the Civil Rights Act of 1964, the Voting Rights Act of 1965, the Head Start early-development program for low-income children, the Corporation for Public Broadcasting, new protections for consumers and the environment, immigration reform, the Freedom of Information Act, the National Endowment for the Arts, and more—an astonishing set of achievements that would benefit Americans for generations to come.

In early 1964, the fighting in faraway, little-known Vietnam was for many Americans a small thunderhead on the distant horizon. Polls showed that 63 percent of the public was paying little or no attention. But LBJ understood that even small wars can explode into expensive, controversial conflagrations that upend a president's domestic agenda by draining dollars and public support. And while he'd pledged to continue Kennedy's assistance programs in South Vietnam, he knew an expansion of the war would inevitably siphon resources from and perhaps even ruin his Great Society plans.

But as bad news from South Vietnam continued to flood in, Johnson came under pressure to strike harder not only at the Viet Cong but at North Vietnam, which was steadily supplying the guerrillas while denying any involvement. As Air Force chief of staff Curtis LeMay, who directed the devastating World War II firebomb raids on Japan, pungently put it: "We are swatting flies when we should be going after the manure pile." Military attacks on the north, the argument went, would make it costlier for Ho Chi Minh to keep infiltrating arms, trained cadres, and supplies into the south.

In a January 22 memo to McNamara, the Joint Chiefs of Staff urged that the United States throw off its "self-imposed restrictions" and take tougher action against North Vietnam. They wanted to bomb key targets in the north and "commit additional US forces, as necessary, in support of the combat action within South Vietnam." The chiefs further recommended that Washington twist Khanh's arm to let an American commander take over "tactical direction of the war"—a move that would amount to an extraordinary usurpation of South Vietnamese sovereignty.

Such escalatory measures, however, went far beyond where LBJ was willing to go in early 1964. Instead, he approved only some small-scale covert actions, including seaborne raids against North Vietnamese coastal defenses, bridges, and other targets. Directed by the CIA, the attacks were to be carried out by South Vietnamese commandos in high-speed gunboats, although McNamara considered them to be no more than pinpricks.

Johnson also shook up his foreign policy staff. He fired Hilsman, who he blamed for the anti-Diem coup and disliked as a "loudmouthed lightweight," according to William Bundy, who moved over from the Pentagon to replace Hilsman as assistant secretary of state for Far Eastern affairs. Harriman was quietly shunted away from Vietnam decision-making.

Anguished and disillusioned, Nolting resigned from the State Department. In a February 25 letter to LBJ, he reiterated his "strong disapproval" of U.S. encouragement of the Diem coup, and said he'd been "uncomfortable in my association" with the State Department since returning from Saigon.

FACED WITH THE APPROACHING whirligig of the 1964 presidential campaign, LBJ wanted to keep a lid on the war as much as possible. It was just as well, since he and his advisers seemed to be at a loss about how to proceed in Vietnam. "The frank answer is we don't know what's going on out there," McNamara told the president in a March 2 phone call, advising him to "say as little as possible" in public about the war.

LBJ was tired of the political turmoil in South Vietnam, telling his staff he wanted "no more of this coup shit." He hoped to achieve some stability by throwing Washington's full weight behind Khanh, publicly embracing him as "our boy" and signaling the general's political rivals that the United States would tolerate no more government upheavals.

On March 8, Johnson dispatched McNamara and Taylor to Saigon, both to gather fresh information and take Khanh on a barnstorming tour intended to increase his popularity among his own people. "Bob," the president told McNamara before he left, "I want to see about a thousand [newspaper] pictures of you with General Khanh, smiling and waving your arms and showing the people out there that this country is behind Khanh the whole way."

Despite his "endless embarrassment" at having to act like a common pol on the hustings, McNamara did as instructed. From Bac Lieu in the south to Hue in the north, he, Taylor, and Khanh clambered onto speakers' platforms in towns and villages as curious locals gathered around. McNamara held up one of Khanh's arms and Taylor held up the other, as if they were proclaiming him the winner of a prizefight.

McNamara had memorized an inspiring Vietnamese phrase—"Vietnam, one thousand years!"—but he mangled the pronunciation, so his audience instead heard "Vietnam, go to sleep!" (General Don recalled that he and the other Diem coup leaders laughed "until tears came to our eyes" upon hearing of McNamara's malaprop.) But, as one South Vietnamese woman later wrote, the more the foreigners tried to build up Khanh, "the more the people despised him as a puppet."

Returning to Washington, McNamara and Taylor told journalists that Khanh and his new government "are acting vigorously and effectively," unveiling new initiatives that would help the war effort. But McNamara was again masking his real findings as he and Taylor privately reported to LBJ that the situation "has unquestionably been growing worse."

Desertions from the ARVN were "high and increasing," they wrote, and morale among hamlet militiamen was "poor and falling." Many South Vietnamese men were dodging the draft, while the VC recruited "energetically and effectively." Yet the biggest problem was the "uncertain viability of the Khanh government." Khanh's grip on the army was shaky and he seemed to have little appeal in the countryside, where most villagers registered only blank stares when he bounced onstage with his two American sponsors. Khanh also faced frequent threats of assassination or overthrow, although he was taking precautions to protect himself. (Khanh asked his friend Conein to train his bodyguards as well as plan an escape route out of Saigon for him.)

Indeed, McNamara was starting to think America's basic strategy in Vietnam wasn't working. As he later explained, it was becoming clear in the first months of 1964 that Washington's efforts to advise and assist the ARVN were a "likely failure." As a result, he and LBJ's other civilian counselors "tilted gradually—almost imperceptibly" toward the Joint Chiefs' demands to bomb the north and introduce U.S. combat forces in the south. "We did so," McNamara later wrote, "because of our increasing fear—and hindsight makes it clear that it was an exaggerated fear—of what would happen if we did not."

While in Saigon, McNamara had held lengthy discussions with the embassy staff over whether to bomb North Vietnam. Most embassy officers, including Lodge, favored bombing, even though they realized it might not significantly reduce Ho Chi Minh's ability to reinforce the VC and ran the fearful risk of drawing China into the war. But they wanted to go ahead anyway because they couldn't think of any better alternatives.

"This," McNamara later admitted, "was the sort of desperate energy that would drive much of our Vietnam policy in the years ahead."

In his report to LBJ, McNamara recommended developing contingency plans to bomb in the future, if the president deemed it necessary. LBJ quickly approved the planning—thus taking a fateful step toward direct American participation in the war.

THE VC, MEANWHILE, BEGAN aiming terror attacks at Americans. In February, enemy agents set off a bomb during a Sunday softball game, killing two Americans and wounding forty-one, including five children. A week later, a bag laden with TNT exploded in a Saigon movie theater frequented by Americans. Three died and fifty-one were injured, most of them U.S. dependents. (Among the dead was Marine Captain Donald Koepler, who, spotting the VC with the bag, ran into the theater shouting, "Bomb! Hit the deck!")

In a spectacular action on May 2, a VC agent working as a stevedore at Saigon's port crawled through a sewer pipe, swam a short distance in the river, and attached two homemade mines to the hull of the USNS *Card*, a World War II–era escort carrier delivering helicopters and fighter-bombers. No one was killed in the massive 3 a.m. blast, but it opened a large hole below the waterline and the 495-foot-long ship sank to the river bottom. That same day, a terrorist threw a bomb into a group of Americans, wounding eight.

Like many in Washington, Khanh believed that a change in war strategy was needed. He was sick and tired of the bloodletting in South Vietnam, and had little patience with the long-lead social programs at the heart of the counterinsurgency effort. The ARVN, he felt, was simply not capable of fighting a successful counterguerrilla war, and should thus revert to what it knew best: conventional military tactics. Although he initially opposed air strikes against the north, he came to view them as necessary.

But the sharp-toothed maw of South Vietnamese politics already was consuming the inexperienced new leader. When McNamara and Taylor visited him again in May, he told them his biggest and most time-consuming problems were political, and religion was usually at their core. His government already was ensnared in a deepening tug-of-war between Buddhists and Catholics. Catholics accused him of being pro-Buddhist; Buddhists charged that he favored Catholics. Emotions were running so high that he worried the strife would spill over to the ARVN, destroying its unity.

Although Khanh and a number of his cabinet ministers were Buddhist, some Buddhist activists were turning against him. Tri Quang had pledged after Diem's demise to give up politics, but he resurfaced in Hue, telling acolytes that Khanh's regime was merely a vehicle for Catholics and the Can Lao Party to regain power. Khanh, the monk claimed, was ignoring ongoing abuses against Buddhists and oppressing them in many of the same ways Diem supposedly had.

Khanh did win some political points with Buddhists by not halting the execution of Diem's brother Can, despite Lodge's plea to grant him clemency and avoid creating another Catholic "martyr." The once-feared political boss had been convicted of murder, extortion, and misuse of power and sentenced to the guillotine.

Severely ill with diabetes, the fifty-three-year-old Can collapsed from a heart attack during his trial. Khanh insisted to Lodge that he was lobbying various religious leaders to publicly appeal for mercy for Can, but Tri Quang was a holdout. The ambassador went to Hue to ask the monk in person to support clemency; he refused. (Although he'd once sheltered Tri Quang, Lodge now found him "ambitious, anti-Christian, full of hatreds.")

On May 9, Can was carried on a stretcher to a soccer field at Saigon's Chi Hoa prison. The Khanh regime had made one concession: he'd die by firing squad rather than guillotine. Can was so feeble he had to be lifted to his feet by two guards and strapped to a post, hands tied behind his back.

A black blindfold was placed over his eyes. Ten military policemen aimed their U.S.-supplied carbines and fired a ragged volley. Can slumped as blood ran down his black tunic and white pantaloons. A military police captain stepped forward and delivered the coup de grâce shot to his head.

Photographers snapped pictures that soon appeared in Saigon newspapers, to the delight of many readers.

IN WASHINGTON, LBJ'S ADVISERS peppered him with ideas for taking the war to the north.

The Pentagon on May 24 submitted a draft of its "Scenario for Strikes on North Vietnam." It envisioned an initial wave of air attacks by South Vietnamese bombers against transportation-related facilities such as ports, railroads, and bridges. Next to be hit were "targets which have maximum psychological effect on the North's willingness to stop insurgency." These would be military as well as industrial assets, including oil tanks, barracks, airfields, and communication centers. The attacks could be expanded by adding American aircraft, either disguised or bearing U.S. markings.

But could bombing persuade Ho Chi Minh to stop reinforcing the Viet Cong? A top secret war game in April concluded that the answer was no.

Designed by the RAND Corporation, a California-based think tank, the game involved fifty-six high-level officials from the White House, Defense and State departments, CIA, and armed services. Participants were divided into three teams: red, representing the VC and North Vietnam; blue, representing South Vietnam and the United States; and yellow, representing China. McCone led the blue team, playing the role of LBJ. Taylor headed the reds, playing Ho Chi Minh with obvious relish. Code-named SIGMA I-64, the exercise took place over four days in a special game room at the Pentagon.

Taylor's reds were instructed to employ guerrilla tactics, absorb heavy casualties, exploit weaknesses in conventional military doctrine, and disrupt government operations with terrorism and propaganda. One red player, William Sullivan, Harriman's special assistant, mounted a surprise attack on the Bien Hoa Air Base in which multiple U.S. bombers were blown up. (In a grisly case of life imitating military art, the VC carried out a real attack on the base less than seven months later.)

Although many individual sorties against the north were rated as effective, the game director judged the overall impact of bombing on VC operations as "negligible." It would have been more accurate, however, to label it as perilously counterproductive. By the end of the game, the air strikes had drawn both China and the USSR into the war. The Chinese sent MiG-17 jet fighters to defend Hanoi, and Soviet technicians began building antiaircraft missile batteries to protect the communist capital and nearby port of Haiphong. Ho Chi Minh stepped up his training of VC cadres and his civilian labor battalions quickly repaired damaged bridges and rail lines.

The game's outcome was so disturbing that McNamara, Rusk, McGeorge Bundy, and other LBJ advisers convened at the Pentagon to go over the results. Yet the dire prognosis did little to dampen the drumbeat within the administration for bolder action against the north.

Bundy urged the president in a May 25 memo to deploy U.S. forces to Southeast Asia on a "very large scale . . . to maximize their deterrent impact and their menace." But he warned that such action might push South Vietnam toward neutralism or lead the United States into a land war or even the use of nuclear weapons.

THE PRESIDENT, HOWEVER, WAS anxious to find an exit from the conflict, which, as he admitted to Bundy, "worries the hell out of me." LBJ vented his anxiety in a lengthy phone call with his trusted friend, Senator Richard Russell of Georgia.

Russell said he didn't think Americans were ready to send troops to Vietnam, and expressed concern that doing so would bring China into the war. South Vietnam, he insisted, "isn't important a damn bit" to U.S. strategic interests.

Russell urged the president to decide whether to "move in or move out . . . in the near future," but noted that there was a good case for withdrawing. When Johnson asked, somewhat plaintively, if Congress would impeach him for "run[ning] out," Russell said he didn't think so.

LBJ complained about Lodge, saying "he ain't worth a damn" and "can't work with anybody." But he worried that if he fired his Republican ambassador, he'd be "campaigning against us on this issue every day."

Johnson was certain about one thing: Harkins needed to be jettisoned. Kennedy had extended the general's stay in Saigon a few months, thumbing his nose at *The New York Times* for its biting coverage of his Vietnam commander. But that extension had lapsed, and Bundy and Forrestal were eager to get rid of Harkins, whose continued presence in Saigon was a painful reminder of the advisory program's lack of success.

LBJ summoned Harkins to Washington to receive a medal and the general left South Vietnam on June 20, relinquishing command of MACV to General William Westmoreland, his deputy. Nearly two years later, Bundy lamented to the president that Harkins's "prolonged tenure was one of our major mistakes."

The tension with Lodge resolved itself when the ambassador announced his resignation on June 18, after his presidential bandwagon came to an abrupt halt. Thanks to a write-in campaign by a small band of energetic volunteers, Lodge had scored a remarkable victory in New Hampshire's first-in-the-nation primary, beating Goldwater and New York governor Nelson Rockefeller, both of whom campaigned vigorously in the state, while Lodge remained in Saigon. The ambassador also won the New Jersey and Massachusetts primaries, again without campaigning. By spring, his picture was in newspapers and magazines across the country, and he led in GOP polls.

But Lodge wasn't fated to capture his party's presidential nomination on the strength of a heroic image as a brave ambassador helping to fight communists in Asian jungles and rice paddies. As the campaign season wore on, and one news story after another described the crumbling of South Vietnam, Lodge's support faded. Goldwater beat him in Illinois, Texas, and Nebraska. After losing to Rockefeller in Oregon on May 15, Lodge was finished.

He left Saigon to campaign for Pennsylvania Governor William Scranton, the last hope of Eastern Establishment Republicans to stop Goldwater. But the ultraconservative Arizona senator locked up the nomination at the party's raucous national convention in San Francisco in July.

A jut-jawed major general in the Air Force Reserve, Goldwater was the perfect foil for Johnson in a campaign that was often to focus on issues of war and peace. At a time when moviegoers flocked to see *Dr. Strangelove*, Stanley Kubrick's black comedy about an unhinged Air Force general who orders a preemptive nuclear attack on the Soviet Union, Goldwater repeatedly made comments about nuclear weapons that frightened many voters.

There were moments when Goldwater sounded like the movie's demented General Jack D. Ripper. "I want to lob one into the men's room of the Kremlin and make sure I hit it," the candidate quipped at one point. He also suggested using "low yield atomic weapons" to bomb Chinese supply lines into North Vietnam. *Time* magazine ran a list of his distressful gaffes, including his statement that "I think brinkmanship is a pretty good word." When he minted the campaign slogan "In your heart, you know he's right," LBJ supporters retorted with "In your guts, you know he's nuts." Throughout the campaign, Johnson worked to cement an image of himself as a sensible, restrained man of peace while depicting Goldwater as a trigger-happy cowboy, if not an outright warmonger.

Goldwater and other Republican politicians in turn attacked Johnson for his "no-win policy" in Vietnam, demanding that he bomb the north and pursue a clear-cut military victory. But when North Vietnamese torpedo boats supposedly attacked two U.S. Navy destroyers in the Gulf of Tonkin in early August, LBJ used the episode to outmaneuver Goldwater.

The USS *Maddox*, which had been collecting electronic intelligence off the North Vietnamese coast, reported on August 2 that three communist PT boats had opened fire on it. But no Americans were injured, and Johnson and his aides concluded that an overeager communist naval commander might have been at fault and decided not to retaliate.

The *Maddox* was then joined by another destroyer, the *Turner Joy*. On August 4, the vessels radioed that another communist attack was underway. But the night was moonless, the sea was rough, and U.S. patrol aircraft reported no enemy sightings. The destroyers' commander later blamed "overeager sonarmen" for reports that torpedoes had been fired at the ships. (A detailed study of "the Gulf of Tonkin incident" by National Security Agency historian Robert Hanyok, declassified in 2005, flatly stated that no second attack took place.)

LBJ swung into action nevertheless. He called Goldwater and said he'd soon announce that U.S. aircraft were conducting retaliatory bombings against North Vietnam. "You've got a good statement, Mr. President," Goldwater said. "I don't know what else you can do."

The raid by sixty-four Navy aircraft against an oil storage facility and moored naval vessels paid big political dividends for Johnson, effectively taking Vietnam off the table as an issue in the presidential race.

By securing Goldwater's advance approval, and publicizing it on national TV, LBJ made it harder for his Republican rival to keep criticizing him over the war. The strikes demonstrated that while he sought to be a man of peace, the president was a resolute leader who didn't hesitate to unsheathe U.S. power when events compelled him, although not in a reckless manner that might plunge the country into nuclear war. The Republican charge that he was "soft on communism" was drained of potency.

Indeed, when LBJ accepted the Democratic presidential nomination in Atlantic City three weeks later, his speech didn't even mention Vietnam.

OVER BUNDY'S OBJECTIONS, JOHNSON decided to replace Lodge with Maxwell Taylor. While the national security assistant had begun to favor tougher military measures, such as bombing the north, he felt that Taylor wouldn't be able to apply the nuanced counterinsurgency tactics and sociopolitical reforms he believed were also necessary. In a tense phone conversation with LBJ, Bundy declared that he didn't think Taylor had "ever understood that war." He complained that the sixty-two-year-old general was "a man of ebbing energy" with possible heart problems. And installing a military man as ambassador, Bundy argued, "is a bad signal, both internationally and in some ways locally."

The president, however, was adamant. "That's a military job, though," he said. "And I think it's gonna show that we mean business without having to bluff and bluster a lot. . . . From what I've seen of [the] seven months I've been in here, the most challenging and the most dangerous military problem we have is out there. He's our top military man."

Tayor arrived in Saigon backed by a presidential directive giving him full control over the entire U.S. Mission, civilian and military components alike. Johnson also gave Taylor a highly experienced new deputy: U. Alexis Johnson, a former undersecretary of state who'd also served as ambassador to Thailand and as a ranking member of the American delegation to the 1954 Geneva Conference.

They made an impressive team that faced a head-spinning array of problems—military, political, and social—in a nation of weary, war-drained people. Some in Saigon who'd hoped that the departures of Lodge and Harkins would lead to dramatic change in U.S. policy were dismayed by Taylor's appointment, despite his years of military experience and familiarity with South Vietnam. "Although he had a reputation as an intellectual, at heart he was a very traditional and often rigid military thinker, imbued with the formal hierarchy of command and wanting always to be in control," wrote Rufus Phillips.

Almost as soon as he settled into his new Saigon office, Taylor was swept into the cyclone of South Vietnamese military and political crises.

The VC unleashed an unprecedented wave of battalion-size attacks against the ARVN. Over and over, the enemy employed the same tactic, assaulting a remote outpost and then ambushing the relief column. In the first three weeks of July, the communists launched eight attacks in battalion strength and three of company size.

Taylor raised the estimate of enemy main-force strength to between 23,000 and 34,000. The VC now had sufficient manpower to operate full regiments in the delta, Central Highlands, and Annamite Mountains. Mimicking the Viet Minh strategy against the French, they had advanced through the subversion and guerrilla stages of revolutionary warfare to the mobile phase, characterized by quick concentration of larger units against targets of opportunity.

Within days of the U.S. air strikes in the Tonkin Gulf, Khanh, in a "fairly euphoric" mood, declared a state of emergency that gave him broad dictatorial powers. These included censorship, a ban on labor strikes and mass meetings, government control of food distribution, more latitude to detain VC suspects, and an 11 p.m. to 4 a.m. curfew.

A measure of wartime austerity descended on high-living, pleasure-loving Saigon. On the night the curfew took effect, fashionable restaurants escorted their guests out the door in the middle of their multicourse meals. As the eleven o'clock deadline approached on subsequent nights, late-night revelers poured out of bars and nightclubs, frantically trying to hail cabs. (Cabbies responded by jacking up their rates and driving even faster and more crazily than usual.)

Khanh also decided to draw up a new constitution that not only gave him sweeping executive authority, but contained fewer enumerated rights for citizens than the old Diem constitution. In addition, it abolished Big Minh's position as chief of state, conveniently knocking Khanh's leading rival out of the government. Taylor warned Khanh that he might face "renewed instability," since many South Vietnamese would see the new charter as an "unduly permanent formalization of [the] military takeover."

Khanh nevertheless got his fellow generals on the Military Revolutionary Council to approve the constitution and elect him as president. On August 16, he announced publicly that he'd ascended to supreme power and Big Minh was out.

BUT, AS TAYLOR PREDICTED, angry citizens soon took to the streets to protest Khanh's usurpations. At one rally, students tore up and burned a copy of the new charter. In heavy rain on August 23, hundreds of students pushed past police and sacked the national radio station in response to a newscast saying their grievances against the government had been resolved.

The next day, as many as forty thousand people stormed through Saigon and three other cities, demanding Khanh's resignation. Alarmed, the general held a late-night conference with Tri Quang and other Buddhist leaders amid reports that they planned all-out protests against him. The monks demanded the immediate replacement of Khanh's constitution with a provisional one under which the Military Revolutionary Council would select a new president. The MRC would then dissolve itself and the new president would form a temporary government of "patriotic and capable" people. The Buddhists also demanded that all "Can Lao elements" be purged from Khanh's government and the armed forces.

Khanh promised in a radio speech that he'd revise his constitution and ease up on the emergency measures, but protesters with banners and bullhorns surged back into the streets anyway. When some 25,000 people gathered outside Gia Long Palace, he bravely came out, protected only by a small circle of bodyguards, to address them, but found himself forced to chant their slogans: "Down with military power! Down with dictatorships! Down with the army!"

Hours after that humiliating performance, Khanh withdrew his charter and resigned as president. He told the other generals they faced the choice of making concessions to Tri Quang and his followers or "shooting their own youngsters." The MRC then pledged to pick a provisional president and disband itself—fulfilling the Buddhists' demands and giving them a stunning political victory.

As new governments rose and fell in coming months, Tri Quang turned his supporters against almost every new leader who appeared. "He was very good at negative politics, but had no concept of positive politics," observed James Rosenthal, the U.S. embassy's chief liaison officer with the monk. "He had this basic irresponsible trait, where you couldn't count on him to support anything. You could always count on him to oppose a lot of people, but you couldn't count on him to support anybody."

The Buddhists' triumph over Khanh, however, heightened the fears of Catholics that they were losing their privileged position in society. Fear turned to anger, and the hideous genie of religious warfare escaped its bottle. Catholics and Buddhists began to attack one another in the streets with knives, clubs, stones, and grenades.

William Sullivan, Harriman's former assistant now working for Taylor, sat sweltering in a traffic jam when he spotted Buddhist and Catholic schoolboys scuffling near Saigon's central market.

Six kids surrounded a boy and began stabbing him with knives. None of the attackers looked older than fifteen. Sullivan didn't realize what was happening until the victim let out a piercing scream and began gushing blood. "Again and again those small arms struck and slashed, until the scream stopped, the face turned ashen, and the body slumped," Sullivan recounted. He and other adults jumped out of their cars, but the young assailants ran off.

In Danang, Buddhists and Catholics clashed repeatedly. About three hundred Buddhists beat a man to death and hung him from a tree with barbed wire. On his body they put a sign that needed no elaboration: "Can Lao." After people wounded in the fighting went to an American-staffed hospital, rioters dragged out four patients and killed them.

Buddhists attacked and burned the Catholic hamlet of Thanh Bo, leaving only fifty of its five hundred houses standing. The hamlet's two churches were razed and its one thousand inhabitants—mostly refugees from North Vietnam—fled. Many were seen putting to sea in fishing boats.

Violence spread in Saigon. On August 27, thousands of Catholics massed outside Joint General Staff headquarters, demanding that the generals end the crisis. Demonstrators angrily pushed against concertina-wire barricades as soldiers with fixed bayonets warned them to stay back. Eventually the troops opened fire, killing six people.

Shortly afterward, the Military Revolutionary Council, which had been meeting at JGS, announced that Khanh, Big Minh, and General Khiem, Khanh's defense minister, would run the country on a temporary basis. This unworkable triumvirate was a panicky attempt to balance several powerful groups: Minh represented Buddhists; Khanh was backed by the Americans (and as a result was South Vietnam's most powerful figure); Khiem, a Catholic, was a leader of the Dai Viet Party, a nationalist organization founded in 1939 and said to have as many as ten thousand members and sympathizers, many holding key jobs in the government. Although outlawed by Diem, the party enjoyed a resurgence after his death.

The generals, along with Buddhist and Catholic leaders, pleaded for calm. But crowds kept fighting in several downtown locations as helicopters dropped leaflets urging them to disperse.

With the exception of the shootings outside military headquarters, Khanh and the other generals—perhaps mindful of the Americans' reaction to Diem's repression the previous summer—hesitated to use force against the protesters. After days of chaos and bloodshed, they finally acted. Paratroopers in trucks raced around the capital, snatching up demonstrators and taking them away. In one night, five hundred people were arrested, including fifteen suspected VC agents.

The drift toward full-blown religious war was halted.

U.S. OFFICIALS IN SAIGON were appalled, however, at how quickly Khanh had capitulated to Buddhist strong-arming.

The CIA station, in a report to its headquarters, castigated him for "in effect put[ting] his government completely in the hands of Tri Quang." By doing so, the station said, Khanh "has similarly bound over to Tri Quang's safekeeping our own government's equity, commitment, and policy in this country. . . . In any event, a new and dangerous period has begun."

Taylor was particularly disgusted. He and his deputy, Alexis Johnson, went to visit Khanh in Dalat, where he'd retreated after the uproar in Saigon. (A government official explained that he'd "suffered a physical and mental breakdown.") The American diplomats found Khanh "suffering from hemorrhoids, high blood pressure, and an obsession over the preponderant strength of the Dai Viet" party, which he'd recently denounced publicly. In a cable to Washington, Taylor complained that Khanh did nothing in Dalat "other than receive medical treatment and enjoy the sunshine. He seems oblivious to the need for getting his government going again."

Khanh emerged from his hideaway on September 4 and announced that civilians would assume control of the government within two months. He produced a letter from Tri Quang pledging that the Buddhists would back him. (Sources told American journalists the letter had been paid for with at least $200,000.) Nonetheless, as Robert Shaplen, the *New Yorker* correspondent, wrote, "almost everyone was glad to have him back," since he seemed to be the only leader with any chance of holding South Vietnam together.

Not all military men were happy to have him back, however. On September 13, a group of Catholic and Dai Viet army officers tried to overthrow Khanh, surrounding the palace with tanks. But it soon became apparent that they had little support from the rest of the military.

The air force commander, the flamboyant Nguyen Cao Ky, remained loyal to Khanh and ordered his planes, conspicuously armed with rockets and bombs, to make menacing, rooftop-level passes over rebel tanks, trucks, and troops clustered at strategic intersections.

Idolized by his pilots, the slightly built, thirty-four-year-old Ky was a thrill seeker who loved drinking, gambling, cockfights, nightly games of mah-jongg, and Hollywood cowboy movies. He had a string of girlfriends and often appeared in a formfitting black flying suit, his hair slicked back, his mustache finely trimmed, and a lavender-colored silk scarf tied at his throat. (He reminded journalist Jean Lacouture of either "a daring pilot or a tango dancer.") While acknowledging his top-notch flying skills, the CIA had a low opinion of Ky, describing him as "childish and often irresponsible . . . not particularly intelligent or sophisticated."

With Taylor in Washington for consultations, his deputy, Alexis Johnson, summoned the coup leaders to his office and, in a heated, three-hour wrangle, made it clear that the United States firmly backed Khanh. Less than twenty-four hours after it began, the attempted putsch collapsed and rebel forces withdrew from Saigon.

Though brief, the rebellion again underscored South Vietnam's chronic instability. It also made Ky and other younger military officers major political players. This group—known as "Young Turks"—would be instrumental in keeping Khanh in power over the next few months, although they ultimately turned against him. And Ky in particular would excel in the murky, turbulent world of Saigon politics.

THE SERIAL UPHEAVALS IN Saigon hardened the consensus among Johnson administration officials that tougher action had to be taken. They began to seriously discuss the idea of using U.S. combat forces to prop up the sagging south.

A particularly aggressive proposal came from John McNaughton, a top McNamara aide and former Harvard law professor. Arguing that there was "no likelihood" that a Saigon government strong enough to win the guerrilla struggle would ever emerge, McNaughton concluded that the U.S. advisory and assistance program was doomed to failure. "Major new elements" had to be injected into U.S. policy, he wrote, suggesting construction of a U.S. naval base, perhaps at Danang, and the introduction of a "large number of US special forces, divisions of regular combat troops, US air, etc., to 'interlard' with or to take over functions or geographical areas from the South Vietnamese armed forces."

In a dismal cable to Rusk, Taylor warned that the Saigon government was incapable of doing much more than "maintaining a holding operation against the Viet Cong." With luck and "strenuous American efforts," it might be able to push the enemy out of the provinces adjacent to Saigon. But, the ambassador said, many South Vietnamese leaders felt that the United States should take over the war while they concentrated on resolving internal political problems. As Taylor observed morosely: "Only the emergence of an exceptional leader could improve the situation, and no George Washington is in sight."

A national intelligence estimate—representing a consensus of all U.S. intelligence agencies—echoed Taylor's pessimism. It noted that the fall of the Diem regime had released a torrent of powerful political forces that previously had been tightly stoppered. These included a jostling array of religious groups, labor organizations, military officers, students, intellectuals, and politicians at home and abroad who demanded quick satisfaction of their long-suppressed aspirations.

The struggle for dominance among these factions could be expected to continue, the estimate said, "until an acceptable balance is struck . . . or the fabric of central government is torn apart."

Facing such grim assessments as the presidential campaign entered its peak season, LBJ convened his inner circle in the Cabinet Room on September 9. McNamara reported that two members of the Joint Chiefs of Staff—Marine Corps commandant Wallace Greene and General Curtis LeMay, the Air Force chief and a bombs-away hawk on the war—were urging the president to "execute extensive U.S. air strikes" against North Vietnam immediately. (In his 1965 autobiography, LeMay said that Washington should warn the North Vietnamese that unless they halted their aggression against the south, "we're going to bomb them back into the Stone Age.")

But McNamara, Rusk, McCone, and Taylor all agreed that the southern government was still too weak to withstand the retaliation from North Vietnam and possibly China that might follow such drastic American action. Johnson concurred, saying he "did not wish to enter the patient in a 10-round bout, when he was in no shape to hold out for one round."

The president asked if there was anything Americans could do to stop the endless feuding among South Vietnamese leaders. Taylor replied that "these people simply did not have the sense of responsibility for the public interest to which we were accustomed, and regularly estimated matters in terms of their own personal gains and losses." When LBJ asked how Khanh compared with Diem in terms of public affection, Taylor said the South Vietnamese "did not care for either one."

LBJ closed the meeting by approving several actions that fell far short of the large-scale bombing sought by Greene and LeMay. Covert maritime raids and electronic surveillance of the North Vietnamese coast were to resume; South Vietnamese troops and aircraft would conduct "limited" attacks on communist infiltration routes. Preparations were to be made for "tit-for-tat" air raids against the north in retaliation for assaults on U.S. personnel.

But while Johnson was repeatedly proclaiming in campaign speeches that "we seek no wider war," he turned more and more to those advocating military solutions: McNamara, the Joint Chiefs, and Eisenhower, with whom he had a good relationship. "Johnson was listening to the hawks," recalled Hilsman. "He wouldn't adopt a policy of a political solution."

Although there was nothing unusual about a president relying on military leaders for advice during a war, Vietnam was a war unlike any other Americans had fought. Political factors were at least as important, if not more so, than military factors. Rusk should have been an important source of information and advice on political matters. But early on, he'd chosen to take a back seat to the Pentagon, believing that the State Department's main work would begin once military victory had been achieved. As a result, he did little to prepare for the possibility of negotiations to end the war. Taciturn and unassertive, he often didn't speak at White House meetings, preferring to offer his advice privately to the president afterward.

LBJ's reliance on military advisers was an approach that tended to freeze out Vice President Hubert Humphrey as well as Forrestal (who'd left the White House to become Rusk's special assistant in July) and other civilian experts. By contrast, if Kennedy had lived, said Hilsman, "We would have pushed hard for a strategic hamlet program. If it had worked, everybody would have been happy. If it hadn't worked, we would have gone to Geneva and negotiated a Laos-type [neutrality] agreement."

SOUTH VIETNAM CONTINUED TO unravel. Another national intelligence estimate predicted further erosion in the Saigon regime's determination and effectiveness, pushing it toward "increasing defeatism, paralysis of leadership, friction with Americans, exploration of possible lines of political accommodation with the other side, and a general petering out of the war effort."

South Vietnam "is almost leaderless at the present time," the October 1 assessment said, as Saigon fonctionnaires waited to see whether Khanh would make good on his promise to turn power over to civilians. The ARVN's chief of operations complained that it was "pointless even to discuss pacification plans" with his U.S. counterparts, and local army commanders shrank from intervening in riots in Hue, Danang, Qui Nhon, and elsewhere on grounds of not receiving proper orders from Saigon.

After an ARVN infantry division was shifted to the Saigon area from Central Vietnam, the VC began to take the initiative there. Even more ominous were the multiplying reports that North Vietnamese army regulars were entering the south, signaling a dangerous escalation of the war.

An enemy offensive in the central coast region generated a host of frightened refugees—up to sixty thousand of them—who streamed into Qui Nhon from the surrounding countryside. "These were Catholic Vietnamese fleeing the North Vietnamese Army units," remembered John Negroponte, a young U.S. embassy officer who later served as U.S. ambassador to Honduras, Iraq, and other nations as well as director of national intelligence. "The NVA were strong there. They were really tearing the place up."

As grim as these tidings were, there was some hope that a transition to civilian government was possible. Two weeks after the September coup attempt against Khanh, Big Minh appointed the members of a provisional legislature, called the High National Council, that was to draft a new constitution, select a new head of state, and create the framework for National Assembly elections. Though broadly representative of South Vietnam's political and religious groups and geographic regions, the HNC was composed of seventeen elderly professional men, leading wags to label it the "High National Museum."

The council nevertheless tackled its mission with vigor. It completed work on the new constitution at the end of October and appointed seventy-one-year-old Phan Khac Suu, a French-trained agricultural engineer, as chief of state. A longtime opponent of both the French and Diem, he'd been imprisoned twice on Poulo Condor Island and was in frail health. Suu then chose sixty-one-year-old Tran Van Huong, Saigon's tough, honest mayor, as his prime minister. A passionate nationalist and ex-schoolteacher, Huong quipped after his selection: "I'm not sure whether I should be congratulated or offered condolences." Khanh resigned as promised, although he kept his position as commander in chief of the armed forces.

But Huong had little success as he tried to establish himself as an honest broker, above the fray of factional in-fighting and self-seeking. Buddhist and Catholic leaders alike were upset when he chose his cabinet ministers without consulting them. Buddhists were further alienated by his public insistence that they confine themselves to religious matters. (A Confucian, Huong believed in strict separation of church and state.)

Saigon soon exploded in a fresh round of anti-government fury. On November 22, a mob led by students and splinter-group politicians marched toward Gia Long Palace following a Buddhist memorial service for President Kennedy. Outside the palace, the crowd—swollen to seven thousand to eight thousand—howled for the prime minister to come out as they pushed and shoved against a cordon of troops.

More trouble broke out on November 24 as students bashed their way through troop lines and severely beat a soldier. At first, the Buddhists stood apart from the street demonstrators, but now they joined the anti-government cause. A Buddhist communiqué declared that the Huong government "does not command the sympathy of the population" and called on the ARVN and the police to defy Huong's orders and take no action against protesters. On November 25, about two thousand youths furiously pounded police and paratroopers with bricks and clubs outside the National Buddhist Center.

Huong declared martial law and closed the city's schools. The government warned that further rioting would be put down by soldiers firing live ammunition. In an interview with Marguerite Higgins, who'd returned to Saigon amid the chaos, Huong declared that Tri Quang was bent on creating a Buddhist "state within a state."

On November 27, two battalions of cops and heavily armed soldiers surrounded the National Buddhist Center, the point of origin for much of the rioting, with orders to shoot anyone who violated a 10 p.m. curfew. The disorders finally subsided, although the Buddhists pledged a new campaign of resistance against the regime.

ON DECEMBER 1, LBJ'S advisers gathered at the White House to go over options for putting more military pressure on North Vietnam.

The president had demolished Goldwater on Election Day by 16 million votes, the biggest margin ever for a presidential candidate. The landslide generated Democratic majorities in both chambers of Congress, giving LBJ the power to ram through the rest of his Great Society agenda—if the rising costs of the war didn't derail it.

The day he was elected, Johnson secretly convened an interagency panel, chaired by William Bundy, to investigate ways to attack the north. Johnson had insisted for months that he didn't want to expand the war until South Vietnam showed signs of developing some political stability. He pushed Taylor to persuade the battling factions to come together in the interests of national unity. But that goal was rapidly receding into the realm of the unattainable.

Just back from a Thanksgiving holiday at his Texas ranch, the president settled into his high-back black leather chair in the Cabinet Room, flanked by principals including Taylor, McNamara, Rusk, McCone, McGeorge Bundy, and General Earle Wheeler, who'd ascended from Army chief of staff to chairman of the Joint Chiefs.

Taylor, in particular, was deeply distressed at the endless political setbacks and baffled by the VC's ongoing gains.

After a year of "changing and ineffective government," South Vietnam was in worse shape than ever, he'd written in a lengthy update. The counterinsurgency program was bogged down and would require "heroic treatment to assure revival." Nearly free of the VC a year ago, the northern provinces "are now in deep trouble," as the communists continuously sabotaged the coastal railroad and Highway 1, threatening to cut the region off, economically and physically, from the rest of the country.

Despite heavy losses inflicted by Saigon's forces, the VC continued to grow in numbers and competence, the ambassador wrote. Not only did they replenish their losses, they adopted effective new tactics, including heavy mortar attacks like the one they executed on November 1 against the U.S. air base at Bien Hoa, where B-57 jet bombers were parked in the open, wingtip to wingtip.

A thirty-minute barrage of shells shortly after midnight reduced the base to a shambles. Four American servicemen were killed and seventy-two wounded. Five of the thirty-odd light bombers were destroyed and fifteen more damaged, effectively putting the whole squadron out of action. (Playing in the SIGMA I-64 war game in April, William Sullivan had imagined just such an attack on the vulnerable base.)

Long admired for his military astuteness, Taylor was perplexed by VC resiliency. "The ability of the Viet-Cong continuously to rebuild their units and to make good their losses is one of the mysteries of this guerrilla war," he wrote. "We still find no plausible explanation of the continued strength of the Viet-Cong if our data on Viet-Cong losses are even approximately correct. Not only do the Viet-Cong units have the recuperative powers of the phoenix, but they have an amazing ability to maintain morale."

For Taylor and the other men seated around the long conference table, the world had recently become a more threatening place. On October 16, Beijing successfully tested its first atomic bomb, inflaming Washington's long-held apprehensions of an aggressive China looming over the smaller nations of Southeast Asia. At about the same time, the Soviet premier, Nikita Khrushchev, was ousted by other Soviet leaders who rejected his strategy of "peaceful co-existence" with Washington. Concerned about a possible resurgence of Soviet imperialism, many experts believed the United States needed to reaffirm its commitment to defend allies around the world, including South Vietnam.

William Bundy's group warned that guaranteeing South Vietnam's continued existence as a noncommunist state might eventually require a "Korean-scale" commitment of U.S. troops as well as the use of nuclear weapons to win a war against North Vietnam and probably China as well. Having been involved in the Cuban Missile Crisis in 1962, LBJ and McNamara understood how easily a nuclear cataclysm could be triggered, and both men deeply feared such an outcome.

Bundy's team came up with three alternatives for proceeding. Option A was to continue the present policy of advising and assisting Saigon's forces, with little hope of defeating the VC. Option B was to undertake a massive but short-term bombing campaign against North Vietnam, hitting ninety-four targets selected by the Joint Chiefs, with the goal of forcing Hanoi to stop helping the VC. Option C was to conduct the same bombing campaign, but in a gradual way less likely to provoke the Chinese or Soviets into counteraction. No "devil's advocate" choices—a U.S. pullout or negotiations with the communists—were offered.

LBJ's advisers, even the military men, disagreed on which was the best option. Westmoreland, the MACV commander, wanted to keep going with Option A for the next six months, in hopes that the Saigon government could be strengthened. The Joint Chiefs wanted to hit the communists fast and hard with B. Taylor wanted to move slowly from current policies (A) to graduated bombing (C).

Complicating matters was fresh advice that bombing wouldn't work. A second SIGMA war game, played in September, and a more recent intelligence study both concluded that an air campaign wouldn't do enough damage to persuade Hanoi to stop infiltrating men and supplies into the south.

Despite all the work put in by Bundy and his colleagues—the background studies, the military estimates, the earnest discussions and debates—important questions remained unanswered. What was the factual basis for the assertion that bombing would compel Hanoi to stop helping the VC? How many U.S. troops would be needed to protect newly expanded air bases in the south, or to deter retaliation by either the VC or North Vietnam? How would the American public react to a drawn-out bombing campaign?

Grappling with such uncertainties, Johnson "became totally frustrated" at the December 1 meeting, McNamara recalled: "He confronted an intractable situation. His anxiety and desperation poured out in a stream of questions and comments."

He conceded that a "day of reckoning" for dramatic action was coming. Before the United States began dropping bombs on North Vietnam, though, he wanted Taylor to "try everything" to buttress the Saigon regime.

Johnson eventually approved a two-phase plan: more small-scale, covert attacks against the north and bombing in Laos, followed, if conditions warranted, by a slow ramp-up to a heavy bombing campaign against North Vietnam. He then repeated his demand that Taylor "do [his] damnedest" to build up South Vietnam's government before Washington shifted to phase two.

Even though his decision could lead to war with North Vietnam in the near future, the president said nothing about it publicly. Instead, the White House issued an anodyne statement that Taylor had been instructed "to consult urgently with the South Vietnamese Government as to measures that should be taken to improve the situation in all its aspects."

BACK IN SAIGON AGAIN, Taylor plunged into the Sisyphean task of persuading angry Buddhists, alienated minor-party politicians, and other malcontents to get behind Prime Minister Huong.

The ambassador met with Huong, Suu, cabinet members, the High National Council, military leaders, and newspaper editors. Over steak and red wine at Westmoreland's villa on December 8, Taylor spoke with several

Young Turks, including Ky, the air force chief, and Nguyen Van Thieu, now a general and commander of IV Corps in the delta, warning that the ongoing unrest in South Vietnam had dismayed even its staunchest friends in America. He made it clear that while the U.S. government was prepared to deepen its involvement in the war, it couldn't do so until the South Vietnamese stood solidly behind their government.

The CIA quietly pressed associates of Tri Quang to get him to ease up on Huong. But by then the Buddhists were openly committed to toppling the prime minister. They published a letter pleading for Taylor to get rid of him—a striking manifestation of the widespread belief among South Vietnamese that their leaders were mere puppets on Washington's strings.

On December 12, Tri Quang and two other prominent monks launched a forty-eight-hour hunger strike; hundreds of other monks and nuns followed suit a few days later. The Buddhists indicated they were ready to launch mass protests and begin burning themselves again. They attacked Huong as "anti-revolutionary and anti-Buddhist," although they didn't seem to have a specific issue to bludgeon him with.

Despite Taylor's admonishment, Khanh and the Young Turks carried out what amounted to another coup on December 20, arresting members of the High National Council, who'd refused to forcibly retire Big Minh and other senior generals so younger officers could move up.

The Young Turks abolished the HNC and formed a new military "advisory" body, the Armed Forces Council, headed by Khanh. They also arrested Big Minh, Don, and three other generals, whisking them off to confinement at Pleiku in the Central Highlands. According to Don, the HNC refused to push out Minh and other senior officers because its members felt that "the army already was suffering from a pitiful lack of competent leaders."

Taylor, usually calm and collected, was beside himself with exasperation. This latest military power grab was exactly what LBJ didn't want. The ambassador quickly paid a visit to Huong, who looked despondent. He reported that Khanh and ten Young Turk generals had awakened him at 2 a.m. to tell him what they'd done and ask him to remain as premier.

Taylor summoned Ky, Thieu, and two other Young Turk generals to his office and addressed them as peremptorily as he would a group of disorderly shavetails: "I thought I made it clear that all our military plans depend on government stability. Now *you*"—he looked straight at Ky—"have made a real mess. We cannot carry you forever if you do things like this."

Ky tried to explain that the Turks had acted because they believed that Big Minh and the other arrested ARVN leaders "had their chance and did badly." The High National Council, said Ky, needed to be purged of "disruptive elements." Taylor was having none of it. "I don't know whether we will continue to support you after this," he fumed. "You people have broken a lot of dishes and now we have to see how we can straighten out this mess."

Taylor met with Khanh the next day at Joint General Staff headquarters and the two quickly crossed swords.

"Khanh dropped his customary cherubic facade and belligerently took the offensive in the conversation, accusing Max of insulting Khanh's colleagues," recalled Alexis Johnson. An angry dialogue ensued. The ambassador said it would be "difficult, if not impossible" for Washington to collaborate with a civilian government that operated with a "military shadow hanging over them." He told Khanh he'd lost confidence in him. Khanh retorted that "loyalty was a reciprocal matter and that Vietnam was not a vassal of the United States." Taylor, he snapped, should "keep to his place as ambassador" and not complain to South Vietnam's commander in chief "on a political matter."

To the Americans' surprise, the general, rather than keep the blowup with Taylor quiet, went public with his grievances, risking his primary asset: his carefully groomed image as the one Vietnamese leader who could parley effectively with the Americans. In an interview with the *New York Herald Tribune*, Khanh insisted that Taylor was "not serving his country well" and that if he "does not act more intelligently, the United States will lose Southeast Asia and we will lose our freedom." He refused to reinstate the arrested High National Council members, as the Americans wanted.

He then doubled down, insisting that the ambassador's effrontery toward South Vietnam's military leaders could only be rectified by his swift recall from Saigon.

There were grumbles at the White House that the scholarly but martial-minded Taylor might not possess sufficient finesse to handle the complex diplomatic and political challenges that lay ahead. But there was little chance that an American ambassador would be withdrawn based on some foreign general's chest-beating.

After quiet talks between Alexis Johnson and the Young Turks, a compromise was struck between the military and the High National Council. A few weeks later, a smiling Khanh and a composed-looking Taylor were photographed shaking hands at a tea party at Gia Long Palace.

BUT AS 1964 CAME to a close, South Vietnam seemed to be in free fall.

From the provinces to Gia Long Palace, the Saigon government was knotted with dysfunction. The counterinsurgency program was at a standstill. The Buddhists again were threatening to take down the nation's political leadership. Exhausted by endless bloodshed and political turmoil, the South Vietnamese seemed more open to neutralism than ever. Worst of all, North Vietnamese regular troops were entering the south.

On Christmas Eve, the Viet Cong struck again at Americans, blowing up a Saigon hotel that served as officer quarters for U.S. military advisers. VC agents dressed as ARVN officers drove a car loaded with explosives beneath the five-story Brink Hotel in the center of town. The subsequent blast killed two Americans and wounded sixty-four. Several American nurses arriving for a holiday celebration found themselves helping the wounded, their party dresses spattered with blood.

On December 28, the VC drew government troops into a set-piece battle at the village of Binh Gia, about forty miles southeast of Saigon. In four days of fighting, about a thousand guerrillas fended off three ARVN battalions backed by tanks, artillery, and helicopters piloted by Americans. When it was over, some five hundred government soldiers were dead, wounded, or missing in what the Associated Press described as "by far the costliest fight of the war up to that date." Five American advisers also died.

Besides infiltrating men and supplies down the Ho Chi Minh Trail, North

Vietnam was now sending regular combat units into the south. Radio intercepts showed elements of the 325th Division moving into Quang Tri Province, just below the demilitarized zone, and later all the way to the Central Highlands. It was the first regular North Vietnamese army division to enter South Vietnam, and it marked the advent of a new and more dangerous phase of the war.

The time was ripe for a thorough rethinking of the American investment in Vietnam. LBJ had tried to limit U.S. involvement during his election campaign, but MACV's roster still rose to 23,300 by the end of 1964—a 43 percent jump over the previous year. The public had little taste for expanding the conflict; a Harris poll in January 1965 showed that 40 percent of those surveyed were willing to do no more than "hold the line," while another 23 percent wanted to "negotiate and get out."

Comfortably situated atop a mountain of political capital and public goodwill following his runaway election victory, LBJ could have pivoted in almost any direction he chose in late 1964 or early 1965.

If he wanted to begin pulling out of South Vietnam, this was the time to do it. He'd promised repeatedly during his campaign that American boys wouldn't be sent to do the job that Asian boys should be doing. He could have invoked JFK's legacy, saying the martyred president had intended to withdraw a thousand advisers in 1963, and then kept gradually raising that number.

Taylor would have been happy to support him. In a New Year's Eve cable to Johnson, the ambassador proposed a major U.S. pullback, given the likelihood of more government upheavals and instability in the future. Washington could disengage by "withdrawing the bulk of our advisers and turning over a maximum number of functions now performed by Americans," Taylor wrote. The United States could still deliver enough military and economic aid to keep the Saigon regime going at current levels, while using U.S. air and sea power to protect it from North Vietnamese incursions.

"By this means we might hope somewhat to disengage ourselves from an unreliable ally and give the [Saigon government] the chance to walk on its own legs and be responsible for its own stumbles," he added. "The hope would be that, having to accept full responsibility, [South Vietnam] would rise to the challenge and 'pull up its political socks.'"

But Johnson seemed to view South Vietnam as a trap with no exit: staying the course was doomed to failure and escalating the war was dangerous, but getting out had its own perils. In an interview with three journalists, the president likened himself to a man trying to keep his balance while standing on a newspaper floating on the Atlantic Ocean. "If I go this way," he said, tilting his hand to the right, "I'll topple over. And if I go this way"—he banked his hand to the left—"I'll topple over. And if I stay where I am, the paper will be soaked up and I'll sink slowly to the bottom of the sea."

A cold warrior to his marrow, LBJ embraced the domino theory and had vowed not to be the first president to lose a war. He wanted to strengthen the "containment dike" that held back communist expansionism. He saw China as an aggressive foe and didn't want to create a power vacuum in Southeast Asia that Beijing could fill. And he wanted no doubts in the minds of the Kremlin's new, post-Khrushchev leaders, Leonid Brezhnev and Alexei Kosygin, about American strength and resoluteness.

Back in Texas for the Christmas season, the president chided Taylor in a lengthy cable for "our lack of progress in communicating sensitively and persuasively with the various groups in South Vietnam." He wanted to enlist Buddhists, labor groups, and anyone else he could in the struggle against the communists, but told Taylor, "I still do not feel that we are making the all-out effort of political persuasion which is called for."

LBJ further complained that while the Pentagon offered nothing but plans for large-scale bombing, "I have never felt that this war will be won from the air." Then, in a suggestion that McNamara said "came from out of the blue," Johnson told Taylor that a more effective course of action than withdrawal would be the deployment of U.S. Marines, airborne infantry, and Green Berets to fight the Viet Cong on the ground.

"I am ready to look with great favor on that kind of increased American effort, directed at the guerrillas and aimed to stiffen the aggressiveness of Vietnamese military units up and down the line," the president wrote. "Any recommendation that you or General Westmoreland make in this sense will have immediate attention from me, although I know that it may involve the acceptance of larger American sacrifice. We have been building our strength to fight this kind of war ever since 1961, and I myself am ready to substantially increase the number of Americans in Vietnam if it is necessary to provide this kind of fighting force against the Viet Cong."

Lyndon Johnson was edging ever closer to some of the most calamitous decisions of his presidency.

CHAPTER 23

"YOU HAVE TO GO ALL OUT!"

THE NEW YEAR brought little to cheer about. U.S. intelligence delivered the alarming news that three regiments of North Vietnamese regulars—as many as eight thousand men—had entered the south, headed for the Central Highlands. Together with the ARVN's recent large-scale losses at Binh Gia, the invasion intensified McNamara's fear that Hanoi and the Viet Cong were readying an all-out offensive that Saigon's army wouldn't be able to withstand.

The crisis atmosphere was exacerbated by five lengthy cables from Taylor to LBJ on January 6, 1965, which concluded: "We are presently on a losing track and must risk a change." But he argued strongly against bringing in U.S. combat troops, saying their political liabilities outweighed their military usefulness. "The Vietnamese have the manpower and the basic skills to win this war," the ambassador stated. "What they lack is motivation. The entire advisory effort has been devoted to giving them both skill and motivation. If that effort has not succeeded there is less reason to think that U.S. combat forces would have the desired effect." ARVN commanders would be likely to hang back and let GIs carry the burden of the fighting, Taylor insisted, putting the Americans in the same position as the French, "occupying an essentially hostile foreign country."

Taylor instead wanted permission to inform Huong's government that if it "reaches a certain level of performance," the United States would begin bombing the north in a slowly escalating fashion. "I know that this is an old recipe with little attractiveness," Taylor wrote, "but no matter how we reexamine the facts, or what appear to be the facts, we can find no other answer which offers any chance of success." In the meantime, he said, Washington should be ready to retaliate swiftly with air raids if Americans were attacked again.

But Johnson, the self-described peace president, was still reluctant to bomb.

At a White House meeting on the day Taylor's cables arrived, LBJ told McNamara, Rusk, and Bundy that he didn't think tit-for-tat bombing would help stabilize Huong's government, or that sustained bombing would improve southern morale. Nevertheless, he cabled Taylor the next day that he was "inclined" to adopt a policy of prompt retaliatory bombings, if American dependents were evacuated beforehand. Johnson also said he was ready to conduct joint planning with the South Vietnamese for sustained bombing, but would base his final decision on Huong's ability to achieve political steadiness and rack up some military gains.

The president said little publicly about his plans. In a lengthy State of the Union address on January 4, he devoted just 132 words to South Vietnam, simply reiterating his commitment to defend it. As his speechwriter Richard Goodwin observed: "There was no note of alarm, no hint that a crucial decision to enlarge the war was already on the president's desk, being ardently urged on the president by McNamara, Bundy, and members of the Joint Chiefs of Staff."

Despite LBJ's secrecy, word of the slow march toward war leaked to the press. "The time has come to call a spade a bloody shovel," James Reston angrily declared in his *New York Times* column of February 13. "This country is in an undeclared and unexplained war in Vietnam. Our masters have a lot of long and fancy names for it, like escalation and retaliation, but it is war just the same."

SOUTH VIETNAM'S BUDDHISTS, meanwhile, ignored Washington's yearning for stability and redoubled their efforts to bring down the Huong government.

Tri Quang and several other monks kicked off the latest onslaught with a hunger strike, pledging to fast unto death. The campaign quickly took on strong anti-American overtones as posters denouncing Taylor appeared throughout Hue. On January 23, a mob sacked the U.S. Information Service library there, burning eight thousand books and forcing local Americans to huddle inside the MACV compound for protection. Buddhist leaders in Saigon called on followers to begin burning themselves, charging melodramatically that Huong and Taylor were trying to "exterminate Vietnamese Buddhism."

Two days later, 15,000 protesters marched in silence through Hue, carrying banners demanding Huong's resignation and Taylor's recall. Martial law was imposed on the city. In Saigon, a rally by 450 monks and nuns outside the U.S. embassy degenerated into a melee, with shouting Buddhists hurling stones at combat police trying to protect the building. Dispersed by clubs and tear gas, the rioters reassembled and raced toward the U.S. Information Service's Abraham Lincoln Library four blocks away.

The mob smashed windows and doors at the library until paratroopers drove them off with tear gas and truncheons. Outside a secondary school, a monk plunged a knife into himself during a demonstration by 2,000 students.

And once again the Buddhists succeeded in fatally undermining a government they didn't like. On January 27, Khanh and the Young Turks ousted Huong and took power in a bloodless coup. Citing Huong's "inability to cope with the present critical situation," the generals said they were entrusting Khanh with the task of resolving it. They didn't even have to deploy any troops to push Huong out of the way, given his inability to rally public support. According to Ky, the air force commander, when Huong was informed of the generals' decision to remove him, "he accepted it gracefully (and probably thankfully!)."

Taylor was more irate than ever at Khanh, convinced that Huong had

had the Buddhists "on the ropes and would probably have survived their attacks had the military stood by him."

In any event, Khanh's machinations over the past twelve months had inflicted a good deal of damage on U.S.–South Vietnamese relations. As a State Department report summed up: "Khanh's overriding ambition, coupled with his repeated maneuvers against known US positions, have in the span of one year precipitated five major crises in Saigon. In the process, he has seriously reduced if not almost eliminated any public respect for US political advice or for those who accept it. Moreover, his actions, coupled with those of the Buddhists, have fostered a rising crescendo of anti-American feelings."

ON THE SAME DAY that Khanh again grabbed power, McNamara and Bundy tried to nudge LBJ toward strategic bombing of North Vietnam with what became known as the "fork in the road" memo.

The president met them for "a very private discussion" of their memo in the White House Treaty Room, where Lincoln consulted his cabinet during the Civil War. Drafted by Bundy, the memo said he and McNamara "are now pretty well convinced that our current policy can lead only to disastrous defeat." They noted that the present goal was to withhold major U.S. military action until Saigon had established a stable government. But given the events of recent weeks, "there is no real hope of success in this area."

Johnson had two choices, his advisers said. The first was "to use our military power in the Far East and to force a change of Communist policy." The second was to "deploy all our resources along a track of negotiation, aimed at salvaging what little can be preserved with no major addition to our present military risks." Bundy and McNamara preferred the first course.

Rusk, they said, disagreed, arguing that since the consequences of either escalating or pulling out were so unacceptable, a way had to be found to make current policies work. Bundy and McNamara didn't think that was possible.

Even as Vietnam came to a boil, Johnson's priority was pushing through Congress the dozens of bills that formed the spine of his Great Society. He knew that plunging deeper into the war would inevitably corrode support for his cherished domestic agenda. "If I left the woman I really loved—the Great Society—in order to get involved in that bitch of a war on the other side of the world, then I would lose everything at home, all my programs," he told Doris Kearns.

The short but explosive fork-in-the-road memo left him depressed and uncertain. As White House aide Douglass Cater recalled: "I'd never seen the man in as dejected a mood. He said, 'I don't know what to do. If I send more boys in, there's going to be killin'. If I take them out, there's going to be more killin'. Anything I do, there's going to be more killin'. . . . Then he got up and walked out of the room, leaving us in a somewhat shattered state."

Caught between the push by McNamara, Bundy, and Taylor for bold new action and Rusk's insistence on staying the course, Johnson decided to send Bundy to Saigon for yet another look at the situation.

On the last day of Bundy's visit, February 7, the VC attacked Camp Holloway, a U.S. air base outside Pleiku. Beginning at 2 a.m., enemy sappers placed explosives on Huey helicopters, Caribou transport aircraft, and tents and shacks where hundreds of American servicemen lay sleeping. Nearby mortar crews began pouring shells into the base.

About two miles away, more communists opened fire with machine guns on a villa housing U.S. advisers attached to the ARVN's II Corps.

The half-hour attack devastated Camp Holloway. Explosions dismembered some servicemen, scattering their body parts. Wrecked billets were splashed with blood. Eight helicopters and one plane were destroyed and another eight aircraft damaged. Between the assaults there and at II Corps headquarters, eight Americans were killed, 126 wounded.

LBJ called an emergency session of his National Security Council, promising his advisers retaliation would be swift.

"We have kept our gun over the mantel and our shells in the cupboard for a long time now," he said angrily. "And what was the result? They are killing our men while they sleep in the night. I can't ask our American soldiers out there to continue to fight with one hand tied between their backs." Had the United States been more forceful in dealing with aggressors prior to the two world wars, it wouldn't have had to fight in either one, the president said, adding: "Cowardice has gotten us into more wars than response has." He said he realized the risks of involving the Chinese and Soviets, but that "the problem is to face up to them both."

Within hours, bomb-laden A-4 Skyhawks and F-8 Crusaders catapulted off the decks of U.S. aircraft carriers in the Gulf of Tonkin in an operation dubbed Flaming Dart. About 120 planes attacked three North Vietnamese army barracks, while South Vietnamese aircraft bombed a fourth. But when LBJ and his men met the following morning to review the results, they learned that only one of the targets had been hit; the other three had been fogged in. (Navy jets hit the big Dong Hoi barracks with 250-pound bombs and rockets, but destroyed or damaged only 22 of the 275 buildings in the complex.)

Fresh off his flight from Saigon, Bundy rushed to the White House. He handed Johnson an eight-page report, written by him and his team on the plane, along with a five-page annex titled "A Policy of Sustained Reprisal."

Even though he'd participated in both SIGMA war games, which cast serious doubt on the effectiveness of bombing, Bundy urged "graduated and continuing reprisal" air raids as the "most promising course available." The annex, written by John McNaughton, warned that such bombing "implies significant U.S. air losses."

Bundy later briefed members of Congress on his bombing recommendation, which if implemented would make the United States a full-fledged belligerent, not just an adviser, in the war.

Viet Cong agents struck back on February 10, blowing up a hotel that housed U.S. service personnel in the central coast port city of Qui Nhon. The toll was even worse than Pleiku. The hotel collapsed, killing twenty-three GIs, seven Vietnamese civilians, and two of the attackers. LBJ reacted with another large air raid, Flaming Dart II, in which more than a hundred Navy warplanes blasted North Vietnamese barracks and staging areas at Chanh Hoa, just north of the demilitarized zone.

AT THE SAME TIME, influential administration voices began warning the president against expanding the war.

In a February 15 memo to Johnson, Vice President Humphrey noted that during the Korean War, Eisenhower—confronted with massive intervention by Chinese troops, the limited effectiveness of airpower, and the difficulties of fighting a land war in Asia—had chosen not to enlarge the conflict, but to end it by negotiating an armistice. Humphrey warned that Americans would find it "increasingly hard to understand" why LBJ, facing similar problems, was willing to risk World War III with China and possibly the USSR by attacking North Vietnam. Nor would Americans understand the president's willingness to take such grave risks on behalf of a country that is "totally unable to put its own house in order."

It was always difficult to cut losses, Humphrey went on, but LBJ, basking in a monumental election victory, was in an excellent position to do so, with "minimum political risk," in 1965.

George Ball, the undersecretary of state, also weighed in. A tall, bearlike figure with wavy white hair, Ball was a forceful speaker and eloquent writer who regarded Southeast Asia as peripheral to U.S. interests and consistently advised JFK and LBJ against sending more troops. He was well respected in Washington, having urged Kennedy to impose a naval quarantine on Cuba, while demanding a withdrawal of Soviet missiles during the 1962 crisis, a course of action that proved successful. As the former director of the United States Strategic Bombing Survey in the last years of World War II, Ball was well aware of the limits of bombing.

Ball viewed the war as unwinnable and had cast himself in the role of in-house devil's advocate, frequently challenging the premises and assertions of those who favored greater U.S. involvement. In a sixty-seven-page memo to LBJ, he ridiculed the idea that bombing could be applied in a gradual and controlled manner, as other advisers insisted. Ball thought bombing would only lead to more communist infiltration and more attacks on the bases from which the planes were launched. Washington, in turn, would dispatch more troops to protect the bases, and an unstoppable and unpredictable cycle of escalation and counter-escalation would be born, eventually drawing the United States into another ground war in Asia.

Still undecided about what course to pursue, the president met with

Eisenhower at the White House on February 17. As Senate majority leader during Eisenhower's second term as president, Johnson had forged a strong bipartisan relationship with the World War II hero and regarded him as both a sage and a friend.

Ike agreed with LBJ's advisers that reprisal strikes—which he said had "helped the situation a great deal"—should now give way to a campaign of unrelenting attacks on the north. The seventy-four-year-old ex–supreme commander of Allied forces in Europe acknowledged that bombing wouldn't stop infiltration, but it could discourage Hanoi's leaders by exacting a price for their continued aggression.

The Flaming Dart strikes had lifted the south's morale, he said, and Washington should do everything possible to lift it further. He quoted Napoleon's maxim that "in war, morale is to the material element as three is to one," and said that public confidence and determination were even more important in a guerrilla war, since a government fighting insurgents needed the whole population on its side. Targets picked for bombing should have a direct connection to infiltration, making them easier to justify before the world, Eisenhower said. He stressed that if LBJ switched to sustained bombing, he should clearly inform the American public of what he was doing and why.

When Johnson asked what he should do if Chinese forces entered the war, Ike said he doubted they would. But if they did, the United States should hit them with "any weapons required," including tactical nuclear explosives. During the Korean War, Eisenhower said, he'd sent back-channel warnings to North Korea and China that unless they promptly signed a satisfactory armistice, he'd "remove the limits we were observing as to the area of combat and the weapons employed"—a clear threat to employ nuclear weapons against both communist nations. LBJ, he said, should deliver similar warnings to the Chinese and Soviets about intervening in Vietnam.

FOR MONTHS, NO MATTER how hard the bombing enthusiasts pushed, Johnson had been reluctant to go along. The Pentagon had been ready to rain high explosives on North Vietnam since the November election. But the president "just kept asking more and more questions," recalled Joseph Califano, a Defense Department official who later joined the White House staff. "In the eyes of the Pentagon, he was a querulous wallflower, disappointingly reluctant to join the war dance."

As the ARVN struggled, Saigon governments fell, and more Americans died, the war dance became a frenzy.

McNamara's greatest fear at the beginning of 1965 was "that he might not be able to talk the president into the bombing," according to Richard Goodwin. "He spent all his time preparing arguments and lining up allies." His forcefulness began to bear fruit as, one by one, LBJ abandoned the key premises that underlay Washington's policies on Vietnam.

First to go was the original concept that the United States should confine itself to an advisory and assistance role. Next was the idea that a stable Saigon government was an essential prerequisite to U.S. action against the north. Campaign promises to "seek no wider war" and not to send American boys to do the job of Asian boys faded. The postelection wiggle room for reducing U.S. personnel was disappearing. Most of LBJ's advisers insisted there was only one viable option: war with North Vietnam.

Johnson finally relented on February 19, signing off on a strategic bombing program named after a Christian hymn: Rolling Thunder.

Eisenhower's unhesitating counsel to move forward with such bombing no doubt affected Johnson's thinking. But LBJ ignored his predecessor's admonition to inform the public that sustained air strikes were underway and explain why they were necessary. His lack of candor was to cost him dearly as public faith in his credibility and judgment dropped steadily over the next three years, ultimately contributing to his 1968 decision not to seek another term in the White House.

Rolling Thunder began on March 2, as land- and carrier-based aircraft pounded North Vietnam. The first round of targets included ammunition depots, radar sites, barracks, and a naval base. Then roads, bridges, railroads, and ships were hit. The White House kept a tight rein on targeting decisions to avoid provoking China or the USSR by striking near the Chinese border or where Soviet ships might be docked. American planes later went after industrial facilities, oil storage tanks, and power-generating plants, and LBJ eventually approved bombing Hanoi and the nearby port of Haiphong.

But the attacks failed to persuade Ho Chi Minh to reduce support for the VC or sit down at the negotiating table. On the contrary, bombing only hardened Hanoi's resolve and spurred creation of one of the world's most sophisticated air defense networks, built with massive aid from Moscow and Beijing. At the height of China's effort, it had more than 300,000 antiaircraft, engineering, and medical personnel in North Vietnam. The Soviets provided 3,000 military advisers and technicians along with sophisticated weapons. North Vietnamese pilots began flying modern MiG jet fighters; air defense crews fired at U.S. aircraft with the help of the latest radars, antiaircraft artillery, and surface-to-air missiles.

ON THE SAME DAY LBJ authorized Rolling Thunder, yet another coup erupted in Saigon, this one aimed at removing Khanh as commander in chief. Always worried about being captured, he'd been sleeping at different military bases, never in Saigon. But his luck was about to run out.

The latest coup forces were headed by General Lam Van Phat, one of the leaders of the abortive September putsch, and the omnipresent Colonel Thao, the communist agent. Their tanks converged on Tan Son Nhut airport as Khanh emerged from a meeting there. According to General Don, the coup leaders and their troops chased Khanh in his green Mercedes "all over Saigon like Keystone Cops," but were unable to nab him.

Khanh contacted Ky for help, and the air force chief personally flew him to safety in Dalat. Phat and Thao later met with Ky and agreed to hold their fire on condition that Khanh be forced to step down as armed forces chief and leave South Vietnam. The coup fell apart the next day, February 20, as Phat and Thao put on civilian clothes and sunglasses and fled from Tan Son Nhut in an unmarked car.

By then Ky and other generals were fed up with Khanh. They'd tired of his divisive politics and knew his all-important relationship with the Americans was badly frayed. On February 21, the Armed Forces Council voted to oust their commander in chief.

But Khanh, then at the beach resort of Cap St. Jacques, which had been renamed Vung Tau, was much too wily to surrender without a fight. The other generals threatened that "blood would flow" unless he capitulated. His former U.S. adviser, Colonel Jasper Wilson, was dispatched to "try to talk some reason into him." Wilson reached Vung Tau at 1 a.m. on February 22, just as Khanh was about to take off in a C-47 piloted by a veteran of commando drops over North Vietnam. Wilson hurried aboard and off they flew into the night.

For the next several hours Khanh ping-ponged madly around South Vietnam trying to rally military support. From Vung Tau he went to My Tho in the delta, but local forces there refused to refuel his plane. Khanh then flew two hundred miles north to Nha Trang, where he was again denied gas. He headed for Tan Son Nhut, only to find the runways blocked. With fuel running low, he landed at an unlit hilltop airstrip near Dalat. The C-47 touched down in the pitch-black stillness at 5 a.m., without enough gas even to restart its engines.

After one additional attempt to get colonels and lower-ranking officers behind him, Khanh gave up, telling Don, "I've already spread my share of mud around this country." He eventually reached a face-saving compromise with the other generals: he'd be appointed "ambassador-at-large" and leave South Vietnam forever.

A week after the coup began, Khanh was given a formal farewell ceremony with full military honors at Tan Son Nhut. Then, theatrically clutching a bag of soil from his native land, he boarded a commercial jet to Paris with his family.

Watching the scene, Alexis Johnson observed sardonically: "There was not a wet eye in the crowd."

LBJ TOOK ANOTHER FATEFUL step on March 8, ordering two Marine battalions—about 3,500 men—to go ashore near Danang to protect an air base from which Rolling Thunder sorties were launched. By sending in the Marines, the president broke one of the foremost commandments of U.S. foreign policy: thou shalt not engage in an Asian land war. He overruled

Taylor, who'd persistently opposed ground forces, arguing that the American GI, a "White-faced soldier armed, equipped, and trained as he is," wasn't suited for fighting guerrillas in Vietnamese forests and jungles.

Johnson believed that grunts in the mud, not airpower, were the way to push back the VC, to the extent they could be pushed back at all. But the ground war was going poorly and the president wanted more options, more ideas for making headway. He decided to send the Army chief of staff, General Harold Johnson, to South Vietnam to investigate.

General Johnson delivered his report to LBJ, McNamara, and the other service chiefs on March 15, estimating that it could take 500,000 American troops and five years to beat the VC. "His estimate shocked not just the president and me but the other chiefs as well," McNamara recalled. "None of us had been thinking in anything approaching such terms." (The number of U.S. soldiers in Vietnam peaked at 536,100 in 1968.)

McNamara's qualms about the war seemed to grow by the day. He'd recently expressed to Bundy his fear that "the Pentagon and the military have been going at this thing the wrong way round from the very beginning: they have been concentrating on military results against guerrillas in the field, when they should have been concentrating on intense police control from the individual villager on up."

Speaking privately with McCone on March 18, the defense secretary said he was worried that Rolling Thunder was having little effect on Hanoi's will to fight. "He expressed concern over the effectiveness of bombing, distress over the fact that many women and children would be killed, and that guerrilla wars could not be won from the air," McCone wrote afterward in a memo to himself. "McNamara stated that he felt . . . it would not be long until we ran out of worthwhile targets in the north."

The pressure for more military action rose sharply on March 30 when the VC detonated a car bomb next to the U.S. embassy, killing at least 13 people and wounding more than 180 in and around one of the most prominent symbols of American power in South Vietnam.

Most of the embassy's windows overlooked a side street, and there a small gray Renault rolled to a stop. The driver stepped out, complaining of engine trouble to one of the half dozen Vietnamese policemen guarding the building. When the cop ordered him back into his car, he opened fire with a revolver. A nearby man on a motor scooter began shooting, too.

Embassy employees rushed to the windows at the sound of the gunshots. Someone in the ground-floor consular section realized what was happening and yelled at everyone to get down seconds before about three hundred pounds of plastic explosives went off.

The enormous blast left the streets strewn with burning cars and dead and wounded Vietnamese. From the badly damaged, six-story embassy came a stream of dazed, blood-streaked Americans, riddled with wounds caused by flying glass and other shrapnel. Two CIA agents were permanently blinded. Peer de Silva, the station chief, was rushed to the U.S. Navy hospital, his throat perforated by chunks of metal. James Rosenthal, the embassy officer who frequently talked to Tri Quang, was led out to the street drenched head to toe in his own blood from glass cuts. Among the dead were Barbara Robbins, a twenty-one-year-old CIA secretary, and one other American.

Washington recoiled in horror and rage. Some U.S. officials believed the bombing was retaliation for Rolling Thunder; they advocated air attacks on North Vietnamese government buildings. Caution prevailed, however, and air raids continued to be limited to military targets away from population centers.

But, as Bundy's aide, Chester Cooper, noted, "If the Communists had wanted to do something to strengthen the administration's determination to press on with the war, they could not have selected a better target for attack."

COOPER WAS RIGHT. LBJ met for more than two hours on April 1 with McNamara, Rusk, McCone, the Bundy brothers, and others. The mood was bitter and vengeful.

"Get plenty more targets," the president demanded, referring to the Rolling Thunder campaign. "We got to find 'em and kill 'em."

But only a month after Rolling Thunder began, there were signs it wasn't working as planned. On April 6, General Wheeler informed McNamara that the strikes "have not curtailed [North Vietnamese] military capabilities in any major way," nor had they significantly damaged its economy.

On the contrary, the attacks spurred the north to build up its antiaircraft defenses and channel more people into military activities. Wheeler added that Hanoi's small air force had "exhibited considerable daring" in recent dogfights, with North Vietnamese pilots in Soviet-built MiG fighters downing two American planes and damaging a third.

Instead of reducing its infiltration of the south, Hanoi boosted it. Down the Ho Chi Minh Trail came more troops, political cadres, and civilian porters, young and old, men and women, in black pajamas, rubber sandals, or bare feet, carrying ammunition, food, and medical supplies on bicycles or their backs, hidden beneath thick jungle canopy, ghostlike and determined. Infiltration tripled, to about five thousand per month. As the *New York Times* writer Tom Wicker observed: "The bombing could not make something American and technological out of the war, which was profoundly Asian and intensely human."

With the air war in the north faltering, the ground war in the south took on new importance. On April 20, McNamara, Wheeler, McNaughton, and others met at U.S. Pacific Command headquarters in Honolulu to examine a potential troop buildup with Taylor, Westmoreland, and Admiral Ulysses S. Grant Sharp, the new commander of American forces in the Pacific.

Over Taylor's objections, McNamara decided to recommend that two Army brigades plus three more Marine battalions be deployed. McNamara also wanted logistical preparations to be made for the future arrival of two Army divisions—nearly 50,000 more soldiers.

On April 22, LBJ approved the recommendation, which would bring the total number of U.S. troops in South Vietnam to almost 82,000—a 150 percent increase in a matter of weeks. Again seeking to conceal the scale of his decisions, LBJ emphasized in a cable to Taylor that "it is not our intention to announce whole program now but rather to announce individual deployments at appropriate times."

The growing violence and visibility of the war generated a backlash from stateside peace groups. A small antiwar movement emerged and began to grow rapidly among young people, clergy, academics, and entertainers who viewed American actions in South Vietnam as immoral.

Pennsylvania Avenue in Washington became a focal point for antiwar protests, crowded with clamorous picketers day and night. Lafayette Park, across the avenue from the White House, was a virtual campground for demonstrators. Night after night, LBJ and his family could hear their angry chant: "Hey, hey, LBJ, how many kids did you kill today?"

As domestic opposition to the Rolling Thunder attacks mushroomed, Johnson decided to pause them for a few days.

The May 12 stand-down, code-named Mayflower, was one of a series of temporary bombing halts during the war intended to nudge Hanoi toward peace talks. Even this move LBJ kept secret, fearing a right-wing backlash if it became public knowledge (although the press soon found out). The moratorium, however, failed to produce the desired results. The night before it was to take effect, an American diplomat delivered a secret démarche to the North Vietnamese embassy in Moscow, saying Washington expected "equally constructive actions" from Hanoi. The message was returned to the U.S. embassy without comment the following morning. "Hanoi spit in our face," McNamara complained angrily in a conference with LBJ. The air strikes resumed on May 18, again with no public announcement.

Sensing that victory might be within reach, the communists were more interested in battlefield gains than peace talks. They launched an offensive that coincided with the start of monsoon season, when heavy rains and cloud cover would impede U.S. air operations.

Just before midnight on June 9, up to two thousand guerrillas equipped with mortars, machine guns, and flamethrowers attacked a town in Phuoc Long Province, on the Cambodian border north of Saigon. A nearby Green Beret base was also hit. ARVN reinforcements rushed to the scene, but the communists clobbered two government battalions as they piled out of helicopters, and nearly destroyed three more sent on the ground to relieve them. By the time the VC pulled back on June 14, more than nine hundred South Vietnamese soldiers had died, the ARVN's worst loss in a single battle. Of the twenty Americans at the Green Beret base, five were dead and all but one of the rest wounded.

AS ARVN BLOOD DRENCHED the countryside, the newest Saigon government was in danger of capsizing amid a rising gale of criticism from religious, military, and civilian factions still vying for power despite the communist offensive.

The new prime minister, Phan Huy Quat, a gentle, French-trained doctor, was endowed both with extensive government experience (he'd served as Bao Dai's defense minister and Khanh's foreign minister) and the approbation of U.S. officials, who thought he'd performed well in his brief time in office. For one thing, he managed to persuade the generals to dissolve the Armed Forces Council, eliminating their main instrument for meddling in government affairs.

By late spring in 1965, however, Quat, like his predecessors, was surrounded by political enemies with daggers drawn. Some critics complained of weak and corrupt officials in his administration; others demanded national elections. And South Vietnamese couldn't resist expressing their chronic impatience with the government for failing to achieve sweeping successes in a short period.

Quat's most vociferous critics were Catholics, who charged that he was in league with Buddhists and too eager to negotiate with communists. Priests in Saigon encouraged their parishioners to arm themselves in anticipation of a neutralist deal between Buddhists and the Viet Cong.

On May 20, security agents arrested forty military officers and civilians for plotting to overthrow Quat. The chief organizer was Colonel Thao, the wily, walleyed VC agent. A military tribunal had recently sentenced him and General Phat to death for trying to unseat Khanh in February, and both men went underground.

The incident that eventually brought Quat down at first appeared to be a relatively trivial conflict between him and the elderly chief of state, Phan Khac Suu. Under pressure from the Americans, Quat fired his ministers of economic affairs and the interior. Both had performed poorly during a recent crisis over rice supplies and were considered incompetent. "We harassed Quat about these two ministers, about getting rid of them," recalled Alexis Johnson. "And Quat said, 'Leave it to me. I'll have to do it in my own time.'

But as a result of our pushing him on this, Quat acted on this sooner than he otherwise would have."

Quat neglected to obtain formal resignations from the two ministers before he announced their termination and Suu, sensing an opportunity to increase his own nominal powers, refused to sign an order dismissing them. Backed by Catholics, southerners, and out-of-power politicians, Suu refused to budge, arguing that Quat had violated the provisional constitution.

The generals became restive as the standoff dragged on with no resolution in sight. At 1 a.m. on June 11, Quat summoned Johnson to his office, where two prominent Young Turks, Ky and Thieu, were waiting. Quat said the trio had been discussing the situation and didn't see any way out except for him to resign and for the military to take over once again.

The American diplomat was dumbfounded. "I turned to Quat and said, 'Are you fully satisfied on this? There's just no other way out of this?' And he said, 'No, there's just no other way out of it.'" Quat soon announced he was quitting. Ky replaced him as prime minister; Thieu took over as chief of state.

Ky was South Vietnam's sixth prime minister in the nineteen months since Diem's assassination.

Imposing a raft of new authoritarian measures, Ky moved quickly to "shake and shock the country out of its lethargy." In his first few days in office, he declared martial law and shut down twenty newspapers. He ordered a captured VC executed and slapped price controls on rice, sugar, condensed milk, and other foodstuffs. Against U.S. wishes, he severed diplomatic relations with France, charging that "de Gaulle has always, indirectly or directly, assisted our enemies."

American officials were unimpressed by the showy, impulsive air marshal turned politician, who foolishly told a British newsman of his admiration for Hitler. "We need four or five Hitlers in Vietnam," Ky proclaimed. Alexis Johnson regarded him as "an unguided missile." McNamara disliked that he "drank, gambled, and womanized heavily." William Bundy later remarked disgustedly that Ky and Thieu represented "the bottom of the barrel, absolutely the bottom of the barrel!"

AT THE TIME KY and Thieu took over, the ARVN had lost five infantry battalions in three weeks. Intelligence indicated the Viet Cong were capable of organizing regiment-size operations in all four ARVN corps areas, and at least battalion-size attacks in virtually every province. Larger enemy attacks were now sometimes supported by 75-millimeter artillery. Westmoreland cabled that ARVN commanders "do not believe that they can survive without the active commitment of U.S. ground combat forces."

The combination of ARVN setbacks and enemy advances jolted McNamara. His shock was compounded when on June 7 Westmoreland requested a big new commitment of American troops. The MACV commander wanted 41,000 more soldiers right away, and 52,000 more later—pushing the total number of U.S. forces from 82,000 to 175,000. Westmoreland said the conflict was "moving to a higher level," as more northern regulars entered the south. ARVN battalions were being destroyed faster than they could be reconstituted. The Saigon army, he warned, "cannot stand up successfully to this kind of pressure without reinforcement."

The urgency of Westmoreland's request was underscored in a cable from Taylor, who'd consistently argued against introducing American combat troops. But he'd changed his mind in the face of ARVN desertion rates so high and leadership so weak that the Saigon army was threatened with collapse. The situation was so bad, Taylor wrote with grim resignation, that "it will probably be necessary to commit U.S. ground forces to action."

Yet LBJ still agonized over ordering more and more young Americans into harm's way in swamps and jungles thousands of miles away. Speaking with McNamara by phone on June 21, the president said: "It's going to be difficult for us to very long prosecute effectively a war that far away from home with the divisions that we have here and particularly the potential divisions. . . . I'm very depressed about it because I see no program from either Defense or State that gives me much hope of doing anything except just praying and grasping to hold on during monsoon [season] and hope they'll quit. And I don't believe they're ever goin' to quit."

MORE MEETINGS WERE HELD. Memos, position papers, and telegrams flew among the White House, Pentagon, Saigon embassy, and MACV. Johnson ordered three key aides—McNamara, Ball, and William Bundy—to draw up more options for him.

On July 1, McNamara proposed a vast enlargement of the U.S. war effort. He urged LBJ to boost the total number of U.S. troops to 175,000 "within the next few months"; extend duty tours; call up reservists; nearly triple bombing and armed reconnaissance sorties against the north (from 1,800 per month to 5,000); destroy bridges and rail lines between Hanoi and China; mine Haiphong harbor and three other ports (effectively imposing a naval quarantine on the north); and begin attacking VC havens in the south with eight hundred B-52 bomber sorties a month.

McNamara also wanted to deploy an additional thirteen U.S. helicopter companies and more American artillery batteries and engineers to strengthen the ARVN. The north's war-making capacity could be destroyed, he said, by bombing an explosives plant, five supply depots, seven ammunition depots, nine oil storage facilities, twelve military barracks or headquarters, thirteen power plants, two communications facilities, six naval bases or ports, airfields, roads, ferries, and surface-to-air missile sites.

McNamara's recommendations left McGeorge Bundy aghast. In a memo to the defense secretary, Bundy assailed his ideas as "rash to the point of folly."

Bundy said McNamara's plan "seems to me to have grave limitations. . . . It proposes this new land commitment at a time when our troops are entirely untested in the kind of warfare projected. It proposes greatly extended air action when the value of the air action we have taken is sharply disputed. It proposes naval quarantine by mining at a time when nearly everyone agrees the real question is not in Hanoi, but in South Vietnam."

Bundy faulted McNamara for not stating "the upper limit of US liability. If we need 200 thousand men now for these quite limited missions, may we not need 400 thousand later? Is this a rational course of action? Is there any real prospect that US regular forces can conduct the anti-guerrilla operations which would probably remain the central problem in South Vietnam?"

While Bundy had thrown his support behind bombing the north and dispatching the Marines, he now seemed to recognize the intense pressures for open-ended escalation that those previous actions had set in motion. He feared that the United States was being sucked into a serious war alongside an allied government that lacked popular support and might easily fall apart.

Ball submitted his own paper, warning that the South Vietnamese "are losing the war" and there was no guarantee the VC could be defeated or forced to negotiate regardless of "how many hundred thousand white foreign (US) troops we deploy." A few days earlier, Ball had recommended a U.S. withdrawal, but backed off after other advisers criticized his suggestion as "the worst way to lose if it came to that." Ball now urged instead that American forces be firmly capped at the 72,000 already announced, and that they be restricted to providing only combat support for the ARVN.

The alternative to a firmly limited U.S. commitment, he wrote, "is almost certainly a protracted war involving an open-ended commitment of US forces, mounting US casualties, no assurance of a satisfactory solution, and a serious danger of escalation at the end of the road." Ball wanted Washington to reach out to Hanoi and try to jump-start talks leading to a peace conference.

William Bundy argued that the president should pause U.S. deployments at 85,000 and then evaluate how well they performed during the monsoon season.

McGeorge Bundy forwarded the three proposals to Johnson with a cover note from which he withheld his scorching criticism of McNamara's recommendations for massive escalation. "My hunch," Bundy wrote, "is that you will want to listen hard to George Ball and then reject his proposal. Discussion could then move to the narrower choice between my brother's course and McNamara's."

LBJ spent much of July trying to figure out what to do. He reached out far and wide for advice, speaking with Democrats and Republicans, and people in and out of government. On July 2, he telephoned Eisenhower to ask what he thought about bigger troop deployments. The ex-president remained stridently hawkish. "You have to go all out!" he declared. "This is war, and as long as the enemy are putting men down there, my advice is to do what you have to do!"

SIX DAYS LATER, LBJ convened a meeting of the so-called wise men, an informal group of distinguished Americans who'd made their mark in foreign policy, the military, politics, and business. They represented the cream of the "Greatest Generation," men whose smarts, determination, and confidence helped propel the United States to victory in World War II and global dominance in the early Cold War era.

They included Dean Acheson, Truman's secretary of state and a key architect of U.S. Cold War policy; retired five-star general Omar Bradley, who led more than a million soldiers of the U.S. Twelfth Army Group into Germany in World War II and later served as chairman of the Joint Chiefs of Staff; John Cowles, the liberal Republican publisher of *Look* magazine and the *Minneapolis Star* and *Tribune* newspapers; Robert Lovett, a former defense secretary and undersecretary of state in Truman's administration; and John McCloy, Truman's high commissioner for occupied Germany, former president of the World Bank, and disarmament adviser to Eisenhower and Kennedy.

Johnson joined the wise men in the Cabinet Room and voiced "a long complaint" about the resistance he faced from Congress, the press, and intellectuals. The supremely self-confident Acheson, with his clipped mustache and haughty manner, recounted his reaction to LBJ's griping in a letter to Truman two days later:

"Finally I blew my top & told him that he was wholly right [in Vietnam], that he had no choice except to press on, that explanations were not as important as successful action . . . ," Acheson wrote. "With this lead my colleagues came thundering in like the charge of the Scots Greys at Waterloo. They were fine; old Bob Lovett, usually cautious, was all out, &, of course, Brad[ley] left no doubt that he was with me all the way. I think . . . we scored."

But it was Ball who really blew his top that day. Sitting in the meeting along with McNamara, Rusk, and Bundy, he was taken aback by what he considered the wise men's ill-considered and wrongheaded opinions. When the conference ended, he stalked over to Acheson and one of his cohorts.

"You goddamned old bastards," he berated them. "You remind me of nothing so much as a bunch of buzzards sitting on a fence and letting the young men die. You don't know a goddamned thing about what you're talking about."

EVEN AS AMERICAN POLICIES in Vietnam began to shred, Johnson's Great Society legislation was moving briskly ahead on Capitol Hill. By mid-July, Congress was close to approving the landmark Medicare bill. The Voting Rights Act was making progress as well. Combined with the likely passage of his anti-poverty and housing programs, LBJ stood to match or exceed Roosevelt's dazzling legislative accomplishments during the early months of the New Deal.

Congressional conservatives, meanwhile, were pushing for up to $2 billion in additional appropriations to cover the rising costs of the war. They also wanted to mobilize 200,000 reservists. Major pieces of Great Society legislation were yet to be acted on, including the Clean Air Act, immigration reform, and aid to Appalachia. But the calls for more money for Vietnam reinforced LBJ's anxiety that his grand vision for improving life for all Americans was in jeopardy.

As the president labored under the mind-bending pressures of simultaneously navigating the complexities of the war and his Great Society reforms, two of his closest aides began to worry about his mental state.

Both Bill Moyers, now the White House press secretary, and speechwriter Richard Goodwin concluded that Johnson was sliding into paranoia. "I became convinced that the president's always large eccentricities had taken a huge leap into unreason," related Goodwin, a JFK holdover who coined the phrase "Great Society" and penned LBJ's powerful "We shall overcome" speech urging congressional passage of the Civil Rights Act. "Not on every subject, and certainly not all the time. During this same period, Johnson was skillfully crafting some of the largest triumphs of his Great Society."

Moyers and Goodwin had witnessed some troubling episodes, however. In mid-June, Johnson learned that Bundy was to appear on network TV to debate five college professors about the American role in the war. The president was incensed, telling Moyers to fire the national security assistant. Moyers didn't carry out the order, but telephoned Goodwin at midnight. As the speechwriter noted in his diary, Moyers "said he was extremely worried, that as he listened to Johnson he felt weird, almost felt as if he really wasn't talking to a human being at all."

On July 5, LBJ told Goodwin in all seriousness: "You know, Dick, the communists are taking over the country." A few days earlier, Moyers had walked into Goodwin's office, visibly shaken. "I just came from a conversation with the president," the press secretary said. "He told me he was going to fire everybody that didn't agree with him, that Hubert [Humphrey] could not be trusted and we weren't to tell him anything." Johnson also insisted that the "communist way of thinking had infected everyone around him, that his enemies were deceiving the people and, if they succeeded, there was no way he could stop World War III."

For the next hour, Moyers and Goodwin discussed "the intermittent, but clearly visible signs of Johnson's instability, the transformation of personality, which, far from total, was clearly accelerating." The two aides then separately consulted multiple psychiatrists, describing LBJ's words and behavior. The doctors, Goodwin wrote later, gave the same diagnosis: "a textbook case of paranoid disintegration, the eruption of long-suppressed irrationalities." A few weeks later, sitting around the pool at his Texas ranch with Goodwin and other staffers, Johnson absurdly proclaimed: "The communists already control the three major networks and the forty major outlets of communication."

Goodwin resigned from the White House not long afterward, saying nothing publicly about his former boss's apparent mental fraying.

HAVING LISTENED TO HOUR upon hour of discussion and debate among his advisers, and having read a blizzard of memos, papers, and studies, Johnson seemed resigned to a bigger war despite his reservations. He sent McNamara back to Saigon to determine the exact number of additional troops that would be needed.

The defense secretary arrived on July 16 and was whisked to MACV headquarters under heavy security. There Westmoreland reiterated that he needed 175,000 American troops by the end of 1965, and predicted that another 100,000 would be needed in 1966.

Westmoreland and the Joint Chiefs of Staff believed that the VC were on the verge of entering what Hanoi's chief military strategist, General Vo Nguyen Giap, called "the third stage," in which guerrillas transform themselves into a conventional army, assembling in large units and fighting as regular soldiers. U.S. military leaders expected that American troops—by virtue of their superior firepower and mobility, coupled with "search and destroy" tactics—could wipe out communist conventional forces. Even if the VC stayed in the guerrilla phase, Westmoreland and the Joint Chiefs assumed U.S. troops could beat them at that game, too.

But, as McNamara acknowledged years later, "all these assumptions proved incorrect." U.S. forces weren't able to lure the Viet Cong and North Vietnamese into set-piece battles fought on American terms. Nor was Westmoreland able to wage an effective anti-guerrilla campaign. Bombing the north failed to force the enemy either to reduce infiltration of cadres and supplies into the south or to talk peace at the conference table.

Before he came to the Pentagon, McNamara's reputation rested on his skills as corporate America's hardest-driving inquisitor, capable of divining flaws in complex business plans and forcing executives to make necessary changes. His discussions with Westmoreland and MACV felt superficial, but McNamara failed to dig deeper. "Looking back," he admitted in his 1995 memoir, "I clearly erred by not forcing—then or later, in either Saigon or Washington—a knock-down, drag-out debate over the loose assumptions, unasked questions, and thin analyses underlying our military strategy in Vietnam."

McNamara submitted his depressing report to LBJ within hours of returning to Washington on July 21.

"The situation in Vietnam is worse than a year ago (when it was worse than a year before that)," he wrote. "After a few months of stalemate, the tempo of the war has quickened. A hard VC push is now on to dismember the nation and to maul the army. . . . Without further outside help, the ARVN is faced with successive tactical reverses, loss of key communication and population centers particularly in the highlands, piecemeal destruction of ARVN units . . . and loss of civilian confidence."

He continued: "There are no signs that we have throttled the inflow of supplies for the VC or can throttle the flow while their material needs are as low as they are. . . . The [VC and North Vietnamese] seem to believe that South Vietnam is on the run and near collapse; they show no signs of settling for less than a complete take-over."

McNamara argued that the United States should undertake a major war against the communists. Westmoreland's troop requests should be granted. The defense secretary also urged LBJ to intensify Rolling Thunder strikes; add 375,000 personnel to the armed forces by stepping up draft calls and extending tours of duty; and mobilize 235,000 reservists and National Guardsmen. The price tag for his proposals was later pegged at a staggering $8 billion (nearly 7 percent of the 1965 federal budget of $116.8 billion).

Events were closing in on LBJ with breathtaking speed. He was under intense pressure to make one of the most momentous decisions of his presidency. But he remained deeply ambivalent about expanding the war, fearing the domestic as well as international repercussions.

McNamara's aggressive proposals triggered a weeklong series of White House meetings at which, despite the risks, the president's civilian and military advisers alike coalesced behind the idea of jumping into the war with both feet.

THERE WAS ONE EXCEPTION: George Ball. On July 21, the undersecretary of state made what became known as "Ball's last stand," arguing long and hard against further escalation in an audience with LBJ.

Ball knew the president was reluctant to plunge deeper into the war and desperate to find a different course. He lined up his notes, cleared his throat, and began. "We can't win," he declared, adding that the best Washington could hope for was a "messy conclusion" to a long, painful war. Ball then displayed a chart that traced U.S. public opinion during the Korean War, indicating that as casualties rose, public support sank.

Ball was familiar with France's losing struggle against the Viet Minh in the 1940s and '50s and knew the VC wouldn't be "so considerate" as to concentrate their forces in large formations, making them sitting ducks for U.S. bombers, helicopter gunships, and artillery. He viewed Ky's new government as "a travesty" and thought the best course was for Washington to cut its losses in Vietnam.

LBJ listened attentively, chin cupped in hand.

"No great captain in history ever hesitated to make a tactical withdrawal if conditions were unfavorable to him," Ball went on. "We can't even find the enemy in Vietnam. . . . He's indigenous to the country, and he always has access to much better intelligence. He knows what we're going to do but we haven't the vaguest clue as to his intentions. I have grave doubts that any Western army can successfully fight Orientals in an Asian jungle."

Ball then suggested a way out that echoed a scheme President Kennedy had toyed with. Washington, said Ball, should make demands so blatantly unacceptable to the South Vietnamese that they ordered the Americans to leave and then adopted a neutralist stance. Such a scenario, Ball said, would undoubtedly lead to an eventual communist takeover, but at least there'd be no further loss of American blood and treasure.

Johnson asked about the impact of a U.S. departure on allies as well as enemies around the globe: "Wouldn't we lose all credibility by breaking the word of three presidents?" Ball didn't think so, replying: "We'll suffer the worst blow to our credibility when it is shown that the mightiest power on earth can't defeat a handful of miserable guerrillas."

But LBJ's three most valued and trusted advisers—McNamara, Rusk, and Bundy—all rejected Ball's ideas.

Calling Ball's proposed pullout a "radical switch" in policy, Bundy argued that it was contrary to everything the United States had done so far in Vietnam. Rusk said getting out would only encourage communist expansionism. McNamara criticized Ball for underestimating the costs of withdrawing and overestimating the costs of intensifying the war, which he thought was winnable given enough time and enough troops.

LBJ agreed, later writing that Ball "had not produced a sufficiently convincing case or a viable alternative." A U.S. retreat in Southeast Asia, he believed, would encourage communist efforts to expand throughout the world, paving the way to another world war.

The next day, Johnson summoned the top ranks of the Pentagon—including McNamara, the Joint Chiefs, and all of the service chiefs—and polled them about what to do. No one objected to McNamara's plans for a colossal ramp-up of combat troops and bombing. General Wallace Greene, the Marine Corps commandant, argued that LBJ should escalate even more.

ON FRIDAY, JULY 23, LBJ took a helicopter to Camp David, the presidential retreat nestled in western Maryland's Catoctin Mountains, to make his final decision on McNamara's recommendations for plunging headlong into war.

Before taking off, the president invited McNamara and another tried-and-true adviser, Clark Clifford, to join him over the weekend.

Clifford was widely respected in Democratic Party circles. A courtly Missourian who spoke with a gentle drawl, the prosperous, fifty-eight-year-old Washington lawyer had been an adviser and confidant to Harry Truman and JFK. He masterminded the famous "give-'em-hell Harry" whistle-stop campaign that led to Truman's upset victory over Republican Thomas Dewey in 1948. As Truman's speechwriter and special assistant, Clifford crafted legislation establishing the Central Intelligence Agency and the Defense Department.

Kennedy's personal lawyer in his Senate years, Clifford had led his presidential transition team. Shortly after JFK's assassination, Clifford conferred with LBJ for four hours about the enormous task of taking over and running the government.

McNamara and Clifford arrived at Camp David on July 24. They represented opposite poles in the White House debate over whether to flood

South Vietnam with American soldiers. McNamara, of course, was in favor; Clifford saw such a move as a dangerous mistake. Torn between their contrary viewpoints, but strongly confident in the judgment of both men, Johnson wanted them at Camp David to argue their respective cases face-to-face.

On Sunday, July 25, Johnson had breakfast and went for a solitary walk around the secluded camp. At noon, he attended services conducted by an Episcopalian minister from Washington and then retired to his quarters in Aspen Lodge for a few hours of private reflection.

At 5 p.m. he summoned McNamara and Clifford, along with a couple of White House aides and Arthur Goldberg, his United Nations ambassador. The group sat at a small dining table with views of the wooded hills beyond.

Clifford went first. He'd spoken with Ball and fully agreed that the least harmful option for the United States was to get out of South Vietnam. Expanding the war, he believed, would ultimately wreck not only Johnson's Great Society but his presidency as well.

"What happened in Vietnam is no one person's fault," he said. "The bombing might have worked, but it hasn't. A commitment like the one that we have made in Vietnam can change as conditions change. A failure to engage in an all-out war will not lower our international prestige. This is not the last inning in the struggle against communism. We must pick those spots where the stakes are the highest for us and we have the greatest ability to prevail."

Clifford didn't think the United States could prevail in Vietnam. "I hate this war," he explained. "If we send in 100,000 more men, the North Vietnamese will match us. If the North Vietnamese run out of men, the Chinese will send in volunteers. Russia and China don't intend for us to win the war. If we won, we would face a long occupation with constant trouble."

The lawyer suddenly paused, then slammed both of his fists on the table:

"If we don't win after a big buildup, it will be a huge catastrophe. We would lose more than 50,000 men in Vietnam. It will ruin us. Five years, 50,000 men killed, hundreds of billions of dollars—it is just not for us."

He closed by urging the president to stick with the current course until the end of the year and then begin quietly searching "for an honorable way out.

Let us moderate our position in order to do so, and lower our sights—lower the sights of the American people—right away. Let the best minds in your administration look for a way out, not ways to win this unwinnable war."

The president told Clifford that no one was more concerned about the bad consequences of the war than he was, but that "we could not simply walk out." Nor was he prepared to "accept just any settlement as a cover-up for surrender." He insisted that he would keep searching for a way to begin "real negotiations" with the enemy.

Meantime, he wanted to downplay the war as much as possible. He, too, worried that any U.S. escalation would be matched by Hanoi, possibly with help from the Chinese and the Soviets. He also feared that if congressional right-wingers—the "great beast," as he called them—found out how badly things were going in South Vietnam, they'd demand much heavier bombing or even a U.S. invasion of the north.

Thus, Johnson wouldn't call up the reserves or ask Congress for a declaration of war. And he'd refuse to publicly acknowledge the mammoth increase in U.S. troop levels he contemplated as a significant change in U.S. policy.

LBJ asked McNamara to state his case. The Pentagon leader did so with his usual forceful concision. South Vietnam couldn't stand up to the communist onslaught without the help of more U.S. troops. Its fall would be a disaster for American security and credibility around the world.

The president left the lodge and drove around Camp David for an hour by himself. He came back at dusk and then set out for a solo stroll as night closed in on the midsummer day.

After a lifetime spent in pursuit of greater political power, LBJ was tantalizingly close to realizing his youthful vision of improving the lives of more Americans in more ways than any other elected leader. As he later told Doris Kearns: "I was determined to keep the war from shattering that dream. . . . I was determined to be a leader of war *and* a leader of peace. I refused to let my critics push me into choosing one or the other. I wanted both, I believed in both, and I believed America had the resources to provide for both."

JOHNSON ANNOUNCED HIS DECISION during a nationally televised press conference on July 28. About two hundred journalists filled the East Room as the president stood at a podium, brilliantly illuminated by klieg lights. About 28 million Americans tuned in to the broadcast.

"We intend to convince the communists that we cannot be defeated by force of arms or by superior power," Johnson slowly intoned. "They are not easily convinced. In recent months they have greatly increased their fighting forces and their attacks and the number of incidents. I have asked the commanding general, General Westmoreland, what more he needs to meet this mounting aggression. He has told me. And we will meet his needs."

Although he'd authorized 100,000 more U.S. combat soldiers by the end of 1965, with the possibility of another 100,000 in 1966, LBJ downplayed the increase. He was raising the number of troops, he said, "from 75,000 to 125,000 men almost immediately. Additional forces will be needed later and they will be sent as requested." He also planned to double monthly draft calls, to 35,000 from 17,000.

"I do not find it easy to send the flower of our youth, our finest young men, into battle," Johnson said. "I have spoken to you today of the divisions and the forces, the battalions and the units, but I know them all, every one. I have seen them in a thousand streets of a hundred towns in every state in this Union—working and laughing and building and filled with hope and life. And I think I know, too, how their mothers weep and how their families sorrow. And this is the most agonizing and the most painful duty of your President."

Johnson spoke of his lifelong desire to raise up the poor and disadvantaged—and promised not to let that dream be "drowned in the wasteful ravages of cruel wars." Sitting in the front row, Sarah McClendon, a reporter for small-town Texas newspapers, cried openly. LBJ's wife, Lady Bird, and daughter Lynda daubed their eyes. Others in the audience seemed close to tears as well.

MOVING AS HIS SPEECH may have been, Johnson's decision to pump large numbers of American soldiers into South Vietnam marked the beginning of the end of his presidency.

By the end of 1965, more than 185,000 U.S. troops were in South Vietnam. Two years later, the number had soared to 485,600. As opposition to the war intensified, LBJ stunned the nation in March 1968 by announcing that he wouldn't run for reelection. He pledged to instead devote the remainder of his presidency to trying to bring peace to Vietnam.

He failed, and Americans continued to die in Vietnam for five more years.

EPILOGUE

ABETTED BY THE Kennedy administration, the anti-Diem coup opened the door to much deeper U.S. involvement in the fiasco of the Vietnam War.

By the time the last U.S. combat units pulled out of Vietnam in March 1973—nearly a decade after the coup—58,220 Americans were dead, 306,606 had been wounded, and our national psyche was scarred in ways that took decades to heal.

The war had much grimmer consequences for the two Vietnams, Laos, and Cambodia. As many as 2 million Vietnamese civilians and about 1.1 million North Vietnamese soldiers and Viet Cong guerrillas died between 1954 and 1975, according to the Vietnamese government, which released the figures in 1995. The U.S. military estimated that between 200,000 and 250,000 South Vietnamese soldiers also perished before the war finally ended with a communist victory in 1975.

The Rolling Thunder raids inflicted substantial damage on North Vietnam, wrecking industrial facilities and disrupting transportation and agriculture. By the end of 1967, 864,000 tons of bombs had been dropped on North Vietnam and nearly 76,000 people had been killed or wounded, two-thirds of them civilians. Yet neither the physical damage nor human losses yielded "any significant weakening of North Vietnam's military capabilities" or the determination of its government and people to keep fighting, according to the CIA. President Johnson halted Rolling Thunder on Halloween in 1968.

A parallel U.S. bombing campaign in Laos—during which more than 2 million tons of ordnance were dropped—lasted five years longer than Rolling Thunder and killed about 200,000 people, or roughly 10 percent of the country's population. Another 400,000 Laotians were wounded during Operation Barrel Roll; 750,000 were forced to flee devastated villages and other areas.

Since 1973, when Barrel Roll ended, 20,000 more Laotians have been killed or wounded by unexploded cluster bombs, which can detonate with even slight pressure. Many victims were farmers plowing their fields or children picking up what looked like a brightly colored toy. As of this writing, less than 1 percent of the unexploded ordnance has been cleared. Laos remains the most heavily bombed country in history, including Japan and Germany during World War II.

Heavy American bombing of communist supply routes and bases in Cambodia helped to give momentum to Pol Pot and his murderous Khmer Rouge guerrillas, who seized control of the country in 1975. The Khmer Rouge are thought to have killed as many as 2.8 million Cambodians, or nearly 40 percent of the population.

U.S. aircraft sprayed herbicides in an attempt to destroy foliage in forests and jungles that provided cover to VC guerrillas. Begun under President Kennedy, the spraying program, Operation Ranch Hand, grew to gigantic proportions, coating 3.6 million acres in South Vietnam and Laos with nearly 19 million gallons of Agent Orange and other defoliants between 1962 and 1971. Researchers later linked the chemicals to various cancers, Parkinson's disease, birth defects, leukemia, type 2 diabetes, and other serious ailments suffered by American veterans and Vietnamese and Laotian civilians.

The coup certainly wasn't the only development that led to full-blown Americanization of the war later in the 1960s. JFK's assassination eliminated a commander in chief who was opposed to deploying U.S. combat forces and indicated that he wanted to withdraw from South Vietnam. He was succeeded by Lyndon Johnson, who proved to be far more susceptible to Pentagon pressure to widen the war. The Viet Cong launched bloody attacks against American servicemen in 1964 and early 1965 that could have provoked almost any president into some form of military response. The pressure for U.S. intervention rose further with repeated battlefield setbacks for the ARVN and the introduction of regular North Vietnamese troops into the south. But the coup did unleash the relentless political chaos in South Vietnam that caused Washington policymakers to lean increasingly toward direct American military involvement.

Diem's overthrow had adverse effects even before it took place, as planning and hand-wringing over it distracted top military and civilian leaders, South Vietnamese as well as American, for months on end.

Rather than focusing on how to improve their ability to fight an increasingly dangerous insurgency, South Vietnam's generals were preoccupied with how to beat Diem's loyal forces and run his government, an enormously complex task for which they had no experience.

Diem and Nhu were forced to spend as much if not more time fending off rebellious generals, their American enablers, and Buddhist and student protesters as they did fending off the VC. By the summer of 1963, the brothers were effectively fighting on four fronts. Under tremendous pressure, they paid less attention to the strategic hamlet program, which became moribund. Nhu had been the driving force behind the fortified hamlets; when he died, they died with him.

From the White House to the Saigon embassy and MACV, key American policymakers, diplomats, and military officers were drawn into the coup sideshow. The Kennedy administration wasted innumerable hours trying to undermine rather than help Diem, while failing to notice the alarming deterioration of the strategic hamlets.

But the coup's real impact was felt after Diem and Nhu were murdered.

By tearing down Diem's relatively stable government, Big Minh and his fellow mutineers opened a Pandora's box of competing factions that plunged South Vietnam into rioting, religious warfare, and more coups. Feeble new regimes rose and fell, none of them able to win the support of the people or organize a better war effort.

The chronic chaos and governmental weakness then provided a rationale for the United States to bomb North Vietnam. The Joint Chiefs of Staff originally argued that bombing was necessary to make Ho Chi Minh pay a price for infiltrating men and arms into the south. But proponents later claimed that air attacks on the north would buck up South Vietnamese morale, galvanize public support for the government—and tamp down the disorder the coup had engendered. Indeed, Eisenhower made this argument to LBJ.

Had Diem and Nhu remained in power, it's likely they would have strongly resisted the introduction of large numbers of U.S. troops in 1965. The brothers were convinced they were winning the war, and that the Americans had become a hindrance to their progress. They understood the neocolonial stench that would attach to the sudden reappearance in their country of tens of thousands of foreign troops, and how the resulting popular resentment would damage their ability to govern.

Nhu would have stayed busy building and refining the strategic hamlets. Assuming its flaws were corrected, the program might have begun to work, shielding the rural population from VC marauders. Consolidating the hamlets and making sure peasants were adequately paid for their labor on them could have yielded more effective results.

In his 1972 memoir, *Swords and Plowshares*, Maxwell Taylor called the coup "one of the great tragedies of the Vietnamese conflict and an important cause of the costly prolongation of the war into the next decade." William Colby, always a perceptive observer, regarded it as the "worst mistake of the Vietnam War." Arthur Schlesinger, in *A Thousand Days*, his bestselling account of the Kennedy administration, concluded that the president undoubtedly knew Vietnam "was his great failure in foreign policy, and that he had never really given it his full attention."

JFK'S LACKADAISICAL ENCOURAGEMENT of the fatal overthrow of a close ally during wartime was the product of shortsightedness, indecision, and paralyzing bureaucratic quarrels. It's one of the ironies of his presidency that while he hoped to get the United States out of Vietnam, he failed to perceive that the coup could produce the opposite result: deeper American entanglement in the war.

There was nothing preordained about the coup. Diem might not have survived much beyond November 2, 1963, even without Washington's connivance. More than a few of his army officers were ready to shoot him "right in the back of the neck," as he feared. Buddhists and students were doing their best to push him out of his palace, alive or dead.

On the other hand, South Vietnam's bold, durable president had survived crises before, warding off Binh Xuyen gangsters and religious sects in 1955 and outmaneuvering rebel paratroopers in 1960. He might well have weathered the political storms that whirled around him in the summer and fall of 1963. By September 1963, he seemed to have defanged both the Buddhist and student groups that were trying to upend him.

Nolting, for one, thought he could have carried the day.

"My view is that the Diem government would have made it, and would have gradually succeeded in pacifying the country and making a reasonably viable place out of South Vietnam," the ex-ambassador said in a 1971 interview. "With the amount of aid that we were giving them, with the type of equipment that we were giving them—perhaps some modifications but not great ones—if we'd persisted and stuck with that original program and had not changed towards the end of President Kennedy's term and gone for what was supposed to be a quicker solution—we would have made it."

What sealed Diem's fate was Washington's covert promise to his generals of full American military and economic support if they got rid of their commander in chief and his brother.

Big Minh and his co-conspirators might have gone forward with their coup without that pledge, but it's also likely that Washington could have stopped them in their tracks by the simple expedient of firmly threatening to cut off the U.S. aid on which Saigon so heavily relied.

That tactic was successfully used in 1967 by Ambassador Ellsworth Bunker after Nguyen Van Thieu, who'd taken power with Nguyen Cao Ky two years earlier, was elected president in what was considered a reasonably fair election. When Bunker learned that the National Assembly might refuse to certify Thieu's victory, he called together his embassy political officers. He told them to pass the word to their Vietnamese contacts that if the assembly didn't confirm Thieu, the United States would regard that as a formal request to cancel economic aid and withdraw its forces, leaving the South Vietnamese to confront the communists on their own.

"This quickly ended that kind of maneuver," recalled Thomas Conlon, a State Department officer then stationed in Saigon.

AS IT BECAME CLEAR what a disaster the coup was, the finger-pointing began among the prominent and ambitious men who served as counselors and courtiers to JFK and LBJ.

In his confessional memoir *In Retrospect*, McNamara castigated himself for not forcing more internal discussion and debate about the merits of a putsch. He wanted Diem to stay in power, and he regretted not pushing harder for answers to such basic questions as whether the war could be won with him in charge. If the answer was yes, his overthrow wasn't necessary. If the answer was no, the next question was whether a replacement could do a better job. But that issue, too, received little attention.

McNamara also believed he and other presidential advisers should have given careful thought to working with de Gaulle and Nhu toward neutralization, or even getting out of South Vietnam altogether on grounds that its perpetual political disarray made winning the war impossible.

He criticized Rusk for "fail[ing] utterly to manage the State Department and to supervise Lodge," and for not "participat[ing] forcefully" in White House discussions. Taylor came in for reproach for not resolving the contradictory reports on military progress, or the lack thereof, that streamed into Washington from MACV and the embassy.

McNamara faulted JFK the least, citing his preoccupation with other important matters including civil rights and the partial nuclear test ban treaty. He did point out, however, that Kennedy failed to pull together a bitterly divided U.S. government and "remained indecisive far too long."

Yet, as president and commander in chief, Kennedy must bear the greatest weight of responsibility.

Even some of his closest advisers felt Kennedy was largely at sea about how to handle Diem and the war. "I think the president was very uncomfortable with decision making in Far East matters. I don't think he had any real feel for it," said Roswell Gilpatric, who served as deputy secretary of defense from 1961 to 1964. Victor Krulak, the Pentagon's counterinsurgency expert, put it more bluntly: "I saw the president often during the Vietnam years. He was impatient; he wanted things to happen; he wanted progress to be made. He didn't understand the war any more than the rest of us did; we were all monumentally ignorant."

Kenneth O'Donnell, JFK's aide and confidant, once asked him how he expected to exit South Vietnam without damaging U.S. prestige in Asia. "Easy," the president said. "Put a government in there that will ask us to leave." But such a government was already in place: Diem's.

In a front-page *Washington Post* interview in May 1963, Nhu had called for a 50 percent reduction in U.S. forces, saying the presence of foreign troops played into VC propaganda. A few months later, he told the Australian author Morris West that he wanted *all* American military personnel out, claiming they didn't know how to fight the VC. Nhu's words, along with his wife's vitriolic attacks on American "little soldiers of fortune," provided a golden opportunity to engineer a U.S. pullback. Why should Americans expend their blood and treasure for a country that didn't want them?

JFK may have missed another chance to back out of the war when Nhu claimed he'd discussed with the Polish diplomat Maneli a possible ceasefire with the north. Rather than demonize Nhu, the administration could have encouraged him and Diem to make some sort of deal with Hanoi, at a time when the brothers believed they were winning the war and could finish the job on their own.

Diem's foot-dragging in the face of Washington's repeated demands for reforms generated years of friction between the two allies. His refusal to jettison Nhu led directly to the Kennedy administration's encouragement of the coup. But Diem's resistance raised a fundamental question about U.S. policy: Could a poverty wracked, largely illiterate society like South Vietnam's realistically be expected to convert itself into a functioning, Western-style democracy amid an existential war?

Washington was able to use the tremendous leverage of its economic and military aid to nudge South Korea toward democracy. But that progress came after the Korean War ended, not while it was underway. Kennedy would have been well-advised to stop hammering Diem to get rid of Nhu and let the brothers do their best to win the war. Free and fair elections could never be held, nor strong democratic institutions established, until the Viet Cong were largely cleared out of the country. At that point, Diem might have been markedly less resistant to U.S. prodding.

Nhu argued that Washington needed to stop pressuring South Vietnam and provide aid on a no-strings-attached basis. He cited the precedent of the Lend-Lease Act, under which the United States shipped large amounts of war matériel and food to Britain, the Soviet Union, China, and other allies during World War II.

In his conversation with the State Department's Robert Manning, Nhu pointed out that Washington made no "moral commitment" to the governments receiving its help during World War II, including Stalin's. But it attached all sorts of conditions to its assistance to Diem, demanding that he make changes to his government as well as his army. Diem had no choice but to defy many of those demands lest he be caricatured, by the VC and the rest of the communist world, as a U.S. puppet no better than the discredited emperor Bao Dai.

JFK'S HANDLING OF THE coup reveals other striking deficiencies: his lax control of subordinates; his failure to seriously examine the possible consequences of the coup; his ambivalence and indecisiveness as the generals drew closer to executing their plot.

Kennedy was also far too sensitive to press criticism. The negative newspaper articles coming out of South Vietnam galled him to no end. Kennedy not only read the papers too much, as Hilsman put it, he reacted to them too much. That led him to extend the incompetent Harkins's stay in Vietnam for several months. It also prompted him to make a preposterous request to the publisher of *The New York Times* to yank Halberstam out of Saigon.

The chorus of U.S. press opposition to Diem—especially its condemnations after the pagoda raids—undoubtedly made JFK more receptive to dumping Diem. But while getting rid of an irksome foreign leader may have seemed like a good short-term fix, it turned into a long-term disaster.

American support for toppling Diem originated not with Kennedy, but with Hilsman, a third-tier State Department bureaucrat who, with his green light cable, commandeered the president's Vietnam policy and enmeshed the United States in the generals' conspiracy. JFK recognized the cable as a mistake, but never overrode it.

The infighting, press leaks, and personality clashes that broke out in the summer and fall of 1963 ("My god, the government is coming apart!") reflected Kennedy's less-than-firm grip on his own bureaucracy. But the most vivid example was the Agency for International Development's suspension of the Commercial Import Program, so vital to South Vietnam's infirm economy, without presidential knowledge or consent.

The vague assertion by Hilsman and other coup touts that Diem's ouster would lead to a more effective Saigon government amounted to a political Hail Mary based not on evidence, but on the thin hope that things would somehow shake out in Washington's favor. No in-depth analysis was conducted of what sort of regime would emerge, or how the war was to be won if Diem and Nhu suddenly disappeared. At a White House conference in August 1963, Edward R. Murrow, the famous CBS newsman then running the U.S. Information Agency, posed a penetrating question: If military leaders replaced Diem, would they be any better able than him to bring the Buddhists into the government fold? No one knew, yet that issue was to become a primary driver of South Vietnam's unending post-coup turmoil.

Another salient aspect of the administration's myopic debate over the coup was the absence, as Senate Foreign Relations Committee chairman William Fulbright later noted, of "any questioning by U.S. officials of the U.S. Government's right to reform the Vietnamese government or to replace it. The right to manipulate the destiny of others [was] simply assumed."

JFK and his men seemed to overlook or discount even the most obvious short-term consequences of a failed coup. Who would lead South Vietnam's armed forces if Diem imprisoned or executed all of the generals and other high-ranking officers implicated in the plot? The hunt for traitors would've consumed months of effort and turned South Vietnam upside down. Diem and Nhu would never have trusted Washington again, and might well have thrown the Americans out of their country. (This, ironically, would have been a good outcome for the United States, although Kennedy would probably have faced withering criticism from conservatives and the press.)

Kennedy may have gotten a chuckle out of entangling Lodge, his longtime rival, in the Vietnam morass, but it turned out to be another costly mistake. Lodge's haughty, lone-wolf persona asserted itself again and again as he feuded with Harkins and Richardson, and ignored White House orders to resume communication with Diem prior to the coup and protect Diem's brother Can afterward. When Lodge's help was most needed—to stand up Big Minh's new government—he was mostly missing in action.

Then there were JFK's vacillations. He veered from telling Lodge in August that a coup might be necessary to his eleventh-hour hand-wringing over the generals' capacity to defeat Diem. He compounded his hesitancy by leaving the final decision over whether to restrain the generals to Lodge, who'd never wavered in his eagerness to see Diem, Nhu, and Madame Nhu pushed overboard.

Lastly was Kennedy's appalling negligence in not offering to get Diem safely out of Saigon when the military uprising began or telling the generals to spare his life if they wanted more U.S. help.

Kennedy didn't want Diem harmed and appeared to be genuinely grieved when he learned of his murder. Prior to the coup, he'd sent an obscure congressman, Torbert Macdonald, to urge Diem to seek sanctuary in the U.S. embassy. But on the day of the coup, no offer of protection came from Lodge or any other U.S. official. Diem, a brave patriot, might well have refused any concrete attempt to fly him to exile in Paris or New York. But an effort should have been made, if only out of common decency and appreciation for an old ally. The fact that it wasn't left the White House spattered with blood when Diem was slain.

Despite Lodge's denials, the Kennedy administration was deeply implicated in the coup. The green light cable was an accelerant for the generals' revolt. So were JFK's televised upbraiding of Diem and the suspension of U.S. aid. When the generals backed away from their first attempt to upend Diem, Washington assured them it supported their second attempt.

Had Kennedy been willing to withstand the heat, he could've pursued a very different course, explaining to the American public—over and over, if necessary—that a noncommunist ally struggling to survive an existential war needed security more than democracy, and unflinching support rather than unceasing criticism. The president, cabinet members, and congressional allies could have made speeches, given TV and radio interviews, and written op-eds saying that once Diem defeated the VC, he'd have breathing room to make the democratic reforms that Washington sought. Winning counterguerrilla wars and building democratic institutions takes time, and Diem needed more of it, probably much more.

Instead of obsessing about Nhu and his wife, Kennedy and his advisers could have concentrated on making sure that strategic hamlets were properly configured and that U.S. aid yielded maximum value in the form of more health clinics, schools, farm assistance, and physical security for the rural population. If JFK demanded anything from Diem, it should have been a vigorous and generous land reform program designed to deprive the communists of that overarchingly important issue.

What about the generals? Could they have been held back? Perhaps not forever, given their resentment over Diem and Nhu's political meddling with the ARVN and clumsy handling of the Buddhist uproar. But rather than induce them to mutiny, the Kennedy administration could have firmly told them to stand down while the Americans worked with Diem to strengthen his armed forces and civil bureaucracy.

Confronted with the alarming reality of the U.S. aid cutoff, Diem seemed to knuckle under at last, suggesting to Lodge on the morning of the coup that he might be ready to make changes that Washington wanted.

By then, it was too late—for Diem, for South Vietnam, and for the United States.

ACKNOWLEDGMENTS

KENNEDY'S *COUP* COULDN'T have been written without the help of many people.

Ambassador James D. Rosenthal spent many hours with me describing his work as a young State Department officer in South Vietnam from 1961 to 1965. We met on Sundays in the sunny living room of his apartment in San Francisco's elegant Pacific Heights neighborhood as his wife, Britta, kept us going with coffee and pastries.

Fluent in Vietnamese, Rosenthal was the U.S. embassy's primary liaison with Tri Quang, the charismatic Buddhist leader. He hoped to write a memoir about his time in Vietnam and, through the Freedom of Information Act, acquired numerous State Department cables to and from the American embassy in Saigon.

Jim wasn't able to complete his manuscript, but he generously gave me his entire document collection, which formed a pile of paper about two feet high. This material was enormously helpful to me, especially in reconstructing the Hue massacre of May 1963 and the escalating tensions between Buddhists and Diem in the summer of 1963.

John J. Helble walked me through his many adventures as U.S. consul in the lovely old imperial capital of Hue in the early 1960s. He also gave me a copy of his unpublished memoir, *Anecdotes of a Foreign Service Career:*

1956–1985. His narrative helped unravel the mystery of how Ngo Dinh Can, Diem's brother and Hue's onetime political boss, was granted asylum by the United States but was later turned over to the rebel generals and executed.

Jane Nolting Meniktos gave me marvelous insights into the personality of her father, Ambassador Frederick Nolting, and his warm relationship with Diem.

John H. Richardson and Charles Trueheart provided me with photos of their fathers that I could not have obtained otherwise. Both of them also wrote excellent books about their dads' work in Vietnam that I borrowed from liberally.

Through scores of declassification requests under former President Bill Clinton's Executive Order 13526, I acquired more than 1,100 pages of coup-related documents from the Central Intelligence Agency, National Security Agency, and State Department. The CIA was especially helpful, releasing hundreds of pages with very few redactions. The material included CIA Inspector General J. S. Earman's detailed, eighty-four-page compendium of CIA actions in Vietnam from August 1963 to September 1964. The agency also gave me "The Coup d'Etat of November 1963 and Its Aftermath," a twenty-five-page paper by David Smith, the acting CIA Saigon station chief, and CIA agent Lucien Conein's seventeen-page report, "The Anti-Diem Coup."

CIA director John McCone had the habit of compiling detailed notes of his private conversations with presidents, government officials, and journalists. The CIA turned over a number of these memos, which, among other things, shed light on the clash between the agency's Saigon station chief, John Richardson, and Ambassador Henry Cabot Lodge that culminated in Richardson's dismissal less than a month before the coup.

The National Security Agency released documents indicating that it secretly intercepted phone calls between the Nhus and between the coup generals, as well as cables between the Saigon government and South Vietnamese embassies in several foreign countries, including the United States.

Tony Lake, Rufus Phillips, Hedrick Smith, Joan Helble, Vladimir Lehovich, Dr. Jan Berlin, Beverly McKeever, and George Clee gave me valuable details about life in Saigon and Hue in 1963 and the events that led to and followed the anti-Diem coup.

John Buquoi, Harvey Kline, and Peyton Bryan, young Vietnamese-language translators assigned to the Army Security Agency, recounted their long days and nights of tapping the phones of Diem's generals as they plotted and then carried out the coup.

Kennedy's Coup owes its existence in no small part to Brent Howard, who superbly edited my first book, *Act of War: Lyndon Johnson, North Korea, and the Capture of the Spy Ship* Pueblo. Brent purchased *Kennedy's Coup* for Dutton, but the publisher later canceled it. After the book was then rejected by about thirty other publishers, Brent suggested that I reach out to Robert Messenger, who acquired it for Simon & Schuster.

Robert subsequently left Simon & Schuster but, amazingly, insisted on editing *Kennedy's Coup* on his own time. His work was nothing less than stellar. Besides helping me straighten out my chronology and eliminate repetitive passages, Robert saved me from several factual errors. I'm also indebted to Mindy Marqués Gonzalez, Simon & Schuster's executive editor and vice president, for her excellent final edit, which compressed and sharpened the book, and for shepherding it to publication.

My agent, Mel Berger of William Morris Endeavor, has been expertly advising me on how to draft book proposals and then selling my books since 2002. He is a marvel.

Finally, I'd like to thank my fellow authors Max Boot, Michael Connelly, Christopher Goscha, and James M. Scott. Let's just say that when the chips were down for me, these guys came through.

NOTES

ABBREVIATIONS USED IN THE NOTES

ADST: Association of Diplomatic Studies and Training
CIA CREST: Online collection of declassified Central Intelligence Agency documents
FRUS: *Foreign Relations of the United States*, Vietnam volumes
JFKL: John F. Kennedy Presidential Library
JRC: James Rosenthal Collection (State Department cables provided to author)
LBJL: Lyndon Baines Johnson Library
LoC: Library of Congress
MSU: Michigan State University Archives and Historical Collections
NARA: National Archives and Records Administration
NYT: *New York Times*
ToV: *Times of Vietnam*
TTU: Texas Tech University's Virtual Vietnam Archive
UVA: University of Virginia, Special Collections Library, Frederick E. Nolting Papers

CHAPTER 1: A MASSACRE IN EDEN

3 *His assistant at the consulate*: Author interview with George Clee.
4 *The lieutenant then marched up*: John Helble oral history interview, ADST, 44.
5 *One of the advisers exclaimed*: Ibid., 57.
6 *It took him a while to adjust to the sight*: Helble, "Anecdotes of a Foreign Service Career, 1956–1985," 15.
7 *"We have," a Hue resident wryly told an American journalist*: Schecter, *The New Face of Buddha*, 151.
7 *In the nineteenth century, Emperor Minh Mang put eight thousand soldiers to work*: Vu, *Royal Hue*, 139.
8 *"He had his agents everywhere"*: James D. Rosenthal oral history interview, ADST.
8 *He told one associate that his family had salted away $7 million*: Tran Van Don, *Our Endless War*, 65.
9 *The last U.S. consul who managed to get inside Can's home*: *FRUS, 1958–1960*, vol. 1, *Vietnam*, doc. 94.
10 *The men drank cognac*: Author interview with Dr. Jan Berlin.
10 *"Father, that was a delicious dish"*: John Helble oral history interview, ADST, 56.
11 *The games had a dual purpose*: Author interview with John Helble.
11 *They explained to Helble*: Helble, "Anecdotes of a Foreign Service Career, 1956–1985," 14.
12 *Hue University faculty members*: Department of State Airgram A-20 from Hue, June 3, 1963, JRC, 6.

13 *In a lengthy cable to the State Department*: Ibid.
14 *"They were amazed"*: Ibid., 17.
18 *Helble's report warned*: Ibid.

CHAPTER 2: STRANGER IN A STRANGE LAND

21 *"We were often hopelessly baffled"*: Dockery, *Lost in Translation*, 23.
22 *On a wall inside the U.S. embassy was a* Peanuts *cartoon*: Miller, *Vietnam and Beyond*, 56.
22 *In one village he visited, the communists had murdered some peasants*: Nolting, *From Trust to Tragedy*, 29.
23 *"There was," noted a younger colleague, "an appealing, elemental decency"*: Phillips, *Why Vietnam Matters*, 121.
23 *"He had a little bit of a gloomy side"*: Author interview with Jane Nolting Meniktos.
23 *"I threw it out"*: Trueheart, *Diplomats at War*, 43.
23 *"We here are unanimous"*: *FRUS, 1961–1963*, vol. 1, *Vietnam, 1961*, doc. 86.
24 *"Lt. Nolting is cool under fire"*: Letter from Walter M. Christiansen, Nolting Papers, box 30, August 22, 1944, UVA.
25 *But what Trueheart called "this beautiful friendship"*: William Trueheart oral history interview, ADST.
27 *But one U.S. official who knew him well*: Author interview with Rufus Phillips.
27 *When the men finally finished*: Nolting, *From Trust to Tragedy*, 23.
28 *"There was a real rapport"*: Higgins, *Our Vietnam Nightmare*, 162.
29 *Nolting and Nhu immersed themselves*: Schecter, *The New Face of Buddhism*, 202.
30 *As Nhu told a U.S. newsman*: Halberstam, *The Best and the Brightest*, 225.
31 *After Nolting reported the results of his survey*: Nolting, *From Trust to Tragedy*, 60.
31 *The ambassador told friends that when he pestered Diem*: William Sullivan oral history interview, JFKL.
32 *"If you bring in the American dog"*: Jacobs, *Cold War Mandarin*, 98.
33 *Although they constituted only 5 percent*: Fall, *Viet-Nam Witness*, 191.
35 *"The Americans . . . have put an army at my back"*: Catton, *Diem's Final Failure*, 154.
35 *Farther on, he saw a blind beggar woman*: Bert Fraleigh memo to Rufus Phillips, July 11, 1963, Rufus Phillips Collection, TTU.
36 *"Monsieur Diem's position is quite difficult"*: Jacobs, *Cold War Mandarin*, 188.
37 *Incredulous at Walton's blunt remarks*: Frederick Nolting letter to Averell Harriman, March 11, 1963, Nolting Papers, box 12, UVA.
37 *Chatting with a young embassy officer*: John T. Bennett oral history interview, ADST.
38 *Anspacher then snapped*: John Anspacher oral history interview, ADST.
40 *Blaming others for his loss*: Abramson, *Spanning the Century*, 569.
41 *Diem noticed Harriman's inattention*: Nolting, *From Trust to Tragedy*, 83.
43 *His hearing-aid antics*: Thomas L. Hughes oral history interview, ADST.
43 *"I must confess to being somewhat astonished"*: Frederick Nolting letter to Averell Harriman, February 27, 1963, Nolting Papers, box 12, UVA.
44 *"Fritz Nolting is one of the finest human beings"*: Stanley Karnow, "The Newsmen's War in Vietnam," *Nieman Reports*, December 1963, 5.
44 *When the Buddhists asked him to guarantee*: David Halberstam, "Buddhists Mourn Vietnam Victims," *NYT*, May 29, 1963.
45 *Looking back in sorrow*: Nolting, *From Trust to Tragedy*, 109.

CHAPTER 3: "A BASKET OF CRABS": SAIGON 1954

48 *In the evenings, the children knelt together*: "The Autobiography of Mgr. Pierre Martin Ngô-dinh-Thuc, Archbishop of Hué," CathInfo, January 10, 2024, https://www.cathinfo.com/the-library/autobiography-of-archbishop-thuc/.

48 *He made daily inspection tours*: Miller, *And One for the People*, 85.

48 *"He had to really pull himself together"*: "The Autobiography of Mgr. Pierre Martin Ngô-dinh-Thuc, Archbishop of Hué," CathInfo.

49 *Diem often listened to the men's hopeful talk*: "Ngo Dinh Diem of Viet-Nam," 1957 information booklet published by Diem's press office, TTU.

49 *He supervised nearly three hundred villages*: Robert Shaplen, "Nine Years after a Fateful Assassination," *NYT*, May 14, 1972.

50 *"Here we give refuge"*: Farrère, *Les Civilises (The Civilized Ones)*, 94.

51 *"The most common forms of punishment"*: Tran Tu Binh, *The Red Earth*, 24.

51 *He also broke up a communist plot*: Miller, *Misalliance*, 25.

53 *Diem made his way to Saigon*: Ibid., 30.

53 *Still in Saigon, he disguised himself*: Miller, *And One for the People*, 481.

53 *In February 1946, Diem was brought to Hanoi*: Shaplen, "Nine Years after a Fateful Assassination."

55 *Mike Mansfield, a Democratic senator from Montana*: Edward Miller, "Vision, Power and Agency: The Ascent of Ngo Dinh Diem: 1945–54," *Journal of Southeast Asian Studies* 35, no. 3 (October 2004): 446.

56 *American officials generally approved of Diem*: Morgan, *The Vietnam Lobby*, 10.

57 *Lansdale wanted to gauge the crowd's reaction*: Lansdale, *In the Midst of Wars*, 156.

57 *On the eve of Lansdale's departure*: Phillips, *Why Vietnam Matters*, 14.

57 *"In this critical situation"*: Miller, *Misalliance*, 5.

58 *South Vietnam's treasury was nearly empty*: Hammer, *A Death in November*, 60.

58 *He flew to Hanoi*: Ibid., 97.

59 *The U.S. Navy assembled*: Naval Historical Center, "Report of Operation Passage to Freedom," Operational Archives Command File, Post 1, January 1946, box 141—PHIBGRP1 serial: 4, January 3, 1955.

60 *But many others drowned*: Ibid.

61 *Confronting the general at a party*: Demery, *Finding the Dragon Lady*, 83.

62 *Lansdale apologized for the short notice*: Lansdale, *In the Midst of Wars*, 175. In his official report at the time, Lansdale told a less colorful story, writing that he invited General Hinh & Co. to observe the Philippine army's campaign against the Hukbalahap rebels, not to visit nightclubs.

64 *He also funneled a slice of his profits*: "Night of Despair," *Time*, April 11, 1955.

65 *Vien uttered something in Vietnamese*: Bloodworth, *An Eye for the Dragon*, 210.

65 *Diem not only ignored the ultimatum*: "NSC Briefing, 'Background—Crisis in South Vietnam,'" April 5, 1955, CIA CREST.

67 *Casualties were relatively light*: "Situation in Vietnam," March 31, 1955, CIA CREST.

68 *The CIA reported that Diem's own commanders*: "Current Intelligence Bulletin," March 18, 1955, CIA CREST.

68 *The Cao Dai pope . . . received a new Cadillac*: "NSC Briefing, 'Background—South Vietnam O/B,'" March 23, 1955, CIA CREST.

68 *More than half of the Binh Xuyen Sûreté's seven hundred employees*: "Situation in Saigon," April 28, 1955, CIA CREST.

68 *Ely warned Diem*: *FRUS, 1955–1957,* vol. 1, *Vietnam*, doc. 146.
69 *An elderly woman*: A. M. Rosenthal, "Saigon Is Swept by Civil Warfare; Big Area Is Afire," *NYT*, April 29, 1955.
70 *"This fellow is impossible"*: Jacobs, *Cold War Mandarin*, 74.

CHAPTER 4: "DIEMOCRACY" AND ITS DISCONTENTS

72 *"At that time, we were all behind Diem"*: Tran Van Don, *Our Endless War*, 62.
73 *Returning from such forays*: Lansdale, *In the Midst of Wars*, 237.
73 *His anti-vice drive kicked off*: Fishel, *Problems of Freedom*, 29.
74 *One Saigon newspaper memorably labeled him*: Jessica M. Chapman, "Staging Democracy: South Vietnam's 1955 Referendum to Depose Bao Dai," *Diplomatic History* 30, no. 4 (September 2006): 684.
75 *When the votes were tallied*: Simpson, *Tiger in the Barbed Wire*, 172.
75 *Dr. Dan's arrest caused even Lansdale*: Ahern, *CIA and the House of Ngo*, 94.
77 *The Can Lao also operated secret jails*: Race, *War Comes to Long An*, 19.
78 *"If one hundred people would come in"*: Author interview with Rufus Phillips.
79 *And while the constitution contained some progressive features*: Bouscaren, *The Last of the Mandarins*, 54.
80 *Rice production almost doubled*: Scigliano, *South Vietnam: Nation Under Stress*, 107.
80 *By 1956, U.S. assistance came to $270 million*: Goscha, *Vietnam: A New History*, 289.
80 *Gushing that "a wholly unexpected political miracle"*: William Henderson, "South Viet Nam Finds Itself," *Foreign Affairs*, January 1957, 283.
81 *The next day, Diem addressed a joint session*: Cooper, *The Lost Crusade*, 153.
81 *Prior to his arrival*: Jacobs, *America's Miracle Man in Asia*, 254.
82 *Prisoners were often held*: Fall, *Viet-Nam Witness*, 207.
83 *Editors were told*: Wesley R. Fishel Papers (UA 17.95), box 1192, folder 4; Memorandum, Subject: Press censorship, February 15, 1956, MSU.
83 *In 1958, the publisher*: Duy Hinh and Nguyen Tho, "The South Vietnamese Society," paper published by U.S. Army Center of Military History, 1980, 131.
84 *Diem's security chief warned*: Memorandum, "A Review of Election Processes in South Vietnam," March 9, 1966, 15, TTU.
84 *A subsequent CIA analysis:* Ibid., 13.
86 *In 1958, the National Assembly passed*: Colby, *Lost Victory*, 36.
86 *The palace banished*: Demery, *Finding the Dragon Lady*, 109.
87 *French journalist Jean Lacouture*: Lacouture, *Vietnam: Between Two Truces*, 80.
87 *"Intelligence breeds ambition"*: Demery, *Finding the Dragon Lady*, 127.
92 *Peasants had to pay*: Scigliano, *South Vietnam: Nation Under Stress*, 123.
94 *But his broken promise*: Nguyen Thai, *Is South Vietnam Viable?*, 153.
94 *"You must tell me everything"*: "Vietnam Coup," typewritten notes, box 2, folder 2, Rufus Phillips Collection, TTU.
95 *In the early 1960s, their main-force units*: Pike, *Viet Cong*, 238.
96 *The Pentagon warned Williams*: Samuel T. Williams oral history interview, LBJL.
96 *Williams continued to beef up*: Ahern, *Vietnam Declassified*, 28.
98 *A U.S. pilot recalled*: Ian Thompson, "John Takeuchi Went from WWII Internee to Air Force Officer," *Daily Republic* (Fairfield, CA), September 5, 2018.
99 *Colonel Daniel Boone Porter*: Daniel Boone Porter oral history interview, LBJL.

100 *From a mid-1959 low*: "The Historical Setting and Evolution of the Indochina Struggle," July 27, 1971, CIA CREST.

100 *Madame... "is as brilliant, vivacious, bitchy"*: *FRUS, 1961–1963*, vol. 2, *Vietnam*, doc. 69.

102 *the agency found "no verification whatsoever"*: Elbridge Durby oral history interview, ADST.

102 *The CIA trained its members*: "Republican Youth Movement (RYM) and Women's Paramilitary Force," March 19, 1963, record group 59, General Records of the Department of State, Bureau of Far Eastern Affairs, 1963–1966, box 2, NARA.

103 *But in a private moment with General Harkins*: Paul Harkins oral history interview, LBJL.

CHAPTER 5: A FIERCE TRIBE OF TRUTH SEEKERS

105 *"He was quite different"*: "Reporters Remember Halberstam in Vietnam," *Today*, April 24, 2007.

106 *"Never as in that moment"*: David Halberstam, "A Letter to My Daughter," *Parade*, May 2, 1982.

107 *"Why, Monsieur Sully"*: Prochnau, *Once Upon a Distant War*, 50.

110 *He especially liked Brodard's*: Ibid., 156.

111 *He was smart and funny*: Bass, *The Spy Who Loved Us*, 2.

113 *Despite the risk of ambush or capture*: Sheehan, *A Bright Shining Lie*, 61.

114 *"This is a political war"*: Prochnau, *Once Upon a Distant War*, 162.

115 *As the son of a surgeon*: David Halberstam oral history interview, LBJL.

116 *Even while smiling demurely*: Browne, *The New Face of War*, 255.

118 *"Aircraft carrier?"*: Browne, *Muddy Boots and Red Socks*, 108.

119 *Browne appended a list*: Arnett, *Live from the Battlefield*, 77.

120 *"I'm an alcoholic"*: Prochnau, *Once Upon a Distant War*, 99.

121 *"No story, kid?"*: Ibid., 54.

122 *While the VC were "lean and hungry"*: David Halberstam, "U.S. Deeply Involved in the Uncertain Struggle for Vietnam," *NYT*, October 21, 1962.

123 *When a reporter asked Nolting*: Halberstam, *The Making of a Quagmire*, 17.

124 *In early November, the regime kicked out*: Mecklin, *Mission in Torment*, 137.

125 *In discussions with journalists*: *FRUS, 1961–1963*, vol. 1, *Vietnam, 1961*, doc. 92.

125 *In a cable to the State Department, he condescendingly described*: *FRUS, 1961–1963*, vol. 3, *Vietnam, January–August 1963*, doc. 30.

125 *Halberstam in turn believed that Nolting*: David Halberstam interview with WGBH-TV, 1979.

126 *The ambassador erupted*: David Halberstam, "Innocents Abroad: Or How a Corps of Young, Underpaid Reporters Sought the Truth in Saigon in a Different Age," *Neiman Reports*, Fall 1994.

127 *"After Ivan came in"*: Prochnau, *Once Upon a Distant War*, 206.

128 *Malcolm Browne once survived*: Browne, *Muddy Boots and Red Socks*, 121.

129 *Halberstam's letter began*: Roger Hilsman Papers, Country Files 1961–64, box 003, Vietnam: Hilsman trip, December 62–January 63: related documents, JFKL.

130 *"With one or two exceptions"*: Mecklin, *Mission in Torment*, 124.

131 *In other words, as Mecklin put it*: Roger Hilsman Papers, Country Files 1961–64, box 003, Vietnam: Hilsman trip, December 62–January 63: related documents, JFKL.

132 *"It's a funny thing, the Oriental mind"*: Paul D. Harkins oral history interview, U.S. Air Senior Officers Oral History program, 1972.
132 *He favored bombing with napalm*: *FRUS, 1961–1963,* vol. 3, *Vietnam, January–August 1963*, doc. 5.
133 *Shortly after taking over MACV*: Gregg, *Pot Shards*, 65.
134 *The general also drew the mistaken*: Paul Harkins oral history interview, LBJL.
134 *As wine flowed*: Richard Holbrooke, "A Loss for All of Us," *Washington Post*, May 1, 2007.
136 *"All we had was the story"*: Halberstam interview with WGBH-TV, 1979.

CHAPTER 6: "A MISERABLE DAMN PERFORMANCE": THE BATTLE OF AP BAC

138 *Thanks to weapons captured*: Sheehan, *A Bright Shining Lie*, 205.
143 *"I've got a problem, Topper Six"*: Ibid., 228.
149 *A dazzling tongue of flame*: Ibid., 254.
150 *During one operation in which his artillery*: Ibid., 76.
152 *They suffered eighteen killed*: Ibid., 262.
152 *"He fed me the initial story"*: Bass, *The Spy Who Loved Us*, 137.
153 *The reporter did something*: Halberstam, *The Making of a Quagmire*, 78.
155 *As Halberstam later wrote: "The enemy was long gone"*: Ibid.
156 *"It was a miserable damn performance"*: Sheehan, *A Bright Shining Lie*, 276.
156 *Halberstam's January 4 story*: David Halberstam, "Vietnamese Reds Win Major Clash," *NYT*, January 4, 1963.
156 *A State Department analysis*: "Alert on Viet-Nam: Current American Concern and Misunderstanding," record group 59, General Records of the Department of State, Files of the Office of Public Opinion Studies, U.S. Policy on S. Vietnam, April–December 1963, NARA.
157 *Felt believed, oddly*: Memo from Harry Felt to Arthur Sylvester, assistant secretary of defense for public affairs, November 26, 1962, TTU.
157 *In a memo to Harriman*: "Press Reporting from Viet Nam," March 23, 1963, TTU.
158 *Wheeler wrote that U.S. press coverage*: *FRUS, 1961–1963,* vol. 3, *Vietnam, January–August 1963*, doc. 26.
158 *Major Robert Bayless*: "The Advisors in Vietnam Who Served before the Thousands Died," unpublished manuscript by Robert Bayless, TTU.
159 *"We'd sit there every day"*: Prochnau, *Once Upon a Distant War*, 277.

CHAPTER 7: BEHOLD A BURNING MONK

164 *One of the monks poured*: Browne's account of Quang Duc's burning is drawn from his *The New Face of War* and *Muddy Boots and Red Socks*.
165 *Twelve hundred captured*: Goscha, *Vietnam: A New History*, 57.
166 *The French gave tax breaks*: *CQ Researcher*, August 3, 1966.
166 *Buddhists observed bitterly that Vietnamese Catholics*: Memorandum for the CIA Director, "The Motivation, Objectives, and Influence of Thich Tri Quang," September 11, 1964, CIA CREST.
166 *South Vietnam, he told an American friend*: Conversation with President Diem on July 19, 1963, Rufus Phillips Collection, TTU.
167 *As the country's first constitution*: Gheddo, *The Cross and the Bo-tree*, 143.

167 *In 1957, when the regime unwisely ordered*: Nhat Hanh, *Lotus in a Sea of Fire*, 27.

168 *About 70 percent of South Vietnamese*: Some writers and historians have disputed this, putting the actual figure as low as 30 percent. The author isn't aware of any authoritative census of religious affiliation in South Vietnam in the early 1960s. South Vietnamese held a wide variety of beliefs, including animism, Taoism, ancestor worship, Confucianism, and Caodaism. The 70 percent figure came from a 1961 survey by the Asia Foundation, a respected, New York–based nonprofit organization. That survey estimated that 10 to 11 million of South Vietnam's 14.5 million people considered themselves Buddhists; of those, 5 or 6 million were "practicing Buddhists."

168 *Even the influential Catholic journal*: The *Informations Catholiques Internationales* article is quoted in Roberts, "Buddhism and Politics in South Vietnam," *World Today*, June 1965, 240.

169 *When Buddhists hung*: "Memorandum of Conversation, Views on the South Vietnamese Situation," September 18, 1963, Averell Harriman Papers, Special Files, Public Service, JFK-LBJ, Subject file: Vietnam, general, September–November 1963, LoC.

170 *In the 1940s, he said, the Viet Minh forced him*: "An Analysis of Thich Tri Quang's Possible Communist Affiliations, Personality, and Goals," CIA Intelligence Information cable, August 28, 1964, TTU.

171 *"the perfect conspirator"*: "Vietnam's Political Buddhism and the War," *Time*, April 22, 1966.

171 *"He is one of that rare breed"*: "Memorandum for the (CIA) Director: The Motivation, Objectives and Influence of Thich Tri Quang," September 11, 1964, CIA CREST.

171 *But the officials were dismissed*: Saigon embassy cable to State Department, June 11, 1963, JRC.

173 *An informant told the U.S. embassy*: *FRUS, 1961–1963*, vol. 3, *Vietnam, January–August 1963*, doc. 146.

173 *He was horrified*: Halberstam, *The Making of a Quagmire*, 112. Interestingly, Browne later claimed he was the only Western newsman to witness Quang Duc's suicide.

175 *Vietnamese Buddhists viewed setting oneself afire*: Thich Nhat Hanh, "In Search of the Enemy of Man (Letter Addressed to Rev. Martin Luther King)," *Dialogue*, 1965.

175 *"As shock photography goes"*: Ferrari and Tobin, *Reporting America at War*, 101.

176 *Sheehan wrote a letter*: Saigon embassy cable to State Department, June 14, 1963, JRC.

177 *The two newsmen*: Maneli, *War of the Vanquished*, 132.

CHAPTER 8: KENNEDY IN THE QUAGMIRE

178 *"Jesus Christ!"*: Reeves, *President Kennedy*, 517.

179 *"Who are these people?"*: Roger Hilsman oral history interview, JFKL.

180 *Surveying a group*: Guthman and Shulman, *Robert Kennedy in His Own Words*, 350.

182 *The administration's relentless activism*: Wofford, *Of Kennedys and Kings*, 426.

183 *"He'd get a lot of people in"*: U. Alexis Johnson oral history interview, ADST.

184 *Discussing the Joint Chiefs*: Bradlee, *Conversations with Kennedy*, 122.

185 *"What is crucial"*: James Burnham, *National Review*, April 22, 1961.

185 *He eagerly read the writings of Mao Zedong*: Reeves, *President Kennedy*, 232.

187 *At the conclusion of one unsatisfying update*: Victor Krulak oral history interview, JFKL.

188 *Another U.S. officer went so far*: Lind, *Vietnam, the Necessary War*, 103.

188 *The foot-dragging*: Krepinevich, *The Army and Vietnam*, 31.

188 *As communist assaults escalated*: "Challenge to SEATO," *Time*, October 13, 1961.

190 *Everywhere he turned, Taylor sensed*: Taylor, *Swords and Plowshares*, 229.
190 *But Rostow doubted*: Unpublished Walt Rostow manuscript, National Defense University, 584.
191 *"They want a force of American troops"*: Schlesinger, *A Thousand Days*, 547.
192 *That "very disturbing question"*: Nolting, *From Trust to Tragedy*, 40.
192 *In a memo to Kennedy*: *FRUS, 1961–1963*, vol. 1, *Vietnam, 1961*, doc. 227.
193 *Roger Hilsman*: Roger Hilsman oral history interview, JFKL.
194 *In a memo to JFK, Bundy noted*: *FRUS, 1961–1963*, vol. 1., *Vietnam, 1961*, doc. 342.
194 *"I can't do it"*: Roger Hilsman oral history interview, JFKL.
195 *"Practically the first words out of his mouth"*: Nolting, *From Trust to Tragedy*, 54.
196 *The winners in this revolutionary reshuffling*: Ahern, *Vietnam Declassified*, 77.
197 *By July 1962*: "CIA Memorandum for the Secretary of Defense, 13 July 1962." The CIA declassified this document at the author's request.
198 *"The only thing for the government to do"*: "The Vietnamese 'Strategic Hamlets': A Preliminary Report," RAND Corporation, August 1962, 30.

CHAPTER 9: "WE'RE GOING TO GET OUR ASSES THROWN OUT OF VIETNAM"

200 *"He wasn't the Diem I knew"*: Oberdorfer, *Senator Mansfield*, 191.
201 *JFK later told an aide that he "got angry at Mike"*: O'Donnell and Powers, *"Johnny We Hardly Knew Ye,"* 15.
202 *Because of a map-reading error*: Hilsman, *American Guerrilla*, 268.
203 *He once went so far as to snatch*: Michael Forrestal oral history interview, JFKL.
205 *He informed Kennedy that he'd never been*: Ibid.
206 *Diem also donated*: *FRUS, 1961–1963*, vol. 3, *Vietnam, January–August 1963*, doc. 96.
207 *"They simply rounded up"*: Michael Forrestal oral history interview, JFKL.
208 *"We are probably winning"*: "Memorandum for the President: A Report on South Vietnam," n.d., Roger Hilsman Personal Papers, Country Files, 1961–64, box 003, JFKL.
210 *Wheeler's assessment*: *FRUS, 1961–1963*, vol. 3, *Vietnam, January–August 1963*, doc.11.
211 *Reflecting on the damaging report*: Nolting, *From Trust to Tragedy*, 98.
211 *"In 1965, I'll become one of the most unpopular presidents"*: O'Donnell and Powers, *"Johnny, We Hardly Knew Ye,"* 16.
211 *The communist diplomat*: Sullivan, *Obbligato*, 177.
212 *But if Diem's government couldn't succeed*: Roger Hilsman oral history interview, JFKL.
212 *At one point, Kennedy told Bartlett*: Charles L. Bartlett oral history interview, LBJL.
213 *"Eisenhower had read the newspapers too little"*: Hilsman, *To Move a Nation*, 458.
213 *Mecklin was having more trouble*: Mecklin, *Mission in Torment*, 148.
214 *Reelected to the Senate in 1946*: Whalen, *Kennedy versus Lodge*, 51.
215 *But no one was warier than Robert Kennedy*: Guthman and Shulman, *Robert Kennedy in His Own Words*, 400.
215 *Kennedy simply couldn't resist*: O'Donnell and Powers, *"Johnny, We Hardly Knew Ye,"* 16.

CHAPTER 10: A SHARPENING OF KNIVES

217 *If there was to be any chance*: *FRUS, 1961–1963*, vol. 3, *Vietnam, January–August 1963*, doc. 165.
218 *But he pleaded with the State Department*: Trueheart, *Diplomats at War*, 81.

218 *If he refused*: *FRUS, 1961–1963*, vol. 3, *Vietnam, January–August 1963*, doc. 167.
219 *Learning of it*: Ibid., doc. 169.
221 *Nhu, however, told a regime official*: Memorandum of Conversation, September 18, 1963, record group 59, General Records of the Department of State, Pol 27 S Viet, NARA.
221 *Two days later*: "Documents on the Buddhist Issue in Viet-Nam," Embassy of Viet-Nam, Washington, D.C., July 1963, TTU.
223 *"He is running on nerves"*: Trueheart, *Diplomats at War*, 157.
223 *At the cemetery*: "A Message from Viet-Nam," a film produced by the National Motion Picture Center, Saigon, n.d.
223 *Wonderment spread*: Schecter, *The New Face of War*, 267.
224 *During a family lunch*: Halberstam, *The Making of a Quagmire*, 212.
224 *In a communiqué to his Republican Youth*: "Communique No. 3 of the Movement of the Republican Youth," June 26, 1963, TTU.
225 *"The pictures in the press"*: Hilsman, *To Move a Nation*, 477.
226 *As the CIA pointed out*: *FRUS, 1961–1963*, vol. 3, *Vietnam, January–August 1963*, doc. 190.
227 *"How many concessions"*: Hammer, *A Death in November*, 151.
227 *Discussing with a Diem aide*: *FRUS, 1961–1963*, vol. 3, *Vietnam, January–August 1963*, doc. 198.
227 *Rumors were afoot*: Letter from the Venerable Thich Tinh Khiet to the President of the Republic, June 26, 1963, TTU.
228 *"To David, they were not just fools and liars"*: Neil Sheehan, "The Combatant," *New York Times Magazine*, December 30, 2007.
228 *When Trueheart and other diplomats raised*: Prochnau, *Once Upon a Distant War*, 324.
229 *After the party, Conein joined Don*: Ahern, *CIA and the House of Ngo*, 169; Lucien Conein interview with WGBH-TV, 1981.
230 *But, as Conein noted*: "Report of Jedburgh Team Mark, 16 August–23 November 1944." The CIA made this document public in 2017.
231 *Meeting him for the first time*: Phillips, *Why Vietnam Matters*, 19.
232 *But when Don reported all this*: Tran Van Don, *Our Endless War*, 84.
234 *The listening devices*: Denis Warner, "Vietnam: A Dynasty in Disorder," *The Reporter*, September 12, 1963.
234 *A secret memo circulated*: "Subject: Emergency Planning," July 10, 1963, Rufus Phillips Collection, TTU.
235 *Kennedy asked whether the drugging story*: *FRUS, 1961–1963*, vol. 3, *Vietnam, January–August 1963*, doc. 205.
238 *"Get back"*: Sheehan, *A Bright Shining Lie*, 352.
238 *Trueheart cabled Washington: "Given extreme emotional involvement"*: *FRUS, 1961–1963*, vol. 3, *Vietnam, January–August 1963*, doc. 210.
240 *"I feel very happy"*: "Suicide in Many Forms," *Time*, July 19, 1963.
241 *"The various opposition groups are sharpening their knives"*: "CIA Reporting on the Political Situation in South Vietnam, 1 June 62–21 August 63." The CIA declassified this document at the author's request.
241 *"C'est un panier de crabes"*: Saigon embassy cable to State Department, July 6, 1963, National Security Files, box 198, folder: Vietnam: General, July 1963: 1–20, JFKL.

CHAPTER 11: CITY ON THE BRINK

243 *The ambassador met with a testy*: Nolting, *From Trust to Tragedy*, 113.

243 *The ambassador couldn't resist*: *Executive Sessions of the Senate Foreign Relations Committee, Historical Series*, vol. 15, *1963*, 388.

244 *When the ambassador later read the telegram*: Frederick Nolting oral history interview no. 2, JFKL.

245 *He later criticized his friend*: "Final report, William C. Trueheart," August 17, 1963, Nolting Papers, box 13, UVA.

245 *Trueheart also had newfound respect*: William C. Trueheart oral history interview, ADST.

247 *If soldiers surrounded*: Circular from Thich Tinh Khiet to members of the Inter-sect Committee, July 15, 1963, JRC.

248 *A cop told one Western newsman*: David Halberstam, "Vietnam Orders Rein on Protests," *NYT*, July 18, 1963.

248 *As a woman voluntarily climbed*: "Observation of Buddhist-Police Incident 17 July 1963 at 582 Phan Thanh Gian Near the Giac Minh Pagoda," JRC.

249 *After Nolting left on vacation*: CIA memo, October 18, 1963, CIA CREST.

250 *Taken aback by his remarks*: "Memorandum for the Record: Conversation with President Diem on 19 July 1963," Rufus Phillips Papers, TTU.

250 *The most remarkable report*: CIA Information Report, July 13, 1963, National Security Files, box 198, folder: General, July 1963: 1–20, JFKL.

251 *He felt that the "heat is slowly going out"*: Saigon embassy cable to State Department, July 25, 1963, JRC.

251 *"Halberstam and I and the other correspondents"*: Sheehan, *A Bright Shining Lie*, 346.

252 *Every night he loaded*: Prochnau, *Once Upon a Distant War*, 363.

253 *Harkins's command wanly reported*: MACV to CINCPAC, Air Force Historical Research Agency, message 513, July 23, 1963.

253 *Asked by Rusk*: Mark Feeney, "Robert Manning, a Writer and Innovative Editor of the Atlantic," *Boston Globe*, September 29, 2012.

254 *He insisted that despite the negative news*: *FRUS, 1961–1963*, vol. 3, *Vietnam, January–August 1963*, doc. 226.

257 *Egged on by the monk*: Marguerite Higgins, "Fact and Fiction: Why the Buddhist Fury," *New York Herald Tribune*, August 27, 1963.

258 *Duc Nghiep told journalists*: Higgins, *Our Vietnam Nightmare*, 23.

259 *He cabled one: "if you mention that woman's name"*: Sheehan, *A Bright Shining Lie*, 349.

260 *Disturbed by the ghoulishness*: Schechter, *The New Face of Buddha*, 192.

261 *Nolting later cabled Washington*: Saigon embassy cable to State Department, July 23, 1963, JRC.

261 *"There was a trace of thickness in his speech"*: Mecklin, *Mission in Torment*, 177.

262 *Incensed, Harriman telephoned Hilsman*: Telephone Conversations, September 3, 1963, Averell Harriman Papers, LoC.

263 *Before it started*: Halberstam, *The Making of a Quagmire*, 119.

CHAPTER 12: A WILD ALARM IN THE HOT NIGHT

265 *It seemed, noted Hilsman, as if "all the fates of Asia"*: Hillsman, *To Move a Nation*, 480.

265 *To top off the debacle*: Mecklin, *Mission in Torment*, 179.

266 *"Why overthrow my brother?"*: Reuters, "Anti-U.S. Coup Hinted," *NYT,* August 4, 1963.
267 *Khiet said the monks discovered*: Letter from Thich Tinh Khiet to Ngo Dinh Diem, August 7, 1963, JRC.
267 *The Buddhists kept up their campaign*: "Memorandum of Grievances" to the United Nations, n.d., MSU.
267 *"Don't you think it will help our cause"*: Denis Warner, "Vietnam's Militant Buddhists," *The Reporter,* December 3, 1964.
268 *"The whole place is going sky high!"*: Arnett, *Live from the Battlefield,* 105.
268 *Asked why he did it*: Mecklin, *Mission in Torment,* 168.
268 *From his Foggy Bottom perch*: *FRUS, 1961–1963,* vol. 3, *Vietnam, January–August 1963,* doc. 246.
270 *Nolting replied skeptically*: Ibid., doc. 247.
271 *Hoi said Nhu wanted to set up*: Saigon embassy cable to State Department, National Security Files, Country File, box 204, top secret cables, tab A/B, 10/63, Saigon 655, October 7, 1963, JFKL.
272 *According to Nhu, however, Luan had turned*: Saigon embassy cable to State Department, National Security Files, Country File, box 198, folder: Vietnam 8/21–8/30/63, CIA Information Report, August 23, 1963, JFKL.
273 *Some residents believed that Archbishop Thuc*: Hammer, *A Death in November,* 164.
274 *"They are almost cocky about it"*: David Halberstam, "Vietnamese Reds Gain in Key Area," *NYT,* August 15, 1963.
274 *"Vouchers were not being signed"*: Michael Forrestal oral history interview no. 3, JFKL.
276 *"They're going to plastique your office"*: Prochnau, *Once Upon a Distant War,* 365.
277 *He and the other generals proposed*: *FRUS, 1961–1963,* vol. 3, *Vietnam, January–August 1963,* doc. 275.
277 *He added that a martial law declaration*: CIA Information Report, August 23, 1963, National Security Files, box 198, Vietnam, General, August 1963: 21–23, JFKL.
278 *"This is a helluva costly mistake"*: Letter to Neil Sheehan from Earnest Hoberecht, June 17, 1963, Dateline-Saigon.com.
279 *The Buddhists tried to defend*: U.S. Army Saigon cable to Washington, August 21, 1963, National Security Files, box 198, Vietnam, General, August 1963: 21–23, JFKL.
280 *"Why didn't you tell us?"*: Halberstam, *The Making of a Quagmire,* 127.
280 *But, without informing the newsmen*: See handwritten note on Saigon embassy cable to State Department, August 20, 1963, National Security Files, box 198, Vietnam, General, August 1963: 1–20, JFKL.
282 *John Helble, the Hue consul, cabled*: Saigon embassy cable to State Department, September 18, 1963, JRC.
286 *Worse, Diem and Nhu had done it*: Hilsman, *To Move a Nation,* 482.
287 *"We just didn't know"*: Halberstam, *The Making of a Quagmire,* 130.
288 *In a short explanatory note*: "Two Versions of the Crisis in Vietnam: One Lays Plot to Nhu, Other to Army," *NYT,* August 23, 1963.
288 *The CIA reported Nhu's contrary claim*: CIA Information Report, August 23, 1963, National Security Files, Country File, box 198, folder: Vietnam 8/21–8/30/63, August 23, 1963, JFKL.
289 *From his rocking chair he could reach*: "The JFK White House Tape Recordings," JFKL, September 8, 2022, https://www.jfklibrary.org/learn/about-jfk/jfk-in-history/white-house-tape-recordings.

289 *"The time may come"*: Henry Cabot Lodge–President Kennedy meeting on Vietnam, August 15, 1963, Meetings: Tape 104/A40, JFKL.

291 *"Unlike his predecessors"*: Browne, *Muddy Boots and Red Socks*, 152.

292 *The day he returned to Washington*: Chronology of Events Affecting the Joint Chiefs of Staff Related to the Vietnam Crisis, David Lifton Collection, Memorandum for the Record, Subject: Vietnam; August 21, 1963, TTU.

293 *But there was no clear consensus*: President's Intelligence Checklist, August 24, 1963, CIA CREST.

294 *When a subordinate pointed out*: John Helble oral history interview, ADST. Hilsman was quoted by Thomas F. Conlon, a former member of the State Department's Vietnam Working Group, who conducted the Helble interview.

294 *Felt told Hilsman*: Michael Forrestal oral history interview no. 3, JFKL.

295 *"US government cannot tolerate situation"*: State Department cable to Saigon embassy, August 24, 1963, Roger Hilsman Personal papers, Country Files 1961–64, box 003, Vietnam, August 1963: 22–26, JFKL.

296 *Secretary of Defense Robert McNamara was climbing*: *Executive Sessions of the Senate Foreign Relations Committee, Historical Series,* vol. 15, *1963*, 752.

296 *When Forrestal later sent Kennedy the text*: National Security Files, Vietnam: General, August 1963: 24–31, State cables, box 198, August 24, 1963, JFKL.

297 *"He asked me what I really thought"*: George Ball oral history interview no. 1, LBJL.

298 *Taylor, who opposed ousting Diem, read the text*: *FRUS, 1961–1963,* vol. 3, *Vietnam, January–August 1963*, doc. 282.

298 *After Hilsman asserted that he'd discussed the message*: Ford, *CIA and the Vietnam Policymakers*, 33.

CHAPTER 13: "WE HAVE TO MAKE THIS WORK"

303 *"Jack Kennedy would never approve"*: Mecklin, *Mission in Torment*, 194.

304 *Although the message didn't explicitly mention*: CIA, "Memorandum for the Record, Meeting in DCI's Office, 7 October 1963." The CIA declassified this document at the author's request.

305 *Nonetheless, he advised Richardson*: Ford, *CIA and the Vietnam Policymakers.*

306 *The generals would be on their own*: Presidential Office Files, box 128a, Vietnam: Security, 1963, August 26, 1963, JFKL.

306 *Khanh was less than enthusiastic*: National Security Files, Vietnam General, August 1963: 24–31, State cables, August 26, 1963, box 198, JFKL.

306 *As one of their first acts*: *FRUS, 1961–1963,* vol. 3, *Vietnam, January–August 1963*, doc. 299.

307 *On the same day that Lodge met Diem*: Saigon embassy cable to State Department, August 26, 1963, National Security Files, Vietnam General, August 1963: 24–31, State cables, box 198, JFKL.

307 *While the president had signed off*: Schlesinger, *A Thousand Days*, 991.

307 *"He passed it off too quickly"*: Robert F. Kennedy oral history interview, February 29, 1964, JFKL.

308 *"When we move to eliminate a government"*: Meeting on Vietnam, August 26, 1963, Meetings: Tape 107/A42, JFKL.

309 *"We have our prestige"*: Ibid.

311 *"This shit has got to stop!"*: Bird, *The Color of Truth*, 254.

311 *Hilsman said he thought he could "bring Nolting around"*: Averell Harriman Papers, Kennedy-Johnson Administrations, 1958–1971, box 581, telephone conversations, Dec. 61–Oct. 63, telecon of August 27, 1963, LoC.

312 *In his slow, stentorian, southern-gentleman voice*: Meeting on Vietnam, August 27, 1963, Meetings: Tape 107/A42, JFKL.

312 *Nolting evidently didn't know*: Saigon embassy cable to State Department, August 24, 1963, Roger Hilsman Papers, Country Files, 1961–64, box 003, Vietnam, Aug 63: 22–26, JFKL.

313 *Nolting noted that if Washington now chose*: Meeting on Vietnam, August 27, 1963, JFKL.

314 *"I have very grave reservations"*: Meetings: Tape 108/A43. Vietnam (Tape 107. Meeting on Vietnam, Continued), August 28, 1963, JFKL.

314 *He warned that Diem and Nhu were "perfectly aware"*: Ibid.

315 *"Shut up!"*: Hilsman, *To Move a Nation*, 492; Nolting, *From Trust to Tragedy*, 128; Roswell Gilpatric oral history interview, JFKL.

315 *After the president found out that Taylor*: Thomas L. Hughes notes of conversations with Michael Forrestal and Roger Hilsman, August 24–28, 1963, National Security Archive, George Washington University.

316 *Apprehensive about knowing so little*: Hanyok, *Spartans in Darkness*, 168; "B2, 26 August 1963/CCH Series VI.HH.6.75," NSA document. The National Security Agency declassified the NSA document at the author's request.

316 *The message ended, "Love, Mamma"*: "Madam Chuong Urges Daughter to Come to USA," National Security Agency intercept, August 20, 1963. The NSA declassified this document at the author's request.

317 *"Prudence demands that we assume some bloodshed"*: Saigon embassy cable to State Department, August 28, 1963, National Security File, box 198, Vietnam General, 8/24/63–8/31/63, CIA cables, JFKL.

318 *"Situation here has reached point of no return"*: "Memorandum for the Director, Subject: Record on Vietnam," by CIA Inspector General J. S. Earman, 8. The eighty-four-page Earman report, a detailed compendium of CIA actions in Vietnam from August 1963 to September 1964, was declassified at the author's request. Earman named Richardson as the author of this cable, but condensed his text; the CIA released the full text to the author under a separate declassification request.

319 *His son called him "the humble warrior"*: Richardson, *My Father the Spy*, 123.

319 *Buddhist monks had to exorcise*: de Silva, *Sub Rosa*, 211.

320 *"He finds particular pleasure"*: Ahern, *Vietnam Declassified*, 83.

321 *When Lodge learned what had happened*: Ahern, *The CIA and House of Ngo*, 180; Earman Report, 27.

322 *He reported on French shipping schedules*: CIA Intelligence Information Cable, August 29, 1964, TTU.

322 *Touring Thao's watery domain*: Colby, *Lost Victory*, 92.

322 *He had a walleye*: Browne, *The New Face of War*, 1.

323 *In fact, Thao was a VC agent*: Truong Nhu Tang, *A Viet Cong Memoir*, 42.

323 *The CIA quickly got in touch*: CIA cable to State Department, August 30, 1963, National Security File, box 198, Vietnam General, 8/24/63–8/31/63, CIA cables, JFKL.

325 *"First, try to calm American opinion"*: Saigon embassy cable to State Department, August 30, 1963, National Security File, box 198, Vietnam General, August 1963, 24–31, State cables, JFKL.

326 *"This is not . . . going to be a matter of public record"*: Meetings: Tape 108/A43, Vietnam, August 29, 1963, JFKL. JFK's taping system didn't pick up any audible response from him to Bundy's recommendation that coup records be concealed.

326 *"Until the very moment of the go signal"*: *FRUS, 1961–1963*, vol. 4, *Vietnam, August–December 1963*, doc. 18.

328 *Lodge chimed in*: Telegram from Saigon embassy to State Department, August 31, 1963, National Security File, box 198, Vietnam General, August 1963: 24–31, State cables, JFKL.

328 *"I was sure"*: Taylor, *Swords and Plowshares*, 295.

CHAPTER 14: VISIONS, PROPHESIES, AND CELESTIAL PORTENTS

329 *"Let me in!"*: Saigon embassy cable to State Department, September 1, 1963, JRC.

330 *By the time the melee was over*: David Halberstam, "Saigon's Forces Seize 1,000 More in School Battle," *NYT*, September 10, 1963.

331 *"By late afternoon, desperate parents were searching"*: Arnett, *Live from the Battlefield*, 112.

333 *Thuan, told Rufus Phillips that virtually all work had stopped*: *FRUS, 1961–1963*, vol. 4, *Vietnam, August–December 1963*, doc. 76.

333 *Tuyen lived in a walled villa across the street from William Trueheart*: Saigon embassy cable to State Department, September 12, 1963, Rufus Phillips Collection, TTU.

334 *The CIA reported that disaffection*: "The Situation in South Vietnam, 12 September 1963," CIA Memorandum, CIA CREST.

334 *"Even the heavens are protesting"*: Arnett, *Live from the Battlefield*, 119.

335 *Then there was the very large carp*: "Throngs of Vietnamese Pilgrims Visit Pond of 'Miraculous Fish,'" *NYT*, September 1, 1963.

336 *As the representative of America's first Catholic president*: Henry Cabot Lodge oral history interview, JFKL.

337 *Nhu pledged to retire*: *FRUS, 1961–1963*, vol. 4, *Vietnam, August–December 1963*, doc. 44.

337 *Reporters were tailed*: Malcolm Browne, "Vietnam Reporting: Three Years of Crisis," *Columbia Journalism Review*, Fall 1964.

338 *"Sure, we were paranoid"*: Prochnau, *Once Upon a Distant War*, 423.

339 *Nhu told the CIA*: *FRUS, 1961–1963*, vol. 4, *Vietnam, August–December 1963*, doc. 72.

340 *One night he dreamed*: Mecklin, *Mission in Torment*, 204.

341 *Conein found Dinh's men*: Ahern, *CIA and the House of Ngo*, 187.

342 *"Use your elbows"*: Frederick W. Flott oral history interview, LBJL.

342 *"We seem to have reached the point"*: Memorandum for the Director, Subject: Record on Vietnam, by CIA Inspector General J.S. Earman. The CIA declassified this document at the author's request.

343 *In a note to himself*: Papers of Henry Cabot Lodge II, Vietnam Papers, folder: "Preparatory papers before becoming Ambassador," Massachusetts Historical Society.

344 *The first indication came*: CIA, "The Demise of the House of Ngo," in "Central Intelligence: 50 Years of the CIA." The CIA declassified this twenty-nine-page document at the author's request.

344 *Still eager to see Diem overthrown*: Papers of Henry Cabot Lodge II, Vietnam Memoir, II–6, Massachusetts Historical Society.

346 *Trueheart told the visiting CIA executive*: Top secret report from Huntington Sheldon to John McCone, September 13, 1963, CIA CREST.

347 *He told his interviewers*: Interview with Thich Tri Quang, September, 2, 1963, JRC.

CHAPTER 15: "YOU BOTH WENT TO THE SAME COUNTRY?"

349 Time *magazine labeled it*: "Diplomacy by Television," *Time*, September 13, 1963.

349 *Robert then asked*: National Security Files, box 316, Meetings on Vietnam: General, September 1963: 1–10, September 6, 1963, JFKL.

350 *"I'll give you 48 hours"*: Victor Krulak oral history interview, JFKL.

352 *Many of these men*: *FRUS, 1961–1963,* vol. 4, *Vietnam, August–December 1963*, doc. 82.

353 *When they'd both finished*: Meetings: Tape 109, Meeting on Vietnam, September 10, 1963, JFKL.

353 *Strategic hamlets there were being "chewed to pieces"*: *FRUS, 1961–1963,* vol. 4, *Vietnam, August–December 1963*, doc. 83.

355 *Even selective cuts*: Top secret report from Huntington Sheldon to John McCone, September 13, 1963, CIA CREST.

356 *"We're stuck with that"*: Michael Forrestal oral history interview no. 3, JFKL.

356 *Church reiterated*: *Congressional Record (Senate)*, September 12, 1963, 17377.

358 *"The leak is the prerogative of the ambassador"*: Blair, *Lodge in Vietnam*, 52.

358 *In 1954, he throttled*: Lodge, *As It Was*, 134.

358 *"Visiting Diem . . . is an extremely time-consuming procedure"*: *FRUS, 1961–1963,* vol. 4, *Vietnam, August–December 1963*, doc. 102.

359 *The opium rumor*: National Security Council Executive Committee meeting, Meeting on Vietnam, September 16, 1963, MaryFerrell.org.

360 *Although Kennedy had secretly tried*: William Bundy oral history interview, JFKL.

361 *"Even during the most ferocious battle"*: Maneli, *War of the Vanquished*, 146.

362 *Trueheart, for one, regarded the idea*: William C. Trueheart oral history interview, ADST.

362 *Hilsman, who figured Nhu was trying to blackmail*: *FRUS, 1961–1963,* vol. 4, *Vietnam, August–December 1963*, doc. 90.

363 *"This is impossible"*: Newman, *JFK and Vietnam*, 375.

364 *He "appeared critical of Hilsman"*: CIA, "Discussion with Secretary Rusk at lunch at DCI residence," September 3, 1963. The CIA declassified this document at the author's request.

365 *In a September 3 phone call*: *FRUS, 1961–1963,* vol. 4, *Vietnam, August–December 1963*, doc. 52.

365 *As Nolting told McCone over lunch*: CIA, DCI and Ambassador Nolting, September 4, 1963. The CIA declassified this document at the author's request.

367 *Lodge cabled the president*: *FRUS, 1961–1963,* vol. 4, *Vietnam, August–December 1963*, doc. 126.

367 *As Hilsman continued to fuss*: Roger Hilsman oral history interview, LBJL.

367 *Talking to the two Pentagon officials in person*: Meetings: Tape 112, Vietnam, September 23, 1963, JFKL.

368 *JFK was none too impressed*: Miller, *Misalliance*, 299.

368 *As McNamara strode*: Prochnau, *Once Upon a Distant War*, 437.

369 *That encouraged other advisers*: Michael Forrestal oral history interview no. 3, JFKL.
369 *The president had "aged terribly"*: *FRUS, 1961–1963,* vol. 4, *Vietnam, August–December 1963*, doc. 150. Although McNamara didn't identify the professor he spoke with in his report to JFK, he named him in his memoir, *In Retrospect.*
369 *Honey believed that a small group*: Honey, *Genesis of a Tragedy*, 76.
370 *The Americans had been told*: *FRUS, 1961–1963,* vol. 4, *Vietnam, August–December 1963*, doc. 162.
371 *Chain-smoking as always*: McNamara, *In Retrospect*, 75.
371 *Taylor subsequently wrote that he left*: Taylor, *Swords and Plowshares*, 299.
372 *Lodge, he later wrote, "was beyond control"*: Colby, *Lost Victory*, 146.
374 *McCone believed that Lodge*: CIA, "Memorandum: CIA Activities in South Viet Nam," September 26, 1963. The CIA declassified this document at the author's request.
374 *Hilsman told Marguerite Higgins*: Gibbons, *The U.S. Government and the Vietnam War, Part II: 1961–1964*, 165.
375 *In a reply that fairly reeked*: National Security Files, box 200, Vietnam: General, September 1963: 18–21, State cables, September 21, 1963, JFKL.
376 *McCone went so far*: Robarge, *John McCone as Director of Central Intelligence*, 186.
376 *For example, it falsely charged that the Saigon station*: *Executive Sessions of the Senate Foreign Relations Committee, Historical Series*, vol. 15, *1963*, 758.
377 *Wisner soon reported that the CIA*: CIA, "Memorandum: Report of Origins and Underlying Motivation of Anti-CIA Campaign in re Vietnamese Situation," October 11, 1963. The CIA declassified this document at the author's request.
377 *Not long afterward, Lodge took over*: Frederick W. Flott oral history interview, LBJL.
378 *"The president wants her to have a cold shoulder"*: Averell Harriman Papers, Kennedy-Johnson Administrations, 1958–1971, box 581, telephone conversations, December 61–October 63, telecon of September 13, 1963, LoC.
379 *When he called JFK to explain*: Clarke, *JFK's Last Hundred Days*, 178.
380 *"H said they had better start as she would be a headache"*: Averell Harriman Papers, Chronological File, August–September 1963, telephone conversations, LoC.
381 *When a staffer brought in a wire-service story*: *FRUS, 1961–1963,* vol. 4, *Vietnam, August–December 1963*, doc. 87.
381 *On October 2, the National Security Agency*: "Madame Nhu's proposed itinerary in U.S.," National Security Agency, October 2, 1963. The NSA declassified this document at the author's request.

CHAPTER 16: "ARROGANT UPSTARTS" VERSUS THE "SPECIALS"

383 *"You must tell Mr. Kennedy"*: Arnett, *Live from the Battlefield*, 117.
383 *The police encircled the journalists*: *New York Times* Company Records, Foreign Desk Records, David Halberstam, October–December 1963, New York Public Library.
386 *He felt the American newspapermen*: Alsop, *"I've Seen the Best of It,"* 459.
388 *Driving back to Saigon*: Salisbury, *Vietnam Reconsidered*, 115.
388 *"I want to tell you that the story is a bunch of shit!"*: Prochnau, *Once Upon a Distant War*, 395.
389 *The rides home*: Author interview with John Buquoi.
390 *Visiting the French embassy*: Maneli, *War of the Vanquished*, 140.
390 *Minh said he needed to know*: *FRUS, 1961–1963,* vol. 4, *Vietnam, August–December 1963*, doc. 177.

391 *He suggested that "we do not set ourselves irrevocably"*: CIA, "Report on CIA and U.S. Government Involvement in the Vietnamese Generals' Coup of 1 November 1963," JFK Assassination Records, Record No. 104-10214-10035, NARA.

392 *But the plastic explosive*: "Continued Operation of Tran Kim Tuyen's Coup d'Etat Group," CIA Information Report, September 17, 1963. The CIA declassified this document at the author's request.

392 *Thao had an alternative plan*: "Progress of Huynh Van Lang and Pham Ngoc Thao with Plans for Coup d'Etat," CIA Information Report, September 11, 1963. The CIA declassified this document at the author's request.

393 *The CIA cautioned*: CIA Saigon cable to CIA headquarters, "Plans of Government to Assassinate Ambassador Lodge, Other High Embassy Officials, and Thich Tri Quang, and Burn the Chancery," Report No. TDCS DB-3/657,149, October 9, 1963. The CIA declassified this document at the author's request.

393 *"If I am assassinated"*: *FRUS, 1961–1963,* vol. 4, *Vietnam, August–December 1963,* doc. 193.

394 *State Department security officers agreed*: Averell Harriman Papers, Special Files, Public Service, JFK-LBJ, Subject file: Vietnam, General, September–November 1963, LoC.

395 *He assigned a squad*: Don, *Our Endless War,* 102.

396 *Significantly, JFK and his advisers backed away*: State Department cable to Saigon embassy, October 5, 1963, National Security Files, Vietnam, box 204, top secret cables, tabs A/B, 10/63, JFKL.

396 *Chatting with a small circle*: CIA, "Further Notes on SVN Controversy," October 7, 1963, draft memo from Wisner to McCone. The CIA declassified this document at the author's request.

399 *The bickering was so intense*: Henry Cabot Lodge oral history interview, JFKL.

400 *But he found the extended discussions*: Robarge, *John McCone as Director of Central Intelligence,* 183.

401 *"We need a dictator in time of war"*: *Executive Sessions of the Senate Foreign Relations Committee, Historical Series,* vol. 15, *1963,* 737.

403 *"The world . . . is divided into two classes"*: *Newsweek,* October 7, 1963.

404 *Senator Stephen Young*: *Congressional Record,* October 7, 1963, Senate proceedings, 17787.

406 *"We are very proud people"*: *New York World Telegram,* October 10, 1963.

407 *Kennedy followed Madame's high-profile visit*: Sorenson, *Kennedy,* 659.

409 *"I had my doubts"*: "Vietnamese Summary Supplement," October 24, 1963, CIA CREST.

CHAPTER 17: KENNEDY'S BIG SQUEEZE

410 *With the flow of imports drastically curtailed*: CIA memorandum, October 30, 1963, CIA CREST.

411 *"Pressures should be continued"*: Saigon embassy to State Department, October 19, 1963, National Security Files, Vietnam, box 204, top secret cables, tabs A/B, 10/63, JFKL.

411 *So provocative was the political counselor's diatribe*: Confidential memo from Bundy to JFK, October 19, 1963, National Security Files, box 201, Vietnam, General, Oct 63: 15–28, State cables, JFKL.

414 *Browne told them*: Browne, *Muddy Boots and Red Socks,* 15.

415 *He also "expressed regret"*: Lodge cable to State Department, October 23, 1963, National Security Files, Vietnam, box 204, Top secret cables, tabs A/B, 10/63, JFKL.
416 *And the ambassador made it clear*: "NBC News White Paper: Vietnam Hindsight, Part II; The Death of Diem (1971)," 32.
417 *When CIA officers finally reached Thao*: Ahern, *CIA and the House of Ngo*, 201.
418 *He was surrounded*: CIA, Saigon station cable to CIA headquarters, October 25, 1963. The CIA declassified this document at the author's request.
419 *When the incendiary white paper came out*: John Helble oral history interview, ADST.
419 *"He's tough and intelligent"*: Sheehan, *A Bright Shining Lie*, 366.
420 *"Earnie! The reporters are not plotting"*: Prochnau, *Once Upon a Distant War*, 456. Emphasis in original.
421 *"He seems so lonely here"*: O'Donnell and Powers, *"Johnny, We Hardly Knew Ye,"* 438.
422 *Kennedy was confident*: Ibid., 445.
422 *"The first thing I do"*: Clarke, *JFK's Last Hundred Days*, 241.
422 *"He was relentless"*: Prochnau, *Once Upon a Distant War*, 454.
423 *Within minutes, thirty ARVN men*: Confidential report from General Harkins to Commander in Chief, Pacific Forces, U.S. Air Force Historical Research Agency, October 21, 1963.
424 *The CIA, however, discerned a deeper meaning*: President's Intelligence Checklist, October 22, 1963, CIA CREST.
425 *Two days later, Rusk wrote back*: Louis Sarris, "McNamara's War, and Mine," *NYT*, September 5, 1995.
425 *"We are now in a position"*: *Times of Vietnam Magazine*, October 13, 1963.
426 *In a separate report, Chester Cooper*: "Viability of the GVN," Memorandum for the Director, CIA, October 30, 1963. The CIA declassified this document at the author's request.
427 *"We're like a bunch of amateurs"*: Meeting on Vietnam, October 25, 1963, Meetings: Tape 117/A5, JFKL.
428 *"Let's see where [Lodge] can get"*: Ibid.
428 *The president also directed McCone*: "Memorandum for the Record: Meeting with the President," CIA, October 25, 1963. The CIA released this document at the author's request.
429 *Don did drop one hint*: Cosmas, *MACV*, 100.
429 *"Diem was at his best"*: *FRUS, 1961–1963*, vol. 4, *Vietnam, August–December 1963*, doc. 221.
430 *"I believe that if we cover up"*: Collection: Saigon embassy files kept by Ambassador Graham Martin, box 8, folder: Henry Cabot Lodge, including Diem coup, 1963–65, Gerald Ford Library.
431 *While Lodge was disappointed*: Miller, *Misalliance*, 317.
432 *"So far they have allowed them to meet everyone"*: *FRUS, 1961–1963*, vol. 4, *Vietnam, August–December 1963*, doc. 245.
432 *Instead, they described harassment*: "Report of the United Nations Fact-Finding Mission to South Viet-Nam, Dec. 7, 1963," Document A/5630, 34.

CHAPTER 18: "WE'RE WORKING PRETTY MUCH IN THE DARK"

435 *When Lodge ran into General Don*: Lodge cable to State, SAIG 2003, CIA, October 28, 1963. The CIA declassified this document at the author's request.
436 *Don said he wasn't involved*: *FRUS, 1961–1963*, vol. 4, *Vietnam, August–December 1963*, doc. 225.

436 *If a face-to-face meeting*: CIA station to McCone, SAIG 2042, October 29, 1963. The CIA declassified this document at the author's request.
437 *"Should we cool off the whole enterprise?"*: *FRUS, 1961–1963,* vol. 4, *Vietnam, August–December 1963*, doc. 232.
438 *Kennedy didn't like the rebels' chances*: Meeting on Vietnam, October 29, 1963, Meetings: Tape 118/A54, JFKL.
440 *"We can discourage a coup"*: *FRUS, 1961–1963,* vol. 4, *Vietnam, August–December 1963*, doc. 235.
442 *"Gen Harkins has read this"*: Ibid. doc. 242.
443 *He bluntly told Diem*: Parmet, *JFK: The Presidency of John F. Kennedy*, 335.
444 *"I did not like being told"*: *Look*, January 28, 1964.
444 *They even paid a fortune teller*: Halberstam, *The Making of a Quagmire*, 161.
445 *The missive instructed General Tri*: "The Coup D'état of November 1, 1963," a series of articles published in the Saigon newspaper *Lap Truong* between June 4 and July 31, 1971, John M. Echols Collection on Southeast Asia, Cornell University Library.
447 *Boiling with affected rage*: Ibid.
448 *Lodge believed that most of the pro-coup forces*: Lodge to Washington, SAIG 2114, CIA, October 31, 1963. The CIA declassified this document at the author's request.
448 *Dinh insisted that the lives*: Tran Van Don, *Our Endless War*, 99.
448 *Lodge, the president added, "knows that we've been rather negative"*: Meeting on Vietnam, October 20, 1963, Meetings: Tape 118/A54 (reel 3), JFKL.
449 *"Rightly or wrongly"*: *FRUS, 1961–1963,* vol. 4, *Vietnam, August–December 1963*, doc. 240.
450 *"I told you he was going to be trouble"*: Reeves, *President Kennedy*, 642.
451 *"The sun is spinning!"*: Elliott, *Vietnamese Days*, chap 2.
453 *He felt like crying*: Phillips, *Why Vietnam Matters*, 201.

CHAPTER 19: DAY OF THE DEAD

454 *Even at this late stage*: Tran Van Don, *Our Endless War*, 103.
455 *Don made small talk*: *FRUS, 1961–1963,* vol. 4, *Vietnam, August–December 1963*, doc. 267.
455 *Rebel marines*: Goscha, *Vietnam: A History*, 305.
456 *As Lodge stood up*: *FRUS, 1961–1963,* vol. 4, *Vietnam, August–December 1963*, doc. 262.
457 *As dessert was served*: David Smith, "The Coup d'Etat of November 1963 and Its Aftermath," lecture to the Foreign Service Institute, October 27, 1964. The CIA declassified this twenty-five-page document at the author's request.
459 *His Presidential Guard*: *FRUS, 1961–1963,* vol. 4, *Vietnam, August–December 1963*, doc. 254.
460 *When the deputy mayor*: Miller, *Misalliance*, 319.
460 *Listening on their earphones*: Hanyok, *Spartans in Darkness*, 163. The National Security Agency declassified page 163 of this report, which describes Nhu's call to his wife, at the author's request.
460 *"Why didn't you tell me that yesterday?"*: Hammer, *A Death in November*, 287.
461 *Some units have made a rebellion*: *FRUS, 1961–1963,* vol. 4, *Vietnam, August–December 1963*, doc. 259.
462 *Trueheart, however, contradicted Lodge's account*: Strober, *"Let Us Begin Anew,"* 421.

465 *"Once you are into the attack"*: *NBC News White Paper: Vietnam Hindsight Part II, The Death of Diem.*
466 *Hovis heard the telltale grind*: Hovis, *Station Hospital Saigon*, 84.
467 *But when he got a phone call through*: Rust, *Kennedy in Vietnam*, 175.
467 *Less than two hours later*: *FRUS, 1961–1963,* vol. 4, *Vietnam, August–December 1963,* doc. 266.
469 *"For many of these conversations"*: Meeting on Vietnam, Discussion on the Dominican Republic, November 1, 1963, Meetings: Tape 118/A54, JFKL.
470 *Two infantry battalions*: CIA Saigon to State Department, November 1, 1963, National Security Files, box 201, Vietnam, General, November 1963: 1–2; CIA reports; CRITIC 3, JFKL.
470 *As the rebels closed in*: William C. Trueheart oral history interview, ADST.
471 *"Mr. Minister, we know only what we have heard"*: Mecklin, *Mission in Torment*, 265. Although Mecklin didn't identify the U.S. diplomat who took Thuan's call, Trueheart's son, Charles, named him in his book *Diplomats at War*, 266.
471 *"I've saved you motherfuckers"*: Goscha, *Vietnam: A History*, 308.
475 *"If you want to go, you can go"*: Miller, *Misalliance*, 323.
475 *Don was to claim years later*: Tran Van Don, interview with WGBH-TV, 1981.
476 *"This aircraft was available"*: Lucien Conein, "The Anti-Diem Coup," n.d. The CIA declassified this seventeen-page document at the author's request.
477 *"There was just a manic, frenetic pace going on"*: Author interview with John Buquoi.
477 *"To kill weeds"*: *NBC News White Paper: Vietnam Hindsight, Part II; The Death of Diem.*
477 *"Have courage; we face difficulties"*: Fox Butterfield, "Man Who Sheltered Diem Recounts '63 Episode," *NYT*, November 4, 1971.
478 *According to a CIA report, Big Minh's bodyguard*: CIA, "Unsanitized Copy of Diem Report," May 31, 1967, 44, https://www.archives.gov/files/research/jfk/releases/2018/104-10214-10036.pdf.
478 *Apparently unaware of Don's presence*: Tran Van Don, *Our Endless War*, 111.
478 *"I will give you publicly an order"*: Nguyen Ngoc Huy, "Ngo Dinh Diem's Execution," *Worldview*, November 1976.
479 *According to a CIA account, Nhu taunted*: Smith, "The Coup d'Etat of November 1963 and Its Aftermath."
480 *Conein told the coup leader*: Conein, "The Anti-Diem Coup."
480 *"Goddamn bastards"*: Phillips, *Why Vietnam Matters*, 205.
481 *"Goddamn it"*: Thomas F. Conlon oral history interview, ADST.
481 *"Oh, come on now, Maggie"*: Higgins, *Our Vietnam Nightmare*, 225.
482 *"Kennedy leaped to his feet"*: Taylor, *Swords and Plowshares*, 301.
483 *"Did Big Minh order the execution?"*: Meeting on Vietnam, November 2, 1963, Meetings: Tape 119/A55, JFKL.
483 *"Deaths of Diem and Nhu, whatever their failings"*: *FRUS, 1961–1963,* vol. 4, *Vietnam, August–December 1963*, doc. 278.
484 *"That goddamn bitch"*: Paul B. Fay oral history interview, JFKL.
485 *"In twenty-two years of public service"*: Nolting, *From Trust to Tragedy*, 132.

CHAPTER 20: THE GENERALS TAKE OVER

486 *"Every Vietnamese has a grin"*: *FRUS, 1961–1963,* vol. 4, *Vietnam, August–December 1963*, doc. 270.

487 *"Here were the guys"*: James D. Rosenthal oral history interview, ADST.
488 *"I could spit upon the world"*: Higgins, *Our Vietnam Nightmare*, 224.
488 *It turned out that the kids had left*: Demery, *Finding the Dragon Lady*, 202.
489 *Because they lacked passports*: Lodge, *The Storm Has Many Eyes*, 210.
490 *The next day, Hilsman released a cable*: State Department to U.S. embassy Rome, November 6, 1963, National Security Files, box 202, Vietnam, General, November 1963: 11–15: State cables, JFKL.
491 *"We are not here to present our condolences"*: Don, *Our Endless War*, 111.
492 *When Harkins asked Don about the purported graves*: *FRUS, 1961–1963*, vol. 4, *Vietnam, August–December 1963*, doc. 298.
492 *The White House agreed*: State Department to Saigon embassy, November 4, 1963, National Security Files, box 201, Vietnam, General; November 1963: 3–5: State cables, JFKL.
493 *"I was now meeting the man"*: Helble, "Anecdotes of a Foreign Service Career: 1956–1985."
493 *Can boarded the CIA aircraft*: Helble cable to State Department, November 5, 1963, record group 59, General Records of the Department of State, Pol 30-1, S Viet, Hue 17, NARA.
494 *Conein reappeared*: Helble oral history interview, ADST.
494 *"Giving him asylum, as I understand it"*: Saigon embassy to State Department, November 5, 1963, National Security Files, box 201, Vietnam, General; November 1963: 3–5: State cables, JFKL.
494 *Six months later, as Can was about to be executed*: Associated Press, "U.S. Seeks to Save Brother of Diem," *NYT*, May 7, 1964.
495 *"I knew I had been double-crossed"*: Helble, "Anecdotes of a Foreign Service Career."
496 *"Just for this fleeting, golden moment"*: Bloodworth, *An Eye for the Dragon*, 217.
497 *"The military holds the reins"*: President's Intelligence Checklist, November 5, 1963, CIA CREST.
498 *"He appears more politically sophisticated"*: Forrestal memo to Bundy, November 12, 1963, President's Office Files, box 128, Vietnam: General, 1963, JFKL.
500 *A source later told the CIA that Big Minh*: CIA information report, November 4, 1963, National Security Files, box 201, Vietnam, General; November 1963: 3–5: CIA reports, JFKL.
501 *Another problematic figure*: President's Intelligence Checklist, November 4, 1963, CIA CREST.
501 *"To have compelled Diem to abdicate"*: Denis Warner, "Vietnam: The Awful Choice," *The Reporter*, February 27, 1964.
502 *But he was informed that Minh "did not like doing that kind of thing"*: *FRUS, 1961–1963*, vol. 4, *Vietnam, August–December 1963*, doc. 309.
503 *Although the generals twice asked*: Ahern, *The CIA and the Generals*, 2, CIA CREST.
504 *"They chose to report what they saw as the truth"*: James Wechsler, *New York Post*, November 6, 1963.
505 *But Harkins opposed the changes*: Memorandum for the ambassador from Rufus Phillips, November 13, 1963, Rufus Phillips Collection, TTU.
506 *Over the weekend*: President Kennedy Dictates His Thoughts on the Coup in Vietnam, November 4, 1963, text transcript, JFKL.
507 *JFK replied that because the United States had encouraged*: *FRUS, 1961–1963*, vol. 4, *Vietnam, August–December 1963*, doc. 304.

508 *"What is it that we can [do to] make them decide"*: Meeting on 1964 Democratic Convention Plans, November 12, 1963, Meetings: Tape 120/A56, JFKL.

508 *"It may thus become necessary"*: *FRUS, 1961–1963,* vol. 4, *Vietnam, August–December 1963*, doc. 310.

509 *As Forrestal was getting ready*: *NBC News White Paper: Vietnam Hindsight, Part II; The Death of Diem.*

510 *Prior to leaving*: O'Donnell and Powers, *"Johnny, We Hardly Knew Ye,"* 13.

CHAPTER 21: "LET US CONTINUE"

512 *As he later lamented to Democratic Senator Eugene McCarthy*: Conversation Tape WH6602-01-9601-9602, February 1, 1966, LBJL.

512 *Kennedy and his inner circle*: Guthman and Schulman, *Robert Kennedy in His Own Words*, 417.

512 *As he later told his biographer Doris Kearns*: Kearns, *Lyndon Johnson & the American Dream*, 177.

513 *The vice president noted France's inability*: *FRUS, 1961–1963,* vol. 1, *Vietnam, 1961,* doc. 60.

514 *But Lodge, usually the embodiment of patrician aplomb*: Kennedy-Johnson Administrations, 1958–1971, box 581, telephone conversations, Dec. 61–Oct. 63, telecon of December 4, 1963, Averell Harriman Papers, LoC.

515 *"I am not going to lose Vietnam"*: Wicker, *JFK and LBJ*, 205.

515 *But at that moment, he said, his predicament*: Bill Moyers, "Flashbacks," *Newsweek*, February 10, 1975.

516 *"The political impetus"*: James D. Rosenthal oral history interview, ADST.

517 *In his home province, An Giang*: *FRUS, 1961–1963,* vol. 4, *Vietnam, August–December 1963*, doc. 314.

518 *"The Communists," wrote Chester Cooper*: Ibid., doc. 349.

519 *Arnett described it as "a victory party"*: Arnett, *Live from the Battlefield*, 128.

519 *The junta, the CIA's William Colby concluded*: Colby, *Honorable Men*, 222.

520 *After Tho engaged in a heated confrontation*: *FRUS, 1961–1963,* vol. 4, *Vietnam, August–December 1963*, doc. 368.

521 *When Marguerite Higgins interviewed him*: Higgins, *Our Vietnam Nightmare*, 238.

522 *"On the basis of the evidence"*: Alba Zizzamia, "UN Says No Persecution in Vietnam," *Catholic Northwest Progress*, December 27, 1963.

523 *Lodge asked Gunewardene*: Blair, *Lodge in Vietnam*, 78.

525 *Reading Bumgardner's survey results*: Earl Young memo to Michael Dunn, December 15, 1963, Rufus Phillips Collection, TTU.

525 *In a December 17 memo*: Smith to McCone, December 17, 1963, CIA. The CIA declassified this document at the author's request.

526 *"I'm totally dissatisfied"*: Gregg, *Pot Shards*, 73.

527 *The ARVN's Ninth Division*: Briefings of Secretary McNamara and Mr. McCone in Saigon, CIA Memorandum for the Record, December 19–20, 1963. The CIA declassified this document at the author's request.

527 *Meeting with Big Minh*: Tran Van Don, *Our Endless War*, 133.

528 *"I cannot overemphasize"*: CIA Inspector General J. S. Earman, "Memorandum for the Director, Subject: Record on Vietnam," CIA, 39.

528 *De Silva and Smith studied*: de Silva, *Sub Rosa*, 211.

529 *Lodge claimed he "had no ambitions"*: "Discussion with Ambassador Lodge at his residence," McCone Memorandum for the Record, December 21, 1963. The CIA declassified this document at the author's request.
529 *"Ah, les statistiques!"*: Hilsman, *To Move a Nation*, 523.
531 *"I sat there amazed"*: de Silva, *Sub Rosa*, 210.
533 *"the report was never seen again"*: David Halberstam, "The Ugliest Man in Vietnam," *Esquire*, November 1964.
533 *"He was quite notorious"*: Erland Heginbotham oral history interview, ADST.
533 *The generals were "indecisive and drifting"*: *FRUS, 1961–1963*, vol. 4, *Vietnam, August–December 1963*, doc. 374.
534 *"we should watch the situation very carefully"*: Ibid., doc. 374.
535 *"What national interests in Asia"*: Gibbons, *The U.S. Government and the Vietnam War, Part II*, 215.
536 *In 1962, he'd signed a peace agreement*: Sullivan, *France's Vietnam Policy*, 71.
537 *While the president treated Mansfield*: Oberdorfer, *Senator Mansfield*, 239.
538 *Widely considered a French agent*: CIA, Background Data, South Vietnam, November 6, 1963. The CIA declassified this document at the author's request.
538 *Harkins said in a 1974 interview*: Interview with General Paul D. Harkins, U.S. Army Senior Officers Debriefing Program, Military History Research Collection.

CHAPTER 22: SOUTH VIETNAM IN FREE FALL

541 *His mother ran a bar*: Shaplen, *The Lost Revolution*, 228.
542 *In a cable to the State Department*: *FRUS, 1964–1968*, vol. 1, *Vietnam, 1964*, doc. 30.
544 *As Air Force chief of staff Curtis LeMay*: Goscha, *Vietnam: A History*, 326.
544 *In a January 22 memo to McNamara*: *FRUS, 1964–1968*, vol. 1, *Vietnam, 1964*, doc. 17.
544 *He fired Hilsman*: William J. Jorden, "Talk with President Johnson," oral history interview, August 12, 1969, LBJL.
545 *LBJ was tired of the political turmoil*: Halberstam, *The Best and the Brightest*, 430.
546 *As a result, he and LBJ's other civilian counselors "tilted gradually"*: McNamara, *In Retrospect*, 107.
549 *The Pentagon on May 24 submitted*: *FRUS, 1964–1968*, vol. 1, *Vietnam, 1964*, doc. 171.
549 *One red player, William Sullivan*: Sullivan, *Obbligato*, 180.
549 *Although many individual sorties*: "Final Report, SIGMA I-64," National Security File, box 30, agency file, JCS—war games, vol. 1, LBJL.
550 *Bundy urged the president*: *FRUS, 1964–1968*, vol. 1, *Vietnam, 1964*, doc. 173.
551 *Nearly two years later*: *FRUS, 1964–1968*, vol. 4, *Vietnam, 1966*, doc. 77.
553 *"You've got a good statement, Mr. President"*: Goodwin, *Remembering America*, 357.
553 *He complained that the sixty-two-year-old general*: Conversation with McGeorge Bundy, June 15, 1964. Citation Number 3748, Miller Center, University of Virginia.
554 *"Although he had a reputation as an intellectual"*: Phillips, *Why Vietnam Matters*, 235.
558 *The CIA station, in a report to its headquarters*: *FRUS, 1964–1968*, vol. 1, *Vietnam, 1964*, doc. 326.
560 *As Taylor observed morosely*: Ibid., doc. 339.
561 *But while Johnson was repeatedly proclaiming*: Ibid., doc. 343.
561 *"Johnson was listening to the hawks"*: Roger Hilsman oral history interview, JFKL.
562 *Another national intelligence estimate*: *FRUS, 1964–1968*, vol. 1, *Vietnam, 1964*, doc. 368.
562 *"These were Catholic Vietnamese"*: John D. Negroponte oral history interview, ADST.

563 *On November 22, a mob*: Schecter, *The New Face of Buddha*, 208.
564 *about two thousand youths*: Peter Grose, "New Saigon Riots by the Buddhists Bring Crackdown," *NYT*, November 26, 1964.
565 *Nearly free of the VC a year ago*: *FRUS, 1964–1968*, vol. 1, *Vietnam, 1964*, doc. 426.
567 *the White House issued an anodyne statement*: Department of State *Bulletin*, December 21, 1964.
568 *They attacked Huong as "anti-revolutionary"*: CIA Weekly Report, December 16, 1964, TTU.
569 *"Khanh dropped his customary cherubic facade"*: Johnson, *The Right Hand of Power*, 418.
569 *There were grumbles*: Cooper, *The Lost Crusade*, 236.
572 *"If I go this way"*: Wise, *The Politics of Lying*, 295.
572 *in a suggestion that McNamara said "came from out of the blue"*: McNamara, *In Retrospect*, 165.

CHAPTER 23: "YOU HAVE TO GO ALL OUT!"

574 *Together with the ARVN's recent large-scale losses*: McNamara, *In Retrospect*, 166.
575 *"I know that this is an old recipe"*: *FRUS, 1964–1968*, vol. 2, *Vietnam, January–June 1965*, doc. 9.
575 *As his speechwriter Richard Goodwin observed*: Goodwin, *Remembering America*, 364.
576 *According to Ky*: Ky, *Twenty Years and Twenty Days*, 59.
578 *White House aide Douglass Cater*: Goldstein, *Lessons in Disaster*, 154.
578 *"We have kept our gun over the mantel"*: Johnson, *The Vantage Point*, 125.
579 *Navy jets hit the big Dong Hoi barracks*: Marolda, *The Approaching Storm*, 88.
582 *"In the eyes of the Pentagon, he was a querulous wallflower"*: Califano, *The Triumph & Tragedy of Lyndon Johnson*, 32.
584 *He overruled Taylor*: *FRUS, 1964–1968*, vol. 2, *Vietnam, January–June 1965*, doc. 153.
585 *Speaking privately with McCone*: Ibid., doc. 206.
586 *Peer de Silva, the station chief*: de Silva, *Sub Rosa*, 268.
586 *"We got to find 'em and kill 'em"*: *FRUS, 1964–1968*, vol. 2, *Vietnam, January–June 1965*, doc. 229.
587 *As the* New York Times *writer Tom Wicker observed*: Wicker, *JFK and LBJ*, 271.
588 *By the time the VC pulled back*: VanDeMark, *Into the Quagmire*, 163.
589 *"We harassed Quat"*: U. Alexis Johnson oral history interview, ADST.
590 *Imposing a raft*: "Ten Days of Action," *Time*, July 2, 1965.
591 *Westmoreland cabled*: *FRUS, 1964–1968*, vol. 3, *Vietnam, June–December 1965*, doc. 1.
592 *He urged LBJ to boost*: Ibid., doc. 38.
593 *The alternative to a firmly limited U.S. commitment*: Ibid., doc. 40.
593 *"My hunch"*: McNamara, *In Retrospect*, 195.
594 *"Finally I blew my top"*: "Acheson Correspondence (1964–1971)," Post Presidential Papers, Name File, letter from Acheson to Truman, July 10, 1965, Truman Presidential Library.
595 *"You goddamned old bastards"*: George Ball oral history interview, LBJL.
595 *"I became convinced"*: Goodwin, *Remembering America*, 393.
597 *"Looking back"*: McNamara, *In Retrospect*, 203.
599 *"No great captain in history"*: Ball, *The Past Has Another Pattern*, 400.

601 *"What happened in Vietnam is no one person's fault"*: VanDeMark, *Into the Quagmire*, 205.

602 *The president told Clifford*: Johnson, *The Vantage Point*, 148.

602 *As he later told Doris Kearns: "I was determined"*: Kearns, *Lyndon Johnson & the American Dream*, 282.

603 *"We intend to convince the communists"*: "Transcript of the President's New Conference on Foreign and Domestic Affairs," *NYT*, July 29, 1965.

EPILOGUE

605 *The Rolling Thunder raids*: "An Assessment of the Rolling Thunder Program Through December 1967," CIA Intelligence Memorandum, March 1968.

609 *"My view is that the Diem government"*: Frederick Nolting oral history interview, Air Force Historical Program.

610 *"This quickly ended that kind of maneuver"*: Thomas Conlon oral history interview, ADST.

611 *Victor Krulak, the Pentagon's counterinsurgency expert*: Strober, *"Let Us Begin Anew,"* 407.

613 *Another salient aspect*: "U.S. Involvement in the Overthrow of Diem, 1963: A Staff Study Based on the Pentagon Papers," U.S. Senate Foreign Relations Committee, U.S. Government Printing Office, Washington, 1972.

BIBLIOGRAPHY

BOOKS

Abramson, Rudy. *Spanning the Century: The Life of W. Averell Harriman, 1891–1986*. William Morrow, 1992.

Allen, George W. *None So Blind: A Personal Account of the Intelligence Failure in Vietnam*. Ivan R. Dee, 2001.

Alsop, Joseph, with Adam Platt. *"I've Seen the Best of It": Memoirs*. W. W. Norton, 1992.

Arbuckle, Les. *Saigon Kids: An American Military Brat Comes of Age in 1960's Vietnam*. Mango, 2017.

Arnett, Peter. *Live from the Battlefield: From Vietnam to Baghdad, 35 Years in the World's War Zones*. Simon & Schuster, 1994.

Ball, George W. *The Past Has Another Pattern: Memoirs*. W. W. Norton, 1982.

Bass, Thomas A. *The Spy Who Loved Us: The Vietnam War and Pham Xuan An's Dangerous Game*. PublicAffairs, 2009.

Beech, Keyes. *Not without the Americans: A Personal History*. Doubleday, 1971.

Bird, Kai. *The Color of Truth: McGeorge Bundy and William Bundy: Brothers in Arms*. Simon & Schuster, 1998.

Blair, Anne. *Lodge in Vietnam: A Patriot Abroad*. Yale University Press, 1995.

Blaufarb, Douglas S. *The Counterinsurgency Era: U.S. Doctrine and Performance, 1950 to the Present*. Free Press, 1977.

Bloodworth, Dennis. *An Eye for the Dragon: Southeast Asia Observed, 1954–1970*. Farrar, Straus and Giroux, 1970.

Bouscaren, Anthony T. *The Last of the Mandarins: Diem of Vietnam*. Duquesne University Press, 1965.

Bradlee, Benjamin C. *Conversations with Kennedy*. W. W. Norton, 1975.

Brandon, Henry. *Anatomy of Error: The Secret History of the Vietnam War*. Andre Deutsch, 1970.

Browne, Malcolm W. *Muddy Boots and Red Socks: A Reporter's Life*. Times Books, 1993.

———. *The New Face of War*. Bantam, 1986.

Bui Diem, with David Chanoff. *In the Jaws of History*. Indiana University Press, 1999.

Bui Tin. *From Enemy to Friend: A North Vietnamese Perspective on the War*. Naval Institute Press, 2002.

Buttinger, Joseph. *Vietnam: The Unforgettable Tragedy*. Horizon, 1977.

Califano, Joseph A. *The Triumph & Tragedy of Lyndon Johnson*. Simon & Schuster, 1991.

Catton, Philip E. *Diem's Final Failure: Prelude to America's War in Vietnam*. University Press of Kansas, 2002.

Chapuis, Oscar. *The Last Emperors of Vietnam*. Greenwood Press, 2000.

Charlton, Michael, and Anthony Moncrieff. *Many Reasons Why: The American Involvement in Vietnam*. Scholar Press, 1978.

Clarke, Thurston. *JFK's Last Hundred Days*. Penguin, 2013.

Colby, William E., and Peter Forbath. *Honorable Men: My Life in the CIA*. Simon and Schuster, 1978.

Colby, William E., with James McCargar. *Lost Victory: A Firsthand Account of America's Sixteen-Year Involvement in Vietnam*. Contemporary, 1989.

Collins, J. Lawton. *Lightning Joe: An Autobiography*. Presidio, 1994.

Cooper, Chester L. *In the Shadows of History: 50 Years behind the Scenes of Cold War Diplomacy*. Prometheus, 2005.

———. *The Lost Crusade: America in Vietnam*. Dodd, Mead, 1970.

Currey, Cecil B. *Edward Lansdale: The Unquiet American*. Houghton Mifflin, 1988.

Dallek, Robert. *Flawed Giant: Lyndon Johnson and His Times, 1961–1973*. Oxford University Press, 1998.

———. *An Unfinished Life: John F. Kennedy, 1917–1963*. Little, Brown, 2003.

Demery, Monique Brinson. *Finding the Dragon Lady: The Mystery of Vietnam's Madame Nhu*. PublicAffairs, 2013.

de Silva, Peer, *Sub Rosa: The CIA and the Uses of Intelligence*. Times Books, 1978.

Doan Bich and Le Trang. *Saigon in the Flesh*. Le Trang, 1965.

Dockery, Martin J. *Lost in Translation: Vietnam, A Combat Advisor's Story*. Presidio, 2003.

Dommen, Arthur J. *Conflict in Laos: The Politics of Neutralization*. Frederick A. Praeger, 1964.

Duiker, William J. *Ho Chi Minh: A Life*. Hyperion, 2000.

Elliott, David. *Vietnamese Days*. Pressbooks, 2019. https://pressbooks.pub/vietnamesedays.

Elliott, Duong Van Mai. *The Sacred Willow: Four Generations in the Life of a Vietnamese Family*. Oxford University Press, 1999.

Ellsberg, Daniel. *Secrets: A Memoir of Vietnam and the Pentagon Papers*. Viking, 2002.

Fall, Bernard B. *Viet-Nam Witness, 1953–66*. Frederick A. Praeger, 1966.

Farrère, Claude *Les Civilises (The Civilized Ones)*. Librairie Paul Ollendorff, 1905.

Ferrari, Michelle, and James Tobin. *Reporting America at War: An Oral History*. Hyperion, 2003.

Field, Michael. *The Prevailing Wind: Witness in Indo-China*. Methuen, 1965.

Fishel, Wesley R., ed. *Problems of Freedom: South Vietnam since Independence*. Free Press of Glencoe, 1961.

Freedman, Lawrence. *Kennedy's Wars: Berlin, Cuba, Laos, and Vietnam*. Oxford University Press, 2000.

Gelb, Arthur. *City Room*. Penguin, 2004.

Gheddo, Piero. *The Cross and the Bo-tree: Catholics & Buddhists in Vietnam*. Sheed and Ward, 1970.

Gibbons, William Conrad. *The U.S. Government and the Vietnam War: Executive and Legislative Roles and Relationships, Part II: 1961–1964*. Princeton University Press, 1986.

Goldstein, Gordon M. *Lessons in Disaster: McGeorge Bundy and the Path to War in Vietnam*. Henry Holt, 2008.

Goodwin, Richard. *Remembering America: A Voice from the Sixties*. Little, Brown, 1988.

Goscha, Christopher. *Vietnam: A New History*. Basic Books, 2016.

Grant, Zalin. *Facing the Phoenix: The CIA and the Political Defeat of the United States in Vietnam*. W. W. Norton, 1991.

Gregg, Donald P. *Pot Shards: Fragments of a Life Lived in the CIA, the White House, and the Two Koreas*. New Academia / Vellum, 2014.

Guthman, Edwin O., and Jeffrey Shulman, eds. *Robert Kennedy in His Own Words: The Unpublished Recollections of the Kennedy Years*. Bantam, 1988.

Halberstam, David. *The Best and the Brightest*. Penguin, 1983.

———. *The Making of a Quagmire: America and Vietnam during the Kennedy Era*, rev. ed. Alfred A. Knopf, 1988.

Hall, M. Clement. *Viet Nam 1963: Memoirs of a Civil Surgeon*. Lulu, 2009.

Hallin, Daniel C. *The "Uncensored War": The Media and Vietnam*. Oxford University Press, 1986.

Hammer, Ellen J. *A Death in November: America in Vietnam, 1963*. Oxford University Press, 1987.

———. *The Struggle for Indochina*. Stanford University Press, 1954.

Hannah, Norman. *The Key to Failure: Laos and the Vietnam War*. Madison, 1987.

Hersh, Seymour M. *The Dark Side of Camelot*. Little, Brown, 1997.

Higgins, Marguerite. *Our Vietnam Nightmare: The Story of U.S. Involvement in the Vietnamese Tragedy, with Thoughts on a Future Policy*. Harper & Row, 1965.

Hilsman, Roger. *American Guerilla: My War Behind Japanese Lines*. Potomac, 2005.

———. *To Move a Nation: The Politics of Foreign Policy in the Administration of John F. Kennedy*. Doubleday, 1967.

Honey, P. J. *Genesis of a Tragedy: The Historical Background to the Vietnam War*. Ernest Benn, 1969.

Hovis, Bobbi. *Station Hospital Saigon: A Navy Nurse in Vietnam, 1963–1964*. Naval Institute Press, 1991.

Howland, Carol. *Hue: Vietnam's Last Imperial Capital*. Mynah Bird, 2018.

Humphrey, Hubert H. *The Education of a Public Man: My Life and Politics*. Doubleday, 1976.

Jacobs, Seth. *America's Miracle Man in Asia: Ngo Dinh Diem, Religion, Race, and U.S. Intervention in Southeast Asia, 1950–1957*. Duke University Press, 2004.

———. *Cold War Mandarin: Ngo Dinh Diem and the Origins of America's War in Vietnam, 1950–1963*. Rowman & Littlefield, 2006.

Johnson, Lyndon B. *The Vantage Point: Perspectives of the Presidency, 1963–1969*. Holt, Rinehart and Winston, 1971.

Johnson, U. Alexis, with Jef Olivarius McAllister. *The Right Hand of Power: The Memoirs of an American Diplomat*. Prentice Hall, 1984.

Kahin, George McTurnan. *Intervention: How America Became Involved in Vietnam*. Anchor, 1987.

Kaiser, David. *American Tragedy: Kennedy, Johnson, and the Origins of the Vietnam War*. Belknap, 2000.

Karnow, Stanley. *Vietnam: A History*. Penguin, 1984.

Kearns, Doris. *Lyndon Johnson & the American Dream*. Harper & Row, 1976.

Keever, Beverly Deepe. *Death Zones & Darling Spies*. University of Nebraska Press, 2013.

Kempe, Frederick. *Berlin 1961: Kennedy, Khrushchev, and the Most Dangerous Place on Earth*. Berkley, 2011.

Kern, Montague, Patricia W. Levering, and Ralph B. Levering. *The Kennedy Crises: The Press, the Presidency, and Foreign Policy*. University of North Carolina Press, 1983.

Kiem Do and Julie Kane. *Counterpart: A South Vietnamese Naval Officer's War*. Naval Institute Press, 1998.

Kluger, Richard. *The Paper: The Life and Death of the* New York Herald Tribune. Alfred A. Knopf, 1986.

Krepinevich, Andrew F. *The Army and Vietnam*. Johns Hopkins University Press, 1986.

Lacouture, Jean. *Vietnam: Between Two Truces*. Vintage, 1966.

Lam Quang Thi. *The Twenty-Five Year Century: A South Vietnamese General Remembers the Indochina War to the Fall of Saigon*. University of North Texas Press, 2001.

Lansdale, Edward G. *In the Midst of Wars: An American's Mission to Southeast Asia*. Fordham University Press, 1991.

Lederer, William J., and Eugene Burdick. *The Ugly American*. W. W. Norton, 1958.
Lind, Michael. *Vietnam, the Necessary War: A Reinterpretation of America's Most Disastrous Military Conflict*. Simon & Schuster, 1999.
Lindholm, Richard W., ed. *Viet-Nam: The First Five Years: An International Symposium*. Michigan State University Press, 1959.
Lodge, Henry Cabot. *As It Was: An Inside View of Politics and Power in the '50s and '60s*. W. W. Norton, 1976.
———. *The Storm Has Many Eyes: A Personal Narrative*. W. W. Norton, 1973.
———. *Vietnam Memoir*. Unpublished manuscript. Massachusetts Historical Society, n.d.
Logevall, Fredrik. *Choosing War: The Lost Chance for Peace and the Escalation of War in Vietnam*. University of California Press, 2001.
Maneli, Mieczyslaw. *War of the Vanquished*. Harper & Row, 1971.
Mao Tse-tung. *On Guerrilla Warfare*. Praeger, 1961.
McNamara, Robert S., with Brian VanDeMark. *In Retrospect: The Tragedy and Lessons of Vietnam*. Vintage, 1996.
McPherson, Harry. *A Political Education*. Little, Brown, 1972.
Mecklin, John. *Mission in Torment: An Intimate Account of the U.S. Role in Vietnam*. Doubleday, 1965.
Miller, Anne. *And One for the People: The Life-Story of President Ngo Dinh Diem*. Unpublished biography. Downloaded March 22, 2018, https://www.vietnam.ttu.edu/reports/images.php?img=/images/242/2420502001a.pdf.
Miller, Edward. *Misalliance: Ngo Dinh Diem, the United States, and the Fate of South Vietnam*. Harvard University Press, 2013.
Miller, Robert Hopkins. *Vietnam and Beyond: A Diplomat's Cold War Education*. Texas Tech University Press, 2002.
Morgan, Joseph G. *The Vietnam Lobby: The American Friends of Vietnam, 1955–1975*. University of North Carolina Press, 1997.
Mounier, Emmanuel. *Personalism*. University of Notre Dame Press, 1952.
Neese, Harvey, and John O'Donnell, eds. *Prelude to Tragedy: Vietnam, 1960–1965*. Naval Institute Press, 2001.
Newman, John M. *JFK and Vietnam: Deception, Intrigue, and the Struggle for Power*. Warner, 1992.
Nguyen Cao Ky. *Buddha's Child: My Fight to Save Vietnam*. St. Martin's, 2002.
———. *Twenty Years and Twenty Days: How and Why the United States Lost Its First War with China and the Soviet Union*. Stein and Day, 1976.
Nguyen Cong Luan. *Nationalist in the Viet Nam Wars: Memoirs of a Victim Turned Soldier*. Indiana University Press, 2012.
Nguyen Thai. *Is South Vietnam Viable?* Carmelo & Bauermann, 1962.
Nguyen Van Thai and Nguyen Van Mung. *A Short History of Viet-Nam*. Times Publishing, 1958.
Nhat Hanh. *Vietnam: Lotus in a Sea of Fire*. Hill and Wang, 1967.
Nichter, Luke A. *The Last Brahmin: Henry Cabot Lodge Jr. and the Making of the Cold War*. Yale University Press, 2020.
Nolting, Frederick. *From Trust to Tragedy: The Political Memoirs of Frederick Nolting, Kennedy's Ambassador to Diem's Vietnam*. Praeger, 1988.
Oberdorfer, Don. *Senator Mansfield: The Extraordinary Life of a Great American Statesman and Diplomat*. Smithsonian Books, 2003.
O'Donnell, Kenneth P., and David F. Powers. *"Johnny, We Hardly Knew Ye": Memories of John Fitzgerald Kennedy*. Pocket, 1973.

Parmet, Herbert S. *JFK: The Presidency of John F. Kennedy.* Dial, 1983.
Perret, Geoffrey. *Jack: A Life Like No Other.* Random House, 2001.
Phillips, Rufus. *Why Vietnam Matters: An Eyewitness Account of Lessons Not Learned.* Naval Institute Press, 2008.
Pike, Douglas. *Viet Cong: The Organization and Techniques of the National Liberation Front of South Vietnam.* MIT Press, 1966.
———. *War, Peace, and the Viet Cong.* MIT Press, 1969.
Prados, John. *Lost Crusader: The Secret Wars of CIA Director William Colby.* Oxford University Press, 2003.
Preston, Andrew. *The War Council: McGeorge Bundy, the NSC, and Vietnam.* Harvard University Press, 2006.
Pribbenow, Merle L., trans. *Victory in Vietnam: The Official History of the People's Army of Vietnam, 1954–1975.* University Press of Kansas, 2002.
Prochnau, William. *Once Upon a Distant War: Young War Correspondents and the Early Vietnam Battles.* Times Books, 1995.
Race, Jeffrey. *War Comes to Long An: Revolutionary Conflict in a Vietnamese Province.* University of California Press, 1973.
Reeves, Richard. *President Kennedy: Profile of Power.* Touchstone, 1993.
Reston, James. *Deadline: A Memoir.* Random House, 1991.
Richardson, John H. *My Father the Spy: An Investigative Memoir.* Harper Perennial, 2006.
Rusk, Dean, as told to Richard Rusk. *As I Saw It.* Penguin, 1990.
Rust, William J. *Kennedy in Vietnam.* Scribner, 1985.
———. *So Much to Lose: John F. Kennedy and American Policy in Laos.* University Press of Kentucky, 2014.
Salinger, Pierre. *With Kennedy.* Avon, 1966.
Salisbury, Harrison E. *Vietnam Reconsidered: Lesson from a War.* Harper & Row, 1984.
Schecter, Jerrold. *The New Face of Buddha: The Fusion of Religion and Politics in Contemporary Buddhism.* Coward-McCann, 1967.
Schlesinger, Arthur M. *A Thousand Days: John F. Kennedy in the White House.* Houghton Mifflin, 1965.
Scigliano, Robert. *South Vietnam: Nation Under Stress.* Houghton Mifflin, 1964.
Shaplen, Robert. *The Lost Revolution: The U.S. in Vietnam, 1946–1966.* Harper & Row, 1966.
Shaw, Geoffrey. *The Lost Mandate of Heaven: The American Betrayal of Ngo Dinh Diem, President of Vietnam.* Ignatius, 2015.
Sheehan, Neil. *A Bright Shining Lie: John Paul Vann and America in Vietnam.* Random House, 1988.
Simpson, Howard R. *Tiger in the Barbed Wire: An American in Vietnam, 1952–1991.* Kodansha International, 1994.
Sloyan, Patrick J. *The Politics of Deception: JFK's Secret Decisions on Vietnam, Civil Rights, and Cuba.* St. Martin's, 2015.
Smith, Russell Jack. *The Unknown CIA: My Three Decades with the Agency.* Pergamon-Brassey's, 1989.
Sorenson, Theodore C. *Kennedy.* Harper & Row, 1965.
Strober, Gerald S., and Deborah H. Strober. *"Let Us Begin Anew": An Oral History of the Kennedy Presidency.* HarperCollins, 1994.
Sullivan, Marianna. *France's Vietnam Policy: A Study in French-American Relations.* Greenwood, 1978.
Sullivan, William H. *Obbligato: Notes on a Foreign Service Career.* W. W. Norton, 1984.

Tanham, George K. *Communist Revolutionary Warfare: From the Viet Minh to the Viet Cong.* Frederick A. Praeger, 1967.
Taylor, John M. *An American Soldier: The Wars of General Maxwell Taylor.* Presidio, 2001.
Taylor, Maxwell D. *Swords and Plowshares: A Memoir.* Da Capo, 1972.
Thompson, Kenneth, E., ed. *Diplomacy, Administration, and Policy: The Ideas and Careers of Frederick E. Nolting Jr., Frederick C. Mosher, and Paul T. David.* University Press of America, 1995.
Topmiller, Robert J. *The Lotus Unleashed: The Buddhist Peace Movement in Vietnam, 1964–1966.* University Press of Kentucky, 2002.
Topping, Seymour. *On the Front Lines of the Cold War: An American Correspondent's Journal from the Chinese Civil War to the Cuban Missile Crisis and Vietnam.* Louisiana State University Press, 2010.
Tran Tu Binh. *The Red Earth: A Vietnamese Memoir of Life on a Colonial Rubber Plantation.* Ohio University Center for International Studies, 1985.
Tran Van Don. *Our Endless War: Inside Vietnam.* Presidio, 2008.
Trueheart, Charles. *Diplomats at War: Friendship and Betrayal on the Brink of the Vietnam Conflict.* University of Virginia Press, 2024.
Truong Nhu Tang, with David Chanoff and Doan Van Toai. *A Viet Cong Memoir: An Inside Account of the Vietnam War and Its Aftermath.* Vintage, 1985.
Tubridy, Ryan. *JFK in Ireland: Four Days That Changed a President.* HarperCollins, 2010.
VanDeMark, Brian. *Into the Quagmire: Lyndon Johnson and the Escalation of the Vietnam War.* Oxford University Press, 1991.
Veith, George J. *Drawn Swords in a Distant Land.* Encounter, 2021.
Vu Hong Lien. *Royal Hue: Heritage of the Nguyen Dynasty of Vietnam.* River, 2015.
Warner, Denis. *The Last Confucian: Vietnam, Southeast Asia, and the West.* Penguin, 1964.
———. *Wake Me If There's Trouble.* Penguin Books Australia, 1995.
Weintal, Edward, and Charles Bartlett. *Facing the Brink: An Intimate Study of Crisis Diplomacy.* Scribner, 1967.
West, Morris L. *The Ambassador.* Dell, 1965.
Whalen, Thomas J. *Kennedy versus Lodge: The 1952 Massachusetts Senate Race.* Northeastern University Press, 2000.
White, Theodore H. *The Making of the President 1964.* Atheneum, 1965.
Wicker, Tom. *JFK and LBJ: The Influence of Personality upon Politics.* Ivan R. Dee, 1991.
Winters, Francis X. *The Year of the Hare: America in Vietnam: January 25, 1963–February 15, 1964.* University of Georgia Press, 1997.
Wofford, Harris. *Of Kennedys and Kings: Making Sense of the Sixties.* Farrar, Straus and Giroux, 1980.
Wyatt, Clarence R. *Paper Soldiers: The American Press and the Vietnam War.* W. W. Norton, 1993.

GOVERNMENT PUBLICATIONS AND OTHER DOCUMENTS

Ahern, Thomas L., Jr. *CIA and the Generals: Covert Support to Military Government in South Vietnam.* Center for the Study of Intelligence, Central Intelligence Agency, 1998.
———. *CIA and the House of Ngo: Covert Action in South Vietnam, 1954–1963.* Center for the Study of Intelligence, Central Intelligence Agency, 2000.
———. *Vietnam Declassified: The CIA and Counterinsurgency.* University Press of Kentucky, 2012.
Cosmas, Graham A. *MACV: The Joint Command in the Years of Escalation, 1962–1967.* Center of Military History, United States Army, 2006.

Donnell, John C. *Viet Cong Recruitment: Why and How Men Join.* RAND Corp., 1967.

Executive Sessions of the Senate Foreign Relations Committee, Historical Series. Vol. 15, *1963.* Government Printing Office, 1963.

Ford, Harold P. *CIA and the Vietnam Policymakers: Three Episodes, 1962–1968.* Center for the Study of Intelligence, Central Intelligence Agency, 1999.

Glennon, John P., ed. *Foreign Relations of the United States, 1955–1957.* Vol. 22, *Southeast Asia.* United States Government Printing Office, 1989.

———. *Foreign Relations of the United States, 1958–1960.* Vol. 1, *Vietnam.* United States Government Printing Office, 1986.

———. *Foreign Relations of the United States, 1961–1963.* Vol. 1, *Vietnam, 1961.* United States Government Printing Office, 1988.

———. *Foreign Relations of the United States, 1961–1963.* Vol. 2, *Vietnam, 1962.* United States Government Printing Office, 1990.

———. *Foreign Relations of the United States, 1961–1963.* Vol. 3, *Vietnam, January–August 1963.* United States Government Printing Office, 1991.

———. *Foreign Relations of the United States, 1961–1963.* Vol. 4, *Vietnam, August–December 1963.* United States Government Printing Office, 1991.

———. *Foreign Relations of the United States, 1964–1968.* Vol. 1, *Vietnam, 1964.* United States Government Printing Office, 1992.

Hammond, William M. *The U.S. Army in Vietnam, Public Affairs: The Military and the Media, 1962–1968.* U.S. Army Center of Military History, 1990.

Hanyok, Robert J. *Spartans in Darkness: American SIGINT and the Indochina War, 1945–1975.* National Security Agency, 2002.

Helble, John J. "Anecdotes of a Foreign Service Career, 1956–1985." Unpublished manuscript, n.d.

LaFantasie, Glenn W., ed. *Foreign Relations of the United States, 1964–1968.* Vol. 2, *Vietnam, January–June 1965.* United States Government Printing Office, 1996.

Marolda, Edward J. *The Approaching Storm: Conflict in Asia, 1945–1965.* Naval History & Heritage Command, 2009.

Report of the United Nations Fact-Finding Mission to South Viet-Nam, Document A/5630, December 7, 1963. https://digitallibrary.un.org/record/729703?v=pdf.

Robarge, David. *John McCone as Director of Central Intelligence, 1961–1965,* pt. 1 of 2. Center for the Study of Intelligence, Central Intelligence Agency, 2005.

JOURNAL ARTICLES

Carver, George A. "The Real Revolution in South Vietnam." *Foreign Affairs,* April 1965.

Chapman, Jessica M. "Staging Democracy: South Vietnam's 1955 Referendum to Depose Bao Dai." *Diplomatic History* 30, no. 4 (2006): 671–703.

Gnoinska, Margaret K. "Poland and Vietnam, 1963: New Evidence on Secret Communist Diplomacy and the 'Maneli Affair.'" *Cold War International History Project, Working Paper #45,* Woodrow Wilson Center for International Scholars, March 2005.

Miller, Edward. "Vision, Power, and Agency: The Ascent of Ngo Dinh Diem, 1945–54." *Journal of Southeast Asian Studies,* October 2004.

INDEX

ABOUT THE AUTHOR

JACK CHEEVERS is the author of *Act of War: Lyndon Johnson, North Korea, and the Capture of the Spy Ship* Pueblo, which won the 2014 Samuel Eliot Morison Award for Naval Literature. A Massachusetts native and proud graduate of Berkeley, he was a reporter for the *Los Angeles Times* and other California newspapers for twenty-seven years. He lives on a pond in New Hampshire.

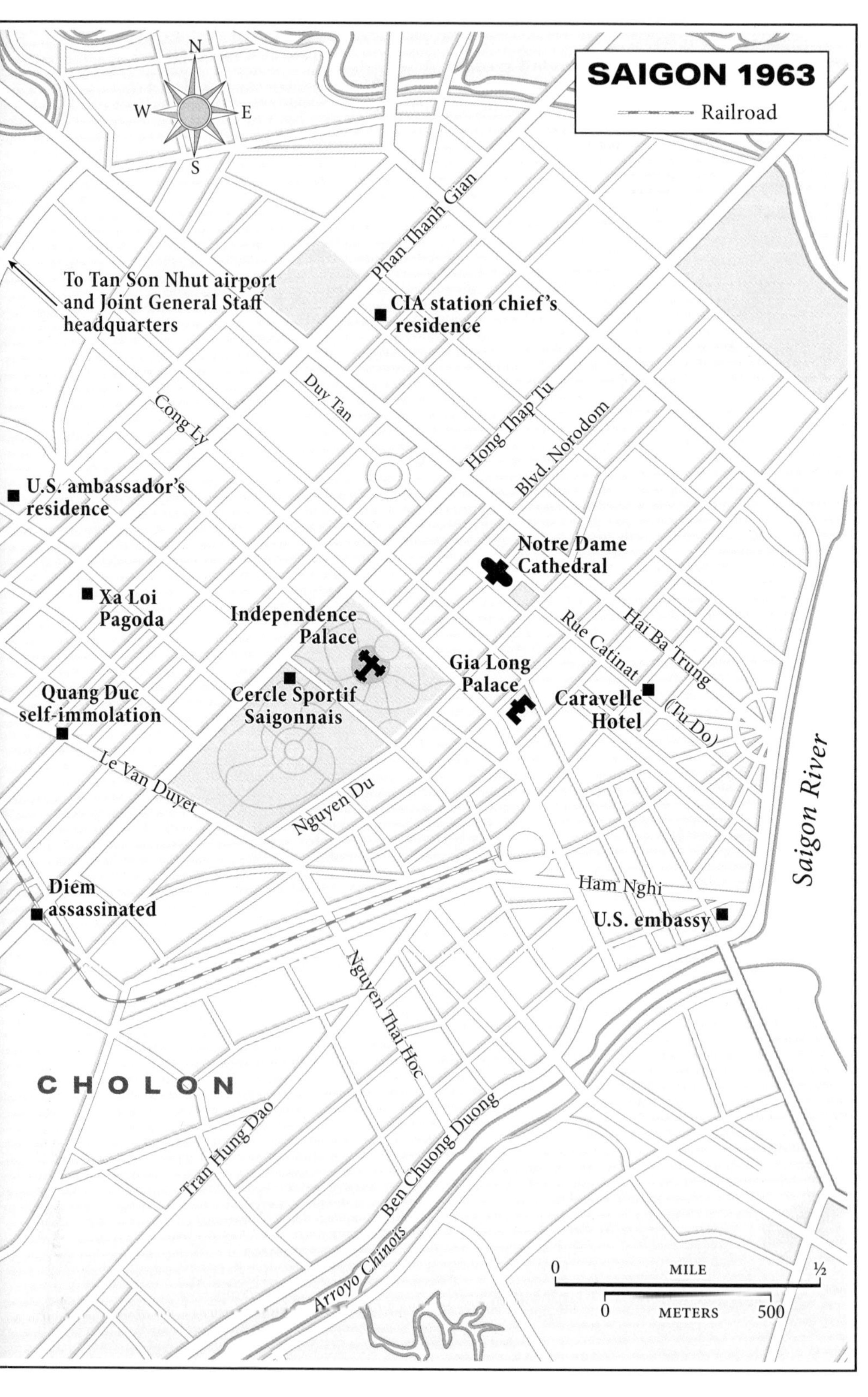
SAIGON 1963
Railroad
N
W
E
S
To Tan Son Nhut airport and Joint General Staff headquarters
Phan Thanh Gian
CIA station chief's residence
Duy Tan
Cong Ly
Hong Thap Tu
Blvd. Norodom
U.S. ambassador's residence
Notre Dame Cathedral
Xa Loi Pagoda
Independence Palace
Rue Catinat
(Tu Do)
Hai Ba Trung
Gia Long Palace
Caravelle Hotel
Quang Duc self-immolation
Cercle Sportif Saigonnais
Le Van Duyet
Nguyen Du
Saigon River
Ham Nghi
Diem assassinated
U.S. embassy
Nguyen Thai Hoc
CHOLON
Tran Hung Dao
Ben Chuong Duong
Arroyo Chinois
0
MILE
½
0
METERS
500